The Routledge Handbook of Language Testing

The Routledge Handbook of Language Testing offers a critical and comprehensive overview of language testing and assessment within the fields of applied linguistics and language study.

An understanding of language testing is essential for applied linguistic research, language education, and a growing range of public policy issues. This handbook is an indispensable introduction and reference to the study of the subject. Specially commissioned chapters by leading academics and researchers of language testing address the most important topics facing researchers and practitioners, including:

- An overview of the key issues in language testing
- Key research methods and techniques in language test validation
- The social and ethical aspects of language testing
- The philosophical and historical underpinnings of assessment practices
- The key literature in the field
- Test design and development practices through use of practical examples

The Routledge Handbook of Language Testing is the ideal resource for postgraduate students, language teachers and those working in the field of applied linguistics.

Glenn Fulcher is Professor of Education and Language Assessment at the University of Leicester in the United Kingdom. His research interests include validation theory, test and rating scale design, retrofit issues, assessment philosophy, and the politics of testing.

Fred Davidson is a Professor of Linguistics at the University of Illinois at Urbana-Champaign. His interests include language test development and the history and philosophy of educational and psychological measurement.

The Routledge Handbook of Language Testing

Edited by
Glenn Fulcher and Fred Davidson

Routledge
Taylor & Francis Group

LONDON AND NEW YORK

First published 2012
by Routledge
2 Park Square, Milton Park, Abingdon, Oxon OX14 4RN

Simultaneously published in the USA and Canada
by Routledge
711 Third Avenue, New York, NY 10017

Routledge is an imprint of the Taylor & Francis Group, an informa business

British Library Cataloguing in Publication Data
A catalogue record for this book is available from the British Library

Library of Congress Cataloging in Publication Data
The Routledge handbook of language testing / edited by Glenn Fulcher and Fred Davidson.
  p. cm.
Includes bibliographical references and index.
1. Language and languages–Ability testing. I. Fulcher, Glenn. II. Davidson, Fred.
P53.4.R68 2011
418.0028'7–dc23
          2011019617

ISBN: 978-0-415-57063-3 (hbk)
ISBN: 978-0-203-18128-7 (ebk)

Typeset in Times New Roman
by Taylor & Francis Books

Printed and bound in Great Britain by
CPI Group (UK) Ltd, Croydon, CR0 4YY

Contents

Contents

Contents

Illustrations

Tables

Figures

Box

Contributors

Jamal Abedi is a Professor at the School of Education of the University of California, Davis, and a research partner at the National Center for Research on Evaluation, Standards, and Student Testing. His research interests include accommodations and classification for English language learners, and comparability of alternate assessments for students with significant cognitive disabilities.

Marta Antón is Associate Professor of Spanish at Indiana University–Purdue University Indianapolis and Research Fellow at the Indiana Center for Intercultural Communication. She has published on classroom interaction, sociocultural theory, dynamic assessment and Spanish sociolinguistics.

Annie Brown is a Principal Research Fellow with the Australian Council for Educational Research. Her research interests include rater and interlocutor behaviour and the assessment of oral proficiency

James Dean (J.D.) Brown, Professor and Chair in the Department of Second Language Studies at the University of Hawai'i at Manoa, has worked in places ranging from Brazil to Yugoslavia, and has published numerous articles and books on language testing, curriculum design, and research methods.

Carol A. Chapelle is Distinguished Professor in Liberal Arts and Sciences at Iowa State University, where she teaches courses in applied linguistics. She is author of books on technology for language learning and assessment.

Andrew D. Cohen is Professor of Second Language Studies at the University of Minnesota. His research interests are in language learner strategies, language assessment, pragmatics, and research methods.

Alan Davies is Emeritus Professor of Applied Linguistics at the University of Edinburgh. His research interests include language proficiency testing; language testing as a research methodology; the role of ethics in applied linguistics and language testing; and the native speaker construct.

Gene B. Halleck is Professor of Linguistics/TESL at Oklahoma State University. She has designed a set of diagnostic tests, the Oral Proficiency Tests for Aviation, to accompany an aviation English curriculum designed for the US Federal Aviation Administration.

Angela Hasselgreen is Professor of Language Didactics at Bergen University College, Faculty for Teacher training, Norway. She has carried out research and published extensively on the subject of assessing young language learners.

Thom Hudson is Professor of Second Language Studies at the University of Hawai'i. His research has concentrated on second language reading, testing, language for specific purposes, and program development.

Eunice Eunhee Jang is Associate Professor at Ontario Institute for Studies in Education, University of Toronto. Her research areas include diagnostic assessment for improving English language learners' English development, validation of English proficiency descriptors-based assessment for K-12 English language learners, evaluation of school effectiveness in challenging circumstances, and fairness issues.

Neil Jones is currently Director of the European Survey on Language Competences within the Research and Validation Unit at the University of Cambridge, ESOL Examinations. His interests include applying IRT to item banking, analysis and computer-adaptive testing, formative assessment, scaling, and cross-language equating and standard-setting within multilingual proficiency frameworks.

Michael Kane holds the Samuel J. Messick Chair in Validity at Educational Testing Service in Princeton, NJ. His main research interests are in validity theory and practice, in test score precision and errors of measurement, in differential performance and bias across racial/ethnic and other groups, and in standard setting.

Dorry M. Kenyon, Vice-President and Director of the Language Testing Division at the Center for Applied Linguistics in Washington, DC, is particularly interested in the application of new technologies to the development and delivery of content and language assessments.

Antony John Kunnan is a Professor of Education at California State University, Los Angeles and Honorary Professor of Education at the University of Hong Kong. His interests include test fairness, test evaluation, structural equation modelling, differential item functioning, and language requirements for immigration and citizenship.

David MacGregor is Manager of the Academic Language Testing Research and Development Team at the Center for Applied Linguistics. His research interests include exploring the construct of academic language and applications of cognitive linguistics to language testing.

Robert J. Mislevy is Professor of Measurement, Statistics and Evaluation and Affiliated Professor of Second Language Acquisition at the University of Maryland at College Park. His research applies developments in psychology, statistics, and technology to practical problems in educational assessment.

Carol Lynn Moder is Professor of Linguistics/TESL at Oklahoma State University. She has designed aviation English assessments for the International Training Division of the US Federal Aviation Administration and for Ordinate Corporation. She served as a consultant to the International Civil Aviation Organization in 2005.

Susan Nissan is a Director of English Language Learning Assessments at Educational Testing Service. Her current research interests include assessing listening, the use of corpora in assessment and standard setting.

Gary J. Ockey is Director of Assessment in the English Language Institute at Kanda University of International Studies in Chiba, Japan. He has published numerous theoretical and quantitative articles in the field of language assessment.

John W. Oller, Jr. is the University of Louisiana Hawthorne Regents Professor IV. His current research focuses on communication disorders attributable to disrupted biological and social control systems from genetics to human languages.

Lia Plakans is Assistant Professor in Foreign Language/ESL Education at the University of Iowa. Her research focuses on assessing integrated skills and connections in L2 reading and writing, language planning and policy, and second language learning.

John Read is an Associate Professor in Applied Language Studies at the University of Auckland, New Zealand. His research interests are in vocabulary assessment and the testing of English for academic and professional purposes.

Steven J. Ross is Professor of Second Language Acquisition at the University of Maryland's School of Language, Literature and Culture. His research interests are focused on assessment of language proficiency and performance, and how assessment methods provide the evidential basis for models of instructed and naturalistic second language acquisition.

Nick Saville is Director of Research and Validation at the University of Cambridge, ESOL Examinations. His research includes the development of Reference Level Descriptions for English to supplement the Common European Framework of Reference (CEFR) and language assessment in the context of migration.

Yasuyo Sawaki is Associate Professor of foreign language education and applied linguistics at Waseda University in Tokyo, Japan. She has research interests in diverse topics in second/foreign language assessment including test validation, diagnosing language ability, test preparation, and using technology in language assessment.

Mary Schedl is a Second Language Test Specialist at Educational Testing Service. Her current research interests include assessing reading comprehension, especially the interrelationship of specific text characteristics and item difficulty.

Rob Schoonen is Associate Professor of Second Language Acquisition at the University of Amsterdam. His main research interests are second and foreign language acquisition, models of language proficiency, language testing and research methodology.

Dong-il Shin is Professor in the Department of English Language and Literature at Chung-Ang University, Seoul, South Korea. His research interests include test development and validation, the interfaces between language testing and other academic disciplines, and the social dimensions of English language assessment in South Korea.

Bernard Spolsky is Professor emeritus in the English Department at Bar-Ilan University. He has published widely in applied linguistics, with a focus on language assessment, language policy and language management.

Carolyn E. Turner is Associate Professor in the Department of Integrated Studies in Education, McGill University. Her main focus and commitment is language testing/assessment within educational settings.

Dianne Wall teaches language testing at Lancaster University (UK), and is Head of Research at Trinity College London examinations board. She specialises in language test construction and evaluation, and the use of innovation theory to study the washback and impact of new tests.

F. Scott Walters teaches L2 assessment at Southern Connecticut State University. His research involves L2 pragmatics testing, conversation analysis and assessment-literacy development.

Xiaoming Xi is a Senior Research Scientist in Educational Testing Service. Her areas of interest include factors affecting performance on speaking tests, issues related to speech scoring, automated scoring of speech, and validity and fairness issues in the broader context of test use.

Chengbin Yin specializes in Second and Foreign Language Education at the University of Maryland at College Park. Her current research focuses on assessment design from a sociocognitive/interactionist perspective and measurement models in educational assessment.

Richard F. Young is Professor of English at the University of Wisconsin-Madison. His research is concerned with the relationship between language and social context, with a particular focus on variation in interlanguage, morphology, talking and testing, language and interaction, and discursive practices in language teaching and learning.

Introduction

Glenn Fulcher and Fred Davidson

Introduction

An understanding of language testing is critical for applied linguists and language teachers. In the early 1980s Alan Davies declared: ' ... language testing has come of age and is now regarded as providing a methodology that is of value throughout applied linguistics and perhaps in core linguistics too' (Davies, 1982: 152). A failure to design or select appropriate instruments threatens the validity of research throughout applied linguistics and second language acquisition (Chapelle, 1994, 1999; Read and Chapelle, 2001). Furthermore, careful construct definition followed by the construction and validation of methodologies to collect data aid innovation in research (e.g. Svalberg, 2009). Language testing is intimately concerned with Validation theory, and so helps researchers to focus on making explicit claims about the meaning of test scores, and the rationales and evidence that can be brought to bear upon the evaluation of these claims. This further strengthens the core values of language testing researchers and practitioners.

It is also crucial for teachers to be able to assess the usefulness of tests that their students may wish to take. Selecting the most appropriate test may be a motivational factor in learning, and preparing learners for tests has been a widespread practice for as long as there have been tests (Latham, 1877: 5–8). There is a danger in using retired test forms as a means of teaching. If learners are to be well served by tests in the ways described in Part II of this volume, and if classroom and dynamic assessment (see Antón) is to play a transformative role in learning, language testing and assessment must be given a more prominent position in teacher training.

As well as its central role in research and learning, the use of language testing in the wider world has become endemic. On the one hand, language tests may be used to protect the public, as in the case of ensuring pilots and air traffic controllers can communicate effectively in English (see Moder and Halleck); on the other they may be used as part of governmental immigration asylum policy (see Kunnan). It is also the responsibility of test providers and researchers to inform test users of the limitations and dangers of the proposed uses, as discussed by contributors such as Davies and Spolsky.

As Davies (1997; this volume) argues, it is the normative role of large-scale language testing that has led to the requirement for a code of ethics and guidelines for practice that establish a professional morality, or the contract that the language testing profession has with the public.

We feel this code should extend to all forms of language assessment. Although it is a profession, language testing is still a young discipline. With the professionalization of language testing has come a growing interest in its history, and the philosophy and principles that underpin practice (Spolsky, 1995; Fulcher, 2010). Young disciplines have a short collective memory, which means that researchers fail to replicate, and do not build upon what is known. This is often exacerbated by postmodern beliefs in the local, temporal nature of co-constructed knowledge. Postmodernism does not cohabit easily with language testing, which by its very nature makes an assumption that knowledge, skills or abilities are stable and can be 'measured' or 'assessed'. It does this in the full knowledge that there is error and uncertainty, and wishes to make the extent of the error and uncertainty transparent. But that does not detract from the fundamentally empirical approach that lies at the heart of a social science that is based on measurement theory as well as language theory.

Finally, we should recall a longstanding argument in favour of normative assessment: to introduce meritocracy to decision making, where otherwise the opportunities and advantages the world has to offer would be distributed according to other criteria such as birth or socioeconomic class, to mention but two. The meritocratic motivation is what Spolsky (1995: 16–24) refers to as the 'Chinese Principle' (Miyazaki, 1981), which resonates with reforms in society and education in Britain during the nineteenth century (Roach, 1971), and subsequently exported around the world. Thus, despite its scientific foundations, like all educational assessment, language testing is fundamentally concerned with social and distributive justice (Rawls, 2001). Its methods may involve quantification, but its goals and motivations are thoroughly human.

Part I: Validity

In this volume we have decided to place the discussion of validity and validation in the very first part, because it remains the central concept to all design and research activity in language testing. Purpose-driven research is required to identify and investigate the evidence needed to build a suitable assessment from which the scores may be interpreted with relevance to intended decisions.

Chapter 1: Conceptions of validity, Carol Chapelle, Iowa State University

In the first chapter of this volume Chapelle provides an historical overview and incisive critique of the concept of validity, and outlines four approaches to examining validation. Arguably, all research in language testing is in some senses about validity and the process of validation. Yet, the concept is slippery and has come to mean very different things for different authors. There are also different validity frameworks in which the scope of the concept is either very limited to technical test design issues, or expansive, including issues of language test use and impact upon institutions and society. Chapelle approaches this complex topic by asking the central question of how we can know what a test score means, and what it can be used for. The claims that we make in these regards, and the evidence that is presented in support of an argument for the claims, is at the heart of the validation process, irrespective of the different epistemologies that are fiercely argued over, alongside the vexed question of the ontological status of our constructs.

Chapter 2: Articulating a validity argument, Michael Kane, Educational Testing Service, NJ

The notion of the interpretive argument and its role in preparing a case for the nature of validity claims is expounded by Kane in this second chapter. He demonstrates how an interpretive argument can be constructed with reference to an illustration from the language assessment literature, and shows that it is evaluated in a validity argument that examines the 'coherence and the plausibility of its inferences and assumptions'. The approach is based firmly in the approach to the development of substantive inferences found in Toulmin (1958; 2003), and which have now become a fundamental tool in thinking about validation. Kane stands firmly in the tradition of Messick (1989), arguing that we validate interpretations of scores rather than the scores themselves, thus placing himself in what Chapelle terms the 'interactionalist' approach. The methodology outlined by Kane provides a flexible framework within which to set out and pursue a validation research agenda. The advantages of the approach, as Haertel (1999: 6) points out, are numerous. First, it avoids the more traditional 'checklist' approach to research (Iwashita *et al.*, 2001) encouraged by hierarchical models that require attention to each heading in a list. Second, it is more resource friendly, as research is directed at potential problems with a specific interpretive argument. Third, because it must take account of rebuttals to claims, it is less inclined to be used to generate only confirmatory evidence, which is always sought by examination boards as a matter of preference. We also note that less flexible checklist approaches tend to lead to claims of validity on grounds that have little to do with test purpose and explicit target domain-related claims of score meaning, such as 'all indirect tests are invalid as they do not replicate the cognitive processes inherent in face-to-face communication'. Kane's approach avoids such over-simplistic interpretations of validation.

Chapter 3: Validity issues in designing accommodations, Jamal Abedi, University of California

The final chapter in this part, by Abedi, deals with accommodations to tests and assessments, which can be defined as changes or alterations to the test in order to compensate a test taker for some disadvantage that they face. These accommodations may compensate for a disability such as a hearing or sight impediment, or in the case of language learners taking content tests (e.g. mathematics or history), provide them with access to the material without language ability impacting on the test score. It is arguably the case that this is where validity theory meets practice head on. The reason is that any accommodation should reduce the impact of construct-irrelevant factors (the disability, or taking the test in a second language) so that the score reflects ability on the construct; yet, if the accommodation alters the definition of the construct, as would be the case if a text in a reading comprehension were read aloud to a blind test taker, validity would be compromised. Second, if the accommodation would raise the scores of test takers who would not normally be eligible for an accommodation, questions may be raised regarding the 'fairness' of the practice. This may be the case with allowing additional time to dyslexics, for example. In some countries, notably the United States, assessment practices in this area are increasingly regulated by equality legislation. Abedi guides us through the validity and legal issues, providing guidance on best practice as well as practical advice on the critical research needed in these areas. The discussion is set within the context of providing accommodations to learners of English with regard to content assessments, but the principles are generalizable to other contexts and problems.

Part II: Classroom assessment and washback

In addition to educational access, labour mobility and employment, language tests are also used to inform teaching, to aid learning, and to diagnose areas where improvement is needed or help required. In this part we have five chapters that represent the diversity of research and test use for these purposes, which also includes a discussion of how assessments can be used to aid and encourage the language development of young learners.

Chapter 4: Classroom assessment, Carolyn Turner, McGill University

In the first chapter of this part, Carolyn Turner argues that far from being an offshoot of traditional normative testing, classroom-based assessment (CBA) should be viewed as an alternative paradigm. There is a question mark over whether the approaches to validity discussed in the first part, and the measurement issues discussed in Part VII, are useful, appropriate, or even relevant, to CBA. Turner recognizes that there is no clear research agenda in a field that is only just beginning to find its feet, despite the research that has built on the pioneering work of Black and Wiliam (1998), which arguably set the ball rolling. It is also argued that a socio-cultural and constructivist approach to learning has also encouraged the evolution of the separate paradigm. However, we live in a state of flux. There is disagreement over issues like the terminology to be used in CBA investigations, and even the purpose of CBA (whether it is to encourage classroom learning, or to record achievement against externally imposed standards). Nevertheless, there is a central concern of CBA research: does the practice of CBA lead to improved learning? This implies an ever-closer relationship with second language acquisition theory, as well as the development of assessment practices that are unique to CBA, and alien to the normative context of the high stakes test.

Chapter 5: Washback, Dianne Wall, Lancaster University

Alderson and Wall (1993) provided (arguably) the first overarching problem statement about the influence of language tests on educational practice. They wrote a seminal paper with a titular question: 'Does washback exist?' The name of the phenomenon—washback—was in use previously, but it was in the early 1990s that serious research attention first arose. In an articulate and informative chapter, Dianne Wall returns to that topic, or, more accurately, she narrates the intervening decades, for she has been closely involved with washback research ever since. Interesting conclusions emerge. First, it is clear that the influence of a language test is not a solitary factor in any form of change. Phenomena like teacher attitudes and beliefs consistently impact research findings on washback. Second, Wall voices a very real frustration that most so-called washback studies are unique and highly contextualized to a given test and its setting; perhaps, as she notes, this is because of the pressure to publish original research. She joins a call for replication, and perhaps this is the one topic in our book most needing that fundamental empirical approach. As Wall notes, there is a problem of linkage among all the various washback research projects that have emerged in the intervening years. The chapter thus provides a fitting reflection to the seminal 1993 paper, so many years later. Maybe the question today should be: 'Yes, it exists, but is washback a theory?'

Chapter 6: Assessing young learners, Angela Hasselgreen, Bergen University College

Perhaps the most powerful statement in this comprehensive chapter comes near the end. The clear question is: how can we improve practices of the assessment of young language learners (YLLs)? Hasselgreen concludes that the first and best step our field can take is to better equip classroom teachers as assessors. Hasselgreen carefully describes variation in YLL testing, from nation to nation. She outlines how the Common European Framework of Reference (CEFR) is influencing YLL testing in Europe, even though its adaptation from adult to younger learners is presumptive. She presents several insights about YLL testing in Norway. She also covers the explosion of YLL testing in the United States in the wake of the 2002 No Child Left Behind legislation.

Chapter 7: Dynamic assessment, Marta Antón, Indiana University-Purdue University at Indianapolis

It is noteworthy that this chapter is the only one to discuss a particular testing technique. We have no chapter on multiple-choice item design, on the structure of an oral interview or on the crafting of essay prompts. The reason is simple: dynamic assessment (DA) is both a suite of techniques and an entire philosophical platform on which language assessments can be reconceived in a very fundamental way. Founded in the work of Vygotsky (1978, *inter alia*), it views testing as part of the growth potential of the learner, not divorced from it. How-to references exist (e.g. Poehner, 2008), and Antón's chapter provides an overview of DA with technical advice, as well. What is far more important—and intriguing—is her treatment of the fundamental philosophical distinctions between this approach and the norm of non-dynamic testing. DA looks at learners under a simple but profound assumption: the most valid measurement is when others intervene in it, when the testing not only acknowledges its fundamental social context (see Young, this volume) but welcomes it and tries to activate and to describe it. We share Antón's closing concerns about promoting DA to a wider user base, and she, in turn, readily acknowledges those criticisms are shared by many others, as well. What will *not* work is to standardize DA, for that would rob it of its very strengths.

Chapter 8: Diagnostic assessment in Language Classrooms, Eunice Jang, University of Toronto

As Eunice Jang makes very clear in this readable and comprehensive chapter, there is a great desire to create educational assessments that provide diagnostic information, which is something that Oller (this volume) is striving for in a clinical setting. Research in language testing has an historical interest in diagnosis, both in a technical and methodological sense (e.g. Buck and Tatsuoka, 1998; Jang, 2009) and in a more general manner, e.g. with regard to the granularity of test specifications (e.g. Davidson and Lynch, 2002: 53–57). Seamlessly, Jang tours both the technical and the theoretical; this is a chapter both about tools and about philosophy. There is a resonant hope voiced by the diagnosticians among us: if we continue to engage test takers' 'deep thinking processes', then we can provide better score reports that are valued by those test takers, as well as valuable to test score users. This chapter has a sense of mission, one with which we are in complete agreement.

Part III: The social uses of language testing

For the public the most obvious use of language tests is in making a variety of high-stakes decisions, many of which are frequently discussed in the popular press. These uses of language tests are designed to protect the public from the potential harm that may be caused through an inability to communicate, as when (for example) an industry (e.g. aviation) wishes to ensure that its staff (e.g. pilots and controllers) are proficient in the agreed-upon language of use (for aviation, English). Language testing is also used in clinical settings to determine the extent of communication disorders, or rather the level of remaining communicative ability as a result of illness. In these cases there is universal agreement that language testing is beneficial. However, when they are used to determine international mobility, or used to make immigration decisions and award citizenship, there is a great deal of controversy, particularly with regard to the ethics of such practices. The chapters in this part deal with all these issues in expert detail, concluding with the chapter by Young that takes an overview of the role of tests in society.

Chapter 9: Designing language tests for specific social uses, Carol Moder and Gene Halleck, Oklahoma State University

A great deal of language testing is conducted to make specific decisions about the ability of individuals to communicate successfully in workplace environments. This is the case with the assessment of medical and legal language, for example. The stakes are particularly high when assessing aviation English, where the consequences of allowing an air traffic controller or pilot to practice without the necessary language and communication skills to do so safely are potentially catastrophic. In this chapter Moder and Halleck dissect the issues surrounding such high-stakes tests with specific reference to assessment in aviation. A thorough analysis of the target domain is essential for the language tester to design instruments that adequately sample from it, and that do not produce scores that under-represent the full range of communicative acts that test takers will be required to use in the real world. Furthermore, the language testers are working in a political environment where they must negotiate the sensitivities of the various stakeholders that make up the International Civil Aviation Organizaton (ICAO) while maintaining the highest possible standards of test design and implementation. Critically, the chapter shows clearly why general English tests should not be used to assess workplace competence in high-stakes contexts.

Chapter 10: Language assessment for communication disorders, John Oller, University of Louisiana at Lafayette

John Oller's contribution to this section provides us with a unique insight into a branch of language assessment that rarely appears in the mainstream language testing literature, despite our interest in providing test accommodations for learners with a range of disabilities. Communication disorders, we are told, have a long-lasting impact on a person's ability to communicate, which can include mild conditions or very serious cases of autism. Oller is concerned with how language tests can help identify communication disorders so that appropriate treatments may be applied or developed. In order to do this the chapter classifies the range of disorders that have been identified to date, considers causal factors and attempts to identify the scale of their effect. Throughout the chapter there is a consistent positive message for both identification and treatment, which is that ' … success is informative while failure, in general, tells next to nothing'. There are implications for both norm and criterion referenced approaches to test development for clinical purpose, as well as developing measures of comparison groups which are necessary to establish the levels of communicative ability that individuals retain. The clinical potential of language testing is surely an area where consequential outcomes may inform treatment, and be of significant benefit to the test takers.

Chapter 11: Language assessment for immigration and citizenship, Antony Kunnan, California State University

Of necessity well explained at the outset, Antony Kunnan has written a chapter that departs from the domain of language testing. He reasons that we cannot understand how language tests are used for political, national and transnational purposes without first exploring the dynamics of those purposes. Therefore, his chapter presents an overview of human migration, citizenship policies, and the historical changes and tensions that have shaped them. Then and only then can he explore how language testing has joined with these phenomena. Kunnan's treatment is both technical and dense as well as critical and provocative, but he ends on a note of hope. To adapt the famous quote from Dr King, Kunnan hopes for a time when all people are granted social privilege not by the language that we speak but by the content of our character. We share that hope.

Chapter 12: Social dimensions of language testing, Richard Young, University of Wisconsin-Madison

'Power is everything', said John Aaron (played by Loren Dean in the film *Apollo 13*). It is easy to say that tests function in a society, and that society is about power, and that power is everything. We have characterized that as a 'counsel of despair' (Fulcher and Davidson, 2007: 158). Richard Young seems to agree, as he takes us on a complex and masterful tour of how tests function in society. The chapter moves seamlessly from linguistic theory of discourse to discussion of language varieties to questions of test use and normative thought. He ends with three speculations about the near future: one about data (there will be a lot of it and it will be hard to handle), one about the English language (its varieties will continue to grow), and one about ethics (we will have them, but will anybody really listen?). 'Remember Red, hope is a good thing, maybe the best of things, and no good thing ever dies', said Andy Dufresne (played by Tim Robbins in the film *The Shawshank Redemption*). Power, when rightly managed, got that errant moon shot back home safely. It *is* everything—and as the social fabric of language testing unfolds in the coming years, let us all listen to rather than ignore the ethical challenges that face us. This chapter is a superb launch for our powerful and hopeful attention.

Part IV: Test specifications

Test specifications are the design documents of tests. Their form and evolution constitutes the history of the decisions made in the test design process, and the reasons for those decisions. As such, they form a critical component of an interpretive argument (see Kane, this volume). This part asks readers to pause and consider the basic creative engines of all language test development: the generative templates by which items and tasks are built. In so doing, we hope these papers (also) join in the growing call to turn the lens of language testing research onto the people who write tests.

Chapter 13: Test specifications and criterion referenced assessment, Fred Davidson, University of Illinois at Urbana-Champaign

Test specifications are the 'blueprints' or design documents of tests, and are therefore a fundamental part of all approaches to test development. They are also a centre piece of any validity argument that wishes to show that test effect and test purpose were considered in the earliest stages of development. They therefore play a critical role as an audit trail of decisions made while building the test, and the reasons for those decisions. Davidson sets his discussion of test specifications against the backdrop of criterion-referenced tests and their legacy of reporting detailed information about what test takers can do. However, they are also used in norm-referenced testing as well; as Davidson reminds us, it is not feasible to produce hundreds (or thousands) of parallel items to populate multiple forms of a large-scale test without these 'generative blueprints', which metaphorically act as the mould to produce the machine parts. Davidson illustrates the use of 'specs' as a central tool in test design and production, highlighting the iterative nature of their consensual evolution as we learn more about the nature of what we wish to test, and how best to do it.

Chapter 14: Evidence-centered design in language testing, Robert Mislevy, University of Maryland, and Chengbin Yin, Center for Applied Linguistics

Evidence-centered design (ECD) is, as the authors say, 'a conceptual framework for the design and delivery of educational assessments'. At the heart of the framework is the requirement to provide evidence for design decisions that supports the claims to be made about score meaning. It is not surprising that ECD has been used in conjunction with an argument-based approach to validation, as described by Kane (this volume), that the two are often presented as 'part of a package' (Fulcher and Davidson, 2007) and used in tandem in practical test development (Chapelle *et al.*, 2008). This chapter explains the key principles, components and operations of ECD. Like all argument-centred approaches it is flexible enough to be applied to many kinds of educational assessments as well as language tests, avoids a checklist approach and focuses very firmly on the claims that are made for score meaning within explicit statements of test purpose. Indeed, the prior position of domain analysis and the 'central role of context' gives appropriately high priority to test purpose that has been watered down in other frameworks in recent years (see Fulcher *et al.*, 2011 for a discussion). Mislevy and Yin illustrate the possibilities of ECD by reference to a number of test development and design projects that have used the system, and explain how the modular approach results in efficiency through the ability to reuse parts of a design. ECD, like the argument-based approaches with which it is allied, is a flexible tool that holds significant possibilities for future development in the design of language tests that take validity into account from the earliest planning phases through implementation, and beyond.

Chapter 15: Claims, evidence, and inference in performance assessment, Steven Ross, University of Maryland

In Chapter 15 Ross discusses the issues facing performance assessment in the context of theories of validation as argument, involving claims and evidence as outlined in Kane and in Mislevy and Chengbin Yin (this volume). Tests of performance inevitably involve undertaking tasks that are modelled on some communicative activity in the real world, and thus introduce into the testing context a number of problems. Ross investigates issues of domain analysis for performance tests, assessing task difficulty and establishing usable criteria for rating task-based performances (also see Annie Brown, this volume). The chapter illustrates the issues at stake with regard to speaking tests, and the oral proficiency interview (OPI) in particular. A validity argument is outlined and critiqued with reference to a sample performance on a role play task. The chapter concludes with a look into the future of performance testing and assesses what might be required to make automated assessment more feasible.

Part V: Writing items and tasks

In educational institutions across the world directors and head teachers expect their staff to write tests and assessments at short notice, and usually with few resources. The three chapters in this part reveal the complex issues that item writers face, both practical and theoretical. There is also consideration of how test takers respond to items. Item writers assume that test takers' responses are indicative of the constructs they intend to measure, but this may not always be the case.

Chapter 16: Item writing and writers, Dong-il Shin, Chung-Ang University, South Korea

In a pithy and provocative chapter, Shin unpacks what is often seen as a straightforward part of language testing: writing items and tasks. He develops four historically motivated schools of item writing: psychometric, systematic, authentic and critical. The chapter stays true to its title, because Shin examines the real world of item writers: often undertrained, often underpaid, often over-worked, these souls who drive test construction may or may not be doing what test development supervisors think that they are doing. This chapter is a critical reality check on item writing, and it should serve both as a trigger and as a roadmap for a nascent but growing (e.g. Kim *et al.*, 2010) research question: just how do language tests actually get created?

Chapter 17: Writing integrated items, Lia Plakans, University of Iowa

For a long time it has been argued that skills should be tested in isolation so that scores are not contaminated. By 'contamination' the critics meant (for example) that an ability to read should not cause a score on a speaking or writing test to vary. Recently, however, there has been a renewed interest in integrated items. The rationale is that such items more precisely reflect the kinds of holistic tasks that are undertaken in the 'real world'. Students do not simply write essays from prompts. They read texts, listen to lectures, discuss ideas and then come to the writing task. Plakans addresses the issues of complex constructs, how they are operationalized in integrated tasks, and the problems surrounding score interpretation. This is an area that is currently ripe for further research as these task types are being utilized in ever more high-stakes contexts. Her erudite treatment of the topic is well illustrated with new task types from a range of language tests.

Chapter 18: Test-taking strategies and task design, Andrew Cohen, University of Minnesota

Cohen places his discussion of test-taker strategies in a psychometric context. A fundamental question is posed: what is, and what is not construct-relevant variance? If a test taker utilizes particular strategies to handle test items and tasks, how do we know if those are part of the skill set being measured? This powerful thematic question unites the entire chapter, as he returns to it at several key points. Cohen's exploration of strategies is historical, because researchers have been investigating this question for several decades. In careful detail, he charts studies and findings going back some thirty years, synthesizes those findings, and then summarizes them for today's reader. He includes a careful dissection of perhaps the most common strategy research technique: verbal reports. The lists of suggested research topics and advice to test takers at the end of the chapter benefit from this extensive literature review.

Part VI: Prototyping and field tests

Test design and development is in itself a research enterprise. One of the critical questions that test designers ask is: how do I know that the items and tasks that I have designed genuinely elicit responses that are directly related to the meaning I wish the scores to have, and the decisions I wish to make? Extensive trialling can be undertaken before taking the decision to roll out an operational test. The process usually begins with prototyping new items on small groups of people drawn from the target population of test takers. This saves time and resources by discovering at the earliest stages which ideas will not work. Those that do are taken forward to larger-scale trials, and ultimate field tests. The chapters in this part provide a masterly overview both of the processes and the kinds of research questions that arise as a result.

Chapter 19: Prototyping new item types, Susan Nissan and Mary Schedl, Educational Testing Service, NJ

'Prototyping' has frequently been used interchangeably with 'piloting' or 'pre-testing', but is now seen as a phase of pre-operational testing that precedes the larger-scale piloting or pre-testing that serves the purposes outlined in Kenyon and MacGregor (this volume). Nissan and Schedl show that many of the questions facing researchers who are developing new item types, or looking at new delivery systems, can often work with much smaller sample sizes, unless of course it is necessary to have a wide range of abilities (when investigating the suitability of new scoring rubrics, for example). A key word that crops up in the discussion of prototyping is 'viability'. Given a construct definition, how 'viable' is the item or task that has been designed to elicit data that is relevant to that construct, and can it be scored? Furthermore, is it feasible to produce as many of the new items as necessary to create an item pool for large-scale testing programmes? The chapter also brings to our attention the importance of prototyping on samples drawn from a clearly defined population for which the test is designed, as the usefulness of items and scores for decision making quickly erodes if there is a mismatch.

Chapter 20: Pre-operational testing, Dorry Kenyon and David MacGregor, Center for Applied Linguistics, Washington, DC

In this chapter Kenyon and MacGregor bring considerable experience to describing the two essential components of pre-operational testing, which is defined as 'collecting and analysing evidence to support the validity of an assessment *prior* to the assessment's operational use'. This consists of two phases: investigative pilot testing to trial components of the test, followed by field testing, which is a final larger-scale tryout to ensure that everything is working as intended. The discussion is framed within the creation of an assessment use argument (Bachman and Palmer, 2010), and so is couched within a similar philosophical approach adopted by many others in this volume. Further, pre-operational testing is seen as critical to investigating claims made by the test designers in an argument-based approach (Kane, this volume). Kenyon and MacGregor provide a worked example with an academic writing test, linking the kinds of claims made to the studies that might be conducted during pre-operational testing. Along with guidelines for practice, the chapter provides a framework within which language test developers could begin to plan such studies within a carefully planned research agenda.

Chapter 21: Piloting vocabulary tests, John Read, University of Auckland, New Zealand

The final chapter in this part has been given a very deliberate dual focus. On the one hand it is about the practice and process of piloting tests, which is why it appears alongside the chapters by Nissan and Schedl, and Kenyon and MacGregor. It does so using the example of discrete vocabulary testing. We decided on this example because in recent years the assessment of vocabulary has almost achieved the status of a sub-field within language testing. This is partly because stand-alone vocabulary tests are widely used as placement instruments because of their ability to predict many other language abilities such as reading, and because they are used to research how the brain stores lexical items and meaning. It is therefore crucial that these tests are piloted with care, and, as John Read observes, the literature really does not tell us how piloting is carried out. With reference to the word associates format he guides the reader through the process of piloting a vocabulary test in particular, and also provides a generic template for piloting other tests as well.

Part VII: Measurement theory and practice

Language testing brings together two fields: language and measurement. While language testers usually have a major background in one of these areas, it is essential for them to have a good working knowledge of the other. The chapters in this part describe the major measurement models in current use. These models are used to generate scores from responses to items or tasks. Some are purely statistical, while others require human judgement regarding performances on communication tasks. We also expect scores to be reliable; that is, we expect the outcomes of an assessment should be consistent across time, administration, and human raters (Lado, 1961: 330–331), and that we expect the scores are generalizable to a universe of items or tasks that do not appear in a particular test form, but are part of the domain in which we are interested. Arguably this is the most technical area of language testing, and these chapters provide an accessible and comprehensive introduction.

Chapter 22: Classical test theory, J. D. Brown, University of Hawai'i.

Perhaps the oldest psychometric toolkit available to language testing is 'CTT' or 'classical test theory'. As J.D. Brown carefully points out, these tools are not obsolete and, in fact, are only 'classical' in historical comparison to other techniques like IRT (see Ockey's chapter) or G-theory (see Schoonen's chapter). CTT is in widespread and perhaps pervasive use, because it provides test developers a means to carefully monitor the contribution of each test item to the overall test score distribution. Its goal is to improve test reliability and the precision of measurement of the construct of interest. Brown takes care to position his exegesis in the modern era, when he discusses recent advances in validity theory and posits a growing and greater role for content experts and item specifications. Nevertheless, readers of this book will benefit greatly from this succinct unpacking of a 'classical' toolbox.

Chapter 23: Item response theory, Gary Ockey, Kanada University of International Studies

Item-level analysis of language test data continues to be a valuable component of test development and score interpretation. Ockey surveys the dominant modern school of item analysis: item response theory (IRT). The chapter is accessible and can serve easily as an introduction to the topic. Textbooks—some of them classic—exist on this topic, but they are often rather dense and in need of interpretation, even though IRT has influenced general educational measurement for many years (e.g. Lord and Novick, 1968). IRT provides extremely useful and efficient information to test developers, as Ockey illustrates. The chapter provides a sample dataset and gives the basic formulae of the most widespread IRT models: one-, two- and three-parameter. The exposition about the sample dataset is particularly well-suited to explaining the fundamentals of IRT. Ockey shows how a fully articulated three-parameter item analysis is extremely insightful about test data. He also explores the Rasch model, which in both the original form and in its modern multifaceted derivatives has been extremely influential in language testing (McNamara, 1996). At the same time, Ockey reflects on the rather constrained growth of IRT as a tool in language testing, perhaps due to its complexity and, he reckons, certainly due to the slow growth of accessible IRT software.

Chapter 24: Reliability and dependability, Neil Jones, University of Cambridge ESOL

In a measured and comprehensive chapter, Neil Jones explores what is perhaps the oldest notion in psychological and educational testing, including testing of languages: score consistency. This chapter is a very fitting complement to others in the volume (e.g. those by J.D. Brown and by Schoonen) which delve into the techniques of psychometrics. Here, Jones takes a decidedly more philosophical approach. For unidimensional exams (which are very much still the norm), that which the test measures most consistently is its trait. In a carefully worded and nuanced conclusion, he endorses that worldview (precisely because it is the norm of how tests are still constructed); but he still leaves open some doors to creative progress from advances in cognitive models of language ability and in the rendering of those models in language test design (see Jang, this volume). We also see a general reluctance to look beyond them because of many decades of inertia. Beyond are things of intrigue, and there and only there will we see true challenges to the oldest and most dominant concept in all of testing: reliability.

Chapter 25: The generalisability of scores from language tests, Rob Schoonen, University of Amsterdam

Schoonen presents a thorough and detailed introduction to generalisability theory and its tools and techniques. G-theory explores contributions of different sources of variance in language assessment, such as rater, occasion and task. It is a very influential technique, because of its ability to investigate questions of test quality and efficiency (e.g. 'how better would things be if I added more raters?'). The chapter is a sound and readable technical introduction to the topic, and, as such, it balances nicely with both general measurement expositions (e.g. Cronbach *et al.*, 1972; Brennan, 2001) and with applications of the technique to language test settings (e.g. Lee, 2006; Sawaki, 2007). However, the paper is not purely psychometric. Schoonen also delves into deeper methodological and philosophical issues, and in particular, he draws on Deville and Chalhoub-Deville (2006) in an extended discussion of the nature of language test score variability.

Chapter 26: Scoring performance tests, Glenn Fulcher, University of Leicester

Taking an historical and philosophical view on language rating scales, Fulcher presents a close discussion of issues and methods in the crafting of rating scales. The chapter carefully outlines details and techniques of scale development, and in a nuanced manner it presents critical discussion of approaches that have garnered wide attention (such as the extended-binary approach first proposed by Upshur and Turner, 1999). Fulcher also highlights certain tensions in scale development, such as that between scales derived from language performance samples in comparison to scales that exist on the inertia of widespread acceptance (compare, *inter alia*, Fulcher, *et al.*, 2011 with Lowe, 1985; 1986). To Fulcher, it is absolutely essential to see the social and political backdrop for any scale. Life-altering decisions can result, as when the Common European Framework of Reference determines permission to work in a particular country.

Part VIII: Administration and training

This part is concerned with two aspects of language testing that until relatively recently have gone unmentioned in textbooks. The first is the process of test administration, which covers not only the rituals associated with administering the test itself, but also the host of quality assurance and test preparation processes carried out by examining boards and testing agencies. In this category we also include activities related to the training of interlocutors who elicit rateable samples of speech from test takers and raters who make judgements about the quality of speech and writing. The second aspect is the growing use of technology in language testing. It is now more common for tests to be delivered on computer than pen and paper, which presents unique validity and security issues. Then there is the matter of automated scoring. This is not a problem for traditional closed-response items like multiple choice, but is much more hotly debated for the automated scoring of writing and speech.

Chapter 27: Quality management in test production and administration, Nick Saville, University of Cambridge ESOL

In the first chapter of this part Saville brings to the description of quality management systems a great deal of experience in managing and supervising the systems and processes of a large examination board that produces and delivers high-stakes international tests. The most important thing we can learn from his treatment is the fact that good administrative processes are actually a part of a validation argument. Quality management procedures at all stages of the operation remove—or at least limit—the possibility that errors of various kinds might constitute alternative hypotheses for score meaning. While Saville is primarily concerned with large operations there is also much here to be learned by schools and institutions that run their own assessment programmes upon which decisions about students are made.

Chapter 28: Interlocutor and rater training, Annie Brown, Australian Council for Educational Research

As with Saville, Brown begins by placing the practice of training interlocutors for speaking tests, and raters for both speaking and writing tests, within the context of validity. If we are to draw appropriate inferences from scores on performance tests it is essential that all test takers have a similar experience and are scored in the same way. This is where training comes in, but, as Brown notes, it is inevitable that there will be some variability within and between human beings. This can be addressed by automated scoring (see Xi, this volume), but in some contexts human interlocutors and raters are required if the assessment is going to replicate some real-world human encounter or the construct is not going to be under-represented. Brown considers the processes involved in training and investigates what we know about rater and interlocutor variability, and in the process raises key questions about whether variation is seen as pernicious (within a psychometric tradition) or indeed desirable (from a constructivist perspective).

Chapter 29: Technology in language testing, Yasuyo Sawaki, Waseda University, Japan

If there is one area in which language testing seems to change on a daily basis it is in the use of computers, not only for test delivery, but in test design and analysis. Sometimes it seems that whatever we write today is out of date before it gets into the public domain. We are reminded of a quotation from an early review of technology in language testing: 'The memory capacity of most modern delivery systems is evolving rapidly. Most microcomputer workstations now have half to two megabytes of random access memory' (Bunderson et al., 1989: 371). Or even this from an earlier generation of technophiles: ' … we have encountered some cases of mike-fright or similar terror on the part of the examinee upon finding himself face-to-face with the revolving reels and gentle hum of the modern tape recorder' (Stabb, 1955: 235). Sawaki wisely avoids the temptation to focus on the technology itself, and engages instead with the fundamental issues of language testing: whether and to what extent the functionality that computers offer can be utilized to enhance score meaning. She does this with reference to the different types of computer-based tests available, and the contexts in which they are used.

Chapter 30: Validity and the automated scoring of performance tests, Xiaoming Xi, Educational Testing Service, USA

There is no longer any question. It's here. Computer scoring of language performance tests (most notably writing, but also speaking) is widely operational, and for one major test (the Pearson Test of English/Academic), all scoring is by computer. In a wide-ranging chapter with a remarkably detailed historical backdrop, Xiaoming Xi presents a state-of-the-art review. Her overriding theme is that automated scoring should develop a sound basis in test validation. The real challenge at hand is to build sound and standardized validity arguments about the use and impact of automated scoring systems. As she makes quite clear, these arguments will include the most canonical form of evidence: comparison to human raters. However, these arguments will go well beyond that: into studies of acceptance by test users, into studies on 'tricking out' the system, and a host of other pressing agenda items. Her chapter is a very complex and careful endorsement of automated scoring, but more importantly, it ends with a paramount question: how can such research ensure value to its most important target of attention, the all-too-human test users? We agree. Much of this future is here, already. Xi has charted the rest.

Part IX: Ethics and language policy

Like discussions of validity, considerations of ethics and fairness with reference to language policy seem pervasive in the language testing literature, and certainly in many of the chapters of this book. Perhaps this is fitting. Language testers live with ethical decisions on a daily basis and, we believe, are well aware of it. The intended effect of the test in relation to its purpose should drive design decisions from the very start of a test development project: 'The task for the ethical language tester is to look into the future, to picture the effect the test is intended to have, and to structure the test development to achieve that effect' (Fulcher and Davidson, 2007: 144). The four chapters in this part address these issues from a number of different perspectives, bringing new questions and insights to how we create the conditions for 'fairness'.

Chapter 31: Ethical codes and unexpected consequences, Alan Davies, University of Edinburgh

As a point of thematic departure and unity (for a massive topic), Davies explores the concept of ethical codes. These are sets of guidelines issued by a professional organization for its members. The purpose of such guidelines is to assist members in making ethical choices, and in particular, the codes set forth or imply what the correct choices should be. As Davies notes, we have seen a growth of these codes in language testing in recent years from agencies such as ILTA (the International Language Testing Association), EALTA (the European Association for Language Testing and Assessment), JLTA (the Japan Language Testing Association) and ALTE (the Association of Language Testers in Europe). Why that has happened is but one of several deeper questions that Davies explores in the chapter. Perhaps these organizations craft these codes to assuage themselves of some kind of collective worry or, at worst, guilt about possible misuse of tests. This chapter is usefully read alongside that of Kunnan. Together these two chapters unpack how language testing has always been a problem of equitable practice.

Chapter 32: Fairness, F. Scott Walters, Southern Connecticut State University

Walters presents a carefully crafted and closely reasoned treatise on the meaning of the word 'fairness'. He documents several competing definitions, and in particular, he explores Kunnan's (2009) Test Context Framework and the discussion of fairness presented by Xi (2010). The chapter also treats a currently unresolved philosophical question: how is fairness different from validity? He posits that a resolution to that conundrum will surface in the future, and we tend to agree that some kind of rapprochement is feasible. Having one would certainly help everybody. This is a chapter written as an exposition of its central charge—fairness—and so to close the chapter Walters leaves the reader with several carefully constructed thought exercises. As he makes clear, the meaning of the word is evolving. We encourage readers to study this chapter early in their encounter with this book. It sets the stage nicely for a theme found in many other topics: language testing is highly contextualized to each reader's own educational ecology.

Chapter 33: Standards-based testing, Thom Hudson, University of Hawai'i

In language test development and use standards are statements of expected language ability or performance at given levels. They function as foundations for language test development and score interpretation. This seems—at first glance—to be a very commonsense idea. As Thom Hudson shows, it is not. There are multiple (perhaps competing) documents that purport to show language standards. These are evolving and continue to evolve. The origin of standards is also at question, and Hudson shows how two major standards documents came from rather different origins: the Common European Framework of Reference (CEFR) and the American Council on the Teaching of Foreign Language (ACTFL)/Foreign Service Institute (FSI). The chapter contains multiple detailed examples from various standards, and so in addition to being a very readable and comprehensive overview of the topic, it could serve as the catalyst for discussion among readers of this book; for example, a reader could ponder exactly what the following claim means and how to develop tests that assess it: 'Begin to speak with a few words or sentences by using a few standard English grammatical forms and sounds (e.g. single words or phrases)' (California Department of Education, 1999). How does one assess that a learner can 'begin to' perform language? This fascinating chapter is but the tip of a critical iceberg.

Chapter 34: Language testing and language management, Bernard Spolsky, Bar-Ilan University, Israel

The final chapter in the book may at first glance appear to offer a rather pessimistic conclusion, with its discussion of the use of tests in language management, and to achieve policy ends for which language tests are unsuitable. It concludes with a warning against test misuse. But this is not really as negative as it might appear. Our awareness of the social and policy issues that surround testing has been growing since Messick (1989) placed the consequences of test use firmly within validity theory. The use of tests has an impact on individuals, institutions and society (McNamara and Roever, 2006); and they are used for political ends within policy contexts (Fulcher, 2009; this volume). It is this awareness that leads to theories of ethical test practice (see Davies, 1997; this volume), and therefore to an increasing professionalization of language testing. It is also part of the call for the continuous examination of what we do with language tests to ensure that we are benefitting all stakeholders, rather than causing harm (Shohamy, 2001: 161).

Conclusion

The chapters in this volume constitute state-of-the-art coverage of all the critical issues facing everyone who is engaged in language testing and assessment today. It is relevant to academic language testers, to those who work for testing agencies and teachers who have to create their own classroom tests and prepare their learners to take large-scale tests. We also think that it is relevant to other stakeholders, and policy makers in particular.

The breadth of topics covered is unique, but also benefits from depth of analysis. The reader will note, however, that in these chapters different voices emerge. This is to be expected, and it is indeed healthy. There is much in the theory and practice of language testing that is not settled, despite wide areas of agreement. As editors we have not attempted to change these voices, even where our own approach may have been somewhat different. This is because we agree with J. S. Mill (1859: 24–26) that the only path to knowledge and progress is through discussion and the testing of different points of view. Discussion, experience, the advancement of theory, and empirical research, lead us to the point at which we admit that ' … there is no such thing as absolute certainty … [but] there is assurance sufficient for the purposes of human life.'

References

Alderson, J. C. and Wall, D. (1993). Does washback exist? *Applied Linguistics* 14: 115–29.

Bachman, L. F. and Palmer, A. S. (2010). *Language Assessment in Practice*. Oxford, UK: Oxford University Press.

Black, P. and Wiliam, D. (1998). Inside the black box: raising standards through classroom assessment. *Phi Delta Kappan* 80: 139–48.

Brennan, R. L. (2001). *Generalizability Theory*. New York, NY: Springer.

Buck, G. and Tatsuoka, K. (1998). Application of the rule-space procedure to language testing: examining attributes of a free response listening test. *Language Testing* 15: 119–57.

Bunderson, C. V., Inouye, D. K. and Olsen, J. B. (1989). The four generations of computerized educational measurement. In R. L. Linn (ed.), *Educational Measurement*, 3rd edn. London, UK: Collier Macmillan, 367–407.

California Department of Education (CDE) (1999). *English-language development standards for California Public Schools: kindergarten through grade twelve*. [Listening and Speaking, Beginning Level.] www.cde.ca.gov/be/st/ss/documents/englangdevstnd.pdf (accessed 23/4/10).

Chapelle, C. A. (1994). Are c-tests valid measures for L2 vocabulary research? *Second Language Research* 10: 157–87.

—— (1999). Construct definition and validity inquiry in SLA research. In Bachman, L. and Cohen, A. (eds), *Interfaces between Second Language Acquisition and Language Testing Research*. Cambridge, UK: Cambridge University Press.

Chapelle, C. A., Enright, M. K. and Jamieson, J. M. (eds), (2008). *Building a Validity Argument for the Test of English as a Foreign Language*. New York, NY: Routledge.

Cronbach, L. J., Gleser, G. C., Nanda, H. and Rajaratnam, N. (1972). *The Dependability of Behavioral Measurements: theory of generalizability for scores and profiles*. New York, NY: John Wiley & Sons, Inc.

Davidson, F. and Lynch, B. K. (2002). *Testcraft: a Teacher's Guide to Writing and Using Language Test Specifications*. London, UK: Yale University Press.

Davies, A. (1982). Language testing 2. In Kinsella, A. (ed.), *Surveys 1: eight state-of-the-art articles on key areas in language teaching*. Cambridge, UK: University of Cambridge Press, 141–159.

—— (1997). Demands of being professional in language testing. *Language Testing* 14: 328–39.

Deville, C. and Chalhoub-Deville, M. (2006). Old and new thoughts on test score variability: Implications for reliability and validity. In Chalhoub-Deville, M., Chapelle, C. A. and Duff, P. (eds), *Inference and Generalizability in Applied Linguistics. Multiple perspectives*. Amsterdam, The Netherlands: John Benjamins Publishing Company, 9–25.

Fulcher, G. (2009). Test use and political philosophy. *Annual Review of Applied Linguistics* 29: 3–20.

—— (2010). *Practical Language Testing*. London, UK: Hodder Education.

Fulcher, G. and Davidson, F. (2007). *Language Testing and Assessment: an advanced resource book*. London, UK: Routledge.

Fulcher, G., Davidson, F., and Kemp, J. (2011). Effective rating scale design: performance decision trees. *Language Testing* 28: 5–29.

Haertel, E. H. (1999). Validity arguments for high-stakes testing: in search of the evidence. *Educational Measurement: Issues and Practice* 18: 5–9.

Iwashita, N., McNamara, T. and Elder, C. (2001). Can we predict task difficulty in an oral proficiency test? Exploring the potential of an information processing approach to task design. *Language Learning* 51: 401–36.

Jang, E. E. (2009). Cognitive diagnostic assessment of L2 reading comprehension ability: Validity arguments for applying Fusion Model to LanguEdge assessment. *Language Testing* 26: 31–73.

Kim, J., Chi, Y., Huensch, A., Jun, H., Li, H. and Roullion, V. (2010). A case study on an item writing process: Use of test specifications, nature of group dynamics, and individual item writer's characteristics. *Language Assessment Quarterly* 7: 160–74.

Kunnan, A. J. (2009). Testing for citizenship: the U.S. naturalization test. *Language Assessment Quarterly* 6: 89–97.

Lado, R. (1961). *Language Testing*. London, UK: Longman.

Latham, H. (1877). *On the Action of Examinations Considered as a Means of Selection*. Cambridge, UK: Dighton, Bell and Company.

Lee, Y.-W. (2006). Dependability of scores for a new ESL speaking assessment consisting of integrated and independent tasks. *Language Testing* 23: 131–66.

Lord, F. M., and Novick, M. (1968). *Statistical Theories of Mental Test Scores*. Reading, MA: Addison-Wesley.

Lowe, P. (1985). The ILR proficiency scale as a synthesizing research principle: The view from the mountain. In James, C. J. (ed.), *Foreign Language Proficiency in the Classroom and Beyond*. Lincolnwood, IL: National Textbook Company, 9–53.

—— (1986). Proficiency: panacea, framework, process? A reply to Kramsch, Schulz, and particularly Bachman and Savignon. *Modern Language Journal* 70: 391–97.

McNamara, T. F. (1996). *Measuring Second Language Performance*. London, UK: Addison Wesley Longman Limited.

McNamara, T. and Roever, C. (2006). *Language Testing: the social turn*. London, UK: Blackwell.

Messick, S. (1989). Validity. In Linn, R. L. (ed.), *Educational Measurement*. New York, NY: Macmillan/ American Council on Education, 13–103.

Mill, J. S. (1859; 1998). *On Liberty*. In Gray, J. (ed.), *John Stuart Mill's On Liberty and Other Essays*. Oxford, UK: Oxford University Press.

Miyazaki, I. (1981). *China's Examination Hell: the civil service examinations of imperial China*. New Haven, CT: Yale University Press.

Poehner, M. (2008). *Dynamic Assessment: a Vygotskian approach to understanding and promoting L2 development*. Boston, MA: Springer Science.

Rawls, J. (2001). *Justice as Fairness: a restatement*. Cambridge MA: Harvard University Press.

Read, J. and Chapelle, C. A. (2001). A framework for second language vocabulary assessment. *Language Testing* 18: 1–32.

Roach, J. (1971). *Public Examinations in England 1850–1900*. Cambridge, UK: Cambridge University Press.

Sawaki, Y. (2007). Construct validation of analytic rating scales in a speaking assessment: reporting a score profile and a composite. *Language Testing* 24: 355–90.

Shohamy, E. (2001). *The Power of Tests*. Harlow, UK: Longman.

Spolsky, B. (1995). *Measured Words*. Oxford, UK: Oxford University Press.

Stabb, M. (1955). An experiment in oral testing. *The Modern Language Journal* 39: 232–36.

Svalberg, A. (2009). Engagement with language: interrogating a construct. *Language Awareness* 18: 242–58.

Toulmin, S. (1958; 2003). *The Uses of Argument*. Cambridge, UK: Cambridge University Press.

Upshur J. and Turner C. E. (1999). Systematic effects in the rating of second-language speaking ability: test method and learner discourse. *Language Testing* 16: 82–111.

Vygotsky, L. S. (1978). *Mind in Society: the development of higher psychological Processes* (M. Cole, V. John-Steiner, S. Scribner, and E. Souberman, eds). Cambridge, MA: Harvard University Press.

Xi, X. (2010). How do we go about investigating test fairness? *Language Testing* 27: 147–70.

Part I
Validity

1
Conceptions of validity

Carol A. Chapelle

Introduction

For many test users, validity is seen as an essential quality of a language test because to them "a valid test" means "a good test." Accordingly, test users frequently explain their search for a new test or their choice of a test by citing their desire for a test that "has been validated." In using the passive voice, "has been validated," users reveal their assumption that validity is a quality of a test that is bestowed by testing experts to make a test measure what it is supposed to. This conception of validity, which requires test users to take little or no responsibility for validity, is at odds with the majority opinion of specialists in educational measurement. In fact,

> to claim that validity refers simply to demonstrating that a "test measures what it purports to measure" or that it is an inherent property of a test is to ignore at least seventy years of research on validity theory and test validation as well as the consensus Technical Recommendations and Standards that have existed since 1954.

> *(Sireci, 2009: 28)*

Many language test users might be surprised that professionals work with a different conception of validity than they do. In view of the fact that validity is considered by all to be of paramount importance in language testing, it is worth exploring what validity means.

Such an exploration needs to examine how test users can know what a test score means and what it can be used for. For example, if a student achieves a score of 75, B2, or NOVICE HIGH, how can test users know what the score means and how it can be used? The focus is the test score, or the results of the test, because this is what is used to make an interpretation about test takers' ability and typically a decision. "Test score" refers to the results of a testing or assessment process even though such results might be in the form of a descriptor (rather than a number) and they might refer to more than one single score as in the case of diagnostic information. If validity entails demonstrating the meaning of test scores and justifying their use, the issues are how one goes about doing this and who is responsible for getting it done. In other words, what are the rules of the validity game?

In language testing the rules are outlined in text books, which draw upon authoritative sources in educational measurement in such a way that language testers do not find themselves playing by a different set of rules from those responsible for tests in other areas. Sireci referred to one such authoritative source, the *Standards for Educational and Psychological Measurement*, published jointly by the American Psychological Association, the American Educational Research Association, and the National Council on Measurement in Education (AERA, APA and NCME, 1999). A second authoritative source is an edited collection called *Educational Measurement*. These sources and the research and practice that informed their development create the context in which books on language assessment present concepts and practices, which they interpret and apply to the specific challenges of language assessment.

This chapter outlines the conceptions of validity that have appeared in language testing over the past fifty years, relying primarily on some of the influential text books in language testing. It outlines critical issues that remain in need of exploration, and notes areas providing impetus for development. This examination of the conceptions of validity reveals that professionals in language testing today would agree with test users that validity is essential, but rather than equating "valid" with "good," most would recognize that the conception of validity encompasses complex principles and practices for validation research.

Historical perspectives

From the first books on modern language testing in the 1960s, most have had something to say about validity, although precisely how validity is conceived and presented varies. Four conceptions of validity are evident over the past fifty years; all have a foundation contemporary work in educational measurement and each contains some treatment of how language ability or performance intersects with validity in language testing.

Does the test measure what it claims to measure?

Early language testing books define validity through a question such as this or a statement such as the one that appears in Valette's 1967 book: "It must measure what it is supposed to measure" (Valette, 1967: 30). Harris (1969) defined validity with reference to two questions: "(1) What precisely does the test measure? And (2) How well does the test measure?" The questions are to be addressed though demonstrating content validity, and empirical validity, but face validity is introduced as well. Heaton (1975) defined the validity of a test as "the extent to which it measures what it is supposed to measure *and nothing else*" (italics in original; 153). He presented the types of validity as face validity, content validity, construct validity, and empirical validity (concurrent and predictive). In Finocchiaro and Sako's 1983 book, validity appears in the glossary where it is defined as follows: "The degree to which a test measures what it is designed to measure. The validity is always specific to the purpose of the test. Different kinds of tests require different evidences of validity" (1983: 311). They introduced four types of validity—content validity, concurrent validity, predictive validity, and construct validity—as did Hughes (1989). Oller (1979) introduced construct validity, content validity, and concurrent validity and discussed these in terms of assessing the validity of tests as measures of the construct "pragmatic expectancy grammar" (1979: 50).

In Lado's *Language Testing* in 1961 validity is defined as "essentially a matter of relevance. Is the test relevant to what it claims to measure?" (Lado, 1961: 321). He recommended six steps for achieving maximum validity in a language test:

- Begin from a linguistically accurate list of learning problems of the students. This ensures better content validity.

- Select or create a type of item that is practical and has validity with relation to content and conditions of problems.
- Edit the items for possible extraneous factors that may be more difficult than the linguistic problems the test is to measure.
- Administer the test experimentally to native speakers of the language of comparable education and language experience as the students for whom the test is intended, or to non-native speakers who are known to have mastered the language. Eliminate or edit the items missed by significant proportions of these speakers of the language. This increases validity making the test more purely a matter of language proficiency.
- Administer the test experimentally to a representative sample of the students for whom the test is intended and correlate their scores with scores by the same students on a valid criterion. If the criterion is another test or the grades made by students in college, reduce the data to a numerical scale and apply the appropriate correlation method. The coefficient of correlation between the scores on the test and the scores on the criterion is the validity coefficient of the test.
- Present the data in the form of a correlation coefficient followed by its standard deviation, or expectancy tables and graphs or both (Lado, 1961: 328–29).

Most applied linguists would recognize the datedness of the assumptions about language in these procedures, i.e., that predictable learning problems could and should be the source of test content, that native speakers can be defined and are always relevant as norms for performance, that pure language proficiency is possible and desirable to measure, and that criterion measures exist against which a new test can be compared. In like fashion, anyone in educational measurement will recognize the datedness of use of the expressions "content validity" (step 1) and "validity coefficient" (step 5). In addition to these particular signals of datedness, however, is the overarching issue of the decontextualized conception presented here (of language and validity).

Nevertheless, Lado's approach to constructing procedures for validation is important: he arrived at them by combining his own perspectives and findings from contrastive linguistics with the contemporary work in educational measurement (e.g., Anastasi's 1954 *Psychological Testing*). Moreover, the terms and concepts Lado used still remain in some text books and appear regularly in the test manuals of commercial tests. The ideas of the native speaker model and the succinct definition of validity, for example, fit well with public, common sense notions, and therefore remain. The field, however, has moved on.

Appropriateness of interpretations and actions

In 1990, Bachman's *Fundamental Considerations in Language Testing* introduced applied linguists to the conception of validity as it had been outlined in the third edition of *Educational Measurement*. In that volume, Messick (1989) defined validity as "an overall evaluative judgment of the degree to which evidence and theoretical rationales support the adequacy and appropriateness of interpretations and actions based on test scores" (1989: 13). To those accustomed to defining validity as "Does the test measure what it is supposed to?" Messick's definition was met with mixed reactions, but in fact Messick had not radically changed the conception of validity held by many researchers in educational measurement. In fact the seminal work by Cronbach asnd Meehl (1955) had put forth a number of the key concepts which had been expanded upon by others (e.g., Wainer and Braun, 1988). Messick's paper extended the complex conception of validity that had been evolving for years.

Four characteristics are useful for summarizing Messick's 1989 conception of validity:

- Validity is not a property of tests themselves; instead, it is the interpretations and uses of tests that can be shown to be more or less valid.
- Validity is best thought of as one unitary conception, with construct validity as central, rather than as multiple validities such as "content validity," "criterion-related validity," or "face validity."
- Validity encompasses the relevance and utility, value implications and social consequences of testing. This scope for validity contrasts with the view that validity refers only to technical considerations.
- The complex view of validity means that validation as an ongoing process of inquiry. The focus on the process of investigation contrasts with a product-oriented perspective of a validated test—one for which the research has been completed.

Despite the initial mixed reception in language testing, this conception of validity has ultimately affected the research in language assessment. Messick's paper is regularly cited in language testing research in the main language assessment journals, in overviews presenting language testing research (e.g., Chapelle and Douglas, 1993; Cumming, 1996; Kunnan, 1998), and in other textbooks on language testing. Importantly for language testing, the central place of construct validity required a substantial discussion of the construct, which Bachman (1990) provided through a reformulation of prior work on communicative competence.

The other significant outcome was what Davies and Elder (2005) retrospectively called the social turn in the conception of validity in language assessment. The challenge laid out by Messick and presented by Bachman was to include critical forms of inquiry as part of the validation process in order to be able to analyze the values and social consequences underlying test interpretation and use. Analysis of values requires researchers to question whether test interpretations are defensible from both technical and ethical perspectives. Critical language testing questions would include the following: What are the assumptions about language underlying this test? Should language be measured in the manner that it is in the test? What are the effects of measuring such a construct in this way? Who benefits and who loses when this test is used as proposed? Such context interested forms of analysis helped to usher in "critical language testing" (Shohamy, 2001).

Indeed, for some researchers in language testing and educational measurement more broadly, the scope of concerns raised for validation by Messick's paper was simply too much. With users needing test scores for decision making, how could test developers and researchers be charged with a never-ending research agenda encompassing both the scientific questions about construct interpretations and the ethical questions of values and social consequences? From a pragmatic perspective of getting the validation job done, Messick's framework made validation seem unapproachably complex for some (Shepard, 1993). At the same time, however, many researchers, including many in language testing, found the complexity appropriately captured the challenges inherent in validation. From the latter point of view, the issue is how to capture the complexity in concepts that can be operationalized and procedures that can actually be accomplished. Many text books continued to use the more manageable explanation of "types of validity" from the earlier era. Alderson *et al.* (1995) handled the complexity by introducing types of validity (from the 1960s and 1970s), but they pointed out that "these 'types of validity' are in reality different methods of assessing validity" (1995: 171). Bachman and Palmer (1996), in contrast, introduced a new term and manner for conceiving validity, "test usefulness."

Test usefulness

To address the gap between theory and practice in language testing, Bachman and Palmer (1996) aimed to interpret validity theory in a manner that could be understood and used by those responsible for developing language tests and justifying their use. Framing the issue as an eva-luation of usefulness (rather than justifying interpretations and uses of test scores), Bachman and Palmer were able to communicate to a wide audience including graduate students and practi-tioners that tests have to be evaluated in view of the particular uses for which they are intended. They defined six criteria for test evaluators to investigate:

- Reliability: The consistency of test performance that is reflected in the test scores.
- Construct validity: The appropriateness of the inferences about test takers' ability made on the basis of test scores.
- Authenticity: The correspondence between the test tasks and the tasks students will engage in outside the test context.
- Interactiveness: The extent of the involvement of test takers' engagement in completing the test tasks using the same capacities they would use in other contexts.
- Impact: Positive consequences the test might have on individuals and institutions within the immediate test setting and beyond.
- Practicality: The extent to which resources support the design and development of the test as well as its ongoing use.

Targeting an audience in need of concrete practices for evaluating language tests, Bachman and Palmer's usefulness framework helped practitioners to move beyond thinking of validity as a characteristic of a test to a more contextualized, use-focus evaluation. This framework is used in papers describing test evaluation projects, test reviews, and other books on language testing. It is also used in a widely disseminated book published by TESOL in the United States for describing to teachers and others wishing to evaluate tests for adoption (Stoynoff and Chapelle, 2005).

On the surface, it may appear that Bachman and Palmer's conception of test usefulness represented a departure of language testing from mainstream educational measurement approa-ches to validity. In retrospect, however, it actually forecasted key concepts that are played out in the more praxis-oriented approach to validity that appears in the most recent edition of *Educa-tional Measurement*. The forecast is apparent if one sees the qualities of test usefulness as claims that one would like to be able to make concerning a test (e.g., that the test tasks have a high degree of the authenticity; that evidence exists for construct validity, etc.). The claims would also need to be seen as additive in a way that allows for an overall conclusion resulting from a validity argument.

Validity argument

The editor of the fourth edition of *Educational Measurement* introduced the chapter on validation relative to Messick's by indicating that the current chapter "aims at making validation a more accessible enterprise for educational measurement practitioners" (Brennan, 2006: 3). The title of the chapter is "Validation," the nominalization of the verb "validate," which suggests that the chapter describes the process of making validity arguments. The emphasis on the detail of constructing arguments is the praxis step which makes concrete the expression (i.e., validity argument) that had been used for many years (e.g., Cronbach, 1988). The praxis orientation to validity arguments is developed according to these principles as outlined by Kane (1992; 2001; 2006; this volume):

- A validity argument is structured through claims that one would like to make about test score meaning.

- The first step in developing a validity argument is to lay out the claims that one would want to be able to make about the test scores including the intended use. This set of claims about score meaning is an interpretive argument.
- The validity argument is intended to specify score meaning, which can include technical aspects of meaning such as level of response consistency as well as social aspects of meaning such as the value and policy implications of score use.
- The conclusion for the interpretive argument is a statement about the utility of the test score for a specific purpose.

Kane's (2006) conception calls for a reflective process requiring the test developer to have an understanding of what a test score can and should mean as well as the knowledge to draw upon theoretical rationales and empirical methods to support score meaning and use. Kane provides examples of how interpretive arguments can be developed, but for any particular test, the researcher is responsible for outlining the interpretive argument.

Kane's perspective on the interpretive argument and validity argument is proving useful in language assessment (see Kane, this volume). Bachman's recent work presents validation by drawing upon the same principles of argument as Kane does (Bachman, 2005). The validation research for a major international language testing program, the Test of English as a Foreign Language (TOEFL), was framed on the basis of an interpretive argument as outlined by Kane (Chapelle *et al.*, 2008), in conjunction with evidence-centered design (see Mislevy, this volume). The language assessment textbook, *Language Testing and Assessment: an advanced resource book* (Fulcher and Davidson, 2007) presents validity argumentation based on this approach and Bachman and Palmer's book, *Language Assessment in Practice*, presents an approach to validity argument specifically for language assessment. Research in the professional journals also draws upon Kane's work in formulating validation research (e.g., Chapelle *et al.*, 2010).

These important indicators suggest that validity in mainstream language assessment may be moving forward in harmony with educational measurement. Most would agree that this is a positive development in language assessment; however, it should not be seen as an indication that all thorny issues associated with defining validity and conducting validation research are approaching eminent solution. On the contrary, within educational measurement, the conception of validity is not a settled matter, but rather a source of continuing discussion, particularly as the new edition of the *Standards* is under development. At least equally important for language assessment are the challenges that remain in the program that Lado initiated to combine the concepts and practices from educational measurement with those in linguistics. These two broad areas intersect with needs in language testing to create a number of issues.

Critical issues

Because of the importance and complexity of validity, it would be possible to identify a long list of critical issues that remain on the table today. I have selected just five of these which pertain to how research is conducted and interpreted in applied linguistics.

Epistemology and validity

Conducting and interpreting validation research requires researchers to explore their own knowledge and beliefs about score meaning. The connection between validity and epistemology was evident at a conference on validity at the University of Maryland in 2008, from which a volume entitled *The Concept of Validity* was published (Lissitz, 2009). The aim of the conference was to assemble researchers with diverse views of validity, and accordingly, in the edited volume, readers find authors with views as diverse as Sireci's (quoted in the second paragraph of this chapter) and Borsboom's, whose view directly opposes Sireci's. Borsboom argued in this volume, as he has elsewhere (Borsboom, 2006), that validity is the property of a test. The dialectic created by expression of opposing views forces the discussion to the level of epistemology and in particular assumptions about the ontological status of the constructs that underlie assessment.

Messick (1989) introduced the dialectic by outlining the various positionings one might take in defining and interpreting constructs. Taking a realist's perspective, a construct can be viewed as a trait that really exists in an individual. Alternatively, a construct can be treated as a convenient construction created by the researcher, a constructivist view. Messick also defined an intermediate position of the constructivist-realist who sees a construct as summarizing the performance consistency that is caused by a real trait. The realist position allows for the idea that validity is something that a test either has or does not depending on whether or not it measures the real trait possessed by the test takers. A constructivist and constructivist-realist position are more consistent with validity pertaining to inferences and uses, but the point is that even to make sense of the issue, it is very useful to understand that there are different ways of understanding what constructs are.

In applied linguistics multiple epistemological stances co-exist (Bachman, 2006), but in language assessment, most researchers, at least implicitly, tend to be satisfied with a constructivist or constructivist-realist position. It has been some time since the idea has been taken seriously that a single unidimensional language trait is—or should be—the target of all language assessments because it reflects reality. The question today is how the language capacities of interest can be modeled in a manner that is useful for particular purposes. Starting from a constructivist-realist position, Mislevy (2009) points out that models (such as constructs) do not have to be psychologically true or accurate in order to be useful. They simply need to capture relevant response consistencies. Since models are always simplifications of complex phenomena, the question is not whether they are accurate, but rather how wrong they have to be in order to not be useful. This pragmatism is productive for language assessment, which is at risk of being held hostage to intractable theoretical disputes about the nature of language in which opponents argue on the basis of what is theoretically correct rather than pragmatically useful.

Language constructs

The construct definition underlying score interpretation is the focal point of intersection between measurement and linguistics because a conception of language ability has to be formulated in a manner that can serve as a basis for score interpretation. McNamara and Roever (2006) characterize the relationship historically as one in which "psychometrics became the substrate discipline, prescribing the rules of measurement, and language was virtually poured into these pre-existing forms" (2006: 1). In the days of Lado, when language was defined as discrete units independent from other knowledge, at least in the United States, the fit within the pre-existing forms was plausible. However, as perspectives on language in applied linguistics evolved and uses for a range of language constructs arose, the need to reconceptualize language ability constructs became evident (e.g., Stansfield, 1986). If a test is intended to measure communicative competence, models relevant to communicative competence have to be conceptualized. In other words, models have to be capable of capturing response consistency reflective of the many sources of knowledge, strategies, and contextual factors responsible for communicative performance. McNamara (1996) described the complexity of such a program as "opening Pandora's box."

While many language testers declined to look in the box, those grappling with testing language for specific purposes had no choice but to do so (McNamara, 1996; Douglas, 2000). The test score in such testing contexts needs to be interpreted as indicating the test taker's ability to use language to perform in a particular domain such as a medical office or in aviation. The construct definition has to include the domain of language use as well as the ability to make appropriate linguistic choices and interpretations in order to make meaning.

Although tests of language for specific purposes provide the clearest examples of the need for a perspective on language that links language and context, in fact many test scores are intended to indicate the test taker's ability to use language. The construct underlying score interpretation, would usefully draw from functional linguistic theory which connects language use to context, as systemic functional linguistics does (Halliday and Hasan, 1989). Systemic functional linguistics is a theory of language, however, and what is needed for score interpretation is a construct definition that makes sense for score interpretation.

The framework for building constructs is sketched out in educational measurement by Messick (1981; 1989), who identifies three ways of defining constructs: as samples of behavior in particular contexts; as signs of underlying traits; and as a combination of the two, i.e., as signs of traits as they are sampled in particular contexts. It is the latter, the interactionalist construct definition that seems to be particularly relevant for many of the types of interpretations in which applied linguistics often are interested (Chapelle, 1998). Bachman's (2007) analysis of the possibilities for definition of language constructs includes at least seven perspectives that have appeared. This array of possibilities could fruitfully be examined in view of the linguistic perspectives informing them and in view of Mislevy's observations on useful models as a means for interpreting response consistency. If a good model is a useful simplification, it would be ideal for professionals to be able to articulate the linguistic detail of which a construct definition is a simplification, but this is a project in need of additional work.

Language development

In some language testing contexts, the test taker's score is intended to index a particular level of language development, and therefore the construct that should form the basis of the construct validity argument needs to be interpreted from a developmental perspective. Such score meanings are implied when scores are indexed to the American Council on the Teaching of Foreign Languages (ACTFL) scale or to a scale developed based on the Common European Framework of Reference (CEFR). In other words, score meaning is not the amount of a particular construct or an indicator of the level of an ability. It is the position on a trajectory of language development. In such cases, any given score is to be interpreted relative to the scores below and above on the scale in such a way that one would expect learners to move along the scale as their language developed. Ideally, such scale descriptors would make sense relative to perspectives and findings from research on second language development. In fact, however, it is difficult to find such links in descriptions of such scales and frameworks.

One reason for the gap that has sometimes been cited is that second language acquisition research is narrowly focused on development of morphosyntax whereas descriptions of levels used in educational settings refer to broad functional abilities in contexts. This reason, however, has become less credible over the years as second language acquisition theory and research has expanded to encompass multiple perspectives. The issue today is not that Second Language Acquisition (SLA) findings are too narrow to be useful but rather that SLA research is so rich, diverse, and complex that it is not clear precisely how and what the connections should be. This challenge is exacerbated by the lack of shared knowledge base between researchers in language assessment and those in second language acquisition. Yet, at some point, it is likely to become more difficult to maintain developmental score meanings that are completely unrelated to any empirical and theoretical bases in the study of second language acquisition.

Analysis of linguistic performance

One way in which validity is investigated for language tests includes the analysis of test takers' written or oral language produced during test performance. Such performance is used (1) as an indicator of their ability to write or speak the language, (2) as a sample of linguistic performance that would be expected to be similar under certain conditions beyond the test setting, or (3) both. One way of examining the validity of inferences made on the basis of such performances is through analysis of the language produced in view of the test score awarded and the opportunities the test tasks provide for the production of a particular register of language use. This is therefore an area where a register-sensitive approach to discourse analysis is critically important for understanding the constraints presented by the test tasks. As Mohan (2011) points out, however, the frameworks motivating discourse analysis of language in validation research do not include categories of analysis for describing the lexicogrammatical features that are relevant for developing register-specific language:

> Conversation Analysis (Schegloff *et al.*, 2002), as a field of sociology, is concerned with describing the interactional practices used to accomplish social action through conversation, including such matters as turn-taking and repair. ... But as a sociological approach to grounded analysis of interactional meaning, it does not deal with the linguistic question of a systematic account of how lexicogrammar builds meaning in discourse. ... Discourse analysis conducted within the framework of Vygotskyan sociocultural theory of mind points analysts to aspects of dialogue theorized to be relevant to second-language learning such as scaffolding used in collaborative dialogue and miscommunication in cross-cultural communication (e.g., Swain *et al.*, 2002). But as a sociocultural theory, it does not attempt to deal systematically with the linguistic question of how lexicogrammar builds meaning in discourse.
>
> *(Mohan 2011: 755–56)*

Without an analytic framework for describing how meaning in constructed through use of the lexicogrammatical resources of the language, such research remains at some distance from understanding the quality of test tasks for providing relevant contexts for test takers to construct meaning through their language. The challenge is to draw upon professional knowledge in linguistics to develop relevant methods for analysis of discourse in language assessments.

Values and consequences of language testing

Messick (1989) challenged researchers to justify the values underlying test interpretation and use as well as to include the consequences of test use within the scope of validation research: "Given the pervasiveness and the subtlety of the impact of values and ideologies on test interpretation, we need to explore some ways and means of uncovering tacit value premises and of coping with their consequences for test validation" (Messick, 1989: 62). The issue, which is not immediately obvious to many researchers, is frequently exemplified with a discussion of the cultural biases inherent in the intelligence testing of the 1950s. The construct of intelligence was operationalized in a manner that favored examinees who grew up in affluent circumstances, and test scores were used to place those with high scores in advantageous positions. Rectifying the situation requires researchers to examine such issues as the values underlying the construct definition and the beneficiaries of test use.

In language assessment, value-laden issues emanate from such practices as the use of the native speaker as a norm for assessment, selection of privileged varieties of a language as a standard, and interpretation of test scores for learners with different learning biographies (e.g., heritage learners vs. classroom learners). In all of these cases, the manner in which language constructs are defined and operationalized in tests holds the potential of systematically advantaging particular test takers on the basis of their background. Language constructs can be defined in many different ways, and so the point of the values analysis is to examine the value implications of choosing one construct definition over another. Like defining intelligence, the problem is insidious because the constructs are defined and the test scores are used by people who themselves operate on the basis of their implicit values. Moreover, McNamara (2006) points out that the more praxis-oriented approaches to validation risk de-emphasizing analysis of values at precisely the time when such analyses are increasingly important in language assessment. The challenge for validation remains to make explicit the values at work in this process of test design and use.

Current contributions

The push to improve the clarity and usability of conceptions of validity in language assessment comes first and foremost from the unrelenting need for methods of evaluating and justifying testing practices that affect millions of test takers each year. A comprehensive example for a high stakes language test appears in Chapelle *et al.* (2008), which charts the process of revising the test to show how the research and development results serve as backing in a validity argument for test use. Examination of the making of a validity argument for a real test brings a concept of validity to validation practice. A look at validation practice demonstrates the extent to which new opportunities for test design and delivery (i.e., though computer technology) and test analysis (i.e., item response theory, confirmatory factor analysis, and generalizability theory) actually affect validation as it is carried out in testing programs.

In both high-stakes and low-stakes settings, researchers, developers, and users aim to increase the quality of assessments and, particularly in high-stakes assessment, the validity of inferences and uses needs to be demonstrated. Such a demonstration takes place in a social context, in which acceptable procedures need to be agreed upon, i.e., the rules of the game need to be understood by the professionals. In some cases adherence to the rules are aired more broadly as questions about validity find their way to court, but the daily venue for setting professional norms is the research that appears at conferences and in professional journals.

As documented in this paper, perhaps the most important force contributing to conceptions of validity in language assessment are the applied linguistics books that consolidate knowledge while presenting principles and procedures for validation. Current work filling this role provides detailed guidance on developing a validity argument in a manner that is consistent with the presentation provided by Kane (e.g., Bachman and Palmer, 2010). Like in their previous volume, Bachman and Palmer (2010) aim to emphasize that what is needed is evidence that justifies test use, and they therefore lay out how the test developer can present a chain of argumentation in an "assessment use argument." The chain in an assessment use argument specifies the connections from the performance of a test taker, to the records resulting from a scoring process, to the interpretations made of those records, to the decisions that will be made on the basis of the interpretations, and finally to the consequences that will result from the decisions. In other words, the aim is to fill in the middle part of what happens between the test takers' responses and the positive consequences that are intended to happen as a result.

Future directions

The conception of validity as an argument emphasizes the role of the socio-academic community. An argument is made to an audience, and therefore success is determined on the basis of how well the argument succeeds with the audience, as Cherryholmes (1988) pointed out many years ago. From this vantage point, the community is a critical part of the validity question: Who is the audience for a validity argument and what knowledge and values do they hold that affect their judgment? Obviously, the non-specialist test users will view a validity argument from a different perspective than will specialists in language testing. Therefore, one important issue is how to express a validity argument in a manner that communicates the depth and aptness of the support for test interpretations and uses to a general audience. Users are typically happy to count on the experts for the specifics of the technical backing in the validity argument. However, at the same time, test users need to be able to see their role in judging the appropriateness of a test for their particular context and use.

But if users depend on specialists, who is the specialist community for language assessment? Who is the audience for whom the technical quality of validity arguments are presented and by whom they are judged? The chronology of validity conceptions in language assessment demonstrates that language assessment researchers draw upon work in educational measurement extensively. Long gone are the days when professional practice condoned simply claiming a language assessment is valid or inventing criteria for good assessments that have no foundation in the broader field of educational measurement. However, it is not clear to what extent international practices in language testing need to speak to a largely North American community of educational measurement. It may be a coincidence but the two papers comprising the "relatively divergent" section of the book *The Concept of Validity* were imported from outside North America, whereas the four papers in the part called "relatively mainstream" were all from scholars in North America. In a world where audiences are characterized by hybrid influences of culture, academic traditions, and disciplinary affiliations, the idea of a single conception of validity may be as much of an abstraction as the conception of the native speaker.

Further reading

Bachman, L. F. and Palmer, A. S. (2010). *Language Assessment in Practice*. Oxford: Oxford University Press. This book takes readers through the process of building a validity argument from current perspectives of inferences, assumptions, warrants, backing, etc. It is aimed at readers wishing to take validity argumentation into account from the beginning stages of test design. It emphasizes the use of validity arguments for justifying test design decisions to stakeholders.

Chapelle, C. A., Enright, M. E. and Jamieson, J. (2010). Does an argument-based approach to validity make a difference? *Educational Measurement: Issues and Practice* 29: 3–13. This paper describes four points of distinction that can be made between that approach to validation described by Messick and the more praxis-oriented argumentation outlined by Kane. It draws upon experience in developing a validity argument for a high-stakes language test drawing upon both approaches.

Kane, M., Crooks, T. and Cohen, A. (1999). Validating measures of performance. *Educational Measurement: Issues and Practice* 18: 5–17. This paper describes an argument-based approach to developing a validity argument using the analogy of bridges that must be traversed as support (or backing) is found for each of the inferences in the argument. Focusing on performance assessment, it demonstrates a validity argument built without a theoretical construct, and it describes, in particular, evaluation, generalization, and extrapolation inferences, without suggesting that these would be the only inferences contained in validity arguments.

Messick, S. (1989). Validity. In R. L. Linn (ed.), *Educational Measurement*, 3rd edn. New York, NY: Macmillan Publishing Co, 13–103. This is the seminal paper on validity, which consolidates and extends work on theory and practice in validation of educational and psychological assessments while con-textualizing validation within philosophy of science. It defines validity in terms of interpretations and uses of tests while including relevance and utility, value implications and consequences of testing. It contains extensive discussion and examples of validation research in addition to definition and discussion of concepts that remain fundamental conceptions of validity.

References

AERA, APA and NCME. (1999). *Standards for educational and psychological testing*. Washington, DC: AERA.

Alderson, J. C., Clapham, C. and Wall, D. (1995). *Language Test Construction and Evaluation*. Cambridge, UK: Cambridge University Press.

Anastasi, A. (1954). *Psychological Testing*. New York, NY: Macmillan.

Bachman, L.F. (1990). *Fundamental Considerations in Language Testing*. Oxford, UK: Oxford University Press.

—— (2005). Building and supporting a case for test use. *Language Assessment Quarterly*, 2: 1–34.

—— (2006). Generalizability: A journey into the nature of empirical research in applied linguistics. In M. Chalhoub-Deville, C. Chapelle and P. Duff (eds), *Inference and Generalizability in Applied Linguistics: multiple perspectives*. Amsterdam, The Netherlands: John Benjamins, 165–207.

—— (2007). What is the construct? The dialectic of abilities and contexts in defining constructs in language assessment. In J. Fox, M. Wesche and D. Bayliss (eds), *What are we measuring? Language testing reconsidered*. Ottawa, Canada: University of Ottawa Press, 41–71.

Bachman, L. F. and Palmer, A. S. (1996). *Language Testing in Practice*. Oxford, UK: Oxford University Press.

—— (2010). *Language Assessment in Practice*. Oxford, UK: Oxford University Press.

Borsboom, D. (2006). The attack of the psychometricians. *Psychometrika* 71: 425–40.

Brennan, R. L. (ed.), (2006). Perspectives on the evolution and future of educational measurement. In R. Brennen (ed.), *Educational Measurement,* 4th edn. Westport, CT: Greenwood Publishing, 1–16.

Chapelle, C. A. (1998). Construct definition and validity inquiry in SLA research. In L. F. Bachman and A. D. Cohen (eds), *Interfaces between second language acquisition and language testing research*. Cambridge, UK: Cambridge University Press, 32–70.

Chapelle, C. and Douglas, D. (1993). Foundations and directions for a new decade of language testing. In D. Douglas and C. Chapelle (eds), *A New Decade of Language Testing Research*. Arlington, VA: TESOL Publications, 1–22.

Chapelle, C. A., Enright, M. E. and Jamieson, J. (eds), (2008). *Building a Validity Argument for the Test of English as a Foreign Language*. London, UK: Routledge.

Chapelle, C.A., Yoo-Ree Chung, Y.-R., Hegelheimer, V., Pendar, N. and Xu, J. (2010). Designing a computer-delivered test of productive grammatical ability. *Language Testing* 27: 443–69.

Cherryholmes, C. (1988). *Power and Criticism: poststructural investigations in education*. New York, NY: Teachers College Press.

Cronbach, L. (1988). Five perspectives on validity argument. In H. Wainer and H. Braun (eds), *Test Validity*. Hillsdale, NJ: Lawrence Erlbaum, 3–17.

Cronbach, L. J. and Meehl, P. E. (1955). Construct validity in psychological tests. *Psychological Bulletin* 52: 281–302.

Cumming, A. (1996). Introduction: the concept of validation in language testing. In A. Cumming and R. Berwick (eds), *Validation in Language Testing*. Clevedon, UK: Multilingual Matters, 1–14.

Davies, A. and Elder, C. (2005). Validity and validation in language testing. In E. Hinkel (ed.), *Handbook of Research in Second Language Teaching and Learning*. Mahwah, NJ: Lawrence Erlbaum Associates, 795–813.

Douglas, D. (2000). *Assessing Language for Specific Purposes*. Cambridge, UK: Cambridge University Press.

Finocchiaro, M. and Sako, S. (1983). *Foreign Language Testing: a practical approach*. New York, NY: Regents Publishing Company.

Fulcher, G. and Davidson, F. (2007). *Language Testing and Assessment: an advanced resource book*. London, UK: Routledge.

Halliday, M. A. K. and Hasan, R. (1989). *Language, Context, and Text: Aspects of language in a social-semiotic perspective*. Oxford, UK: Oxford University Press.

Harris, D. P. (1969). *Testing English as a Second Language*. New York, NY: McGraw Hill.

Heaton, J.B. (1975). *Writing Language Tests*. London, UK: Longman.

Hughes, A. (1989). *Testing for Language Teachers*. Cambridge, UK: Cambridge University Press.

Kane, M. T. (1992). An argument-based approach to validity. *Psychological Bulletin* 112: 527–35.

—— (2001). Current concerns in validity theory. *Journal of Educational Measurement* 38: 319–42.

—— (2006). Validation. In R. Brennen (ed.), *Educational Measurement,* 4th edn. Westport, CT: Greenwood Publishing, 17–64.

Kunnan, A. J. (1998). *Validation in Language Assessment: selected papers from the 17th Language Testing Research Colloquium, Long Beach*. Mahwah, NJ: Lawrence Erlbaum Associates.

Lado, R. (1961). *Language Testing: the construction and use of foreign language tests*. New York, NY: McGraw-Hill.

Lissitz, R. W. (ed.), (2009). *The concept of validity: revisions new directions and applications*. Charlotte, NC: Information Age Publishing, Inc.

McNamara, T. (1996). *Measuring Second Language Performance*. London, UK: Longman.

—— (2006). Validity in Language Testing: The Challenge of Sam Messick's Legacy. *Language Assessment Quarterly* 3: 31–51.

McNamara, T. and Roever, C. (2006). *Language Testing: the social dimension.* Malden, MA: Blackwell Publishing.

Messick, S. A. (1981). Constructs and their vicissitudes in educational and psychological measurement. *Psychological Bulletin* 89: 575–88.

—— (1989). Validity. In R.L. Linn (ed.), *Educational Measurement,* 3rd edn. New York, NY: Macmillan Publishing Co, 13–103.

Mislevy, R. J. (2009). Validity from the perspective of model-based reasoning. In R. W. Lissitz (ed.), *The Concept of Validity: revisions new directions and applications.* Charlotte, NC: Information Age Publishing, Inc, 83–108.

Mohan, B. (2011). Qualitative research methods in second language assessment. In E. Hinkle (ed.), *Handbook of Research on Second Language Teaching and Learning,* 2nd edn. London, UK: Routledge.

Oller, J. (1979). *Language Tests at School.* London, UK: Longman.

Schegloff, E., Koshik, I., Jacoby S. and Olsher, D. (2002). Conversation analysis and applied linguistics. In M. McGroarty (ed.), *Annual Review of Applied Linguistics* 22. New York, NY: Cambridge University Press, 3–31.

Shepard, L. A. (1993). Evaluating test validity. *Review of Research in Education* 19: 405–50.

Shohamy, E. (2001). *The power of Tests: a critical perspective on the uses of language if language tests.* Harlow, UK: Pearson Education.

Sireci, S. (2009). Packing and unpacking sources of validity evidence: History repeats itself again. In Lissitz, R. W. (ed.), *The Concept of Validity: revisions new directions and applications.* Charlotte, NC: Information Age Publishing, Inc, 19–38.

Stansfield, C. W. (ed.), (1986). *Toward Communicative Competence Testing: Proceedings of the second TOEFL invitational conference. TOEFL Research Reports,* No. 21, Princeton, NJ: Educational Testing Service.

Stoynoff, S. and Chapelle, C. A. (2005). *ESOL Tests and Testing: a resource for teachers and program administrators.* Alexandria, VA: TESOL Publications.

Swain, M., Brooks, L. and Tocalli-Beller, A. (2002). Peer-peer dialogue as a means of Second Language Learning. In M. McGroarty (ed.), *Annual Review of Applied Linguistics,* 22 New York: Cambridge University Press, 171–85.

Valette, R. A. (1967). *Modern Language Testing.* New York, NY: Harcourt, Brace and World.

Wainer, H. and Braun, H. I. (eds), (1988). *Test Validity.* Hillsdale, NJ: Lawrence Erlbaum Associates.

Articulating a validity argument

Michael Kane

Introduction

Validation involves an evaluation of the plausibility and appropriateness of the proposed interpretations and uses of test scores. As the Standards for Educational and Psychological Testing put it:

> Validity refers to the degree to which evidence and theory support the interpretations of test scores entailed by proposed uses of test scores.
>
> *(AERA, APA, and NCME, 1999: 9)*

It is the interpretations and uses of the test scores that are to be validated rather than the test or the scores themselves, and, therefore, it is critical that the proposed interpretations and uses be clearly stated: 'Ultimately, the need for validation derives from the scientific and social requirement that public claims and decisions be justified' (Kane, 2006).

To the extent that the interpretation is vague or implicit, any validation will necessarily be incomplete and fragmentary.

Framework

An argument-based approach to validation imposes two basic requirements: state the claims that are being made, and evaluate the credibility of these claims. One way to specify the proposed interpretation and uses in some detail is to lay out a chain or network of inferences and supporting assumptions that would get us from the test scores to the proposed interpretations and uses of the scores, if the inferences and assumptions could be shown to be plausible. Given an explicit statement of the proposed interpretation and use, along with strong evidence supporting the underlying assumptions, it would be reasonable to accept the accuracy of the inferences and the appropriateness of the uses. I refer to the network of inferences and assumptions that specify the proposed interpretation and use as an *interpretive argument*. Once the interpretive argument is in place, it can be evaluated in a *validity argument*, which examines its coherence and the plausibility of its inferences and assumptions. The validity argument is also expected to provide an evaluation of the plausibility of alternative possible interpretations.

The interpretive argument

The *interpretive argument* specifies the proposed interpretations and uses of the test scores, and, in doing so, lays out the claims being made in some detail. The inferences take the form of "if–then" rules. For example, a scoring rule might indicate that if a performance has certain characteristics (e.g., it responds fully and accurately to the question), it should get a certain grade. A less complete or accurate response would get a lower grade. The scores on a sample of such performances might be averaged to get an estimate of the student's expected level of performance over a larger domain of similar tasks. This inference from the score summarizing a sample of performances to the mean over the domain of possible performances rests on statistical theory and assumptions about sampling.

An inference from a student's score to a claim that the student is proficient in some area is based on a rule that if a student's score is above some cutscore (associated with the "proficient" category), the student will be classified as proficient. In this case, another level of interpretation involving categorical descriptions (e.g., proficient, advanced) is superimposed on the test scores.

Each inference involves an extension of the interpretation or a decision. For the inferences to be considered reasonable, they have to be either highly plausible *a priori* or be supported by appropriate evidence; that is, the inferences should be warranted in some way.

The inferences rely on a large number of assumptions, but many of these assumptions can ordinarily be taken for granted; for example, on standardized college admissions tests, we typically assume that students understand the instructions and the questions, and can record their responses, unless there is some reason (e.g., a physical disability, a language issue) to think otherwise. For any questionable assumption, we are expected to provide support. It is particularly important to identify the inferences that are most likely to fail in a particular case and to subject these assumptions to scrutiny.

The interpretive argument is intended to make the reasoning inherent in the proposed interpretations and uses explicit, so that they can be evaluated in the validity argument. The interpretive argument thereby serves three important functions. First, it provides a framework for the validity argument, which is expected to evaluate the plausibility of the claims in the interpretive argument. Second, it can help to identify alternative possible interpretations that merit scrutiny by identifying inferences and assumptions that may be questionable. Third, it can provide guidance in developing an assessment that is likely to support the proposed interpretation and use.

The validity argument

The *validity argument* provides an overall evaluation of the proposed interpretations and uses, as outlined by the interpretive argument. To claim that the proposed interpretations and uses are valid is to claim that the interpretive argument is complete and coherent, that its inferences are reasonable given the assumptions that are made, and that the assumptions are either inherently plausible or are supported by adequate evidence for the population of interest. The validity argument incorporates the interpretive argument, and it "should make clear and, to the extent possible, persuasive the construction of reality and the value weightings implicit in a test and its application" (Cronbach, 1988: 5).

Different kinds of inferences require different kinds of support. Scoring rules that take us from observed performances to a score generally rely on expert judgment about the criteria to be used in scoring and on quality control of scoring procedures (and possibly on data regarding rater accuracy and consistency). Generalizations from a sample of observations to expected performance over domains of possible observations rely on evidence that the sampling was consistent with the statistical model being employed, and on generalizability (or reliability) analyses indicating that the sample was large enough to control sampling errors. Inferences to different kinds of performance in different contexts rely on empirical evidence (e.g., from an empirical regression analysis) and/or on analyses of the overlap in the skills required for the different kinds of performances in different contexts.

As noted above, some of the assumptions in the interpretive argument may be accepted *a priori*, or with minimal support, but some assumptions may require extensive empirical support. In particular, strong claims (e.g., causal inferences, or predictions of future performance in different contexts) would typically require strong empirical support. The most questionable assumptions should get the most attention in the validity argument.

The development and appraisal stages of validation

The validation of a proposed interpretation and use typically involves two stages, which can overlap quite a bit, but involve somewhat different kinds of evaluative analyses.

In the *development stage*, the goal is to develop (or adopt) an assessment and to develop an interpretive argument that represents the proposed interpretations and uses of the scores. Initially, a preliminary interpretive argument is outlined, and an assessment plan is developed. The interpretive argument makes some assumptions about the assessment and about the resulting scores, and the assessment procedures would be designed in ways that make it likely that the assumptions in the interpretive argument will hold.

If some assumptions are found to be violated during test development, the assessment or the interpretive argument, or both can be modified to remove the discrepancies. This process of development and revision continues until the test developers are satisfied with the fit between the test and interpretive argument. The evidence produced during the development stage tends to support the validity of the proposed interpretations and uses, because, if any evidence indicates a weakness in the assessment design or in the interpretive argument, the problem is likely to be fixed in some way. For example, if the generalizability/reliability of the scores is found to be inadequate, the test might be lengthened, thereby improving the generalizability of the scores.

The development stage is expected to deliver a clear statement of what is being claimed in terms of an explicit interpretive argument linking test performances to the proposed interpretations and uses of the scores. For low-stakes applications involving relatively plausible inferences and assumptions (e.g., a teacher-made test used for formative assessment), the evidence derived from the development phase may be sufficient for the validation of the interpretation and use.

For high-stakes applications, a more extensive and arm's-length evaluation of the proposed interpretation and use is called for. In the *appraisal stage*, the interpretive argument is subjected to challenge, preferably by a neutral or skeptical evaluator. If the validity of the proposed interpretive argument is to be evaluated by the assessment developers, as is often the case, they should seek to identify and examine the challenges that might be posed by a skeptical critic.

The appraisal stage would begin with a critical review of the interpretive argument, with particular attention to identifying any hidden assumptions, and alternative plausible interpretations of the test scores, and would provide a critical evaluation of the assumptions built into the interpretive argument. Without the discipline imposed by an explicit statement of the claims being made, it is easy to take much for granted.

The appraisal stage would also focus on empirical investigations of the most questionable assumptions in the interpretive argument. As Cronbach (1980: 103) has suggested:

> The job of validation is not to support an interpretation, but to find out what might be wrong with it. A proposition deserves some degree of trust only when it has survived serious attempts to falsify it.

To the extent that the interpretive argument survives these challenges, confidence in the claims being made increases. If these analyses reveal serious weaknesses, either the assessment or the interpretive argument has to be revised or abandoned.

It is appropriate for test developers to adopt a confirmationist approach during the development stage, where the goal is to develop a plausible interpretive argument, based on an appropriate assessment. During the appraisal stage, it is appropriate to adopt a more critical stance.

The argument-based approach to validation was developed mainly as a way of facilitating the process of validation. By the 1990s, a general unified model of construct validation had been developed (Cronbach, 1971; Cronbach and Meehl, 1955; Loevinger, 1957; Messick, 1989), but the model did not outline a specific strategy for conducting validations, and there was a widespread perception that validation was a daunting and potentially endless process. The argument-based approach was designed to retain the generality inherent in the theoretical frameworks, while proposing a more straightforward approach to the implementation of validation efforts (Cronbach, 1988; Kane, 2006; Chapelle, 1999; Chapelle *et al.*, 2008; Xi, 2008; Bachman, 2005; Bachman and Palmer, 2010). The process outlined in the argument-based approach is basically quite simple. First, state the claims that are being made (explicitly or implicitly) in a proposed interpretation or use (the interpretive argument), and, second, evaluate these claims (the validity argument).

Developing the interpretive argument and the validity argument

The testing procedure and the interpretive argument are interwoven and are best developed in tandem. It is also possible, of course, to develop an interpretive argument and a validity argument for an existing assessment, but in these cases, the choices to be made in developing the interpretation will be constrained by the properties of the existing assessment.

An effective way to develop an assessment and an associated interpretive argument starts with the conclusions and decisions included in the proposed interpretation or use and works backward to the kind of assessment and the inferences required to support the proposed conclusions and decisions (Bachman and Palmer, 2010; Kane, 2006). For example, if the goal is to measure student mastery of spoken English, we can begin by identifying the range of performances and contexts that are of interest. We could then develop an assessment plan specifying the kinds of tasks to be included in the assessment and the criteria to be used in evaluating responses to these tasks.

We have several options in developing the assessment and the interpretive argument. The most direct approach would involve observing extended performances in which the examinee is required to use the language effectively in one or more real or simulated situations. A less direct approach would involve observing a large number of brief, structured performances in which the examinee is required to use the language to achieve some specific goal. Either of these or some combination of these or other approaches might work well in a particular case.

This approach keeps the goal in view. We start with the interpretation and uses that are of interest and then figure out how to get to these interpretations and decisions. And, as we move backwards from the conclusions and decisions to the observations on which they are based, we develop a chain or network of inferences, and we identify the assumptions on which these inferences depend. The claims to be made (i.e., the conclusions to be drawn and the decisions to be made) define the end point of the interpretive argument but do not specify how to get there. There may be several interpretive arguments that could support the same kinds of conclusions and decisions, starting from different kinds of assessment procedures. Some of these assessment procedures and interpretive arguments are likely to be more appropriate or plausible than others.

The development of the assessment and the associated interpretive argument is likely to be iterative. First, we develop a preliminary assessment plan and a general version of the interpretive argument that would lead from the observed performances to the conclusions and decisions to be made. Second, we develop a validity argument by evaluating the plausibility of the interpretive argument in terms of the coherence of the argument and the plausibility of its inferences and assumptions (particularly its more questionable assumptions) in light of all available evidence. If gaps or weak links are identified, it may be necessary to adjust the interpretation and/or the assessment or to conduct additional research.

Third, we restate the interpretive argument and the validity argument and repeat the evaluation of the interpretive argument until the validity argument provides adequate support for the plausibility of the interpretive argument, or the interpretive argument is rejected. An interpretive argument that survives all reasonable challenges to its inferences and assumptions can be accepted (with the caveat that new challenges may arise in the future).

Once the interpretive argument has been specified, it can be played forward, using the network of inferences to draw conclusions based on each test taker's performances and to make decisions based on the conclusions.

The interpretive argument will generally contain a number of inferences and assumptions, and the studies to be included in the validation effort are those studies that are most relevant to the inferences and assumptions in the specific interpretive argument under consideration (Chapelle *et al.*, 2008). It is the content of the interpretation that determines the kinds of evidence that are most relevant, and, therefore, most important in validation.

Some examples

As indicated above, the development of assessments and interpretive arguments linking the assessment scores to the proposed interpretation and use is a critical component of effective validation. If we don't know what is being claimed, it is hard to evaluate the plausibility of the claims. Although certain types of interpretations or uses (e.g., placement testing systems) have a common structure, each interpretive argument is unique in many ways (e.g., the specific claims made, the contexts, the populations assessed), and, therefore, the associated validity argument is also unique.

In order to make the discussion above more concrete, it is useful to consider a few examples of what is involved in developing interpretive arguments, their associated assessments, and the validity arguments.

Observable attributes/performance assessments

Simple inductive inferences can be used to draw general conclusions about people based on samples of their performance. If we observe a child riding a bicycle with ease, we can reasonably conclude that the child can ride a bicycle. If we observe a student solving quadratic equations, we might conclude that the student can solve quadratic equations. This is a very basic and useful way to draw conclusions about competencies, skills, and dispositions.

Observable attributes can be defined in terms of how well persons can perform some kind of task or how they respond to certain situations (e.g., how persistent they are in trying to perform an assigned task). Cronbach and Meehl (1955) refer to this kind of attribute as an "inductive summary" and suggest that such variables can be defined entirely in terms of descriptive dimensions, and need not involve any theory.

For quantitative observable attributes, the observed performances are scored using some scoring rules, which reflect the intended interpretation of the observable attribute. The value of the observable attribute can be defined in terms of the average score over some domain of possible performances. The attribute is observable in the sense that its interpretation is specified in terms of a domain of possible observations.

Observable attributes are basically simple inductive summaries from observed performances to a larger domain of possible performances. Yet, the definition of observable attributes raises many questions about how the target domain should be defined (Bachman and Palmer, 2010; Chalhoub-Deville, 2009).

Target domains

The domain of performances over which the observable attribute is defined will be referred to as a *target domain* for the observable attribute, and a person's expected score over the target domain is the value of the observable attribute for the person (Kane, 2006). The target domain involves some range of possible tasks, performed under some range of possible conditions, and it defines what we mean by the observable attribute, as an observable attribute. The decisions made in defining the interpretive argument can rely on tradition, on experience, on structural similarities in the tasks and contexts, or on assumptions about the processes involved in the performances, but once the domain is specified, it defines the observable attribute.

A major determinant of the target domain is, of course, the purposes for which estimates of the target variable are being sought. In educational contexts, where specific skills are being taught, a target domain could focus on relatively simple tasks requiring the use of some skill. The skill of forming plural nouns could be defined in terms of a target domain in which the tasks involve taking a singular noun and turning into a plural noun. Note that even this narrowly defined domain contains a very large number of possible tasks (involving all nouns in the English language, and perhaps a number of simple task formats).

A much broader target domain could be specified for reading comprehension in English. In the context of college admissions, the reading tasks that are of interest would probably emphasize the kinds of prose found in textbooks, literature, and perhaps journals and other documents, and would typically not assume any specific prior knowledge. For admission to more specialized programs (medicine, law, graduate programs), the target domain could include more specialized reading materials, requiring prior knowledge and familiarity with the conventions in the field. In adult literacy classes for immigrants, most of the attention might be on everyday reading materials like signs, menus, timetables, newspapers, etc. Note that in defining these target domains, the tasks are not restricted to test items. In drawing conclusions about reading comprehension for college admissions, we want to draw inferences about a student's ability to read a text (e.g., a chapter, a textbook, a novel), and the target domain includes these extended tasks. In a test of reading comprehension, we may restrict ourselves to short passages followed by multiple-choice questions, but the target domain for the observable attribute is not restricted to any kind of test task.

In some cases, the content of the target domain for language use may be determined by the operational requirements of a particular kind of activity and/or context (e.g., resolving customer complaints). The tasks in this domain would involve samples of the activity, and success in these tasks might require a wide range of skills, including linguistic competence, content knowledge, interpersonal skills, and personal qualities (e.g., patience). In other cases, the domain definition may reflect a set of related skills and abilities that are not tied to any particular setting or any particular kind of goal (e.g., the ability to understand a variety of spoken utterances in a language and to respond appropriately).

The argument-based approach does not suggest that the target domain for an observable attribute be defined in any particular way. It does suggest that the target domain be defined clearly, and that assessments of the observable attribute be evaluated in terms of how well they represent the corresponding target domain. In particular, it is important to avoid the tendency to define the target domain in one way (e.g., narrowly) for validation, while implicitly adopting a different kind of target domain (e.g., a more broadly defined and ambitious domain) as the basis for score use.

Note that observable attributes are not operational definitions. Operational definitions focus on specific measurement operations and tend to be narrowly specified. The target domains for observable attributes are intended to be defined broadly enough to include the full range of performances associated with the attribute label.

We can add additional meaning to an observable attribute by assuming that the behavioral regularities in the target domain are due to an underlying *trait* of the person. A trait is not observable; its existence is inferred from observed regularities in performance, but the trait, *per se*, is not observable. General assumptions about the trait and its relationship to other traits and to the performances in the target domain can play a significant role in interpreting test scores and in defining the boundary of the target domain, but it is not necessary to make this kind of assumption in order to define the observable attribute.

The target domains for the observable attributes that are of most interest in language assessment are not restricted to standardized assessment tasks or to assessment contexts, although they include this kind of structured performance as a subset. A person's level of literacy in a language depends on his or her ability to perform a variety of reading tasks in a variety of contexts, ranging from the casual reading of a sign to the careful reading of text. The fact that it might be difficult to include some of these activities (reading the menu and discussing the options with several people in a restaurant) in an assessment does not indicate that they be removed from the target domain for the attribute.

The target domain is likely to be very large and not very precisely defined. Whether a particular kind of document or a particular situation should be included in the target domain may be questionable, but some ambiguity at the edges is not a fatal flaw. The point is not to develop a tidy domain or one that is easy to assess, but to identify the range of performances associated with the attribute of interest.

Performance assessments

An obvious way to assess a person's level of competence in performing a certain kind of task is to observe the person's performance on the task. We can estimate a person's expected performance over the target domain by obtaining a sample of performances for the person, and using the average score on this sample of performances to estimate the person's expected score over the target domain. For example, we could use observed performance on a sample of reading tasks drawn from a domain of reading tasks to estimate proficiency on this kind of task. If the observed performances can be considered a random or representative sample from the target domain, this generalization from the sample to the target domain would be a straightforward statistical inference.

If the observed performances can be considered a random or representative sample from the target domain, the interpretive argument would involve two main inferences, an evaluation of the observed performances, and a generalization of the observed results to a much larger target domain of possible performances (Kane *et al.*, 1999).

The scoring inference takes us from the observed performances to an observed score, which represents an evaluative summary of the observed performances. The scoring rule needs to be consistent with the intended interpretation and use of the scores, and the scoring rule has to be implemented accurately and consistently, if the proposed interpretation is to be plausible.

The observed score can then be used as an estimate of the expected value over the target domain. In generalizing from the observed score to the target score, the score does not change, but the interpretation is extended from the observed performance to the expected performance over the target domain.

The evidence supporting the evaluation of the examinee's performances would involve justifications for scoring rubrics and administration procedures. The evidence for the generalization to the mean over the universe of possible performances defining the observable attribute would involve procedural evidence supporting the representativeness of the sampling and an empirical estimate of the reliability or generalizability of the statistical inference from the observed score to the target score.

Standardized assessments

Assessments are generally standardized in a number of ways and for a number of reasons, and, therefore, the observed performances are sampled from a small subset of the target domain. Some performances from the target domain are likely to be excluded for practical reasons; the assessment has to be completed in a reasonable period of time and at modest cost. Some performances may be ruled out for reasons of fairness; we would generally not want to include tasks or situations that might make some examinees very uncomfortable, or that might give some candidates an unfair advantage or subject them to an unfair disadvantage.

The observations are actually sampled from a *universe of generalization* for the measurement procedure, and a person's expected score over the universe of generalization is the person's *universe score* (Brennan, 2001).

While the target domain for adult literacy would include a very wide range of written material (e.g., novels, instructional manuals, magazines, memos, signs), responses (answering specific questions, giving an oral or written summary, taking some action based on the manual or sign), and contexts (e.g., at home, in a library, at work), the universe of generalization for a measure of literacy may be limited to responses to a set of questions following short passages while sitting at a desk or computer terminal. The performances involved in standardized reading tasks are legitimate examples of literacy, but they constitute a very narrow slice of the target domain for literacy. That is, the universe of generalization from which the observed performances are drawn is a relatively small and non-random subset of the target domain.

Because the samples of tasks included in measurements are not random or representative samples from the target domain, it is not legitimate to simply generalize from the observed score to the target score. It is, however, often reasonable to generalize from the observed score to the universe scores for the universe of generalization associated with the measurement procedure.

The interpretive arguments for the standardized assessments of observed attributes require three main inferences. The scoring inference goes from the test results to an observed score, the observed score is generalized to the universe score, and the universe score is extended, or extrapolated, to the target score.

Extrapolation from the universe of generalization to the target domain extends the interpretation from the universe score to the target score. The extrapolation inference assumes that the universe score is related (rationally and/or empirically) to the target score and that the extrapolation is relatively free of systematic and random error (Bachman and Palmer, 2010). Again, the score does not change, but the interpretation of the score is extended from the universe of generalization to the target domain.

Target domains and universes of generalization for language proficiency

The definition of the target domains can raise a number of serious issues. We tend to think that we know the kinds of performances subsumed under terms like language proficiency and literacy, but identifying the range of performances to include in the target domain, and on the emphases to be given to different kinds of performance, tends to get complicated once we attempt to specify the domain well enough to use it as a guide in developing an assessment plan. These issues get progressively more complex as we move from the mechanics of language use to general conceptions of communicative competence (Bachman and Palmer, 2010; Fulcher and Davidson, 2007).

For example in assessing competence in a language (first or second language), the target domain can focus on skills needed for basic interpersonal communication or on the skills needed for academic settings at various levels. The cognitive/academic competency domain is likely to include vocabulary and grammatical structures that are not generally used in everyday conversations (Chalhoub-Deville, 2009).

On a more pragmatic level, we have a range of options in deciding on the kinds of performances to use in the assessment, and in the relationship between the universe of generalization for the assessment and the target domain. As noted above, one option is to sample randomly or representatively from the target domain. Under this approach, the performances that could be observed are likely to be quite varied, and, at least in some cases, quite complicated and lengthy. The observed performances may be considered to be relatively authentic, but they also have at least two potential disadvantages. First, in drawing performances from a broadly defined and diverse target domain, the sampling variability is likely to be quite large, and in evaluating the generalization inference, this variability will be considered to be a major source of errors of measurement. This problem can be addressed by drawing large samples of performance, and possibly by adopting efficient sampling plans, but the cost of these options tends to be high.

The second problem associated with sampling directly from the target domain arises because the effectiveness of a person's performance in various tasks will depend in part on knowledge and skills that go beyond what we usually think of as language skills, and performance can vary substantially from task to task and context to context. To the extent that the goal is to assess facility in using a language, specific content knowledge, or lack of such knowledge that might have an effect on performance on specific tasks or in specific situations, is said to be construct-irrelevant variance (Messick, 1989), and it can lead to biased results for individuals and groups.

The standard way to address this problem without using very large samples of performance is to select relatively neutral performances, neutral in the sense of not introducing emotional factors in cognitive tests, and not requiring any knowledge or skills not explicitly associated with the intended interpretation and use of the test scores.

In some cases, we may be interested in assessing how well individuals can communicate in contexts where effective communication requires specialized knowledge and vocabulary, specialized skills (e.g., interpreting graphical representations of data), or specialized conventions, and in these cases employing tasks and contexts from the domain of interest will tend to enhance the accuracy of extrapolation from the assessment to the target domain (Bachman and Palmer, 2010). If the target domain is defined in terms of tasks that require specialized knowledge or skills, it is appropriate that the assessment tasks also require the relevant knowledge or skills. This kind of target domain defines a kind of communicative competence that is different from general linguistic competence, and it is important to be clear about the difference (Widdowson, 2001).

Placement testing

In a sequence of language courses (e.g., foreign language courses in a university), the goal is to develop increasing proficiency in the use of the language in some range of contexts. Each course builds upon the previous courses in the sequence. The first course would typically be designed for novices, with little or no skill in the language, and would aim to develop some rudimentary proficiency in the use of the language. Success in the first course allows students to move on to the second course, where the competencies are developed further. Similarly, the third course builds on the first two, and so on.

If all students entered the language program as complete novices, there would be no need for a placement testing program: in this case all students would start in the first course and continue in succeeding courses until they completed the sequence, or stopped for some reason. However, many of the incoming students may have acquired some proficiency in the language (e.g., in high school courses, at home, or by spending time in locations where the language is used), and it would be useful to be able to place each student into a course that would be most appropriate for the student. The intended use of the placement program is to place each student into a course in which she or he will be challenged but will have a good chance of success (Frisbie, 1982).

We already have a placement system for students who have started out in the first course. If these students complete the first course successfully, say with a grade of B or better, they are allowed (or encouraged) to take the second course. Students who get a B or better in the second course are allowed/encouraged to take the third course, etc.

This system does not apply to new students who have some competence in the language, because they do not have grades in any of the courses. However, if we can develop an assessment that reflects the competencies developed in the courses, and can get the students who are currently completing the various courses to take this test, we can use scaling methods to link specific test scores to the level of competence indicated by scores of B in each of the courses (Frisbie, 1982). The test scores can be used as proxies for grades of B in the courses.

Identifying the test score that corresponds to the achievement level associated with a grade of a B or better in a course can be difficult, because the test scores will not be perfectly correlated with course grades (which are not perfect measures of achievement in a course), and some students with a grade of C in a course may have higher test scores than students with a grade of B in the course. One way to get around this difficulty would be to form test score distributions for students with a B and with a C; these distributions can be smoothed to iron out some of their variability, and the cutscore can be set at the point on the test-score scale where the two distributions cross.

In addition to the basic scoring inference (from performances to the observed score), placement testing systems involve two inferences and a decision rule that depends on these inferences. The first inference is from scores on the test to conclusions about level of achievement in the competencies developed in the sequence of courses. The second inference is from competency, as measured by the test, to conclusions about level of achievement relative to performance at the end of courses in the sequence. The third inference is a decision about suggested course placement, based on cutscores on the test-score scale. This is not the only way to think about placement systems, but it is a useful framework.

Inference from test scores to level of achievement

The inference from scores on the test to conclusions about level of achievement in the competencies developed in the sequence of courses depends on at least four assumptions:

1. The courses are designed to develop a cluster of competencies, with a student's overall level of competency expected to increase from one course to the next in the sequence.

This assumption is likely to be supported by the judgment of those involved in running the courses. If the courses do not have this kind of sequential, hierarchical structure, a simple placement test of the kind outlined here would not make much sense.

2.   The test assesses the competencies developed in the courses over the range covered by the courses.

This assumption is likely to be supported by an analysis of the competencies evaluated by the assessment relative to those developed in the courses. Assuming that the assessment is developed to reflect the competencies developed in the courses, much of the work done in test development will contribute evidence in support of this assumption. The test may not cover all of the competencies developed in the courses, but it should cover most of the competencies.

3.   Scores on the test are generalizable across tasks, scorers, occasions, etc.

The scores should be generalizable enough for dependable conclusions about each student's level of competence. This assumption is likely to be supported empirically in reliability or generalizability studies, indicating that the scores do not fluctuate too much over samples of tasks, scorers, and perhaps occasions, etc.

4.   There are no sources of systematic error that would interfere with the intended interpretation.

There are at least two main sources of systematic errors in the assessments: construct-irrelevant variance and construct underrepresentation. Any source of score variability that does not reflect the competencies to be assessed is a source of construct-irrelevant variance. For example, an assessment that employed formats that were not familiar to the students could underestimate student achievement, and students with disabilities may need accommodations.

Language courses generally seek to develop competencies that involve listening and speaking, as well as reading and writing and at least some of the course may focus the ability to communicative effectively in various contexts. To the extent that the assessment does not fully cover all of these competencies, it may suffer from construct underrepresentation. Some omissions may not cause problems, especially if the omitted competencies do not play a large role in the courses in which most placements occur, and if level of achievement in the tested competencies is highly correlated with level of achievement in the non-tested competencies, but the tradeoffs involved in covering most competencies vs. the cost in time and resources deserve serious consideration.

If these four assumptions can be supported in a convincing way, it would be reasonable to accept the claim that scores on the placement test can be interpreted as measures of the competencies developed in the courses. The analyses of this first inference rely on methods traditionally categorized under the heading of content-related validity evidence.

Inference from test score to end-of-course grade

The second inference is from competency as measured by the test to levels of achievement corresponding to a grade of B or better in the courses in the sequence.

5.   The levels of achievement needed to get a B or better in the courses increase across the sequence, and the assessment scores are positively related to these levels of achievement.

This assumption would be supported by evidence indicating that students completing higher-level courses generally get higher scores on the assessment, and in particular, that students completing higher-level courses with a B or better get higher scores on the assessment.

Placement decisions

The final inference is a decision about suggested placement of students into courses, based on level of achievement, as indicated by test scores, relative to cutscores on the test-score scale. The courses in the sequence require increasing level of competence as prerequisites, and students whose assessment scores indicate that they have mastered the competencies developed in a course well enough to get a B or better in that course are generally prepared to do well in the next course.

6. Students are placed in the highest-level course for which they seem to be prepared, because they have a level of achievement comparable to the achievement of students getting a B or better in the previous course in the sequence.

As indicated earlier, the cutscores can be determined empirically by administering the assessment to students completing the courses and identifying points on the assessment score scaled corresponding to boundary between students who get a B or better and students who get grade lower than B. The procedures used to develop the assessment and to set the cutscores can provide strong support for this inference.

In addition, the decisions being made can be evaluated by investigating how well the students who are placed in various courses do in these courses, student self-evaluations of how well prepared they were for the course, and faculty evaluations of whether the placement seemed appropriate.

The point of this exercise is not to develop a definitive outline for placement testing, but rather, to illustrate an argument-based framework in which the intended interpretation and use of the assessment scores are outlined in some detail (i.e., as an interpretive argument), with an emphasis on the inferences being made and the assumptions required for these inferences to be plausible. The assessment is developed to satisfy the requirements inherent in the proposed interpretation and use (i.e., the development phase), and the effectiveness of the assessment system in use is evaluated (the appraisal phase).

Concluding remarks and future directions

The argument-based model provides a relatively pragmatic approach to validation. The goal is to develop a measurement procedure that supports the proposed interpretations and uses of test scores and an interpretive argument that is plausible, given the measurement procedure and the proposed interpretations and uses.

An explicitly stated interpretive argument serves three functions. First, it provides a framework for test development by indicating the assumptions that need to be met. A measure of competence in the use of a language for every day activities would be different in many ways from the development of a language test for a particular academic or work setting, in which specialized concepts and terms are especially important.

Second, the interpretive argument provides a framework for the validation of the proposed interpretation and use, as specified in the interpretive argument. The evidence called for in the validity argument is that needed to support the specific inferences and assumptions in the interpretive argument.

Third, the interpretive argument provides a basis for evaluating the adequacy of the validity argument. If the validity argument provides adequate support for the coherence of the interpretive argument, and for the plausibility of its inferences and assumptions, the proposed interpretations and uses are warranted. If the interpretive argument is incomplete or some of its inferences or assumptions are shaky, the proposed interpretations and uses are not fully justified.

The theory of validity has evolved quite a bit over the last century, especially since the publication of Cronbach and Meehl's (1955) seminal article on construct validity, but arguably, the practice of validation has not changed that much. Validity theorists have tried to attend to the range of issues that arise in practice, but in doing so they tended to make validity theory progressively more general and abstract, and as a result, the relevance of the theories to practice became less obvious.

The argument-based approach to validation was intended to reverse this trend by making the theoretical framework for validation more responsive to the details of proposed interpretations and uses of assessment scores in particular contexts and with particular populations. However, in some ways, the argument-based approach to validation is even more general than other validity frameworks. In particular, it does not propose any particular kind of interpretation or use. Rather it suggests that the proposed interpretations and uses and the intended contexts and target populations be specified in the form of an interpretive argument, and that the appropriateness of the claims being made in this interpretive argument be evaluated. However, implementing these suggestions is, in most cases, no easy task, and expositions of the argument-based framework do not generally specify who is to do this work, the assessment developer or user, or some third party.

The analysis of practical arguments plays out in very different ways in different areas and for different kinds of arguments (Bachman and Palmer, 2010; Kane, 2006; Toulmin, 1958). So in addition to a general argument-based theory of validity, more specific frameworks for the evaluation of interpretive arguments for different kinds of interpretations and uses (placement, certification, diagnosis), in different areas (language learning, science), and in different contexts are needed to facilitate applied work in assessment development and validation. That is, we need validity frameworks at various levels of generality between the abstract, general models and specific applications. In language testing, much conceptual work has been done on how to support the development and validation of different kinds of assessments for different purposes (Bachman and Palmer, 2010; Chapelle et al., 2008), but there is always a lot more to do.

Further reading

Bachman, L. (2005) Building and supporting a case for test use. *Language Assessment Quarterly* 2: 1–34. Bachman (2005) provides a very clear and concise introduction to an argument-based framework for validation, with an emphasis on the evaluation of test uses in terms of the consequences of such use. He examines the kinds of warrants and evidence needed for a utilization argument over and above those typically needed for the validations of a score interpretation per se.

Chapelle, C. A., Enright, M. and Jamieson, J. (2008). Test score interpretation and use. In C. Chapelle, M. Enright, and J. Jamieson (eds), *Building a Validity Argument for the test of English as a Foreign Language*. New York, NY: Routledge, 1–25. Most of the examples of interpretive arguments and validity arguments in the literature are quite simple and quite general, and have been developed for illustrative purposes. Chapelle, Enright, and Jamieson (2004) developed and documented an interpretive argument and a validity argument for a large and complex testing program, and in doing so, have pushed the argument-based methodology forward in a dramatic way by applying the approach to an existing assessment program.

Cronbach, L. J. and Meehl, P. E. (1955). Construct validity in psychological tests. *Psychological Bulletin* 52: 281–302. It took a while for the sophisticated framework introduced by Cronbach and Meehl to gain traction, but it became the base for most work on the theory of validity from the 1980s to the present. It had less impact on the practice of validation, in part because it was written at a very abstract level and was framed in terms of a philosophy of science (logical positivism) that has been largely rejected, but it introduced a conceptualization of score interpretation and validation that was much broader and more sophisticated than those that had been in use up to that point. This article is over 50 years old and does not provide specific guidance for validation, but it is essential reading for anyone who wants to follow current debates on validity and validation.

Kane, M. T. (2006). Validation. In R. Brennan (ed.), *Educational Measurement*, 4th edn. Westport, CT: American Council on Education and Praeger, 17–64. Kane (2006) provides an overview of an argument-based approach to validation and indicates how some common interpretations and uses of test scores can be specified in terms of interpretive arguments. He starts with relatively simple interpretations involving a limited set of inferences and moves on to interpretations and uses that require increasingly complex interpretive arguments for their explication, and as a result, require increasing levels of evidential support. Kane (2006) also discusses some fallacies that tend to interfere with effective validation.

References

American Educational Research Association, American Psychological Association, and National Council on Measurement in Education (AERA, APA, and NCME) (1999). *Standards for Educational and Psychological Testing*. Washington, DC: American Psychological Association.

Bachman, L. F. (2005). Building and supporting a case for test use. *Language Assessment Quarterly* 2: 1–34.

Bachman, L. F. and Palmer, A. (2010). *Language assessment in practice: Developing language assessments and justifying their use in the real world*. Oxford, UK: Oxford University Press.

Brennan, R. (2001). *Generalizability Theory*. New York, NY: Springer-Verlag.

Chalhoub-Deville, M. (2009). Content validity considerations in language testing contexts. In R. Lissitz (ed.), *The Concept of Validity*. Charlotte NC: Information Age Publishing, 241–63.

Chalhoub-Deville M. and Deville C. (2006). Old, borrowed, and new thoughts in second language testing. In R. Brennan (ed.), *Educational measurement*, 4th edn. Westport, CT: Praeger Publishers, 517–30.

Chapelle, C. A. (1999). Validity in language assessment. *Annual Review of Applied Linguistics* 19: 254–72.

Chapelle, C. A., Enright, M. and Jamieson, J. (2008). Test score interpretation and use. In C. Chapelle, M. Enright and J. Jamieson (eds), *Building a Validity Argument for the Test of English as a Foreign Language*. New York, NY: Routledge, 1–25.

Cronbach, L. J. (1971). Test validation. In R. L. Thorndike (ed.), *Educational Measurement*, 2nd edn. Washington, DC: American Council on Education, 443–507.

—— (1980). Validity on parole: how can we go straight? In *New Directions for Testing and Measurement: measuring achievement over a decade*, 5. San Francisco, CA: Jossey-Bass, 99–108.

—— (1988). Five perspectives on validity argument. In H. Wainer and H. Braun (eds), *Test Validity*. Hillsdale, NJ: Lawrence Erlbaum, 3–17.

Cronbach, L. J. and Meehl, P. E. (1955). Construct validity in psychological tests. *Psychological Bulletin* 52: 281–302.

Frisbie, D. A. (1982). Methods of evaluating course placement systems. *Educational Evaluation and Policy Analyses* 4: 133–40.

Fulcher, G. and Davidson, F. (2007). *Language testing and assessment: an advanced resource book*. London, UK: Routledge.

Kane, M. (2006). Validation. In R. Brennan (ed.), *Educational Measurement*, 4th edn Westport, CT: American Council on Education and Praeger, 17–64.

Kane, M. T., Crooks T. J. and Cohen, A. S. (1999). Validating measures of performance. *Educational Measurement: Issues and Practice* 18: 5–17.

Loevinger, J. (1957). Objective tests as instruments of psychological theory. *Psychological Reports, Monograph Supplement* 3: 635–94.

Messick, S. (1989). Validity. In R. L. Linn (ed.), *Educational Measurement*, 3rd edn New York: American Council on Education and Macmillan, 13–103.

Toulmin, S. (1958). *The Uses of Argument*. Cambridge, UK: Cambridge University Press.

Widdowson, H. G. (2001). Communicative language testing: the art of the possible. In C. Elder, A. Brown, E. Grove, *et al.* (eds), *Experimenting with Uncertainty, Essays in Honor of Alan Davies*. Cambridge, UK: Cambridge University Press, 12–21.

Xi, X. (2008). Methods of test validation. In E. Shohamy and N. Hornberger (eds), *Encyclopedia of Language and Education*, 2nd edn, Vol. 7: *Language Testing and Assessment*. New York, NY: Springer, 177–96.

3

Validity issues in designing accommodations for English language learners

Jamal Abedi

Introduction

Different accommodations are used in the assessment of students who are English language learners (ELLs). However, many of these accommodations were originally created and used for students with disabilities (see Oller, this volume); therefore, the utility of such accommodations for ELL students is questionable. To help reduce the impact of construct–irrelevant sources in the assessment of ELL students, accommodations should be used that (1) are effective in making assessments more accessible for ELL students, (2) provide assessment outcomes that are valid, i.e., comparable with those of non-ELLs, and (3) are sensitive to student background. These three characteristics are vital in determining the validity of accommodated outcomes. First, if an accommodation is not helpful in reducing the performance gap which is partly due to the impact of construct-irrelevant sources, then the accommodation is not doing what it is intended to do. For example, if an accommodation does not help ELL students with understanding the complex linguistic structure of the assessment, which is unrelated to the content being measured, then that accommodation may not be relevant. Second, if an accommodation alters the construct being measured, then the validity of the accommodated assessment could be at risk. An accommodation that provides unfair advantage to the recipients may impact the measurement of the construct. Third, if an accommodation does not address each individual student's educational needs, then the outcome of the accommodated assessment many not present a good picture of what the student truly knows and is able to do. For instance, providing a native language assessment to an ELL student who has been predominantly instructed in English may not produce a desirable outcome. In this chapter, we introduce the concept of accommodation for ELL students, discuss major issues concerning accommodations, and elaborate on the limitations of the currently used accommodations for ELL students. The chapter also discusses the methodology for conducting studies to examine the effectiveness and validity of accommodated assessments and provides recommendations on best practices of accommodations.

Historical perspectives

In order to provide fair assessment for every child in the United States, both federal (No Child Left Behind Act of 2001, P.L. 107–10) and state legislation require the inclusion of all students, including ELLs, in state and national assessments. There are, however, major technical issues in including ELL students in large-scale assessments. The limited English proficiency of these students may create unequal opportunities for them to benefit from the teacher's instructions and fully demonstrate their knowledge and abilities (Abedi and Herman, 2010). In an attempt to level the playing field, current legislation requires that these students receive accommodations—changes in the test process, in the test itself, or in the test response format. The objective of accommodations is to provide a fair opportunity for English language learners to demonstrate what they know and what they are able to do, without giving them an advantage over students who do not receive accommodations.

Many states currently use accommodations for ELL students (Abedi, 2007; Abedi *et al.*, 2004; Francis *et al.*, 2006; Rivera *et al.*, 2000; Willner *et al.*, 2008; Sireci *et al.*, 2003; Wolf *et al.*, 2008). The widespread use of accommodations, however, raises a number of issues and questions. Does the use of accommodations provide more valid inferences about ELL students' content knowledge? Which students should be eligible for receiving accommodation(s) and what criteria should be used to decide their eligibility? What type of accommodation should be used? Are some accommodations more effective than others for individual students with different background characteristics? Do accommodations provide an unfair advantage to the recipients? Is it meaningful to aggregate accommodated and non-accommodated scores? When we look for answers to these questions throughout studies of content area assessments, we are confronted with a striking lack of empirical research.

Critical issues and topics

The questions and concerns that were presented above can be organized into the following four questions, all of which need to be fully addressed before one chooses to use accommodations in the assessments of ELL students.

1. How effective are the accommodations in making assessments more accessible for ELL students? (Effectiveness)
2. Are the accommodated assessments as valid as the non-accommodated assessments? (Validity)
3. Do accommodations work the same for all ELL students, despite their different backgrounds and their differences in the levels of English proficiency? (Differential impact)
4. How relevant are the accommodations that are used for ELL students to their specific needs? (Relevance)

To shed light on these questions, one must examine these issues using studies that are based on a sound research methodology. Among the necessary conditions for such experiments are random assignments of ELL and non-ELL students to different accommodation conditions.

The most commonly used accommodations for ELL students within the United States are extended time (42 of the 48 states); use of a glossary (26 states), an English dictionary (33 states) or bilingual dictionary (22 states); and linguistically simplified test items (12 states) (Rivera, 2003). Willner *et al.* (2008) distinguished between accommodations that are relevant for ELLs and those that may be irrelevant for these students. Research results are available only for a few forms of accommodations, while others have yet to be examined. For example, research has shown that providing an English dictionary (Abedi *et al.*, 2003a) and extra time (Abedi *et al.*, 2004; Hafner, 2001; Thurlow, 2001) affects the performance of all students, including those for whom the accommodations are not intended (see also, Maihoff, 2002; Thurlow and Liu, 2001). To aggregate the results of accommodated and non-accommodated assessments, one must have enough evidence on the validity of accommodations.

Results of research on the assessment and accommodations of ELL students have indicated that some accommodations are not effective in making assessments more accessible to ELL students while others have been shown to have a more positive impact on the assessment outcomes for ELL students. Among them are linguistic modification of assessments, English dictionary/glossary and bilingual dictionary/glossary, and testing in the student's native language. In the next section of this chapter, we will present a summary of research on some of the most commonly used accommodations in the nation and will then briefly present methodological issues for examining major characteristics of these accommodations based on the four research questions presented above.

Current contributions and research

As indicated earlier, accommodations are meant to assist ELL students in the area where they need the most help, i.e., language, in order to "level the playing field" for these students. Accommodations are strategies intended to reduce threats to validity of test scores. Students' performance on content-based assessments, such as mathematics and science, can be confounded by language, which is considered to be irrelevant to the construct being measured. In other words, the test may unintentionally measure students' language abilities, rather than their content knowledge in areas such as math or science. Accommodations can help ELL students demonstrate their content knowledge by reducing the confounding of language with the content knowledge. However, accommodations are not intended to give ELL students an unfair advantage over students not receiving accommodations. Therefore, research must be conducted to determine not only if an accommodation helps ELL students score better on an assessment than without it, but also that the accommodation *does not* alter the construct being measured. Below is a brief presentation of research findings for the following most commonly used accommodations for ELLs:

- extended time
- English dictionary
- English glossary
- bilingual dictionary or glossary
- customized dictionary
- native language testing
- linguistically modified test
- computer testing.

Extended time

This accommodation provides students with additional (or extended) time to complete an assessment. This is one of the most commonly used accommodations for ELL students and students in different categories of disabilities (Rivera *et al.*, 2000) possibly due to its ease of administration relative to other accommodations. Some studies found extended time to be an effective accommodation for ELLs and students with disabilities (Abedi *et al.*, 2000; Hafner, 2001; Thurlow, 2001; Chiu and Pearson, 1999).

However, other studies did not show extended time to be effective for ELLs and students with disabilities (Munger and Loyd, 1991; Fuchs *et al.*, 2000; Marquart, 2000). A major issue is that extended time may affect the performance of non-ELL students positively as well, therefore making the validity of an assessment using this accommodation suspect (Abedi *et al.*, 2000, 2004; Wolf *et al.*, 2008).

English dictionary

Providing a published English dictionary for students to use during a test is another commonly used accommodation for ELL students (Abedi *et al.*, 2000; Sireci *et al.*, 2003; Willner *et al.*, 2008). However, a dictionary must be provided in combination with extended time in order to avoid the problem of information overload. Some studies have found that the dictionary and extended time affect the performance of all students (Abedi *et al.*, 2000; Hafner, 2001; Thurlow, 2001; Maihoff, 2002; Thurlow and Liu, 2001; Wolf *et al.*, 2008), casting doubt on the validity of the assessment outcomes under this accommodation.

Furthermore, by having access to the definitions of content-related terms, recipients of a dictionary may be advantaged over those who do not have access to dictionaries, which may compromise the validity of assessment. Consequently, the results of accommodated and non-accommodated assessment may not be aggregated. Providing a dictionary is also difficult and burdensome for test administrators, which makes it less feasible to implement (Abedi *et al.*, 2001).

English glossary

An English language glossary can be provided as an alternative to a dictionary. In this case, only terminology that appears in the test appears in the glossary, making a glossary less burdensome than providing a dictionary. In some studies the English glossary with extended time raised the performance of both ELL and non-ELL students. For example, the results of a study by Abedi *et al.* (1998, 2000) showed ELL students' performances increased by 13% when they were given a glossary with extended time. While this seemed promising, the non-ELL students' performances increased by 16% (Abedi *et al.*, 2004), indicating a change in construct from the non-accommodated test version. That is, rather than decreasing performance gap between ELLs and non-ELLs, this accommodation actually increased the performance gap between the two groups. Thus, the outcomes of assessments under this accommodation may not be aggregated with the non-accommodated outcomes.

Bilingual dictionary/glossary

Bilingual dictionaries and glossaries are also among widely used accommodations for ELL students. As with an English dictionary, by having access to definitions of content-related terms, recipients of a published bilingual dictionary may be advantaged over those who did not have access to one (Abedi *et al.*, 2000, 2003b) Another major limitation with a bilingual dictionary is the content equity issue. Different published bilingual dictionaries present a substantial range of content coverage. Furthermore, students who speak another language at home may not be literate or fully literate in their home language, and would not find a bilingual dictionary helpful. They may also be unaccustomed to using one in the classroom, making it unfamiliar, and therefore not useful.

Customized dictionary

In one study, a customized English dictionary was introduced and used as a more valid alternative to English/ bilingual dictionaries (Abedi *et al.*, 2001). The customized dictionary was a literal cut-and-paste of the actual dictionary entries, which only included terms that were (1) in the test and (2) non-content related. Results of studies suggested that it is a highly effective and valid accommodation for ELL students.

Native language testing

Translating tests into a student's native language is an accommodation used by many states across the country (Abedi *et al.*, 2001; Rivera *et al.*, 2000). However, translating a test can make the instrument easier or harder in another language, and some cultural phrases and idioms can be difficult to translate (Hambleton, 2001). Furthermore, students may be only proficient in *speaking* their home language, not in reading it, particularly if the students have not received formal instruction in the home language. Translating assessment tools into a student's native language may not produce desirable results if the language of instruction and assessment are not aligned (Abedi *et al.*, 2000). Given the large number of languages spoken in public schools, translating tests also raises many feasibility issues due to the resources needed.

Linguistically modified test

Some accommodations help ELL students with their English language needs without compromising the validity of assessment. Studies suggest that a linguistically modified version of the test items is an effective and valid accommodation for ELL students (Abedi *et al.*, 2000; Maihoff, 2002; Rivera and Stansfield, 2001). We will elaborate more on this form of accommodation for two reasons. First, as indicated above, a linguistically modified version of a test is a good example of an effective, valid, and relevant accommodation for ELL students, and, second, the impact of linguistic factors in the assessment of ELL students is clearly being demonstrated by this accommodation.

Linguistic modification involves modifying the linguistic features on existing assessments of any item that may include unnecessary complexity. For example, something as simple as switching from passive voice to active voice is considered linguistic modification. Some research refers to this as linguistic simplification, but it is not necessarily simplifying a test, but rather reducing linguistic complexity that is not related to the construct.

To provide a more contextual framework for this accommodation, we start with the concept of language as a source of construct-irrelevant variance for content areas in which language is not the primary construct being measured. Research has identified 14 major categories of linguistic features that appear to contribute to the difficulty of comprehending text (Abedi, 2006, 2007, 2010; Abedi *et al.*, 1997; Shaftel *et al.*, 2006). These features may slow the reader down, increase the likelihood of misinterpretation, or add to the reader's cognitive load, thus interfering with concurrent tasks. Indexes used to measure language difficulty include unfamiliar (or less commonly used) vocabulary, complex grammatical structures, and discourse that include extra material, abstractions, and passive voice (Abedi *et al.*, 1997).

In the linguistic modification approach, sources of unnecessary linguistic complexity, such as those mentioned above, are identified. A team of content, linguistic, and measurement experts determine which linguistic features, among the 14 major categories that were identified in research (Abedi, 2010), are present in the text and how to reduce their impacts. First, each item in the test is examined for the presence and intensity of each linguistic feature by rating these features in the item. A five-point Likert-type rating rubric (with 1 indicating little or no complexity of the item on that feature and 5 suggesting that the item was seriously impacted by the feature) is used to generate ratings on all items. Items that were rated high (rating of 3 or higher) can then be marked for either deletion or revision. The same group of experts who identified these features would then guide the revision process, changing or eliminating items when necessary. The goal would be for all items to have a rating of 2 or below on the test.

This accommodation may have great potential to be effective and help provide valid assessment outcomes for ELL students. It appears to be quite relevant for ELL students, since it provides the type of assistance (linguistic assistance) that ELL students need, is based on consistent results from experimentally controlled experiments, and does not alter the construct being measured (Abedi, 2010).

Computer testing

Research findings suggest that computer testing is an effective and valid accommodation for ELL students. In a study by Abedi (Abedi, 2009; Abedi *et al.*, 2003), ELL students showed higher levels of motivation on the assessment when it was administered by computer. The study used a computer to implement a customized English "pop-up" glossary, which was also found to be effective and valid for ELL students. The "pop-up" glossary aspect of the system was set up to only gloss terms that were unrelated to the content being measured (mathematics in this study). The system kept track of how often the glossary terms were utilized and how much time each student spent on the glossary terms. In a modified second version of this study (currently being conducted), several additional accommodation features have been added to the system. These new features include variation in font size, read aloud test items and adaptive testing based on the students' level of English proficiency, which is tested at the start of the session.

Main research methods

The summary of literature presented above clearly shows mixed results on the effectiveness and validity of many forms of the accommodations currently used for ELL students. There might be several issues with the design of these studies that could lead to such mixed findings. First and foremost are the issues regarding samples of students for these studies. If the sample size is small or the sample is not representative of the population in question, then inconsistent results could be obtained. The inconsistencies in the outcomes of the studies described above may also be due to the impact of extraneous variables on the study that are considered as threats to internal and external validity of the study that may not have been properly controlled (Gay, 1981). To help understand methodological issues in the use and interpretation of accommodations, we will discuss the methodological issues concerning accommodations that were reflected in the four research questions presented earlier.

Question 1: examining the effectiveness of accommodations for ELL students

The concept of accommodation was developed and applied mainly in the assessment of students with disabilities, and some of the accommodations that are used for ELL students were originally designed and implemented for students with disabilities (Willner *et al.*, 2008). Therefore, they may be irrelevant for ELLs and may not be effective at improving ELL student performance. For example, among the 73 accommodations used for ELL students across the nation (Rivera, 2003), only 11 (15%) of them were found to be relevant for ELL students (Abedi, 2006). The rest of these accommodations (62) did not seem to be relevant or did not even have face validity for ELL students.

An accommodation is effective for ELL students if it helps reduce the sources of construct-irrelevant variance and make the assessment more accessible to these students. Therefore, it is imperative to assess ELL students' needs and the ways that accommodations could help them when selecting effective accommodations. Unlike students with disabilities, who are grouped under several different categories with different types of disabilities and different needs, ELL students share a common characteristic: they all need linguistic assistance. Therefore, accommodations that could directly address their linguistic needs would be the most relevant accommodations for this group.

Effective accommodations for ELL students should help to provide assessments that are more accessible to these students by reducing unnecessary linguistic complexity of assessments. The effectiveness of accommodations for ELL students can be examined through an analysis of performance differences between ELL students assessed under the accommodation conditions (the treatment group) and ELL students tested under the standard testing condition with no accommodations provided (the control group). This comparison should be done through a randomized experiment in which students are assigned randomly to the treatment (accommodated) and control (non-accommodated) groups. Such random assignment (assuming a large enough sample size) would control for many sources of threats to internal validity of the design for testing effectiveness of accommodations. By assigning students randomly to the treatment and control groups students' initial differences can also be controlled.

Unfortunately, however, results of studies on the effectiveness of accommodations have illustrated that some of the accommodations that are shown to be effective may alter the construct being measured (Abedi *et al.*, 2000; Sireci *et al.*, 2003). Therefore, it is essential that evidence on the effectiveness of accommodations be interpreted in light of the validity evidence for the accommodations.

Research design for examining effectiveness of accommodations for ELLs

ELL students should be randomly assigned to either a treatment group in which they receive accommodations or to a control group in which they are tested under the standard testing condition in which no accommodation is provided. Evidence of improvement in the performance of ELL students under the accommodated condition may be an indication of the effectiveness of the accommodation used. However, as indicated above, the study of how effective each accommodation is must be conducted under experimentally controlled conditions by assigning subjects randomly to the treatment and control groups so that any possible initial differences that may affect the outcome of the study could be controlled. It is also important to control for any other sources of variations that could affect the outcome of the effectiveness study. For example, studies on accommodations are often conducted in intact classrooms. There are some expected sources of variability due to classroom characteristics (e.g., teacher background, average socioeconomic status, percentage of ELLs, percentage of students with disabilities) and school and district characteristics and resources that can be controlled statistically with a hierarchical linear modeling approach and other statistical methodologies.

Question 2: examining the validity of accommodations for ELL students

Accommodations are provided to ELL students to reduce construct-irrelevant variance from the assessment outcomes; thus making assessments more accessible to ELL students. A major source of construct-irrelevant variance is due to language factors in the assessments of ELL students. Unnecessary linguistic complexity in the assessment introduces an additional dimension into the assessment model, which may be unrelated to the target construct being measured. However, in the use of accommodation one must be extremely careful that the accommodations used do not alter the construct being measured. Therefore, one approach in examining the validity of accommodations is to compare the performance of non-ELL students under the accommodated and non-accommodated conditions. If the performance of non-ELL students, for whom accommodations are not intended, changes significantly under the accommodated condition, then the accommodations is believed to do more than what is intended to do. The accommodated outcomes under such situation may not be valid. Another approach in examining the validity of accommodations is to compare the structural relationship of the assessment outcomes with a set of valid external criteria under accommodated and non-accommodated conditions.

While there is not enough evidence to judge the validity of all the accommodations used for ELL students, results of existing research suggest that some of the accommodations used for ELL students and students with disabilities may alter the construct being measured (Abedi, 2007; Bielinski *et al.*, 2001; Meloy *et al.*, 2000). For others, however, there is not much evidence to judge the validity of assessments under those accommodations. Such lack of evidence puts states in a very difficult position. They may have to use accommodations without having evidence on their validity and comparability.

Research design for examining validity of accommodations for ELLs

Both effectiveness and validity of accommodations depend, to a large extent, on the content being measured. Accommodations that may be effective and valid for one content area may not be so for other content areas. Therefore, it is important to examine the validity of accommodations for each particular content and testing situation. To provide more valid and consistent results on the validity of accommodations, an experimental study can be conducted where large samples of students are randomly assigned to the accommodated and non-accommodated conditions and sources of extraneous variables that affect validity of the outcomes are controlled to the extent possible. Then, the validity of the accommodations can be examined using two different yet complementary approaches: (1) performance difference and (2) the criterion-related validity approach.

Performance difference

If accommodations do not alter the construct being measured, then performance of non-ELL students— for whom accommodations are NOT intended—should remain the same under both the accommodated and non-accommodated assessments. Thus, a significant performance change under accommodated assessment for the non-ELL students may suggest that accommodations are doing more than what they are supposed to do. The null hypothesis on the validity of the accommodated assessments can be examined separately for each accommodation. To test this hypothesis, the mean scores of non-ELL students are compared across the accommodation conditions (accommodated/non-accommodated). If the null hypothesis of no performance difference between the accommodated and non-accommodated assessments is rejected, then one can conclude that the accommodations are affecting the constructs being measured and that the validity of those accommodations may have been compromised.

Criterion-related validation approach in examining validity of accommodations

Some researchers argue that increased performance of non-ELL students under accommodations may not be enough to suggest that the accommodated assessment outcome is invalid, especially when the ELL group benefits more from the accommodations (the interaction effect). Therefore, examining the validity of accommodated assessments using the criterion-related validity approach may provide more convincing evidence for judging the validity of accommodated assessments. It would be helpful to apply both approaches in the study of the validity of accommodations.

To assess the validity of accommodation through an external criterion approach, additional information from the participating students would be needed. Students' state assessments scores, as well as some relevant background variables, may be used as the criterion variables. These variables can then be correlated with the accommodated assessment scores using a latent-variable modeling approach. Using a multiple-group confirmatory factor analysis approach, the structural relationships across the accommodated and non-accommodated assessments can be compared (Abedi, 2002). Hypotheses of differences between the two groups (non-ELL accommodated and non-ELL non-accommodated students) can be examined by testing the invariance of the relationships between the accommodated assessment outcomes and the external criteria.

The following hypotheses of invariance can then be tested:

1. Factor loading of item parcels with the latent variables for math would be the same across the accommodated and non-accommodated assessments.
2. Correlations between the math test and the state assessment latent variables (math) would be the same across the accommodated and non-accommodated assessments
3. The fit indices would be similar between the treatment and the control groups.

If these hypotheses of invariance are not rejected, then the comparability of accommodated and non-accommodated assessment outcomes can be established.

In summary, there are concerns over the validity of accommodations used in the assessment of English language learners. For many of the currently used accommodations there is not sufficient evidence on how they perform in term of validity of assessment outcomes. Without convincing evidence on the validity of accommodations used in practice, it would be difficult to aggregate the accommodated and non-accommodated assessment outcome for assessment and/or accountability purpose.

Question 3: examining the differential impact of accommodations for ELL students

The level of impact accommodations have on student performance may depend on a student's academic background. That is, a single accommodation may not work for all students. As indicated earlier in this chapter, ELL students share a common need and that is the need for assistance with their language. However, even within this population with a common need, there are major differences in their academic backgrounds. For example, ELL students differ in their level of English language proficiency (see, for example, Abedi et al., 2003). Some of these students are as proficient in English as their native English-speaking peers while some are transitioning from full proficiency in another language. For ELL students at the higher levels of English proficiency, accommodations such as "linguistically modified tests" might be more relevant whereas for those students at the lower level of English proficiency (but who have a higher level of native language proficiency), native language or bilingual assessments might be more relevant.

However, native language accommodations may not be relevant for all students who are proficient in their native language. Thus, a student's academic background should be considered for assigning appropriate accommodations. For example, for bilingual students who are quite proficient in their native language but are being instructed in English, the native language or bilingual assessments may not be a relevant accommodation since they have learned all of the content terms in English (Abedi et al., 2004).

Another important background variable that could help with the appropriate assignment of accommodation is the experience students have with the accommodations in their instructional history. Students perform better under accommodations that they have used in their classrooms.

Question 4: assessing the degree of relevance of accommodations for ELL students

As indicated earlier in this chapter, the concept and application of accommodation was first introduced in the assessment literature for students with disabilities. There are many different categories of disabilities with different background characteristics and different needs; therefore, accommodations should be relevant to each of these students in addressing their needs. For example, accommodations that are used for blind and visual impaired students (e.g., Braille) would not be relevant for deaf and hard of hearing students. For ELL students, however, the situation might be quite different. While their level of English proficiency might be different, all ELL students share a common need for assistance with their language. Therefore, many of the accommodations currently used for ELL students that are adopted from the field of students with disabilities are not relevant for these students. For example, accommodations such as "one-on-one testing," "small group testing," "multiple breaks," "writing the response on the text booklet" may not have any relevance to ELL assessments. None of these accommodations specifically address their particular language needs. Providing such irrelevant accommodations may prevent students from receiving the accommodations that they actually need.

To assess the relevance of accommodations for ELL students in absence of credible experimental-based evidence, an accommodation expert panel at the state level could be formed to discuss the accommodations that are used at the state level and judge their relevance for ELLs. Willner *et al.* (2008) conducted an expert-group study to identify relevant accommodations for ELL students through a Delphi approach. The expert group selected a small set of accommodations that they recommend to use for ELL students.

Recommendations for practice and future directions

Accommodations are used for English language learners and students with disabilities to "level the playing field" by making assessments more accessible for these students. Unlike students with disabilities who are in different categories of disabilities with different needs, ELL students have a common need of language assistance. Therefore, accommodations that are created and used for students with disabilities for different purpose may not be relevant for ELL students. Willner *et al.* (2008) discussed direct-linguistic accommodations and indicated those accommodations may be more relevant for ELL students than the accommodations that are developed and used for students with disabilities. Unfortunately, there is not enough research support for many of the accommodations that are currently used for ELL students, even those that are under the category of "direct-linguistic accommodations." The only way to judge the efficiency and validity of these accommodations is to use them in experimentally controlled situations on both ELL and non-ELL students and examine their validity, effectiveness, and differential impact under well-controlled experimental designs.

Based on the summary of research presented in this chapter, there is not enough evidence to help decide which accommodations to use for ELL students. In terms of research evidence, accommodations can be grouped into three categories. Category 1 includes accommodations that may alter the construct being measured. These accommodations are often referred to as "Modifications." The outcome of assessments under these accommodations may not be aggregated with the non-accommodated assessment outcomes. As an example of these accommodations *read-aloud* test items in reading and providing full dictionary may be mentioned. For example, a dictionary may provide an unfair advantage to the recipient by helping them with the correct response to the questions. Category 2 includes accommodations for which research findings are mixed. For these accommodations more research is needed to shed light on their effectiveness and validity. Examples include extended time accommodations and providing glossaries. For accommodations in category 3, there is enough research support that could help to use them without much concern over their use. Linguistically modified tests are examples of these accommodations.

In summary, providing accommodations for ELL students helps not only to make assessments more accessible for these students but also to provide more valid assessments in general. However, in selecting accommodations for ELL students several major criteria must guide us. The purpose of accommodation is not to give unfair advantage to the recipients but to provide equal assessment opportunity to everyone; therefore, accommodations must be able to play this important role. In selecting accommodations one must clearly consider the purpose and use those accommodations that are relevant for such purpose.

Future developments

Issues concerning the use and validity of accommodations are gaining international momentum. Given the growth in the population of immigrants in the world and considering education issues of ELLs, accommodations are among the important concerns in the international education community. For example, it is likely that the United Kingdom may go down a route akin to the United States in coming years given the growing numbers of ELLs in state schools, and similarly in Germany with its Turkish or Kurdish communities. Educational researchers and policy makers have given their highest attention to these issues since accommodation issues are of major concern in the United States due to the increasing population of ELL students. There is much to be learned from the research amassed on accommodations in the United States as well as that from other countries facing the same situation.

Since accommodations are likely to become a major part of curriculum, instruction, and assessment in the future world's educational system, examining their validity and effectiveness should have a high priority within each nation's educational agenda. It is important to understand that ELLs have the knowledge and ability to learn the content knowledge at the same level as their native English-speaking peers, and accommodations should be used to "level the playing field," i.e., give them opportunity to learn and opportunity to be fairly assessed as their peers as they are learning academic content in a language in which they may not still be quite proficient.

The international community can share and benefit from research on the accommodations for ELL students. It is therefore imperative to have an effective communication channel to collaborate with the research in accommodations and share the outcomes of such studies.

Acknowledgements

I wish to acknowledge the help of Kimberly Mundhenk and Nancy Ewers in reviewing and editing drafts of this chapter.

Further reading

Abedi, J. (2007). Utilizing accommodations in the assessment of English language learners. In N. H. Hornberger (ed.), *Encyclopedia of Language and Education:* Volume 7: *Language Testing and Assessment.* Heidelberg, Germany: Springer, 331–48. Concerns over the validity of accommodations for ELL students have surfaced as the international education community moves toward inclusion of all students (including ELLs and SDs) in national and local assessments. The results of accommodated and non-accommodated assessments cannot be aggregated if the validity of accommodations has not been established. This paper summarizes results of research on the effectiveness and validity of accommodations for ELLs and will examines research findings to determine if there is sufficient evidence to inform decision-makers on the provision of accommodations and reporting of accommodated assessments. While the main thrust of this paper is on accommodation issues for ELL students, some references have been made to accommodations for students with disabilities since ELL accommodation practices are highly affected by accommodation policies and practices for SDs.

Abedi, J., Hofstetter, C. and Lord, C. (2004) Assessment accommodations for English language learners: Implications for policy based research. *Review of Educational Research* 74: 1–28. Decisions about which accommodations to use, for whom, and under what conditions, are based on limited empirical evidence for their effectiveness and validity. Given the potential consequences of test results, it is important that policymakers and educators understand the empirical base underlying their use. This article reviews test accommodation strategies for English learners, derived from "scientifically based research." The results caution against a one-size-fits-all approach. The more promising approaches include modified English and customized dictionaries, which can be used for all students, not just English language learners.

Francis, D., Rivera, M., Lesaux, N., Kieffer, M. and Rivera, H. (2006). Practical Guidelines for the Education of English Language Learners: Research-Based Recommendations for the Use of Accommodations in Large-Scale Assessments. (Under cooperative agreement grant S283B050034 for U.S. Department of Education). Portsmouth, NH: RMC Research Corporation, Center on Instruction. Available online at http://www.centeroninstruction.org/files/ELL3-Assessments.pdf. Language is a key component of individual student success yet English language learners are often unprepared for the rigors of academic language in content areas. This meta-analysis examines the effectiveness and validity of selected accommodations, familiar to the student through daily instructional use and applied during assessments. The results suggest the importance of linguistically appropriate accommodations, ones that have been used effectively in the classroom, and are appropriately selected to match individual student needs. Although no single accommodation has been shown to level the playing field, the most effective ones may be the use of a dictionary or glossary with extra time, provided that the student has previous classroom experience with dictionary or glossary use. Ensuring the opportunity to learn during instruction combined with accommodations that are familiar and useful to individual students in the classroom can increase the chance of academic success for all students.

Kieffer, M., Lesaux, N., Rivera, M. and Francis, D. (2009). Accommodations for English language learners taking large-scale assessments: A meta-analysis on effectiveness and validity. *Review of Educational Research* 79: 1168–1201. Accommodation use is an important consideration in improving assessments for English language learners and warrants continued research. However, these researchers hypothesize that the performance gap between English language learners and native speakers of English may be due to the impact of necessary language skills rather than unnecessary language demands which accommodations address. They suggest that academic language and content knowledge intersect and are highly dependent on classroom opportunities to learn, without which accommodation use will not result in improved academic performance. They recommend that assessment accommodation research continue but that a strong focus is placed on instruction and academic language that is so important for academic success.

Sireci, S., Li, S. and Scarpati, S. (2003). *The Effects of Test Accommodation on Test performAnce: a review of the literature* (Report No. 485). Amherst, MA: School of Education, University of Massachusetts, Center for Educational Assessment. These authors call into question the interaction hypothesis that only students who need an accommodation benefit from it, and those for whom it is not intended will not. The focus on four accommodations: customized dictionaries or glossaries, extra time, test translation/adaptation into native language translations, and simplified English accommodations results in mixed findings. The authors attribute the inconclusive results to the fact that both accommodations and groups of students are heterogeneous. They further discuss the four accommodations in detail together with potential in the concept of Universal Design for Learning (UDL) to increase test accessibility for the widest number of students; possibly reducing or eliminating the need for accommodations. Research in the challenging arena of accommodations has produced positive results for many groups of students and will continue to improve assessment practices.

References

Abedi, J. (2002). Assessment and accommodations of English language learners: issues, concerns, and recommendations. *Journal of School Improvement* 3: 83–89.

—— (2006). *Accommodations for English Language Learners that May Alter the Construct Being Measured*. Paper presented at the Annual Meeting of the American Educational Research Association, San Francisco.

—— (2007). English language learners with disabilities. In C. Cahlan-Laitusis and L. Cook (eds), *Accommodating Students with Disabilities on State Assessments: what works?* Arlington, VA: Council for Exceptional Children.

—— (2009). Computer testing as a form of accommodation for English language learners. *Educational Assessment* 14: 195–211.

—— (2010). *Linguistic Factors in the Assessment of English Language Learners.* In G. Walford, E. Tucker and M. Viswanathan (eds), *The Sage Handbook of Measurement.* Oxford, UK: Sage Publications.

Abedi, J. and Herman, J. L. (2010). Assessing English language learners' opportunity to learn mathematics: issues and limitations. *Teachers College Record* 112: 723–46.

Abedi, J., Lord, C. and Plummer, J. (1997). *Language background as a variable in NAEP mathematics performance* (CSE Technical Report No. 429). Los Angeles, CA: University of California, National Center for Research on Evaluation, Standards, and Student Testing.

Abedi, J., Hofstetter, C., Lord, C. and Baker, E. (1998). *NAEP Math Performance and Test Accommodations: interactions with student language background.* Los Angeles, CA: University of California, National Center for Research on Evaluation, Standards, and Student Testing.

Abedi, J., Lord, C., Hofstetter, C. and Baker, E. (2000). Impact of accommodation strategies on English language learners' test performance. *Educational Measurement: Issues and Practice* 19: 16–26.

Abedi, J., Courtney, M., Mirocha, J., Leon, S. and Goldberg, J. (2001). *Language Accommodation for Large-scale Assessment in Science.* Los Angeles, CA: University of California, National Center for Research on Evaluation, Standards, and Student Testing.

Abedi, J., Courtney, M. and Leon, S. (2003a). *Effectiveness and validity of accommodations for English language learners in large-scale assessments* (CSE Technical Report No. 608). Los Angeles, CA: University of California, National Center for Research on Evaluation, Standards, and Student Testing.

Abedi, J., Leon, S. and Mirocha, J. (2003b). *Impact of students' language background on content-based assessment: analyses of extant data.* Los Angeles, CA: University of California, National Center for Research on Evaluation, Standards, and Student Testing.

Abedi, J., Hofstetter, C. H. and Lord, C. (2004). Assessment accommodations for English language learners: implications for policy-based empirical research. *Review of Educational Research* 74: 1–28.

Bielinski, J., Thurlow, M., Ysseldyke, J., Freidebach, J. and Freidebach, M. (2001). *Read-aloud accommodation: effects on multiple-choice reading and math items.* Technical Report: Minneapolis, MN: National Center on Educational Outcomes.

Chiu, C. W. T. and Pearson, D. (1999). *Synthesizing the effects of test accommodations for special education and limited English proficient students.* Paper presented at the Paper presented at the National Conference on Large Scale Assessment, Snowbird, UT.

Francis, D., Lesaux, N., Kieffer, M. and Rivera, H. (2006). *Research-based Recommendations for the Use of Accommodations in Large-scale Assessments.* Houston, TX: Center on Instruction.

Fuchs, L. S., Fuchs, D., Eaton, S. B., Hamlett, C., Binkley, E. and Crouch, R. (2000). Using objective data sources to enhance teacher judgments about test accommodations. *Exceptional Children* 67: 67–81.

Gay, L. R. (1981). *Educational Research: competencies for analysis and application,* 2nd edn. Columbus, OH: Charles E. Merrill.

Hafner, A. L. (2001). *Evaluating the Impact of Test Accommodations on Test Scores of LEP Students & Non-LEP Students.* Los Angeles, CA: California State University.

Hambleton, R. H. (2001). Setting performance standards on educational assessments and criteria for evaluating the process. In G. J. Cizek (ed.), *Setting Performance Standards: concepts, methods, and perspectives.* Mahwah, NJ: Lawrence Erlbaum, 89–116.

Maihoff, N. A. (2002). *Using Delaware Data in Making Decisions Regarding the Education of LEP Students.* Paper presented at the Paper presented at the Council of Chief State School Officers 32nd Annual National Conference on Large-Scale Assessment, June, Palm Desert, CA.

Marquart, A. (2000). *The Use of Extended Time as an Accommodation on a Standardized Mathematics Test: an investigation of effects on scores and perceived consequences for students of various skill levels.* Paper presented at the Paper presented at the annual meeting of the Council of Chief State School Officers, Snowbird, UT.

Meloy, L. L., Deville, C. and Frisbie, D. (2000). *The Effect of a Reading Accommodation on Standardized Test Scores of Learning Disabled and Non Learning Disabled Students.* Paper presented at the Annual Meeting of the National Council on Measurement in Education (New Orleans, LA, April 24–28, 2000). Available: http://eric.ed.gov/PDFS/ED441008.pdf.

Munger, G. F. and Loyd, B. H. (1991). Effect of speediness on test performance of handicapped and nonhandicapped examinees. *Journal of Educational Research* 85: 53–57.

Rivera, C. (2003). *State Assessment Policies for English language learners.* Paper presented at the Presented at the 2003 Large-Scale Assessment Conference.

Rivera, C. and Stansfield, C. W. (2001). *The effects of linguistic simplification of science test items on performance of limited English proficient and monolingual English-speaking students.* Paper presented at the Paper presented at the annual meeting of the American Educational Research Association, April, Seattle, WA.

Rivera, C., Stansfield, C. W., Scialdone, L. and Sharkey, M. (2000). *An Analysis of State Policies for the Inclusion and Accommodation of English Language Learners in State Assessment Programs during 1998–99.* Final Report. Paper presented at the Annual Meeting of the American Educational Research Association (Seattle, Washington, April 12, 2001). Available: http://deepwater.org/bioteacher/12-Review%20and%20SOLs/SOL-Delaware-simplification.pdf

Shaftel, J., Belton-Kocher, E., Glasnapp, D. and Poggio, J. (2006). the impact of language characteristics in mathematics test items on the performance of English language learners and students with disabilities. *Educational Assessment* 11: 105–26.

Sireci, S. G., Li, S. and Scarpati, S. (2003). *The Effects of Test Accommodation on Test Performance: a review of the literature* (Center for Educational Assessment Research Report No. 485). Amherst, MA: School of Education, University of Massachusetts, Amherst.

Thurlow, M. L. (2001). *The effects of a simplified-English dictionary accommodation for LEP students who are not literate in their first language.* Paper presented at the Paper presented at the annual meeting of the American Educational Research Association, April, Seattle, WA.

Thurlow, M. and Liu, K. (2001). *State and District Assessments as an Avenue to Equity and Excellence for English Language Learners with Disabilities.* Minneapolis, MN: University of Minnesota, National Center on Educational Outcomes.

U.S. House of Representatives (2001). No Child Left Behind Act of 2001, 107th Congress 1st Session, Report 107–334. Washington, DC.

Willner, L. S., Rivera, C. and Acosta, B. D. (2008). *Descriptive Study of State Assessment Policies for Accommodating English Language Learners.* Arlington, VA: George Washington University Center for Equity and Excellence in Education.

Wolf, M. K., Herman, J. L., Kim, J., Abedi, J., Leon, S., Griffin, N., *et al.* (2008). *Providing Validity Evidence to Improve the Assessment of English Language Learners.* CRESST Report 738: National Center for Research on Evaluation, Standards, and Student Testing (CRESST).

Part II
Classroom assessment and washback

Classroom assessment

Carolyn E. Turner

Introduction and definitions

For a long time classroom-based assessment (CBA, i.e., assessment internal to the classroom and managed by the teacher) was only viewed as an offshoot of traditional large-scale testing (i.e., assessment external to the classroom such as school board exams, standardized international exams). This was reflected in the language testing literature, in the conference presentations concerning language testing and even in the language testing textbooks available to teachers. In other words it was taken for granted that the types/tasks of testing and the interpretation/use/reporting of results employed in large-scale testing also applied to classroom assessment. The field of language testing/assessment is evolving and is beginning to see the importance and uniqueness of the classroom learning context and the teacher factor in interpreting the true role of assessment in classroom settings (i.e., to provide information to help inform teaching and learning). In the 1990s, textbooks for pre-service and in-service teachers began to appear that considered CBA as a unique paradigm (e.g., Genesee and Upshur, 1996) and as time passed, research in such settings began creeping into the language testing literature (e.g., Leung, 2004; Rea-Dickins, 2006). Well-known language testing resources online also began to include references to CBA (Fulcher, 2010a). The assessment focusing on teaching and learning has increasingly become of interest to the research world (both in general education and more specifically in language education for the purposes of this chapter) and the teacher's role has been the focus. A research agenda separate from the paradigm of traditional large-scale testing remains to be identified, but a consensus is growing that more research is needed and that the "theorization" of CBA (Davison and Leung, 2009) is overdue.

The literature demonstrates a variety of terms (see 'Historical perspectives' below). There is a need to come to agreement on definitions, but this appears to be part of the process as CBA becomes recognized as a separate paradigm from psychometrically based large-scale testing. In the meantime for this chapter, concepts from Genesee and Upshur (1996), Colby-Kelly and Turner (2007), and Yin (2010) have been combined to define characteristics of CBA. It involves strategies by teachers to plan and carry out the collection of multiple types of information concerning student language use, to analyze and interpret it, to provide feedback, and to use this information to help make decisions to enhance teaching and learning. Observable evidence of learning (or lack of learning) is collected through a variety of methods (e.g., observation, portfolios, conferencing, journals, questionnaires, interviews, projects, task sheets, quizzes/tests), and most often embedded in regular instructional activities. In other words, CBA comprises a repertoire of methods and the reflective procedures that teachers and students use for evidence to gauge student learning on an ongoing basis. In this way teaching is adjusted to meet student needs. In addition, CBA is a contextually bound and socially constructed activity involving different stakeholders in learning. Within the classroom it is mainly teachers and students working together (e.g., teacher, peer or self-assessment), but additional participants can be parents, school administrators, and others in the educational context. Within CBA there is potential for overlap with psychometrically based large-scale testing if teachers choose to use such information when interpreting their quiz or test results, but this would only be one source of information among many others with the latter falling into the category of assessment without tests. Teachers most often have external criteria/standards to meet concerning their students' performance. Ideally CBA should complement such criteria and the external tests that accompany it. Teacher mediation between these criteria/standards and CBA is a challenge, however, and the call for synchronized assessment across internal and external assessment to the classroom within educational systems is becoming more prominent (Pellegrino et al., 2001).

Within this context this chapter will provide an overview of CBA, which in the broader scheme of things is still in its infancy as an independent domain and paradigm. Even though language teachers have been assessing for decades, the reality of how such activity unfolds in the classroom has not been well documented nor have the resources to teachers been that useful until more recently.

Historical perspectives

In order to make sense of CBA's emerging profile, it is important to situate it within a historical framework. To date a substantial amount of research has been carried out concerning the method of large-scale testing external to the classroom. This is important information that has contributed to the increasing quality of tests and has provided salient criteria by which to judge the validity of high-stakes decisions concerning language ability of individuals. What has been confusing during this period, however, is to what extent such studies are related to classroom activity. Initially, such concepts as norm-referencing, psychometrics, validity theory, reliability, generalizability (to only name a few) were also thought to be part of CBA in their current interpretations. In some situations they were even imposed on teachers causing a gap between theory and actual classroom practice. There was no ill intention. It is just that in general and language education the focus had been on measurement theory for large-scale testing and little attention had been paid to CBA. This was partially due to the assumption that large-scale testing qualities also applied to CBA (Shephard, 2000).

With the increased attention towards constructivist/socio-cultural theories of learning and the influence of Vygotsky's work (1978) (e.g., *zone of proximal development* where learning takes place through social interaction), the call to expand traditional educational measurement to view CBA as a different paradigm slowly began to gain momentum (see James, 2006 for a discussion on assessment, teaching, and theories of learning). Reflection on this direction is clearly articulated in Moss (1996): 'It would enable us to support a wider range of sound assessment practices, including those less standardized forms of assessment that honor the purposes teachers and students bring to their work … ' (20). The assessment approach internal to the classroom as opposed to the approach employed in large-scale testing has evolved into a current discussion of two distinct paradigms (Leung, 2004). Different terms have been used to describe the two approaches which can be confusing at times, but each term comes with a specific rationale. This chapter uses the terminology CBA versus large-scale assessment/testing (Pellegrino et al., 2001), but other examples are teacher assessment versus formal assessments (McNamara and Roever,

2006); formative and summative assessment (Brookhart, 2003); and assessment for learning (AFL) versus assessment of learning (AOL) (Black and Wiliam, 1998a, 1998b; Gardner, 2006). What remains is to develop a research agenda for CBA. Literature is abundant concerning large-scale testing, and now that CBA is emerging as a different paradigm, there is much to learn. (See Fulcher and Davidson (2007) and Fulcher (2010b) for expanded discussions on 'pedagogy and the measurement paradigm.')

Critical issues and topics

Since describing CBA is still in its initial stages, there are many aspects that need investigating and clarification as with any new paradigm. Some of the salient issues will be mentioned here.

Terms: Do we need one umbrella term for assessment internal to the classroom?

As the awareness of classroom assessment as an activity to support learning grows, grappling with what to call it has become apparent. Various labels and approaches with overlapping characteristics can be found in the literature. This can be perplexing, because each of them claims some relation to the classroom, but the question remains, which one can serve as a comprehensive or umbrella term? There is no consensus to date because some terms have unique characteristics that may not generalize to all classrooms, so a question may be: Do we need an umbrella term? There is much overlap among the terms that have evolved and one learns quickly that they are often used interchangeably in some of the literature. Davison and Leung (2009: 395) summarize the situation well when saying:

> all [the terms] tend to be used to signify a more teacher-mediated, context-based, classroom-embedded assessment practice, explicitly or implicitly defined in opposition to traditional externally set and assessed large scale formal examinations used primarily for selection and/ or accountability purposes.

It is important to note here that parallel to the recognition of CBA, there is another discussion taking place in the literature which pits the traditional 'testing culture' against a new 'assessment culture' (Lynch, 2001); the latter overlapping with CBA. The two opposing perspectives argue as though there is only room for one paradigm. Others focusing on educational concerns (e.g., Pellegrino *et al.*. 2001) provide a more pragmatic view in stating a variety of assessments are needed and it's the purpose of the context that should dictate the type employed. (For an informative discussion of these opposing views, see Fox, 2008).

Some of the names found in the literature and used in conjunction with classroom assessment include: alternative (Fox, 2008), authentic (O'Malley and Valdez Pierce, 1996), dynamic (Lantolf and Poehner, 2008) (also see Antón, this volume), diagnostic (Alderson, 2005; also see Jang, this volume), performance (McNamara, 1996), classroom-based (Genesee and Upshur, 1996), teacher-based (Davison and Leung, 2009), school-based (Davison, 2007), and AFL (Black and Wiliam, 2003). To date, several of these terms when related to classroom activity are used simultaneously with and considered to be an extension of the more general term formative evaluation (Brookhart, 2005). Scriven (1967) coined the term formative evaluation in education meaning that assessment could be used to form acquisition of learning through ongoing assessment procedures to support learning. In other words, in this role it could enhance learning rather than just being used to calculate final grades (i.e., as in summative evaluation). One of its main objectives was to cultivate greater learner responsibility through motivation, teacher feedback, self- and peer assessment. The most recent iteration of formative assessment and the one gaining attention in research and practice is AFL (see 'Current contributions and research' below). It will be the main focus in this chapter.

Reliability and validity: Do we need to revisit these qualities for CBA?

Another issue concerns reliability and validity and whether these qualities as they are known in the large-scale testing context (i.e., measurement paradigm) are relevant to CBA. The purpose of CBA is to support learning and through feedback to help learners understand where they are in their learning, where they need to go and how best to get there (ARG, Assessment Reform Group, as cited in Gardner, 2006: 2). This involves a very local context where teachers know their students and work with them, where student reflection and performance promote and encourage further learning via self, peer and teacher feedback. Awareness is growing in the literature that these phenomena in the CBA context unfold uniquely and that the assessment characteristics are different than traditional large-scale testing (Arkoudis and O'Loughlin, 2004; Moss, 2003). Fulcher and Davidson (2007: 24–25) explain that the main difference between CBA and large-scale testing is the "context of the classroom" which is a learning setting as described above. They state that this is not part of large-scale testing where context (e.g., the room, the invigilators) is considered construct-irrelevant variance (Messick, 1989), that is, the context is not relevant to the test. It's the test taker's ability in relation to the test construct that generates a score.

Early attempts were made to reconceptualize reliability and validity in CBA (Moss, 1996), but others (Brown and Hudson, 1998) expressed concerns from a measurement viewpoint. Over time, however, the proponents of CBA made their case that applying psychometric theory to assessment internal to the classroom had not really worked (Black and Wiliam, 1998a, 1998b; Brookhart, 2003; Moss, 2003). They demonstrated how CBA served learning in that the participants (teacher, students) discussed and interpreted the evidence to enhance the progression across the necessary learning phases. They endorsed the concepts of reliability and validity as important, but felt revisiting these concepts was in order due to the contextualized nature of information generated in classrooms (Brookhart, 2003). This line of thought was running parallel in second language education.

> The traditional positivist position on language testing, with the tendency to map the standard psychometric criteria of reliability and validity onto the classroom assessment procedures, has been called into question, and the scope of validity has been significantly broadened and taken further by a number of researchers.
>
> *(Rea-Dickins, 2006: 512)*

The known overlap across CBA and large-scale testing is the need for evidence, but the context and use of this evidence are different. Fulcher (2010b: 75–77) attempts to explain the differences through a discussion of understanding change and states that the "whole purpose of 'feedback' or 'mediation' in CBA is to cause change," whereas the purpose of large-scale tests is "certainly not to cause change." It is assumed that a "learner's state will remain stable." It has become apparent that before the concepts of reliability and validity can be adequately reconceptualized, however, more research is needed to fully understand the realities of assessment practice in the classroom.

Alignment: In educational systems, what is needed to align internal and external-to-the-classroom assessment?

As awareness grows concerning different approaches to and different purposes for assessment in educational systems, discussion has turned to the need for alignment across CBA and large-scale assessments. In the United States, the Committee on the Foundations of Assessment, National Research Council stated:

> A vision for the future is that assessments at all levels … will work together in a system that is comprehensive, coherent, and continuous. In such a system, assessments would provide a variety of evidence to support educational decision making. Assessment at all levels would be linked back to the same underlying model of student learning and would provide indications of student growth over time.
>
> *(Pellegrino* et al.*, 2001: 9)*

Cumming (2009) points out that educational systems internationally are reforming their policies concerning student language achievement by way of setting criteria (i.e., standards, benchmarks, competencies) for a unified system across tests, curricula and pedagogy (see Hudson, this volume). Examples of this can be seen in the *Common European Framework of Reference for Languages: Learning, Teaching, Assessment* (Council of Europe, 2001) and the *PreK-12 English Language Proficiency Standards* (TESOL, 2006). (See Cumming, 2009 for references that discuss the "dilemmas of transposition" of curriculum standards into assessment instruments). This is unfolding in the form of criterion-referenced approaches (as opposed to the traditional norm-referenced approaches) and provides criteria for teaching and large-scale testing alike.

In support of alignment, there are increasing claims that "assessment can support learning as well as measure it" (Black and Wiliam, 2003: 623). Discussion on the benefits of aligning formative and summative assessment is increasing. For example, teachers' formative work would not be undermined by summative pressures, and summative requirements might be better served by taking full advantage of improvements in teachers' assessment work (Black and Wiliam, 2003: 623–24). This discussion is informed by the washback research which explores the potential effects of high-stakes tests on language teaching and learning (Cheng *et al.*, 2004; Turner, 2009; Turner *et al.*, 2010; Wall, 2000). At the same time we need to back up and examine what is actually happening in practice. CBA has been described in conjunction with the term "assessment bridge" which means "the place where assessment, teaching and learning interweave in the classroom" (Colby-Kelly and Turner, 2009: 12), but as this activity is taking place teachers continue to grapple with the relationship between what they are doing in the classroom and the specifications of the external large-scale tests their students will eventually need to take. It is not clear how individual systems will implement educational policies to promote alignment and whether in practice they will be viable. For example, in the UK where AFL has its roots, a new strategy labeled Assessing Pupil's Progress (APP) has been introduced by the government (Guiver, 2010). Those promoting AFL see APP as completely distinctive from AFL, and feel it resembles summative assessment in that its focus is on recording progress and achievement, rather than on how students learn and the processes to help them learn. Elsewhere attempts have been made to describe practices that might accompany a standards-aligned classroom (e.g., see Gottlieb, 2006, for the US context). The issue of alignment is far from being a straightforward procedure. Many further questions remain. For example: How do teachers and students distinguish in practice ongoing assessment for student learning towards a goal and assessment for recording achievement of that goal? How does this relationship manifest itself in instructional contexts? How do teachers mediate between routine classroom assessment activity and preparing students for upcoming external exams? What will the teachers' role be within the context of an alignment policy?

Assessment literacy and teacher training: How do we reach a balance between CBA strategies and technical test development strategies?

With the burgeoning awareness of the need for diverse approaches to assessment contingent on purpose and for the complementary components of assessment internal and external to the classroom, there has also been an increasing consensus on the importance of assessment literacy for pre-service and in-service teachers at all levels. Assessment literacy refers to knowledge, skills, and understanding of assessment principles and practice (Taylor, 2009). This can include classroom assessment strategies, mediation between assessment activity internal and external to the classroom, and understanding of test development strategies and interpretation of test scores. Malone (2008) points out, however, that the scope of assessment literacy that is actually needed by teachers and/or specific groups of teachers still must be identified. There are varying perspectives throughout the literature (Davison and Leung, 2009; Pellegrino *et al.*, 2001; Taylor, 2009) as to what this might encompass, and this would naturally vary across different contexts. Even though research is needed, Malone (2008) points out that an abundance of information sources have evolved and are now available to teachers (e.g., text-based materials, self-access materials including workshops and internet-based resources). Turner (2006) in exploring teachers' "professionalism" in assessment learned that secondary level teachers displayed knowledge concerning several important elements that abound in the language testing/assessment literature (e.g., method effect, the assessment bridge). Her survey results indicated that teachers want to do their part in moving the education system into a position where curriculum, their teaching and assessment, and the system's high-stakes exams correspond, but that they struggle with aligning assessments for different purposes (i.e., classroom-based assessment and high-stakes provincial exams). This comes back to the preceding issue of alignment, which points toward the need to potentially include guidance in this area to help teachers become and be viewed as agents and not instruments in their assessment practices (Yin, 2010: 193).

Current contributions and research

Much of the research on CBA is relatively recent (1990s to present) for many of the reasons discussed above concerning the gradual emergence of CBA as a distinct paradigm. It is in fact some of this research that led to the recognition of CBA. The research has been mainly in general education, but studies specific to second/foreign/additional language education are increasing (henceforth called L2 studies). Inquiry has been diverse and segmented, but with the evolving importance of CBA, there is an increasing call for a research agenda to help consolidate its definition to date and to help relate its activity to theory. One finds in the literature numerous studies from different international contexts. There are some that have had a general impact and others that are case studies dealing with individual contexts. The focus here is on language education contexts, but first one of the most salient contributions needs to be mentioned. It is that of the Assessment Reform Group (ARG) in the UK and its ongoing examination of the benefits of what is now labeled as assessment for learning (AFL) in the classroom. Gardner (2006) provides an in-depth view into the work of the ARG explaining the processes and international contexts that have contributed to the research. The ARG considers the AFL process beneficial, but complex, and puts forth 10 principles that serve as the underpinnings of their research. AFL

- is part of effective planning;
- focuses on how students learn;
- is central to classroom practice;

- is a key professional skill;
- is sensitive and constructive;
- fosters motivations;
- promotes understanding of goals and criteria;
- helps learners know how to improve;
- develops the capacity for self-assessment;
- recognizes all education achievement (Gardner, 2006: 3).

In their milestone review of 250 studies of formative assessment in mathematics, science, and other subjects taught in the UK and elsewhere, Black and Wiliam (1998a, 1998b), members of the ARG, found that the common characteristic across the studies they surveyed was that attention to classroom-based formative assessment led to significant gains in learning. They considered this type of assessment to be a salient contributor to successful learning. Even though the research contexts did not include language education, Harlen and Winter (2004) describe how the research in science and mathematics settings can be useful to language learning contexts. As Colby-Kelly (2010) discusses, the disciplines of science and mathematics lend themselves well to AFL strategies (e.g., guided, deductive questioning techniques and scaffolding of learner knowledge through an anticipated linear learning progression). AFL application has proven to be challenging, however, in light of the non-linear nature of L2 acquisition, but increasing research into CBA demonstrates that several of its features appear to have benefits.

A majority of the L2 studies to date report CBA within the context of educational reform and standard-based language policy in education systems (see 'Alignment' above). The L2 studies focus on teachers and their inclusion and application of more learner-centered, formative, and AFL-styled approaches to CBA. At the same time, teacher decision making and reflection on such assessment demonstrates variation contingent on context (Llosa, 2007). This has made it problematic to articulate within a theoretical framework. Recently, however, the discussion has been expanded to find common themes in the research due to mounting evidence that CBA has benefits for learning (Davison and Leung, 2009: 410).

In order to move in the direction of developing a theoretical framework, it is important to realize how much the field of language testing/assessment has actually learned. Even though L2 studies may appear segmented to date, the combination of their findings serve as an important starting point. They have taken place simultaneously and in some instances have drawn upon the work of the ARG when examining the nature of AFL-related classroom processes. They have also confirmed the central role that context plays (the internal teaching and learning socio-cultural context and the external educational socio-political context). The studies have dealt with different but overlapping areas of CBA. Some of the main contributions (but by no means a comprehensive overview) are mentioned here.

- *Teacher processes to support learning:* As L2 studies examining CBA become increasingly visible in the literature, the line between formative assessment and SLA becomes blurred. This is apparent in studies from contexts around the world (e.g., Butler and Lee, 2010, in Korea at the elementary school level; Colby-Kelly and Turner, 2007, in Canada at the pre-university level; Davison, 2004, in Hong Kong and Australia at the secondary school level; Leung and Scott, 2009, in Wales and Scotland at the elementary school level; Rea-Dickins and Gardner, 2000, in England at the primary school level). The common thread across these studies is that teachers consider a wide range of evidence to inform their judgments on student ability. This happens in an ongoing manner within the instructional setting. The combination of information is drawn upon in order to determine what instruction is needed next so further learning can take place. Research designs generating these findings have drawn on multiple methods. Initially much of the research employed qualitative methods to examine teacher processes (e.g., observation, verbal protocol analysis, ethnography, discourse analysis, interviews). As studies continued, quantitative methods were added such as surveys and the quantifying of data used with earlier procedures (Llosa, 2007). In conjunction with these findings comes the increasing recognition of the social character of assessment as it takes form in the classroom (McNamara and Roever, 2006; Rea-Dickins, 2008). When taken individually these contextualized studies may show variation in classroom activity, but when taken as a whole they have furthered our understanding of CBA by confirming the inter-face of SLA and language assessment and the importance of teacher and student interaction, feedback, uptake, and reflection to support learning.

- *Specific methods employed in CBA:* Another area of research that has helped describe CBA pertains to the variety of methods employed by teachers in the instructional context. Brown and Hudson (1998) discuss the complexity of CBA in that teachers have an increasingly wide array of choices in terms of the methods they use. They suggest these "alternatives in assessment" are only tools and should be used in combination to support teacher decision making. In a comparative study across tertiary levels in Canada, Hong Kong, and China, Cheng *et al.* (2004), by way of a self-reporting survey, go further and identify the actual methods (in addition to purposes and procedures) that teachers use in their CBA. They conclude that even though there is diversity across methods, assessment plays a central role in classrooms, and once again it is the context that helps determine the type of assessment method. They, along with others, stress the challenges teachers have in terms of mediating between CBA and external high-stakes tests.

- *Teacher judgments and decision making and the contributing factors:* The two areas of inquiry mentioned thus far could be labeled as precursors for this third area. Drawing on them and "teacher thinking" research, Yin (2010) studied teacher thought processes when assessing students. Using a case study approach with teachers at a UK university language center, she collected data through classroom observation, interviews, and simulated recalls. Her results demonstrate the importance of teacher agency (Rea-Dickins, 2004) as teachers "constantly make decisions related to assessment in the midst of conflicting demands and numerous considerations" (Yin, 2010: 193). Brindley (2001) and Leung and Lewkowicz (2006) discuss the concerns about teacher variability in decision making and in the diverse ways teachers interpret their students' language abilities. "Unless greater attention is given to providing adequate time allocation and appropriate forms of professional development, the many potential benefits of involving teachers in assessment will not be realized" (Brindley, 2001: 403). In her study validating a standards-based classroom assessment of English language proficiency, Llosa (2007) provides a comprehensive literature review of the numerous factors that contribute to teacher decision making in assess-ment (e.g., teacher characteristics, the educational framework in which teachers work, their stu-dents' characteristics). Commonly found is the fact that these decisions "are often affected by factors that are not related to the construct of the assessment" and "are often mediated by competing forces and purposes" (Llosa, 2007: 492).

The three areas of research contributions discussed here have furthered our understanding of the nature of CBA. Teacher diversity in CBA at first caused concern, but as more is learned about the effects inherent to a context for learning (internal and external to the classroom) defining an independent CBA research agenda (as opposed to an agenda similar to that of large-scale tests) appears within reach. Davison and Leung (2009: 410) express their cautious optimism by saying

... TBA [teacher-based assessment], in all its incarnations, has been around English language teaching long enough to demonstrate its powerful potential to improve learning and teaching in a range of different contexts. What it has lacked until recently has been sufficient engagement with theory and a sense of a research agenda ... TBA appears to be gaining enough critical mass and common interest to generate a new level of discussion about core concepts.

Recommendations for practice

An extensive review of the literature does not reveal a common list of ideal "how to" steps for CBA implementation in the classroom itself, and certainly not a list of "how to" select methods. More importantly, a variation of frameworks, principles, strategies, and questions to consider concerning CBA events and selecting methods are provided which will be expanded on in this section (for examples of frameworks which suggest teacher processes/events in carrying out components of CBA, see Davison and Leung, 2009; Genesee and Upshur, 1996; Harlen, 2006; Rea-Dickins, 2001). In addition, there are case studies from around the world that have been reported and serve as useful examples of CBA approaches. Several of them maintain active websites (e.g., School-Based Assessment Projects in Hong Kong, 2010; Scotland's National Assessment Resource, 2010; World Language Assessment in Wisconsin, 2010). As can be seen by perusing these case studies, CBA approaches to support learning may take on diverse forms in different places, but the basic practice characteristics are similar.

One of CBA's main principles (also exemplified by these case studies) is that the assessment information elicited in the classroom should be used as a basis for interaction between teachers and students. When put into practice this should include the following: effective questioning to engage students in reflection concerning the topic and their related work; the use of feedback to assist students in understanding the criteria for high-quality work and what they need to do to achieve it; training in and the use of peer and self-assessment; and when pertinent-making formative use of summative tests. Several recommendations for specific procedures in these areas can be found in Black *et al.*, (2004), but it is made clear in this publication and elsewhere that there are no "uniform recipes." Instead (to reiterate what was earlier stated) the ARG summarizes by providing a process-oriented definition of AFL which is contingent on context: "the process of seeking and interpreting evidence for use by learners and their teachers, to identify where the learners are in their learning, where they need to go and how best to get there" (as cited in Gardner, 2006: 2).

There is a growing range of methods available for CBA. What research is demonstrating is that teachers use multiple sources to gain information concerning learners' language proficiency (e.g., see Cheng *et al.*, 2004 for higher education; Hasselgreen, 2005, for young learners; also see Hasselgreen, this volume). In addition, assessment books for teachers increasingly recommend that a variety of methods be employed to build learner profiles to support language learning in the classroom (e.g., Coombe *et al.*, 2007; Genesee and Upshur, 1996; Ioannou-Georgiou and Pavlou, 2003). As with procedures, however, no "uniform recipes" are put forward for method selection. Instead, teachers are advised that having a list of methods may contribute to CBA practice, but more importantly it is the context and culture in which they employ the methods that define them (see James and Pedder, 2006 for "professional learning"). In order to classify a method as being useful for CBA and to relate it to AFL (the most recent iteration of formative assessment), teachers need to plan and consider the following questions:

- Why would the method be used?
- How would the method be used?
- Who would the participants be?

- Who would assess the results?
- How would the results be recorded and interpreted?
- What type of feedback and reflection would be generated?
- What decision would be made in the process to further learning?

Much remains to be done in terms of defining/describing how best to select methods that will enhance CBA, but enough is known that teacher training (pre-service and in-service) materials are beginning to base their recommendations for practice on the research literature (Malone, 2008). In this process, we have learned concepts that seem quite basic, but in reality appear to be sometimes misunderstood in educational settings. Two salient concepts concerning methods are (1) methods with the same label can represent many variations, and (2) there is no "best" method. First, method labels are generic (e.g., portfolio, observation, open group discussions, teacher-student conferences, peer assessment), but in practice each one has several variations. Each variation or approach has specific characteristics or facets (see questions above) which distinguishes it from others in its category (Bachman and Palmer, 1996). Therefore, assumptions cannot be made by looking at the label of a method that it will be a procedure that is supportive of teaching and learning. For example, portfolios have been used in both formative and high-stakes summative situations; therefore, in order for portfolio use to be classified as CBA to support learning, characteristics consistent with CBA would need to be defined from the outset. Second, there is no "best" method. This has been confirmed by the central role "context" plays in any assessment situation (Fulcher and Davidson, 2007). Context brings with it variation (in the learners, teachers, course specifications, socio-cultural factors, etc.) and therefore assumptions cannot be made that one method will provide all the information that is needed to support learning in a particular context. In addition, diverse contexts involve different types of decisions, resulting in the reality that "one size does not fit all." What is important, however, is that those involved in CBA have knowledge of a repertoire of diverse methods and have the knowledge to develop, adapt or adopt them to specific classroom situations.

A starting point for teachers is to become aware of the methods and procedures that have become associated with CBA. Davison and Leung (2009: 400) put forth a "Typology of Possibilities". They do not list methods *per se* (only examples), but more importantly they describe the characteristics of assessment possibilities across a continuum ranging from informal to formal including classroom tests. Textbooks (see Malone, 2008; Taylor, 2009), websites, and journal articles (see References) provide explanations of methods including within their definitions the task, the procedure, and a recording mechanism whether done by teacher and/or students in self- or peer-assessment situations (e.g., written anecdotal comments, response comments on written work, checklists, rating scales/rubrics, observation grid, audio or video-recorded oral responses). A comprehensive textbook example is Genesee and Upshur's (1996) *Classroom-based Evaluation in Second Language Education*. They begin by describing the importance of context, the participants and the quality of methods. They then explain how to collect information with and without tests. In the latter category they include observation, portfolios, conferencing, journals, questionnaires, and interviews. Other sources expand the CBA repertoire by describing video-recorded group work for self- and peer reflection, projects, pair work reflection on written work, the use of concept maps in learning (Brown, 2004; Colby-Kelly, 2010; Ioannou-Georgiou and Pavlou, 2003).

Further to such pedagogical guidance is the need for research on specific assessment methods and procedures associated with CBA. Owing to the only recent emergence of CBA as a separate paradigm, classroom assessment methods have benefited less from extensive research, and from the development of frameworks that can bring together the research that has been carried out. An example of a current study concerning portfolio use demonstrates how research is able to inform CBA practice. The portfolio has been defined in many ways, but at its simplest is a collection of student work (Hamp-Lyons and Condon, 2000). It has been seen as a source of information for quite some time in L2 classrooms and has the potential to serve as a forum for teacher and student interaction through feedback and reflection. The lack of substantial evidence for its contribution to learning, however, has been an issue (Hamp-Lyons and Condon, 2000). Fox and Hartwick (2011) decided to take up this challenge within the context of English for academic purposes (EAP) courses at the university level. Their research design included a systematic diagnostic approach to portfolio pedagogy in the classroom. A context for learning was generated and preliminary results indicate that teachers and researchers were able to assess language learning progress. Other research on methods to engage students in their own learning through self-reflection, pair–group–teacher interaction and feedback can also be identified (e.g., Little, 2005).

Future directions

This chapter has attempted to consolidate the various research, practices and views concerning the emerging paradigm of CBA. It has situated CBA in a historical background which provides some rationale for the delayed recognition of the differences between the measurement paradigm of external large-scale testing and what takes place in classrooms in terms of ongoing assessment to support learning. The chapter demonstrates that a portion of CBA research appears segmented. Pulling it together has been challenging in that CBA-related research is not always identified as such. As mentioned at the outset of this chapter, for many years it has been considered an offshoot of traditional large-scale testing; therefore, mention of it in the earlier literature is limited. Moving forward, however, and if we take this body of research as a whole, we are beginning to learn about CBA. At the same time, as with any emerging paradigm, the more we learn, the more the complex issues are unveiled. This overview reveals that CBA's time as a paradigm appears to have come, and with that it presently needs and merits its own theoretical and applied set of procedures which in turn can further our understanding of the importance generated from this type of assessment. The time is ripe to begin to formulate a research agenda. This chapter concludes by mentioning some salient questions to be included in such an agenda. They are generated from the above overview and are considerations for future directions.

- What are the quality criteria for assessment for learning contexts? How can reliability and validity be reconceptualized within the socio-cultural framework of CBA?
- What are the characteristics of assessment methods (tasks and procedures) that appear to provide a context for learning? What is the evidence that indicates that these interventions bring about change in learning?
- What is the nature of teacher/student feedback and reflection that influences the effort towards and outcome of further learning?
- What defines the role(s) of "assessor" and the accompanying responsibilities within CBA? How do teachers and students interpret their roles in this process? What are the underlying factors of their decision making?
- How do teachers mediate between CBA and preparing students for external tests? What are the underlying commonalities needed to create coherence across the different assessment components in an education system (i.e., across internal and external-to-the-classroom assessment procedures)?
- What elements should be included in training and supporting pre-service and in-service teachers so they can effectively engage in assessment that supports learning?

CBA activity has existed for many years. It is encouraging to see the recent efforts toward trying to explain it and to identify the conditions that are required to make it beneficial for teaching and learning. The socio-cultural framework of classrooms and the variability of context across classrooms have brought research challenges. Out from under the influence of the theory and practice of large-scale testing, and within its own paradigm, however, we are already beginning to witness an evolving definition of CBA.

Further reading

Broadfoot, P. (2005). Dark alleys and blind bends: testing the language of learning. *Language Testing* 22: 123–41. Broadfoot recommends the reconsideration of cognitive dimensions that are assessed. She stresses the importance of the process of learning itself ("learning power") in assessment procedures and introduces the Effective Lifelong Learning Inventory (ELLI). She argues for the inclusion of the affective domain in formative assessment (i.e., dimensions such as confidence, collaboration, critical curiosity and creativity to support and enhance learning). She explains that the present pattern in schools appears to make learners increasingly less creative and self-motivated and increasingly dependent on teachers.

Stobart, G. (2006). The validity of formative assessment. In J. Gardner (ed.), *Assessment and learning*. London, UK: SAGE Publications. Stobart argues that the validity issue for formative assessment can be stated very simply, that is, did learning take place as a consequence. In other words, further learning is the criterion. His consequential approach places the emphasis on the trustworthiness of the inferences drawn from the results. He considers the learning context to include the socio-cultural, the political environment and the classroom activity.

Teasdale, A. and Leung, C. (2000). Teacher assessment and psychometric theory; A case of paradigm crossing? *Language Testing* 17: 163–84. Teasdale and Leung make a case for a separate paradigm for what they label as "alternative assessment", but in essence they are referring to CBA. They use the context of second language or additional language (ESL, EAL) primary school children in England and Wales to discuss theoretical and practical issues to demonstrate why the needs of classroom assessment activities are not served well by psychometric approaches.

References

Alderson, J. C. (2005). *Diagnosing Foreign Language Proficiency: the interface between learning and assessment*. London, UK: Continuum.

Arkoudis, S. and O'Loughlin, K. (2004). Tensions between validity and outcomes: Teacher assessment of written work of recently arrived immigrant ESL students. *Language Testing* 21: 284–304.

ARG (2002) *Assessment for Learning: 10 principles*. Cambridge, UK: University of Cambridge, Assessment Reform Group.

Bachman, L. F. and Palmer, A. S. (1996) *Language Testing in Practice: designing and developing useful language tests*. Oxford, UK: Oxford University Press.

Black, P. and Wiliam, D. (1998a). Assessment and classroom learning. *Assessment in Education: Principles, policy and practice* 5: 7–74.

—— (1998b). Inside the black box: raising standards through classroom assessment. *Phi Delta Kappan* 80: 139–48.

—— (2003). In praise of educational research: formative assessment. *British Educational Research Journal* 29: 623–37.

Black, P., Harrison, C., Lee, C., Marshall, B. and Wiliam, D. (2004). Working inside the black box: assessment for learning in the classroom. *Phi Delta Kappan* 86: 8–21.

Brindley, G. (2001). Outcomes-based assessment in practice: some examples and emerging insights. *Language Testing* 18: 393–407.

Brookhart, S. (2003). Developing measurement theory for classroom assessment purposes and uses. *Educational Measurement: Issues and Practices,* 22(4): 5–12.

—— (2005). *Research on formative classroom assessment*. Paper presented at the American Educational Research Association, Montreal, April.

Brown, H. D. (2004). *Language Assessment: principles and classroom practice*. White Plains, NY: Longman/ Pearson Education.

Brown, J. D. and Hudson, T. (1998). The alternatives in language assessment. *TESOL Quarterly* 32: 653–75.

Butler, Y. G. and Lee J. (2010). The effects of self-assessment among young learners of English. *Language Testing* 27: 5–31.

Cheng, L., Rogers, T. and Hu, H. (2004). ESL/EFL instructors' classroom assessment practices: Purposes, methods, and procedures. *Language Testing* 21: 360–89.

Cheng, L., Watanabe, Y. and Curtis, A. (eds), (2003). *Washback in Language Testing: research contexts and methods*. Mahwah, NJ: Lawrence Erlbaum Associates.

Colby-Kelly, C. (2010). *Using 'assessment for learning' practices with pre-university level ESL students: a mixed methods study of teacher and student performance and beliefs*. Unpublished doctoral dissertation, McGill University.

Colby-Kelly, C. and Turner, C. E. (2007). AFL research in the L2 classroom and evidence of usefulness: Taking formative assessment to the next level. *Canadian Modern Language Review* 64: 9–38.

Coombe, C., Folse, K. and Hubley, N. (2007) *A Practical Guide to Assessing English Language Learners*. Ann Arbor, MI: The University of Michigan Press.

Council of Europe (2001) *Common European Framework of Reference for Languages: learning, teaching, assessment*. Cambridge, UK: Cambridge University Press.

Cumming, A. (2009). Language assessment in education: tests, curricula, and teaching. *Annual Review of Applied Linguistics* 29: 90–100.

Davison, C. (2004). The contradictory culture of teacher-based assessment: ESL teacher assessment practices in Australian and Hong Kong secondary schools. *Language Testing* 21: 305–34.

—— (2007) Views from the chalkface: School-based assessment in Hong Kong. *Language Assessment Quarterly* 4: 37–68.

Davison, C. and Leung, C. (2009). Current issues in English language teacher-based assessment. *TESOL Quarterly* 43: 393–415.

Fox, J. (2008) Alternative assessment. In E. Shohamy and N. H. Hornberger (eds), *Encyclopedia of Language and Education,* Vol. 7. *Language Testing and Assessment*, 2nd edn. New York, NY: Springer Science + Business, 97–109.

Fox, J. and Hartwick, P. (2011) Taking a diagnostic turn: reinventing the portfolio in an English for academic purposes (EAP) classroom. In D. Tsagari and I. Csepes (eds), *Classroom-Based Language Assessment*. Frankfurt, Germany: Peter Lang.

Fulcher, G. (2010a) *Language Testing Resources Website*. languagetesting.info/features/afl/formative.html (accessed 22/11/10).

—— (2010b) *Practical Language Testing*. London, UK: Hodder Education.

Fulcher, G. and Davidson, F. (2007) *Language Testing and Assessment: an advanced resource book*. London, UK: Routledge.

Gardner, J. (2006) *Assessment and Learning*. Thousand Oaks, CA: SAGE Publications.

Genesee, F. and Upshur, J. A. (1996) *Classroom-based Evaluation in Second Language Education*. Cambridge, UK: Cambridge University Press.

Gottlieb, M. (2006) *Assessing English Language Learners: bridges from language proficiency to academic achievement*. Thousand Oaks, CA: Corwin Press.

Guiver, C. (producer) (2010) *Afl and APP: What's going on with assessment* (video). www.teachers.tv/videos/afl-and-app-what-is-going-on-with-assessment (accessed 22/11/10).

Hamp-Lyons, L. and Condon, W. (2000) *Assessing the Portfolio: principles for practice, theory, and research*. Cresskill, NJ: Hampton Press.

Harlen, W. (2006). On the relationship between assessment for formative and summative purposes. In J. Gardner (ed.), *Assessment and Learning*. London: SAGE Publications.

Harlen, W. and Winter, J. (2004). The development of assessment for learning: Learning from the case of science and mathematics. *Language Testing* 21: 390–408.

Hasselgreen, A. (2005). Assessing the language of young learners. *Language Testing* 22: 337–54.

Ioannou-Georgiou, S. and Pavlou, P. (2003) *Assessing Young Learners*. Oxford, UK: Oxford University Press.

James, M. (2006). Assessment, teaching and theories of Learning. In J. Gardner (ed.), *Assessment and Learning*. London, UK: SAGE Publications.

James, M. and Pedder, D. (2006). Professional learning as a condition for assessment for learning. In J. Gardner (ed.), *Assessment and Learning*. London, UK: SAGE Publications.

Lantolf, J. and Poehner, M. (2008). Dynamic assessment. In E. Shohamy and N. H. Hornberger (eds), *Encyclopedia of Language and Education*. Vol. 7. *Language testing and assessment*, 2nd edn, New York: Springer Science + Business, 273–84.

Leung, C. (2004). Developing formative teacher assessment: knowledge, practice and change. *Language Assessment Quarterly* 1: 19–41.

Leung, C. and Lewkowicz, J. (2006). Expanding horizons and unresolved conundrums: Language testing and assessment. *TESOL Quarterly* 40: 211–34.

Leung, C. and Scott, C. (2009). Formative assessment in language education policies: Emerging lessons from Wales and Scotland. *Annual Review of Applied Linguistics* 29: 64–79.

Little, D. (2005). The Common European Framework and the European Language Portfolio: Involving learners and their judgements in the assessment process. *Language Testing* 22: 321–36.

Llosa, L. (2007). Validating a standards-based classroom assessment of English proficiency: a multitrait-multimethod approach. *Language Testing* 24: 489–515.

Lynch, B. (2001). Rethinking assessment from a critical perspective. *Language Testing* 18: 351–72.

McNamara, T. (1996) *Measuring Second Language Performance*. London, UK: Longman.

McNamara, T. and Roever, C. (2006) *Language Testing: the social dimension*. Malden, MA: Blackwell Publishing.

Malone, M. (2008). Training in language assessment. In E. Shohamy and N. H. Hornberger (eds), *Encyclopedia of Language and Education*, Vol. 7. *Language testing and assessment*, 2nd edn. New York, NY: Springer Science + Business, 225–39.

Messick, S. (1989). Validity. In R. L. Linn (ed.), *Educational measurement*, 3rd edn. New York, NY: Macmillan, 13–103.

Moss, P. A. (1996). Enlarging the dialogue in educational measurement: voices from interpretive research traditions. *Educational Researcher* 25: 20–28.

Moss, P. (2003). Reconceptualizing validity for classroom assessment. *Educational Measurement: Issues and Practices* 22: 13–25.

O'Malley, J. M. and Valdez Pierce, L. (1996). *Authentic assessment for English language learners: Practical approaches for teachers*. Reading, MA: Addison-Wesley.

Pellegrino, J. W., Chudowsky, N. and Glaser, R. (eds), (2001). *Knowing What Students Know: the science and design of educational assessment*. Washington, DC: National Academy Press.

Rea-Dickins, P. (2001). 'Mirror, mirror on the wall.' Identifying processes of classroom assessment. *Language Testing* 18: 429–62.

—— (2004). Understanding teachers as agents of assessment. *Language Testing* 21: 249–58.

—— (2006). Currents and eddies in the discourse of assessment: A learning-focused interpretation. *International Journal of Applied Linguistics* 16: 163–88.

—— (2008). Classroom-based language assessment. In E. Shohamy and N. H. Hornberger (eds), *Encyclopedia of Language and Education,* Vol. 7. *Language testing and Assessment*, 2nd edn. New York, NY: Springer Science + Business, 257–71.

Rea-Dickins, P. and Gardner, S. (2000). Snares or silver bullets: Disentangling the construct of formative assessment. *Language Testing* 17: 215–44.

School-Based Assessment Projects in Hong Kong (2010). sba.edu.hku.hk/new_sba/index.html (accessed 22/11/10).

Scotland's National Assessment Resource (2010). www.ltscotland.org.uk/learningteachingandassessment (accessed 22/11/10).

Scriven, M. (1967). The methodology of evaluation. In R.W. Tyler (ed.), *Perspectives of curriculum evaluation*. Chicago, IL: Rand McNally, 39–83.

Shephard, L. (2000). The role of assessment in a learning culture. *Educational Researcher* 29: 4–14.

Taylor, L. (2009). Developing assessment literacy. *Annual Review of Applied Linguistics* 29: 21–36.

Teachers of English to Speakers of Other Languages (TESOL) (2006) *PreK-12 English Language Proficiency Standards*. Alexandria, VA: TESOL.

Turner, C. E. (2006). Professionalism and high stakes test: Teachers' perspectives when dealing with educational change introduced through provincial exams. *TESL Canada Journal* 23: 54–76.

—— (2009). Examining washback in second language education contexts: A high stakes provincial exam and the teacher factor in classroom practice in Quebec secondary schools. *International Journal on Pedagogies and Learning* 5: 103–23.

Turner, C. E., Tan, M. and Deschambault, E. (2010). 'Development and field-testing of the writing task for Quebec's Secondary Five provincial ESL exit exams: Using the washback effect to create an assessment bridge. Poster presented at the Canadian Association of Applied Linguistics (CAAL), Montreal, June.

Vygotsky, L. (1978). *Mind in Society: the development of higher psychological processes*. Cambridge, MA: Harvard University Press.

Wall, D. (2000). The impact of high-stakes testing on teaching and learning: Can this be predicted or controlled? *System* 28: 499–509.

World Language Assessment in Wisconsin (2010). www.ecb.org/worldlanguageassessment/index.htm (accessed 22/11/10).

Yin, M. (2010). Understanding classroom language assessment through teacher thinking research. *Language Assessment Quarterly* 7: 175–94.

5

Washback

Dianne Wall

Introduction

It is now well accepted that tests can have important consequences – for students, whose future may be determined by their test results, and for their teachers, whose self-esteem, reputation and even career progression may be affected by how successful they are at preparing their students to cope with test requirements. If the test is 'high stakes', defined by Madaus as a test 'whose results are seen – rightly or wrongly – by students, teachers, administrators, parents, or the general public, as being used to make important decisions that immediately and directly affect them' (1988: 87), a phenomenon known as 'washback' may occur. Washback is the term that is used when students and teachers 'do things *they would not necessarily otherwise do* because of the test' (Alderson and Wall, 1993: 117). They might, for example, pay more attention to certain parts of the teaching syllabus at the expense of other parts because they believe these will be emphasised on the test. They might practise certain types of questions rather than others for the same reasons. The washback of a test

> can either be positive or negative to the extent that it either promotes or impedes the accomplishment of educational goals held by learners and/or programme personnel.
>
> *(Bailey, 1996: 268)*

There has been growing interest in washback over the last two decades, for theoretical, practical and political reasons. Messick (1996) claimed that washback is a particular instance of the consequential aspect of construct validity, which suggests a corollary that investigating washback and other consequences is a crucial step in the process of test validation. The practical and political interest stems from the use that policy-makers make of high-stakes tests to influence educational practices. Educational advisors such as Heyneman and Ransom argue that tests 'can be a powerful, low-cost means of influencing the quality of what teachers teach and what students learn at school' (1992: 105). This view is shared by educators such as Popham (1987), who proclaimed the advantages of 'measurement-driven instruction', and language educators such as Pearson (1988), who used the term 'lever for change' to describe the influence he hoped a new national test of English would have on language teaching. Opponents to this view include Madaus, who claimed that using high-stakes testing to effect change leads to 'teaching to the test' and the use of past test papers as teaching material, and that it 'transfers control over the curriculum to the agency which sets or controls the exam' (1988: 97).

The idea of washback takes on more complexity when we consider not only whether the effect of tests are positive or negative but also whether they are immediate or delayed, direct or indirect, or apparent or not visible – e.g. changes in attitude that do not manifest themselves in overt behaviour (Henrichsen, 1989: 80). There are also methodological challenges in determining whether washback has occurred, such as deciding on procedures to establish whether the classroom practice that appears after the introduction or revision of a test is actually test washback, or rather the effect of other factors in the educational context.

Historical perspectives

There are many accounts of the use of high-stakes testing in education and other realms of public life. Eckstein and Noah (1993: 5–17) discuss a number of functions that such tests have served in society: ending the monopoly over government jobs held by the privileged classes (e.g. competitive examinations in China during the Han Dynasty), checking patronage and corruption (the Indian Civil Service examination in nineteenth-century Britain), encouraging 'higher levels of competence and knowledge' (entry examinations to the professions in France and Germany), allocating sparse places in higher education (university entrance examinations in Japan), and measuring and improving the effectiveness of teachers and schools (the 'Payment by Results' system established in Britain in the 1860s, where state funding of schools was partly determined by the results students received in tests administered by school inspectors). It is not difficult to imagine the influence that these tests might have had on the learning goals and methods of the candidates preparing for them. There is little empirical evidence available, however, to provide a link between these tests and the teaching and learning that are said to have resulted from them.

There was considerable discussion of the effects of high-stakes testing in educational settings in the twentieth century. Fredericksen and Collins introduced the notion of 'systemic validity', which occurred when a test

> induces in the education system curricular and instructional changes that foster the development of the cognitive skills that the test is designed to measure.
>
> *(1989: 27)*

These changes were not to be seen as automatic, however. Improvements in educational standards depended not only on well-constructed tests representing the full range of educational objectives, but also on a clear articulation and exemplification of the standard desired, sensitive training of markers, and ample opportunity for teachers and students to understand and practise using the criteria for evaluating performance. Airasian (1988) was cautious in his views of whether tests could bring about changes in teaching and learning, emphasising the need to consider the level of cognitive skills assessed in the test and the likelihood that teachers could successfully train students in high-level operations such as reasoning, problem-solving and critical thinking. Educators such as Haladyna *et al.* (1991) signalled some of the dangers of using tests to change standards, including threats to validity caused by test preparation practices which 'increase or decrease test performance without connection to the construct represented by the test' (4). They ranked different types of preparation activity according on a scale from ethical to highly unethical. An example of an ethical practice was motivating students to study by discussing how important the test was to them. An example of unethical practice was using material in the classroom that was very similar to the material used in the test (see Mehrens and Kaminsky, 1989, for further discussion of the ethics of test preparation).

It was not until the early 1990s that discussions regarding the washback of high-stakes testing began to appear in the field of language testing. Until this time there were general claims about the influence of tests on the curriculum, but little discussion of whether this influence was real or imagined. Alderson and Wall (1993) provided the first critical analysis of the notion of washback. They explained that washback was not the same as the general pressure caused by important tests – for example, the feeling that one should spend more time studying. The washback of a test was specific to that test alone, manifesting itself in decisions about how much attention to pay to certain aspects of the domain in question (e.g. the teaching syllabus), depending on the importance given to these aspects in the test. They proposed a number of 'washback hypotheses' to illustrate the types of influences that a test could conceivably have: on what teachers taught and learners learned; on how teaching and learning took place; on the rate, sequence, degree and depth of teaching and learning; and on the attitudes of teachers and learners. They stressed how important it was for test designers to make explicit the type of washback they intended to create with their tests, and for researchers to be explicit about the types of activity they were investigating in their attempts to discover whether washback had occurred. Alderson and Wall further argued that there was a need to expand the range of research techniques used to study washback, and to draw on the insights gained in other fields of research (such as innovation and motivation) in order to not only describe washback but also to account for its nature.

Other early contributions to the understanding of washback came from Hughes (1994) and Bailey (1996, 1999). Hughes introduced an important distinction between washback on the participants in an educational system (e.g. teachers, learners, administrators, materials writers, curriculum designers), on processes (the types of thinking and activities the participants engaged in) and on products (for example, the amount and quality of learning that resulted). Bailey, among her other contributions, created a 'basic model' to illustrate the mechanism by which washback developed. She also proposed a series of questions to ask of any external examination (one which was not created within the institution where it was being administered). These questions probed the participants' understanding of the purpose of the test and how the results were to be used, the theoretical bases of the test, the use of authentic texts and tasks, the manner in which test results were provided, and other features she believed could influence the appearance and nature of washback.

The next important milestone appeared in 1996, with the publication of a special issue of *Language Testing* devoted to washback. Issue 13: 3 included two discussions of the nature of washback and four case studies. The first discussion was by Messick (1996), who first reviewed the notion of a unified version of construct validity, and then argued that washback was one (but not the only) manifestation of the consequential aspect of validity. It was important to investigate washback when attempting to establish the validity of a test. Messick also warned that just because certain features appeared in the context where a test was operating, this did not mean that those features constituted washback. In his words

> it is problematic to claim evidence of test washback if a logical or evidential link cannot be forged between the teaching or learning outcomes and the test properties thought to influence them.
>
> *(Messick, 1996: 247)*

If a link could be found between the test and the teaching or learning outcomes, and the outcomes were not considered desirable then it would be necessary to analyse the test design and see whether it required adjustments. It was preferable, however, to concentrate on creating desirable washback to begin with,

> ... rather than seeking washback as a sign of test validity, seek validity by design as a likely basis for washback.

Messick advocated incorporating authenticity and directness in the test design, and to minimise 'construct under-representation' and 'construct-irrelevant difficulty' (1996: 252).

The second discussion of the nature of washback was by Bailey (1996), who provided a comprehensive review of the literature on washback up to that point, and presented the model of washback referred to above.

Four case studies provided the type of empirical evidence for washback that was often missing in publications before the 1990s. Alderson and Hamp-Lyons (1996) used teacher and student interviews and classroom observations to investigate the washback of the Test of English as a Foreign Language (TOEFL) on teaching in a private language school in the United States. They followed two teachers as they conducted 'normal' language lessons and TOEFL preparation lessons, and found that although there were differences between the two types of lessons for each teacher, there were differences that were at least as great between the two teachers themselves. Watanabe (1996) also designed a comparative study, with the aim of determining whether there was a relationship between university entrance examinations in Japan (which are very high stakes) and the amount of grammar-translation teaching taking place in private examination preparation centres. He carried out observations and interviews with two teachers who were teaching preparation classes for one examination which emphasised grammar-translation and for one which did not. He predicted that both teachers would include more grammar-translation teaching in the first type of class than in the second. He found, however, that while one teacher seemed to be influenced by the type of examination he was preparing his students for, the other explained grammar and employed translation no matter which type of examination he was dealing with. Both Alderson and Hamp-Lyons, and Watanabe concluded that tests do not affect all teachers in the same way: that the personal characteristics of the teachers, including their beliefs and attitudes, are key factors in how they react to test pressures.

Shohamy et al. (1996) and Wall (1996) investigated the washback of high-stakes tests on teaching in state secondary schools. Shohamy et al. compared the effects of two tests in Israel, a test of English as a Foreign Language (EFL) and a test of Arabic as a Second Language (ASL), both when they were introduced and after they had been in place for some time. They found that while the washback of the EFL test increased over the years, the washback of the ASL test decreased 'to the point where it has no effect: no special teaching activities are introduced in preparation for the test, no special time is allotted, no new teaching materials have been developed, awareness of the test is minimal ... ' (Shohamy et al., 1996: 312). The researchers attributed these changes to a variety of factors, including the status of the two languages within the country, the purposes of the tests, the test formats that were used and the skills that were tested.

Wall (1996) reported on the washback of a major EFL test on secondary school teaching in Sri Lanka. Her study involved repeated observations at many schools over a two-year period, and in-depth interviews with the teachers whose classes were observed. She found that the test in question influenced the content of the classes in both positive and negative ways, but it had no influence on the methods the teachers used to deliver this content. Wall presented a number of reasons for these findings, relating not only to the test itself but also to other factors in the educational and social setting. These included a lack of understanding on many teachers' part of the test construct, a lack of official feedback to teachers about their students' test performance, and inadequate teacher support systems. Wall's analysis was underpinned by insights from innovation theory (e.g. Fullan and Stiegelbauer, 1991).

Interest in washback grew quickly in the 1990s, with explorations into many dimensions of the phenomenon and the use of many frameworks and methods to gather and analyse data. The next decade witnessed a further growth in the number of investigations into washback and into the wider educational and social impact of high-stakes testing.

The second important collection of washback studies was edited by Cheng and Watanabe (2004). This volume contained three comprehensive reviews of different aspects of the topic: the impact of testing on teaching and learning (Cheng and Curtis, 2004), the methods (mainly qualitative) used in washback studies (Watanabe, 2004) and the relationship between washback and curricular innovation (Andrews, 2004). It also contained eight studies of the washback of different kinds of assessment (school tests, university entrance tests, tests for immigration purposes, international proficiency tests) in different education settings (the United States, New Zealand, Australia, Japan, Hong Kong, China and Israel) and on different aspects of teaching, including the design of course books to support test preparation.

A number of monographs on washback and other forms of impact have also been published. Cheng (2005) investigated how teachers and students in Hong Kong secondary schools reacted to changes in the English component of the Hong Kong Certificate of Education. Wall (2005) developed further her ideas concerning the relevance of innovation theory to washback studies (as noted in Wall, 1996, reviewed above) and provided a more complete treatment of examination reform in Sri Lanka. Green (2007) investigated the effects of the Academic Writing Module of the International Language Testing System (IELTS) examination on preparation for academic study. Hawkey (2006) presented two separate studies: one into the impact of the IELTS, and one into the impact of a foreign language education improvement programme in the state school system in Italy (the 'Progetto Lingue 2000'). These volumes, along with the case studies presented in the Cheng and Watanabe (2004) volume, provided further support for the arguments emerging from earlier work in the field: that washback is not easy to predict or control, and that the shape it assumes is influenced not only by tests but by the interaction of numerous factors, including characteristics of the teachers and students involved, characteristics of the educational context and characteristics of the wider social, political and cultural setting. They also reveal the variety of quantitative and qualitative research methods that are now being used to probe the existence of washback and to explain the appearance it takes in different contexts.

A recent survey of washback studies by Spratt (2005) sets out to inform teachers (rather than testers or researchers) 'of the roles they can play and the decisions they can make concerning washback' (2005: 5). Spratt looks at approximately 20 studies and discusses what they reveal about washback on the curriculum (e.g. the content of the curriculum, when it is offered, and whether time is taken away from normal teaching to emphasise the areas believed to be assessed in the test), teaching materials (for instance, the use of course books, past papers and other materials), teaching methods (which methods to use and in which measure, the teaching of test-taking skills), feelings and attitudes (which attitudes to promote in learners) and student learning (the appropriacy of student outcomes). She also provides a clear account of the many types of factors now known to influence the nature of washback.

Critical issues and topics

The language testing community has discussed washback for nearly two decades, but there are a number of issues which have yet to be resolved. The first has to do with the difficulty of separating out the influence of tests from the effects of other variables at work in the educational context. Some of the early references to washback in the language testing field assumed a direct cause and effect relationship between a test and the effects it would have in the classroom. Heaton, for example, wrote that

> If it is a good examination, it will have a useful effect on teaching; if bad, then it will have a damaging effect on teaching.
>
> *(1990: 17)*

Research has now shown that the introduction or revision of a test will not automatically cause changes to occur in teaching and learning. While tests may have an influence on attitudes and behaviour, it is not easy to predict how much influence they will have or what this will look like in concrete terms. Even if a test carries high stakes, it is but one factor amongst many that are interacting in any educational setting. It is important to understand all these factors in order to be able to gauge whether the washback intended by the test designers is likely to appear as envisaged or whether it will be diluted or distorted beyond recognition. A good example of how complex the situation can be is provided by Wall (2000, 2005), who compared classroom practice before and after the introduction of a high-stakes test of English in the state school system in Sri Lanka. The test was meant to reflect and reinforce an innovative approach to teaching (new objectives, new content and new teaching methods) embodied in a series of textbooks introduced several years earlier. Observations of classrooms over time and in-depth interviews with teachers after the launch of the test revealed that while some changes had come about in *what* the teachers were teaching (more emphasis on reading and writing, for example), there was little change in *how* they were teaching (more evidence of a word-for-word approach to dealing with reading, for example, than of efforts to develop enabling skills and strategies). Wall's analysis, which was informed by a diffusion-of-innovation framework devised by Henrichsen (1989), showed that the type of teaching that was taking place after the introduction of the test was due not only to the characteristics of the test itself (there were strengths and weaknesses in its design), but also to conditions in place in the educational setting before the test was introduced (e.g. traditional ways of teaching) and factors at play when the test was introduced and for some time thereafter (e.g. inadequate teacher support, and problems in communication and resourcing).

Later studies have also emphasised the importance of looking at factors beyond the test when attempting to predict what form washback will take in new surroundings. Green (2007: 25), for example, points to the need to take the test users' characteristics into account:

> Differences among participants in the perceptions of test importance and difficulty, and in their ability to accommodate to test demands, will moderate the strength of any effect, and, perhaps, the evaluation of its direction.

Spratt (2005: 29) presents a long list of factors which have been shown to influence a test's washback. These include teacher-related factors (beliefs, attitudes, education and training), resourcing (with a focus on teacher-made and commercial materials), the conditions at the school where teaching and test preparation is taking place and the attributes of the test in question (e.g. its proximity, its purpose, the status of the language it tests, the formats it employs, the weighting of the different sections and how familiar the test is to teachers). Unfortunately, however, the fact that we are now more aware of the complexity of washback does not necessarily lead to greater success in predicting its coverage or intensity.

The second issue has to do with the dilemma many teachers face when they are preparing their students for a test that has important consequences. Most teachers work in a system with a curriculum that is to be honoured and a syllabus that should be adhered to. If a test is introduced which is known (or believed) to sample only some of the syllabus then the teacher must decide whether to cover the whole syllabus or whether to 'teach to the test'. When educators such as Popham promoted the idea of 'measurement-driven instruction' they envisaged a system where tests were 'properly conceived and implemented' (1987: 680). The term 'teaching to the test' implies that the test is not so conceived, and that the teachers are 'doing something in teaching that may not be compatible with (their) own values and goals, or with the values and goals of the instructional program' (Bachman and Palmer, 2010: 108). Teachers may well understand that they are not serving their students' long-term interests by narrowing their teaching to address what they perceive to be the demands of the test. However, they are also likely to feel pressured to ensure that their students perform well, and this can lead to what Spratt (2005: 24) calls 'a tension between pedagogical and ethical decisions'. The most effective solution to this problem is for test designers to 'sample widely and unpredictably' (Hughes, 2003: 54), in order to encourage teachers to teach all the points in the syllabus. Unless this occurs, teachers will still be faced with hard decisions, and some may find themselves, without devious intentions, engaging in the sort of activities that researchers such as Haladyna *et al.* (1991) might see as less than ethical.

The third issue has to do with the responsibilities of test developers with regard to the washback of their tests and/or any impact that extends beyond the classroom, into the educational system or even greater society. If the test is having a beneficial influence then there is no problem, but if teachers or institutions narrow their teaching too drastically or if there are other unintended consequences should the blame be placed on the test developers? In Messick's view

> washback is a consequence of testing that bears on validity only if it can be evidentially shown to be an effect of the test and not of other forces operative on the educational scene.
>
> *(1996: 242)*

As stated in 'Historical perspectives' above, Messick sought to minimise construct under-representation and construct-irrelevant difficulty, so it follows logically that the test designer would be responsible for negative consequences if the test design suffered from either of these sources of invalidity. It is more difficult to assign responsibility in cases where unintended consequences stem not from poor test design but from the misuse of tests, when tests are used for purposes they were not intended for (see Davies, this volume). An example of such unintended (and generally considered to be negative) consequences would be the exclusion of immigrants from a country as a result of low scores on a language test not designed for this type of screening. The Standards for Educational and Psychological Testing state that 'If a test is used in a way that has not been validated, it is incumbent on the user to justify the new use' (AERA/APA/NCME, 1999 Standard 1.4: 28); however, there is much debate in the language testing community about how much warning test developers should give to the users and what other actions they might take to prevent their tests from being used inappropriately.

Current contributions and research

As can be seen in the preceding sections, the study of washback has expanded greatly over a relatively short period of time. Among the most recent areas to be explored are those of teacher beliefs, washback on learners and washback over time.

Spratt (2005) lists the types of teacher beliefs that have been seen as important mediators of washback. These includes beliefs about

- the reliability and fairness of the exam
- what constitutes effective teaching methods
- how much the exam contravenes their current teaching practices
- the stakes and usefulness of the exam
- their teaching philosophy
- the relationship between the exam and the textbooks, and
- their students' beliefs.

Only recently, however, have attempts been made to systematically study the nature of teachers' beliefs and the influence that these can have on their classroom behaviour. Huang (2009) used insights from social psychology, in particular the Theory of Planned Behaviour (Ajzen, 2006), to analyse data she had obtained through teacher diaries, observations, and in-depth interviews. Her purpose was to distinguish between teachers' behavioural beliefs (what they believed about the four types of teaching behaviour that a new high-stakes test was meant to encourage), their normative beliefs (what they believed important people around them – district inspectors, their head teacher, their peers, their students and the students' parents – expected of them with regard to the behaviours) and their control beliefs (what they believed was achievable given the possibilities and the constraints of the situation they were working in). Huang showed how the interaction between these different types of beliefs led to intentions about how to how to teach, and how these intentions were modified by actual circumstances before being transformed into observable behaviour. Huang's study provides a good example of how insights from other disciplines can contribute to our understanding of important concepts in language assessment. (See also Burrows, 2004, for an analysis of teachers according to whether they are adopters, adapters or resisters to innovation, and how this type of categorisation allows predictions of how they will react to changes in assessment policy.)

Another relatively new focus of study has to do with the washback of tests on learners, as seen through the eyes of learners. Washback studies have often been concerned with how tests influence teachers, perhaps because of the central role that teachers play in the classroom but also because of the practical difficulties of investigating student attitudes and behaviour. Notable exceptions include Gosa (2004) and Tsagari (2009), who looked at students' reactions to tests as recorded in their diaries, and Watanabe (2001), who used interviews to explore the ways in which tests motivated learners. A recent and innovative approach was described in Huhta *et al.* (2006), who studied a group of students for four months, from the time they started preparing for a high-stakes national school test to after they received their results. The researchers asked the students to keep an oral diary as they prepared for the test, and got them to discuss their reactions with fellow students after they had taken it. The data were analysed using a type of discourse analysis from the field of social psychology, focusing on

> how stakeholders (e.g. test-takers or raters) come to talk or write about a test in attempts to make sense of taking it or rating it ... at the same time evaluating aspects related to it, including actions, thoughts and feelings.
>
> *(Huhta et al., 2006: 331)*

The researchers were particularly interested in the roles that the students adopted as they talked about their relationship with the test – whether they saw or portrayed themselves as hardworking or lazy, well or poorly skilled, lucky or unlucky, or 'cool' or nervous. They found that the students adopted different roles at different stages of the report period, and sometimes even changed roles during the same situation. They concluded that the relationship between any student and a test is an individual and sometimes emotional one. This suggests that studies which talk about washback to 'the learners' may be simplifying matters unduly. (See also Ferman, 2004, for a detailed account of learner test preparation strategies.)

A third new area of interest concerns the detailed tracking of washback over a long period of time. Longitudinal studies are not in themselves new. Shohamy *et al.* (1996), for example, compared the washback occurring soon after the introduction of two national language tests in Israel and the washback of the same tests a number of years later. They found that there were differences in the way the washback of the two tests had developed, and that these were due to differences in the purposes of the tests, the status of the languages involved and features having to do with the tests' internal structure. Such 'before and after' studies have been helpful in shaping our understanding of how washback can change from one period to another, but what they have not given us is an understanding of how it is developing at various points along the way. Wall and Horák (2011) report on a five-year study of the impact of changes in the TOEFL on teaching in a sample of test-preparation institutions in different countries in Europe. The study was divided into four phases: a baseline study which looked at teaching practices before the teachers and institutions involved were aware that a new test was on the horizon; a 'transition phase' which tracked the teachers' reactions as they began learning about changes in the test and had to think about rede-signing their preparation courses; a further transition phase, which analysed the course books that the teachers had selected and the use they made of them as they planned and delivered their early redesigned courses; and a final phase which looked at the teachers' classes once the new test had had some time to 'settle' in their countries and compared the teaching then with the teaching that had been taking place in the baseline phase. The unique feature of this study was that it traced several teachers from the start to the finish of the project, probing their awareness and understanding of the new (and old) tests, their developing abilities to cope with the new test demands, their questions about how best to help their students, and their decisions about the materials and teaching methods that would be most appropriate for their own circumstances. The continuous and in-depth communication with the teachers allowed the researchers to feel confident in their claim that 'an evidential link' had been established between the test and the teaching practice in place after its introduction. Although there are considerable resourcing demands in this kind of project there is also the potential to feed information back to the testing agency on a regular basis, and thereby to enable adjustments in communication about the test and in arrangements for teacher support.

Main research methods

Hawkey (2006) reminds us that if one of the aims of a test development project is to create positive impact (in our case, positive washback), then a key part of the process of test validation is to investigate whether the test has achieved its intended purpose. Hawkey states that the purpose of such studies is

> to measure and analyse both outcomes, for example test results or subsequent performance on the criteria the test is measuring, and processes, for example the learning and teaching approaches and activities of programmes preparing candidates for a test.
>
> *(Hawkey, 2006: 21)*

It is important to add that a further product of such studies should be an understanding of why the test has *not* produced the desired washback, so that this information can be fed back into the test design process and/or the testing agency's communication with the test users, in particular with teachers and learners.

Bailey (1996) questions the notion of 'measuring' washback, since this term is associated with experimental research and 'identifying, operationally defining and controlling the variables that impinge upon the desired measurements' (1996: 272). Bailey stresses the difficulty of isolating washback from other variables that may affect teaching and learning, and the fact that washback must be studied in naturally occurring settings (rather than laboratory conditions), with a non-random sample of subjects. Although some washback outcomes (e.g. test results) can be measured, other outcomes and most processes can only be analysed and described. Bailey advises that such analysis should involve methodological 'triangulation' – looking at the situation from various angles, using, for example, more than one data set, or more than one type of informant or more than one type of method.

Wall and Horák (2007) state that there are two types of washback studies: those that investigate the effects of tests which are already operational (e.g. Green, 2007, which looked at the effects of the IELTS test on teaching in different contexts), and those that investigate the effects of a new test or a test which has been revised substantially. They focus on the second type of study, and describe the procedures that they followed when setting up an investigation to identify changes in classroom practice that may have been brought about by the introduction of a much-revised TOEFL (Wall and Horák, 2011). The essential steps are as follows:

- identify the sorts of washback the test designers originally intended, and the means they planned to use to ensure that this washback actually appeared;
- analyse the new test in detail, to see how it differs from the test it is replacing;
- predict what washback may occur (intended and unintended), using information from the first two steps;
- design a baseline study, to find out what teaching and/or learning look like before participants are aware of the new test demands;
- carry out the baseline study, to document the educational setting and practices before the test is introduced;
- disseminate the results of the study, to inform the test developers of any features in the setting or established practices that might negatively affect the participants' understanding and ability to accommodate the new test demands.

The key component in this kind of investigation is the baseline study, which can serve as a point of comparison when attempts are made after the launch of the test to describe whether it has produced any washback. After carrying out the baseline study researchers need to keep track of the process leading up to the test launch and what happens as the test becomes established in its context. The amount of detail that is possible will be determined by the resources the researchers have access to. The final stage is to describe the teaching and/or learning that are taking place at the end of a time period agreed at the beginning of the project, and then to explain whether any of the features present in the 'after' period can be evidentially linked to the introduction of the test. As stated earlier, it is also important to try to investigate what other factors may be working in the environment to facilitate or hinder the appearance of the desired washback (Wall, 2005).

The process described above is essentially a 'compare and contrast' exercise, usually using the same research instruments and procedures and the same analytical frameworks in both stages of the study. If the purpose of a washback study is to describe the influence of a test which is already embedded in an educational context then it is also necessary to compare and contrast classroom practices. In this case, however, the comparison may be between the 'ordinary' teaching and the test-preparation teaching presented by the same set of teachers, or the teaching that takes place for two or more different tests. Watanabe (2004: 28) presents a detailed scheme of how to organise such comparisons in order to investigate various kinds of washback. Watanabe also offers advice on general research matters such as how to select a sample of teachers and institutions to participate in a study; how to gain access to them; whether to reveal the purpose of the research; how to organise observations and interviews; how to analyse data; and how to interpret and discuss the results of the analysis.

In addition to deciding on the general approach to a washback study researchers need to consider carefully the specific methods they will use to gather and analyse data. Among methods commonly used are questionnaires and interviews (for teachers, students, principals, inspectors, policy-makers, etc.), focus groups, document analysis (policy documents, test papers, lesson plans, teaching materials and so on), observations, diaries (written or oral, by teachers or learners), and analysis of test scores. Examples of instruments (questionnaires, textbook analysis frameworks, interview protocols, observation forms, and marking rubrics) can be found at the end of most of the case studies in Cheng and Watanabe (2004), and in the appendices of Cheng and Watanabe (2004), Wall (2005), Hawkey (2006), Green (2007), Tsagari (2009) and Wall and Horák (2011).

Future directions

This survey of the literature on washback shows that a great deal of energy and effort has gone into the study of this phenomenon since the first critical questioning began in the early 1990s. Considerable discussion has taken place about the nature of washback, the factors that can facilitate or hinder its appearance and intensity, and the steps that testing agencies should take to ensure that the effects of their tests are viewed as positive by teachers, learners and others who are affected by test results and the use made of them. Numerous case studies have been undertaken which have commented in detail on the characteristics of particular tests and how they have or have not produced the washback their designers originally intended. While it is encouraging to see the amount of interest washback has generated over the years, it can also be frustrating to see how many directions the research has gone off into and how little connection there seems to be between researchers working on the same types of questions. Although most researchers include references to 'classic' washback studies and will review more recent studies if they happen to relate to the theme they are interested in, it is rare to see research that truly builds on work that has been done previously, which replicates or only slightly adapts the work of others. The washback literature is full of interesting individual studies but it seems to lack an overall coherence. This may be inevitable, given the need for researchers to display originality in order to gain their doctorates or to have their articles accepted by prestigious journals. It may also be a function of the relative newness of this area in the field of language assessment – while 20 years can seem a long time in some ways, it is still only 20 years.

Cheng (2008) expresses similar reservations about the coherence of the washback literature, and she argues that while individual studies of different tests in different contexts have their value,

> [i]t would be the best use of resources if a group of researchers could work collaboratively and cooperatively to carry out a series of studies around the same test within the same educational context.

> *(Cheng, 2008: 360)*

Cheng envisages a situation where researchers would look at different aspects of the same situation and would be able to cross-reference their findings to build up a comprehensive picture of the washback operating therein. Spratt (2005) seems to be thinking along the same lines, although she advocates using 'parallel methodologies' in different contexts, to investigate 'some of the apparent contradictions in the findings to date'.

I concur. I would hope to see a consolidation of the many research findings we already have in the near future, so that we can produce confident statements about how tests affect participants, processes and products (especially learning outcomes) over the next 20 years. My personal interests are in helping testing agencies to create the best possible washback with the least waste of anyone's effort, and in helping researchers to understand how to design the most effective investigations for the tests and the contexts they wish to study. I would therefore also hope to see two very practical outcomes from the collaboration of many researchers: a set of evidence-based guidelines for creating positive washback, and a set of authoritative but user-friendly guidelines on how to design a washback study.

Further reading

Chapman, D. W. and Snyder, C. W. (2000). Can high-stakes national testing improve instruction: Re-examining conventional wisdom. *International Journal of Educational Development* 20: 457–74. Chapman and Snyder review five propositions for how to use high-stakes national testing to improve classroom teaching practices and student learning. They argue that such propositions often fail because policy-makers do not understand the links that must be present (e.g. increased resources to low-achieving schools, teacher and parent concern about poor scores, parent and community pressure on teachers to improve their practices) to convert strategy into the desired outcomes. A model of these linkages is presented to guide future policy-makers in their attempts to improve teaching through testing.

Rea-Dickins, P. and Scott, C. (2007). Washback from language tests on teaching, learning and policy: Evidence from diverse settings. *Assessment in Education: Principles, Policy & Practice* 14: 1–7. Rea-Dickins and Scott provide an overview of the notion of washback and associated issues in this editorial for a special issue of *Assessment in Education*. They summarise six papers commissioned for the issue, which include investigations into washback in settings which differ not only in terms of the groups being studied but also geographically. The authors/editors conclude that washback should be re-defined as a 'context-specific shifting process, unstable, involving changing behaviours in ways that are difficult to predict'.

References

AERA/APA/NCME (1999). *Standards for Educational and Psychological Testing*. Washington, DC: American Educational Research Association.

Airasian, P. (1988). Measurement-Driven Instruction: A Closer Look. *Educational Measurement: Issues and Practice* Winter: 6–11.

Ajzen, I. (2006). Constructing a TpB Questionnaire: Conceptual and Methodological Considerations. www.people.umass.edu/aizen/pdf/tpb.measurement.pdf (accessed 4/1/11).

Alderson, J. C. and Hamp-Lyons, L. (1996). TOEFL preparation courses: a study of washback. *Language Testing* 13: 280–97.

Alderson, J. C. and Wall, D. (1993). Does Washback Exist? *Applied Linguistics* 14: 115–29.

Andrews, S. (2004). Washback and Curriculum Innovation. In L. Cheng and Y. Watanabe (eds), *Washback in Language Testing*. Mahwah, NJ: Lawrence Erlbaum Associates, Publishers, 37–50.

Bachman, L. and Palmer, A. (2010). *Language Assessment in Practice*. Oxford, UK: Oxford University Press.

Bailey, K. (1996). Working for washback: a review of the washback concept in language testing. *Language Testing* 13: 257–79.

—— (1999) *Washback in Language Testing*. TOEFL Monograph No. MS-15. Princeton, NJ: Educational Testing Service.

Burrows, C. (2004). Washback in classroom-based assessment: a study of the washback effect in the Australian adult migrant English Program. In L. Cheng and Y. Watanabe (eds), *Washback in Language Testing*. Mahwah, NJ: Lawrence Erlbaum Associates, Publishers, 113–28.

Cheng, L. (2005). *Changing Language Teaching Through Language Testing: a washback study*. Cambridge, UK: Cambridge University Press and Cambridge ESOL.

—— (2008). Washback, Impact and Consequences. In E. Shohamy and N. H. Hornberger (eds), *Encyclopedia of Language and Education*, 2nd edn. Vol. 7. *Language Testing and Assessment*. New York, NY: Springer Science+Business Media LLC, 349–64.

Cheng, L. and Curtis, A. (2004). Washback or backwash: a review of the impact of testing on teaching and learning. In L. Cheng and Y. Watanabe (eds), *Washback in Language Testing*. Mahwah, NJ: Lawrence Erlbaum Associates, Publishers, 3–17.

Cheng, L. and Watanabe, Y. (eds), (2004). *Washback in Language Testing*. Mahwah, NJ: Lawrence Erlbaum Associates, Publishers.

Eckstein, M.A. and Noah, H. J. (1993). *Secondary School Examinations: international perspectives on policies and practice*. New Haven, CT: Yale University Press.

Ferman, I. (2004). The washback of an EFL national oral matriculation test to teaching and learning. In L. Cheng and Y. Watanabe (eds), *Washback in Language Testing*. Mahwah, NJ: Lawrence Erlbaum Associates, Publishers, 191–210.

Fredericksen, J.R. and Collins, A. (1989). A systems approach to educational testing. *Educational Researcher* 18: 27–32.

Fullan, M. G. and Stiegelbauer, S. (1991). *The New Meaning of Educational Change*, 2nd edn. London, UK: Cassell Educational Limited.

Gosa, C. M. C. (2004). *Investigating washback: a case study using student diaries*. Unpublished PhD Thesis, Lancaster University, UK.

Green, A. (2007). *IELTS Washback in Context: preparation for academic writing in higher education*. Cambridge, UK: Cambridge University Press and Cambridge ESOL.

Haladyna, T. M., Nolen, S. B. and Haas, N.S. (1991). Raising Standardized Achievement Test Scores and the Origins of Test Score Pollution. *Educational Researcher* 20: 2–7.

Hawkey, R. (2006). *Impact Theory and Practice: Studies of the IELTS Test and Progetto Lingue 2000*. Cambridge, UK: Cambridge University Press and Cambridge ESOL.

Heaton, J. B. (1990). *Classroom Testing*. Harlow, UK: Longman.

Henrichsen, L. E. (1989). *Diffusion of Innovations in English Language Teaching: The ELEC Effort in Japan, 1956–1968*. New York, NY: Greenwood Press.

Heyneman, S. P. and Ransom, A.W. (1990). Using examinations and testing to improve educational quality. *Educational Policy* 4: 177–92.

Huang, L. (2009). *Washback on Teachers' Beliefs and Behaviour: Investigating the Process from a Social Psychology Perspective*. Unpublished PhD Thesis, Lancaster University.

Hughes, A. (1994). *Backwash and TOEFL 2000*. Unpublished manuscript, commissioned by Educational Testing Service.

—— (2003). *Testing for Language Teachers*, 2nd edn. Cambridge, UK: Cambridge University Press.

Huhta, A., Kalaja, P. and Pitkänen-Huhta, A. (2006). Discursive construction of a high-stakes test: the many faces of a test-taker. *Language Testing* 23: 326–50.

Madaus, G. F. (1988). The influence of testing on the curriculum. In L. N. Tanner (ed.), *Critical Issues in Curriculum: eighty-seventh yearbook of the National Society for the Study of Education*. Chicago, IL: University of Chicago Press, 83–121.

Mehrens, W. A. and Kaminsky, J. (1989). Methods for Improving Standardized Test Scores: Fruitful, Fruitless or Fraudulent? *Educational Measurement: Issues and Practices* 8: 14–22.

Messick, S. (1996). Validity and washback in language testing. *Language Testing* 13: 241–56.

Pearson, I. (1988). Tests as levers for change. In D. Chamberlain and R. Baumgardner (eds), *ESP in the Classroom: practice and evaluation*. ELT Documents 128. London, UK: Modern English Publications, 98–107.

Popham, W. J. (1987). The merits of measurement-driven Instruction. *Phi Delta Kappan* 68: 679–82.

Shohamy, E., Donitsa-Schmidt S. and Ferman, I. (1996). Test impact revisited: washback effect over time. *Language Testing* 13: 298–317.

Spratt, M. (2005). Washback and the classroom: the implications for teaching and learning of studies of washback from exams. *Language Teaching Research* 9: 5–29.

Tsagari, D. (2009). *The Complexity of Test Washback*. Frankfurt, Germany: Peter Lang.

Wall, D. (1996). Introducing New Tests into Traditional Systems: Insights from General Education and from Innovation Theory. *Language Testing* 13, 3: 334–54.

—— (2000). The impact of high-stakes testing on teaching and learning: can this be predicted or controlled? *System* 28: 499–509.

—— (2005). *The Impact of High-Stakes Examinations on Classroom Teaching: A Case Study Using Insights from Testing and Innovation Theory*. Cambridge, UK: Cambridge University Press and Cambridge ESOL.

Wall, D. and Horák, T. (2007). Using baseline studies in the investigation of test impact. *Assessment in Education* 14: 99–116.

—— (2011). *The Impact of Changes in the TOEFL on Teaching in a Sample of Countries in Europe*: phase 3, the role of the coursebook, and phase 4, describing change. TOEFL iBT Reports series. Princeton, NJ: Educational Testing Service.

Watanabe, Y. (1996). Does grammar translation come from the entrance examination? Preliminary findings from classroom-based research. *Language Testing* 13: 318–33.

—— (2001). Does the university entrance examination motivate learners? A case study of learner interviews. In Akita Association of English Studies (ed.), *Trans-Equator Exchanges: a collection of academic papers in honour of Professor David Ingram*. Akita, Japan: Akita Association of English Studies, 100–10.

—— (2004). Methodology in washback studies. In L. Cheng and Y. Watanabe (eds), *Washback in Language Testing*. Mahwah, NJ: Lawrence Erlbaum Associates, Publishers, 19–36.

6

Assessing young learners

Angela Hasselgreen

Introduction

Young language learners (YLLs) are defined here as being primary school pupils up to about 12 years who are learning a second, additional or foreign language. This group includes children attending school where the language of instruction is not their L1, as well as those studying another language as a school subject. The assessment of YLLs is distinct in many ways from that of older learners, who for a long time comprised the 'default' subjects in the literature and research in language assessment. This is due to both the characteristics of YLLs themselves and the assessment they are most often subjected to, being largely informal and formative in purpose. This chapter will show how this YLL group has gradually been highlighted on the stage of language assessment, and will present some principal issues confronting those involved in their assessment, as well as the extent to which these issues have started to be tackled.

Historical perspectives

The term *language assessment* has only in the last decade or so taken a place alongside, or even instead of, *language testing*. In the 1980s and 1990s, language testing came into its own as a research field, focusing on the understanding and production of good tests in a world where these were being seen to have consequences not only for education and employment, but for such matters as citizenship or safety. During the 1990s, concern for the effects of national language testing in schools, among younger pupils, was voiced, e.g. Shohamy (1997). In 2000, a special issue of *Language Testing* (17) was devoted to YLLs. In her editorial, Rea-Dickins comments: 'In spite of the lack of formal reporting in the area of assessment of young language learners, the field is active in several ways.' (Rea-Dickins, 2000: 245). This recognition of YLL assessment as a field of research went hand in hand with the emergence of 'alternative assessment', culminating in a further special issue of *Language Testing* on this topic (Volume 18, 2001). In his editorial, McNamara cites two defining characteristics of papers which he deemed as belonging to the area *alternative assessment*:

- They articulated the theoretical challenge to mainstream interests in testing research.
- They focused on classroom contexts of assessment, involving either adult or school-based learners.

(McNamara, 2001: 229–330)

In short, by the start of the new millennium, a place had been established in the research field for young learners, and the types of assessment generally associated with them, now incidentally no longer regarded as an alternative to 'normal' assessment, but commonly referred to as 'classroom assessment' (which is the subject of Chapter 4 of this volume). In 2006, McKay's seminal book on the assessment of YLLs appeared, providing a comprehensive insight into issues, principles and practices in the field. In her chapter on research, she identifies four main purposes for research into YLL assessment:

- to investigate and share information about current assessment practices
- to find ways to ensure fair and valid assessment tasks and procedures
- to find out more about the nature of young learner language proficiency and language growth
- to investigate and improve the impact of assessment on young language learners, their families, their teacher and their school.

(Mackay, 2006: 65)

Certain of these areas have attracted more research than others, e.g. the second area; Mackay maintains: 'Assessment carried out by the teacher in the classroom is a rapidly growing area of research … Research interest in this area has developed as standard documents require teacher-based assessment and reporting' (Mackay, 2006: 96). However, echoing the words of Rea–Dickins (2000: 245), she remarks: 'Research into the assessment of young learners is a new field of endeavour, and whilst there has been relatively little published research to date, a growing amount of work is being undertaken by researchers and teachers around the world' (Mackay, 2006: 61).

Reports of YLL research have emerged as a trickle rather than a flood. A glance through collections of articles on language testing and assessment over the past decade reveals relatively few relating to younger learners. Similarly, articles on YLL research rarely focus on assessment, as can be illustrated in Moon and Nikolov's (2000) collection of research articles on the teaching of English to YLLs, where not one article addresses this topic.

Much is happening to change this situation, however. The traditional university structure in some countries (such as Scandinavian countries) whereby postgraduate students were unlikely to enter primary education, is yielding to more open systems, offering postgraduate studies with a didactic focus for trained teachers. Organisations such as EALTA (European Association for Language Testing and Assessment) are explicitly catering for school teachers in their events. In the USA, the No Child Left Behind legislation has led to a considerable research focus on English language tests for young learners, as exemplified in Ferrara (2008). The widespread adoption of the Council of Europe's European Language Portfolio in primary schools has inspired researchers, e.g. Little (2009). And a tendency for formal language learning to start earlier, combined with increased mobility and immigration, has meant that there are many more YLLs to assess.

Critical issues and topics, and how recent research has shed light on these

A number of critical issues impact on the assessment of YLLs. The first and most central is the complex nature of children themselves. The second involves the language skills we can expect YLLs to acquire. The third takes account of the situation of the teachers of YLLs, and their competence in language assessment. Some less obvious issues, but still deserving of mention, include the effect of language assessment policy on the status of languages, the role of digital media in assessment and the use of assessment in SLA research. This section will expand on these issues, taking into account what recent research has contributed to their understanding.

Young learners themselves

Young learners are generally rather different from adults. This is perhaps most apparent in their behaviour (good and bad), reactions, interactions, emotion and concentration spans. It also manifests itself in what they are capable of, linguistically and cognitively, raising the question of how much support children should be given in the assessment process. These characteristics have particular repercussions for any tasks we can expect them to do as part of an assessment process. It has also to be borne in mind that age and maturity play a great part in the extent to which these characteristics apply, and the teacher has to judge this for each child.

Some of the characteristics of YLLs identified by Hasselgreen (2000) are:

- they have a particular need and capacity for play, fantasy and fun;
- they have a relatively short attention span;
- they are at a stage when daring to use their language is vital, and any sense of 'failure' could be particularly detrimental.

(Hasselgreen 2000: 262)

As language assessment, for whatever purpose, involves giving a learner the optimal chance to show what he/she can do, tasks need to be designed which capture – and hold – the interest of the child. The use of pictures and game-like elements are a feature of YLL assessment tasks, as exemplified in Ioannou-Georgiou and Pavlou (2003). Cameron (2001) warns of tasks placing demands – linguistic and otherwise – that may prevent a child from performing optimally; she lists six such demands:

- cognitive (involving the degree of contextualisation of the language and the child's readiness to deal with the concepts involved)
- language (involving the familiarity/complexity of the language used, and the 'skills' involved, such as reading or conversing)
- interactional (involving the child's ability to take part in the interactions involved)
- metalinguistic (involving the 'technical' language used about the task)
- involvement (involving factors such as the time needed, the degree of interest etc., which may influence the level of engagement with the task)
- physical (involving any actions needed, or sitting still, as well as motor skills required)

(adapted from Cameron, 2001: 25)

A teacher needs to consider these demands when designing and giving tasks to children, and in deciding what level of support to give. Clearly, the non-linguistic demands should be reduced to a minimum if we are primarily interested in assessing the child's language, but the question arises of how much linguistic support we should give. From the perspective of Vygotsky (1962), the child will perform best when supported by a helpful adult, suggesting that assessment may benefit from children performing in interaction with the teacher. However, the situation is far from clear cut. Oliver *et al.* (2008) gave two groups of children (10–12 years and 5–7 years) information-gap and picture-based oral activities, with pre-task instructions. For some tasks the pupils also received teacher guidance during the task. The authors demonstrate that the older children (ages 10–12) appeared better able to respond and adapt to teacher input while doing a task than the 5–7 year olds, who appeared best left to their own devices, and who actually performed significantly less well with teacher support.

In formative assessment, classroom interactions play a major role, both in eliciting what a child knows, or can do, and in giving feedback. In Torrance and Pryor's (1998) investigation of formative assessment in UK infant classes, primarily based on the analysis of teacher–pupil interactions in a range of subjects/topics, a number of salient observations are made and conclusions drawn. The authors are able to demonstrate that 'many of the practices that are routinely employed by teachers as "positive reinforcement" to enhance motivation may actually result in children avoiding intellectual tasks, approaching them with limited confidence, and not persisting in the face of difficulties' (ibid.: 84). This is discussed with reference to psychological theories concerning *attributions*, *goals* and *rewards*.

It is posited that a child who attributes success to stable factors, such as high ability, rather than unstable factors, such as luck or effort, will have higher expectations and confidence. On the other hand, if failure is attributed to stable factors, such as ability, this can result in a lowering of expectations and self-esteem (ibid.: 84). So a child who performs badly on a task, but is praised for trying hard may suffer more, in terms of self-esteem, than one who is admonished for not making an effort.

Goals are distinguished as belonging to two orientations: *learning goals*, where the pupil aims to learn or master something, and *performance goals*, where the aim is to get a favourable judgement on his/her performance. Children who are generally oriented towards learning goals will choose challenging tasks, make every effort to succeed and not be put off by the prospect of failing. They will accumulate learning from the task. Children who are oriented towards performance goals will avoid or even sabotage challenging tasks. They will attribute failure to low ability, and will give up easily (ibid.: 85). One way of encouraging learning goals can be by bringing criteria in line with the true aim of a task. If a pupil knows s/he will be judged positively for evidence of having managed what is essential to learning, s/he is more likely to tackle the task in a positive way.

Rewards are seen as either intrinsic to the task itself, or extrinsic, such as stars and points. There is evidence that intrinsic rewards generally support learning, while extrinsic rewards can demotivate pupils from doing tasks without a reward, and are not shown to be generally beneficial, although they may be the only way to motivate pupils with no real interest in a task (ibid.: 86–87).

And it is not only pupils who are the object of rewards. As Cameron (2001: 26) points out, there is a strong desire in young learners to please their teachers. While this can make children a delight to teach, it can lead them to find any way to get a task 'right', producing what they think the teacher expects, and, at worst, hiding the fact that they do not understand the task or know the deeper 'thing' being assessed.

The intention in this section is not to attempt an account of the psyche of children, on which I have no expertise. It is rather to highlight some of the complexity in the ways children respond to situations arising during everyday assessment practices. While many of the factors touched on will of course have some relevance for adults, who are also complex, the difference is that, in the case of children, they play such a dominant role that we ignore them at our (and their) peril.

The language skills we can expect YLLs to acquire

The language skills we can expect a YLL to acquire vary considerably. Factors such as age/ maturity, 'world experience' and L1 literacy are among those that are particularly influential on YLL ability. It is probably safe to say that a 'ceiling' for what a child can say, write or understand in an L2 will be no higher than in his/her L1. The question of how to describe the language ability of children has been the subject of some major research and development work in the past decade, and two distinct areas are identified: (1) where the language is a second, or additional language, and the language of mainstream schooling; (2) where the language is taught as a foreign language and not used as the main language of instruction.

The first area is perhaps the most pressing one; not mastering the language can have implications for every aspect of school life, and educational success generally. A special issue of *Educational Assessment* (13: 2, 2008) is devoted to the assessment of English language learners in the context of the implementation of the No Child Left Behind (NCLB) legislative Act of 2002, in the United States. This act was the latest re-authorization of the Elementary and Secondary Education Act (ESEA), whereby the needs of children with L1s other than English have been addressed for several decades. The NCLB Act requires 'all states to assess the English proficiency of English language learners each year', and, further, 'to measure the annual growth of students' English language development in reading, listening, writing and speaking and in comprehension towards full English proficiency' (Ferrara, 2008: 132). This requires instruments for measurement based on valid standards for what might be expected of learners on their paths to proficiency. Ferarra describes the design of the speaking component of one such assessment tool, ELDA (the English Language Development Assessment). ELDA has separate assessment components for each skill, at three grade clusters: 3–5, 6–8 and 9–12. The content of the tests are taken from three academic areas: English language arts, maths, science and technology as well as one non-academic topic. The tests do not assess content knowledge, but rather the linguistic ability to function within these areas. Proficiency is defined at five levels, and tasks are designed for each of the grade clusters. Very simply put, in placing pupils at a level of proficiency, the assessment covers a range of skills and topics salient for coping in school, as well as taking regard to age. The outcome of the assessment informs decisions relating to assessment in other subjects.

The complexity of this assessment reflects much of what Mackay (2000) argues for in her analysis and discussion on ESL (English as a second language) standards for school learners. Mackay's concern is for children, primarily in the Australian context, whose English skills have been commonly assessed using the same yardstick as for ESB (English-speaking background) children. Mackay lists some of the problems ensuing from this, and outlines requirements for designing ESL standards, which include separate descriptors for younger learners, which are appropriate to the purpose of ESL assessment and which 'convey a sense of what we know about second language learning of school ESL learners in mainstream contexts' (2000: 197). These demands are embodied in the Australian (NLLIA) ESL Bandscales, presented in Mackay (2006). Developed in 1994, these Bandscales are developed for three distinct age groups, approximately 5–7, 8–11 and 12–18 years. The scales are made of up of holistic descriptors for reading, writing, speaking and listening, with eight levels, from beginning to near native. They 'include reminders about the characteristics of second language acquisition of young learners (e.g. of the possible presence of the silent period) and reminders about the role of the first language in second language learning. They reflect the cognitive demand and the maturity of each broad age group, and also the types of tasks that young learners are expected to carry out in the mainstream classroom' (Mackay, 2006: 311).

Thus, in contexts with large-scale second language learner groups, such as those in Australia or the USA, much has been done to ensure that the language assessment takes regard to age, school demands and the situation of the learners, recognising importantly that the learners may enter mainstream schooling at different points. However, there are many situations where second language learners are being assessed in ways that take no regard to these considerations and that use the same yardstick as for native speakers, e.g. in the Norwegian National Tests of reading ability (www.udir.no/Tema/Nasjonale-prover).

The second area, involving foreign language assessment, has, until relatively recently, been more straightforward. School curricula were traditionally able to define aims which assumed a grade-related progression from beginner to higher levels. The language learnt would normally be one commonly taught in the region. Problems typically encountered would be uniform across the class, who would mostly share an L1. However, this has changed in recent decades, clearly exemplified in Europe, with its great linguistic diversity. The Council of Europe (1998) extends it aim of plurilingualism to children from the start of schooling.

Coupled with a high level of migration and mobility, as well as with the influence of multimedia, this had led to a situation in Europe where few would feel able to define a norm for the ability of a school class in a given language. In anticipation of this situation, the Council of Europe (1998) encourages its members to use the *Common European Framework of Reference for Languages* (CEFR) (Council of Europe, 2001) and its offshoot, the *European Language Portfolio* (ELP), (Council of Europe, 1998: Appendix, Section G). Each of these instruments was originally designed for adults, and while the CEFR remains in a standard form, the ELP now exists in numerous forms, for adults and YLLs, across Europe.

The adaptation of the ELP in European schools has acted as a catalyst for defining what YLLs 'can do' in both second and foreign languages. The member countries have designed their own ELP versions to suit their countries' needs, usually with separate portfolios for primary and secondary schools. The flexibility within a list of 'can do' statements usually makes it possible to use with second/additional language learners or foreign language learners. An example of a YLL-oriented ELP, which has been widely used directly, and as a model for other national versions is the CILT portfolio (www.primarylanguages.org.uk), where the 'can do' statements are based on the CEFR levels up to B1, arguably the highest level a YLL can cognitively reach (although B1 has not been recognised as an 'end point' for YLLs). Designing national ELPs has given researchers the opportunity to examine in depth the way YLLs use their language ability, as they progress through the CEFR levels. An example of this research is seen in the ECML's (European Centre for Modern Languages) 'Bergen can do' project (Hasselgreen, 2003), which drew directly on what learners themselves reported to be doing in their foreign languages, and where they and their teachers jointly placed them on a modified CEFR scale.

The CEFR itself has also provided a basis for national curricula, e.g. in the Finnish core curriculum, where performance objectives at key stages, including the end of primary school, for second and foreign languages, are directly expressed as sublevels of CEFR levels (see www.oph.fi/download/47672_core_ curricula_basic_education_3.pdf). The adaptation of the CEFR level descriptors to YLLs has been the object for research, as exemplified in the ECML's AYLLIT project (www.ayllit.ecml.at), where a CEFR-based scale of descriptors for the assessment of writing has been developed in a longitudinal study of YLL writing over two years. The AYLLIT scale is provided in the appendix to this chapter.

An advantage of using the CEFR as a basis for describing the language ability of YLLs, whether in ELPs or as scales of descriptors, is that they can ideally be used regardless of the L2 being assessed. Much work remains, however, on the validation of such adapted instruments, particularly in the context of L2s other than English.

The situation of the teachers of YLLs, and of their competence in language assessment

Recent trends in language education, such as a lowering of the age of starting languages, together with increasing numbers of children who have to function in school in a language other than their own, has put a great responsibility on the teachers of YLLs, many of whom have not been initially trained as language teachers. The assessment needs of school teachers, teacher trainers and 'experts' was addressed in a survey conducted by EALTA in 2004 (Hasselgreen *et al.*, 2004). A total of 914 respondents submitted answers to the survey. Most of these were European, representing 37 countries, while 50 respondents were from non-European countries. While the informants in the survey were not typically 'grassroots' teachers, many having had some training in language assessment, they were clearly able to identify areas in which they had need of training. The most notable were:

- using ELP/other portfolios
- conducting peer/self assessment
- interpreting results and giving feedback
- carrying out informal continuous assessment.

Perhaps not surprisingly, the teacher trainers had very similar needs, and most admitted to teaching many areas of assessment, with no training in these. It has to be concluded that the teachers of YLLs are generally having to carry out assessment with very little training or support. This finding has been corroborated by a recent survey, conducted by Vogt *et al.* (2010) based on an adaptation of the EALTA questionnaire. A total of 781 language teachers from seven countries were questioned on their training and needs in language assessment, and the results showed a distribution of particular needs similar to the EALTA survey and an overwhelming need for training generally in assessment. Although the number of primary school teachers was not reported, it can be assumed that their needs, in relevant areas, will be at least as great as for teachers generally.

A number of research reports seem to corroborate those conclusions. Leung and Rea-Dickins (2007) examine the situation in the UK, whereby teachers of English as an additional language (EAL) are expected to carry out formative assessment in the primary school as part of national policy. However, in 2003 teachers received guidelines from the DfES (Department for Education and Skills) which seem suited to more formal, one-off summative assessment, neglecting the central role of day-to-day interactions. Moreover, the guidelines fail to present teachers with an account of what makes up communicative language ability. As many teachers of language in the primary school are not language specialists, they need support and training in what makes up the ability to communicate in a language.

Torrance and Pryor (1998) consider the extent to which teachers need guidance in classroom questioning. They demonstrate that the traditional teacher-pupil exchange pattern, initiate-respond-feedback, does not give the child the opportunity to show WHAT s/he knows, but simply IF s/he knows whatever is on the teacher's mind. They advocate a move from the 'convergent', closed form of assessment, where the question targets a specific point with a pre-determined answer, to a more 'divergent', open form where questions are authentic, in which and the child can reveal what s/he can do or knows and where more support is needed (1998: 152).

Edelenbos and Kubanek-German (2004) investigate the extent to which primary school language teachers demonstrate skills in diagnosing pupils' weaknesses and strengths, and conclude that support and material are needed in order to build this competence. They maintain this competence includes the teacher's skill in performing certain activities, including such diverse ones as the ability to:

- guess what a child wants to say from his/her fragmentary and possibly linguistically infelicitous utterances, to complete them or motivate the child to do this;
- give concrete examples of an individual child's language growth over a period of, for example, 3 months;

- recognize from a child's face if he/she has understood an instruction or a key point in a story.

(Edelenbos and Kubanek-German, 2004: 277–79)

What has been presented in this section about the assessment needs of primary school teachers involved in second, additional or foreign language shows that these needs are wide-ranging. Yet these are very basic needs, involving activities that most teachers would regard as fundamental to classroom practice. To be able to assess YLLs, teachers recognise that they need knowledge of language ability, basic language testing, peer/self assessment and portfolio use. However, what has been revealed here shows the great importance of teacher-pupil interactions, how these can be conducted, and how the teacher interprets and uses them in the process of assessment. It cannot be assumed that teachers are aware of these skills, or that they will acquire them without training and support.

Other issues

While a wide range of issues impact on the assessment of YLLs, a handful are identified here as being particularly worthy of mention. These include the effect of language assessment policy on the status of languages, the role of digital media in assessment and the use of assessment in SLA research.

While the discussion so far has overwhelmingly focused on the major purpose of YLL assessment, formative assessment, and has assumed it to be in the hands of the classroom teacher, we cannot ignore the fact that summative, external assessment of YLLs occurs to a not inconsiderable degree. It has already been commented that children may be disadvantaged if their L1 is not that being assessed as a mainstream classroom language; but there are cases where languages themselves may be disadvantaged, and neglected or reduced in status. While Council of Europe countries are encouraged to diversify in their language teaching from an early age, national testing policy may work against this. This is particularly true in the case of national testing of English, in countries, such as Norway, where the national language is little known outside the country, and English is considered essential for study, work and social purposes. The pressure on Norwegian teachers to get good external test results acts as a boost for English, at the expense of other languages, which are rarely taught in the primary school, although national policy ostensibly adopts the Council of Europe aims. Shohamy (2007) argues that testing can itself create de facto policy, which may override actual policy. She maintains that in the Israeli context, the 'tested language' becomes the most important language to acquire and master. Indeed, since tests are often more powerful than any written policy document, they lead to the elimination and suppression of certain languages in societies (Shohamy, 2007: 120). She also cites the NCLB legislation in the USA, where the testing of English as a second language has had a major negative impact on the choice of other languages as subjects of study (ibid.: 123).

The role of digital media in assessment will increasingly be an issue in testing YLLs. A pioneer of this is the National testing of English reading in Norway, reported in Schlanbusch and Moe (2006). All fifth and eighth grade pupils in Norway are tested on-line yearly, and scored automatically, with scores linked to bandscales. The tests contain items which are largely picture-based for the younger group, involving matching, colouring, dragging and clicking on texts and pictures. A disadvantage of the computer is that it has proved impossible to include open-ended items. However, it has allowed the use of many formats with considerable 'child appeal' which could otherwise not have been used; furthermore it has made it possible to have very large groups for on-line piloting, resulting in high reliability coefficients, of around 0.85 for the fifth grade and over 0.90 for the eighth grade (Schlanbusch and Moe, 2006: 11–12). Initial fears that lacking computer skills may affect performance have been allayed in local trials, and correlations between teacher ratings of their pupils' reading and test scores, range from 0.508 to 0.552 for the fifth grade and from 0.581 to 0.656 for the eighth grade (ibid.: 11–12). Given that the fifth grade teachers generally professed to find it difficult to rate reading, these correlations must be regarded as positive indications that the tests are testing reading ability rather than computing skills. The question of whether reading on-line is 'genuine reading' is probably becoming less salient, as more YLL reading is actually done on computer.

Finally, there is the subject of the use of tests in SLA research. While it is the case that reports on research in YLL assessment are not abundant, there is a growing amount of literature on research in SLA relating to children (e.g. Philp *et al.*, 2008). It is common, especially when analysing the effect of a teaching style or method, to use pre- and post-tests, sometimes with a control group being given the same tests. Clearly, in such cases, the quality of the testing is fundamental to the value of the findings; it is notoriously difficult to design parallel tests for pre- and post-testing. The point being made here is that YLL research is often dependent on competence in YLL testing, underscoring the need for expertise in this field for researchers as well as teachers.

Recommendations for practice

Three principal issues were identified in the previous section: the complex nature of YLLs themselves, the language skills we can expect them to acquire and the situation of their teachers and their competence in language assessment. While we cannot change the nature of YLLs or the language skills they need to acquire, we can, hopefully, do something about the situation of their teachers, so that they are in a better position to cater for the language assessment needs of their pupils.

Language teachers acknowledge their need for considerable training and support in assessing language ability. What has perhaps not been sufficiently highlighted is the fact that (a) many language teachers who find themselves in YLL classrooms may not have specialist YLL training, and (b) many teachers who are responsible for assessing the language needs of younger pupils have little background as linguists, especially in the case of mainstream class teachers with children with L1s other than the language of instruction. Added to this is the fact that classroom interaction, a major part of formative assessment, is very challenging to carry out successfully.

On the other hand, there are few groups of people more dedicated than primary school teachers. My own experience with Norwegian teachers is that those in primary school are keen to join in research projects and sign up for courses. Rea-Dickins and Gardner (2000) demonstrate how, with the right kind of support, UK class teachers with young pupils with EAL are able to carry out the kind of successful assessment to which they aspire, but are not always in a position to achieve.

A basic knowledge of YLLs and the language and skills they need to acquire should be accessible to any YLL teacher. Support or training in assessment practices, including classroom interaction, should be provided for all those involved in YLL assessment. Bringing this about is in the hands of many. In the Early Years Intervention Project, described by Rea-Dickins and Gardner (2000), class teachers in each project school worked in collaboration with a language support coordinator, as well as each other and bilingual assistants. This kind of support is exemplary and, sadly, rare, but much help can also be given through other means. Textbook writers, materials producers, teacher trainees, and professional organisations are among those who have a role to play, if YLLs are to be given the assessment they deserve, by teachers who strive to give this.

In addition, policy makers need to be made aware that learning objectives for children in any language, particularly the mainstream language of the region or country, must take regard to the L1 of the individual child. They must also be aware that by testing any language, this language may be given a status which is at the expense of other languages, possibly running contrary to ostensive language policy.

Finally a brief mention of those carrying out YLL research is in order. This group of researchers consists typically of individuals working largely on their own. While organisations such as IATEFL have special interest groups for YLL teachers, and YLL conferences have taken place (see Moon and Nikolov, 2000), these are the exception rather than the rule. As research into teaching methods or SLA often involves some form of assessment, and as researchers cannot be experts in everything, there is a great need for networking among YLL researchers, both those who work in YLL assessment and those who do not. If competence in assessment itself can be shared and exploited, we may ensure that faulty testing will not mar otherwise valuable results.

Future directions

Following what has been discussed above, it is apparent that there is a need for further surveying of YLL teachers' assessment practices, beliefs and knowledge, both of language ability and assessment, and of the guidance and support they are offered. The focus of research, I believe, is likely to be on less traditional methods of assessment, such as testing with computers, and YLL self- and peer-assessment. The question of how much support YLLs should be given in the assessment process also needs investigation. And hopefully, we will see more studies on teacher-pupil interaction, to measure the extent to which this is fulfilling its potential as a means of assessment in the YLL language classroom.

But perhaps the most radical direction I would predict involves the describing of second or foreign language development in YLLs. This has been tackled in various ways; examples of tailor-made YLL descriptors from Australia and the USA have been presented here, while in Europe, with the CEFR/ELP playing a dominant role, adult scales have been adapted for YLLs, with the dilemma of whether or not to set a 'ceiling' on the level reachable by children. However we design our descriptors, the problem remains of deciding what we can reasonably expect a young, cognitively immature, learner to 'do' in his/her L2. The answer I believe can only be found by looking at what s/he can do in the L1. The parallel study of both L1 and L2 ability could lead to descriptors which truly represent the range of what YLLs are cognitively capable of, and to scales on which a learner could be placed for both language categories, giving rise to a more reasonable assessment of both his/her mother tongue and foreign or second language ability.

Appendix

Writing descriptors, AYLLIT (Assessment of Young Learner Literacy) Project (www.ayllit.ecml.at)

	Overall structure and range of information	Sentence structure and grammatical accuracy	Vocabulary and choice of phrase	Misformed words and punctuation
Above B1	Is able to create quite complicated texts, using effects such as switching tense and interspersing dialogue with ease. The more common linking words are used quite skilfully.	Sentences can contain a wide variety of clause types, with frequent complex clauses. Errors in basic grammar only occur from time to time.	Vocabulary may be very wide, although the range is not generally sufficient to allow stylistic choices to be made.	Misformed words only occur from time to time.

(continued)

	Overall structure and range of information	Sentence structure and grammatical accuracy	Vocabulary and choice of phrase	Misformed words and punctuation
B1	Is able to write texts on themes which do not necessarily draw on personal experience and where the message has some complication. Common linking words are used.	Is able to create quite long and varied sentences with complex phrases, e.g. adverbials. Basic grammar is more often correct than not.	Vocabulary is generally made up of frequent words and phrases, but this does not seem to restrict the message. Some idiomatic phrases used appropriately.	Most sentences do not contain misformed words
A2/B1	Is able to make reasonable attempt at texts on familiar themes that are not completely straightforward, including very simple narratives. Clauses are normally linked using connectors, such as *and, then, because, but*.	Sentences contain some longer clauses, and signs are shown of awareness of basic grammar, including a range of tenses.	Vocabulary is made up of very common words, but is able to combine words and phrases to add colour and interest to the message (e.g. using adjectives).	Clear evidence of awareness of spelling and punctuation rules, but misformed words may occur in most sentences.
A2	Can write short, straightforward, coherent texts on very familiar themes. A variety of ideas are presented with some logical linking.	Is able to make simple independent sentences with a limited number of underlying structures.	Vocabulary is made up of very frequent words but has sufficient words and phrases to get across the essentials of the message.	Some evidence of knowledge of spelling and punctuation rules.
A1/A2	Can adapt and build on to a few learnt patterns to make a series of short and simple sentences. This may be a short description or set of related facts on a very familiar personal theme.		Can use some words which may resemble L1, but on the whole the message is recognisable to a reader who does not know the L1.	
A1	Can write a small number of learnt words and fixed phrases in an easily recognisable way.			
Approaching A1	Makes an attempt to write some words and phrases.			

Further reading

Cameron, L. (2001). *Teaching Language to Young Learners*. Cambridge, UK: Cambridge University Press. This is a sound introduction to YLL teaching and learning for teachers, students and those involved in YLL research. Cameron takes her starting point in theoretical and empirical research, and builds on this to present very practical advice for the YLL classroom.

Clark, S. (2001). *Unlocking Formative Assessment Practical Strategies for Enhancing Pupils' Learning in the Primary Classroom*. London, UK: Hodder Education. While set in the context of the UK National curriculum for literacy and numeracy, this book has much to offer those directly involved in the formative assessment of

YLLs. It provides practical advice and materials for carrying out central aspects of formative assessment, such as target setting, self assessment, teacher feedback and sharing learning objectives.

Ioannou-Georgiou, S. and P. Pavlou (2003). *Assessing Young Learners*, Oxford, UK: Oxford University Press. This book offers concrete, copy-ready tasks for the assessment of a wide range of aspects of language learning. While not having general application to classroom assessment, this book provides a ready-made toolkit for the YLL teacher to draw on.

MacKay, P. (2006). *Assessing Young Language Learners*. Cambridge, UK: Cambridge University Press. A comprehensive overview of the issues involved in YLL assessment, this book has value to those who wish to embark on research into YLL assessment, or who wish to carry out assessment. MacKay takes pains to present 'the special case' of YLLs and their assessment, and shows how far research has been able to shed light on the topic. She gives detailed exemplification and advice on many aspects of assessment, and highlights issues which need further investigation.

Torrance, H. and J. Pryor (1998). *Investigating Formative Assessment*. Milton Keynes, UK: Open University Press. Based on empirical research within UK infant schools classrooms, this book analyses the formative assessment embodied in teacher-pupil interactions. While supportive of teachers, the book demonstrates how teachers' assessment actions can actually influence pupils' responses and behaviour. A conceptual framework of convergent and divergent assessment is offered, with practical classroom implications.

References

Cameron, L. (2001). *Teaching Language to Young Learners*. Cambridge, UK: Cambridge University Press.

Council of Europe (1998). *Recommendation no. R (98) 6 of the Committee of Ministers to Member States Concerning Modern Languages*. wcd.coe.int/wcd/com.instranet (accessed 2/8/11).

—— (2001). *Common European Framework of References for Languages: learning, teaching, assessment* Cambridge, UK: Cambridge University Press.

Edelenbos, P. and Kubanek-German, A. (2004). Teacher assessment: the concept of diagnostic competence. *Language Testing* 21: 259–83.

Ferrara, S. (2008). Design and psychometric considerations for the assessment of speaking proficiency: the English language development Assessment (ELDA) as illustration. *Educational Assessment* 13: 132–92.

Hasselgreen, A. (2000). The assessment of the English ability of young learners in Norwegian schools: an innovative approach. *Language Testing* 17: 261–77.

—— (2003). *The Bergen-Cando Project*. Graz, Austria: ECML.

Hasselgreen, A., Carlsen, C. and Helness, H. (2004). *European Survey of Language Testing and Assessment Needs. Report Part One: general findings*. www.ealta.eu.org/documents/resources/survey-report-pt1.pdf (accessed 2/8/11).

Ioannou-Georgiou, S. and Pavlou, P. (2003). *Assessing Young Learners*. Oxford, UK: Oxford University Press.

Leung, C. and Rea-Dickins, P. (2007). Teacher assessment as policy instrument: contradictions and capacities. *Language Assessment Quarterly* 4: 6–36.

Little, D. (2009). Language learner autonomy and the European Language Portfolio: Two L2 English examples. *Language Teaching* 42: 222–33.

Mackay, P. (2000). On ESL standards for school-age learners. *Language Testing* 17: 185–214.

—— (2006). *Assessing Young Language Learners*. Cambridge, UK: Cambridge University Press.

McNamara, T. (2001). Rethinking alternative assessment. *Language Testing* 187: 329–32.

Moon, J. and Nikolov, M. (2000). *Research into Teaching English to Young Learners*. Pécs, Hungary: University Press Pécs.

Oliver, R., Philp, J. and Mackey, A. (2008). The impact of teacher input, guidance and feedback on ESL children's task-based interactions. In Philp, J., Oliver, R. and Mackey, A. (eds), *Second Language Acquisition and the Younger Learner*. Amsterdam, The Netherlands: John Benjamins.

Philp, J., Oliver, R. and Mackey, A. (2008). *Second Language Acquisition and the Younger Learner*. Amsterdam, The Netherlands: John Benjamins.

Rea-Dickins, P. (2000). Assessment in early years language learning contexts. *Language Testing* 17: 115–22.

Rea-Dickins, P. and Gardner, S. (2000). Snares and Silver Bullets: Disentangling the Construct of Formative Assessment. *Language Testing* 17: 215–43.

Schlanbusch, H. and Moe, E. (2006). *Rapport: nasjonal prøver i Engelsk*. Unpublished report, University of Bergen.

Shohamy, E. (1997). Testing methods, testing consequences: Are they ethical? Are they fair? *Language Testing* 14: 340–49.

—— (2007). Language tests as language policy tools. *Assessment in Education: principles. Policy and Practice* 14: 117–30.

Torrance, H. and Pryor, J. (1998). *Investigating Formative Assessment*. Milton Keynes, UK: Open University Press.

Vogt, K., Sahinkarakas, S., Tsagari, D., Pavlou, P., Migdal, U., Afiri, Q. and Guerin, E. (2010). *Assessment Literacy of Foreign Language Teachers: Findings of a European Survey*. Unpublished.

Vygotsky, L. (1962). *Thought and Language*. New York, NY: Wiley.

7

Dynamic assessment

Marta Antón

Introduction

Dynamic assessment (DA) is defined as an interactive alternative type of assessment that integrates assessment and instruction. Its aim is to gauge and advance the learning potential of individual learners and to devise appropriate educational strategies. Conceptually, it is based on sociocultural theory, particularly on Vygotsky's notion of Zone of Proximal Development (ZPD), as well as on European and American psychology of the 1920s and 1930s (Grigorenko, 2009). This chapter intends to familiarize the reader with DA, particularly with its application to the assessment of second language abilities. I will discuss first the theoretical roots of DA and its early development in cognitive psychology. Then I will present some key characteristics of DA, different approaches to DA, and outcomes. I will consider some criticisms that have been raised from psychometric perspectives, and I will discuss fundamental differences with similar types of assessment. Much of the chapter is devoted to applications of DA to second language contexts, particularly the role of mediated language experiences in assessment, the use of DA as a diagnostic tool, program and peer/group assessment, and DA delivered through technology. Finally, I delineate some recommendations for practice and future developments for DA.

Theoretical background and historical perspective

DA practices are rooted in Vygotsky's theory of cognitive development and his notion of ZPD (Vygotsky, 1978; Minick, 1987). Vygotsky's proposals for the use of ZPD in assessment are based on his conception of ZPD as the place where learning occurs. The ZPD reflects development because "It is not what one is but what one can become; it is not what has developed but what is developing" (Grigorenko and Sternberg, 1998: 78). The ZPD comes into existence through social interaction. Vygotsky called for a change from *symptomatic assessment*, which focuses on present behavior of a particular developmental stage, to *diagnostic assessment*, which focuses on future behavior and on developing recommendations to foster development (Minick, 1987). Vygotsky hypothesized that intervention would benefit learners with a broad ZPD, that is, with a high degree of readiness. The fundamental link between the notion of ZPD and DA is the central idea that assessment which is entirely based on what the child is able to do independently ignores important differences in mental functioning that come to light when the child's interaction with an expert is analyzed (Minick, 1987: 120). For Vygotsky, the application of ZPD to assessment allows for a more complete picture of the learner's actual stage of development and of the proximal phase. He was mostly concerned with qualitative assessment of psychological processes and the dynamics of their development. However, Minick (1987) points out that, with the exception of Feuerstein, applications of the ZPD to DA have had a tendency to produce quantitative measures of learning potential.

DA was first articulated and developed by Feuerstein and his colleagues in the early 1950s in Israel to estimate the learning potential of low-performing children (Feuerstein *et al.*, 1979). Since then it has continued to be mainly applied to the assessment of cognitive development potential by psychologists. While some followed Feuerstein's interactionist model of DA (Haywood and Lidz, 2007; Lidz, 1987, 1991; Tzuriel, 1997), other new approaches of an interventionist quantitative nature developed. Approaches to DA will be further discussed in the next section.

Critical issues and topics

Grigorenko (2009) points to three basic assumptions that underlie the various methodologies known as DA. First, traditional testing may fail to capture the level of cognitive development of learners from dissimilar cultural backgrounds. Second, the focus of assessment should be not only what learners can do now, but also what they may be able to do tomorrow. Third, assessment should be integrated with intervention and should have selecting or modifying intervention as a goal. A major focus of the proponents of DA is the ability to identify those students who are likely to experience difficulties and to provide rich descriptions of the abilities of these students so that remedial programs may be developed (Campione and Brown, 1987).

Lidz (1987) defined DA as "an interaction between an examiner-as-intervener and a learner-as-active participant, which seeks to estimate the degree of modifiability of the learner and the means by which positive changes in cognitive functioning can be induced and maintained" (p. 4). The goal of DA is to measure, intervene, and modify behaviors by concentrating on the process of learning. *Activity* on the part of examiner and learner, and *modifiability* of behavior through *mediation* are crucial characteristics of DA (Lidz, 1991). Mediation in DA refers to the intervention of the assessor in order to select, amplify, and interpret objects and processes to the learner during the assessment. Thus, DA is above all social, interactive, and qualitative (Lidz and Elliott, 2000).

Approaches to DA

According to Sternberg and Grigorenko (2002), there are three fundamental methodological differences between DA and non-DA approaches to assessment. One is that non-DA focuses on past, matured abilities while DA projects towards the future by trying to discern and nurture emergent abilities. The second difference refers to the role of the examiner. While non-DA expects examiners to have a neutral role so as not to affect the testing situation, DA is characterized by the intervention of the examiner, who integrates teaching within the assessment itself. Finally, providing qualitative feedback during assessment is a distinguishing feature of DA, whereas in non-DA no feedback is provided until the end. Any assessment format may be dynamic so long as mediation is included in the assessment procedure (Lantolf and Thorne, 2006). What is distinctive about DA is the intention to uncover what lies next in an individual's proximal development by regulating and refocusing the learner in the interaction (*intentionality*), the attention to high quality *mediation* that provides systematic and contingent graduated assistance during the intervention, and the focus on the achievement of individual performance (self-regulation) and transfer of skills (*transcendence*).

The methods employed in DA educational psychology studies and second language learning studies are presented here along the interactionist versus interventionist paradigm (Lantolf and Poehner, 2004). Interventionist studies follow a test–intervene–retest format and thus tend to focus on quantitative results of the intervention while interactionist studies rely on qualitative analysis and interpretation of key features of the interaction blending learning and assessment. Interventionist approaches may be more appropriate when applied to large groups while an interactionist approach may be more useful in a classroom situation.

Procedurally, interventionist approaches are carried out following what has been called *the sandwich format* or *the cake format*. The first one has three stages. First, the learner is tested in order to establish the level of independent performance. Second, there is an intervention in the form of teaching what is included in the test. In the final stage, the learner is tested again to assess the degree and the nature of the change. Intervention (second stage) follows a predetermined script and thus the procedure is standardized. In this approach there is a tendency to devise quantitative formulae of calculating scores for learning potential derived from gains from the pre-test to the post-test as a result of the intervention stage. In the cake model, assessment and mediation are interspersed in layers, one depending on how the other evolves. Examples of interventionist approaches to DA are Budoff's (1987) *measures of learning potential* or Campione and Brown's (1987) *graduated-prompts approach*. In this approach, learners are provided with a supportive framework of graduated help in test problem-solving with the aim to transfer what is learned to other contexts. Other interventionist approaches are based on manipulation of the test itself. In Europe, Guthke's *Lerntest* consists of a battery of learning potential tests that include repetitions, prompts and systematic feedback as an intervention between pre- and post-test. Carlson and Wiedl's *testing-the limits approach* is also based on different manipulations of the test designed to compensate for deficits and improve performance (see Grigorenko and Sternberg, 1998, and Poehner, 2008b, for a review of these approaches to DA).

Interactionist approaches, on the other hand, make use of unscripted mediation and depend on the mediator's judgment as well as on the learner's response to the mediation during the assessment. Proponents of the interventionist approach object to the interactionist approach because the procedure makes it difficult to discern the learner's understanding and ability from the tester's effect on the learners' performance (Budoff, 1987). However, interactionist DA seems to be closer to Vygotsky's original views on assessment and his concept of ZPD (Minick, 1987). Among the first to employ interactionist DA was Feuerstein, who with his colleagues developed the Mediated Learning Experience (MLE) and Learning Propensity Assessment Device (LPAD). In the MLE there is "reciprocal, emotional, affective and motivational aspect of the interaction that melds the activity into a meaningful and structural whole, leading to self-awareness, structural change and cognitive development" (Feuerstein *et al.*, 2002: 75). The MLE includes eleven components, among them, *intentionality* of the assessor, *reciprocity*, referring to how the learner responds to the mediation in learner-mediator interaction, and *transcendence* or the ability of the learner to move beyond a task and transfer what has been learned to a new activity. Learners perform a series of tasks that increase in complexity in order to observe the learners' ability to transcend what has been learned. The mediator–assessor interacts individually with the learner paying attention to the learner's reciprocity to decide what degree of assistance is necessary. In mediated learning experiences the examiner may guide learners in highlighting important content, making connections, setting goals, planning, regulating, and controlling behavior. A key element of successful mediation is "contingent responsivity" (Lidz, 1991: 85), that is, the ability of the mediator to respond to the learner's behavior timely and appropriately. DA studies show that verbalization and elaborated feedback are two of the most powerful elements of mediated learning experiences.

Poehner (2008a) argues against interventionist approaches to DA because their practice of scripting mediation adheres too closely to standardized testing and ignores the important role of learner reciprocity (cf. Lidz, 1991). Poehner underscores the importance of the quality of dialogic mediation and the role of the learner through reciprocity for effective collaboration within the ZPD. Analyzing interaction of university students of French during mediation sessions, Poehner showed how learners negotiated mediation, used the mediator as a resource, sought approval from the mediator, and even rejected the mediation. What is important, Poehner argues, is that it is not possible to understand the full range of the learner's potential if mediation is detached from its dialogic context and if learners' contributions to the mediation are not interpreted within the whole interaction.

DA outcomes

There are two main outcomes of DA procedures. On one hand, DA improves our understanding of what a learner is able to do in a particular learning/testing situation. Contrary to traditional, static, assessment, DA puts more emphasis on the process rather than the product. On the other hand, from the DA experience we can derive "suggestions for intervention that appear successful in facilitating improved learner performance" (Lidz, 1991: 6). DA studies also indicate that mediation is associated with improvement in performance, particularly in learners experiencing difficulties, which addresses the important issue of fairness in education.

Criticisms of DA

Research related to DA models in educational psychology has concluded that mediation is associated with improved performance, that verbalization and elaborated feedback seem to be the most powerful components of mediation, that low performing children benefit from mediated intervention more than other groups, and that DA contributes significantly to variability in achievement (Lidz, 1991). However, the empirical validity of much of this research has been questioned. Overall, DA is still struggling with the question of how to measure change and establish a causal relation with educational intervention. In addition, concerns about validity and reliability of DA techniques have been raised (Grigorenko and Sternberg, 1998; Sternberg and Grigorenko, 2002) regarding a lack of standardization in the methodology (particularly in interactionist approaches) and a lack of empirical validation of results. Results from one DA study may not be generalized to other situations since the effect of mediation is dependent upon the context and quality of the interaction between mediator and student. Grigorenko and Sternberg (1998) remark on the dearth of empirical data on the reliability and validity of dynamic testing and on insufficient detail on methods, which makes it difficult to replicate studies.

In the psychometric non-dynamic tradition in testing, any change in performance during testing would undermine the reliability of the test (Lantolf and Thorne, 2006). Yet, modifiability is precisely a goal of DA. Poehner (2008b) argues extensively against psychometric criticisms of DA claiming that non-DA constructs are not suitable to the interactionist model of DA because DA represents a very different perspective on human mind functioning. In DA the human mind cannot be separated from the environment in which it operates. The dialectic relation between mind and culture makes DA incompatible with other approaches that try to observe mental functioning independently from the environment. However, Poehner (2008b) adds that this difference does not make DA an inappropriate means of assessment. It simply evidences that DA researchers need to delineate their own methods and criteria for understanding individuals, not measuring them.

DA and similar approaches

Philosophically and procedurally, DA has certain similarities with approaches to assessment such as Response to Intervention (RTI) and Formative Assessment (FA). Grigorenko (2009) compares RTI with DA concluding that "both approaches belong to one family of methodologies in psychology and education whose key feature is in blending assessment and intervention in one holistic activity" (p. 111). Both RTI and DA were developed to respond to the practical needs of children in special education (children with cognitive impairments) or diverse educational experiences (new immigrants and socially disadvantaged children). Both approaches assume a close relation between instruction and assessment with DA placing a major focus on assessment and RTI emphasizing instruction. Grigorenko concludes that the two are fundamentally two sides of the same coin and that the considerable overlapping should, at least, be acknowledged.

FA also resonates with DA because it occurs through interaction in educational settings. However, despite superficial similarities, there are marked differences between these two approaches. In contrast to summative assessment, FA provides teachers with useful information for planning curriculum by diagnosing the effectiveness of pedagogy based on students' learning (Rea-Dickins, 2004; Rea-Dickens and Gardner, 2000). Current use of internal incidental FA, which takes place during instructional conversations in the classroom and provides feedback to the learner during the activity, is mostly constrained to informal unsystematic procedures. According to Poehner and Lantolf (2005), a fundamental difference between DA and FA is that while FA focuses on the completion of the task, DA aims at cognitive development and transfer of skills to future tasks through intentional and systematic mediation. Importantly, Lantolf and Thorne (2006) add that DA is derived from a well-developed theory of learning while FA is mostly experiential. FA most often is not systematic and therefore any development that it may promote is incidental instead of intentional, as is the case in DA. To sum up the differences then, DA is intentional, systematic, and it focuses on development. FA is generally incidental and unsystematic, but even when it is formal and systematic its focus is on the completion of the task.

Current contributions and research

Many years ago, McNamara (1997) argued for the need "to recognize the intrinsically social nature of performance" (p. 446) thus calling for a social perspective in testing. McNamara referred specifically to assessment in a Vygotskian sense, bringing up the challenges that co-construction of interaction, contextual variability, and social constraints on assessment pose for traditional psychometric testing. Swain (2001) suggested also that the analysis of learners' collaborative dialogue could provide valuable information for language testers on "targets for measurement" (p. 297). As collaboration among learners entails distributed performance and joint construction of outcomes, testers must devise fair ways to evaluate group performance. One way to do this, Swain suggests, is to create post-tests based on learners' co-constructed knowledge. Minimally, analysis of learners' interaction may provide validation evidence for test results. More recently, in their introduction to a special issue of *Language Testing*, Taylor and Wigglesworth (2009) acknowledged recent developments in language education towards a better integration of learning and assessment activities, particularly regarding DA.

Second/foreign language dynamic assessment studies

This section reviews applications of DA to second and foreign language contexts over the last decade for different purposes and with different types of learners.

Learners with L2 learning problems and at risk learners

One of the first applications of DA to L2 contexts was related to the instruction of students experiencing L2 learning problems. Schneider and Ganschow (2000) encouraged teachers to teach and assess students' awareness of metalinguistic skills through dialogue. They recommended guiding students through self-discovery with assisting questions and other verbal and non-verbal hints in the use of such strategies as recognizing similarities/differences within language patterns, developing mnemonic devices, etc.

Kozulin and Garb (2002) conducted a study of text comprehension by at-risk EFL adult students in Israel. Following an interventionist model, they assessed the students' ability to learn and use reading comprehension strategies. A pre-test was reviewed by teacher and students together focusing on the strategies called forth by each item, process models, and transfer of strategies from one task to the next. A post-test revealed that many students' scores had improved, but not all. The authors devised a formula which differentiated between high and low learning potential students. They noted that some students with high and low learning potential obtained the same scores in the pre-test, showing that DA adds important information that remains hidden in static testing. However, Kozulin and Garb noted some limitations to their study, mainly the questionable reliability of learning potential assessment. The results of the study have a high instructional value in identifying students in need of further instruction and developing action plans according to individual students' needs.

Mediated L2 learning experiences

Several studies have highlighted the important role of interaction in mediated language learning experiences. Transcendence is a method developed by DA practitioners in which there is collaboration with the learners on tasks with increasing complexity. Poehner (2007) explores transcendence in mediated learning experiences with advanced learners of French. Fourth-year university learners of L2 French met with a mediator for individual tutoring during six weekly sessions in order to improve their speaking ability in French. Mediating sessions based on movie narrations in French focused on past verb forms and aspect. At the end of the sessions, the initial assessment was given to the learners followed by two transcendence assessments that required learners to transfer and to apply the concepts learned to different tasks. Mediation during transcendence sessions demonstrated differences between learners that were not apparent in assessment sessions, thus providing a richer picture of the level of development attained by the learners in the study. As illustrated below, one of the learners ("D"onna) had internalized her conceptual understanding of tense/aspect, through previous interactions, to a degree that allowed her to function almost independently in the transcendence session. Transcendence occurred not only in the performance of different tasks but also from one linguistic feature to another. In this particular case, the learner was able to transfer internalization of tense/aspect differences between *passé composé* and *imparfait* to the past perfect.

1 D: … elle devenait uh elle avait elle devenait fâchée elle devenait elle a été
   … *she was becoming uh she was having she was becoming she was*
2 elle était en colère quelle était la mieux?
   she was angry which was the better one?
3 M: well uh—
4 D: she became angry
5 M: she well uh do you want to use *imparfait* or *passé composé* how do you
6 want to do it?

7 D: she became angry she was being angry she became angry that's what I
8   want to say
9 M: right well um you could use the verb *se fâcher* [but would it change
    to be angry
10   sort of how you
11 D: (to self) it's a verb]
12 M: you know what you're emphasizing if you're using *imparfait* or *passé*
13   *composé* like um if you were saying just here a second ago she got angry
14 D: there was a definite point where she became angry so that would be
15   *passé composé*
16 M: yeah
17 D: elle s'est fâchée? Elle s'est fâchée et uh juste après ça …
    she got angry? She got angry and uh just after that …
18 D: il savait bien qu'il y a quelqu'un qu'il y avait quelqu'un qu'il y avait
    he knew well that there is someone that there was someone that there was
19   quelqu'un dans l'atelier mais le soldat ne peut* trouver donc tout à fait—
    someone in the attic but the soldier can't find therefore completely
20 M: il savait bien qu'il y avait quelqu'un dans l'atelier mais il?
    he knew well that there was someone in the attic but he?
21 D: il ne pouvait pas trouver il ne pouvait pas le trouver, c'est mieux que il
    he couldn't find he couldn't find him, that's better than he
22   n'a pas pu le trouver?
    couldn't find him?
23 M: I guess it depends on the meaning right? il ne pouvait pas trouver or il
24   n'a pas pu trouvé, either is grammatical …
25 D: je peux faire l'imparfait je crois
    I can do the imperfect I believe
26 M: all right
27 D: il ne pouvait pas trouver—
    he couldn't find—
28 M: you see the difference in meaning between the two?
29 D: well he couldn't find him and then he stopped looking for him would
30   be the *passé composé*, *l'imparfait* would be he couldn't find him but
31   there's no it doesn't imply a time when the soldier stopped looking for
32   him
33 M: right so it kind of like depends I think on what you follow it up with

(Poehner, 2007: 329–30)

Ableeva (2008) reported on a DA intervention to develop listening skills in learners of L2 French. During the intervention section, mediation revealed two main problems in comprehending the oral test. One was the inability to recognize words that they knew and could use in oral production. The other problem was the learners' inability to guess the meaning of new words in the oral text. Learners encountered phonological, lexical, and cultural difficulties in different degrees. A post-test consisted of a DA session in which learners summarized the text. Learners' summaries indicated that mediation indeed had a positive effect in comprehending the text. Learners required different degrees of mediation in terms of the number of times they needed to listen to the text as well as the number and explicitness of hints required. Thus, even when learners are seemingly at the same level, mediation uncovers important differences in their abilities and potential for learning.

Summers (2008) explored the effects of teachers' DA training and created a taxonomy of behaviors displayed by mediators and L2 French students during DA sessions. Data from interviews, transcriptions of videotaped mediating sessions, and the researcher's journal indicated that training in DA principles and techniques had a positive effect in increasing the use of implicit mediating strategies. A quantitative comparison of strategy use before and after DA training revealed that mediators avoided explicit strategies such as direct translation and providing the correct answer. Instead, implicit strategies increased in use, for instance, eliciting student answers and comprehension checks. Interviews with the mediators revealed some resistance to DA and lack of conviction that DA was conducive to learning. On the other hand, responses to DA were more positive from students. However, student participation in the mediation sessions was low. It is likely that the low frequency of student-initiated strategies by the learners was a reflection of the lack of buy-in of DA by the mediators. This research highlights the importance of assessors' training in the production of high quality mediation, which is essential in realizing the objectives of DA.

Diagnostic assessment

DA procedures have been used in L2 diagnostic assessment. Antón (2009) illustrated the application of DA in assessment of writing and speaking abilities of Spanish language majors. In the writing assessment learners could make revisions under three conditions. First, following Aljaafreh and Lantolf (1994), learners revised their compositions individually albeit in the presence of the evaluator. Further revisions were allowed by consulting cultural artifacts such as a dictionary and a grammar reference. Finally, learners were able to ask the evaluator specific questions about their compositions. Interestingly, independent revisions as well as revisions mediated by cultural artifacts were common and equally effective in improving the quality of the writing. Those students who were unable to improve their compositions with the mediational tools available would call attention to themselves as needing more explicit mediation.

During one section of the oral assessment, a story narration, the evaluator intervened providing opportunities to make corrections and to add details. This is shown in Table 7.1. Qualitative analysis of the interaction between the examiner and the learner during the narrative task revealed important differences among learners regarding their control of verbal tense and aspect, which had not been apparent during the initial independent narration.

The examples illustrate the agentive role of the examiner in the interaction as key in establishing an appropriate diagnosis of the students' linguistic ability. The results of the diagnostic assessment are presented qualitatively, in addition to a numerical score, and future recommendations for improvement, derived from the qualitative assessment report, are provided for each learner.

Program assessment

Erben et al. (2008) reported on the use of DA among faculty and pre-service teachers in the ESOL program at a university College of Education. The progressive introduction of DA techniques, starting with one quiz in one class at the same time that the students were being instructed about the theoretical underpinnings of DA and its pedagogical advantages, gained increasing support to the point of being deployed voluntarily by the majority of the faculty for high-stakes exams (mid-term and final). While faculty are still in the process of experimenting with DA, the program has an established protocol to introduce DA in their exams. Students complete the exam one page at a time providing an individual response, a pair response and a group response, the two last responses involving negotiation among learners. Points are assigned for each, and students receive a combined score for their individual and negotiated responses with

Table 7.1 Examiner–student discourse during DA episodes

Student A	Student B
12. E-¿Quieres intentarlo otra vez usando el pasado? Y me puedes preguntar. Si hay un verbo que no recuerdas está bien *(Do you want to try again using the past? And you can ask me. If there is a verb that you do not remember it's OK.)* 13. S-sí, sí, entonces, ¿desde el principio? *(yes, yes, from the beginning?)* 14. E- quizás desde el medio *(perhaps from the middle)* 15. S- con el pasado, sí, sí *(in the past, yes, yes)* 16. E- ¿Tú te diste cuenta que hiciste el cambio? *(Did you realize that you made the switch?)* 17. S-sí, sí, yo oí. Bueno, ellos estaban en Toledo, ellos estaban mirando la casa del Greco, y probablemente compraban..*muchos..muchos espadas *(Yes, yes, I heard. Well, they were in Toledo, they were looking at the Greco's house, and they were probably buying many..many swords.)*	8. E- posible, muy bien. Te, te había dicho, quizás no oíste, que empezaras la narración con 'ayer' la palabra 'ayer' porque fue el día de ayer y este, bien, me has narrado lo que hace en el presente, ¿crees que podrías ahora hacerlo en el pasado? *(It is possible, good. I I had asked you, perhaps you did not hear, to start the narration with 'yesterday' the word 'yesterday' because it was yesterday and, good, you have told me what she does, in the present, do you think you could do it now in the past?)* 9. S- Ayer Carla..ah.. *comí, *comí con sus con su familia o ..familia a las siete y a las siete ella… … 20. E-¿jugué o jugó? 21. S- jugó 22. E- aha 23. S- a las a la una ella regresó a casa y ..a la .. una y media ella ..*comí

Source: (Antón 2009: 585–89).

their pair and group. Open-ended interviews with students and faculty provided insights into participants' perceptions on the use of DA techniques. Students reported more confidence in content knowledge than students who had not participated in DA and viewed DA as a learning opportunity. For example, one student said "Doing it DA style, well, I guess I feel I know more because the stuff we learned during the DA exam stuck" (p. 102). Instructors had a positive view of DA. However, there were remaining concerns regarding the ability to assess state standards at the individual level, time restrictions regarding individual assessment, and mediating sessions. The authors recommended more training by faculty already using DA to faculty who are still undecided about using DA in order to diffuse educational change. To this end, they highlight the importance of social and institutional support for faculty to decide whether to adopt an innovation such as DA.

Group dynamic assessment and peer assessment

The studies discussed in this section have pushed the boundaries of our understanding of DA as an individual enterprise to explore the possibilities and limitations of realizing DA within groups or as a whole class and using peers instead of teachers as assessors.

Motivated by the question of how the teacher may organize the social environment of learning and concerned with the feasibility of conducting mediation sessions within the class-room, Guk and Kellogg (2007) proposed that learners trained by the teacher act as mediators during group work learning tasks. Differences found in the way teachers and learners mediate tasks, although numerically small, led the authors to conclude that learner-led mediation seems to align well with Vygotsky's notion of internalization. These differences point at an asymmetrical scaffolding orientation in the construction of grammar in teacher-student interaction as opposed to an orientation towards the co-construction of discourse in student-student interaction. While this study does not deal specifically with DA, it brings to our attention differences in the social context of language tasks and suggests the potential for teacher-led and student-led group work transcripts as a means of assessment.

The interrelation between teaching and assessment during teacher-led interaction in the classroom is developed further by Poehner (2009), who stressed the role of teacher's intentionality and group cohesion in whole class discussions. In this study, the role of group DA during teacher–student exchanges in whole-class interaction is proposed as a way to make interaction "more attuned to learners' emergent abilities" (p. 488). Group and individual DA follow the same procedures, but in group DA mediation is geared towards the group ZPD. Central to this idea is the view of the class, not as an aggregate of individuals, but a socially constructed entity. In group DA, teacher's questions and feedback, informed by an understanding of the role of interaction in development, followed a structured, predetermined pattern of increasing explicitness according to learners' needs. In addition to raising awareness of teacher's language when addressed to individual students during whole-class activities, the author stresses the importance of group cohesion to foster development within a group ZPD. An important point made in this study is that cohesion is not a characteristic of the group itself; rather, it is a feature of an activity. Cohesion emerges in a particular activity when the goals, orientation and responsibilities of individuals come together. In the examples of classroom interaction provided in the study, one of the teachers showed intentionality by planning her feedback and keeping track of the degree of explicitness provided to learners during whole-class interaction. In this way, the teacher was able to work in a systematic way within the group ZPD and, as a result, it is argued that learners required less explicit feedback, increased participation, and gained control of the language problem at hand.

Lund (2008) argued in favor of shifting "the locus of assessment from the individual to the intersection of the individual and the collective, mediated by cultural tools" (p. 32). The interaction of learning, instruction and assessment in a collective environment, Lund maintains, provides new opportunities for learning, and thus advancing the ZPD. This point is illustrated by two qualitative accounts of collective assessment. In the first one, a group of EFL student teachers collectively graded exam papers. In the second one peer assessment was performed among young learners. The analysis of overlapping, complementary, and competing contributions to the discourse, together with the cultural artifacts that mediate assessment such as criteria, guidelines and policies provide a view of the inner workings of assessment. Data provided by logs posted by student teacher groups responding to each other's evaluation of student papers revealed that guidelines and criteria were appropriated by the participants in different ways, according to their different experiences and historical insights on the process. Negotiation played a major role in reaching a shared understanding of the assessment. In a second episode of collective assessment, videotaped activity while learners prepared for an oral exam and response to questionnaires by EFL learners engaged in group work and peer-assessment illustrated the interaction and integration between teaching, learning, and assessment. By involving students in the assessment process they came to understand criteria and guidelines for evaluation. Collaborative assessment increases the validity of grades by making criteria explicit and therefore, from a pedagogical standpoint, the opportunities for collective assessment among teachers should be increased. Lund argues that collective assessment represents an expanded interpretation of the ZPD as a practice that is conducive to the creation of new forms with transformative power in the history of societal activity.

Technology

One of the first studies that applied DA to an L2 context through technology was Oskoz (2005), who adopted Aljaafreh and Lantolf's (1994) regulation scale to analyze how learners scaffolded each other during chat sessions in L2 Spanish. The five-point scale distinguishes different developmental stages from other-regulation (Levels 1–3) to self-regulation (Level 5). In other-regulation stages, the learner is guided by the expert or peer in reaching a desired goal while in self-regulatory stages learners self-correct without any external guidance. First- and second-year students of Spanish were engaged in a series of collaborative tasks (jigsaw puzzles, role-play, information gap, and free discussion). Peer-scaffolded interaction in the chat environment provided a window into the learners' potential level of development. By focusing on the process, rather than the product of the interaction, DA complements standard assessment with a more complete picture of the learner's capabilities. Additionally, Oskoz (2005) argues that DA delivered through technology reduces the time investment that has been a major logistic problem for DA administration. The existence of a written transcript of the students' interaction facilitates assessment. Darhower (in progress) is also exploring the use of DA in synchronous communication mediated by computers in the development of past tense narration in Spanish among learners of Spanish.

Darhower analyzed weekly chat interactions among pairs of students and a mediator. He also compiled learners' perceptions on the use of chats in their language development. Learners discussed the content of a movie for six sessions, while the seventh session dealt with the content of a different movie in order to see if transcendence of skills took place. Looking at the interaction against a scale that determined the degree of mediation required showed that DA can be an effective complement to the assessment provided by the Oral Proficiency Interview, which participants had taken at the outset of the study. Specifically, the frequency and degree of mediation required revealed not only that the learners had different ZPD with respect to control of past form and aspect, but that they advanced in a non-linear fashion through the mediation sessions in their use of past in different contexts. In accordance with these results, learners also felt that the chat sessions with a mediator were useful. What is highlighted by this study is the viability of the chat environment as a tool in DA.

The application of technology to DA in the L2 contexts has not been developed to full potential yet. DA via computer in the field of educational psychology provides models of interventionist approaches that may be adapted to second language contexts.

Recommendations for practice

DA promotes an individualized approach to assessment that is both its major strength and its major challenge. Its strength lies in its ability to provide rich and useful information to teachers and educators for the development of pedagogical interventions that will address the needs of particular learners. The challenges are several. Internally, DA approaches are not homogeneous and there are competing views and disagreements on how to materialize the underlying philosophical ideas of DA (Grigorenko, 2009). In particular, interactionist approaches require a high level of training, skills and expertise by the assessor in order to judge in the moment the level of assistance required during the DA. The high degree of training needed limits the reach of its use. One way to overcome these challenges is to move towards standardization of DA, but as it has been noted this solution means "trading one beast (standardized testing) for another (standardized instruction)" (Grigorenko, 2009: 126).

Teachers and administrators who wish to experiment with DA will have to prepare for the practical challenges outlined above. As illustrated by some of the studies discussed here, the creative use of technology may help overcome time and human constraints in imparting DA to large groups of learners. Also the use of group and peer assessment may provide a way to deal with the time challenge. Whether DA is used as a complement to other methods of assessment or as the only means of assessment, appropriate teacher training and institutional acceptance and support for DA are key in its successful implementation.

Future directions

In educational psychology DA is a promising but developing field (Grigorenko, 2009). In L2 learning and teaching it is still in its infancy. The few studies conducted so far have explored the use of DA mostly with the general population of L2 learners. More small- and large-scale studies are needed to explore the potential of DA for diagnostic and curricular purposes in language learning. In particular, interesting work is being conducted on using DA with groups of learners instead of individuals (peer assessment), delivering DA to groups of learners via technology, and understanding the process of mediation and transcendence during DA sessions. As DA becomes more widely used in L2 contexts, standards for DA of second languages should be developed.

Agreeing with Poehner (2008b), I see potentially fruitful lines of research in DA in the areas of computer and peer-mediated assessment, analysis of mediator/learner interaction and learner reciprocity, and, particularly, the development of standardized procedures in interactionist DA so that learners' development may be systematically documented. To this end, Poehner (2008b: 167) suggests a model of reporting DA inspired by sociocultural studies of L2 learner interaction. The model elicits reporting of three stages in the interaction: orientation, execution, and control, as well as the type of verbalization (explicit/implicit) of mediating moves (leading to transcendence) and high/low learner reciprocity in assuming responsibility for performance.

In the coming years, as DA becomes more widely used in second language contexts, it is likely that practitioners will reach consensus on standards and criteria to deliver DA and report its results both in teacher–learner assessment and in peer or collective assessment. The medium and format of delivering DA is also likely to expand to interventionist models of DA via technology, following existing models in educational psychology. However, other issues may still pose challenges to DA in the coming years, in particular, the resolution of practical obstacles to large-scale implementation, the use of DA as a means of assessment on its own right (not as a complement to standardized testing), and the acceptance of DA as a valid means of assessment with fundamental philosophical differences with mainstream testing regarding validity and reliability measures.

Research on DA in L2 contexts has been predominantly interactionist and with a strong focus on sociocultural theory. The larger field of DA may benefit from efforts in L2 research to set DA apart theoretically, methodologically, and comparatively from non-DA, and from the search for new ways to document and report DA results.

Further reading

Grigorenko, E. L. and Sternberg, R. J. (1998). Dynamic testing. *Psychological Bulletin* 124: 75–111. This article provides a thorough critical review of different cognitive and educational approaches to dynamic testing. Strengths and weaknesses of each approach are considered and research results for the different approaches are evaluated from a psychometrical perspective.

Haywood, H. C. and Lidz, C. (2007). *Dynamic Assessment in Practice. Clinical and Educational Applications.* Cambridge, UK: Cambridge University Press. This is an updated practical guide on interactionist DA in the assessment of cognitive and academic skills. This book provides an introduction to the principles and procedures of dynamic assessment in psychology and education. Numerous examples of DA interventions and report writing are presented to demonstrate how DA can be integrated into an overall assessment program.

Lantolf, J. P. and Poehner, M. E. (eds), (2008). *Sociocultural Theory and the Teaching of Second Languages.* London, UK: Equinox Pub. Several chapters in Part I of this book present innovative applications of DA to second language contexts, including classroom- and program-level assessment. These original studies should be of interest to researchers who are interested in the latest developments of DA in L2 settings, as well as to language teaching practitioners who are looking for models of classroom implementation of DA.

Lidz, C. (1991). *Practitioner's Guide to Dynamic Assessment.* New York, NY: Guilford Press. This is a good introduction to practical aspects of interactionist DA. The book summarizes different models of DA in clinical and educational settings, but, most importantly, it provides a step-by-step guide of procedures and tools for conducting DA assessment. The two manuals included in the book provide a good starting point for anyone wishing to start implementing DA.

Poehner, M. (2008). *Dynamic Assessment: a Vygotskian Approach to Understanding and Promoting L2 Development.* Boston, MA: Springer Science. This the first comprehensive review of theoretical and practical aspects of DA in second language. The first part of this book discusses the origins of DA in Vygotsky's sociocultural theory of mind and subsequent development of different approaches to DA. The second part of the book presents current research in DA applications to L2 settings and offers a model for implementing DA in second language classrooms.

References

Ableeva, R. (2008). The effects of dynamic assessment on L2 listening comprehension. In Lantolf, J. and Poehner, M. (eds), *Sociocultural Theory and the Teaching of Second Languages.* London, UK: Equinox Pub, 57–86.

Aljaafreh, A. and Lantolf, J. (1994). Negative feedback as regulation and second language learning in the Zone of Proximal Development. *The Modern Language Journal* 78: 465–83.

Antón, M. (2009). Dynamic assessment of advanced foreign language learners. *Foreign Language Annals* 42: 576–98.

Budoff, M. (1987). The validity of learning potential assessment. In C. Lidz (ed.), *Dynamic Assessment: an interactive approach to evaluating learning potential.* New York, NY: Guilford Press, 52–81.

Campione, J. and Brown A. (1987). Linking dynamic assessment with school achievement. In C. Lidz (ed.), *Dynamic Assessment.* New York, NY: Guilford Press, 82–115.

Darhower, M. (in progress). Dynamic assessment in synchronous computer-mediated communication: A case study of L2 Spanish past narration. Unpublished manuscript, North Carolina State University.

Erben, T., Ban, R. and Summers, R. (2008). Changing examination structures within a college of education: The application of dynamic assessment in pre-service ESOL endorsement courses in Florida. In J. Lantolf and M. Poehner (eds), *Sociocultural Theory and the Teaching of Second Language.* London, UK: Equinox Pub, 87–114.

Feuerstein, R., Rand, Y. and Hoffman, M. (1979). *The Dynamic Assessment of Retarded Performers: the learning potential assessment device, theory, instruments, and techniques.* Baltimore, MD: University Park Press.

Feuerstein, R., Feuerstein, R. S., Falik, L. H. and Rand, Y. (2002). *The Dynamic Assessment of Cognitive Modifiability: The Learning Propensity Assessment Device: theory, instruments and techniques.* Jerusalem, Israel: International Center for the Enhancement of Learning Potential.

Grigorenko, E. (2009). Dynamic Assessment and Response to Intervention. *Journal of Learning Disabilities* 42: 111–32.

Grigorenko, E. L. and Sternberg, R. J. (1998). Dynamic testing. *Psychological Bulletin* 124: 75–111.

Guk, I. and Kellogg, D. (2007). The ZPD and whole class teaching: Teacher-led and student-led interactional mediation of tasks. *Language Teaching Research* 11: 281–99.

Haywood, H. Carl and Lidz, C. (2007). *Dynamic Assessment in Practice. Clinical and Educational Applications.* Cambridge, UK: Cambridge University Press.

Kozulin, A. and Garb, E. (2002). Dynamic assessment of EFL text comprehension of at-risk students. *School Psychology International* 23: 112–27.

Lantolf, J. P. and Poehner M. E. (2004). Dynamic assessment: bringing the past into the future. *Journal of Applied Linguistics* 1: 49–74.

Lantolf, J. and Thorne, S. (2006). *Sociocultural Theory and the Genesis of Second Language Development.* Oxford, UK: Oxford University Press.

Lidz, C. (1987). *Dynamic Assessment*. New York, UK: Guilford Press.

—— (1991). *Practitioner's Guide to Dynamic Assessment*. New York, NY: Guilford Press.

Lidz, C. and Elliott, J. (eds), (2000). *Dynamic Assessment: prevailing models and applications*. Amsterdam, The Netherlands: JAI Elsevier Science.

Lund, A. (2008). Assessment made visible. Individual and collective practices. *Mind, Culture, and Activity* 15: 32–51.

McNamara, T. (1997). Interaction in second language performance assessment: whose performance? *Applied Linguistics* 18: 446–66.

Minick, N. (1987). Implications of Vygotsky's theories for dynamic assessment. In C. Lidz (ed.), *Dynamic Assessment*. New York, NY: Guilford Press, 116–40.

Oskoz, A. (2005). Students' dynamic assessment via online chat. *CALICO Journal* 22: 513–36.

Poehner, M. (2007). Beyond the test: L2 dynamic assessment and the transcendence of mediated learning. *The Modern Language Journal* 91: 323–40.

—— (2008a). Both sides of the conversation: The interplay between mediation and learner reciprocity in dynamic assessment. In J. Lantolf and M. Poehner (eds), *Sociocultural Theory and the Teaching of Second Languages*. London, UK: Equinox Pub, 33–56.

—— (2008b). *Dynamic Assessment: a Vygotskian approach to understanding and promoting l2 development*. Boston, MA: Springer Science.

—— (2009). Group dynamic assessment: mediation for the L2 classroom. *TESOL Quarterly* 43: 471–91.

Poehner, M. and Lantolf, J. (2005). Dynamic assessment in the language classroom. *Language Teaching Research* 9: 1–33.

Rea-Dickins, P. (2004). Understanding teachers as agents of assessment. *Language Testing* 21: 249–58.

Rea-Dickins, P. and Gardner, S. (2000). Snares and silver bullets: disentangling the construct of formative assessment. *Language Testing* 17: 215–43.

Schneider, E. and Ganschow, L. (2000). Dynamic assessment and instructional strategies for learners who struggle to learn a foreign language. *Dyslexia* 6: 72–82.

Sternberg, R. J. and Grigorenko, E. L. (2002). *Dynamic Testing. The nature and measurement of learning potential*. Cambridge, UK: Cambridge University Press.

Summers, R. (2008). Dynamic assessment: towards a model of dialogic engagement. Unpublished PhD dissertation, University of South Florida.

Swain, M. (2001). Examining dialogue: another approach to content specification and to validating inferences drawn form test scores. *Language Testing* 18: 275–302.

Taylor, L. and Wigglesworth, G. (2009). Are two heads better than one? Pair work in L2 assessment contexts. *Language Testing* 26: 325–39.

Tzuriel, D. (1997). The relation between parent-child MLE interactions and children's cognitive modifiability. In A. Kozulin (ed.), *The Ontogeny of Cognitive Modifiability*. Jerusalem, Israel: International Center for the Enhancement of Cognitive Modifiability, 157–80.

Vygotsky, L. S. (1978). *Mind in Society: the development of higher psychological processes*. (M. Cole, V. John-Steiner, S. Scribner, and E. Souberman, eds.), Cambridge, MA: Harvard University Press.

Diagnostic assessment in language classrooms

Eunice Eunhee Jang

Introduction

Testing has become the primary means to drive educational reforms and measure the resulting outcomes for accountability purposes (Jang and Ryan, 2003). However, in classrooms, teachers report little interest in the prototypical information provided by standardized large-scale tests, but seek instead detailed information about individual students' strengths and weaknesses in specific skills taught (Brindley, 1998; Huff and Goodman, 2007). This type of information that teachers seek is *diagnostic*.

The notion of diagnostic assessment is not unheard of. Almost 18 years ago, Spolsky (1992) envisioned that 'diagnostic testing is an art, albeit one informed by the science of testing—an art that has learned from science ways to ensure fairness and reliability in subjective measures that will lead to responsible language testing' (p. 29). Since then, much progress has been made. Several books and special journal issues have been written expressly on diagnostic assessment in language and educational assessment (Alderson, 2005; Frederiksen *et al.*, 1990; Nichols *et al.*, 1995; Leighton and Gierl, 2007; Rupp *et al.*, 2010). Furthermore, the diagnostic potential of various performance assessments is evident in scaled proficiency descriptors, such as the Common European Framework of Reference for Languages (CEFR), the Canadian Language Benchmarks (CLB), the American Council of the Teaching of Foreign Languages (ACTFL), the Steps to English Proficiency (STEP), and the World-Class Instructional Design and Assessment (WIDA) English language proficiency standards. The performance descriptors included in those scales are often translated into learners' self-assessment (Alderson, 2007). Another significant advancement in diagnostic assessment is computer-assisted assessment systems that provide a dynamic interface for integrating assessment into teaching and learning (Chapelle *et al.*, 2008). This interface, afforded by technological advances, makes possible an interactive diagnostic feedback loop, which can lead to differentiated instruction and learning.

Despite the appeal of diagnostic assessment, misconceptions remain. One idea is that *diagnostic* focuses on student knowledge *prior to* instruction, whereas *formative* is an ongoing assessment of students' learning progress. This distinction appears to undermine the potential of the former. Another idea is that diagnostic assessment is interchangeable with formative assessment, because both concepts share the same goal: positive change in student learning (Leighton, 2009). However, not all formative assessments are diagnostic.

Characteristics of diagnostic assessment

Purposes of diagnostic assessment

The goals of diagnostic language assessment are to *make diagnostic inferences* about learners' strengths and weaknesses in skills of interest, and to *utilize* them for positive changes in learning. This pedagogical desire resonates well with formative assessment, in that both can be used to plan differentiated instruction tailored to students' learning needs (Black and Wiliam, 1998; Nichols *et al.*, 2009). Nichols *et al.* (2009) distinguish formative assessment from other assessments by highlighting test score use as a main validity claim over valid score interpretation:

> General validity theory appears to privilege test score interpretation over test score use.... In contrast, validity claims with regard to formative assessment emphasize test score use over test score interpretation. The consequences of formative assessment use, in terms of improved student learning, are arguably accorded more importance than other sources of evidence. The claim for formative assessment is that the information derived from students' assessment performance can be used to improve student achievement. It is how that information is used, not what the assessment tells us about current achievement, that impacts future achievement. Therefore, use, based on a valid interpretation, is the primary focus of the validity argument for formative assessments.
>
> *(Nichols et al., 2009: 15)*

The pedagogical 'backwash' effect is an important validity criterion for both diagnostic and formative assessments, because both hold promise for the service of teaching. Diagnostic language assessment requires further a profound understanding of pathways to language development and evidence for diagnostic inferences and use; formative assessment lacks its attention to theoretical construct representations (Leighton, 2009; Nichols *et al.*, 2009).

Diagnostic language assessment also differs from diagnosis in clinical and psycho-educational fields. The former presupposes no prescribed algorithm for estimating language proficiency that can be easily measurable and classifiable; the latter involves prescribed classifications based on decisive causal determinations. It is difficult to establish causal inferences about what causes weaknesses in the former. Another defining feature for differentiating between the two is *use*. Action is not necessarily a primary concern for a diagnostician in the latter. Action that teachers and students can take as a result of diagnosis is a primary goal of classroom diagnosis.

Diagnostic language assessment takes a mastery criterion-referenced approach that classifies learners into masters and non-masters without quantifiers of achievement (Council of Europe, 2001). This is differentiated from norm-referenced high-stakes proficiency tests (Kunnan and Jang, 2009). The latter is primarily intended to discriminate among students against the unknown norm established by psychometric principles, such as a Gaussian distribution. These tests often multitask by serving diagnostic and placement purposes in addition to their primary selection purpose, despite their inability to measure developmental changes (Fox, 2009). For such tests, pedagogical washback is not a desirable consequence.

Various sources of diagnostic inferences

Identifying sources of discrepancies from expected performance or characterizing patterns of errors can be diagnostically useful (Bejar, 1984). One common source of diagnosis is a *vertical discrepancy* in performance between a current and an expected knowledge state. The primary criterion for determining a student's state of knowledge is specific learning expectations. In this way, diagnostic feedback can direct students to specific points in learning. Diagnosis based on a vertical discrepancy requires the developmental theories of language learning. This vertical discrepancy can be found in mastery-oriented scales of language proficiency, such as the CEFR common reference global scales (Little, 2006).

Content experts, including teachers, are often involved in a standard-setting procedure used to determine criterion levels based on expectations of mastery for target domains (Cizek, 2001). Standards make learning expectations explicit (Cumming, 2009). The resulting performance categories are expressed on the mastery-oriented proficiency scales. For example, the CEFR includes six reference levels such as Basic (Breakthrough, Waystage), Independent (Threshold, Vantage) and Proficient (Effective Operational Proficiency, Mastery). In fact, detailed performance-level descriptors (PLDs) are diagnostic rather than the performance category labels. The PLDs provide a description of students' knowledge and skills within each performance level (Cizek *et al.*, 2004) and can facilitate teachers' *diagnostic judgments* about students' mastery status. In classrooms, a mastery criterion level can be set at any point of instruction wherever teachers need diagnostic information about students' mastery status, instead of relying on final end-of-term performance (Hudson and Lynch, 1984).

However, setting mastery criteria or standards is neither straightforward nor knowable (Cizek *et al.*, 2004). Determining the level of specificity for diagnosis is equally challenging. Furthermore, the development of language standards and proficiency descriptors relies on content experts' (e.g. teachers) intuitive judgments and *ad hoc* statistical scaling (Alderson, 2005, 2007; Cumming, 2009; North and Schneider, 1998). Cizek *et al.* (2004) respond to this criticism by characterizing standard setting as a procedure involving 'artistic, political, and cultural' elements (p. 33) and further note:

> It is now a widely accepted tenet of measurement theory that the work of standard-setting panels is not to search for a knowable boundary between categories that exist. Instead, standard-setting procedures enable participants to bring to bear their judgments in such a way as to translate policy decisions (often, as operationalized in performance level descriptors) into locations that create the effective performance categories. This translation and creation are seldom, if ever, purely statistical, impartial, apolitical, or ideologically neutral activities.
>
> *(Cizek* et al.*, 2004: 33)*

A lack of theoretical foundations underlying existing vertical scales seems a significant obstacle in seeking validity evidence for diagnostic inferences. Not all competing theoretical frameworks are equally relevant to diagnostic assessment, and no single best-fitting theoretical framework for all learning contexts. It is neither desirable nor practical to assume that a single diagnostic assessment can assess the entire spectrum of language development. The viability of any theoretical framework for diagnosis rests on evaluative judgments about its relevance to a specific learning context and assessment purposes.

Consider the issue of whether there is a hierarchical relationship among reading skills underlying the construct of L2 reading comprehension. One can reasonably assume that language and cognitive development follows a hierarchical sequence of stages, and instruction follows the same sequence to promote students' language development. Research evidence exists to support this incremental relationship between the cognitive demands of higher-order reading skills and task difficulty (Jang, 2005). Yet, this observation does not seem to hold for other assessment contexts. Alderson (2005: 137) calls for research on this issue:

It appears not to be the case that as one's reading ability develops, this is associated with an increased ability to make inferences, for example, rather than to understand the main idea. Thus it will be important in the further development of diagnostic tests of reading to establish, first, exactly what does improve as the ability to read in a foreign language increases, and secondly, what subskills or aspects of linguistic knowledge or text processing predict such a developing ability to read.

This issue can have a significant implication for designing a diagnostic reading assessment and instruction accordingly. Therefore, considering the relative cognitive complexities of reading skills and their interactions with other text variables and learner characteristics is integral for a theoretically sound diagnostic assessment.

A source of discrepancy can be *horizontal*. This occurs when achievement in one content or skill area is in discordance with achievement in others. Proficiency tests based on multimodal construct definitions (i.e., reading, writing, oral) without hierarchical or developmental linkage are often used to determine horizontal discrepancies for diagnostic purposes. Mousavi (2002) notes that proficiency tests, such as TOEFL, can be used for diagnosing students' strengths and weaknesses based on subtest scores and concludes that any language tests have diagnostic potential. Subtest scores can be used to diagnose students' abilities; however, the level of specificity is too broad to direct students' learning. Therefore, that any language test has some degree of diagnostic potential is misleading without considering the appropriate level of specificity in diagnosis determined by those who are most affected by the effects of diagnosis (Fulcher and Davidson, 2009).

The expected knowledge state can be emergent, adjacent to the current state of knowledge, instead of being oriented towards distant mastery learning goals. This is the main characteristic of dynamic assessment (Lantolf and Poehner, 2004). In this view, the source of discrepancy is the gap between students' actual and potential development, and the goal of assessment is to gather diagnostic information through careful mediation. An assessor not only assesses the current state of development but also provides mediation, indispensible for a learner's future development. Lantolf and Poehner (2004) point out that 'assessing without mediation is problematic because it leaves out part of the picture—the future—and it is difficult to imagine an assessment context that is *not* interested in the future' (p. 251).

Another source of discrepancy can arise from students' self-assessment of their own abilities. The students' *performed* competencies are compared against their *perceived* competencies. Considering students as agents for change in their own learning, students' self-assessment is pivotal for ensuring the maximal use of diagnostic information. The DIALANG assessment (Alderson and Huhta, 2005) links the assessment results to a test taker's self-assessment results and provides diagnostic feedback focusing on the discrepancy between the two. Jang (2005) notes that students tend to pay attention to the discrepancy when evaluating the validity of diagnostic feedback.

Washback effects of diagnostic assessment

Much research has focused on the negative impact of externally mandated tests on pedagogy (Alderson and Wall, 1993; Cheng *et al.*, 2004). Little research exists on washback issues associated with school-based diagnostic assessments, as Spolsky (1992: 30) points out:

> For those who worked to develop proficiency tests, any influence that the test has on instruction is usually a side effect, which is generally called backwash ... and unfortunately occurs when preparation for the examination causes students to concentrate on unwanted skills, such as memorizing possible essays or practicing multiple-choice techniques. This

concern for curriculum-fair testing then deflected attention from the fundamental instructional relevance of language tests.

Fulcher and Davidson (2007, 2009) emphasize an 'effect-driven' approach as an important principle to test design and validation. Unlike high-stakes proficiency tests, pedagogical changes through a systematic diagnostic feedback loop are part of *intended effects* in diagnostic assessment instead of the *impact* of testing. Because of its strong association with external high-stakes testing, the term washback needs to be reconceptualized in light of *effect* when it is discussed for diagnostic assessment in classroom settings.

Diagnostic assessment can have a negative effect on teaching and learning. For example, whether too fine-grained construct definitions used for diagnostic assessment narrow the scope of pedagogy is subject to debate (Collins, 1990; Jang, 2005; Leighton, 2009).

> One notion afoot is that because we can diagnose the precise errors students are making, we can then teach directly to counter these errors. Such diagnosis might indeed be useful in a system where diagnosis and remediation are tightly coupled... But if diagnosis becomes an objective in nationwide tests, then it would drive education to the lower-order skills for which we can do the kind of fine diagnosis possible for arithmetic. Such an outcome would be truly disastrous. It is the precisely the kinds of skills for which we can do fine diagnosis, that are becoming obsolete in the computational world of today.
>
> *(Collins, 1990: 76–77)*

Collins highlights two issues: *context* and *purpose*. His emphasis on the context where 'diagnosis and remediation are tightly coupled' supports the effect-driven approach to diagnostic assessment deeply grounded in instructional contexts. It is the *purpose* that distinguishes diagnostic assessment from high-stakes tests. I do not mean that the stakes of diagnostic assessment are low. Rather I argue that they are different in kind. The stakes of diagnostic assessment may rise when diagnosis focuses on identifying only deficits, which could have a profound impact on students' self-esteem (Glazer and Searfoss, 1988). Diagnostic profiles need to highlight both what learners can do and what areas need further improvement.

Further issues in diagnostic assessment

How do we determine the level of specificity?

An important step in designing diagnostic assessment is defining and specifying the primary diagnostic criterion specific to a learning context. Diagnostic assessment tends to assess a target range of skills at a time instead of covering a wide range of skills (Alderson, 2005). However, a too narrowly specified skill specification may pose a problem resulting from 'a gross simplification of the reality of cognition' (Mislevy, 1995: 55). How do we then strike a balance? Mislevy (1995) notes that the level of detail at which students' competencies are differentiated needs to be determined based on pedagogical considerations, that is, can the specified detail direct students' learning? There is no absolutely true level of specificity for diagnostic criteria (Davidson and Lynch, 2002). Does the level of specificity serve the diagnostic purpose and instructional goals in a given learning context? We may begin designing diagnostic assessment by asking this question.

What makes tasks more or less diagnostic?

Diagnostic assessment tasks should investigate a unique part of language learning to gather useful information about students' language profiles. Static taxonomies of content specifications are not sufficient for creating diagnostic tasks that reflect 'the dynamic and sequential nature of diagnostic assessment' (Bejar, 1984: 175). Diagnostic tasks require a micro-analysis of learning behaviour, level of cognitive difficulty, and learner background characteristics.

Various task types should be considered. Selected response task types can be cognitively designed to measure partial knowledge and misconceptions. One can gather diagnostic information by analysing students' responses to multiple distracters. Gu and Jang (2009) examined how distracters included in Grade 6 curriculum-based reading comprehension assessment items function across different ability levels and whether they can provide additional diagnostic information. They concluded that approximately half (21 out of 40) exhibited *optimal or partially rich* distracter functioning in differentiating among students at different ability levels. The average difficulty levels (p) of these items ranged from 0.72 to 0.77. Eleven items showed *crossing* distracter functioning in that their functioning was inconsistent across different ability levels. This type of item tended to be more difficult ($p = 0.59$). The items with *binary* distracter functioning (eight items) were the easiest of all ($p = 0.81$), and these distracters exhibited little capacity to differentiate among students at different ability levels. Figure 8.1 illustrates the three different types of distracter functioning (estimated using TestGraf, Ramsay, 2001).

This micro-level item analysis provides some useful information for evaluating the diagnostic potential of items. For example, items with the crossing or binary distracter characteristics curves (DCCs), exhibiting extreme difficulty levels, may serve standardized testing by completing the two tails of the Gaussian distribution; they are not cognitively rich enough to serve a diagnostic purpose. Items that are too difficult or too easy may have little diagnostic capacity for differentiating among students with different skill mastery profiles (Jang, 2005). A diagnostic task should be more useful for differentiating among different skill profiles of students rather than for discriminating among students (Mislevy, 1995).

Verbal protocol analysis offers insights into why moderate task difficulty is ideal for providing diagnostically useful test information. Leighton (2004: 11) notes:

> Tasks of moderate difficulty are ideal because these tasks require a student to engage in controlled cognitive processing; that is, cognitive processing in which knowledge and strategies are selected consciously, thus allowing the student to be aware of his or her thinking as he or she solves a problem. In contrast, tasks that are too easy for students to solve are not good candidates for eliciting verbal reports because these tasks do not require controlled processing for their solution, eliciting rapid recall instead. This rapid recall or automatic cognitive processing leaves the student unaware of how the problem was solved.

If tasks with extreme difficulty levels fail to elicit students' cognitive processing, the effect of diagnostic feedback may remain limited because the learner may be unconscious of the problem solving process or because difficult tasks overload working memory (Robinson, 2001). Therefore, tasks with moderate difficulty that are novel enough to evoke conscious deliberation may be good candidates for designing a diagnostic assessment.

What is cognitive diagnostic modelling?

Traditional approaches to diagnosis in clinical and psycho-educational tests are based on several subtests each of which measures interrelated skills. Scores are reported using proportion-correct scores, percentiles or scores scaled by item response theory. Alternatively, cognitive diagnostic assessment utilizes latent class modelling approaches either by linking students' test item responses to a set of user-determined cognitive skills (Roussos *et al.*, 2009) or by using diagnostic criteria

(a)

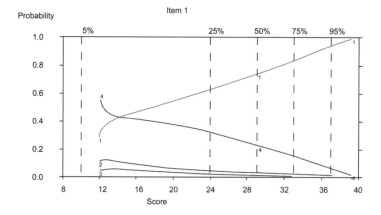

(b)

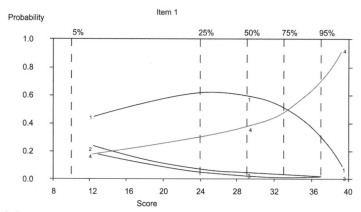

(c)

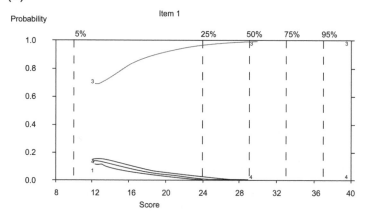

Figure 8.1 Distracter characteristics curves (DCCs)
Note: (a) Optimal DCC (p = 0.7). (b) Crossing DCC (p = 0.38). (c) Binary DCC (p = 0.93)

that summarize response patterns and erroneous misconceptions for statistical classifications (Buck and Tatsuoka, 1998; Tatsuoka, 1983). The resulting diagnostic profiles describe individual students' mastery status for each skill in detail (Jang, 2009; Rupp et al., 2010). Consider the example in Table 8.1 taken from Jang's (2005) classroom research in order to compare incremental granularity in reporting.

First, JK's total test scores prior to and after the instruction indicate improvement, but do not provide information about what aspect of his reading ability was improved. Second, JK's performance on the items grouped by difficulty level provides finer information than the total test scores do. However, the information remains limited in understanding what aspects of his reading ability need further improvement. The last skill mastery profile provides the information about which aspect of his reading was improved. In this profile, his mastery status of each skill is determined by applying a cut-off point to the skill mastery probability estimate.

Nevertheless, that dichotomous determination of skill mastery can be problematic and restrictive. Alternately, a diagnostic standard-setting process can be used to determine the diagnostic rules for classification (Rupp et al., 2010). Henson and Templin (2008) applied it to the development of a diagnostic Algebra 2 assessment for high school students. Once an expert panel specified the performance of students who demonstrated mastery of each skill and estimated the percentage of items answered correctly by a student who has mastered the targeted skill, a set of diagnostic criteria for classification of different skill mastery profiles were established. Henson and Templin (2008) concluded that the skill mastery profiles developed through the standard-setting procedure were congruent with teachers' evaluation of students' mastery levels in classrooms.

Considering that the development of a systematic diagnostic assessment requires financial and human resources in order to bring together content experts and assessment specialists, the further development of cognitive diagnostic assessment is likely to be large scale. Given its current stage of development diagnostic assessment needs to be experimented systematically and empirically both in large and small scales through collaboration among different expert groups.

Classroom-based diagnostic assessment

A survey of various standardized classroom-based diagnostic assessments, mostly in L1 reading, suggests that despite their intended use for diagnostic purposes, they appear to fall short. Despite a

Table 8.1 Incremental granularity in score reporting (for the student JK)

Granularity	Before instruction	After instruction
Total score	18/41	27/42
Performance on items grouped by difficulty level	7/12 easy items 6/17 medium items 5/8 hard items	3/4 easy items 20/26 medium items 4/9 hard items
Fine-grained skill mastery profile	JK needs to improve all of the tested skills. He needs to develop his vocabulary ability in order to comprehend text and relate it to his own experiences. Focus on grammar is also necessary.	JK's skill profile has been improved significantly after the instruction. He needs to develop skills related to comprehending implicit textual information, inferencing, and representing textual information in alternative modes using graphs and tables.

significant amount of financial and human investment, there exists little validity evidence about whether such assessments serve the diagnostic purpose. Little is known about how teachers utilize the test information for their own teaching and students' learning.

A close review of a few K–12 diagnostic assessment tools helps us understand the status quo of contemporary diagnostic assessments available for classroom teachers. For example, two diagnostic assessments that are being widely implemented in elementary schools across Ontario, Canada, are the Developmental Reading Assessment (DRA; Beaver, 2001) for Kindergarten to Grade 3, and the Comprehension, Attitude, Strategies, Interest (CASI; Gibson, 2007) for Grades 4–8. Both are commercial, standardized reading assessments. Both claim to serve multiple purposes including: diagnosing students' strengths and learning needs; planning instructional interventions with reference to the provincial reading expectations; tracking student growth on core skills and strategies that effective readers would use; determining students' reading achievements relative to their grade-specific norm; and supporting decision making procedures taking place among divisions, schools and parents. These are comprehensive, yet possess quite ambitious purposes, which I will revisit later in this section.

The DRA is administered individually through a one-on-one conference. During the individual conference, the teacher administers a running record (Clay, 2000) by introducing a text and recording the numbers of errors and self-corrections while the child is reading the text. The DRA results (reported as percentiles) are used to determine the child's independent reading level and profile students in terms of their reading levels (below, at, or above the grade level proficiency).

In contrast to the DRA, the CASI is administered to a group of students. It includes several subtests including reading interviews, a reading attitude survey, a reading interests inventory, a student self-assessment, and a reading comprehension test. The reading comprehension test includes 10 reading passages (five fiction and non-fiction each) per grade each of which includes eight multiple-choice questions. The results are reported in four levels of performance related to the tested elements. A positive aspect of the CASI reading assessment is its inclusion of measures that assess students' attitudes and values toward reading and their interest in reading.

Though those assessments are widely used in classrooms for diagnostic and tracking purposes in Ontario, surprisingly there is no publicly available research evidence supporting their validity. Based on interviews with teachers in Grades 3–5 who used those assessments, Jang (2010) reports that teachers' use of information from the assessments is limited to individual students' overall performance level or a percentile score. The following interview excerpt with a Grade 3 teacher who uses the DRA in her classroom illustrates its limited use.

> Many students in my class speak other languages than English at home. They are proficient in English when they speak, but jeez, they just can't write. Not only that, they are not motivated, they simply don't care. For example, Jason's reading level is only 6 on DRA. It took two months to figure out what's wrong… It's the fifth year in my teaching, and I'm getting better with this, but it's so hard to know exactly what they are struggling with and support them with individualized instruction.

Agency in diagnostic assessment

Teachers' diagnostic assessment competence

On a daily basis, teachers prefer to use questioning, observations, and frequent quizzes to understand what students know and do not know (Black and Wiliam, 1998; Rea-Dickins, 2001). However, research shows that teachers often do not design and implement such activities with diagnostic assessment in mind and spend a small amount of time assessing individual students (Edelenbos and Kubanek-German, 2004). Most teachers commence their careers with relatively less training in assessment issues than other subject-specific domains. Assessment topics in pre-service and in-service teacher training programmes are elective rather than core curriculum. For example, on the first day of my graduate-level assessment course, I heard a student (also a full-time secondary school teacher) saying:

> I did my pre-service teacher program at this institution, have taught students since then, and am head of the history department at my school. I am passionate about my teaching. But still I have no idea of what is good assessment practice and how to tell what my students' needs are in systematic and fair ways.

She is not alone. Many teachers express their desire to develop (diagnostic) assessment competencies, the ability to assess students' learning progress, interpret the results from various sources of assessment, and intervene the areas of improvement for individual students (Edelenbos and Kubanek-German, 2004; Stiggins, 1997). One way to develop teachers' diagnostic assessment competencies is through their systematic reflections of learners' performance guided by relevant knowledge in a variety of learning contexts (Cumming, 2009; McNamara, 2000). The use of on-going diagnostic assessment affords teachers the opportunity to target their students' specific needs and promote curricular renovations. Teacher education programs should integrate assessment into their core curriculum to promote teachers' assessment competencies and to make their own professional judgments based on evidence gathered from assessment (Cumming, 2009; Fulcher and Davidson, 2007).

Involving teachers in the development and validation of a proficiency descriptor-based assessment can enhance teachers' assessment competencies. Descriptors of these kinds are likely derived from teachers' intuitive judgments and actual teaching practice, and therefore, they can be beneficial for classroom assessment (Byrnes, 2007). However, as I noted previously, they lack theoretical foundations precisely for the same reason. Developing teachers' assessment competencies is key to overcoming such criticism and establishing a strong theoretical base for diagnostic assessment.

The following description illustrates how teachers can benefit from the use of proficiency descriptors in classrooms. Ms. Roussos was one of 32 teachers who were introduced to the Steps to English proficiency (STEP) descriptor scales and used them to assess their students individually during validation research (Cummins et al., 2009).

> Ms. Roussos is pleased that Sam, a Grade-6 new comer speaking Tagalog at home, demonstrated rapid growth in reading proficiency in the past year. He can now read and comprehend informational, graphic, and literary texts with visual support. He has developed comprehension strategies for connecting his prior learning to new textual information. His teacher notes that his oral and writing proficiency development is relatively slower than his reading given that Sam writes a limited range of familiar text forms using personally relevant vocabulary. Ms. Roussos plans to design some activities that will encourage Sam to focus on those aspects.

This illustrates how teachers can systematize their own assessment practice by using proficiency descriptors to infer students' competence from their daily performance.

Students as a change agent

One crucial assumption about the beneficial effect of diagnostic assessment on student learning concerns students' views about diagnostic information and their roles in making changes. Research shows that not all students use similar strategies in processing their language skills to solve tasks. If diagnostic assessment measures only known skills and strategies but fails to incorporate multiple pathways to completing given tasks, the resulting diagnostic outcomes may be of little use (Alderson, 2007). Students from different socio-linguistic and cultural backgrounds are more likely to approach tasks differently, which makes it difficult for assessors to anticipate all pathways.

Students tend to react to diagnostic feedback by comparing it with their own self-assessment and decide whether or not to focus their learning on the areas of improvement (Jang, 2005, 2009). Regardless of whether or not students' self-assessment is reliable and accurate, students' beliefs about their own competencies should be consulted in tailoring instructional intervention and evaluating the effect of diagnostic feedback. Yang (2003) reports that when their self-assessment is incongruent with the DIALANG assessment results, students tend to pay more attention to feedback. She further notes that students' normative beliefs about the purpose of assessment also affect their reactions to feedback.

While the focus of diagnosis is students' cognitive competence, the parameter of diagnostic assessment involves more than a cognitive dimension. Black (2009: 521) notes:

> However, more is involved than a merely cognitive exercise, for the response may be controlled by a desire to protect one's own sense of well-being. For example, a learner may refuse to engage for fear of appearing stupid… One implication is that a focus on marks and grades, on written work or in a regime of frequent testing, can do positive harm by developing obstacles to engagement, effects which can be as harmful to the high achievers as to the low.

The view of students as change agents in diagnostic assessment should consider non-cognitive learner characteristics. Positive learning outcomes attributable to formative feedback are correlated with students' attitude to learning, especially mastery learning (Black and Wiliam, 1998; Dweck, 1986). More research is necessary for understanding what non-cognitive variables mediate students' use of diagnostic feedback for improving their own learning.

Future directions

> The task is not simple, but if we can succeed, we will surely be on the way to developing responsible postmodern language testing.
>
> *(Spolsky, 1992: 36)*

We have begun to pay full attention to the nature of diagnostic assessment, and to experiment with its potential to bring close theories of language learning and assessment. In closing, I call for research in three main areas for diagnostic language assessment to reach its full fruition in the next 10 years.

First, teachers and students will play central roles in diagnostic assessment. Diagnostic assessment signals a shift from testing for selection to assessment for learning, and this, in turn, brings forward teachers and students as critical agents of assessment. Future research needs to focus on how to increase teachers' diagnostic assessment competencies and develop students' autonomy.

Second, research on diagnostic assessment will contribute to developing various theoretical models of language ability, vital for characterizing what to diagnose. While there are competing theories of language ability, we do not know much about their viability for diagnostic assessment. Fully functional models of language development for diagnosis require a micro-level analysis of both cognitive and non-cognitive characteristics of language learning taking place in classrooms. We will benefit from active classroom research that experiments with various theoretical models of language development and provides a thick description of learners' language use.

Lastly, the principled diagnostic assessment design will contribute to enhancing the quality of diagnostic assessment in language classrooms. Existing excellent test design frameworks, such as evidence-cantered design (Mislevy *et al.*, 2002) and effect-driven test development (Fulcher and Davidson, 2007), can guide research on diagnostic assessment construction and validation. Furthermore, the principles can help us develop criteria for evaluating the quality of diagnostic assessment tasks. Students' deep thinking processes should be micro-analysed to understand how tasks elicit their processing skills. Diagnostically rich tasks are likely to evoke students' conscious deliberation. Granularity (or specificity) underlying diagnostic assessment is an exciting issue that links among theory of language, assessment purpose, task, scoring, and use. Diagnostic assessment is not a simple task, yet the complexity that it illuminates and the promise that it holds for teachers and students are a compelling argument for future research.

Further reading

Alderson, J. C. (2005). *Diagnosing Foreign Language Proficiency: the interface between learning and assessment.* London, UK: Continuum. This book is an excellent resource for understanding the theoretical underpinnings of diagnostic language testing. The book provides detailed accounts of the development of the DIALANG language assessment system that assesses 14 European languages in five skills including grammar, vocabulary, writing, reading, and writing.

Black, P. J. and Wiliam, D. (1998). Assessment and classroom learning. *Assessment in Education* 5: 7–74. The article provides a comprehensive review of over 500 publications related to formative assessment in classrooms. The authors pay close attention to the role of feedback and its interactions with learners' mastery learning and task difficulty.

Kunnan, A. and Jang, E. E. (2009). Diagnostic feedback in language testing. In M. Long and C. Doughty (eds), *The Handbook of Language Teaching*. Oxford, UK: Blackwell Publishing, 610–25. This book chapter discusses the role of diagnostic feedback in language assessments. The authors examine the feasibility of diagnostic feedback for proficiency and achievement tests. The chapter reviews several examples of diagnostic feedback in language assessment and discusses challenges concerning theoretical, pedagogical, ideological, and technological barriers.

Spolsky, B. (1992). The gentle art of diagnostic testing revisited. In E. Shohamy and A. R. Walton (eds), *Language Assessment for Feedback: testing and other strategies*. Dubuque, IA: Kentall/Hunt, 29–41. In this chapter, Spolsky attributes a lack of attention to diagnostic assessment to commitments to proficiency testing devoid of curricular matters. He then discusses various approaches to diagnostic testing from three different perspectives including pedagogical, linguistic, and processing, as well as conflicts associated with test form and content, the competency–performance divide, and teachers' and students' roles in diagnostic testing.

References

Alderson, J. C. (2005). *Diagnosing Foreign Language Proficiency: the interface between learning and assessment.* London, UK: Continuum.

—— (2007). The challenge of (diagnostic) testing: Do we know what we are measuring? In J. Fox, M. Wesche, D. Bayliss, L. Cheng, C. Turner, and C. Doe (eds), *Language Testing Reconsidered*. Ottawa, Canada: University of Ottawa Press, 21–39.

Alderson, J. C. and Huhta, A. (2005). The development of a suite of computer-based diagnostic tests based on the Common European Framework. *Language Testing* 22: 301–20.

Alderson, J. C. and Wall, D. (1993). Does washback exist? *Applied Linguistics* 14: 115–29.

Beaver, J. (2001). *Developmental Reading Assessment K-3 Teacher Resource Guide*. Parsippany, NJ: Pearson Learning.

Bejar, I. I. (1984). Educational diagnostic assessment. *Journal of Educational Measurement* 21: 175–89.

Black, P. (2009). Formative assessment issues across the curriculum: The theory and the practice. *TESOL Quarterly* 43: 519–23.

Black, P. J. and Wiliam, D. (1998). Assessment and classroom learning. *Assessment in Education* 5: 7–74.

Brindley, G. (1998). Outcomes-based assessment and reporting in language learning programmes: a review of the issues. *Language Testing* 15: 45–85.

Buck, G. and Tatsuoka, K. (1998). Application of the rule-space procedure to language testing: Examining attributes of a free response listening test. *Language Testing* 15: 119–57.

Byrnes, H. (ed.), (2007). Perspectives. *Modern Language Journal* 91: 641–85.

Chapelle, C. A., Chung, Y.-R. and Xu, J. (eds), (2008). *Towards Adaptive CALL: natural language processing for diagnostic language assessment*. Ames, IA: Iowa State University.

Cheng, L., Watanabe, Y. and Curtis, A. (2004). *Washback in Language Testing*. Mahwah, NJ: Lawrence Erlbaum Associates.

Cizek, G. (ed.), (2001). *Setting Performance Standards*. Mahwah, NJ: Lawrence Erlbaum Associates,

Cizek, G. J., Bunch, M. B. and Koons, H. (2004). Setting performance standards: Contemporary methods. *Educational Measurement: Issues and Practice* 23: 31–50.

Clay, M. M. (2000). *Running Records for Classroom Teachers*. Auckland, New Zealand: Heinemann Publishers.

Collins, A. (1990). Reformulating testing to measure learning and thinking. In N. Frederiksen, R. Glaser, A. Lesgold and M. Shafto (eds), *Diagnostic Monitoring of Skill and Knowledge Acquisition*. New Jersey, NJ: Lawrence Erlbaum Associates, Publishers, 75–88.

Council of Europe (2001). *Common European Framework*. Cambridge, UK: Cambridge University Press.

Cumming, A. (2009). Language assessment in education: tests, curricula, and teaching. *Annual Review of Applied Linguistics* 29: 90–100.

Cummins, J., Jang, E. E., Clark, J. B., Stille, S., Wagner, M. and Trahey, M. (2009). *Steps to English Proficiency (STEP): validation study*. Ontario, Canada: Research report for the Literacy and Numeracy Secretariat, Ministry of Education.

Davidson, F. and Lynch, B. K. (2002). *Testcraft: a teacher's guide to writing and using language test specifications*. London, UK: Yale University Press.

Dweck, C. S. (1986). Motivational processes affecting learning. *American Psychologist* 41: 1040–48.

Edelenbos, P. and Kubanek-German, A. (2004). Teacher assessment: the concept of 'diagnostic competence'. *Language Testing* 21: 259–83.

Fox, J. D. (2009). Moderating top-down policy impact and supporting EAP curricular renewal: Exploring the potential of diagnostic assessment. *Journal of English for Academic Purposes* 8: 26–42.

Frederiksen, N., Glaser, R., Lesgold, A. and Shafto, M. (eds), (1990). *Diagnostic Monitoring of Skill and Knowledge Acquisition*. Mahwah, NJ: Lawrence Erlbaum.

Fulcher, G. and Davidson, F. (2007). *Language Testing and Assessment*. London, UK: Routledge.

—— (2009). Test architecture. Test retrofit. *Language Testing* 26: 123–44.

Gibson, A. (2007). *CASI Grades 4 to 8 Reading Assessment Teacher's Guide*, 2nd edn. Toronto, ON: Thomson Nelson.

Glazer, S. M. and Searfoss, L. W. (1988). Reexamining reading diagnosis. In S. M. Glazer, L. W. Searfoss and L. M. Gentile (eds), *Reexamining Reading Diagnosis: new trends and procedures*. Newark, NJ: International Reading Association, 1–11.

Gu, Z. and Jang, E. E. (2009). *Investigating the diagnostic value of multiple-choice options for cognitive diagnostic assessment*. Paper presented at the Canadian Society for the Study of Education (CSSE), Ottawa, Canada.

Henson, R. and Templin, J. (2008). *Implementation of standards setting for a geometry end-of-course exam*. Paper presented at the annual meeting of the American Educational Research Association, New York.

Hudson, T. and Lynch, B. (1984). A criterion-referenced measurement approach to ESL achievement testing. *Language Testing* 1: 171–210.

Huff, K. and Goodman, D. P. (2007). The demand for cognitive diagnostic assessment. In J. P. Leighton and M. J. Gierl (eds), *Cognitive Diagnostic Assessment for Education: theory and applications*. Cambridge, UK: Cambridge University Press, 19–60.

Jang, E. E. (2005). *A Validity Narrative: effects of reading skills diagnosis on teaching and learning in the context of NG TOEFL*. Unpublished doctoral dissertation, University of Illinois at Urbana-Champaign.

—— (2009). Cognitive diagnostic assessment of L2 reading comprehension ability: Validity arguments for applying Fusion Model to LanguEdge assessment. *Language Testing* 26: 31–73.

—— (2010). Implications of assessment of school age L2 students in Ontario. Symposium at Canadian Association of Language Assessment, Montreal, Canada.

Jang, E. E. and Ryan, K. (2003). Bridging gaps among curriculum, teaching and learning, and assessment [Review of the book *Large-scale assessment: Dimensions, dilemmas, and policy*]. *Journal of Curriculum Studies* 35: 499–512.

Kunnan, A. and Jang, E. E. (2009). Diagnostic feedback in language testing. In M. Long and C. Doughty (eds), *The Handbook of Language Teaching*. Oxford, UK: Blackwell Publishing, 610–25.

Lantolf, J. P. and Poehner, M. E. (2004). Dynamic assessment of L2 development: bringing the past into the future. *Journal of Applied Linguistics* 1: 49–72.

Leighton, J. P. (2004). Avoiding misconception, misuse, and missed opportunities: The collection of verbal reports in educational achievement testing. *Educational Measurement: Issues and Practice* 23: 6–15.

—— (2009). Mistaken impressions of large-scale cognitive diagnostic testing. In R. P. Phelps (ed.), *Correcting Fallacies about Educational and Psychological Testing*. Washington, DC: American Psychological Association, 219–46.

Leighton, J. P. and Gierl, M. J. (2007). *Cognitive Diagnostic Assessment for Education: theory and applications*. Cambridge, UK: Cambridge University Press.

Little, D. (2006). The Common European Framework of Reference for Languages: Content, purpose, origin, reception and impact. *Language Teaching* 39: 167–90.

McNamara, T. (2000). *Language Testing*. Oxford, UK: Oxford University Press.

Mislevy, R. J. (1995). Probability-based inference in cognitive diagnosis. In P. D. Nichols, S. F. Chipman and R. L. Brennan (eds), *Cognitively Diagnostic Assessment*. Hillsdale, NJ: Lawrence Erlbaum Associates, Publishers, 43–72.

Mislevy, R. J., Steinberg, L. S. and Almond, R. G. (2002). Design and analysis in task-based language assessment. *Language Testing* 19: 477–96.

Mousavi, S. A. (2002). *An Encyclopedic Dictionary of Language Testing*, 3rd edn. Taiwan: Tung Hua Book Company.

Nicols, P. D., Chipman, S. F. and Brennan, R. L. (eds), (1995). *Cognitively Diagnostic Assessment*. Hillsdale, NJ: Lawrence Erlbaum Association, Publishers.

Nichols, P. D., Meyers, J. L. and Burling, K. S. (2009). A framework for evaluating and planning assessments intended to improve student achievement. *Educational Measurement: issues and practice* 28: 14–23.

North, B. and Schneider, G. (1998). Scaling descriptors for language proficiency scales. *Language Testing* 15: 217–63.

Ramsay, J. O. (2001). TestGraf: A program for the graphical analysis of multiple-choice test and questionnaire data [Computer software and manual]. Montreal, Canada: McGill University.

Rea-Dickins, P. (2001). Mirror, mirror on the wall: identifying processes of classroom assessment. *Language Testing* 18: 429–62.

Robinson, K. M. (2001). The validity of verbal reports in children's subtraction. *Journal of Educational Psychology* 93: 211–22.

Roussos, L., DiBello, L., Henson, R., Jang, E. E. and Templin, J. (2009). Skills diagnosis for education and psychology with IRT-based parametric latent class models. In S. E. Embretson and J. Roberts (eds), *New Directions in Psychological Measurement with Model-based Approaches*. Washington, DC: American Psychological Association, 35–69.

Rupp, A., Templin, J. and Henson, R. (2010). *Diagnostic Measurement: theory, methods, and applications*. New York, NY: Guilford.

Spolsky, B. (1992). The gentle art of diagnostic testing revisited. In E. Shohamy and A. R. Walton (eds), *Language Assessment for Feedback: testing and other strategies*. Dubuque, IA: Kentall/Hunt, 29–41.

Stiggins, G. (1997). *Student Centered Classroom Assessment*. Upper Saddle River, NJ: Prentice Hall.

Tatsuoka, K. (1983). Rule space: an approach for dealing with misconceptions based on item response theory. *Journal of Educational Measurement* 20: 345–54.

Yang, R. (2003). *Investigating How Test Takers Use the DIALANG Feedback*. Unpublished Master's dissertation. Lancaster University.

Part III
The social uses of language testing

Designing language tests for specific social uses

Carol Lynn Moder and Gene B. Halleck

Introduction

In language for specific purposes (LSP) testing, the task of the test designer is to mirror as accurately as possible the language, tasks, and contexts of the target language situation in order to accurately predict workplace language performance. In such performance-based testing, best practices demand that the representativeness of the test tasks and the language required be based on a needs analysis of the target language use situation (McNamara, 1996; Douglas, 2000).

For work-related LSP tests, the target language use situation is most often framed within a communicative competence model (Hymes, 1972; Canale and Swain, 1980). In this approach, appropriate language testing requires test takers to engage in extended acts of communication in which they assume social roles and perform authentic tasks common in appropriate real-world settings. In order to determine what roles and tasks must be included in the LSP test, a careful analysis of the work domain is essential. The needs analysis requires a focus on interaction in the work setting to determine what kind of exchanges typically occur, who the participants are, what the physical setting of the interaction is, what the purpose of the interaction is and what communicative functions and linguistic forms are used. However, language testers should also be cognizant of the social and political ramifications of test design and consequent decisions. What is the larger context in which the testing is framed? Who is to be tested and why? What societal pressures have established the need for the test? What cultural norms and values are realized in the formulation of the standards? In high stakes situations, where testing decisions have major consequences for the test takers and for the general public, understanding the socio-political underpinnings of a test situation is essential to ethical and fair test design (McNamara and Roever, 2006).

This chapter traces assessment design practices within a socio-political context for language tests that are employed in work-related contexts where the language competency has direct effects on a large segment of society. We will outline the procedures for determining the target language to be assessed: gathering information from stakeholders, consulting work-related documents and manuals, examining discourse-based research, observing workplace task and language use, corpus generation and analysis, and piloting sample items with various stakeholders. Throughout our discussion we will consider the ways in which social and political concerns affect testing decisions. The domain in which we will illustrate these practices is Aviation English. Aviation English is of particular relevance for our purposes because of the socio-political context in which the language proficiency standards emerge and the distinctiveness of the language required in the domain.

The use of English in aviation is governed by the International Civil Aviation Organization (ICAO), a specialized agency of the United Nations, which creates standards and recommendations governing civil aviation "by and for" its 190 contracting member states (ICAO, n.d.). The inherently political nature of a test situation in which 190 member nations with varying interests and resources must debate and agree on a common policy that balances workplace needs with public safety makes the testing of Aviation English an excellent example of the social uses of language tests.

Critical issues

Any effective approach to LSP testing must begin with a consideration of the social or political issues that have prompted the need for the test, including the ways in which language use interacts with key domain-specific goals.

In the aviation domain, English is used as a lingua franca—a language of communication between those who might not share the same native language. The main international use of English is for radio communication between pilots and air traffic controllers in contexts where one of the parties does not speak the local language of air traffic control. A Spanish-speaking South American pilot flying into Spain may interact with the air traffic controllers in Madrid in Spanish, but if he flies into Paris he will communicate with the French-speaking controllers in English. Because of the wide use of Aviation English by non-native speakers, the professional use of English in this context has a prescribed phraseology with reduced syntax and vocabulary for routine actions. The highly specialized nature of the content and the prescribed syntax make the target language domain especially challenging for language testers with no aviation training. In such restricted LSP contexts, it is essential for the language tester to conduct a thorough analysis, not only of the prescribed language use, but also of the actual use in context. In language testing situations where standards are prescribed by local, national, or international policies, the language tester must be thoroughly conversant with all requirements and with the socio-political imperatives that motivated them.

A first step is to consult relevant information provided by government agencies and by professional groups charged with the language training of the professionals in the target domain. For the aviation domain, the ICAO website and their publication, the *ICAO Journal*, provide extensive information on the standards and the motivations behind them. Of particular interest to the aviation language tester are recent efforts to improve aviation safety worldwide by raising English proficiency standards. A full discussion of the new standards appears in ICAO Document 9835, *Manual on the Implementation of ICAO Language Proficiency Requirements* (ICAO, 2004)

As these documents reveal, in 1998 in response to a number of aviation accidents in which investigators found that insufficient English language proficiency on the part of the flight crew or an air traffic controller had played a contributing role, the ICAO passed an international resolution that would put in place new requirements for Aviation English (Mathews, 2004: 4). ICAO member nations were charged with reviewing and strengthening the English language testing and training of air traffic control personnel and flight crews working in airspaces where the use of English is required. In the review, public concerns about air safety had to be balanced against practical concerns about whether and how soon international aviation professionals could meet the new standards. ICAO imposed the new standards in 2003 and member nations were to implement them by 2008. The way the new standards were formulated speaks of the way in which the political process can have large consequences for language testing (see Moder and Halleck, 2009). In order to preserve the autonomy of the member nations, ICAO did not prescribe any particular test or test design, rather the policy defined the uniform minimum English proficiency level, Operational Level 4, in terms of a cutoff on a prescribed rating scale.

The policy engendered extensive international efforts in Aviation English testing and teaching to try to meet the standards within the five-year period. The enormity of the tasks of establishing Aviation English tests to implement the new policy and training tens of thousands of air traffic controllers worldwide to meet the new standard in only five years sent countries and commercial businesses scrambling. Many member nations turned to English teaching professionals, most of whom had little or no familiarity with the aviation domain. Most countries had no established Aviation English programs or teachers, and the few trained in teaching Aviation English had little background in workplace LSP testing. Initially, few countries engaged established LSP testers or consulted professional testing organizations like the International Language Testing Association. Some countries asked the aviation professionals charged with personnel licensing and standards to address the new English proficiency requirement. These professionals were intimately familiar with the aviation domain, but generally had no background in LSP testing or teaching. At the start of the five-year policy implementation phase, very few professionals had the requisite combination of knowledge of the workplace domain and LSP testing expertise.

As Alderson (2009) has detailed, during this period, member nations adopted tests of widely varying validity and reliability, and many states did not meet the new standard by the deadline. ICAO then extended the compliance deadline to March 2011, provided that the member states not in compliance post language implementation plans to the ICAO website (ICAO, 2007).

The new ICAO proficiency standards detailed in Document 9835 specify that an appropriate language test must test listening and speaking in a context appropriate to aviation based on the ICAO Rating Scale and holistic descriptors, and it must test language use in a broader context than in the use of ICAO phraseologies alone (ICAO, 2004: 6–5). The ICAO Proficiency Rating Scale—a product of collaborative compromise between aviation professionals, applied linguists, and politicians—specifies descriptors for six levels of proficiency in each of the areas of pronunciation, structure, vocabulary, fluency, comprehension, and interaction.

The descriptors clearly reference a communicative approach to language use, highlighting the importance of interaction and the negotiation of meaning, as illustrated by descriptor statements that include phrases like "Initiates and maintains exchanges" and "Deals adequately with apparent misunderstandings by checking, confirming, or clarifying" (ICAO, 2004: A-8–9). However, the descriptors make little mention of the Aviation English domain, other than requiring the ability to communicate about or comprehend "common, concrete, or work-related topics" (ICAO, 2004: A-8–9). Another noteworthy aspect of the descriptors that emerges from the socio-political context is the repeated reference to unusual or unexpected contexts. These requirements reference the societal concerns that motivated the increased standards—the need to insure that the language of aviation professionals will be adequate to attenuate future emergency situations in which standard phraseology would not be sufficient.

By studying these documents, the aviation English tester can glean some of the essential aspects of the domain, as specified by ICAO. All aviation professionals must be able to speak and understand English, to negotiate meaning through clarification and confirmation, to employ standard phraseology effectively, and to go beyond phraseology as required in emergencies.

In order to delineate the communicative functions and language structures that define the testing domain, further study of available resources is necessary. In the aviation context, professional manuals provide needed information about the actions and events that are part of the work situation. ICAO Document 4444, *Air Traffic Manual*, establishes the training and licensing standards for air traffic controllers and pilots. It includes extensive information about the work domain and prescribes the formulaic language to accompany particular actions and requests. The manual states that established phraseologies should be used whenever possible in order to avoid confusion. If circumstances differ from the routine, aviation personnel may use "plain language" but such language should be as "clear and concise as possible" (ICAO, 2001: 12–1). An example of the phraseology prescribed in the manual is given in Example 1.

Example 1

CLIMB (*or* DESCEND)
TO (level)
REPORT REACHING (significant point)

(ICAO, 2001: 12–13)

In Example 1 we see the schematic nature of the language—action verbs in bare imperative form and key prepositions, supplemented by lexical items designating flight levels or specified locations on a route. The assumption is that an aviation professional will use the formulae, filling the slots as appropriate in all routine contexts. The manual lists over 30 pages of phraseologies, which all aviation professionals should be able to fluently adapt to the appropriate contexts. Familiarity with the appropriate use of such prescribed language is absolutely essential to the appropriate design and evaluation of language used in work-related contexts.

Recommendations for practice

Once the LSP tester has gained a thorough understanding of the domain-specific issues surrounding language, he or she must go beyond published materials to examine the actual language use situation. One key step is for the tester to consult stakeholders about key communicative functions. Especially in highly political contexts, such measures can provide important insights into the priorities of the various stakeholders. Aviation test designers have used varying approaches to gain information from stakeholders. Estival and Molesworth (2009) conducted a survey with pilots to determine the types of problems that they had encountered in using English with air traffic controllers. Kim and Elder (2009) conducted focus groups in an attempt to identify specific problems that arise during radiotelephony exchanges between pilots and controllers. Their informants listened to recordings and commented on the perceived difficulties that they heard. Such issues as limited English proficiency, pronunciation, verbosity, and word choice were cited as having contributed to the misunderstandings that took place.

Below we outline the procedures we used in designing and evaluating the aviation curricula and test items described in Moder and Halleck (2009). After our examination of the situations in the ICAO documents, we consulted with personnel who train air traffic controllers, asking them to list the key communicative functions that pilots and air traffic controllers must perform in various stages of flight. Based on their responses, we designed a written survey which listed the functions and asked large numbers of aviation professionals to rate their importance on a five-point scale. Compiling these ratings allowed us to construct a list of the communicative functions that the pilots and air traffic controllers considered to be most important. Given the social context for the increase in proficiency standards, we asked them to rate those functions that would be most critical in emergency situations, as well.

We also interviewed aviation professionals about the language used in radiotelephony. These interviews revealed strong beliefs about the language use situation which directly affected testing practices. For example, although more proficient pilots and controllers tolerated the use of plain language instead of the more direct standard phraseologies, it was typical for those with lower general English proficiency to vehemently support the requirement that all aviation professionals use phraseology, except in highly unusual situations. Furthermore, many international air traffic controllers expressed their disdain for the way that native English-speaking pilots disregarded established phraseology, using plain language even for routine activities. In their view, this unnecessary use of plain language placed an unreasonable burden on non-native-speaking aviation professionals. They further asserted that the comprehensibility of these pilots was exacerbated by their rapid and imprecise delivery and by the use of non-standard accents.

The question of the need for native speakers of particular varieties of English to comply with established international norms is part of the broader socio-political context of the ICAO implementation. The ICAO standards apply to all aviation professionals, even native speakers of English, but most member nations where English is a standard language have not imposed the same testing requirements on native speakers. In part this is because of the focus on plain language, rather than its combination with phraseology in the workplace context. Language testers concerned with the ethical uses of tests need to be cognizant of the relation of such attitudes and practices to the fairness of the test implementation procedures.

The interview discussions of phraseology and plain language revealed another significant belief held by aviation professionals. Many aviation professionals, especially those charged with licensing standards, were adamant that non-licensed personnel were completely unqualified to rate any language sample that included the use of phraseology. They were less likely to believe that aviation professionals were not fully qualified to rate language testing samples. These strongly held views about the use of phraseology in tests that would be rated by language specialists informed extensive debates at ICAO and elsewhere about the appropriateness of work-related tasks that used phraseology in English proficiency tests. Following best practices in LSP test design, the tasks on the language test should reflect as closely as possible the actual target language situation. However, when influential aviation professionals refuse to sanction tests in which language testers rate English in a task that uses phraseology, the quality of the test can be severely compromised. The role of the tester is to make a cogent and persistent case for the need for authentic work-related language and tasks in a valid LSP test, but the concerns of powerful stakeholders must also be addressed if the test is to be successfully implemented.

Examining published manuals and other documentation can establish a clearer understanding of the scope of the target language domain. Surveys and interviews can reflect the values and beliefs of the stakeholders about the proper use of language in context. However, as with all language use in context, there is often a great variation between what is prescribed and what is actually used. In order to get a complete view of the target language situation, especially in interactional contexts, an examination of actual discourse usage is essential.

In many domains, the language tester may rely on previously conducted discourse-based research to help delineate the features of the language used in the target context. In the aviation domain, this research is limited but still revealing. A number of discourse-based studies have highlighted the socio-technical setting of aviation communication in which the co-presence of equipment and instrumentation plays a major role in the cognition and task-oriented communication of aviation professionals. They also discuss the large amount of information the participants share and the way that their discourse roles are coded in the use of specific language features (Goodwin, 1996; Linde, 1988; Nevile, 2004). Concerning the use of phraseology or plain language, studies of authentic pilot–air traffic controller communication have consistently found that plain language is not only very common, but, more importantly, they find that it contributes significantly to the local coherence and effectiveness of the interactions (Linde,

1988; Sänne, 1999; Nevile, 2004; Wyss-Bühlmann, 2005; Hinrich, 2008). For example, one aspect of plain language use that aviation professionals often assert is not part of the domain is the use of questions, but Hinrich (2008) found them to occur frequently in pilot–controller communications (28 per hour). The questions were often used to clarify, check, or repair information—key abilities for the new ICAO standards. Such information about actual use should guide task design and may also be useful in discussions with doubtful stakeholders.

In addition to reviewing existing research, the language tester may conduct more specific targeted analyses of samples of authentic language from the target context. An example of this kind of analysis is Mell (2004), in which he uses an aviation corpus in order to delineate communicative functions and target language structures that must be included in authentic Aviation English tests.

Ideally, the analysis of LSP communicative functions and tasks should also be based on observations and data recorded in the workplace. Recorded samples may be available from the stakeholders or the tester may need to collect them. In either case, the samples should be transcribed in order to allow a detailed examination of task and language features. Studies that have collected data from actual controller–pilot communications to use as the basis for item design include Teasdale (1996), Kim and Elder (2009), Moder and Halleck (2009), and Van Moere *et al.* (2009).

To illustrate the information that may be gained from transcripts of authentic language, we discuss two transcribed examples of work-related communication from Moder and Halleck (2009).

Example 2

CC: Alfa Juliet Tango one four two, radar service terminated, maintain flight level three-niner-zero, contact Peachtree Controller one-two-five decimal five, So long

AJT: one-two-five decimal five, Alfa Juliet Tango one four two

The exchange in Example 2 is a routine interaction communicated following standard phraseology. This single transcript provides extensive evidence of the communicative functions and language of Aviation English. The example is a routine radiotelephony exchange between an area or en route air traffic controller and the pilot of a small plane with the call sign AJT 142 (Alfa Juliet Tango one four two). The plane is progressing along its established flight path and has reached the position where it will be turned over to the controller for the next area. The controller first identifies the aircraft that is the recipient of the communication. The use of speaker and recipient identifiers is an essential aspect of the communicative situation, since a controller is in communication with multiple pilots at any given time and all use the same frequency. Indeed, pilots must continually monitor the controller's communication with the other planes in order to ensure safety by maintaining awareness of other planes and events in the airspace. The controller informs the pilot that he is terminating his radar contact with her and provides her with the identifier (Peachtree Controller) and the radio frequency (125.5) for the next area controller. The key information in this exchange is the radio frequency, which the pilot reads back to the controller to verify that she received the information correctly. Since the routine readback is accurate the controller does not respond further.

We see in Example 2 the use of distinctive turn-taking identifiers for speakers (the plane's call sign AJT 142), prescribed number and letter readout format ("alfa juliet tango" and "three niner zero"), limited syntax (imperatives, participles, no articles or auxiliaries), and restricted vocabulary ("maintain," "contact," "radar service," "flight level"). The exception to standard phraseology is the signoff greeting "so long." This expression is an instance of a plain language expression used to regulate the interaction, indicating that the controller is ending the exchange with this plane. Such greetings are common in pilot–controller communication as part of the process of opening and closing interactions. The typical abbreviated length of the exchanges is also evident. The brevity of the communication is made possible by the large amount of given information that the pilot and the controller share. Each is already aware of the call sign of the plane and its intended flight path, which were previously specified in a flight plan. The radio frequencies and the navigation points along the path are also known to the pilot and controller in advance. These discourse-based observations provide a foundation for framing the interactional format of the LSP test tasks.

In Example 2 both parties hear the expected information, and there is no need for any negotiation of meaning. As in this example, most exchanges proceed as expected, but it is critical to safety that both the pilot and the controller maintain focus on assuring the information is accurately delivered and acknowledged and on correcting any discrepancies. Indeed, this ability is specifically referenced in the ICAO guidelines for comprehension and interaction. Example 3 illustrates a situation in which more negotiation of meaning is required.

Example 3

A2220:   Airline two-two-two-zero at three-five-zero and about forty miles ahead we'll need to deviate for weather

CC: Airline two-two-two-zero, roger contact, flight level three-five-zero, confirm what side, left or right?

A2220:   uh deviation uh left for weather in about uh probably start in about thirty miles

CC: two-two-two-zero, Center Control, roger, left deviation approved, after deviation fly direct to Casa

A2220:   left deviation approved afterwards cleared direct to Casa Airline two-two-two-zero

CC: two-two-two-zero, affirm

The pilot of Airline 2220 informs the controller that he intends to deviate from the prescribed flight path because of bad weather. Although standard phraseology exists for such a request ("request weather deviation"), the native English-speaking pilot frames the request in plain language, "we'll need to deviate for weather." He also uses plain English numbers ("forty" rather than the prescribed single digit delivery "four-zero"). These are the kinds of instances of a native speaker's use of plain language to which some aviation professionals object. In the actual exchange, the non-native English speaking air traffic controller acknowledges the plane and its position and requests a clarification of the intended direction of the deviation, using a combination of phraseology and a plain language question, "confirm what side, left or right?" Although weather deviations are not entirely unexpected, their occurrence is not predictable in advance. The controller must be certain that the plane's new path will not interfere with other planes in the airspace. Accordingly, we see greater negotiation between the controller and the pilot to ensure that both parties understand the proposed shift. After getting the pilot's reply, the controller identifies the plane ("2-2-2-0"), identifies himself ("Center Control"), indicates his receipt of the communication ("roger"), explicitly states his approval of the direction of the deviation ("left deviation approved") and specifies the subsequent flight path ("after deviation fly cleared direct to Casa"). The pilot reads back the entire clearance and ends the readback with his identifying call sign. In this case, even though the readback is correct the controller specifically confirms it by giving the plane's call sign and using the standard phrase "affirm."

This brief examination of transcribed examples illustrates the wealth of essential information that the language tester can glean from the analysis of transcripts of authentic discourse. Such information about the communicative context, the purposes of the communication, the roles of the participants, the length and type of exchanges, the turn-taking rules, and the specific language used are all essential to the development of authentic, communicative LSP test tasks.

More extensive, targeted analyses are possible if the authentic workplace transcripts can be collected into an LSP corpus and analyzed using a concordance program (see Sinclair 1991 for an overview of the use of corpora in applied linguistics). Moder and Halleck (2010) report on a corpus analysis of authentic pilot–controller communication used to identify common structures necessary for work-related aviation contexts. Van Moere *et al.* (2009) also report on the use of the Oklahoma State University Aviation Corpus to construct the Versant Aviation English Test (VAET).

The Oklahoma State University Aviation Corpus includes 200,000 words of recordings of authentic pilot–controller communication. Because of the emphasis of ICAO policy on the ability of aviation professionals to use language effectively to deal with "unexpected situations," a significant portion of the corpus included transcriptions of cockpit recordings from accidents that were available on the Aviation Safety Net website (aviation-safety.net/index.php). These were supplemented with recordings of the actual workplace performance of practicing international air traffic controllers, as well as transcripts we obtained from other aviation researchers.

One of the ways in which such a corpus can be used to define the workplace domain is to generate the overall frequency of key lexical items and structures. Such information can supplement interviews and surveys with stakeholders in order to establish the language features that should be sampled within a specific workplace domain. For example in the aviation corpus, the 20 most frequent words, in order starting with the most frequent, were *the, to, one, two zero, you, three, five, and, of, four, seven, is, on, six, we, at, it, eight,* and *right.* This list differs dramatically from what one would find in a corpus of general English. For example in the Corpus of Contemporary American English (corpus.byu.edu/coca), the most frequent 20 words are: *the, is, and, of, a, in, to, have, it, I, that, for, you, he, with, on, do, say, this,* and *they.* Notable distinctions in the top twenty words in the aviation corpus when compared to the general English list are the high frequency of numbers, the occurrence of the directional term *right,* the appearance of only three prepositions *of, on,* and *at,* the appearance of only three pronouns *you, it* and *we,* the absence of the article *a,* the absence of verbs, and the absence of the demonstratives *this* and *that.* These distinctions help to highlight how the specialized nature of LSP contexts requires that test tasks be designed in concert with domain-specific analyses of lexicon and grammar.

Going beyond the list of the most frequent words overall, we can use the corpus to analyze the content of the domain. The most common technique for doing so is to compile a list of frequent nouns and verbs in the corpus.

The most frequent nouns in the corpus are *sound, heading, flight, captain, approach, air, tower, time, atc, feet, miles, pilot, level, speed, controller, radio, officer, wind, aircraft, call, voice, number, gear, engine, flaps.* The frequency of these nouns gives the LSP tester an indication of the nature of the domain and the concepts most mentioned. The corpus analysis can be used to formulate the target proportions of content items in the LSP test. Such frequency data, in combination with the information from documents and stakeholders, should inform the design of the task items.

An examination of the most frequent verbs in the corpus is illustrative not only of typical actions in the workplace setting, but also of the structures commonly used in workplace language. The most frequent verbs are *is, are, have, turn, cleared, can, maintain, get, got, hold, going, contact, land, see.* In order to preserve structural variation, we list these words in the forms that actually appeared. The frequent actions include those typically associated with various stages of a flight: *hold*, *turn*, *maintain*, *contact*, *land*, *cleared*, and *going*. In addition there are the verbs of possession *have*, *get*, and *got*; and the perception verb *see*. With respect to structure, the list indicates that verbs most frequently occur in bare imperatives, with some instances of *-ed* and *-ing* participles. An analysis of the fuller context shows that these participles typically occurred without any accompanying auxiliaries. Given the prescribed absence of auxiliaries in phraseology, the high frequency of *is*, *are*, and *can* is of interest, suggesting some deviance from the standard. Further examination of the utterances in the corpus confirms that the most common verb forms are imperatives ("Turn left whiskey, Hold short"), followed by *-ed* forms without auxiliaries ("Cleared Amsterdam via 5-1 November 0-8 Whiskey upper blue 4-0-0") and *-ing* forms without auxiliaries ("Proceeding direct to Selek, maintaining level 3-6-0"). In the corpus, auxiliaries occurred in statements with participles ("AI-182 is cleared to London) only about 20% of the time, and their use in these contexts did not appreciably improve the effectiveness or the flow of communication. Such corpus-based verb frequency analysis can be used as a guide to the writing and selection of lexical and structural items appropriate to the target LSP context.

In the aviation corpus, more critical occurrences of auxiliaries appear in questions, which are significant because of their frequency of use in emergency situations ("Are you dumping fuel?"). The same frequency in emergencies occurs with the modal "can" ("We're maintaining altitude with difficulty uh but uh we can maintain altitude we think"; "Airline two forty three, can you give me your souls on board and your fuel on board?"). If we return to the corpus and search for question words, we find that only three words appear (*what*, *when*, and *how*). As with the other questions, these are used most in critical situations ("What altitude are you descending to at the moment?").

Though these uses of questions and the modal "can" are considerably less frequent than other forms in routine contexts, they appear with much greater frequency in the critical emergency situations that the ICAO proficiency standards are meant to mitigate. The importance of questions in these contexts belies the assertion of many aviation professionals that "There are no questions in aviation English." The analysis of the word frequency and the specific utterance content in the corpus supports the view that in order to maintain public safety standards, aviation tests absolutely must sample these plain language structures in work-related contexts.

Based on all sources of data, a set of domains and item types should be devised that sample representative communicative functions and language in the context of authentic work-related tasks.

In most LSP tests, the design would also include the formulation of rating criteria (see McNamara 1996 for a description of this process for an LSP context). In the aviation context, the rating scale and descriptors have been established by ICAO policy. However, it is imperative that the test designer consider the importance of training raters to use the scale. Such training is particularly important in LSP contexts when the descriptors appear to reference general proficiency criteria that actually require different standards in the target workplace. For example, Moder and Halleck (2009) discuss the problem of evaluating structure using the ICAO descriptor that references the control of "basic grammatical structures." As we have seen from the needs analysis, these basic structures must be interpreted in the context of workplace tasks; general proficiency structures, such as tense sequencing and subject verb agreement, are irrelevant. Training raters to apply the ratings effectively requires that they become familiar with the distinctive use of language in the aviation domain.

In all LSP contexts, the tester should pilot items, but the need for such piloting is more imperative in socio-political contexts in order to establish the validity of the test constructs to stakeholders. In Moder and Halleck (2009), we reported on pilot trials of test tasks that we devised to engage the socio-political issues raised in our needs analysis.

The reluctance of aviation licensing professionals to allow LSP professionals to rate samples including phraseology combined with the discomfort that many LSP teachers felt with the aviation domain led some member nations to consider using general English proficiency test tasks with aviation content. We wished to examine the potential consequences of testing aviation English using only plain English tasks. We administered a set of work-related radiotelephony-based tasks and general English tasks on aviation topics to 14 international air traffic controllers and compared their performance using the ICAO scale.

A sample radiotelephony question, based directly on the transcripts analyzed in the needs assessment, appears in Example 4.

Example 4: radiotelephony question

Below is an exchange between an air traffic controller at Center Area Control and the pilot of a small plane with call sign JAW 4124. The center controller hands the plane off and advises the pilot to contact Peachtree control at the frequency 125.5. The pilot then calls in to the center controller again. Listen to the pilot and respond appropriately.

CC: JAW 4124 radar service terminated, maintain flight level 390, contact Peachtree controller 125.5. So long.
JAW: 125.5 JAW 4124
JAW: Center control, JAW 4124
CC:
JAW: Confirm the frequency is 125.5?
CC:
WJA: 135.5 will monitor and try them again over WPP JAW 4124
CC:
WJA: Thanks for your help.

The test was administered by audiotape. In order to simulate the interactional context of the workplace, test takers wore headphones with microphones, similar to those used in the work setting. The goal of this item was to test the ability to listen to the information in the readback and to provide an appropriate correction as needed. Such items were included in the test because this ability was highlighted in the ICAO proficiency scales and ranked as highly important by all stakeholders. In order to avoid inappropriate memory requirements that are not part of the normal workplace context, the item included the relevant background information about the aviation situation before the listening task began. The item also provided in writing the first three utterances of the exchange to further establish the appropriate context for the interaction. The remaining communications of the pilot were only presented orally.

The general English tasks required students to listen to instructions and describe an aviation situation. The tasks included both common and less expected occurrences.

In the sample item, the test takers saw a picture of a commercial plane partially off the runway in a ditch. They heard the prompt in Example 5 through their headphones.

Example 5: general English in aviation context question

The picture below shows a plane in an unusual position. Describe where it seems to be, how you think it may have gotten there and the condition of any passengers who may have been aboard at the time of the accident.

Because such general description tasks are not a normal part of the controller's work domain, one would expect that the air traffic controllers would perform better on the familiar radiotelephony task. The overall group results indicated that this was the case. The majority of the practicing air traffic controllers that we tested did perform better on the radiotelephony task. Thus, for most controllers, the use of general English tasks in an aviation test would be likely to underestimate their ability to adequately perform in the workplace, resulting in the potential loss of employment. Of greater concern for public safety is that some controllers performed at Operational Level 4 on one of the general description tasks but failed to demonstrate minimum proficiency on the radiotelephony task. For such test takers, the general aviation English task would have inaccurately predicted the controller's performance level on a critical workplace task.

As the needs analysis demonstrated, the communication requirements of pilot–controller communication overlap little with those found in general English, so it is not surprising that the ability to narrate or describe events within the aviation content domain does not show a direct relationship to workplace communication. However, the empirical demonstration of this discrepancy served to alert some stakeholders of the dangers that might result if some stakeholder beliefs were to unduly influence the test design.

For our study, we had the advantage of having access to willing stakeholders with whom we could pilot our test tasks. For the Versant Aviation Test (Van Moere et al., 2009), items were vetted by a paid advisory board of international aviation professionals, who commented on the appropriateness of language and task type. Although the trial items were carefully devised to sample a representative distribution of communicative functions and language based on the Oklahoma State University Aviation English Corpus, the vetting process required extensive negotiation. Some advisory board members commented negatively on any item that did not strictly follow standard phraseology. The applied linguists who designed the items argued strongly for maintaining the authenticity of the language represented in the sample. The resulting item bank was a compromise between these positions, including plain language in more unexpected contexts and adhering more closely to phraseology in routine exchanges.

Other socio-political complications in engaging subjects to trial test items in the development stage are reported by Huhta (2009) and Read and Knoch (2009). These researchers also caution that once the test developer's initial job is finished, the agencies that commissioned their work may not continue to oversee how the test items or the tests themselves are used. The member states or the commercial enterprises that implement the tests will be the ones that determine how ratings are done and whether or not acceptable standards will be maintained. The long-term integrity of the test design remains a significant concern for test designers working in high stakes socio-political contexts.

Conclusions and future directions

McNamara and Roever (2006: 18) have asserted that the validity of socially mandated LSP testing depends on establishing a balance between the responsibility of the test designer to protect the test taker from unfair exclusion and his or her responsibility to the institution that seeks to use the test to assess the test taker's proficiency for a particular social purpose. Given the increasing use of language tests as instruments of social policy and the likelihood that such uses will continue to affect more societies and more test domains in the coming years, language testers must be better prepared to engage with policy makers and stakeholders in order to assure the ethical and fair use of the tests with which they are involved. Language testers will have to develop more transparent ways of communicating the key components of test validity and fairness to stakeholders at various levels of sophistication. A greater use of discourse-based research methods is one means of making testing concepts more intelligible to non-specialists, but these will still need to be supported by appropriate psychometric analyses to meet policy makers' expectations of scientific rigor. The language tester will need to much more effectively deploy social, psychological and discourse considerations in constructing persuasive support for the ethical and productive uses of language tests.

In establishing the balance between responsibility to social institutions and responsibilities to test takers, the LSP tester must effectively combine knowledge of the socio-political context, dialogue with stakeholders, and best practices in workplace needs analysis and task design. He or she must also be prepared to exercise considerable patience and persistence in articulating the potential consequences of specific test design choices. When the political stakes are high, the possibilities for both social harm and social benefit are great. For all social uses of tests, the more informed the tester, the more likely the positive outcome.

Further reading

Douglas, D. (2000). *Assessing languages for specific purposes*. Cambridge, UK: Cambridge University Press. This book provides a comprehensive discussion of the issues related to LSP assessment. The author evaluates high-stakes-specific, purpose tests by investigating target language use domains, and combines insights from applied linguistics with issues related to relevant social/psychological constructs. Specific purpose tests of listening and speaking, such as the Occupational English Test, the Japanese Language Test for Tour Guides, IELTS, and the Professional Test in English Language for Air Traffic Controllers (PELA) are discussed.

ICAO www.icao.int/icao/en/jr/2004. This link provides online access to English, French and Spanish versions of the *ICAO Journal*, an official ICAO publication that includes articles by aviation professionals on issues of current interest. The 2004 Volume 59 Number 1 issue provides background on the ICAO proficiency requirements. The 2008 Volume 63 Number 1 gives an update on policy related to member nations' efforts to meet targeted levels.

McNamara, T. and Roever, C. (2006). *Language testing: the social dimension*. Malden, MA: Wiley-Blackwell. This volume provides a broad-ranging discussion of the need to integrate socio-political considerations into approaches to language testing, with specific reference to test validity, design, and use. Tests of oral proficiency, pragmatics, and those used in educational contexts are discussed in detail.

www.aero-lingo.com. This website contains extensive information on the language of air traffic control. It includes a list of 50 airplane crashes connected to language difficulties and related articles. In addition, it provides information about air traffic control phraseology and a useful link to ICAO Doc 9835 (the *Manual on the Implementation of ICAO Language Proficiency Requirements*), as well as links to audio files of speech samples of pilots and controllers who have been rated at ICAO Levels 3, 4, and 5.

References

Alderson, J. C. (2009). Air safety, language assessment policy, and policy implementation: The case of Aviation English. *Annual Review of Applied Linguistics* 29: 168–87.

Canale, M. and Swain, M. (1980). Theoretical bases of communicative approaches to second language teaching and testing. *Applied Linguistics* 1: 1–47.

Corpus of Contemporary American English (COCA) (n.d.). www.americancorpus.org.

Douglas, D. (2000). *Assessing Languages for Specific Purposes*. Cambridge, UK: Cambridge University Press.

Estival, D. and Molesworth, B. (2009). A study of EL2 pilots radio communication in the general aviation environment. *Australian Review of Applied Linguistics* 32: 24.1–24.16.

Goodwin, M. (1996). Informings and announcements in their environment: prosody within a multi-activity work setting. In E. Cooper-Kuhlen and M. Selting (eds), *Prosody in Conversation: interactional studies*. Cambridge, UK: Cambridge University Press, 436–61.

Hinrich, S. W. (2008). *The Use of Questions in International Pilot and Air Traffic Controller Communication*. Unpublished doctoral dissertation, Oklahoma State University.

Huhta, A. (2009). An analysis of the quality of English testing for aviation purposes in Finland. *Australian Review of Applied Linguistics* 32: 26.1–26.14.

Hymes, D. H. (1972). On communicative competence. In J. B. Pride and J. Holmes (eds), *Sociolinguistics*. Hammondsworth, UK: Penguin, 269–93.

International Civil Aviation Organization (ICAO) (n.d.). *Strategic Objectives of ICAO*. www.icao.int/icao/en/strategic_objectives.htm (accessed 6/9/2009).

—— (2001). *Air Traffic Management Document 4444. ATM/501*. Montreal, Canada: ICAO.

—— (2004). *Manual on the implementation of ICAO Language Proficiency Requirements Document 9835 AN453*. Montreal, Canada: ICAO.

—— (2007). *Working Paper Assembly 36th Session A36-WP/151; TE/36*.

Kim, H. and Elder, C. (2009). Understanding aviation English as a lingua franca. *Australian Review of Applied Linguistics* 32: 23.1–23.17.

Linde, C. (1988). The quantitative study of communicative success: politeness and accidents in aviation discourse. *Language in Society* 17: 375–99.

McNamara, T. (1996). *Measuring Second Language Performance*. London, UK: Longman.

McNamara, T. and Roever, C. (2006). *Language Testing: the social dimension*. Malden, MA: Wiley-Blackwell.

Mathews, E. (2004). New provisions for English language proficiency are expected to improve aviation safety. *ICAO Journal* 59: 4–6.

Mell, J. (2004). Language training and testing in aviation needs to focus on job-specific competencies. *ICAO Journal* 59: 12–14.

Moder, C. L. and Halleck, G. B. (2009). Planes, politics and oral proficiency: testing international air traffic controllers. *Australian Review of Applied Linguistics* 32: 25.1–25.16.

—— (2010). Can we get a little higher? Proficiency levels in Aviation English. Presentation at the Language Testing Research Colloquium, Cambridge, UK.

Nevile, M. (2004). *Beyond the Black Box: talk-in interaction in the airline cockpit*. Aldershot, UK: Ashgate.

Read, J. and Knoch, U. (2009). Clearing the air: applied linguistic perspectives on aviation communication. *Australian Review of Applied Linguistics* 32: 21.1–21.11.

Sänne, J. M. (1999). *Creating Safety in Air Traffic Control*. Lund, Sweden: Arkiv Forlag.

Sinclair, J. (1991). *Corpus concordance collocation*. Oxford, UK: Oxford University Press.

Teasdale, A. (1996). Content validity in tests for well-defined LSP domains: an approach to defining what is to be tested. In M. Milanovich and N. Saville (eds), *Performance Testing Cognition and Assessment: selected papers from the 15th Language Testing Research Colloquium Cambridge and Arnhem*. Cambridge, UK: Cambridge University Press, 211–30.

Van Moere, A., Suzuki, M., Downey, R. and Cheng, J. (2009). Implementing ICAO language proficiency requirements in the versant aviation English test. *Australian Review of Applied Linguistics* 32: 27.1–27.17.

Wyss-Bühlmann, E. (2005). *Variation and Co-operative Communication Strategies in Air Traffic Control English*. Bern, Switzerland: Peter Lang.

Language assessment for communication disorders

John W. Oller, Jr.

Introduction

In language assessment, the task is only made more difficult by the existence of communication disorders. According to Michael Kane (2011), "finding that an examinee had a disability that had not been adequately accommodated could undermine a standard interpretive argument" (also see Abedi, this volume). How should we interpret scores, ratings, or any language assessment for persons with communication disorders? Is it possible to do so based on the expected ranges and milestones associated with persons who do not have any known disorder or disability? For instance, can a "non-verbal" person with severe "infantile autism" be judged with assessment procedures that are designed for application to normally developing individuals of comparable physical and chronological maturity? Is a differently calibrated scale required for the person with autism? If a newly discovered problem could overturn a standard interpretation of a score, rating, or assessment procedure, just how many distinct language assessment procedures should there be and how are they to be determined?

To address these questions and others that flow from them, it is useful to begin with a definition of what communication disorders are.

Definitions and distinctions

> We define *communication disorders as unexpectedly long-lasting, persistent, or recurrent difficulties that interfere with normal, successful, ordinary communication.*
>
> *(Oller et al., 2010: 5)*

An essential goal of this definition is to differentiate genuine disorders from ordinary difficulties that may arise in the normal course of language use and acquisition.

We would not ordinarily think of a two- or three-year-old child as manifesting a communication disorder if the child reduces syllable initial /r/ into a bilabial glide /w/ as in "wabbit" for "rabbit." However, an adult who persists in such simplifications, might well be regarded as having a mild disorder. For example, there was a former Dean of Education from the University of Chicago at the University of New Mexico who once quipped that "duh Univuhsity of Nuh Mexico is not duh Hahvad on duh Wio Gwande, because de' is no Hahvad on duh Wio Gwande!" The Dean also leveled syllable initial /l/ and /r/ into /w/ glides and made /θ/ and /ð/ into /t/ and /d/. Was his speech "disordered" (even "pathological")? Or, to borrow a neologism from a colleague's student, was it just "idiopathetic"?

Of course, more and less extreme disorders are possible. A less extreme case is what is commonly known as "lisping" or, formerly, in the speech–language pathology jargon as "sigmatism." It can involve interdental, lateral, dental, or palatal distortions of common sibilants. More extreme disorders would include degenerative brain diseases (encephalopathies) and traumatic brain injuries. These may gradually, or suddenly, reduce a competent adult to someone who can neither produce nor understand intelligible language and who may not be able to remember family members from one day to the next. The impact can be devastating beyond belief and the emotional cost to all concerned, inestimable. See the true story of Michael Hussey's Wernicke-type aphasia along with written illustrations from Michael himself as he sought to recover lost abilities (Duchan, 2011b).

A critical question in language assessment is how to distinguish the normal fits and starts of language acquisition, the plateaus, ups, and downs from disorders. Equally important, how will the normal fluctuations owed to incidental factors such as how much rest a person has had in the prior 24 hours and whether or not they have had their coffee be distinguished from genuine disorders? How can we tell normal ups and downs from abnormal delays and regressions? There is also the difficulty for monolingual (monodialectal) individuals to distinguish errors and disorders from mere linguistic variations that fall within normal limits.

In the category of a genuine disorder, descent into autism is often preceded by a sudden loss of vocabulary and of all interest in social relations. Commonly, the regression is reported by parents at about the child's 18th month (Brown and Prelock, 1995; Habakus and Holland, 2011; Oller and Oller, 2010; Olmsted and Blaxill, 2010). It is not difficult to distinguish such dramatic regressions from normal plateaux or ordinary forgetting. Changes involving real disorders, however, may be far more subtle. For instance, when a lapse occurs, e.g., as in groping for a word or name, how are we to be certain this is not a sign of the onset of brain deterioration? Could it be an early sign of Alzheimer's? Or just a sign of being over-tired?

The foregoing may be challenging questions, yet they are not the only ones that arise when communication disorders are factored into language assessment. As important as the distinction between disorders and normal difficulties in language use and acquisition may be, the more important question is just how severe is the impact of any given disorder or combination of them? How badly is communication disrupted? Or, turning the question positive side up, what communication skills and abilities are left intact? How well can the individual still function across the whole range of actual communication contexts?

That said, a great variety of distinct types of disorders have been distinguished, too many to list them all here. However, the range and scope of types of disorders can be circumscribed. Communication disorders range across all those associated with (1) physical (bodily) abnormalities (e.g., clefts of the face, palate, as well as other bodily abnormalities); (2) sensory disorders (e.g., deafness, blindness, or other sensory deficits); (3) sensory–motor disorders (e.g., loss of balance, inability to control movements including spasticity, flaccidity, and breakdowns in tactical control systems resulting in everything from paralysis to dysfluencies of speech, signing, and the like); and (4) sensory–motor–linguistic disorders. The last group are among the most important because they are the ones that determine a human being's ability to connect with others. This group of disorders include the aphasias involving loss of the capacity to speak and/or to understand speech; various agnosias having to do with deficits in the processing of images, including prosopagnosia, the ability to recognize faces, which is the most studied of the agnosias; and the apraxias which involve inability to plan and/or carry out complex voluntary movements or actions.

Of course, combinations of the foregoing and subclasses within the various categories are also possible and common. Among the disorders affecting multiple communication systems are the "pervasive developmental disorders." The latter term has come to be synonymous with the "autism spectrum disorders." According to the National Institutes of Mental Health (2010), "The pervasive developmental disorders, or autism spectrum disorders, range from a severe form, called autistic disorder, to a milder form, Asperger syndrome." Such pervasive disorders include sensory, motor, and linguistic disorders (including dysfluencies) along with physical abnormalities, e.g., gut disease, abnormal brain growth, and seizures.

Because of the diffuse effects of commonly known causal factors that can produce communication disorders, factors ranging from genetic or physical injuries to toxins, disease agents, and the complex interactions between them, communication disorders are rarely so focused that a single diagnostic category is sufficient. Although genetic factors are sometimes regarded as if their identification amounts to a final discovery of causation, this is misleading inasmuch as genetic errors, mutations, and the epigenetic disruptions of biological communications within the bodies of affected individuals are themselves not uncaused. Factors that can disrupt embryonic growth, metabolism, and immune defenses, for example, may also be genotoxic and thus capable of damaging germ cells. For this reason, genetic explanations of disease conditions are never the end of the needed etiological research. The looming question after genetic correlates are discovered is always: what has caused the genetic errors to arise? Of course, random mutations are possible, but current genetic research shows that random mutations tend to be corrected by editing processes when the body's systems are working normally. There are literally hundreds of technical articles showing the ubiquitous presence of such processes. A search on the Web of Science on February 12 2011 for "genome stability AND genome repair" yielded 1,197 hits. Therefore, the incorporation of random mutations into the body's germ cells is generally the result of interfering factors that also need to be sorted out. Offending factors include toxins, disease agents, and interactions between them as discussed by Oller and Oller (2010).

For all the foregoing reasons, communication disorders tend to be diffuse and are rarely if ever isolated. The tendency is for multiple disorders to co-occur rather than for just one problem to appear in isolation. In the medical jargon this tendency is referred to as co-morbidity. It is common for strictly logical reasons. A toxin, disease agent, or interaction between various disruptive factors is unlikely to target just one particular gene, biochemical cascade, cycle, or system. So, the discovery of a single genetic disorder in any individual should give rise to the suspicion that there may be others as yet undiscovered. Likewise, although disease agents may have preferred routes of entry to the body and its organs, their impact also tends to be general and diffuse.

Even a physical injury from a blow to the head tends to result in the rupturing of cells and membranes, and may lead to a cascade of subsequent injuries from the release of fluids, germs, viruses, and disease agents (even parasites) into bodily systems where they do not belong and can do additional harm. As a result, communication disorders are rarely focused on just one of the senses, just one aspect of motor capacity, or a single element of language ability (e.g., only memory for names), and so forth. For this reason, medical professionals and clinicians often comment that disorders of different types tend to be found together in the same individual. In other words, co-morbidity is the rule rather than the exception. Also, it is well established that similar symptomatic conditions and syndromes may have a multitude of efficient causes and combinations of factors that can produce them.

As the terms "disorder" and "morbidity" suggest, such conditions are not desirable. Seizures, as in epilepsy, anaphylactic shock, or from whatever cause are never benign (contrary to Deer

2004–11) and are the most frequent cause of death in the increasingly common autism spectrum disorders (Mouridsen *et al.*, 2008). If they were harmless, we would not call them "communication disorders," nor would we refer to them as "morbid" conditions. They are debilitating and/or disruptive or they would not qualify as disorders.

Summing up, the key point in language assessment is that the most important characteristic of any given communication disorder, or complex of them, is the severity of impact on the individual, the family, and interlocutors impacted.

Historical perspectives

As Duchan (2011a) has shown, there is a long and varied history of concern for and treatment of communication disorders. She highlights the history of the study and treatment of communication disorders dating from about 5,000 years ago, until the 21st century. Among the first speech disorders to be noted and described was stuttering. It reportedly affected the Moses of the Old Testament, who said, according to Exodus 4: 10 in the King James Authorized Version, "I am slow of speech, and of a slow tongue," and the Greek orator Demosthenes. Some of the psychological and emotional concomitants can be seen in "The King's Speech," released December 10 2010 by the Weinstein Company in the United States and on January 7 2011 by Momentum Pictures in the UK.

As Duchan shows, there have been many distinct approaches to communication disorders greatly expanding the various terminologies and jargons. No doubt the most interesting development she discusses has to do with what she has termed "The Pragmatics Revolution 1975–2000" (Duchan, 2011c). Critical to that "revolution" is the concept of pragmatic mapping, the association of conventional signs with particular things, persons, and event sequences through dynamic indexical connections. The fundamental question for pragmatic mapping in actual social contexts of experience concerns who the protagonists are, what they are talking or writing about, what their memories, intentions, and expectations are, and how all those elements of experience are connected over time and space.

Language testers and language assessment specialists, for the most part, excepting those schooled in the standard educational measurement tradition, have generally been more influenced by linguistics than by other fields of study. Applied linguists, especially, have tended to see their roots deeply embedded in linguistics, the scientific study of language. However, linguists, for the most part, have had relatively little to say about communication disorders. Linguists have tended to concentrate on normal, even ideal, language learner/users (Chomsky, 1965).

As a result, questions about disorders have generally been left to medical practitioners, clinicians, especially speech–language pathologists (SLPs), and applied language scientists. Sometimes the same disorder has been given several different names while in other instances distinct disorders have been lumped together under a single phrase or term. For instance, the complex of craniofacial deformities formerly designated as "Treacher–Collins syndrome," have also alternately also been called "mandibulofacial dysostosis" and "Franceschetti–Klein syndrome" (Oller *et al.*, 2010: 72). The entire class involves a failure of the bones of the face and jaw to connect correctly, resulting in abnormal junctions between bone plates.

By contrast, some terms such as "dysfluency" and "autism," to pick a couple of examples, cover a multitude of classes of disorders. The underlying question is which disorders are the same and which ones are different? Because of the complexity of the subject matter, comprehensive classification is problematic. Typically disorders have been defined in terms of behavioral symptoms, or other outward manifestations, e.g., the age of persons affected. Commonly, curricula attempt to differentiate "childhood," "adolescent," and "adult" communication disorders.

Of course, these categories overlap on account of the fact that disorders originating in childhood may persist through both adolescence and into adulthood. In some cases, etiological elements may be brought into play. However, in many if not most cases, the causal factors are described as "unknown." For instance, the Centers for Disease Control and Prevention, and their main spokespersons, report that the causes of the vast majority of cases of autism are "a mystery," although they insist that vaccines and components of vaccines cannot possibly be involved (e.g., see Offit, 2010).

Toxicology, by contrast, tells a different story. Certain toxins found in substantial levels in many vaccines, for example, ethyl mercury, aluminum salts, formaldehyde, and phenol to pick just four toxins, not to mention their interactions with each other and with various disease agents such as measles, rubella, polio, and other viruses, in addition to "adventitious" agents such as animal protein fragments and extraneous disease agents such as SV40, are known offenders (Habakus and Holland, 2011; Oller and Oller, 2010; Olmsted and Blaxill, 2010).

Though less controversial, similarly, Alzheimer's disease continues to puzzle the medical profession. It is generally supposed that genetic factors are involved along with critical toxic triggers. The mercury vapors being off-gased from dental amalgam are implicated (Leong *et al.*, 2001) along with organomercurials of the ethyl and methyl varieties which are known to exacerbate neurological disease conditions such as Alzheimer's and Parkinson's disease across the board.

In our own work, we classified disorders on the basis of the systems of communication impacted: (1) bodily; (2) sensory; (3) sensory–motor; and (4) sensory–motor–linguistic. These categories are arranged in a hierarchical rank according to the systems affected. Because higher systems of communication are built with products that are outputs of lower systems, e.g., sensory–motor–linguistic representations, for instance, depend on bodily, sensory, and sensory–motor products, it is clear that cascading effects must be predicted ranging from the foundational systems upward through the higher levels and limited only by the highest attainable levels. The system of classification also implies the principle that we should always judge communication abilities by the highest and best level attainable by the individual being assessed.

Critical issues and topics

It has long been noted in the research literature, for example, by Lev Vygotsky (1962) and A. R. Luria (1947), that communication disorders provide a natural laboratory for the study of normal communication processes. With that idea in mind, disorders may not only involve distinct sign systems, but may also suggest distinct functions of the brain. For instance, sensory dysfunctions mainly impact iconic sign systems. They, in turn, are definitive of the agnosias, which involve inability to recognize bounded entities, or sometimes persons, or their functions. Indexical sign systems are especially critical to the apraxias. The latter involve breakdowns in articulated actions of speech, musical performances, and the like, and in the conventional symbol systems of language that are critically involved in the aphasias.

The most important of the sign systems for human beings are the conventional symbols of language. It was the loss of the capacity to produce fluent speech that led to the discovery of Broca's "speech" area in the left frontal lobe of the brain. The individual he studied had lost the capacity to produce fluent speech prior to his death. The death was attributed to syphilis, but knowing now about the common organomercurials used in treating syphilis (Olmsted and Blaxill, 2010), the destruction of Broca's area, as determined by autopsy (Broca, 1861) may have been more a consequence of the medical treatment common to the period than it was to the syphilis itself. In 1874, by a similar autopsy method, Karl Wernicke (1977) identified a portion of the left temporal lobe which he associated with the capacity to comprehend and produce coherent sequences of meaningful speech. Later, eight distinct varieties of "aphasias" would be described by Ludwig Lichtheim in 1885. Lichtheim's classification scheme still holds today, and his categories are still associated with damage to the dominant hemisphere of the brain. This is the one that Roger Sperry (1981) would term "the speaking hemisphere" as contrasted with "the mute partner."

There is, however, a distinct class of disorders associated mainly with the mute hemisphere. These are the less studied agnosias. While the aphasias pertain to loss of linguistic functions, especially those requiring sensory–motor–linguistic production, as in speaking, signing, and/or writing, the agnosias can be defined as disorders pertaining to the sensory–motor construction of iconic signs. Although both hemispheres of the brain appear to be involved in the constructive processes, the mute hemisphere (the subordinate one) seems to specialize in the recognition of and memory for icons. Among the agnosias that have been most closely examined is the inability to recognize faces, or "prosopagnosia." Sacks (2010) describes his own condition as "face blindness." Persons with this disorder even have difficulty recognizing themselves in a mirror. Sacks reports that he has found himself greeting an unrecognized reflection of himself in a store window.

Between the two hemispheres, there is a large bundle of fibers enabling communication and coordination of the two hemispheres known as the corpus callosum. Damage to the corpus callosum, genetic or otherwise, tends to lead to apraxias of speech and articulated action sequences. Thus, it can be seen from these major classes of disorders that the fundamental process of pragmatic mapping, i.e., of actively connecting referring phrases with the entities (events or sequences) referred to, is evidently ingrained in the neuroarchitecture of the brain itself (Oller, 2010).

In order for a person to describe a sequence of actions, e.g., getting his hat and coat, checking to see that the car keys are in the right-hand coat pocket, walking to the car, unlocking it, getting in and starting the car, and driving home after work, a highly articulated series of actions must be performed in a certain sequence. Conceptualizing and executing such a sequence requires dominant hemisphere involvement as does reporting it after the fact. Carrying out, recalling, and reporting such a sequence also involves the subordinate hemisphere in obvious ways: distinguishing the articles of clothing, hat from coat, the keys from pocket change or a wallet, the right-hand pocket from the left, the car from others parked nearby, the ignition key from others, and so forth. While all that is occurring, or being recalled and reported after the fact, a great deal of communication is taking place between the two hemispheres of the brain.

In his Nobel lecture of 1981, Sperry described outcomes of the radical (and ethically questionable) split-brain surgeries (where the corpus callosum is severed) as follows:

> Each brain half … appeared to have its own, largely separate, cognitive domain with its own private perceptual, learning and memory experiences, all of which were seemingly oblivious of corresponding events in the other hemisphere … The speaking hemisphere [the dominant one] in these patients could tell us directly in its own words that it knew nothing of the inner experience involved in test performances correctly carried out by the mute partner hemisphere [the minor one].
>
> *(Sperry, 1981)*

Current contributions and research

The three main classes of disorders pertaining to articulated volitional actions—the aphasias (loss of speech and/or language functions), the agnosias (loss of iconic capacities), and the apraxias (loss of capacity to coordinate complex mappings of conventional signs onto iconic representations)—

correspond to the essential elements of the dynamic pragmatic mapping process. In every such mapping, one or several referring phrases are mapped through one or more pointing indexes onto one or several arguments consisting in each case of some bounded entity. Referring to the earlier sequence of actions, getting the hat and coat, checking for the keys in the right-hand pocket of the coat, and so on, the arguments in question would be the hat, the coat, the right-hand pocket of the coat, the keys, and so forth. If any of these mappings should fail, the success of the whole articulated sequence of actions could be jeopardized. Without the coat, the keys will not be found, and without the keys the car cannot be started, and so forth. Therefore, it is clear that successful pragmatic mappings of terms onto entities referred to is essential to ordinary (non-disordered) communication.

Another element that comes out in the study of disordered communications, especially, for example in the breakdown of volitional movements, as in apraxias, is what has been variously termed "episodic organization," "meaningful sequence," and "serial ordering." Karl Lashley wrote:

> The organization of language seems to me to be characteristic of almost all other cerebral activity. There is a series of hierarchies of organization: the order of vocal movements in pronouncing the word, the order of words in the sentence, the order of sentences in the paragraph, the rational order of paragraphs in a discourse. Not only speech, but all skilled acts seem to involve the same problems of serial ordering, even down to the temporal coordinations of muscular contractions in such a movement as reaching and grasping.
>
> *(Lashley, 1951: 187)*

It is not difficult to find disorders in which the normal sequential control systems break down. In Parkinson's disease, as in cerebral palsy, the problem of reaching for and grasping an object of interest may present extreme difficulty. Language abilities may also be affected and many complex apraxias of speech, writing, and articulated volitional sequences of actions are possible. Among the disorders involving where the hemispheres can actually disagree with each other is what is known as "alien hand syndrome". While the left brain is intent on eating a meal with the right hand, the subordinate hemisphere may instruct the left hand to push the plate away (Oller *et al.*: 270ff).

Current practices and methods

Typically, the training of SLPs stresses transcription of the surface forms used in a variety of contexts (e.g., see Haynes *et al.*, 2012). For certification clinicians must learn about phonology, morphology, syntax, lexicon, semantics, and pragmatics, but much of the curriculum and training is about phonetics. As noted by Duchan (2011c), in recent decades, attention has shifted somewhat from morphosyntactic and phonologically conditioned functions of surface forms, especially the famed 14 morphemes of Brown (1973) plus an occasional reference to morpho-syntactic variations as in "electric" versus "electricity," to systematic observations of discursive language samples in natural contexts, e.g., symbolic play, videographed conversations, pragmatic functions, and the like.

However, funding agencies prefer diagnoses and treatment protocols that are grounded in standardized published tests which still tend to direct attention to a few surface forms (Shipley and McAfee, 2009: 11–12). An exception requiring the pragmatic mapping of lexical items onto pictured objects is the *Peabody Picture Vocabulary Test* (Dunn and Dunn, 1959–2011), now in its fourth edition, and another test worthy of note, one that looks to nonverbal performances while recognizing the underlying role of linguistic concepts in abstract reasoning, is the *PTONI: Primary Test of Nonverbal Intelligence* (2008) by David H. Ehrler and Ronnie L. McGhee. Both of these tests take the role of pragmatic mapping seriously.

To qualify for the Certificate of Clinical Competence in order to become licensed SLPs, students must complete extensive undergraduate prerequisites plus a proscribed masters program. In the United States, in addition to completing the usual complement of "core" liberal arts courses, the standard curriculum requires at least six hours of university course work in the behavioral sciences, six hours of biology, six hours of physical science, ten hours of a foreign language, one course in computer science, plus college algebra and two more advanced courses in statistics. Besides these "breadth" requirements, clinicians in training will also normally complete 39 additional semester hours of work in communication disorders proper to be followed by a masters degree program consisting of an additional 36 to 40 hours of graduate work in communication disorders. In addition to their course work, clinicians must accumulate 400 "clock" hours of clinical work with clients diagnosed with communication disorders under the supervision of one or more previously certified clinicians.

According to the national accrediting entity in the United States, the American Speech-Language Hearing Association (ASHA), areas of training must include: articulation; fluency; voice and resonance, including respiration and phonation; receptive and expressive language (phonology, morphology, syntax, semantics, and pragmatics) in speaking, listening, reading, writing, and manual modalities; hearing, including the impact on speech and language; swallowing (oral, pharyngeal, esophageal, and related functions, including oral function for feeding; orofacial myofunction); cognitive aspects of communication (attention, memory, sequencing, problem-solving, executive functioning); social aspects of communication (including challenging behavior, ineffective social skills, lack of communication opportunities); communication modalities (including oral, manual, augmentative, and alternative communication techniques and assistive technologies). Although SLPs do not normally have to take a course in language testing, they do coursework on diagnosis and various approaches to research.

In the main, SLPs generally express more confidence in exercises that involve transcription, judgments about phonetic qualities of speech, and treatments pertaining especially to speech and articulation. Among the 15 National Outcomes Measurement System Categories approved by the American Speech-Language Hearing Association (ASHA), the ones most closely associated with language assessment issues are Fluency, Motor Speech, Pragmatics, Reading, Spoken Language Comprehension, Spoken Language Expression, Voice, and Writing. Of the eight categories that have been approved for the ASHA organization by the National Quality Forum (NQF) funded by various pharmaceutical entities and by a grant from the US Department of Health and Human Services (DHHS) in 2009 to "establish a portfolio of quality and efficiency measures for use in reporting on and improving healthcare quality" (www.qualityforum.org/About_NQF/HHS_Performance_Measurement.aspx), the ones most pertinent to language assessment issues are Attention, Spoken Language Comprehension, Spoken Language Expression (speaking not affected by dysarthria), Motor Speech (speaking as affected by some form of dysarthria), Reading, and Writing.

Each of the eight categories approved by the NQF are to be assessed on a seven-point scale arranged from the most disordered to least. Distinctions are not obvious. For example, in the Spoken Language Expression scale, the first position is described as "LEVEL 1: The individual attempts to speak, but verbalizations are not meaningful to familiar or unfamiliar communication partners at any time." Compare this with the same position on the scale for Motor Speech disorder: "LEVEL 1: The individual attempts to speak, but speech cannot be understood by familiar or unfamiliar listeners at any time." Exchange the words "verbalizations" and "speech" as well as "listeners" and "communication partners" and the descriptions are identical, though the categories are supposed to be different.

Similarly, compare the highest level on the two scales. In the Spoken Language Expression scale we find: "Level 7: The individual's ability to successfully and independently participate in vocational, avocational, and social activities is not limited by spoken language skills. Independent functioning may occasionally include use of self-cueing." In the Motor Speech scale for the same level we have: "LEVEL 7: The individual's ability to successfully and independently participate in vocational, avocational, or social activities is not limited by speech production. Independent functioning may occasionally include the use of compensatory techniques." Substitute the words "compensatory techniques" for "self-cueing" and the descriptions are identical, though the categories are supposed to be different.

In present-day speech-language pathology, questions pertaining to cross-language and cross-cultural phenomena tend to be dealt with superficially or not at all. For instance, in a study by Hammer et al. (2004), approximately one-fifth of a sample of 213 participating SLPs could not recall whether or not they had received any training at all touching on "multicultural/multilingual topics" and "respondents lacked confidence when assessing bilingual children whose primary language was Spanish and when working with parents who do not speak English" (p. 91). Clinicians commonly report confidence and better results when treating "articulatory" symptoms of various disorders (Jacoby et al., 2002), but express less comfort, and generally report less success, in dealing with the deeper problems manifested in pervasive developmental disorders such as autism (Schwartz and Drager, 2008).

Recommendations for practice

In doing valid language assessment of persons with communication disorders, as important as a valid diagnosis may be, it is even more vital to effectively gauge the highest and best abilities that are left intact. Where language abilities are insufficiently developed, or may have been completely lost, it is essential to validly assess the level of nonverbal abilities left intact. Such assessments depend entirely on understanding the normal milestones of development and how sign systems are built up from early infancy to maturity (Oller et al., 2006).

While language assessment procedures need to take account of communication disorders that may come into play, the determination of the severity of losses, or alternatively, the levels of remaining abilities, depends entirely on the remaining functionality of existing sign systems. *Therefore, the challenge for testers, assessors, and diagnosticians is to discover the highest and best levels of performance of which the individual under examination is able to perform with icons, indexes, and symbols.*

In effect, the best plan is to cover the full range of authentic contexts of ordinary communication. This requires soliciting information from interlocutors of the individual under examination, and from that individual as well. Rating scales, tests, and observational techniques must be justified and validated against milestones of normal achievement, i.e., by persons and groups who are not affected by any known communication disorders. It is necessary and desirable to calibrate scales, ratings, and scores of individuals with disorders against normally developing persons across the life span.

Future directions

Returning to the case of a "non-verbal" adult who regressed into severe infantile autism at 18 months of age, how can a language assessment apply? Does it make sense to try to gauge such an individual's intellectual ability with tests that require the use of spoken language? For instance, would any of the standardized tests of verbal intelligence apply? Hardly, because the individual to be assessed cannot speak or write.

What if the individual in question is marginally literate, understands some written language, and is able to write with a keyboard? In this instance, the question for the assessor is to find tasks that will enable the determination of the highest and best linguistic performances (in reading and writing) of which the individual is capable at the time of assessment. It makes no sense to judge a person's ability on the basis of tasks not performed at all or that, for whatever reason, fail to elicit the best effort and the highest attainable level of success from the individual being assessed. Simply put, success is informative while failure, in general, tells next to nothing. Failure to perform a given task may indicate nothing more than disinterest, and it may occur quite by chance. Success, by contrast, is unlikely to occur by chance and is, in nearly all cases, indicative of genuine ability.

With respect to language assessment, the greatest need, as pointed out in Oller and Oller (2010), is to expand the understanding of milestones of development at the preverbal end of the scale. When it comes to accurately measuring levels of severity in persons who are "nonverbal" that expansion is essential. The theory of abstraction as described in that book and references given there shows that such an expanded scale is feasible.

Further reading

Haynes, W. O., Moran, M. J. and Pindzola, R. H. (2012). *Communication Disorders in Educational and Medical Settings: An Introduction for Speech-language Pathologists, Educators, and Health Professionals.* Sudbury, MA: Jones and Bartlett. Despite its 2012 copyright, this book nicely demonstrates the traditional surface orientation of SLPs and the professionals who train them. Language is effectively equated with speech, without mention of verbal thought or reasoning, much less of signed languages, and little attention is given to literacy. No attention at all is devoted to nonverbal aspects of linguistic reasoning. Dialect differences are commonly equated with errors and disorders, e.g. reference is made to a child who, though instructed by an SLP to say, "He is my friend" returns "to the classroom and continues to say sentences without including 'is'" (p. 23). The authors suggest that the teacher should remind the child that "this piece of language is important" thus demonstrating the common confusion of dialect with disorder, and the equating of language with speech. Should it surprise us, then, that speech-language pathologists are more confident in dealing with articulation problems than with deeper language and learning issues?

Habakus, L. K. and Holland, M. (2011). *Vaccine Epidemic.* New York, NY: Skyhorse Publishing. Along with the Pragmatics Revolution described by Duchan (2011b) at her excellent website, has come a growing appreciation that eye-witness reports from persons doing hour-by-hour, day-by-day observation are apt to be far more informative than the 5–15 minutes typically spent in the office of a medical doctor, or even a series of hour-long meetings with a speech-language pathologist. In this book, doctors, lawyers, and professionals from all walks of life, but especially the health professions, report their own observations and examine the research on the interactions of toxins, disease agents, and especially ones received at the age of greatest vulnerability through the eye of a needle. Language assessment specialists certainly need to know the symptoms associated with linguistic regression and social withdrawal that commonly precede the diagnosis of a pervasive developmental disorder, and it can only help them in dealing with affected individuals also to be aware of allergies, asthma, auto-immunity, Guillaine–Barré syndrome, petit mal seizures, and other increasingly common disease conditions such as acid reflux, vomiting, diarrhea, gut disease, brain inflammation (commonly associated with self-injurious behaviors) and full-blown grand mal seizures, associated especially with pervasive developmental disorders. This book is a blockbuster.

Oller, J. W. Jr. and Oller, S. D. (2010). *Autism: the diagnosis, treatment, & etiology of the undeniable epidemic.* Sudbury, MA: Jones and Bartlett Publishers. Those involved in assessment and diagnosis may find this book useful on account of its in-depth treatment of various theories of the definition and diagnosis of autism, and of related communication disorders and disease conditions that impact language abilities. A scale of milestones, based on the theory presented in Oller *et al.* (2006), is applied and shown to be both reliable and valid as a basis for differentiating 17 distinct gradations of severity in pervasive developmental disorders.

Because of its grounding in a richer theory of sign systems, finer distinctions and a greater number of them are possible. For instance, the research reported shows it is possible to distinguish 10 levels of severity in the nonverbal range plus an additional seven levels in the verbal range.

Oller, J. W. Jr., Oller, S. D. and Badon, L. C. (2010). *Cases: introducing communication disorders across the life span*. San Diego, CA: Plural Publishing, Inc. This encyclopedic reclassification of communication disorders and related disease conditions relies on systems of communication affected.

Oller, J. W. Jr., Oller, S. D. and Badon, L. C. (2006). *Milestones: normal speech and language development across the life span*. San Diego, CA: Plural Publishing, Inc. Here, readers will encounter the grounding of language acquisition theory in a deeper understanding of the processes that undergird the phonological, morphological, lexical, semantic, syntactic, and pragmatic development of sign systems.

Olmsted, D. and Blaxill, M. (2010). *The Age of Autism: mercury, medicine, and a man-made epidemic*. New York, NY: St. Martin's Press. The most important epidemic of the current century may well turn out to be autism. Understanding its causes, which cannot be purely genetic, is critical to its diagnosis, the assessment of its impact on individuals, and the prognosis for the future of all those affected by it. In order to build sensible treatment programs, to advise parents and professionals about prevention measures, to fully sort out causal factors, valid assessment and diagnosis is critical. Underlying the diagnosis and prognosis based on valid assessment is the question of causation. This book is a must read.

References

Broca, P. P. (1861). Loss of Speech: Chronic Softening and Partial Destruction of the Left Frontal Lobe of the Brain. *Bulletins de la Société d'Anthropologie de Paris* 2: 235–38.

Brown, J. and Prelock, P. A. (1995). Brief report: the impact of regression on language development in autism. *Journal of Autism and Developmental Disorders* 25: 305–9.

Brown, R. (1973). *A First Language*. Cambridge, MA: Harvard University Press.

Chomsky, N. A. (1965). *Aspects of the Theory of Syntax*. Cambridge, MA: MIT Press.

Deer, B. (2004–11). *The MMR–Autism Crisis: Our Story So Far. An investigation by Brian Deer*. briandeer.com/mmr/lancet-summary.htm (accessed 2/11/11).

Duchan, J. (2011a). *Getting Here: A History of Speech Language Pathology*. www.acsu.buffalo.edu/~duchan/new_history/overview.html (accessed 2/11/11).

—— (2011b). *Margaret Hussey's Story of Her Husband's Aphasia Therapies*. www.acsu.buffalo.edu/~duchan/new_history/margaret_on_therapy.html (accessed 2/11/11).

—— (2011c). *The Pragmatics Revolution 1975–2000*. www.acsu.buffalo.edu/~duchan/1975–2000.html (accessed 2/11/11).

Dunn, L. and Dunn, L. (1959–2011). *Peabody Picture Vocabulary Test*, 4th edn. New York, NY: Psychological Corporation.

Ehrler, D. J. and McGhee, R. L. (2008). *PTONI: primary test of nonverbal intelligence*. Austin, TX: Pro-Ed.

Habakus, L. K. and Holland, M. (2011). *Vaccine Epidemic*. New York, NY: Skyhorse Publishing.

Hammer, C. S., Detwiler, J. S., Detwiler, J., Blood, G. W. and Qualls, C. D. (2004). Speech-language pathologists' training and confidence in serving Spanish–English bilingual children. *Journal of Communication Disorders* 37: 91–108.

Haynes, W. O., Moran, M. J. and Pindzola, R. H. (2012). *Communication Disorders in Educational and Medical Settings: an introduction for speech-language pathologists, educators, and health professionals*. Sudbury, MA: Jones and Bartlett.

Jacoby, G. R., Levin, L., Lee, L., Creaghead, N. A. and Kummer, A. W. (2002). The number of individual treatment units necessary to facilitate functional communication improvements in the speech and language of young children. *American Journal of Speech-language Pathology* 11: 370–80.

Kane, M. (2011). Validating Score Interpretations and Uses. *Language Testing*, doi: 10.1177/0265532211417210.

Lashley, K. (1951). The Problem of Serial Order in Behavior. In L. A. Jeffress (ed.), *Cerebral Mechanisms in Behavior*. New York, NY: Wiley.

Leong, C. C., Syed, N. I. and Lorscheider, F. L. (2001). Retrograde degeneration of neurite membrane structural integrity of nerve growth cones following in vitro exposure to mercury. *Neuroreport* 12: 733–37.

Lichtheim, L. (1885). On Aphasia. *Brain* 7: 433–84. (Originally published in 1885 in German as *Ueber Aphasie. Aus der medicinischen Klinik in Bern. Deutsches Archiv für klinische Medicin, Leipzig* 36: 204–68.)

Luria, A. R. (1947). *Traumatic Aphasia*. Moscow, Russia: Academy of Medical Sciences.

Mouridsen, S. E., Hansen, H. B., Rich, B. and Isager, T. (2008). Mortality and causes of death in autism spectrum disorders: an update. *Autism* 1: 403–14.

National Institutes of Mental Health (2010). *Autism Spectrum Disorders (Pervasive Developmental Disorders): Introduction.* www.nimh.nih.gov/health/publications/autism (accessed 2/11/11).

Offit, P. (2010). *Deadly Choices: how the anti-vaccine movement threatens us all.* New York, NY: Basic Books.

Oller, J. W. Jr. (2010). The antithesis of entropy: biosemiotic communication from genetics to human language with special emphasis on the immune systems. *Entropy* 12: 631–705.

Oller, J. W. Jr. and Oller, S. D. (2010). *Autism: the diagnosis, treatment, & etiology of the undeniable epidemic.* Sudbury, MA: Jones and Bartlett Publishers.

Oller, J. W. Jr., Oller, S. D. and Badon, L. C. (2006). *Milestones: normal speech and language development across the life span.* San Diego, CA: Plural Publishing,

—— (2010). *Cases: introducing communication disorders across the life span.* San Diego, CA: Plural Publishing, Inc.

Olmsted, D. and Blaxill, M. (2010). *The Age of Autism: mercury, medicine, and a man-made epidemic.* New York, NY: St. Martin's Press.

Sacks, O. (2010). *The Mind's Eye.* New York, NY: Alfred A. Knopf.

Schwartz, H. and Drager, K. D. R. (2008). Training and Knowledge in Autism among Speech-language Pathologists: A Survey. *Language Speech and Hearing Services in Schools* 39: 66–77.

Shipley, K. G. and McAfee, J. G. (2009). *Assessment in Speech-Language Pathology: a resource manual*, 4th edn. Clifton, NY: Delmar Cengage Learning.

Sperry, R. W. (1981). *Nobel Lecture: some effects of disconnecting the cerebral hemispheres.* nobelprize.org/nobel_prizes/medicine/laureates/1981/sperry-lecture.html (accessed 2/11/11).

Vygotsky, L. S. (1962). *Language and Thought.* (E. Hanfmann and G. Vakar eds and trans.) Cambridge, MA: Harvard University Press. (Original work in Russian published in 1934.)

Wernicke, C. (1977). *Wernicke's Works on Aphasia: a sourcebook and review.* The Hague, The Netherlands: Mouton, 87–283. (Original work published in German in 1874, ed. and trans).

Language assessment for immigration and citizenship

Antony John Kunnan

Introduction

The newest context of interest in language assessment is in the area of immigration, citizenship, and asylum. Although language assessment in this context can be traced back to the infamous Australian dictation test for immigration in the early twentieth century, an explosion of interest, debate, and practice in this area started about twenty years ago. This recent push has meant that language assessment academics and professionals have had to enter a new arena where the explicitly stated purposes and uses of language assessments are not as clear as they could be, and where, in some cases, there are hidden agendas that are discriminatory and detrimental. This chapter will take a broader perspective on this topic than normally done in language assessment and will attempt to bring together many intersecting areas of interest. It is necessary to do this, because insights and perspectives from immigration and citizenship studies, from state ideology and language rights, and from language policy and legal matters enhance our understanding of this complex human topic of study.

Conceptual matters

Modern migration

In the early years of the twenty-first century, migration has continued unabated much like in the previous century. People move from their home country to another in search of better work opportunities, for temporary residence based on work or study, and for family reunification and asylum. But the main difference between migration of the past, even thirty years ago, and the present is that there is very little or even none of the wrenching separation from the home country, family, and culture felt by the migrant. The electronic age we live in today (with e-mail, the internet, global news, and international audio and video communication) and to lesser degree the relative ease of international travel have made it possible for a migrant to be less isolated from his or her homeland, family, and culture. Further, in this era of globalization, and financial globalization, many migrants are economic migrants looking for better opportunities; therefore, they are not necessarily the poor, the downtrodden, and the persecuted of prior decades.

In terms of self-identity too, migrants today are not required to give up their homeland traditions, language, and culture in the same way as was the case decades ago. Today's migrants, in contrast, can most often find people and culture from their homeland in their receiving countries so that they can continue to follow their home languages and traditions. Thus, although citizenship and identity are intertwined in the past they could remain separate in modern immigrants leading to dual or multiple identities and dual or multiple nationalities or citizenships. This rupture of the traditional concept of citizenship (which once fused citizenship and identity) into two separate entities in many communities is symptomatic of early twenty-first-century trends in migration. The question therefore is whether modern migration has changed the way we should think of immigrants and citizens. Put another way, should immigrant-sending and immigrant-receiving communities and countries rethink the identity and aspirations of newcomers and long-staying residents and citizenship holders?

Immigrants and citizenship applicants

Traditionally, immigrants are classified into two types: those who plan to stay or are staying in the receiving or new country for the *short term* (typically, tourists, students, and temporary workers) and those who plan to stay or are staying for the *long term* (typically, those on work permits, those joining their spouses or families, and those who have sought asylum). Except for tourists in the former group, normally most immigrants will need to demonstrate relevant abilities (which may or may not include language abilities) related to their study or employment before they are issued visas to enter the new country (among many other requirements). In some receiving countries, there are requirements such as a minimum level of language ability in the standard variety of the dominant language of the country that have to be met even for short-term stays. In contrast, it is the latter group, the long-term stay group, which after many years of stay in the receiving country (typically three to five years), may consider applying for citizenship based on the *jus sanguine* (by blood principle) or by naturalization (if the new country has such a provision). It is these applicants for citizenship who are required to take language tests, history and civics tests, and/or social integration courses before they can be granted citizenship.

Although these notions of immigrants and citizens have to be rethought because of the era we live in, immigrant behavior and suitability of immigrants to be granted citizenship have been debated for decades in receiving countries. Pickus (2005) argued that in the late eighteenth century and early nineteenth century in the United States, there was disagreement regarding

> how to turn new immigrants into the proper kinds of citizens. What kind of requirements for officeholders or immigrants wishing to be naturalized would best ensure their loyalty and their ability to understand America's civic principles and participate in its public life? Was the simple fact that the immigrant chose to come to the United States sufficient, or should there be a required amount of time before naturalization, variously set between 3 and 14 years? Or would newcomers never be trusted fully and be barred from holding elective office?
>
> *(Pickus, 2005: 15)*

State ideology and language rights: from public monolingualism to multiculturalism

Modern nation-states, including liberal democracies, have debated the state-mandated national language requirements on the one hand as part of political and social integration policies and minority or indigenous languages of minority communities as part of multilingual and multi-cultural rights. In terms of language rights, most countries embrace the idea of a public mono-lingualism with an emphasis on collective rights while a few countries promote a limited public multilingualism with a limited set of individual rights.

This evangelical desire for public homogeneity which includes public monolingualism and social cohesion was best argued in the United States by assimilationist writers like Schlesinger (1992) and Huntington (2005). In *The Disuniting of America*, Schlesinger wrote that the cult of ethnicity

> reverses the historic theory of America as one people—the theory that has thus far mana-ged to keep American society whole ... The national ideal had once been *e pluribus unum* [out of many, one]. Are we now to belittle *unum* and glorify *pluribus*? Will the center hold? Or will the melting pot give way to the Tower of Babel?
>
> *(Schlesinger, 1992: 16–18)*

In practical terms, this ideological bent resulted in the English First movement in the United States in 1930s. It was mainly an Americanization effort that included English language programs for foreign-born adults. These efforts were also promoted by American employers such as Ford, US Steel, and Pennsylvania Railroad. According to Crawford (1992), employers believed that low proficiency in English led workers to socialist propaganda and prevented them from believing in free enterprise. Pavlenko (2002) observed that the main purpose of

> these efforts had solidified the link between English and patriotism in the public consciousness so well that twenty years later Philadelphia's *Evening News* still argued that all aliens "are to be taught the minimum of English necessary to guarantee a belief in democracy."
>
> *(Pavlenko, 2002: 180)*

Alongside these efforts came positioning English with superiority and patriotism; in the words of Pavlenko (2002), English was supposed to have high moral and intellectual values and the lack of English proficiency was equated to inferior intelligence and low moral standards. In this period, US Presidents Wilson and Roosevelt too reflected their strong support for English:

> *Wilson:* You cannot become thorough Americans if you think of yourselves in groups. America does not consist of groups. A man who thinks of himself as belonging to a particular national group in America has not yet become an American ...

> *Roosevelt:* We have room for but one language here, and that is the English language, for we intend to see that the crucible turns our people out as Americans, of American nationality, and not as dwellers in a polyglot boardinghouse; and we have room for but one sole loyalty, and that is the loyalty to the American people.
>
> *(1919; cited in Pavlenko, 2002: 183–84)*

In Europe, in the nineteenth and twentieth centuries, nation-building was most often conceived of as monolingual nation-building; the general concept was "one language, one nation." This was particularly true in some countries like France, where the use of standard French was part of the national consciousness, and modern Germany, even after unification in the late twentieth century.

But since the post-1991 migration, Europe's identity, which has historically been linked to linguistic and cultural homogeneity, has had to undergo some changes. Based on the formation of the European Union and recent globalization, Extra *et al.* (2009) concluded that "major changes in each of these areas have led inhabitants of Europe to no longer identify exclusively with singular nation-states. Instead, they show multiple affiliations that range from transnational to both global and local ones" (p. 9).

Public multiculturalism has its ideological supporters in writers like Kymlicka (1995) and May (2005). Kymlicka argues for individual rights as "group-differentiated rights": "Granting special representation rights, land claims, or language rights to a minority … can be seen as putting the various groups on a more equal footing, by reducing the extent to which the smaller group is vulnerable to the larger" (p. 24, as cited in May, 2008). May (2008), applying Kymlicka's formulation, put it succinctly, "the preoccupation of modern nation-state organization with a single language and culture, and an allied public monolingualism, is both unnecessarily unjust to and exclusive of minority language groups" (p. 24). He further argued along the lines of Kymlicka, by giving examples for this idea from the Welsh in Britain, Catalans and Basques in Spain, Bretons in France, Québécois in Canada, and some Latino groups (e.g. Puerto Ricans) in the United States.

Thus, based on these arguments it could be asserted that it is necessary for modern nation-states to rethink themselves as multilingual, multicultural, and multinational, promoting plurality and inclusivity. As May (2008: 26) observed,

> the aim, in so doing, is to foster the prospect of more representational multinational and multilingual states by directly contesting the historical inequalities that have seen minority languages, and their speakers, relegated to the social and political margins.

Likewise, Bourdieu (1998) stated this ideological view, "Cultural and linguistic identification is accompanied by the imposition of the dominant language and culture as legitimate and by the rejection of all other languages into indignity" (p. 46).

Language policy: from national language to social integration

Given this backdrop, the question of how to make immigrants fit into their new country becomes a much more difficult question today than many decades ago. Let us first take up the case of language, specifically the push by governments to require immigrants and citizenship applicants to learn to a sufficient degree the standard variety of the dominant language or official language of the country. The history of countries with large-scale immigration in the twentieth century has shown that there has been coercion to learn the dominant or official language through legislative actions, court rulings and political and societal attitudes (see Kunnan, 2009a).

The history of the United States in terms of English versus non-English language policy is a case in point. The early decades were dominated by assimilationist thinking with ideas such as making English the sole official language, limiting access to voting and civil rights to non-English speakers and opposing any form of bilingual education. Ricento and Wright (2008) reported that during this time indigenous Native American languages and cultures were stigmatized and later states passed "compulsory ignorance" laws that made it a crime to teach slaves to read or write. In terms of language education, by 1923, 22 states had laws prohibiting the teaching of foreign languages in primary schools in a country that was made of large numbers of first-generation immigrants. Courts intervened and found these laws unconstitutional: the two most important cases were *Meyer* v. *Nebraska* (1923) in which the US Supreme Court decision ruled that a previous Nebraska law that forbade teaching in any language other than English to be unconstitutional, and *Farrington* v. *Tokushige* (1927) in which the US Supreme Court ruled that Hawaii's effort to abolish private Japanese, Korean, and Chinese language schools was unconstitutional. Later in the 1950s, many states imposed English as the sole language of instruction in schools and passed laws banning the teaching of other languages.

Alongside language requirements is the concept of social integration of immigrants and potential citizens with the existing citizens of the receiving country. This situation can be seen in Belgium and the Netherlands where a whole program of social integration is in place. The region of Flanders in Belgium has the best example of social integration courses, also known as the *inburgering* policy. The integration policy's main arm is the integration course which is required of all newcomers under sixty-five years of age, recognized religious workers, and those who plan to stay beyond the first year as immigrant and who plan to seek long residence in Flanders or Brussels. According to van Avermaet and Gysen (2009), the integration course is made up of proficiency in Dutch, the official language of Flanders, and a course in socio-cultural orientation in the mother tongue of the immigrant focusing on practical knowledge and values and norms such as pluralism, democracy, respect, and solidarity. But van Avermaet and Gysen (2009: 122) raise a critical alarm regarding this program:

> A policy of obliging immigrants to first learn the language of the host country as an initial step to interaction calls for critical reflection. Immigrants are seen as having a language deficiency. This deficiency is seen as an obstacle to integration and as a cause of violence and social conflicts. This argument is selective in the sense that it may only apply to a certain category of immigrants. Those 'migrants' belonging to the 'globalized elite' communicate with the indigenous multilingual elite in French, German, English or Spanish.

An illustration of how some of the conceptual matters discussed above are translated into policy and practice in terms of language policy and assessment policy is presented from the US perspective where language policy and assessment policy have swung widely over the centuries. A few short country-based case studies will also be presented.

Illustration: politics, language policy and legislation in the United States

In the last 235 years, the concept of American citizenship in terms of politics, legislation, court rulings, and social attitudes has swung like a pendulum, sometimes favoring inclusion and tolerance, sometimes exclusion and self-righteousness. The debates have been mainly about language and civic nationalism. In terms of language, many political thinkers have argued for a common language or a public monolingualism (see Huntington, 2005; Schlesinger, 1992), because they believe a bilingual or multilingual country could result in ghettoization and social immobility (Pogge, 2003). On the other hand, others have stressed the importance of multiculturalism and individual language rights (Kymlicka, 1995; Kloss, 1977) and tolerance-oriented language rights (May, 2005, 2008).

Early on, varying concepts of citizenship emerged from two political groups: the Federalists, who promoted a strong nationalist government, and the Anti-Federalists, who campaigned for a less powerful role of government. Washington emphatically declared in 1783 that "the bosom of America was open to receive not only the opulent and respectable stranger, but the oppressed and persecuted of all nations and religions" (Washington, 1783). Although Washington's statement came a few years before the Naturalization Act of 1790, the founders were untroubled by the presence of slavery of Blacks and Native Americans as US citizenship was restricted to "free white persons." This racial terminology was used to exclude Blacks and Native Americans in contrast to the much-quoted line from the US Declaration of Independence, "We hold these truths to be self-evident, that all men are created equal."

Social attitudes toward immigration and citizenship too swung from one extreme encapsulated in the words of Emma Lazarus on the pedestal of the Statue of Liberty, "Give me your tired, your poor, your huddled masses yearning to breathe free" (Kennedy, 1964: 45), to the other extreme of indefensible racial intolerance, bigotry, fear, and hatred against the French, Irish Catholics, Jews, southern and eastern Europeans, Chinese, Japanese, and Asian Indian immigrants. All of these together have played a role in formulating immigration policies of successive governments, which have constantly reconsidered and changed these policies to suit their particular positions.

The first federal regulation came through The Naturalization Act of 1790, which stated that

> any alien, who was a free white person and who had resided within the limits and under the jurisdiction of the United States for the term of two years may be admitted to become a citizen on application to any common law court of record, in any one of the States where he had resided for the term of one year at least, and making proof to the satisfaction of such court that he is a person of good character, and taking the oath or affirmation prescribed by law to support the Constitution of the United States.

In 1795, Congress repealed the 1790 Act, raised the residence requirement for citizenship to five years, and required a declaration of intention to seek citizenship at least three years before naturalization.

Several new acts were passed over the decades in the nineteenth century. The most notable change came in 1865 with the 13th Amendment to the US Constitution, abolishing slavery. Following this amendment, Blacks were recognized as citizens in the 14th Amendment in 1868. Yet a little more than a decade after expounding the 14th Amendment's guarantees of equal protection, due process and consent, Congress reverted to a more restrictive immigration policy. Responding to a national xenophobic clamor for the exclusion of Chinese, Congress passed the Chinese Exclusion Act of 1882. This act included several over-restrictive provisions including the suspension of immigration of Chinese laborers (merchants, teachers, students, and tourists were exempt) to the United States for ten years and prohibition of Chinese from becoming citizens through the naturalization process.

Language criteria for naturalization were added for the first time in the 1893 Act, when Congress added *the ability to read and write* (but not specifically in English), and in the 1906 Act, Congress required applicants *to sign their petitions in their own handwriting and speak English*. In 1896, Congress passed the *literacy test bill*, promoted by the Immigration Restriction League, which wanted to have a barrier in place to restrict "undesirable immigrants" who were coming to the United States from southern and eastern Europe and threatening the "American way of life." The test was expected to assess the ability of applicants for immigration to read at least forty words in any language as a requirement for admission to the United States, but this bill was vetoed by President Cleveland. Around 1906, immigration examiners began to develop questions on the understanding of the Constitution; this was a precursor to the current knowledge of history and government test (see Pickus, 2005, for examples).

In 1917, as wartime hysteria fed American xenophobia, Congress passed the *literacy test bill* again, overriding President Wilson's veto this time. This racially oriented bill became the first literacy requirement that required potential citizens and immigrants over sixteen years of age to read at least thirty words and not more than eighty words in ordinary use in any language. The test resulted in effectively restricting immigration of Italians, Russians, Poles, Hungarians, Greeks, Asians, and Irish Catholics. A variant of the literacy test in English was also used in both northern and southern states to determine eligibility for voting, effectively denying voting rights to large numbers of African Americans in many southern states and disenfranchising a million Yiddish speakers in New York (del Valle, 2003). Decades later, the Voting Rights Act of 1965 suspended the literacy test in all states; in 1970, Congress extended the prohibition of the literacy tests and in 1975 made the ban indefinite and national in scope (del Valle, 2003). After World War II, the Immigration and Naturalization Act of 1952 enshrined both the English language and the history and government requirements for citizenship. In the words of del Valle (2003), "in passing the English literacy provision, Congressmen clearly linked the inability to speak or understand English to political suspicion" (p. 93).

Language assessment: citizenship tests and immigration and integration policies

In terms of language assessment, although the Australian government used the infamous "dictation test" in the early part of the twentieth century, many governments have introduced test requirements in the mid-twentieth to early twenty-first centuries.

Illustration: the US Naturalization test

Although the United States has had a language requirement for citizenship (through the naturalization process) since the first decade of the twentieth century, it was enforced as a formal test only in the late 1980s. Overall, the requirement (and the test) is said to promote "civic integration," "political allegiance," "social cohesion," and/or "social harmony." Specifically, in the language of the Immigration and Nationality Act of 1952, applicants for naturalization are expected to demonstrate (1) an understanding of the English language, including an ability to read, write, and speak words in the English language, and (2) a knowledge and understanding of the fundamentals of the history, and of the principles and form of government. Starting in 1952, the requirement was informally enforced by judges and immigration examiners; in 1986, the idea for a standardized test was considered. The first Naturalization test was used until 2007 when it was replaced by a redesigned test.

The redesigned Naturalization test

The US Citizenship and Immigration Service (USCIS) stated that during the redesign process they considered multiple perspectives: the views of professors and experts in history and government, teachers of English to speakers of other languages, experts on adult learning, USCIS officers, and community-based organizations. After considering all these perspectives, USCIS concluded that the format of the revised test would be the same as the old test.

Thus, the format of the test would be as follows: (1) applicants would have three chances to read and write a sentence in English based on a vocabulary list (rather than actual sentences as in the current test); (2) sentences for reading and writing would cover US history and civics; (3) applicants' answers to questions normally asked about their application during the interview would form the English speaking test; (4) 144 new study questions on US history and government would be available; applicants would have to answer six of ten questions correctly to pass this requirement.

The redesigned Naturalization test was expected to address the concerns raised with the old test; therefore, test items were analyzed for their cognitive and linguistic characteristics to see if they met one or more of the following criteria. Does the item involve critical thinking about government or history? Does the item offer an inferred or implicit concept of government, history, or other areas? Does the item provide a geographical context for a historical or current event? Does the item help the applicant better utilize the system? Is it useful in their daily lives? Does the item help the applicant better understand and relate to our shared history?

Is the test meaningful and defensible?

However, based on the purpose, content, administration and consequences of the test, it does not and cannot serve any of the purposes of "civic nationalism" or "social integration." The reasons for this include (1) the test cannot assess English language ability and knowledge of US history and government (not in the way it is conceptualised, administered and scored), (2) the test cannot meet the standards or qualities (APA, AERA, NCME, 1999; Bachman and Palmer, 1996; Kunnan, 2008) recognized by the language assessment community as necessary properties of assessment procedures, and (3) the test cannot bring about civic nationalism or social integration (see Kunnan, 2009b, for a detailed discussion). Therefore, it can be argued that the Naturalization test is an undue burden on non-English-speaking immigrants and only creates a barrier in their application process. A better approach would be to require courses in English language and US history and government to immigrants who need such skills and knowledge.

Short case studies

Australia

Australia has a long history of using language testing to control immigration. Davies (1997) reported that during the infamous "White Australia policy," the government used a dictation test starting in the early decades of the twentieth century. The test was designed as a fifty-word paragraph dictation test in a number of European languages and administered with intent to discriminate against non-whites and undesirables. Two examples of how individuals were targeted are the cases of Egon Kisch and Mabel Freer. Jewish activist Egon Kisch from Czecho-slovakia, who was exiled from Germany for opposing Nazism, arrived in Australia in 1934. The Australian government went to extraordinary lengths to try to exclude Kisch, including using the dictation test. As he was fluent in a number of European languages he passed the dictation test in them but failed when he was tested in Scottish Gaelic. But later a court ruling found that Scottish Gaelic was not within the fair meaning of the law and overturned Kisch's convictions for being an illegal immigrant. He was allowed to remain in Australia. Similarly, in 1936, the government planned to keep out Mabel Freer, a white British woman born in India. She failed the dictation test in Italian twice but as the press and legal matters proceeded, the government was not able to provide convincing reasons for her exclusion and eventually she was admitted into the country. But examining the number of people who passed the test will provide the harshness of the policy and the use of the test: between 1902 and 1903, forty-six people passed the test out of 805; between 1904 and 1909, only six out of 554 passed; and no one was able to pass the dictation test after 1909. The test was not used after the 1930s and formally abolished in 1973 when a less restrictive immigration policy was introduced.

The government's policy in the mid-1980s was more accommodating to immigrants parti-cularly through the Adult Migrant English Program (see Brindley, 1989, for a description of the program). Also, according to McNamara (2009), in the 1980s, non-English-speaking immigrant medical doctors who were subjected to a test similar to the discriminatory dictation test were given the opportunity to demonstrate their English-language ability through the new Occupational

English Test (McNamara, 1996). This test, which replaced the older indefensible English test, assessed health professionals' English-language ability to communicate in the health workplace. However, as McNamara (2009) reported, the government recently subverted established testing practice by making unsupported changes in scoring (by changing the scorers from language professionals to medical examiners).

In terms of citizenship requirements, although the Australian Citizenship Act of 1948, Section 13, required a basic knowledge of English language of all applicants for citizenship, this law was enforced liberally. This liberal attitude has recently given way to much more restrictive citizenship policy that includes passing a formal test of knowledge of society that focuses on Australian institutions, customs, history, and values. This test came into existence in 2007 with some controversial questions such as identifying the national floral emblem and a famous Australian cricketer. After much criticism, the newer version of this test is a computer-administered twenty-item test in a multiple choice format delivered in English; applicants have to get fifteen of the items correct to satisfy this requirement. The content of the test is available through a resource book titled *Australian Citizenship: Our Common Bond* available in thirty-eight languages, although the test itself is administered in English. The topics in the resource book include topics such as Australia's democratic beliefs, laws and government, as well as the responsibilities and privileges of citizenship.

Canada

Canada, like the United States, is considered a country of immigrants as the country was sparsely populated with Inuit and other North American Indian tribes when white settlers emigrated. Vikings, French, and British explorers and later immigrants from Europe, Asia, and the Caribbean were the early inhabitants. After hostilities between the French and British ended with the English as victors, Great Britain ruled Canada until Canada received independence in 1867. It was many decades later though, in 1947, when Canadian citizenships were granted. Like the United States, Canadian citizenship is based on the *jus solis* principle, which means anyone born in Canada is automatically a Canadian citizen.

As of 2011, there was no direct language requirement for immigration but there are other requirements for citizenship applicants. It includes a test that evaluates knowledge of Canada and language abilities in English or French. The knowledge of Canada part includes topics such as the right to vote and the right to run for elected office, procedures related to elections, the rights and responsibilities of a citizen, Canadian political history, social and cultural history and symbols, and Canadian physical and political geography. The language abilities part assesses the applicant's ability to communicate in either English or French by demonstrating ability to understand simple spoken statements and questions and to communicate simple information. The questions in the citizenship test are based on the information in the study guide *Discover Canada: The Rights and Responsibilities of Citizenship*.

Estonia

Estonia, like the other Baltic States—Latvia and Lithuania—emerged from about fifty years of Soviet occupation in 1991. During the period of the occupation, according to Zabrodskaja (2009), not only did the ethnic Russian percentage in Estonia rise to 30.3% overall but in the northeast of the country, the percentage of Estonians dropped to 20% in Kohtla-Jarve and 3–4% in Narva but the Russian language dominated public administration in areas such as banking, railways, the navy and aviation. Therefore, after the restoration of independence to Estonia, the state declared Estonian the sole official language (removing Russian from this status).

Further, the Law of Citizenship first passed in 1993, then revised in 1995, required knowledge of Estonian language for citizenship. The specific requirements include listening to and reading official statements and announcements, notices of danger and warning, news, description of events and explanations; speech in terms of conversation and narration, use of questions, explanations, assumptions and commands, expressing one's opinions and wishes; and writing applications, letters of attorney, explanatory letters, curriculum vitae, filling in a questionnaire, standard forms, and responding to a test. This type of specificity indicates that the level of Estonian expected is probably at the B1 level of the Common European Framework of Reference. In addition, in order to qualify for Estonian citizenship, applicants are also expected to pass a test of knowledge of the Constitution and Citizenship Act.

Alongside the Law of Citizenship, the Alien Law passed in 1993 required non-citizens (read, mainly Russians) to register on a regular basis in order to renew their stays on a short-term basis. Thus, if Russian residents want to stay indefinitely in Estonia, they would need to apply for Estonian citizenship, which would mean learning Estonian. Zabrodskaja (2009) reported the difficulty of teaching Estonian to older Russians thus particularly between the ages of forty and fifty years.

The key question is whether this group of Russian speakers who have been living in Estonia for the last forty to fifty years will be able to continue to live in Estonia, use Estonian, and integrate into Estonian society.

Germany

The reunification of Germany in 1990 brought into focus issues regarding foreign workers and their continuing status. Guest workers from Turkey, Poland, Hungary and Vietnam, among others, had been living in both the Federal Republic of Germany and the German Democratic Republic for decades. These workers classified as foreigners constituted between 8% and 9% of the post-1990 German population. According to Stevenson and Schanze (2009), the task of bringing about integration of this group was one of the problems that confronted the new German government:

> Constructing possibilities of "belonging" in the new state would require major shifts in the political culture and fundamental questions have to be addressed: what does it mean to be German at the beginning of the 21st century? What should German citizenship entail? How can social inclusion be achieved with a highly diverse and constantly changing population?
>
> (p. 88).

These debates resulted in the Foreigners Act passed in 1997 under the watch of the Kohl government introducing tighter control of immigration. But a less conservative Schroder government passed a new Immigration Act in 2004 with new provisions. The most important provision was the introduction of a qualified version of the *jus solis* principle for citizenship: children of foreign parents born in Germany after January 1, 2000, would automatically qualify for German citizenship if one of their parents had lived in Germany legally for at least eight years. Adults too could qualify for German citizenship after eight years of residence in Germany instead of fifteen years previously, but only if they have an "adequate knowledge of the German language."

The task of improving social integration also saw the enactment of a new immigration law of 1996, then revised in 2005, which allowed the migration of ethnic Germans (*Aussiedler*) from former Soviet Union and eastern European countries provided they (and their family members) demonstrated German language ability through a language test. According to Schupbach (2009), "the language test is not a standardized test of language proficiency but a conversation that aims to establish whether the German language and culture has been part of the applicants' upbringing and family tradition" (p. 80). The language test has been criticized from at least two angles: the double function of the test, one to establish ethnicity and the other to predict integration potential; and the role of language in establishing ethnicity (despite the possibility of different dialects of the ethnic Germans).

The Netherlands

The Netherlands is generally perceived as a liberal democracy with social policies resulting in a tolerant society, but this perception would have to be modified with the recent social attitudes and public policies towards would be immigrants, immigrants, and potential citizens. Newcomers to the Netherlands now have to pass three stages of testing in order to become citizens: admission to the country, civic integration after arrival, and naturalization to citizenship. According to Extra and Spotti (2009), "the testing regimes for adult non-native speakers of Dutch and the recent abolition of languages of instruction other than Dutch in the primary schools should be evaluated against an ideological background of demanded cultural and linguistic homogenization at the national level" (p. 125).

The Law on Integration Abroad passed in 2006 described what applicants for admission to the Netherlands need to do—they basically have to take a computerized phone test of the Dutch language called the *Toets Gesproken Nederlands* (using computer-scoring technology) and a test of knowledge of Dutch politics, work, education, health care, history, and living. This type of requirement is the first in the modern world as it clearly presents barriers to family unification (particularly from women in Morocco and Turkey) and has been criticized on grounds of human rights. Extra and Spotti (2009) cite a Human Rights Watch (2008) report that considered this testing regime as discriminatory "because it explicitly applies to particular 'non-Western' countries and because it violates the qualified human right to marry and start a family" (p. 133).

The mandatory integration program for all newcomers in the country called *inburgering* requires attendance at an intake session at the local level to start the integration process, self-financing of the program and completion of the program in three and a half years. According to Extra and Spotti (2009), the new inburgering exam has two parts: language skills (Dutch language) and language in practice (the integration test). This program too has been criticized mainly for its discriminatory ways as the program exempts citizens from European Union countries, Switzerland, Canada, Australia, New Zealand, Japan, and the United States, and its burden on lower income-level residents.

Japan

As Japan is most often erroneously perceived as an ethnic and culturally homogeneous country with monolingual Japanese speakers, there is the impression that there are no demands for citizenship from foreigners and immigrants (from Brazil, Philippines, and Peru), ethnic minorities (Korean and Chinese), or indigenous people (the Ainu and Okinawan). This myth was not sustainable too long after World War II, and increasingly over the decades Japan has become a multicultural country. With several revisions of the Nationality Act that deals with matters of immigration and citizenship, the needs of oldcomers (who were Japanese subjects before 1947 and are now permanent non-national residents in Japan), and newcomers (who are immigrants who came after 1980s) have been addressed as Japan has found a way to offer civil rights, social rights and political rights to oldcomers and newcomers although differentially. Tarumoto (2003) argues that these rights, however, were not granted because of Japanese "internal multicultural logic" but because of bilateral and international pressure put on the Japanese government by the Korean government.

In terms of language and social integration requirements for naturalization, officially there is no information that speaks about a Japanese history and culture although it is expected that naturalization applicants will have a third grade level in Japanese in reading and writing and a basic conversation level. In addition, it is understood that one has to demonstrate an adequate level of assimilation to the culture. This aspect is generally checked by officials from the local prefecture.

Others

Around the world, there are significant differences in the way immigration and citizenship is controlled and the role of language in this process. Belgium, in contrast to the Netherlands, is one of a few countries that promotes linguistic diversity in its federalized state system through Dutch, French, and German languages. The United Kingdom has tightened immigration and citizenship regulations in the last decade, requiring among other requirements a test of English, Welsh, or Gaelic language ability for both long-stay residents and citizenship applicants promoting the notion of linguistic and cultural unification (although English is clearly the main language that is used). In India, citizenship is granted to applicants who demonstrate proficiency in any one of the twenty-two official languages. Japan and Korea have regulations in place for citizenship which include demonstrating Japanese and Korean language ability, respectively, ignoring long-term minority residents who have lived in the countries for decades.

Two countries that are currently considering language requirements for immigration and/or citizenship include Spain and Sweden. Whether these countries implement such a policy depends on whether conservative or liberal politicians gain control of government (see Vigers and Mar-Molinero, 2009; Milani, 2008, for discussions on this point). Israel, in contrast, restricts citizenship to Jews and privileges the use of Hebrew, although Hebrew and Arabic are both official languages of the country (Shohamy and Kanza, 2009).

In summary, language assessments have become the cornerstone of requirements for citizenship in most countries, and for immigration and long stay in a few countries. The primary premise of such policies is that language ability in the standard dialect of the dominant language of the country will bring about national and social cohesion. In the words of Blackledge (2009), writing about the testing regime in the UK (but this point can be made about any country), testing policy is "based on the notion that when we are all able to demonstrate our English language proficiency, we will be able to achieve national unity and a sense of common belonging" (p. 84).

Future directions

Empirical studies

Now that many countries have language assessments as part of the immigration or citizenship process, it would be useful to have evidence that supports the use of the assessments. As stated earlier, the primary purpose of the language requirement, as cited by politicians and legislative actions, is that language proficiency in the standard variety of the dominant language can bring about the goals of social cohesion, civic nationalism, and national unity. Although these terms are difficult to define, it is necessary to find out if these goals are being realized.

Two pilot studies set in California show that these goals are not being realized. Min (2010) studied civic nationalism (defined as a level of political and civic activity) among Korean Americans in Los Angeles before and after the taking of the citizenship tests for US citizenship. The main finding was that there was no statistically significant difference between before and after political and civic activity among these study participants: study participants who were active before taking the test continued to be that way and individuals who were inactive before taking the test continued to be that way. If this result is found in studies across potential citizenship communities in the country, then the US naturalization process is not helping towards reaching the political and civic goals.

Martinez (2010) found in her study with Latinos in the Los Angeles area that there is a significant reluctance in the community in applying for US citizenship. Statistics show that over 25% of the residents who are eligible to apply for US citizenship do not apply (US Department of Homeland Security, 2008). Martinez found that among the many reasons for this reluctance is the educational requirement (the English language and history and government tests), which seem to be a big hurdle for this group of potential citizens who are non-English-speaking adults.

One of the key issues then is whether courses in language, culture and citizenship can work to bring about civic nationalism or social integration. There is no clear empirical evidence as to how much language and how much social integration an immigrant needs in order to become a civic-minded or socially integrated citizen. The only thing that one can say about these courses is that they have been conducted for decades to satisfy public opinion and the feeling that language assessments and social integration programs are ways to do this.

Legal and ethical challenges

Legal and ethical challenges are other ways of checking governments and their policies. A legal challenge in a Dutch court in 2008 is a case in point. In this case, the court provided relief to a Moroccan woman plaintiff who challenged the admission tests in Morocco because she failed the test and thus was not admitted to the country. After an appeal by the state, a higher state court ruled in February 2010 that applicants for admission to the Netherlands will no longer face a Dutch language test and questions about knowledge of Dutch society. The court's decision now will allow immigrants from Turkey and Morocco to apply for temporary residence on the basis of family reunification, and Dutch citizens would be able to bring their spouses from outside the country without having to pass the Dutch language test and Dutch knowledge of society. Such testing was already considered to be in violation of the equality principle because citizens from European countries and others (such as Australia, Canada, Japan, New Zealand, the United States, etc.) do not need to take these tests. But the state is expected to appeal and the case may then go all the way to the Court of Justice of the European Union. Recently, Human Rights Watch had also reported that ethical and human rights violations of the testing regime in the Netherlands.

Garcia (2010) argued that the US Naturalization test can be challenged citing the 14th Amendment to the US Constitution in terms of the way the test is administered—in terms of variability among the examiners in asking the questions, the lack of an appeal process, and the lack of public information regarding pass and fail rates by nationality, native language or ethnicity. All of these she argued violate the equality and due process provisions of the Amendment.

The twenty-first century

A few remaining questions relevant to twenty-first-century citizenship and citizenship tests need to be briefly raised. The main question in an era of transnational citizenship is regarding nationality and identity—an era such as in the European Union where nationals of twenty-seven European member states with very few limits have the right to live, work, study, and invest in all of them—thus creating an unprecedented tension between nationality and supranationality and the related issue of uni- or bi-identity. Similarly, immigrants in the twenty-first century living in a receiving country may continue to be "involved" with their home countries through global investment, travel, and communications to such an extent that the acquisition of citizenship may not include full social integration in the receiving country. As a result, such immigrants may express allegiance to both countries and in many cases, they may also be doubly ambivalent of both countries in terms of their personal identity.

Second, the convergence of policies in Europe towards language ability and social integration programs (as in Belgium following the Netherlands) is probably a trans-governmental effect—like that of the pan-European Union laws—in immigration and citizenship matters. If this continues and also spreads to other groups of countries in the next decade, we will see further convergence of policies and more deep intrusions into social life of immigrants. In the words of Smith and Bakker (2008), " … Appadurai's post-nationalist expectations concerning the waning power of receiving states and societies in this age of cultural globalization" (p. 212) may be off the mark.

Finally, as more and more countries lean towards bringing about a language and social integration regime for immigrants and would-be citizens, it would be absolutely essential that governments make the substance and process transparent—in terms of the language ability level and social integration programs expected. Most would-be immigrants and would-be citizens understand that government policies could be exclusionary and discriminatory (Wright, 2008), but keeping the requirements and procedures ambiguous (as some countries do now) only continues to frustrate immigrants and would-be citizens—promoting the idea that governments introduce such requirements only to obstruct them.

Conclusion

It is obvious that the role of a country's language policy is critical in determining its language assessment policy and practice towards potential immigrants, immigrants, and potential citizens. Many countries position their language policy as public monolingual despite their own multi-lingualism and therefore require the standard variety of the dominant or official language for immi-gration or citizenship. These procedures are set in place in order to ensure civic nationalism, social cohesion and national harmony, once again fusing language proficiency, citizenship and identity. But achieving these goals is not just difficult but perhaps unrealistic in the way it is done now.

The words of Richard Bartholdt, a successful politician whose dreams to run for US Senate were thwarted by the anti-German hysteria of World War I, capture the feelings of many immi-grants and citizens all over the world who are caught in this web of language requirements. In his memoirs published in 1930 (cited in Pavlenko, 2002: 188–89), he asks

> what has mere speech, the twisting of the tongue in one way or the other, to do with the loyalty of a citizen? It is not lip service a country needs, but genuine patriotism, and the source of that is man's conscience and not his tongue. If we have true loyalty in our heart of hearts, we can express it in any other language as beautifully as in English. Why, a man can be a good and true American without even knowing English, the same as a man who is physically unable to speak at all. It is right and proper that every American citizen, male and female, should master the language of the country. Even aside from public considera-tions, this is in their own interest. But from this it is a far cry to the assertion which nowadays is so often made, at least by implication, that a man cannot become a real American, if his mother tongue is a language other than English.

Well said Richard Bartholdt, we might say! If only governments and the public were reading your words, we might be looking at a more nuanced public policy regarding language and social integration.

Further reading

Del Valle, S. (2003). *Language Rights and the Law*. Clevedon, UK: Multilingual Matters. This book is a comprehensive guide to language rights in the US. It presents a history of language rights during nation formation, the 14th Amendment to the Constitution, English literacy, naturalization and voting rights, and nativism and language restrictions at the end of the twentieth century.

Extra, G., Spotti, M. and van Avermaet, P. (eds), (2009). *Language Testing, Migration and Citizenship*. London, UK: Continuum. This collection of essays discusses cross-national developments in the area of language and integration requirements for immigration and citizenship in over twelve countries in Europe and around the world.

Hogan-Brun, G., Molinero, C. and Stevenson, P. (eds), (2009). *Discourses on language and integration: Critical perspectives on language testing regimes in Europe*. Amsterdam: The Netherlands: John Benjamins. This collection of essays introduces the reader to the ideological bases for the current language testing policies for immigration and citizenship legislation in Europe. The chapters problematize the testing regimes and reveal the hidden agenda of a monolingual, monocultura agenda in many European countries.

Shohamy, E. and McNamara, T. (eds), (2009). Language assessment for immigration and citizenship. *Language Assessment Quarterly* 6, 1 (Special Issue). This special issue features articles of a general nature and discussion of language assessment requirements in eight counties from Europe and around the world.

References

American Psychological Association (APA), American Education Research Association (AERA), National Council on Measurement in Education (NCME) (1999). *Standards for Educational and Psychological Testing*. Washington, DC: APA/AERA/NCME.

Bachman, L. and Palmer, A. (1996). *Language Testing in Practice*. Oxford, UK: Oxford University Press.

Blackledge, A. (2009). Inventing English as a complete fiction: Language testing regimes in the U.K. In G. Extra, S. Spotti and P. van Avermaet (eds), *Language Testing, Migration and Citizenship*. London, UK: Continuum, 66–86.

Bourdieu, P. (1998). *Practical Reason*. London, UK: Polity Press.

Brindley, G. (1989). *Assessing Achievement in the Learner-centered Curriculum*. Sydney, NSW: Macquarie University.

Crawford, J. (1992). *Language Loyalties*. Chicago, IL: University of Chicago Press.

Davies, A. (1997). Australian immigrant gate keeping through English language tests: How important is proficiency? In A. Huhta, V. Kohonene, L. Kurki-Suono and S. Luoma (eds), *Current Developments and Alternatives in Language Assessment*. Jyvaskyla, Finland: University of Jyvaskyla and the University of Tampere, 71–84.

del Valle, S. (2003). *Language Rights and the Law*. Clevedon, UK: Multilingual Matters.

Extra, G. and Spotti, M. (2009). Testing regimes for newcomers in the Netherlands. In G. Extra, M. Spotti and P. van Avermaet (eds), *Language Testing, Migration and Citizenship*. London, UK: Continuum, 125–47.

Extra, G., Spotti, M. and van Avermaet, P. (eds), (2009). *Language Testing, Migration and Citizenship*. London, UK: Continuum.

Garcia, J. (2010). Is the U.S. Naturalization Test in violation of the 14th Amendment of the U.S. Constitution? Paper presented at the SCALAR 13 Conference, UCLA: Los Angeles.

Hing, B. (2004). *Defining America through immigration policy*. Philadelphia, PA: Temple University Press.

Human Rights Watch (2008). *The Netherlands: Discrimination in the name of integration*. www.hrw.org/backgrounder/2008/netherlands0508 (accessed 25/7/10).

Huntington, S. (2005). *Who are We? America's Great Debate*. New York, NY: Free Press.

Kennedy, J. F. (1964). *A Nation of Immigrants*. New York, NY: Harper.

Kloss, H. (1977). *The American Bilingual Tradition*. Rowley, MA: Newbury House.

Kunnan, A. J. (2008). Towards a model of test evaluation: Using the Test Fairness and Wider Context frameworks. In L. Taylor and C. Weir (eds), *Multilingualism and Assessment: achieving transparency, assuring quality, sustaining diversity*. Papers from the ALTE Conference, Berlin, (pp. 229–51). Cambridge, UK: Cambridge University Press.

—— (2009a). Politics and legislation in immigration and citizenship testing: The U.S. case. *Annual Review of Applied Linguistics* 29: 37–48.

—— (2009b). The U.S. naturalization test. *Language Assessment Quarterly* 89–97.

Kymlicka, W. (1995). *Multicultural citizenship: a liberal theory of minority rights*. Oxford, UK: Clarendon Press.

McNamara, T. (1996). *Measuring Second Language Performance*. London, UK: Longman.

—— (2009). The spectre of the dictation test: language testing for immigration and citizenship in Australia. In G. Extra, S. Spotti and P. van Avermaet, (eds), *Language Testing, Migration and Citizenship*. London, UK: Continuum, 224–41.

Martinez, J. (2010). Why are eligible Latinos not becoming U.S. citizens? Seminar paper, TESL 567b, California State University, Los Angeles.

May, S. (2005). Language rights: moving the debate forward. *Journal of Sociolinguistics* 9: 319–47.

—— (2008). Language education, pluralism and citizenship. In S. May and N. Hornberger (eds), *Encyclopedia of Language and Education*, 2nd edn. Vol. 1. *Language policy and political issues in education*. Amsterdam, The Netherlands: Springer Science, pp. 15–29.

Milani, T. (2008). Language testing and citizenship: a language ideological debate in Sweden. *Language in Society* 37: 27–59.

Min, K. (2010). Is the U.S. Naturalization Test meaningful in achieving its purposes of 'civic nationalism,' 'social integration,' and 'political allegiance' with citizens of Korean origin? Seminar paper, TESL 567b, California State University, Los Angeles.

Pavlenko, A. (2002). We have room for but one language here: language and national identity in the US at the turn of the 20th century. *Multilingua* 21: 163–96.

Pickus, N. (2005). *True Faith and Allegiance: immigration and American civic nationalism*. Princeton, NJ: Princeton, University Press.

Pogge, T. (2003). Accommodation rights for Hispanics. In W. Kymlicka and A. Patten (eds), *Language rights and political theory*. Oxford, UK: Oxford University Press, 105–22.

Ricento, T. and Wright, W. (2008). Language policy and education in the United States. In S. May and N. H. Hornberger (eds), *Encyclopedia of Language and Education*, 2nd edn. Volume 1: *Language Policy and Political Issues in Education*. Amsterdam, The Netherlands: Springer, 285–300.

Schlesinger, A. (1992). *The Disuniting if America: reflections on a multicultural society*. New York, NY: W.W. Norton.

Schupbach, D. (2009). Testing language, testing ethnicity? Policies and practices surrounding the ethnic German Aussiedler. *Language Assessment Quarterly* 6: 78–82.

Shohamy, E. and Kanza, T. (2009). Language and citizenship in Israel. *Language Assessment Quarterly* 6: 83–88.

Smith, M. and Bakker, M. (2008). *Citizenship Across Borders*. Ithaca, NY: Cornell University Press.

Stevenson, P. and Schanze, L. (2009). Language, migration and citizenship in Germany: Discourses on integration and belonging. In G. Extra, S. Spotti, and P. van Avermaet (eds), *Language Testing, Migration and Citizenship*. London, UK: Continuum, 87–106.

Tarumoto, H. (2003). Multiculturalism in Japan: citizenship policy for immigrants. *International Journal on Multicultural Societies* 5: 88–103.

van Avermaet, P. and Gysen, S. (2009). One nation, two policies: Language requirements for citizenship and integration in Belgium. In G. Extra, S. Spotti, and P. van Avermaet (eds), *Language Testing, Migration and Citizenship*. London, UK: Continuum, 107–24.

Vigers, D. and Mar-Molinero, C. (2009). Spanish language ideologies in managing immigration and citizenship. In G. Extra, S. Spotti, and P. van Avermaet (eds), *Language Testing, Migration and Citizenship*. London, UK: Continuum, 167–88.

US Department of Homeland Security (2008). *2007 Yearbook of Immigration Statistics*. Washington, DC: Author.

Washington, G. (1783). Letter to the members of the Volunteer Association and other Inhabitants of the Kingdom of Ireland who have lately arrived in the City of New York, December 2. In Fitzpatrick (ed.), *The Writings of George Washington*, (1931–44), Vol. 27, p. 254.

Wright, S. (ed.), (2008). Citizenship tests in a post-national era-Editorial. *International Journal on Multicultural Societies* 10: 1–9.

Zabrodskaja, A. (2009). Language testing in the context of citizenship and asylum: the case of Estonia. *Language Assessment Quarterly* 6: 61–70.

12

Social dimensions of language testing

Richard F. Young

Toward the end of the academic year, a man with a clipboard turned up at one of the capital city's best high schools. He sauntered from classroom to classroom, ignoring the students and instead engaged in seemingly trivial chitchat with the teachers, twenty minutes at a time.

Tell me, what subjects are your specialties? How long have you worked here? Can you explain to me a little about how you prepare your lessons? The inspector didn't seem to be particularly interested in what the teachers said. He only cared about how they said it.

Olga Muravyova teaches biology and geography. She laughed nervously as she recalled her meeting with the inspector. 'He wrote a report saying that I understood all the questions, that I answered all the questions, but that I made some errors. That is actually what he claimed,' Ms. Muravyova said. 'Of course that is hard to hear.'

After the inspector told her that she had failed the test, he told her to attend Estonian classes, which she has tried to do. But she is 57, an age when it is not easy to pick up a new language.

This vignette, based on a story in the *New York Times* (Levy, 2010), describes part of a test of spoken Estonian required since 2008 of teachers and other civil servants. In this small former Soviet republic on the Baltic Sea, the government has been mounting a determined campaign to elevate the status of its native language and to marginalize Russian, the tongue of its former colonizer. Public schools, where students have long been taught in Russian, are now linguistic battlegrounds and the test itself is a skirmish between Estonian and Russian. The test and Ms. Muravyova's experience illustrate two social dimensions of language testing: The first is the construct of language knowledge on which the test is built and on which test results are interpreted; the second is what happens to individuals, societies, and institutions when the test is used—the social consequences of assessment. In this chapter, I describe both of these dimensions and argue that, until quite recently, language tests have been built on incomplete knowledge of the social ground of language in interaction and the social consequences of language assessment.

The social life of language

Language testing is a branch of applied linguistics and applied linguistics grew out of earlier work by linguists. Linguists trace the history of their field to ancient India and usually to Pāṇini, who flourished in the fourth century BCE. One of Pāṇini's main concerns was the correct pronunciation of the body of oral chants of ancient poems known as the *Veda* composed in an early form of Sanskrit that was already archaic by the fourth century. About a thousand years earlier in Shang Dynasty China, we have the earliest written records of a language that today we call Chinese. Ancient Chinese writing was found inscribed on animal bones and turtle shells used for divination. In those days when a ruler wanted advice, he would ask the spirits of his ancestors and other supernatural beings a question, which was written by court officials on an oracle bone or turtle shell. This was then heated, and court officials interpreted the pattern of cracks in the bone as an answer to the question.

In these two ancient examples, interpreting language written on bones and correcting the pronunciation of sacred oral chants was done by people whom today we would call linguists. Linguists today do much the same thing; that is, they take a record in some form and consider (and oftentimes correct) its oral form just like Pāṇini in ancient India, or they interpret the meaning of a written record that has been responded to in some way just like the court officials in Shang Dynasty China. Throughout the long history of their field, linguists have been bound by the physical form of the records that they consider data. When a society transitions from one physical form of language to another—from an oral culture to restricted forms of literacy, for instance—people often complain that the written record does not do justice to the hurly-burly of oral social interaction. In the oral culture of Anglo-Saxon England, when only a select few could read or write, there were many metaphors contrasting the written record with the spoken word. Written words were called 'mouthless speakers', 'dead lifegivers', and 'dumb knowledge-bearers'. To the Anglo-Saxons, the written record of interaction was dead, dumb, and limited—a thing. In contrast, spoken interaction itself is not a thing but a live discursive practice, which the technology of writing took and alienated from the world in which it was originally created. As the Anglo-Saxon scholar O'Brien O'Keeffe (1990: 54) wrote, 'The technology which preserves also kills'.

Today we can go beyond the remembrances of speech and written records that constrained ancient linguists and offended ancient readers. In the twenty-first century, we have still pictures, sound recordings, and movies and, thanks to these new records, our understanding of the forms and functions of language in human interaction—the social life of language—extends far beyond what we know about the forms that language takes in speech and writing. To revivify language, to put language back in its social context, a theory is needed which goes beyond records of disembodied and decontextualized records. The response is Practice Theory, developed by anthropologists (Bourdieu, 1977, 1990; Sahlins, 1981, 1985), sociologists (de Certeau, 1984; Giddens, 1984), and applied linguists (Erickson, 2004; Young, 2009), whose aim was to explicate the nature of social interaction in context. Practice Theorists study discursive practices like language tests; this involves understanding not only the production of meanings by participants as they employ the communicative resources at their command, but also how employment of such resources reflects and creates the processes and meanings of the community in which the test occurs. As Erickson (2004) wrote, although the conduct of talk in local social interaction is unique and crafted by local social actors for the specific situation of its use at the moment of its uttering, it is at the same time profoundly influenced by processes that occur beyond the temporal and spatial horizon of the immediate occasion of interaction. The goal of Practice Theory is to describe both the global context of action and the communicative resources that participants employ in local action. When the context of a practice is known and the configuration of communicative resources is described, the ultimate aim of Practice Theory is to explain the ways in which the global context and the local employment of resources are mutually constituted. Features of global context are described later in this chapter, but how does the global context influence the nature of the test? In other words, how does the global context impact social constructs in language tests?

Social constructs in language tests

The format of Ms. Muravyova's Estonian test could be called a conversation, one in which one party asks the questions and the other party responds. The aim of the test is to evaluate one party's knowledge of language. But what is knowledge of language? When language testers and score users interpret people's scores on a test, they do so by implicit or explicit reference to the construct on which the test is based. Almost all the constructs that underlie high-stakes language tests are theories of individual cognition that can be measured in one context (the test) and are stable enough to be ported to other non-testing contexts where the language is used.

This view of the independence of linguistic knowledge from context underlies the history of linguistics as far back as ancient India and China. In the early twentieth century Saussure (1983) stated the distinction between internal linguistics and external linguistics, which was recently summarized by Lantolf (2006: 74). Lantolf wrote, 'In essence Saussure drew a circle around language (Agar 1994: 41) and proposed that inside-the-circle language, the proper and exclusive domain of linguistic science, was restricted to the study of grammar and dictionary.' If the construct of cognitive ability underlying a language test involves linguistic knowledge that is independent of context—internalized language or I-language in Chomsky's (1986) formulation— then the testing context in which it is elicited is only important to the extent that it helps draw out underlying cognitive abilities (Chalhoub-Deville 2003: 371). According to this construct, the knowledge of Estonian grammar and vocabulary that Ms. Muravyova demonstrated in her conversation with the inspector is independent of the manner in which it was elicited, and her ability and knowledge can be generalized to another context in which she might be called upon again to speak Estonian.

By its emphasis on the mutual constitution of local resources and global context in interaction, Practice Theory provides a very different interpretation of the construct of language knowledge, an interpretation that is best approached by considering how communicative resources are employed in different contexts. In place of knowledge and ability, in Practice Theory the per-formance of a person-in-context is construed as a configuration of communicative *resources*— resources that a person employs together with others in a particular configuration. Assessment of a person-in-context is challenging, however, because from a person's performance on a test, not only do we wish to infer specific resources employed in the discursive practice of the test, but we also wish to know how the same person will perform in other practices. The challenge was eloquently expressed by Chalhoub-Deville and Deville (2005: 826):

> Evaluating test-takers' performance according to this model offers a conundrum. Generally speaking, we administer tests to, assign scores to, and make decisions about individuals for purposes such as selection, placement, assignment of grades/marks, and the like. If we view lan-guage as co-constructed, how can we disentangle an individual's contribution to a communicative exchange in order to provide a score or assess a candidate's merit for a potential position?

The conundrum can be solved by considering the relationship between test performance and the construct underlying a test proposed by Messick (1989, 1996) and revisited by Chapelle (1998) and Norris (2008). Chapelle distinguished between three perspectives on construct definition: a construct may be defined as a *trait*, as *behavior*, or as *some combination of trait and behavior*. In a trait definition of a construct, consistent performance of a person on a test is related in a principled way to the person's knowledge and speech production processes. That is to say, a person's consistent performance on a test is taken to index a fairly stable configuration of knowledge and skills that the person carries around with them—and which that person can apply in all contexts. In contrast, in the definition of a construct as behavior, the consistent performance of a person on a test is related in a principled way to the context in which behavior is observed. That is to say, test performance is assumed to say something about a person's performance on a specific task or in a specific context, but *not* on other tasks or in other contexts— unless they can be shown to be related to the task or context that was tested.

Clearly, neither definition of a construct as trait or behavior is satisfactory for theories of language in use because, as Bachman (1990: 84) emphasized, communicative language ability consists of both knowledge and 'the capacity for implementing, or executing that competence' in different contexts of use. For this reason, it is desirable to consider the third of Messick's and Chapelle's definitions of a construct, which they refer to as the *interactionalist definition*. In an interactionalist validation of a test, a person's performance on a test is taken to indicate an underlying trait characteristic of that person and, at the same time, the performance is also taken to indicate the influence of the context in which the performance occurs. The interactionalist definition is, in other words, a way to have your cake and eat it: to infer from test performance something about both practice-specific behavior and a practice-independent, person-specific trait.

If an interactionalist definition is to allow test users to generalize from performance in one context to another—that is, from the discursive practice of a test to other practices—then what is needed is a theory that relates one discursive practice to another in a principled way. We need to know whether testees like Ms. Muravyova have the skill to mindfully and efficiently recognize contexts in which resources are employed and to use them when participating in different practices. If the purpose of her conversation with the inspector is to discover whether Ms. Muravyova is able to use Estonian when teaching, we really need to know whether the communicative resources that she displayed in her conversation are portable to another discursive practice: teaching high school biology and geography, practices which she currently does in Russian. Although the contexts of use are very different, it is an empirical question whether the same resources are required in the same configuration in the two contexts. To answer such an empirical question, McNamara (1997: 457) argued that what is needed is 'a close analysis of naturally occurring discourse and social interaction [to] reveal the standards that apply in reality in particular settings'. Such an analysis of discourse and social interaction is one objective of Practice Theory.

Language testing as discursive practice

An analysis of social constructs in discursive practice is characterized by three features (Young 2011). First, analysis of language in social interaction is concerned with communicative resources employed by persons in specific discursive practices rather than language ability independent of context. Second, it is characterized by attention to the co-construction of a discursive practice by *all* participants involved rather than a narrow focus on a single individual. Mehan (1982: 65) stressed the interactional nature of discursive practice when he wrote, '"Competence" becomes interactional in two senses of the term. One it is the competence necessary for effective interaction. Two, it is the competence that is available in the interaction between people.' Mehan's focus on interaction was taken up later by Kramsch (1986: 367), who wrote:

> Whether it is a face-to-face interaction between two or several speakers, or the interaction between a reader and a written text, successful interaction presupposes not only a shared knowledge of the world, the reference to a common external context of communication, but also the construction of a shared internal context or 'sphere of inter-subjectivity' that is built through the collaborative efforts of the interactional partners.

Intersubjectivity is the conscious attribution of intentional acts to others and involves putting oneself in the shoes of an interlocutor. Originating in the phenomenology of Husserl (Beyer 2007), intersubjectivity was first inferred empirically from studies of infant development by Trevarthen (1977, 1979). Examples include an infant's following the direction of an adult's direction of gaze when she points and recognition by an infant of transition-relevance moments in interaction with others.

Third, analysis of social interaction identifies a set of verbal, interactional, and nonverbal resources that participants employ in specific ways in order to co-construct a discursive practice. The resources employed by participants in social interaction are not the mouthless, dead, and dumb records that the Anglo-Saxons complained about. Communicative resources, like language, are embodied and include a participant's whole body, the physical presence and movement of the body, the muscles of the face, arms, and upper body—in particular gaze and gesture—and yes, of course, a participant's speech and writing.

When the communicative resources employed by all participants in a testing practice are specified, the problem of generalizability is resolved by identifying the particular configuration of resources that participants employ in a particular practice. Then, by comparing the configuration of resources in that practice with others, it is possible to discover what resources are local to that practice and to what extent those same resources are employed in different practices and how common resources are configured.

Definitions of verbal, interactional, and non-verbal resources and examples of how participants configure resources in various interactive practices were provided in Young (2008, 2009, 2011) and are revisited here. *Verbal resources* include the register of the practice, defined as a recognizable repertoire of pronunciation and lexicogrammar that occurs with high frequency in certain practices, the combination of which is associated with a specific activity, place, participants, or purpose. In addition, verbal resources that participants employ create certain kinds of meaning in a practice. In Systemic Functional Grammar, Halliday (1994) identified verbal resources as instantiating *ideational*, *interpersonal*, and *textual* metafunctions. The ideational metafunction is how language mediates participants' construction of their experiences of the external physical and biological world, their own internal thoughts and feelings, and the logical relations among them. The interpersonal metafunction, as its name implies, is how language mediates speakers' and writers' personal and social relationships with other participants such as their interlocutors and readers. The textual metafunction is how participants build sequences of discourse, organize the discursive flow, and create cohesion and continuity within a linear and time-dependent flow. In every communicative exchange, participants employ all three metafunctions, although they may be configured in different ways in different practices. As Schleppegrell (2004) showed for the language of schooling, these three metafunctions are realized by various aspects of linguistic substance, and their configuration defines communicative registers and genres.

Interactional and non-verbal resources that participants use to construct a discursive practice include the selection and sequential organization of actions, the turn-taking system that participants use to manage transitions from one speaker to another and the ways in which participants repair interactional trouble. Sequences of actions realized in speech or nonverbally have been investigated most rigorously within the framework of Conversation Analysis developed in the 1960s. Conversation analysts have observed that certain acts occur in ordered pairs and that the production of the first act of a pair gives rise to participants' expectations of the production of the corresponding second act of the pair in an adjacent turn by a different speaker. Schegloff and Sacks (1973) showed how this expectation works with question-and-answer in American English, but it applies equally to other sequences of two adjacent utterances produced by different speakers, including greeting–greeting, offer–acceptance/refusal, and call–response. Act sequences longer than adjacency pairs are not generally recognized by conversation analysts, but the study of discursive practices of the same type does in fact show that more than two actions occur quite regularly and that they usually occur in a sequence.

The system of turn taking in conversation was first described in detail by Sacks *et al.* (1974), who answered two basic questions about turn taking: How is the next speaker selected? And how do participants know when to end one turn and when to begin another? The question of next speaker selection was answered by Sacks *et al.* by means of the following algorithm.

1. If the current speaker selects the next speaker, then that party has the right and obligation to speak.
2. If no next speaker is selected, then self-selection may (but need not) occur. The first starter acquires rights to the turn.
3. If no next speaker is selected, then current speaker may (but need not) continue.

Sacks *et al.* answered the second question about transitions between turns by invoking the notion of the turn-constructional unit or TCU. Such a unit may be a unit of the lexicogrammar, of intonation, or a pragmatic unit (a complete idea) and, as Ford and Thompson (1996) pointed out, these units often coincide to make a complex TCU. In any given conversation, the moment at which a transition between speakers occurs is not necessarily at the boundary of a TCU, but speakers are able to predict when a boundary is forthcoming and are therefore able to project the completion of the TCU. Transitions between speakers occur at places when participants project the completion of the TCU, projecting not only the form of the next word but also the completion of larger lexicogrammatical, intonational, and pragmatic units. Prediction is thus an important part of what recipients do when listening to talk in progress and the place in an ongoing turn when participants are able to project the completion of the TCU is called a transition-relevance place or TRP. That is to say, participants do not necessarily take a turn *at* a TRP but, if they do, then they are more likely to do so at a TRP than elsewhere.

Repair is the treatment of trouble in talk-in-interaction. Trouble can be anything in talk to which participants in interaction orient as problematic. One participant may use a word that is misunderstood or misheard by another participant; one participant may realize that a phrase that they have just used is less preferable than another phrase. Although the source of trouble is often a word or phrase, it may be anything to which participants orient as repairable. Thus, the absence of the second pair part of an adjacency pair may elicit an apology or, when a listener projects a TCU and takes a turn while the current speaker wishes to continue, this may be oriented to as an interruption. In many cases, however, the source of trouble in a repair is a choice of words or phrasing and, in understanding repair, conversation analysts have focused on two questions about the participants in the repair: In whose turn did the trouble occur? And who initiated the repair sequence? Beyond the participants, the analysis focuses on the sequence of actions in the repair. For example, a repair is called an *other-initiated self repair* if the repair is initiated by a different participant from the one in whose turn the trouble source occurred, and the repair is completed by the same participant in whose turn the trouble source occurred. Excerpt 1 is an example of an other-initiated self-repair in Estonian between a government official and a client who needs information.

Excerpt 1

Pardon? (Gerassimenko, Hennoste, Koit and Rääbis 2004)

   1 Client: aga kallis see tööluba on. (0.5)
                    How much does this work permit cost?

2   official: Kuidas
                Pardon?
3   Client: kallis tööluba on.
                How much does the work permit cost?
4   official: ei, tö- tööluba ei ole vaja.
                No work permit is needed.

In Excerpt 1, Client's question in line 1 is indexed as a source of trouble by the following 0.5-second pause and by Official's repair initiation in line 2. Client concludes the repair by repeating the question in line 3. Client is the other who initiated the repair that is completed by Official (the self). Three other kinds of repair are classified in a similar way according to the participant who initiates the repair and the participant who completes the repair as *other-initiated other repair*, *self-initiated self repair* and *self-initiated other repair*.

In addition to these, one further resource identified by Levinson (1992) is the way in which participants construct boundaries of a practice. In order for participants to establish mutual orientation to how what they say is creating a context in which the meaning of what they say can be interpreted (what Gumperz 1982, 1992, 1995, called *contextualization cues* in a discursive practice), participants must distinguish it from other practices in which contextualization cues are functioning differently. This is done by means of locating the boundaries of the practice—the opening and closing verbal or non-verbal actions in the sequence of a practice. Not all practices begin and end abruptly and, in fact, boundaries of a practice may be vague, may be negotiated, or may be resisted by one or more participants; nonetheless, boundaries are essential for participants to establish mutual orientation to meaning.

In summary, then, we can describe a discursive practice by specifying the ways in which participants avail themselves of the verbal resources of register and modes of meaning together with the interactional and non-verbal resources of action selection and sequencing, turn taking, repair, and boundary construction. Taken together, these six resources are the fundamental building blocks of intersubjectivity in conversational interaction and the means by which participants craft their local identities as social actors in oral and literate practices. In order to describe local construction of identity, Goffman (1979, 1981) developed the concepts of *participation framework* and *footing*. For Goffman, the identity of a participant in interaction can be animator, author, or principal: animator is an individual engaged in the role of utterance production; author has selected the sentiments being expressed and the words in which they are encoded; and principal's position is established by the words being spoken, whose beliefs have been told and who is committed to what the words say. Three important corollaries of Goffman's theory are: (a) not all participants are neces- sarily physically present in the interaction—as McNamara (1997: 459) wrote, there are others 'whose behavior and interpretation shape the perceived significance of the candidate's efforts but are themselves removed from focus'; (b) an individual's identity may change from moment to moment throughout the interaction—recognized by Goffman as changes of footing and much expanded by Bucholtz and Hall (2004) as tactics of intersubjectivity; and (c) the participation structure of the practice is the configuration of the identities of all participants, present or not, official or unofficial, ratified or unratified and their footing in the practice.

If we follow McNamara's call for a close analysis of naturally occurring discourse in order to compare it with the discourse of a testing practice, we will see to what extent the communicative resources employed and their configurations are similar or different. Such a comparison was carried out by Young and He (1998) in their collection of studies analyzing the spoken discourse of lan- guage proficiency interviews. The studies collected by Young and He addressed a simple com- parative question: Is a language proficiency interview an instance of natural conversation? Most studies answered the question in the negative, pointing out that the system of turn-taking and goal orientation of language proficiency interviews reflects the institutional context in which they are embedded, while in ordinary conversation, topics and turns are neither prescribed nor proscribed by a specific speech activity and none of the participants has a predefined role in managing the conversation. Such a comparison may be extended to compare the test of spoken Estonian that Ms. Muravyova took and the discourse of classroom interaction in an Estonian high school. A corpus analysis will identify the features of Estonian vocabulary, grammatical structures, and pronunciations that occur with frequency in both practices. A systemic functional analysis will identify how participants in the test conversation and the classroom make ideational, inter-personal, and textual meanings, and which participants make which meanings. A conversation analysis of both practices will reveal how participants select and sequence social actions, how they manage the turn-taking system including transitions from one speaker to another and the ways in which participants repair interactional trouble. A similar analysis will describe how participants orient to boundaries and transitions in the classroom and in the oral test.

An examination of these social constructs in tests and in the classroom also reveals how the physically present participants—Ms. Muravyova, her students, and the inspector—construct their identities in interaction, in particular how they co-construct relative power. Power is not only the institutional control of people by a powerful group, nor is it just a mode of thought control, nor does knowledge imply liberation. For Foucault (1978; Foucault and Gordon, 1980), power is exercised in every social interaction and its insidiousness lies in its very ordinariness. At his most explicit, Foucault wrote, 'Power is everywhere; not because it embraces everything, but because it comes from everywhere' (1978: 93). In discourse, power often involves controlling and constraining the contributions of non-powerful participants and the system of allocation of turns in conversation is a particularly effective means of doing so. However, powerful partici-pants are not alone in the exercise of power. Power in discourse is co-constructed by all parti-cipants—both the powerful and the non-powerful. For instance, the use of a technical register by one participant constructs power if other participants do not challenge that power by expressing their lack of comprehension. Another example is in Ms. Muravyova's language proficiency interview. She understood and answered all the questions; in other words, the inspector controlled talk by means of allocating the next turn to her, thus constraining her right to speak. Non-powerful participants co-construct power by accepting the constraints imposed upon them. The student who doesn't understand a word may decide to search for the meaning in a dictionary or to ask somebody to explain it; and testees in a language proficiency interview may simply accept the fact that their discursive contributions will be limited.

But the deployment of communicative resources by persons in local interaction does not create these results alone. Power is also created by the system—organized social situations and political institutions that create enduring identities for individuals as testers and testees, as teachers and students, as officials and clients, and expectations for their roles in society. As I argue in the following section, language—more specifically, language testing—is the construction and reflection of these social expectations through actions that invoke identity, ideology, belief, and power.

The social consequences of language tests

After reviewing a variety of nationally mandated tests of language proficiency, McNamara and Roever (2006) concluded that through language tests, political goals affect language learning and the lives of testees at every level. Such influences of the global on the local are to be expected in Practice Theory, the ultimate aim of which is to explain the ways in which the global context and the local employment of resources are mutually constituted.

Mutual constitution means that the actions of a local practice are influenced by the global context *and* the global context is influenced by local actions. In Ms. Muravyova's experience, the influence of the global context is painfully clear: The government of Estonia required her to take Estonian language lessons. It was the government that mandated that she be tested, it was the government that established a National Examinations and Qualifications Centre to administer the tests, it was this body that designed the Estonian language proficiency examinations, it was by this body that the language inspector was trained and paid, and it was this inspector who examined Ms. Muravyova. There is a long political trail before their twenty-minute conversation, and their actions have a long history, a history that goes back long before the 1995 Estonian Law on Citizenship that decreed the test. Modern Estonian is a descendant of one or possibly two of the original Baltic–Finnic dialects. As long ago as the first century CE, the Roman historian Tacitus mentioned a language he called *aestii* (the Estonians' name for their language is *eesti*), but the language has had a long and difficult history with strong early influences from German and Finnish and, in the twentieth century, from Russian. When Estonia was invaded and occupied by the Soviet Union in World War II, the status of the Estonian language changed to the first of two official languages (Russian being the other one). In the second half of the 1970s, the pressure of bilingualism intensified, resulting in widespread knowledge of Russian throughout the country. The Russian language was termed the language of friendship of nations and was taught to Estonian children as early as kindergarten. Although teaching Estonian to non-Estonians in schools was compulsory, in practice, learning the language was often considered unnecessary. The collapse of the Soviet Union led to the restoration of the Republic of Estonia's independence in 1991, and Estonian went back to being the only official language in Estonia.

Given the recent history of Estonia, the government's desire to strengthen and disseminate the Estonian language by requiring teachers and other civil servants to be proficient in it is understandable but it is clearly an example of political goals affecting language testing. In other societies, too, political goals of ruling elites have had significant influence on examinations. Miyazaki (1976) described the long history of the imperial Chinese examination system, which allowed people from all walks of life to enter the prestigious and powerful imperial civil service. At the time it was instituted over fourteen hundred years ago, the system was designed to weaken the power of the hereditary aristocracy at court by requiring aristocrats and commoners to compete on equal terms for positions in imperial service. From a twenty-first-century perspective, the system may appear equitable but it was not designed to be so, for the amount of preparation time required for candidates to study the classical texts on which examinations were based required a degree of economic support simply not available to poor people. Fulcher (2004, 2009) provided many other examples, in societies both ancient and modern, of attempts by political elites to gain control over the education system through testing and to establish norms. Tests are powerful means of political control and tests are effective largely because, as Foucault (1995: 184) wrote, they are a generally accepted 'normalizing gaze, a surveillance that makes it possible to qualify, to classify and to punish. It establishes over individuals a visibility through which one differentiates them and judges them'.

The normalizing gaze of tests affects the lives of individuals like Ms. Muravyova and at the same time it has been effective in changing the status of languages in multilingual societies and, consequently, the power and prestige of their speakers. Shohamy (2006: 95–98) listed three ways in which language policy objectives are achieved by language tests. Tests are instrumental in (1) determining the prestige and status of languages (and thus maintaining the power of speakers of prestigious language varieties); (2) standardizing and perpetuating language correctness (and thus maintaining the subordinate status of speakers of non-standard varieties); and (3) suppressing language diversity (in favor of speakers of the prestigious standard variety).

Language tests preserve the prestige of the national language

In societies that Fulcher (2009) termed collectivist, the identity and value of individuals is equated with their membership in a collective unit such as a state, a nation, or an institution. One way in which membership is maintained is through use of a common language, and it follows that it is in the interest of the collective that a common language be preserved. Just as when the Estonian Soviet Socialist Republic formed part of the Soviet Union, it was in the interest of the collective to uphold Russian as the national language, in the independent Republic of Estonia today, it is in the interest of the collective to develop Estonian as the national language. Such a collectivist dynamic is in tension with a different political philosophy, termed individualism by Fulcher, which was described by Locke (1690: ¶95) as radically different: 'Men being … by nature all free, equal, and independent, no one can be put out of this estate, and subjected to the political power of another, without his own consent.' Tensions between collectivism and individualism abound in the plurilingual, multicultural, highly mobile societies of the early twenty-first century. According to Shohamy (2006), a collectivist ideology drives the requirement in American public schools for students to be tested in English in order to graduate and to be tested, again in English, for admission to higher education. Taking an individualist stance, Canagarajah (2009) argued that in India, communities had developed local varieties of English to the extent that the language had now become 'Plurilingual English' and these varieties were the ones most appropriate for local schooling and testing.

Language tests help maintain standards

In language tests, norms of lexicogrammar and style are enforced by the evaluation of a response to a norm as either correct or incorrect. In the case of languages such as English, which are used in and among many different communities around the world, there are many varieties, both regional and international and both nativized and non-nativized. The role of language tests has generally been to maintain the international standard variety at the expense of regional standards or nativized varieties. As Lowenberg (1993) demonstrated in discussing the Test of English for International Communication (TOEIC), a widely used test of Standard English for international communication developed by the US-based Educational Testing Service, lexicogrammatical or stylistic variants prevalent in regional varieties of English are considered errors on TOEIC. Examples of TOEIC "errors," which Lowenberg argued are acceptable to educated speakers of non-native varieties of English, are the following italicized elements taken from TOEIC tests:

> His proposal met with a lot of *resistances*.
> Chemicals in the home *they* should be stored out of the reach of children.
> We *discussed about* the problem until a solution was found,
>
> *(Lowenberg, 1993: 102)*

The collectivist norms used to evaluate test performance on TOEIC are those of the group that uses standard American, British, or Australian English, no matter whether different groups adopt different norms. The normative gaze of the collective is internalized by speakers of non-dominant varieties of the standard language as a subject position that requires them to accept personal responsibility for the communication problems that they encounter. In prescriptive grammars of English, examples abound of non-standard English "errors" such as *irregardless*, *you could of got one*, and *I could care less*. Those are all "errors" that were supposedly committed by native speakers of English, but the problematic status of the norms of Standard English becomes, *like, ginormous* in plurilingual contexts or when English functions as a lingua franca, as Seidlhofer, Breiteneder, and Pitzl (2006) have described.

Language tests suppress diversity

Perhaps most problematic for language assessment in multicultural settings are differences in discourse pragmatic norms between a socially dominant group and less dominant groups. Such differences are most often found in the contexts in which directness and volubility are evaluated positively and those in which the same degree of directness and volubility are evaluated negatively. Second language pragmatics is often assessed by discourse completion items such as Excerpt 2, in which verbal action is required.

> Excerpt 2
> Apology (Röver 2005: 130)
>
> > Ella borrowed a recent copy of *Time* magazine from her friend Sean but she accidentally spilled a cup of coffee all over it. She is returning the magazine to Sean.
> > Ella: _____
> > Sean: "No, don't worry about replacing it, I read it already."

The pragmatic ideology that Excerpt 2 promotes is that Ella should say something related to her action and she should promise to replace the damaged magazine because of the rejoinder from Sean. In other words, the response of the party who has damaged the possession of another is entirely satisfied *verbally*. No action is required except verbal action, and yet there are occasions when a physical action may be more appropriate and more welcomed by the injured party than any words, although such a test item promotes the pragmatic ideology that verbal action is sufficient.

A critical analysis of language testing practices thus brings to the forefront the social dimension of language testing including speaker subject positions, lexicogrammatical norms, transcultural pragmatic conventions, and many other aspects of societal ideology. Practice Theory proposes that the practices of language testing occur in contexts that are much broader than the testing practice itself, including not only the designers and takers of a particular test, but also the purposes for which the test is designed, the purposes for which people take the test and the ends to which the results of the test are put. McNamara and Roever (2006) have stressed the importance of these broader political questions because, they argue, the requirement to distinguish between *them* and *us* has increased in intercultural societies and in a world of cross-border migration. Distinguishing between them and us is famously recorded in tests such as the password used by American defenders of the Bataan Peninsula against the Japanese in World War II. Stimpson (1946: 51) recounted an Associated Press dispatch from the Bataan front. The Americans discovered an infallible way to distinguish friendly troops from Japanese who attempted to pass the sentries at night dressed in American or Filipino uniforms:

> They simply pick a password with numerous *l*'s, such as *lollapalooza*. Sentries challenge approaching figures and if the first two syllables of *lollapalooza*, for instance, should come back as *rorra*, they open fire without waiting to hear the remainder.

Many more recent and less fatal ways of distinguishing friend from foe are recorded in the language assessment of immigrants, asylum seekers, and those who wish to become citizens. The political context of language testing is just as pertinent in widespread language testing enterprises resulting from the No Child Left Behind (NCLB) Act of 2001 in the United States and the *Common European Framework of Reference for Languages: Learning, Teaching, Assessment* (CEFR) (Council of Europe 2001). Both of these frameworks are designed to achieve collectivist policy goals and do so, as Foucault (1995: 184) predicted, by combining 'the ceremony of power …, the deployment of force and the establishment of truth.'

In the case of NCLB, the policy was designed to improve education for all by allowing communities to distinguish between schools where students do well on tests from schools where students perform poorly, and to direct financial resources to those schools with good testing results and, over the long term, to sanction those with consistently poor results. In the early years of the twenty-first century, NCLB came to be seen as the poster child for assessment-based intervention in language education by the Republican Party; in fact, central political control over education in the United States is neither recent nor partisan. NCLB was actually a reauthorization of the Elementary and Secondary Education Act (ESEA), which had its roots in the 1960s during the administration of Lyndon Johnson, a Democrat, and his Great Society. The first mention of language education was discussion of bilingualism in a reauthorization of the ESEA in the 1970s. Harbingers of NCLB were seen in the reauthorization debates in the early and mid-1990s. The movement to control language education began during a Democratic administration, and legislators on both sides of the aisle have long seen that being strong on education helps get votes. NCLB is part of an evolutionary trajectory toward greater state control over education, a movement that continues under the present Obama administration, which is continuing along the path with 'Race to the Top' designed to spur reforms in state and local public education.

McNamara and Roever (2006) summarized the assessment procedures involved in NCLB as statewide tests of reading/language arts and mathematics in grades 3–8 and at least once during high school. The subjects tested and the grades tested are mandated by NCLB, but states develop their own testing instruments. Aggregate results are reported at the school, district, and state level for the entire student populations at the different grade levels. Speakers of English as a second language, however, are one of the four groups of students whose scores are disaggregated from the population. Each school is required to make *adequate yearly progress* in all parts of the assessment: scores of its entire student body and all its disaggregated subgroups on both reading/language arts and mathematics. Evans and Hornberger (2005) argued that the consequences of NCLB for English as a Second Language (ESL) learners have been mixed. On the one hand, added attention has been paid by school districts to their ESL students and small increases in funding of ESL programs have resulted because of the recognition in NCLB of ESL learners as one of the disaggregated groups, who must also show adequate yearly progress. On the other hand, because students' achievement in foreign languages is not assessed in the NCLB framework, bilingual education programs are disappearing in the push to quickly develop students' proficiency in English. In addition, Rosenbusch (2005) reported that NCLB has resulted in a decrease in instructional time for foreign languages, especially in schools with high minority populations. In effect, NCLB has contributed to the hegemony of English in schools and in US society.

The CEFR was initially designed to facilitate the recognition of language credentials across national boundaries, and the framework promulgated one particular theory of language knowledge and the establishment of a progressive set of standards. It has rapidly become insti-tutionalized throughout Europe but, as Fulcher (2004: 260) has argued, the impact of the CEFR and the adequacy of its underlying construct are in need of debate because 'For tea-chers, the main danger is that they are beginning to believe that the scales in the CEFR represent an acquisitional hierarchy, rather than a common perception. They begin to believe the language of the descriptors actually relates to the sequence of how and what learners learn'.

In both the American and European cases, the establishment of a particular assessment framework has had a very significant effect on teaching and learning.

Because language assessments like these serve the purpose of distributing scarce resources such as jobs, higher education, and financial support to those who desire them, the question of how to distribute those resources fairly is by no means academic. In recent years, the critical theory of Foucault as applied to language testing by Shohamy and Fulcher has set out quite clearly the goals both overt and covert of policy makers and the role of language tests in achieving those goals. No matter how policy is implicated in language tests, no matter whether power is exercised in the service of ends that we admire or ends that we abhor, knowledge of power and how power is exercised is liberating for testees and test designers. It is only by taking this critical perspective on language testing and by implementing proposals such as those by Shohamy (2001, 2004) for democratic assessment and by Fulcher and Davidson (2007) for effect-driven testing that those involved in language testing can assume full responsibility for tests and their uses.

Chapter summary and a look ahead

In recent years, the social dimensions of language testing have received the attention that they deserve largely thanks to the new technologies of recording human interaction that erased the circle around language, which had characterized the linguistic theories of Saussure and his predecessors. Once language is seen as greater than vocabulary and grammar and human meaning making is seen as embodied, theories of language can be expanded to embrace how persons employ communicative resources in social interaction. A theory of the mutual constitution of language and social context permits us to revivify language and to reject a construct of language knowledge that interprets test performance in a disembodied, decontextualized context.

In Practice Theory, social constructs in language tests are seen as a configuration of communicative resources employed by all participants in a test, not just the testee. It is the configuration of communicative resources rather than language knowledge or strategic abilities that characterizes a test as a discursive practice, and the configuration of communicative resources is a means by which participants in a test create local identities and discursive power. Through close analysis of discourse and social interaction, a person's performance in a testing practice can be compared with practices outside the testing room. Testing practice can, however, never be removed from the global context in which powerful elites design and administer language tests and interpret test results. The political context of a newly independent Estonia and the desire of the Estonian government to establish the country's independence from its colonial ruler by language planning and testing have an effect on the lives of teachers like Ms. Muravyova. In communities around the world, the same linguistic battles are fought between local languages and the languages of colonial rulers, between standardized languages and local varieties, and between national languages and the languages of immigrants. The role of language testing in these battles is to maintain the power of speakers of prestigious language varieties and to maintain the subordinate status of speakers of non-standard varieties. It is only recently that critical language testing has made clear the relationship between language and social context, the social consequences of assessment, and the power of language tests.

What are the consequences of this newfound understanding of the social context of language testing? What debates will still be raging and which issues will be unresolved say five or ten years from now? As I gaze into the crystal ball of the future of language testing, I observe three events. One is an image of two psychometricians, experts in the field of educational measurement, sitting in front of a computer monitor scratching their heads as a waterfall of data pours down the screen. I interpret this image to mean that the attempt to measure the rich social context of language will produce so much quantitative data that new means must be developed to analyze and understand it. I also hear audio from a satellite that picks up sounds from the places over which it flies. The sounds are familiar, almost like English, but while I can understand the audio from the satellite as it flies over some countries, the audio coming from other parts of the world I can't understand, although some words sound like English. I interpret this to mean that world languages such as English will continue to spread as they are doing today in China and Korea, but local varieties will diverge further and further from what a native speaker of standard English can understand today. Finally, I see an image of a band of brown-clad brothers and sisters, guardians of a sacred code of ethics by which they wish all language testers should live. Their code is displayed in a temple of shining marble and the brown-clad band recites it every day. They are, however, alone in their recitations and their temple is empty.

Further reading

Davies, A. (ed.), (1997). *Ethics in Language Testing* [special issue of *Language Testing* 14, 3]. The articles in this special issue were presented in a symposium on the ethics of language testing held at the World Congress of Applied Linguistics in 1996. In ten articles, well-known scholars of language testing address the role of ethics (and the limits of that role) in professional activities such as language testing. The authors discuss language testing as a means of political control, the definition of the test construct, the effects of language tests on the various stakeholders who are involved, and criteria for promoting ethicality in language testing.

McNamara, T. F. and Roever, C. (2006). *Language Testing: the social dimension*. Malden, MA: Blackwell. This book focuses on the social aspects of language testing, including assessment of socially situated language use and societal consequences of language tests. The authors argue that traditional approaches to ensuring fairness in tests go some way to addressing social concerns, but a broader perspective is necessary to understand the functions of tests on a societal scale. They consider these issues in relation to language assessment in oral proficiency interviews and to the assessment of second language pragmatics. They argue that traditional approaches to ensuring social fairness in tests go some way to addressing social concerns, but a broader perspective is necessary to fully understand the social dimensions of language testing.

Shohamy, E. (2006). *Language Policy: hidden agendas and new approaches*. London, UK: Routledge. Shohamy illuminates the decisions surrounding language policy and tests and emphasizes the effects of these decisions on different groups within society. Drawing on examples from the United States, Israel, and the UK, Shohamy demonstrates different categories of language policy, from explicit use by government bodies and the media to implicit use where no active decisions are made. She also reveals and examines the mechanisms used to introduce language policy, such as propaganda and even educational material. Her critical exploration of language policy concludes with arguments for a more democratic and open approach to language policy and testing, suggesting strategies for resistance and ways to protect the linguistic rights of individuals and groups.

Young, R. F. (2009). *Discursive Practice in Language Learning and Teaching*. Malden, MA: Wiley-Blackwell. Young sets out to explain Practice Theory and its implications for language learning, teaching and testing. He examines the consequences of considering language-in-interaction as discursive practice and of discourse as social action. Discursive practice is the construction and reflection of social realities through language and actions that invoke identity, ideology, belief, and power. The ultimate aim of Practice Theory is to explain the ways in which the global context affects the local employment of communicative resources and vice versa. In chapters 5 and 6, Young uses Practice Theory to take a new look at how the employment of communicative resources in a specific discursive practice may be learned, taught, and assessed.

References

Agar, M. (1994). *Language Shock: understanding the culture of conversation*. New York: Morrow.

Bachman, L. F. (1990). *Fundamental Considerations in Language Testing*. Oxford: Oxford University Press.

Beyer, C. (2007). Edmund Husserl. In *Stanford Encyclopedia of Philosophy*. plato.stanford.edu/entries/husserl (accessed 18 September 2010).

Bourdieu, P. (1977). *Outline of a Theory of Practice*. R. Nice (trans.). Cambridge, UK: Cambridge University Press.

—— (1990). *The Logic of Practice*. R. Nice (trans.). Stanford, CA: Stanford University Press.

Bucholtz, M. and Hall, K. (2004). Language and identity. In A. Duranti (ed.), *A Companion to Linguistic Anthropology*. Malden, MA: Blackwell.

Canagarajah, S. (2009). The plurilingual tradition and the English language in South Asia. *AILA Review* 22: 5–22.

Chalhoub-Deville, M. (2003). Second language interaction: Current perspectives and future trends. *Language Testing* 20: 369–83.

Chalhoub-Deville, M. and Deville, C. (2005). A look back at and forward to what language testers measure. In E. Hinkel (ed.), *Handbook of Research in Second Language Teaching and Learning*. Mahwah, NJ: Erlbaum.

Chapelle, C. A. (1998). Construct definition and validity inquiry in SLA research. In L. F. Bachman and A. D. Cohen (eds), *Interfaces Between Second Language Acquisition and Language Testing Research*. Cambridge, UK: Cambridge University Press.

Chomsky, N. (1986). *Knowledge of Language: its nature, origin, and use*. New York, NY: Praeger.

Council of Europe (2001). *Common European Framework of Reference for Languages: learning, teaching, assessment*. Cambridge, UK: Cambridge University Press.

de Certeau, M. (1984). *The Practice of Everyday Life*. S. Rendall (trans.). Berkeley, CA: University of California Press.

Erickson, F. (2004). *Talk and Social Theory: ecologies of speaking and listening in everyday life*. Cambridge, UK: Polity.

Evans, B. A. and Hornberger, N. H. (2005). No child left behind: repealing and unpeeling federal language education policy in the United States. *Language Policy* 4: 87–106.

Ford, C. E. and Thompson, S. A. (1996). Interactional units in conversation: syntactic, intonational, and pragmatic resources for the management of turns. In E. Ochs, E. A. Schegloff and S.A. Thompson (eds), *Interaction and Grammar*. Cambridge, UK Cambridge University Press.

Foucault, M. (1978). *The History of Sexuality*, vol. 1, R. Hurley (trans.). New York, NY: Pantheon.

—— (1995). *Discipline and Punish: the birth of the prison*, 2nd Vintage edn, A. Sheridan (trans.). New York, NY: Vintage.

Foucault, M. and Gordon, C. (1980). *Power/Knowledge: selected interviews and other writings, 1972–1977*, C. Gordon *et al.* (trans.). New York, NY: Pantheon.

Fulcher, G. (2004). Deluded by artifices? The Common European Framework and harmonization. *Language Assessment Quarterly* 1: 253–66.

—— (2009). Test use and political philosophy. *Annual Review of Applied Linguistics* 29: 3–20.

Fulcher, G. and Davidson, F. (2007). *Language Testing and Assessment*. London: Routledge.

Gerassimenko, O., Hennoste, T., Koit, M. and Rääbis, A. (2004). Other-initiated self-repairs in Estonian information dialogues: solving communication problems in cooperation. Paper presented at the Association for Computational Linguistics Special Interest Group Workshop on Discourse and Dialogue, Boston, MA, April 30–May 1.

Giddens, A. (1984). *The Constitution of Society: outline of the theory of structuration*. Berkeley, CA: University of California Press.

Goffman, E. (1979). Footing. *Semiotica* 25: 1–29.

—— (1981). *Forms of Talk*. Philadelphia, PA: University of Pennsylvania Press.

Gumperz, J. J. (1982). *Discourse Strategies*. Cambridge, UK: Cambridge University Press.

—— (1992). Contextualization and understanding. In A. Duranti and C. Goodwin (eds), *Rethinking Context: language as an interactive phenomenon*. Cambridge, UK: Cambridge University Press.

—— (1995). Mutual inferencing in conversation. In I. Marková, C. Graumann and K. Foppa (eds), *Mutualities in Dialogue*. Cambridge, UK: Cambridge University Press.

Halliday, M. A. K. (1994). Systemic theory. In R. E. Asher and J. M. Y. Simpson (eds), *The Encyclopedia of Language and Linguistics*, vol. 8. Oxford, UK: Pergamon.

Kramsch, C. (1986). From language proficiency to interactional competence. *The Modern Language Journal* 70: 366–72.

Lantolf, J. P. (2006). Re(de)fining language proficiency in light of the concept of languagculture. In H. Byrnes (ed.), *Advanced Language Learning: the contribution of Halliday and Vygotsky*. London, UK: Continuum.

Levinson, S. C. (1992). Activity types and language. In P. Drew and J. Heritage (eds), *Talk at Work: interaction in institutional settings*. Cambridge, UK: Cambridge University Press.

Levy, C. J. (2010). Estonia raises its pencils to help erase Russian. *New York Times*, June 8: A6.

Locke, J. (1690). *A Essay Concerning the True Original, Extent, and End of Civil Government*. http://jim.com/2ndtreat.htm (accessed 18 September 2010).

Lowenberg, P. H. (1993). Issues of validity in tests of English as a world language: whose standards? *World Englishes* 12: 95–106.

McNamara, T. F. (1997). Interaction in second language performance assessment: whose performance? *Applied Linguistics* 18: 446–66.

McNamara, T. F. and Roever, C. (2006). *Language Testing: the social dimension*. Malden, MA: Blackwell.

Mehan, H. (1982). The structure of classroom events and their consequences for student performance. In P. Gilmore and A. A. Glatthorn (eds), *Children in and out of School: ethnography and education*. Washington, DC: Center for Applied Linguistics.

Messick, S. (1989). Validity. In R. L. Linn (ed.), *Educational Measurement*, 3rd edn. New York, NY: American Council on Education and Macmillan.

—— (1996). Validity of performance assessments. In G. W. Phillips (ed.), *Technical Issues in Large-Scale Performance Assessment*. Washington, DC: US Department of Education, Office of Educational Research and Improvement.

Miyazaki, I. (1976). *China's Examination Hell: the civil service examinations of imperial china*. C. Schirokauer (trans.). New York, NY: Weatherhill.

Norris, J. M. (2008). *Validity Evaluation in Language Assessment*. New York, NY: Peter Lang.

O'Brien O'Keeffe, K. (1990). *Visible Song: transitional literacy in Old English verse*. Cambridge, UK: Cambridge University Press.

Rosenbusch, M. H. (2005). The No Child Left Behind Act and teaching and learning languages in U.S. schools. *The Modern Language Journal* 89: 250–61.

Röver, C. (2005). *Testing ESL Pragmatics: development and validation of a web-based assessment battery*. Frankfurt, Germany: Peter Lang.

Sacks, H., Schegloff, E. A. and Jefferson, G. (1974). A simplest systematics for the organization of turn-taking for conversation. *Language* 50: 696–735.

Sahlins, M. D. (1981). *Historical Metaphors and Mythical Realities: structure in the early history of the Sandwich Islands Kingdom*. Ann Arbor, MI: University of Michigan Press.

—— (1985). *Islands of History*. Chicago, IL: University of Chicago Press.

Saussure, F. de (1983[1916]). *Course in General Linguistics*, R. Harris (trans.). London, UK: Duckworth.

Schegloff, E. A. and Sacks, H. (1973). Opening up closings. *Semiotica* 8: 289–327.

Schleppegrell, M. J. (2004). *The Language of Schooling: a functional linguistics perspective*. Mahwah, NJ: Erlbaum.

Seidlhofer, B., Breiteneder, A. and Pitzl, M.-L. (2006). English as a lingua franca in Europe: challenges for applied linguists. *Annual Review of Applied Linguistics* 26: 3–34.

Shohamy, E. (2001). Democratic assessment as an alternative. *Language Testing* 18: 373–91.

—— (2004). Assessment in multicultural societies: applying democratic principles and practices to language testing. In B. Norton and K. Toohey (eds), *Critical Pedagogies and Language Learning*. Cambridge, UK: Cambridge University Press.

—— (2006). *Language Policy: hidden agendas and new approaches*. London, UK: Routledge.

Stimpson, G. (1946). *A Book About a Thousand Things*. New York, NY: Harper.

Trevarthen, C. (1977). Descriptive analyses of infant communicative behaviour. In H. R. Schaffer (ed.), *Studies in Mother-Infant Interaction: Proceedings of the Loch Lomond Symposium, Ross Priory, University of Strathclyde, September, 1975*. London, UK: Academic Press.

—— (1979). Communication and cooperation in early infancy: a description of primary intersubjectivity. In M. Bullowa (ed.), *Before Speech*. Cambridge, UK: Cambridge University Press.

US Congress (2002). *No Child Left Behind Act of 2001*. Public Law 107–10 (8 January). United States Congress.

Young, R. F. (2008). *Language and Interaction: an advanced resource book*. London, UK: Routledge.

—— (2009). *Discursive Practice in Language Learning and Teaching*. Malden, MA: Wiley-Blackwell.

—— (2011). Interactional competence in language learning, teaching, and testing. In E. Hinkel (ed.), *Handbook of Research in Second Language Teaching and Learning*, vol. 2, London, UK: Routledge.

Young, R. F. and He, A. W. (eds), (1998). *Talking and Testing: discourse approaches to the assessment of oral proficiency*. Amsterdam, The Netherlands: Benjamins.

Part IV
Test specifications

Test specifications and criterion referenced assessment

Fred Davidson

Introduction and historical perspectives

Educational tests yield scores, and a score needs to have a meaning. If a student takes a test and receives a result of "ten," then a natural question arises: what does the "ten" represent? There are two classic answers to this question: norm referencing and criterion referencing.

The earliest work on normative testing dates from the late nineteenth century, when Galton built his Anthropometric Laboratory and addressed the question of why people need to be measured. For example, he wrote about human eyesight: "Measurement would give an indication of the eyesight becoming less good, long before the child would find it out for himself, or before its impairment could attract the observation of others" (Galton 1890: 2). Such a stance is normative because it views eyesight in relative terms: "less good." To return to the opening question, above: the norm referenced meaning of a "ten" on a language test would be the rank of the test taker in a group of peers—the norm group: how many scored above ten? How many scored below? And more crucially: what is the normative score value for some particular decision, such as admission to or exit from a particular language program?

In a classic paper, Glaser (1963) coined the notion of criterion referencing, which nowadays is typically defined in contrast to norm referenced testing. A problem arises when a test is given after an instructional sequence, such as a module or unit in an academic semester-long class. In such a case, the score range may be very narrow. That would be exactly what a teacher wants in an achievement test: very little score spread, because it shows that the teaching was successful. The teacher's chief concern is about the skills and abilities that the students can demonstrate: the criteria against which they will be measured. If the entire group of students can display mastery of the entire suite of criteria for a particular teaching unit or module, then the variation of scores could be even be zero—there may have been ten separate skills in the teaching module, and all of the students performed all ten skills flawlessly, and so all of them scored "ten." In contrast to norm referencing, there would be little reason to rank and to compare the students: if they all achieve, they all get full value.

This distinction led to a body of criterion referenced statistics. If a score of "ten" on a language test is deemed to be a passing mark on a criterion referenced test, the presumption is that a "ten" indicates mastery of a sufficient number of skills in a very well-defined domain of language ability. Unlike normative item statistics (J.D. Brown, this volume), criterion referenced statistics look at the dependability of judging mastery and view that dependability in much the same philosophical light as reliability in normative testing: how trustworthy is that "ten" as an indicator of mastery? (Hudson and Lynch, 1984; Bachman, 1990: 209–20).

Over the years, the chief legacy of criterion referencing seems not to be its body of statistics. Few testing companies utilize or report criterion referenced item analyses, to the knowledge of this author. Rather, the legacy of criterion referencing lies in its impact on communication of test results, because criterion referencing places strong value on clear definitions of the skills to be tested. Today's standards-based educational systems demand that language tests have thick score reports. Figure 13.1 shows a sample modern score report. Many of the modern techniques to calibrate and track the standard descriptive language (in such reports) derive historically from criterion referencing's emphasis on skills rather than the spread of scores in a distribution.

Criterion referenced test development focused attention on particular skills and abilities. Operationalization is the challenge of putting an ability into measurable terms, and it is featured centrally in criterion referenced testing (Davidson et al., 1985). The chief tool for operationalization is a test specification.

Test specifications

A test specification is a generative blueprint from which many equivalent test items or tasks can be produced. Perhaps the earliest mention of test specifications (or "specs") dates to Ruch (1924: 95–99; 1929: 150). Well prior to Glaser's paper that coined the term "criterion referenced," test developers realized that standardized testing needed to control test tasks, so that new and equivalent versions of tests could be developed, trialed, and normed. Early conceptions of test specifications reflected then-prevalent normative views of test development, and the goal of these early specs was to generate tasks of varying difficulty levels. These specs also provided information about the particular skills in a test: how many test items are needed for each skill. Often, this information was set forth in tabular form: a table of specifications. For example, the table may tell the test developer that ten multiple-choice comprehension questions are needed for a test of reading: five texts, two per text, one each to test a main idea and to test a specific textual inference.

A table of specifications is a very valuable tool, and it is still widely used in many test development settings. However, it has a drawback: it does not provide adequate detail to generate test questions that say much about mastery. It is not a tool for operationalizing an ability. What is a "main idea"? What is "textual inference"? Criterion referenced test specifications originated in the 1970s and provide that level of detail (Popham, 1978; Davidson and Lynch, 2002; Fulcher and

Reading Skills	Level	Your Performance
Reading	Intermediate (15–21)	Test takers who receive a score at the **INTERMEDIATE** level, as you did, typically understand academic texts in English that require a wide range of reading abilities, although their understanding of certain parts of the texts is limited. Test takers who receive a score at the **INTERMEDIATE** level typically • have a good command of common academic vocabulary but still have some difficulty with high-level vocabulary; • have a very good understanding of grammatical structure; • can understand and connect information, make appropriate inferences, and synthesize information in a range of texts but have more difficulty when the vocabulary is high level and the text is conceptually dense; • can recognize the expository organization of a text and the role that specific information serves within a larger text but have some difficulty when these are not explicit or easy to infer from the text; and • can abstract major ideas from a text but have more difficulty doing so when the text is conceptually dense.

Figure 13.1 A sample score report for the internet-based TOEFL, Reading Subsection
Note: This is the text information that accompanies a scaled score "17"
Source: www.pl.efsglobal.org/fileadmin/free_resources/polish%20website/Download/TOEFL_iBT_examinee_ score_report_sample_Miki.pdf, downloaded 31 October 2010.

Davidson, 2007: Chapters A4 and C4). Modern test score reports obtain their richness, in part, from their bank of detailed test specs, and if the test still serves a normative function (and many do), then it is no longer accurate to say that detailed test specs are the sole province of criterion referencing. They have become part of all good testing practice.

Detailed test specs can come in many formats and design. All formats share two common elements: sample test tasks and "guiding language" about how to produce such samples (Fulcher and Davidson, 2007: Chapter A4). The following is an example of a detailed test spec.

Box 13.1 A sample test specification

Example of a Detailed Test Specification: Level 2 on the Association of Language Testers in Europe (ALTE). Framework: Social and Travel Contexts

Guiding Language:

At this level of the ALTE Framework ("Threshold") speakers are expected to handle the following types of language:

"In social and travel contexts, Threshold users can understand most of the language on an ordinary menu, routine letters and forms, adverts and brochures related to hotels or other forms of accommodation. They can understand most labels on everyday medical and food products, and follow simple instructions for use of medicines and cooking instructions found on food packaging. As a general point, they can distinguish between personal and promotional mail from institutions such as banks, and get the general meaning of simple articles in newspapers or leaflets produced by post offices and banks."

(ALTE, www.alte.org/framework/level2.php)

This test spec produces a multiple-choice item aligned with the above descriptor. The stem of the item is rendered in the test taker's first language. It stipulates background knowledge to the setting of the item and refers to real-world language sources as quoted in the ALTE-2 descriptor, above ("ordinary menu, routine letters and forms, adverts and brochures related to hotels or other forms of accommodation"). The stem is a stated or implied question that links the background knowledge to the ordinary language source. For instance, in the German example below, the background knowledge stipulated is that the test taker is travelling alone and is considering a particular hotel and would like a view of the river. The overall intent of the stem is to ask the test taker to make an inference that requires use of the target language as utilized in the real-world language use settings mentioned in the ALTE-2 descriptor, above.

The primary source of the target language (given that the item stem is rendered in the test taker's first language) is contained in the choices and the adjacent textual input.

There will be four or five choices in the item. One choice will be clearly correct according to the stipulated background information contained in the stem, the stated question derived from that information, the adjacent text, and the inferential skills involved. The incorrect choices will come directly from the adjacent text. Hence, an important factor to consider (when choosing the adjacent language sample) is whether or not it provides four or five clear choices that can be used in the multiple-choice format. *(Continued on next page)*

The adjacent text should be authentic, but in concert with the test item, it should not require high-level use of the target language. Rather, it should require the typical every-day language use skills needed to understand such sources. Successful completion of the multiple-choice item can involve simple scanning. The test taker can overlook many elements of the adjacent text.

Sample item

You are planning a trip and are considering the hotel shown below. You are travelling alone, and you would prefer a view of the river. Which room is best?

a. €95
b. €125
c. €160
d. €170
e. €195

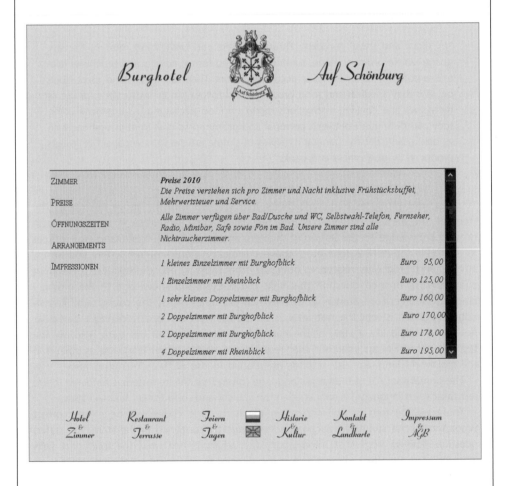

Burghotel *Auf Schönburg*

ZIMMER	**Preise 2010**	
	Die Preise verstehen sich pro Zimmer und Nacht inklusive Frühstücksbuffet,	
PREISE	*Mehrwertsteuer und Service.*	
ÖFFNUNGSZEITEN	*Alle Zimmer verfügen über Bad/Dusche und WC, Selbstwahl-Telefon, Fernseher,*	
	Radio, Minibar, Safe sowie Fön im Bad. Unsere Zimmer sind alle	
ARRANGEMENTS	*Nichtraucherzimmer.*	
IMPRESSIONEN	*1 kleines Einzelzimmer mit Burghofblick*	*Euro 95,00*
	1 Einzelzimmer mit Rheinblick	*Euro 125,00*
	1 sehr kleines Doppelzimmer mit Burghofblick	*Euro 160,00*
	2 Doppelzimmer mit Burghofblick	*Euro 170,00*
	2 Doppelzimmer mit Burghofblick	*Euro 178,00*
	4 Doppelzimmer mit Rheinblick	*Euro 195,00*

Hotel & Zimmer *Restaurant & Terrasse* *Feiern & Tagen* *Historie & Kultur* *Kontakt & Landkarte* *Impressum & AGB*

(*www.burghotel-schoenburg.de/rhein-burg-hotelzimmer/index.html*)

Clearly, this spec needs to improve. For example, the test developer should state the intended correct response (which is b). The guiding language implies that this sample task fits the quoted ALTE-2 descriptor, because it is a hotel advertisement. However, the task is actually rather simple. The test taker really needs just some basic vocabulary ("blick") and needs to know that the Rhine is a major river. Likewise, the test taker is travelling alone, and so the double rooms would be something of a waste of money—the word "doppel" is a cognate with English, making that a relatively easy part of the inferential task. The item may be easy that it is, in fact, not "inferential"? What is the definition of "inferential" as used by the spec, and is it part of the ALTE-2 level? Perhaps this is not an ALTE-2 task at all—perhaps it is too simple for that level and needs to be made more complex. One way to adjust the level of the spec would be to generate items from other travel or everyday sources (e.g. menus or price guides for products other than hotels). As more test items are created from this spec, its developers may fine-tune their intent and come to a consensus about what they do and do not want to measure. Later versions of the spec will reflect this consensus, and as those versions are written, the positioning of the spec against the ALTE-2 descriptor would improve. Furthermore, piloting and trialing of the item would certainly improve the spec (see Kenyon and MacGregor, this volume); however, there is much value in careful discussion of specs, and in many test development settings it is either impossible or very costly to try out tests before they are used. There are also some problematic considerations of language theory at play in this test. What exactly does this ALTE-2 descriptor mean? For instance, if a person is rated an "ALTE-2," can s/he really accommodate the language demands of checking in at this hotel? What actually happens in travel-related discourse? (Fulcher et al., 2011). Healthy criticism of the ALTE Framework can ensue from attempting to write test specs that align to it. Another issue is the scope of operationalization. Test specs are supposed to be generative, and this one plans to generate items from a rather wide range of language use situations, other than hotels. Even if the above test item adequately represents language use for a hotel setting, does it generalize to the other language uses given in the ALTE-2 descriptor—for example, are adverts really similar to hotel price guides? Finally, there are a number of editing considerations which, at first glance, seem like simple problems—but on later reflection may not be. The items choices have omitted the European style decimal numbers shown by a comma and two zeros. Does this threaten authenticity? If not, then how much latitude is the item writer permitted when quoting information from the adjacent text in the choices? In this case, the adjacent text has more than five choices shown—there are six. Is that always permitted? Can item writers locate adjacent language samples with more than the stated number of choices? If so, how many more? It is a far different language scanning skill to look over a list of twenty or thirty elements in an adjacent text to find the five shown in the item than it is to review a list of six, as is the case here. The spec provides some latitude to the item writer, in that four or five choices are required. What is the difference between four and five choices in a multiple-choice item such as this? That particular issue would be very suitable for pilot testing and statistical analysis.

The previous paragraph is quite critical of this detailed test spec. Such criticism is typical practice in spec-driven test development. A spec really does not stabilize until it has been exposed to extensive and reflective criticism among test developers: feedback makes specs better. Furthermore, the team should be able to look at the spec, to reflect on its accumulated expertise and opinions, to critique it, and to improve it—all without trialing the test item. As mentioned previously, it is costly to try out test items, and in some test settings, trialing is not typical. For example, a group of teachers at a language institute may regularly gather to discuss their students and classes and exams. In such a setting, it is doubtful that the institute can invest much time in trying out test items to improve the tests. However, the institute can invest part of its coordination and planning meetings to the planning and refinement of the test—and such discussions can focus on test specs. The institute's tests—its specs, actually—can grow and evolve and improve from feedback obtained at regularly scheduled discussions.

This process is spec-driven test development. Its key characteristics are:

- it is generative: the spec is intended to produce many equivalent test items or tasks;
- it is iterative: the spec evolves over time and proceeds through versions;
- it is consensus-based: the spec is co-authored by a team.

Spec-driven test development is probably standard practice in most large commercial and government testing operations. A primary purpose of this chapter is to help to spread that practice to a wider educational audience, as is the purpose and intent of other writing on this topic (Davidson and Lynch, 1993, 2002; Lynch and Davidson, 1994; Davidson *et al.*, 2007; Fulcher and Davidson, 2007: especially Chapters A4 and C4).

Research topics in spec-driven test development

There are a number of active research topics in spec-driven language test development. The first is the relationship of test specs to validity. Over time, test specifications grow and evolve and improve as feedback from team members is incorporated and as tryout data (if available) is consulted. This growth is one source of evidence for a validity argument (Chapelle, this volume). Li (2006) presents a conceptual diagram of the relationship of evolutionary test specs to validation, shown in Figure 13.2. Particular changes in test specs can be tracked or "audited," and Li's research illustrates how auditing can serve as evidence of test validity. This is a conceptual diagram, and it does not endorse a particular frequency of spec revisions.

Specs also have a potential role in matters of educational policy, and this raises another research challenge. Many of the world's educational systems are, or are becoming, standards driven (see Hudson, this volume). The governing entity sets forth a series of statements about expected student performance at various ability levels. Logically, the spec stands between the test items or tasks and the standards, because it operationalizes the expectations stated in a standard. The test developers can reason that the test matches government policy, because they can document that it was developed with that policy in mind; for example, an external authority may stipulate that language tests align with a framework such as ALTE's, and so the developers of the German spec (above) can claim to meet policy, because the spec directly quotes an ALTE descriptor. The external authority—a government agency, perhaps—may wish to verify the relationship of a test to its standards via independent means, without reference to the spec. This can be done with a test-to-standards alignment project, in which a group of content experts go through a rigorous analysis of the test, of the standards, and arrive at ratings of the degree to which the two are in agreement along three dimensions:

- Match—how well the assessment/standard matches content expectations.
- Depth—the degree of complexity within content expectations that are resident in the test/standard.
- Breadth—how well tests/standards cover content expectations.

("Alignment," www.wida.us/Research/Alignment/index.aspx)

Kim *et al.* (2010) investigated a particularly interesting problem in spec-driven language test development. After a test development team has reached consensus and a spec has gotten to a

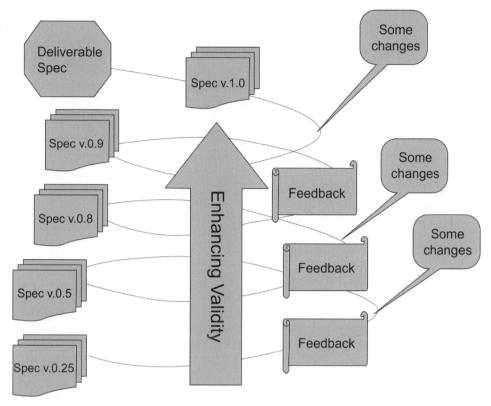

Figure 13.2 The evolutionary role of test specs in test development
Source: Li, 2006: 20.

finalized version, it enters operational production. At that point, it is very likely that a group of item writers will be brought in to produce equivalent items and tasks—this is the classic function of a test spec: it serves as a directive to test writers. The Kim *et al.* study investigates what happens at that point in time: for instance, how do the new item writers react to the spec? What useful feedback do they bring?

Another pressing research issue in spec-driven testing concerns the group of people who work on a spec. Consensus plays an important role during test development. Davidson and Lynch (2002: Chapter 6), Kim (2006) and Kim *et al.* (2010) investigated the role of group dynamics in the creation and revision of test specs. These research projects argue that test developers need to be keenly aware of the roles that test developers take, in order to make progress toward an operational deliverable test.

Another area of research in spec-driven testing is closely allied with the modern paradigm of validity, specifically, with its consequential nature (Messick, 1989). Test impact is part of a validation argument. Fulcher and Davidson (2007) suggest "effect-driven" test development: they argue that testers should build tests with the intended effects in mind, from the outset. These effects could be stated overtly in a test spec. Kim (2008) investigated effect-driven testing in her research. She revised a test along several "effect-driven hypotheses." Her findings suggested that effects can be incorporated into test development—including specs—but that there are mediating factors that impact the visibility of the effect, once the test is launched. These mediating factors form an interesting question for future research: just how much control is ever feasible in any spec-driven testing system, even one which overtly embraces the modern consequentialist view of validity? The ALTE-2 spec, above, does not really discuss its effect. Were it to do so, it might engage the following question: If a test taker is falsely certified at level ALTE-2 based on specs like this, what negative impact might it have on the test taker's life? Considering such a question could help to verify if the spec is at the proper ALTE level.

There are some other areas for future research in test specifications that have not yet been investigated. The first is releasability—how much of a test spec should be made public? Specs reveal generative guidance about how to produce test questions, and so the authors of the spec may not wish to jeopardize their investment. Furthermore, extensive release of test specs may alter the tests results, because doing so may encourage extensive test coaching. On the other hand, test takers and score users naturally wish to understand: how is the test built? What are its questions? What is the rationale behind the questions? In commercial testing situations, there is another motivation to release the specs in some form: marketing. Sales forces need a common message for potential clients, in order to promote the test products. Research is needed on the tolerance of testing systems to the release of specs.

Another area for future research is grain size in test specs. Davidson and Lynch (2002: 53–57) discuss the level of generalization of a test specification. Specs can be written at a very fine-grained level, and in doing so, they both heighten control of the test production process as well as limit the creativity of the item writer. A particularly controlled form of spec is an "item form" or "item shell," in which the test spec becomes a fill-in-the-blank activity (Haladyna 1994: 109–124). At the other end of the extreme, a spec can be written so generally that it encompasses a broad range of item types and offers little fine-grained advice about how to write a particular test question. There are modern models of test development such as Mislevy's evidence-centered design (this volume) which encourage a fine-grained view of test specification. Tradeoffs exist: the finer grained that test specs are, the greater the control. The less grainy the specs, the greater freedom that the item writer has. What is the effect of this phenomenon on test validity?

Fruitful research could also investigate the relationship of cognitive diagnostic analysis (CDA; see Jang, this volume) to specification-driven test development. CDA offers a formal method to link content analysis of tests to performance data and may help to sort out the grain-size problem. Test specs can serve an important role in such analyses: an item should reflect the generative spec from which it was built. However, the precise relationship of test specs to cognitive diagnostic models is, also, still unknown.

Recommendations for practice

Language test specifications are an accessible concept: guiding language plus example(s) of the item to be generated are collected in a document, circulated among colleagues and peers, revised, circulated again and revised again (and perhaps a few more cycles), piloted if resources permit, revised again, until a consensus to halt production is reached. The best way to grasp this process is to try it. For that reason, the following practice exercise is encouraged to readers of this chapter:

Exercise: spec revision

1. Gather a group of colleagues who work in your language teaching setting. Show them the German spec above. Ideally, you should find a German speaker (if you, yourself, do not speak German). However, as noted previously, the item is actually rather easy.
2. Render the sample item in the several languages shared among your peers.

3. Discuss your sample items, the ALTE-2 descriptor, the specs guiding language, and the critical questions about the spec raised above. How should the spec be revised? Should it test a broader range of content from the hotel website, in order to test a wider range of vocabulary? Or do you feel that it is an accurate representation of the ALTE-2 level?

4. Consider the spec as given here to be Version 0.10. Revise it to Version 0.20. Set it aside, and return to it later and discuss it again, possibly rendering further sample items in your various languages. That will be Version 0.30.

5. And so on—hopefully, your team will get an opportunity to try out this spec in operational teaching.

Future directions

This chapter began by discussing the distinction between norm referencing and criterion referencing. Dating from Glaser (1963), criterion referenced testing is most usually defined in comparison to normative testing. Over the years, the distinction has become blended. From a normative standpoint, tests will continue to be used to compare test takers. From the standpoint of criteria, score reports are growing in detail and, more central to this chapter, the detail seen in criterion referenced test specifications has become common industry practice.

What, then, is the overriding reason to separate the two terms: norm referencing and criterion referencing? The distinction has become part of common measurement jargon, but is there a deeper philosophical or ethical good that it serves? Are there measurement situations where it makes sense to speak solely of normative interpretations, and conversely, are there situations in which a normative interpretation seems irrelevant?

A good example of the latter—of the irrelevance of normative score interpretation—would be a language licensure examination to become a court interpreter. Upon completion of the test, it would seem illogical for the score report to say only: "Congratulations! You are equal or better than such-and-so percent of people who have taken this test." Furthermore, and more importantly, the score report should say more than simply: "Congratulations! You are equal or better than such-and-so percent of people who have taken this test, and you are qualified to become a court interpreter." Rather, the score report should state the result, the certification, and some kind of list of skill descriptors in the manner of the TOEFL report shown in Figure 13.1. In effect, the reason to distinguish norm and criterion referenced information is so that a score user sees both in the score report: how does the test taker rank, and what can she or he presumably do? A court interpretation test yields a score report that is evaluated by attorneys, by a judge, or by a licensing entity such as a national government. These score users benefit from two types of information: does the test taker rank high enough to obtain certification or a job and what skills and abilities has the test taker mastered?

The test taker herself or himself also sees the result of the test and may react: "Although I am certified now, I really feel uncomfortable. I'd like to study a bit more and see if I can raise my score the next time around." And if the test taker is not certified, then most likely her or his response will be to think: "What can I do to improve my chances? What must I study? How must I prepare?" Oscarson (1989) pointed out a fundamental axiom of the assessment of language ability:

Seen from the learner's point of view, foreign language skills may be assessed along two fundamentally different lines. They involve:

(a) Assessment in the form of self-report or self-assessment, that is, assessment seen in the learner's own perspective; assessment as an internal or self-directed activity.

(b) Assessment in the form of examinations and administrations of tests, that is, assessment seen in the perspective of an outside agent, typically a teacher or trained examiner; assessment seen as an external or other directed activity.

(Oscarson, 1989: 1)

This essential difference in testing is overlooked by norm referencing and by criterion referencing, because both traditions are determined by people other than the learner. Tests are set by the test developers, and the results are transmitted to and used by various score users and educationalists, and policy makers. All of these stakeholders (of course) have a social need for test-based score information, but so too does the test taker. She or he has a life agenda, and the results on the test can be central to that agenda.

Perhaps, then, there is a future where each score report would contain three minimal sources of meaning—three references. First, the score itself would be stated in normative terms. For example, the TOEFL score report in Figure 13.1 is for a score of 17, and so the report would state where that score stands in the norm group. Score users—e.g., college admissions officers—have such information at hand from their local experience and from consultation of the test publisher's website. So too should the examinee.

The second reference on the score report would be thick and detailed criterion-based information about the abilities of the test taker. This is, in fact, already given on the sample report in Figure 13.1. Very likely, the examinee looks at that, but it has been the (painful) experience of this author that college and departmental admissions personnel do not. Somehow, the value of that thick information needs to improve. Perhaps this is a matter of precision and marketing, and so further research on grain size and CDA will help.

The third and exciting possibility is that the score report would include an active personal investment by the test taker. She or he would receive the score report and then attach a sampling of his or her own work in the target language, perhaps by computer hyper-link. To ensure security, some of those performance samples could be gathered in identity-verified testing locations around the world. This self-referenced addendum would include not only target language samples and test taker reflection about them, but it would include reflection by the test taker as to the standardized score report, itself.

This is a future of "multiple referencing." Score reports would present and would document three sources of meaning: normative, criterion, and self-reflection. How might such a future alter the landscape of language test score use?

Further reading

Downing, S. M. and Haladyna, T.M. (eds), (2006). *Handbook of Test Development*. Mahwah, NJ: Lawrence Erlbaum. This 2006 volume is a comprehensive and broad overview of all aspects of test development. It touches on many important technical problems, including topics such as scaling, computer-adaptive testing, and validation reports. Of keen interest is the book's mention of test specifications, item content, and the creative role of the item writer—these topics receive (frankly speaking) short mention.

Ekbatani, G. and Pierson, H. (eds), (2000). *Learner-directed Assessment in ESL*. Mahwah, NJ: Lawrence Erlbaum. This book is an accessible and useful overview of various self-assessment techniques for language education. If the future holds promise for self-referencing, then scholarship such as this will play a keen role.

Roid, G. H. and Haladyna, T. M. (1982). *A Technology for Test-Item Writing*. Orlando, FL: Academic Press. This seminal volume presents a codified and formalized vision for test production. It is part of a group of modern resources, along with Downing and Haladyna (2006) and Haladyna (1994; cited in the reference list, below). This literature presents the modern techniques of highly controlled, standardized, and largely normative test production.

Yerkes, R. M. (ed.), (1921). *Psychological examining in the United States Army. Memoirs of the National Academy of Sciences,* vol. 15, Washington, DC: U.S. Government Printing Office. In World War I, the US Army pioneered the first true large-scale norm referenced test. This report is fascinating reading. How were some 1.7 million recruits tested and normed? Early visions of standardized and normative thought (e.g., Galton, cited below) appeared here, for the first time, on an industrial scale. Readers of this chapter are encouraged to contact this author to enquire about obtaining a PDF of this famous document.

References

Bachman, L. (1990). *Fundamental Considerations in Language Testing.* Oxford: Oxford, UK: University Press.

Davidson, F., Kim, J., Lee, H.J., Li, J. and Lopez, A. (2007). Making Choices in Academic English Language Testing: Evidence from the Evolution of Test Specifications. In Bailey, A. L. (ed.), *Language Demands of Students Learning English in School: putting academic language to the test.* New Haven, CT: Yale University Press, 157–70.

Davidson, F., Hudson, T. and Lynch, B. (1985). Language testing: operationalization in Classroom Measurement and L2 Research. In M. Celce-Murcia (ed.), *Beyond Basics: issues and research in TESOL.* Rowley, MA: Newbury House, 137–52.

Davidson, F. and Lynch, B. (1993). Criterion referenced language test development: a prolegomenon. In A. Huhta, K. Sajavaara and S. Takala (eds), *Language Testing: new openings.* Jyvaskyla, Finland: University of Jyvasklya, 73–89.

—— (2002). *Testcraft: a teacher's guide to writing and using language test specifications.* New Haven, CT: Yale University Press.

Fulcher, G. and Davidson, F. (2007). *Language Testing and Assessment: an advanced resource book.* Oxford, UK: Routledge.

Fulcher, G., Davidson, F. and Kemp, J. (2011). Effective rating scale development for speaking tests: Performance Decision Trees. *Language Testing* 28: 5–29.

Galton, F. (1890). *Anthropometric Laboratory: notes and memoirs.* London, UK: Richard Clay & Sons.

Glaser, R. (1963). Instructional technology and the measurement of learning outcomes: some questions. *American Psychologist* 18: 519–21.

Haladyna, T. M. (1994). *Developing and Validating Multiple-Choice Items.* Hillsdale, NJ: Lawrence Erlbaum.

Hudson, T. D and Lynch, B. K. (1984). A criterion referenced measurement approach to ESL achievement testing. *Language Testing* 1: 171–201.

Kim, J. T. 2006. *The Effectiveness of Test-Takers' Participation in Development of an Innovative Web-Based Speaking Test for International Teaching Assistants at American Colleges.* Unpublished doctoral dissertation. University of Illinois at Urbana-Champaign, USA: Department of Educational Psychology.

Kim, J. 2008. *Development and Validation of an ESL Diagnostic Reading-to-Write Test: An Effect-Driven Approach.* Unpublished doctoral dissertation. University of Illinois at Urbana-Champaign, USA: Department of Educational Psychology.

Kim, J., Chi, Y., Huensch, A., Jun, H., Li, H. and Roullion, V. (2010). A case study on an item writing process: use of test specifications, nature of group dynamics, and individual item writers' characteristics. *Language Assesment Quarterly* 7: 160–73

Li, J. (2006). *Introducing Audit Trails to the World of Language Testing.* Unpublished Masters thesis. University of Illinois at Urbana-Champaign, USA: Division of English as an International Language.

Lynch, B. and Davidson, F. (1994). Criterion referenced language test development: linking curricula, teachers and tests. *TESOL Quarterly* 28: 727–43.

Messick, S. (1989). Validity. In Linn, R. L. (ed.), *Educational Measurement.* New York, NY: Macmillan/American Council on Education, 13–103.

Oscarson, M. (1989). Self-assessment of language proficiency: rationale and applications. *Language Testing* 6: 13.

Popham, W. J. (1978). *Criterion Referenced Measurement.* Englewood Cliffs, NJ: Prentice-Hall.

Ruch, G. M. (1924). *The Improvement of the Written Examination.* Chicago, IL: Scott-Foresman and Company.

—— (1929). *The Objective or New-Type Examination.* Chicago, IL: Scott-Foresman and Company.

14

Evidence-centered design in language testing

Robert J. Mislevy and Chengbin Yin

Introduction

Evidence-centered design (ECD) is a conceptual framework for the design and delivery of educational assessments, organized around the idea of assessment as evidentiary argument. We want to draw inferences about what learners know or can do in various situations, based on observing what they say, do, or make in a handful of particular situations (Mislevy *et al.*, 2003). Assessment is viewed as five coordinated layers of activities, processes, and elements. Most directly related to test development are the layers called Domain Modeling, in which assessment design and use arguments are developed, and the Conceptual Assessment Framework, in which Student, Evidence, and Task Models specify the pieces that instantiate the argument (such as scoring methods, measurement models, and schemas for tasks). This chapter lays out the basic ideas of ECD and discusses ways it can be gainfully employed in language testing.

Historical perspectives

Assessment as argument

Validity research concerns ways in which we can build and use assessments that support interpretations and uses of results (Bachman, 2005; Bachman and Palmer, 2010; Kane, 2006; Messick, 1994). The elements of an assessment argument articulate well with Toulmin's (1958) argument schema shown in Figure 14.1 (Mislevy, 2006). A *claim* is a proposition we wish to support with data. A *warrant* is a generalization that justifies the inference from the particular data to the particular *claim*. In language testing, we make claims about learners' language proficiency or abilities, within and across language domains, from observing their task performances. Theory and research concerning processes of language acquisition, stages of language development, and instances of language use can all provide *backing* for the warrant. This backing also informs task design and performance evaluation. When using the test, we reason back up through the warrant from the observations to particular claims. Usually we must qualify our inferences because of *alternative explanations*, which further data might support or undercut; for example, that anxiety rather than language difficulties caused a candidate's poor performance in a speaking task.

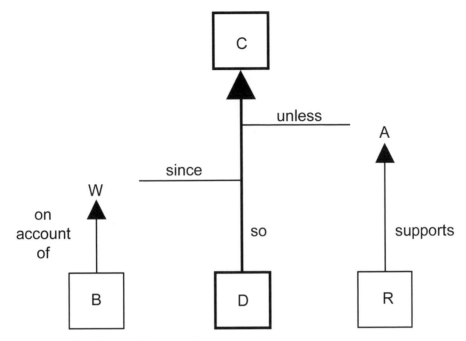

Figure 14.1 Toulmin's general structure for arguments

Assessment design means specifying the kinds of claims we wish to make, then crafting the operational elements of an assessment that allow us to reason in this manner. Messick (1994: 17) outlines the essential structure:

> A construct-centered approach would begin by asking what complex of knowledge, skills, or other attributes should be assessed, presumably because they are tied to explicit or implicit objectives of instruction or are otherwise valued by society. Next, what behaviors or performances should reveal those constructs, and what tasks or situations should elicit those behaviors? Thus, the nature of the construct guides the selection or construction of relevant tasks as well as the rational development of construct-based scoring criteria and rubrics.

Test specifications

Test specifications, also known as test blueprints, have long been used in test development. The original focus was content coverage and item types. Bloom's (1956) taxonomy of learning objectives incorporated considerations of cognition as well. Continued extensions provide additional support for the many specific decisions a test developer must make. In language testing, Bachman and Palmer's (1996) framework of task characteristics describes the features of target language use and assessment tasks. Davidson and Lynch's (2002) book on test specifications helps developers create a detailed blueprint for writing tasks with specified properties to suit the purposes, constraints, and resources of a particular testing context.

Assessment engineering

Another line of research is developing tools to improve the efficiency and quality of task design. Hively *et al.*'s (1968) item shells, Haladyna and Shindoll's (1989) item forms, and Bormuth's (1970) transformational-grammar item generation algorithms were early theory-based approaches to task development. Embretson (1985) illuminated a path toward integrating test theory, task design, and cognitive psychology. Irvine and Kyllonen (2002) provide review articles and illustrative examples of theory-based item generation through 2000. In more recent work, the physical features of tasks that are to be varied reflect the features of tasks that are important cognitively (e.g., Gierl *et al.*, 2008). Embretson's (1998) cognitive assessment design system and Luecht's (2003) integrated test design, development, and delivery approach are two examples of technology supports for principled task design.

Definitions

The terminology in ECD is best understood through its representation of layers in the design and implementation of educational assessment (Mislevy and Riconscente, 2006; Mislevy *et al.*, 2002, 2003). Table 14.1 summarizes the roles and key entities of layers, which are discussed below in the context of language assessment.

Domain analysis

Domain analysis marshals information that has implications for assessment in the targeted domain. In Toulmin's terminology, *domain analysis* provides the backing for assessment arguments. In

Table 14.1 Summary of evidence-centered design layers in the context of language testing (adapted from Mislevy and Riconscente, 2006)

Layer	Role	Key entities	Examples of knowledge representations
Domain analysis	Gather substantive information about what is to be assessed.	Representation forms; analysis of language learning and language use in specific context or content area.	Language framework; language curriculum; proficiency guidelines; syllabi.
Domain modeling	Express assessment argument in narrative form.	Knowledge, skills, and capabilities; task features; potential observations.	Toulmin diagram; design patterns; claims, evidence, and task worksheets.
Conceptual assessment framework	Express assessment argument in specifications for tasks, measurement models, scoring procedures.	Student, evidence, and task model; task model variables; rubrics; measurement models; test specifications.	Task shells; task templates; graphical representation of measurement models.
Assessment implementation	Implement assessment, including writing tasks and fitting measurement models.	Task materials; pretest data for item and task scoring.	Items and tasks; design of test materials and score reports; item parameter data files.
Assessment delivery	Coordinate interaction of students and tasks; task and test-level scoring and reporting.	Task as presented; responses as collected; scores as evaluated.	Rendering of test materials; individual and group-level reports; data files.

language testing, this means forms, meanings, and use, assemblies of knowledge, skills, and competencies that language learners typically engage with in target situations, and features of tasks that invoke them.

The inferences we wish to draw about examinees and the psychological perspective we take on language acquisition and use serve as the starting point for *domain analysis*. If the inferences concern learners' ability to perform certain kinds of real-world tasks, the domain analysis will necessarily involve analysis of prototypical real-world tasks, or needs analysis (Long, 2005), and examine target language use (TLU) situations (Bachman and Palmer, 1996). Task-based tests focus on features of tasks, and characterize examinees in terms of their performance in those situations. In contrast, language aptitude tests are cast in trait terms and support inferences about individuals' possession of capabilities conceptualized as latent traits. The *domain analysis* for these tests is thus an analysis of abilities that capture individual differences in language aptitude. In *domain analysis*, here we draw on perspectives and expertise of language educators and researchers to identify characteristics of knowledge, skills, and competencies that are central to assessment design. Analysis of task features and competency–task relationships also occur in this layer. Curriculum materials and standards, language framework, and national and regional language proficiency standards are potential sources of information as well.

Domain modeling

The *domain modeling* layer is used to articulate the assessment argument. It does not address technical details such as measurement models or data formats, but rather ways to fill in an argument schema using information identified in *domain analysis* and task paradigms, Toulmin diagrams, and design patterns are schematic tools for this purpose. The paradigms are non-technical sketches of those discussed in the section on the next layer.

Figure 14.2 is an extended Toulmin diagram in the context of a task-based language assessment. The claim is an aspect of a language user's capabilities. The evidence is particular things the user says or does in the assessment situation. In this diagram, Student X has completed a number of assessment tasks that approximate the real-world language use situations of interest. A behaviorist perspective characterizes students in terms of what responses are produced under what conditions, and postulates how likely they are to complete real-world tasks (alternative perspectives around which assessment arguments can be cast are trait and interactionist; Bachman, 2007). Backing comes from practical experience and language acquisition research (e.g., Bachman and Cohen, 1998). Patterns of responses across a range of tasks are an indication of what tasks Student X performs well on and those which the student is not able to complete.

Design patterns organize information from *domain analysis* to define a design space for a task designer who needs to write tasks addressing the capabilities at issue (Mislevy *et al.*, 2003). Table 14.2 shows the attributes of a design pattern. Focal knowledge, skills, and abilities (KSAs) are the capabilities about which the tasks will be constructed to assess (i.e., the claims). Characteristic features of tasks must be included in some form in order to evoke evidence of the targeted capabilities, and variable features are ways designers can shift focus or difficulty. Potential Work Products are the kinds of things student can say, do, or make to produce evidence, and Potential Observations are the qualities of the work that constitute evidence (e.g., accuracy, fluency, appropriateness, correctness of inferences). Table 14.3 is an example of a design pattern for an aspect of reading proficiency, namely reasoning through Cause and Effect structures in text.

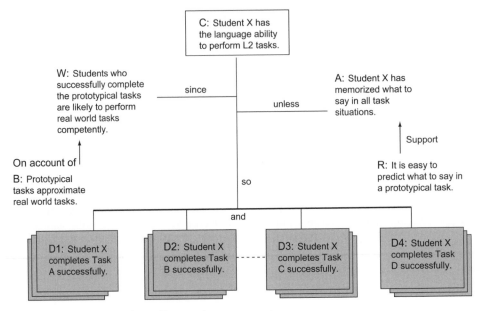

Figure 14.2 Extended Toulmin diagram for assessment

Table 14.2 Design pattern attributes and relationships to assessment argument

Attribute	Description	Assessment argument component
Summary	Overview of design pattern	Warrant
Focal knowledge, skills and abilities (KSAs)	The primary knowledge/skill/abilities targeted by this design pattern.	Student model
Additional knowledge, skills and abilities	Other knowledge/skills/abilities that may be required by tasks generated under this design pattern.	Student model, if construct relevant; alternative explanations, if construct irrelevant.
Characteristic features of tasks	Aspects of assessment situations that must be present in the task situation in order to evoke the desired evidence.	Task model
Variable features of tasks	Aspects of assessment situations that can be varied in order to shift difficulty or focus.	Task model
Potential observations	Characteristics of performance that constitute evidence about KSAs (e.g. accuracy, fluency, correct inference).	Evidence model
Potential work products	Performances by which students can produce evidence about Focal KSAs (e.g., written text, response choice, oral speech)	Task model

Table 14.3 A design pattern for assessing cause and effect reasoning reading comprehension (adapted from Mislevy and Rahman, 2009)

Summary	This design pattern motivates tasks that require students to reason through cause-and-effect schema expressed in the conventions of written English to make inferences, predictions, or provide explanations.
Focal KSAs	Knowledge of how real or imaginary phenomena are connected in terms of causation, what makes an event a cause and what makes an event an effect, and how causal connections are expressed in propositions.
	Skill to distinguish various forms of causal connections, distinguish causal connections from logical or temporal connections, distinguish signal words for cause-effect relation from that of the other relations, organize propositions as indicated by rhetorical structure, marker words.
	Ability to reason in inductive or deductive mode for predictions or explanations, trace relationship among causally connected events whether stated explicitly or implicitly, hypothesize in cause & effect structures, and recognize signal words for cause-effect relationship.
Additional KSAs	Ability to decode and to respond orally or in writing.
	Knowledge of various types of text passages, and notations, signs, and symbols used in specific disciplines.
	Familiarity with the substantive situation being addressed.
Characteristic features of tasks	Prose presentation of a situation involving one or more cause & effect relationships; directive requiring examinee to reason about or through those relationships.
Variable features	Nature of C&E relationship(s) with regard to Lakoff's (1987) canonical C&E schema.
	Structure of C&E relationship(s): simple, chained, multiple effects, multiple possible causes, multiple conjunctive causes.
	C&E relationship(s) implicit, explicit, or mixed?
	Direction of reasoning required—cause to effect or effect to cause.
	Length and complexity of prose passage.
	Degree of substantive knowledge required.
Potential work products	Selection of adverbials or answer choices, completion of table/graphic organizer, sequencing cards or pictures to structure a narrative, oral or written explanations or predictions, identifying missing elements, retell a story.
Potential observations	Is the C&E relationship appropriately explained or distinguished from other forms of relationship, or correctly constructed when the events are not presented in canonical order?
	Were C&E text conventions used appropriately?
	Are there conceptual errors or misunderstandings that indicate the C&E relationship has not been properly constructed?
	Are conventions and rhetorical structures being used appropriately in explanation?

Conceptual assessment framework

The *conceptual assessment framework* (CAF) provides a structure for coordinating the substantive, statistical, and operational aspects of an assessment. The operational elements of assessment machinery are specified in the form of three models, which instantiate the assessment argument. The Student Model operationalizes claims in terms of student variables, which can be as simple as an overall score, or as complex as the person variables in an item response theory or cognitive diagnostic model. Values assigned to student model variables, based on observing performances, correspond to claims about students' capabilities.

The Evidence Model contains two components, the evaluation component and the measurement model. The evaluation component concerns how to identify and characterize salient features of examinee performances—that is, how to score task performances. Through evaluation procedures using answer keys, rating rubrics with examples, and so on, we determine the values of Observable Variables from students' Work Products. What aspects of student work are important and how to evaluate them are governed by the psychological perspective in which the assessment is framed. Tests cast in behaviorist terms, with its focus on stimulus–response bonds, may focus on qualities such as accuracy or complexity of the responses. Tests cast in interactionist/sociocognitive terms highlight the appropriateness and effectiveness of the choices an examinee makes in light of the language use situation. The measurement model provides a mechanism for synthesizing data across tasks and quantifying the strength of evidence for claims, such as reliability coefficients and standard errors of measurement. Psychometric models such as classical test theory, item response theory, and cognitive diagnosis models (Lee and Sawaki, 2009) are used in this step.

The Task Model consists of blueprints for assessment tasks and work products. In applications using design patterns, task models reflect choices from the suggested range of potential work products, and characteristic and variable features and potential work products and observations. This layer specifies work products and narrows down to central and optional task features that evoke evidence about the targeted claims. For example, performance-based assessment of student teachers will necessarily involve observations of a student teaching a language class, and evaluations of qualities of lesson planning and lesson delivery. In contrast, if the claim concerns mastery of content or pedagogical knowledge, a computer-delivered knowledge assessment, in the form of multiple-choice questions or short-essay questions will serve the purpose. Constellations of tasks are brought together as an assessment in the *assembly model* to determine the breadth and depth of the domain being assessed. Test specifications and blueprints are generated in this model on the basis of CAF models.

The implementation and delivery layers

The *assessment implementation* layer includes activities such as authoring tasks, fine-tuning rubrics and examples, and fitting measurement models. It is in this layer that assessment-engineering developments in technology for creating such elements as adaptive testing, interaction in simulation environments, and capture and evaluation of complex performances are effected, in accordance with specifications laid out in the CAF. Williamson *et al.* (2006), for instance, provide worked-through examples of how automated scoring procedures are developed through the ECD framework.

The *assessment delivery layer* includes processes for selecting and administering test items, interacting with examinees, reporting scores, and providing feedback to appropriate parties. The information, structure, and rationale of these processes embody the assessment argument laid out in *domain analysis*, are structured by the blueprint laid out in the CAF, and utilize the operational elements created in assessment implementation. Details of delivery system architecture are provided in Almond *et al.* (2002).

Critical issues and topics

Conceptions of capabilities and competencies shape the assessment argument. A perspective on language learning and language use suggests the kinds of inferences we should draw about examinees, from what kinds of evidence, in what kinds of assessment situations (Mislevy, 2006; Mislevy and Yin, 2009).

Definition of constructs

Claims in language testing are usually phrased in terms of constructs, and reflect our intended ways to construe aspects of examined capabilities and competencies. In language testing, approaches vary as to the nature of the construct to be assessed (Bachman, 2007). From the trait perspective, a construct is defined in terms of aspects of examinees' capabilities that are stable across a range of situations. Constructs in task-based language assessment are cast in the behaviorist perspective, phrased in terms of examinees' capabilities to perform certain kinds of real-world tasks (Norris *et al.*, 1998). An interactionist approach views language activities as discursive meaning co-construction practices that all participants engage in, using a conglomeration of linguistic, interactional, and identity resources (Young, 2008). This last approach is compatible with a sociocognitive perspective on language development, seeing a holistic, adaptive process that integrates the social, the physical, and the cognitive (Atkinson, 2002). A construct of interest in this approach can be phrased in terms of resources that enable the language event.

A construct in an assessment is the assessor's inevitably simplified conception of examinee capabilities, chosen to suit a purpose of a given assessment. We can think of examinee capabilities in terms of resource employment during a language event, and describe them in terms of the extrapersonal linguistic, cultural, and substantive patterns (L/C/S patterns; Mislevy and Yin, 2009) learners can usefully engage with in various contexts (Ellis, 2008; Larsen-Freeman and Cameron, 2008). Approaches to construct definition can all be understood in terms of resource assembly, of L/C/S patterns that relate to language use. From an interactionist perspective, we see people's capabilities, contexts, and performances as intertwined in a constantly evolving process (Chalhoub-Deville, 2003; Chapelle, 1998). Any approach to construct definition necessarily involves all three, explicitly or implicitly. The assessor's intentions determine what the construct is, which in turn holds implications for design decisions in regard to tasks, evaluation procedures, and the measurement models used to aggregate evidence.

The central role of context

Use of language is enmeshed with the context in which a language event takes place. Language use patterns emerge as humans "soft assemble" resources in response to a communicative demand, and are transformed through further usage (Larsen-Freeman and Cameron, 2008). Form–meaning–use mapping occurs as a result of ongoing interaction among the social, cultural, and psychological, as individuals become attuned to linguistic and cultural norms and conventions. A sociocognitive view argues for a coherent coupling of and coordinated interaction between the individual and the context. Context as co-constructed by multiple participants in a communicative event evolves through ongoing meaning negotiation activities; through such interactions do individuals' capabilities develop (Douglas, 2000; Young, 2008).

Unobserved, yet central to assessment, is the examinee's internal perception of the context that presents externally as an assessment task (Douglas, 2000). We wish to examine the extent to which the examinee can assemble resources and activate internal patterns that go with the extrapersonal L/C/S patterns required for an assessment task. The examinee's internal patterns structure and mediate her behaviors, which are evaluated by the standards of the external L/C/S patterns the assessor considers germane. The inference thus concerns the observed "mental context" (Council of Europe, 2001: 50) that combines unique features of the assessment situation with internal patterns at all levels she has built up from her past experiences. Claims and inferences are thus high-level descriptors of (1) the degree to which assessment tasks align with TLUs, and (2) the extent to which targeted patterns are activated across assessment tasks.

Current contributions and research

Language tests developed using ECD

In language testing, ECD has been applied in the Test of English as a Foreign Language internet-Based Test (TOFEL iBT; Pearlman, 2008), the Test of English for International Communication (TOEIC) Speaking and Writing test (Hines, 2010), and the Advanced Placement (AP) Spanish Language Exam (College Board, 2010). The procedures Educational Testing Service used to develop test blueprints for the TOEFL iBT illustrate ECD principles in a large-scale assessment of English language learners (ELLs) (Chapelle *et al.*, 2008). The step of defining the construct to be measured and the claims and subclaims to be made about examinee abilities illustrates a proficiency paradigm from domain modeling. An example of a claim for the speaking test is that the examinee can "communicate effectively by speaking in English-speaking academic environments" (Pearlman, 2008: 232). Subsequent steps characterize observations for grounding them and identify real world tasks to provide evidence, resulting in evidence paradigms and task paradigms from domain modeling. Based upon the results of these steps, templates for generating items or tasks, namely task shells, are constructed to incorporate essential elements of task models in the conceptual assessment framework.

Principled assessment designs for inquiry

The Principled Assessment Designs for Inquiry (PADI) project developed a conceptual framework and software tools to support ECD, including design patterns (Baxter and Mislevy, 2004). Although the project focused on science inquiry, the PADI object model and knowledge representations have been applied in a number of domains, including language testing (e.g., Wei *et al.*, 2008; Mislevy and Rahman, 2009).

Structured measurement models and task design

Connected with work on assessment argument structures and design frameworks has been the development of measurement models that explicitly incorporate features of tasks. Variables representing task features appear in both structured item response theory models (De Boeck and Wilson, 2004) and diagnostic classification models (Tatsuoka, 1983; Rupp *et al.*, 2010) in accordance with theories about their role in both the arguments and the anticipated effects they have on response patterns. Jang (2009; this volume), for example, describes a cognitive diagnosis model for performance on the LanguEdge assessment in terms of nine skills required in various combinations in test items. Two examples are "Determine word meaning out of context with recourse to background knowledge" and "Recognize major contrasts and arguments in the text whose rhetorical structure contains the relationships such as compare/contrast, cause/effect or alternative arguments and map them into mental framework." Examinees' performance would then be reported in terms of the skills they had mastered. Jang concludes that this modeling approach works best for tasks developed around targeted skills, rather than retrofitted to existing tests developed for other purposes.

Main research methods

This section describes ways that ECD has been applied, with processes and representations that vary in details and the foci with which the framework is operationalized.

Claims and evidence

The TOEFL iBT final blueprints and TOEIC speaking and writing tests show how fine-grained pieces of evidence are marshaled to support claims and subclaims (Hines, 2010; Pearlman, 2008). ECD principles guide the various stages and procedures employed in the design of the two tests. Table 14.4 summarizes the steps. Note the effective use of proficiency, evidence, and task paradigms. This work articulated claims and subclaims in the domain and laid out sources of evidence, tasks for eliciting them, and task features that discriminated among a range of capabilities. A particular focus was the more technical step of creating task shells for generating parallel items.

Table 14.4 Steps taken to redesign TOEFL iBT and TOEIC speaking and writing tests and guided by layers in Evidence-Centered Design (adapted from Hines, 2010)

Steps in TOEFL iBT and TOEIC redesign		Components from evidence-centered design	Layers in evidence-centered design
Task design analysis	Reviewing prior theory and research	Domain documents	Domain analysis
	Articulating claims and subclaims about language proficiency in all domains	Proficiency paradigm	Domain modeling
	Listing sources of evidence for each claim and subclaim	Evidence paradigm	
	Identifying real world tasks that provide evidence	Task paradigm	
	Identifying task characteristics affecting task difficulty	Task paradigm	
	Identifying criteria for evaluating performance on the tasks	Task paradigm	
Constructing task shell	*Reiterating claim and subclaims*	*Proficiency paradigm*	*From domain modeling layer*
	Defining aspects of responses that are the focus of evaluation	Measurement model	Conceptual assessment framework
	Specifying fixed elements of tasks	Task model	
	Specifying variable elements of tasks	Task model	
	Composing rubric	Evaluation component	
	Describing example tasks	Task model	

Luecht's (2003) design procedures similarly align a theoretical construct model, a task development model, and a psychometric scoring model. The theoretical construct model defines the knowledge, skills, and ability space to be assessed—in effect a proficiency paradigm. Luecht organized an illustrative theoretical model of language proficiency around the Interagency Language Roundtable (ILR) proficiency scale to define five ability dimensions: vocabulary, grammar, pronunciation, fluency/integrative, and sociolinguistic ability, each organized into five ordered levels. The two components of the task development model are task development specifications and test assembly specifications, both CAF objects from the ECD perspective. Task development specifications provide a detailed schema for stimulus selection, item writing, and expected responses within each proficiency level. The psychometric model specifies the scoring procedures and uses measurement models to relate observations to the underlying construct. Iterative use of these procedures thus aligns constructs with test development practices and psychometric models, to address the complexity of language proficiency assessment.

The PADI tools and representations for working through an evidence centered design are described in Mislevy and Riconscente (2006). The illustrations are in the domain of science, but the approach is applied in the same manner for language testing.

Reusability and modularity

Taking advantage of the common conceptual language and representational forms of ECD can enhance efficiency as well as validity, by exploiting the principles of reusability, modularity, and interoperability. Whenever design and implementation are required, the designer seeks to express the results in forms that are explicit and can be more readily adapted in further work in the same or other assessments.

Laying out assessment arguments and creating design patterns for hard-to-assess aspects of learners' capabilities helps make explicit design choices that assessment has and supports their choices (Mislevy et al., 2003). This is re-use of the conceptual structures that underlie assessments. Developing fragments of measurement models that express recurring evidentiary relationships allows psychometricians and content specialists to work together to design many new tasks with the same underlying measurement models (Mislevy et al., 2002). This modular approach illustrates the concept of re-use for the evidentiary foundation of complex tests: complex tasks that differ on the surface but share the same evidentiary structure can use the same pieces of scoring procedures and measurement models. Creating models for tasks and data structures for implementing and delivering them thus reduces programming and testing time for computer-based tests (Luecht, 2003). For existing assessments, understanding a test in terms of explicit arguments and modular elements makes it easier to adapt and reassemble elements for new purposes (Fulcher and Davidson, 2009). The projects mentioned in this chapter have used ECD in ways that makes explicit the underlying arguments and the role the elements in the operational test play, and expressed the results in forms that support further development.

Assessment use arguments

Assessment use arguments (AUA; Bachman, 2005; Bachman and Palmer, 2010) extend the argument-based approach beyond the ECD design phase, to assessment use and validation. AUA addresses the social context in which an assessment is meant to be used. Claims in an AUA concern intended uses of an assessment and are justified in terms of beneficence of consequences and equitability and value sensitivity of decisions made based on assessment results. For example, results of foreign language proficiency assessment can be an indication of whether language benchmarks have been met, and consequently can be used for purposes such as evaluating outcomes of instruction and program effectiveness. A coherent chain of reasoning connects essential elements in the assessment design argument and AUA. Examples of AUAs for actual assessments can be found in Llosa (2008) and Chapelle *et al.* (2008).

Recommendations for practice

A developer wishing to use ECD to develop a language test should browse both the more conceptual discursions and the illustrative applications cited above. The conceptual references provide a common grounding of the essential elements of ECD, which underlie the variations seen in the applications. The applications show the ideas at work. Adapting the forms and the processes of a prototypical example to one's own project is often a useful way to begin. In all cases, the up-front attention paid to domain modeling more than pays for the time invested.

Claims, framed in terms of constructs, reflect the assessor's psychological grounding and the purpose or intended use of the assessment. As Messick indicated, attending to the nature of claims that are needed to serve an assessment's purpose is the starting point in design. For example, discrete-point grammar or vocabulary tests are designed to identify students' mastery of focused components of a language curriculum; results indicate whether instructional objectives have been met and guide instruction to address learning needs. Claims in general language proficiency tests are phrased in generic terms, such as examinees being able to speak or write at particular levels, with minimal descriptions of context. The purposes these tests are intended for are broad and span any number of TLUs. In contrast, tests specifying context of use are intended for more focused purposes. For instance, the Occupational English Test specifies examinee occupation as context of use and assesses examinee competencies to perform tasks typical of a specific occupation, such as business or medicine (McNamara, 1996). Claims and inferences are contextualized, and relate directly to the context for which they are intended. These considerations should guide test developers as they work through domain modeling, regardless of the particular ECD representations they employ (e.g., paradigms, Toulmin diagrams, design patterns).

Advances in language science inform and transform conceptions of language learning and language use. They call attention to aspects of context and aspects of language use that are inextricably connected and integral to language development. An interactionist perspective highlights the importance of context for language assessment, and of the alignment between assessment tasks and TLUs needed to justify claims about the examinee performance in those TLUs. Focused analysis of features characterizing TLUs, of configurations of knowledge, skills, and competencies that underlie performance with reference to particular TLUs is essential to task design, because it is the representation of TLU features in assessment tasks that elicits the targeted L/S/C patterns in the examinee. Task design requires principled patterning of features that invoke stable states and regularities, amid ongoing variation and change within and across individuals. An important aspect of these features is the "resource-directing dimension," defined as increasing demands on learners' cognitive resources while potentially directing them to aspects of language code to be used to complete the tasks (Robinson, 2009: 199).

The inescapable involvement of L/C/S patterns at all levels in any language event raises a tradeoff in task design, as to how much and what kinds of context to include in tasks. Minimizing context reduces demands for necessary but unrelated knowledge and skills. In argument terminology, such demands introduce alternative explanations for poor performances; in measurement terms they are possible sources of construct irrelevant variance. But decontextualized situations lack fidelity; students can perform well here, yet not apply what would seem to be the same skills in TLU situations (see Ross, this volume). Worse, instruction that emphasizes performances on decontextualized tasks draws attention from learning to use language in real world situations. An alternative strategy that increases fidelity while minimizing alternative explanations is to use contexts that are known to be familiar to examinees. Assessing verb usage in a role-playing scenario of a familiar local festival is an example with younger students. Assessing reading proficiency with medical texts illustrates the idea with prospective healthcare professionals (Douglas, 2000).

Future directions

Our understanding of how people acquire and use language has advanced radically, and new technologies are coming online continually to provide interactive task environments and capture the resulting evidence (see Sawaki, this volume). The challenge is harnessing this new knowledge for practical testing purposes—effectively, validly, affordably. ECD provides a coherent conceptual framework that makes explicit the principles and interacting structures of argumentation, analysis, and operation that underlie assessment. It provides language and concepts to help developers design and coordinate the elements of familiar assessments as well as new ones. It motivates definitions of data structures and operational processes that can be used and re-used flexibly, across projects and organizations.

The work described in this chapter represents initial steps in developing and using ECD. Future work will fill the framework out more fully, provide additional worked examples, and develop software tools and knowledge representations that make it easy for test developers to put the ideas to use. In the Domain Modeling layer, design patterns are needed to provide support performance assessments and simulation-based assessments that focus on interactive capabilities. In the CAF layer, we need task design frameworks, adaptable modules for measurement models, and automated or rubric-based evaluation procedures, all explicated in terms of their relationship to assessment arguments. In the implementation and delivery layers, we need representations and data structures that exploit computer capabilities to build, administer, and evaluate tests. These are ambitious and broad undertakings, spanning years or decades. At the same time, however, the most fundamental ideas of ECD—carefully thinking through what capabilities one wants to assess, and the kinds of things we need to see learners do in what kinds of situations—can be put into action immediately by every teacher and every test designer in the field.

Further reading

Chapelle, C., Enright, M. K. and Jamieson, J. M. (eds), (2008). *Building a Validity Argument for the Test of English as a Foreign Language^{TM}*. New York, NY: Routledge. This volume presents an in-depth discussion of the application of some of the ideas of evidence-centered design and assessment use argumentation to the TOEFL redesign.

Mislevy, R. J., Almond, R. G. and Lukas, J. (2004). *A brief introduction to evidence-centered design*. CSE Technical Report 632, Los Angeles: The National Center for Research on Evaluation, Standards, Student Testing (CRESST), Center for Studies in Education, UCLA. www.cse.ucla.edu/products/reports/r632.pdf. This is a reader-friendly introduction to evidence-centered design. It is the best place for a new reader to start.

Mislevy, R. J. and Riconscente, M. (2006). Evidence-centered assessment design: Layers, concepts, and terminology. In S. Downing and T. Haladyna (eds), *Handbook of Test Development*. Mahwah, NJ: Erlbaum. Online version: *Evidence-centered assessment design: Layers, structures, and terminology* (PADI Technical Report 9). Menlo Park, CA: SRI International. padi.sri.com/downloads/TR9_ECD.pdf. This discussion of ECD is aimed at test developers. It uses representations and terminology from the Principled Assessment Design for Inquiry (PADI) project.

Mislevy, R. J., Steinberg, L. S. and Almond, R. A. (2002). Design and analysis in task-based language assessment. *Language Testing* 19, 477–96. This is a more technical discussion of the application of evidence-centered design to task-based language tests. It addresses issues of construct definition, multivariate student models, and complex tasks.

Mislevy, R. J. and Yin, C. (2009). If language is a complex system, what is language assessment? *Language Learning* 59 (Suppl. 1): 249–67. This article discusses how to build and interpret assessment arguments from an interactionist/ complex systems perspective on language.

References

Almond, R. G., Steinberg, L. S. and Mislevy, R. J. (2002). Enhancing the design and delivery of assessment systems: A four-process architecture. *Journal of Technology, Learning, and Assessment* 1, 5. www.bc.edu/research/intasc/jtla/journal/v1n5.shtml (accessed 6/7/10).

Atkinson, D. (2002). Toward a sociocognitive approach to second language acquisition. *The Modern Language Journal* 86: 525–45.

Bachman, L.F. (2005). Building and supporting a case for test use. *Language Assessment Quarterly* 2: 1–34.

—— (2007). What is the construct? The dialectic of abilities and contexts in defining constructs in language assessment. In J. Fox, M. Wesche, and D. Bayliss (eds), *Language Testing Reconsidered*. Ottawa, Canada: University of Ottawa Press.

Bachman, L. F. and Cohen, A. D. (eds), (1998). *Interfaces Between Second Language Acquisition and Language Testing Research*. New York, NY: Cambridge University Press.

Bachman, L. F. and Palmer, A. S. (1996). *Language Testing in Practice*. Oxford, UK: Oxford University Press.

—— (2010). *Language Assessment Practice: developing language assessments and justifying their use in the real world*. Oxford, UK: Oxford University Press.

Baxter, G. and Mislevy, R. J. (2004). *The case for an integrated design framework for assessing science inquiry*, CSE Technical Report 638. Los Angeles, CA: The National Center for Research on Evaluation, Standards, Student Testing (CRESST), Center for Studies in Education, UCLA.

Bloom, B. S. (ed.), (1956). *Taxonomy of Educational Objectives: the classification of educational goals, Handbook I, cognitive domain*. New York, NY: Longman.

Bormuth, J. R. (1970). *On the Theory of Achievement Test Items*. Chicago, IL: University of Chicago Press.

Chalhoub-Deville, M. (2003). Second language interaction: current perspectives and future trends. *Language Testing* 20: 369–83.

Chapelle, C. (1998). Construct definition and validity inquiry in SLA research. In L. F. Bachman and A. D. Cohen (eds), *Interfaces Between Second Language Acquisition and Language Testing Research*. New York, NY: Cambridge University Press.

Chapelle, C., Enright, M. K. and Jamieson, J. M. (eds), (2008). *Building a validity argument for the Test of English as a Foreign Language*[TM]. New York, NY: Routledge.

College Board (2010). *AP Spanish Language Update on Changes to the Course and Exam*. apcentral.college board.com/apc/members/courses/teachers_corner/50015.html (accessed 6/7/10).

Council of Europe (2001). *Common European Framework of Reference for Languages: Learning, teaching and assessment*. Cambridge, UK: Cambridge University Press. www.coe.int/t/dg4/linguistic/source/Framewor k_EN.pdf (accessed 6/7/10).

Davidson, F. and Lynch, B. K. (2002). *Testcraft: a teacher's guide to writing and using language test specifications*. Newhaven, CT: Yale University Press.

De Boeck, P. and Wilson, M. (eds) (2004). *Explanatory item response models: A generalized linear and nonlinear approach*. New York, NY: Springer.

Douglas, D. (2000). *Assessing Languages for Specific Purposes*. Cambridge, UK: Cambridge University Press.

Ellis, R. (2008). *The Study of Second Language Acquisition*, 2nd edn. Oxford, UK: Oxford University Press.

Embretson, S. E. (ed.) (1985). *Test design: developments in psychology and psychometrics*. Orlando, FL: Academic Press.

—— (1998). A cognitive design system approach to generating valid tests: Application to abstract reasoning. *Psychological Methods* 3: 380–96.

Fulcher, G. and Davidson, F. (2009). Test architecture. Test retrofit. *Language Testing* 26: 123–44.

Gierl, M. J., Zhou, J. and Alves, C. (2008). Developing a taxonomy of item model types to promote assessment engineering. *Journal of Technology, Learning, and Assessment* 7, 2. escholarship.bc.edu/cgi/viewcon tent.cgi?article=1137&context=jtla (accessed 6/7/10).

Haladyna, T. M. and Shindoll, R. R. (1989). Shells: a method for writing effective multiple-choice test items. *Evaluation and the Health Professions* 12: 97–104.

Hines, S. (2010). *Evidence-centered design: the TOEIC® speaking and writing tests*. Princeton, NJ: Educational Testing Service. www.ets.org/Media/Research/pdf/TC-10-07.pdf (accessed 6/7/10).

Hively, W., Patterson, H. L. and Page, S. H. (1968). A "universe-defined" system of arithmetic achievement tests. *Journal of Educational Measurement* 5: 275–90.

Irvine, S. H. and Kyllonen, P. C. (eds), (2002). *Item Generation for test Development*. Mahwah, NJ: Lawrence Erlbaum Associates.

Jang, E. E. (2009). Cognitive diagnostic assessment of L2 reading comprehension ability: Validity arguments for Fusion Model application to *LanguEdge* assessment. *Language Testing* 26: 31–73.

Kane, M. (2006). Validation. In R. J. Brennan (ed.), *Educational measurement*, 4th edn. Westport, CT: Praeger.

Larsen-Freeman, D. and Cameron, L. (2008). *Complex Systems and Applied Linguistics*. Oxford, UK: Oxford University Press.

Lee, Y. W. and Sawaki, Y. (2009). Cognitive diagnosis approaches to language assessment: An overview. *Language Assessment Quarterly* 6: 172–89.

Llosa, L. (2008). Building and supporting a validity argument for a standards-based classroom assessment of English proficiency based on teacher judgments. *Educational Measurement: Issues and Practice* 27: 32–42.

Long, M. H. (ed.), (2005). *Second Language Needs Analysis*. Cambridge, UK: Cambridge University Press.

Luecht, R. M. (2003). Multistage complexity in language proficiency assessment: A framework for aligning theoretical perspectives, test development, and psychometrics. *Foreign Language Annals* 36: 527–35.

McNamara, T. F. (1996). *Measuring Second Language Performance*. New York, NY: Addison Wesley Longman.

Messick, S. (1989). Validity. In R. L. Linn (ed.), *Educational measurement*, 3rd edn. New York, NY: American Council on Education/Macmillan.

—— (1994). The interplay of evidence and consequences in the validation of performance assessments. *Educational Researcher* 32: 13–23.

Mislevy, R. J. (2006). Cognitive psychology and educational assessment. In R.L. Brennan (ed.), *Educational Measurement*, 4th edn. Westport, CT: American Council on Education/Praeger Publishers.

Mislevy, R., Hamel, L., Fried, R. G., Gaffney, T., Haertel, G., Hafter, A., Murphy, R., Quellmalz, E., Rosenquist, A., Schank, P., Draney, K., Kennedy, C., Long, K., Wilson, M., Chudowsky, N., Morrison, A., Pena, P., Songer, N. and Wenk, A. (2003). *Design Patterns for Assessing Science Inquiry* (PADI Technical Report 1). Menlo Park, CA: SRI International. padi.sri.com/downloads/TR1_Design_Patterns.pdf (accessed 6/7/10).

Mislevy, R. J. and Rahman, T. (2009). *A Design Pattern for Assessing Cause and Effect Reasoning in Reading Comprehension (PADI Technical Report 20)*. Menlo Park, CA: SRI International.

Mislevy, R. J. and Riconscente, M. (2006). Evidence-centered assessment design: Layers, concepts, and terminology. In S. Downing and T. Haladyna (eds), *Handbook of Test Development*. Mahwah, NJ: Erlbaum.

Mislevy, R. J., Steinberg, L. S. and Almond, R. A. (2002). Design and analysis in task-based language assessment. *Language Testing* 19: 477–96.

—— (2003). On the structure of educational assessments. *Measurement: Interdisciplinary Research and Perspectives* 1: 3–67.

Mislevy, R. J. and Yin, C. (2009). If language is a complex system, what is language assessment? *Language Learning* 59 (Suppl. 1): 249–67.

Norris, J. M., Brown, J. D., Hudson, T. D. and Yoshioka, J. K. (1998). *Designing Second Language Performance Assessment*. Honolulu, HI: University of Hawai'i Press.

Pearlman, M. (2008). Finalizing the test blueprint. In C. Chapelle, M. K. Enright and J. M. Jamieson (eds), *Building a Validity Argument for the Test of English as a Foreign Language^{TM}*. New York, NY: Routledge.

Robinson, P. (2009). Task complexity, cognitive resources, and syllabus design. In K. V. den Branden, M. Bygate and J. M. Norris (eds), *Task-based Language Teaching: a reader*. Amsterdam, The Netherlands: John Benjamins.

Rupp, A. A., Templin, J. and Henson, R. J. (2010). *Diagnostic measurement: theory, methods, and applications*. New York, NY: Guilford Press.

Tatsuoka, K. K. (1983). Rule space: an approach for dealing with misconceptions based on item response theory. *Journal of Educational Measurement* 20: 345–54.

Toulmin, S. E. (1958). *The Uses of Argument*. Cambridge, UK: Cambridge University Press.

Wei, H., Mislevy, R. J. and Kanal, D. (2008). *An introduction to design patterns in language assessment* (PADI Technical Report 18). Menlo Park, CA: SRI International. padi.sri.com/downloads/TR18_Language_Design_Patterns.pdf (accessed 6/7/10).

Williamson, D. M., Mislevy, R. J. and Bejar, I. I. (eds), (2006). *Automated Scoring of Complex Performances in Computer Based Testing*. Mahwah, NJ: Erlbaum Associates.

Young, R. F. (2008). *Language and Interaction: an advanced resource book*. New York, NY: Routledge.

Claims, evidence, and inference in performance assessment

Steven J. Ross

Introduction

The assessment of performance in understanding and using a second language potentially spans an extraordinary range of domains, tasks, testing techniques, scoring procedures, and score interpretations. The notion of "performance" is usually associated with overt simulation of real-world language use, but it also extends to both recognition of well-formed utterances and sentences, as evidenced in assessment methods such as grammaticality judgments, picture identification, and the ubiquitous multiple-choice item. Performance on these types of instruments is primarily passive and indirect, tapping into learners' declarative knowledge about a second language. Test takers need only indicate their capacity to identify what is well-formed in the target language. Indirect methods of assessing language proficiency have for many decades been found wanting in terms of content, construct, and predictive validity, but have survived primarily because of their relative cost-effectiveness and familiarity.

Demonstrations of procedural knowledge, specifically timed essays, role plays, interviews, and simulations, represent the most direct versions of performance assessment. Direct assessments of language proficiency have been associated with task-based language assessment (Norris *et al.*, 1998), though the transition from the most indirect discrete point forerunners of current task-based assessments was separated by more than a decade of experimentation with testing methods such as translation, cloze, and dictation, which were thought to require an integration of declarative knowledge onto quasi-productive modalities (Oller, 1979). The integrated skills approach was considered an advance over the more discrete-point indirect predecessors, but as Wesche (1987) concluded, integrative tests may not be direct enough to accurately predict proficiency in contexts where language use requires overt performances.

As performance assessment becomes increasingly synonymous with task-based assessment, specification of what an assessment task actually entails is subject to interpretive variability. Norris *et al.* (1998) identify tasks as facsimiles of what occurs in the real world, reproduced in an assessment context. Bachman (2002) in contrast postulates that tasks designed without detailed specifications about the target domain can easily under-represent the construct the tasks are supposed to measure. Claims about language proficiency implied by performance on assessment tasks are thus crucially dependent on how thoroughly they sample and represent the constructs they are designed to measure, how much they entail content felicitous with language use outside the assessment context, and the degree to which performances on such assessment tasks predict proficiency in non-assessment contexts.

Basic to performance task specification and design is the notion of task difficulty. Attempts to design facets of difficulty into tasks (e.g., Robinson, 2001) have been predicated on the idea that particular characteristics of tasks can be proactively and reliably manipulated by designers to calibrate the relative difficulty. The difficulty by design approach has not, however, consistently led to the predictable difference among tasks. As Bachman (2002) has stressed, task difficulty is not solely dependent on analytically derived characteristics of a task, but depends also on the interaction of individual test takers' experiences and abilities to engage in particular tasks. This issue is a core challenge for task-based assessment design. Norris *et al.* (2002), for instance, argue that while some *a priori* estimations about task difficulty are borne out in empirical results, inferences about candidates' performances on other tasks in the same domain might not be considered trustworthy. The implications of their research suggest that the task feature approach to design may be insufficient as a basis for task design. A feature checklist does not well predict actual difficulty, nor does it necessarily satisfy face or content validity expectations.

Central to any validity claim is content domain analysis. Cumming *et al.* (2004) provide an example of how content validity, which is subjectively argued, can be approached. They examined the perceptions of English as a Second Language (ESL) instructors about the authenticity of specimen tasks devised for the performance-oriented revision of the Test of English as a Foreign Language (TOEFL). As the perception of authenticity is central to the evidence-centered design approach adopted for the redesign of the TOEFL, expert judgment is considered essential for supporting claims about the validity of tasks devised to be facsimiles of performance in the target use domain. Content validity is considered by some measurement theorists, e.g., Lissitz and Samuelsen (2007) as essential to defining validity. The issue of content validity for performance assessment is even more crucial, but remains a necessary, but not sufficient, condition for a cohesive validity claim. Bachman and Palmer (1996) and Bachman (2002, 2005) argue for rigorous construct validation of performance assessments in addition to validity claims predicated on correspondences of task content to performance in the target domain. The rationale for test use thus shifts from domain sampling to the interpretation of test outcomes. In this interpretation, the assessment outcomes need to be construct-valid and predict future performances in the target use domain.

Recent efforts to specify the relations among constructs, tasks devised to measure such constructs, and performance characteristics have been applied to a variety of language assessments. The evidence-centered design approach (Mislevy *et al.*, 2002; Chapelle *et al.*, 2008) uses a set of inferential procedures derived from Toulmin's (2003) argument structure for the integration of models of examinee performance, construct validation, and task design specifications, which collectively strengthen the linkage of examinee performance characteristics to the constructs the performances are meant to instantiate. These schematic model formats require a multi-step interlinking chain of arguments from the domain description to the utilization of assessment results. Between each step, evidence-based justifications are required for the ultimate validity claims to be made. For performance assessments, the evidential basis for test score interpretation crucially depends on the validity of arguments linking the body of information or experience (i.e., its backing) to the test data that justifies interpretive claims (i.e., the warrant). Bachman (2005) provides a hypothetical example of a performance task examined under the lens of the Toulmin argument structure. An analogous example is presented here, but with excerpts from an authentic performance assessment specimen, a role play extracted from an oral proficiency interview.

The role play as performance

Speaking performance is the epitome of task-based assessment, for it requires the extemporaneous integration of procedural memory into a real-time performance. The performance, as will be seen, is not, however, independently constructed by the candidate, and is to no small degree co-articulated with an interlocutor whose interjections shape the performance of the candidate, and can potentially influence the formation of proficiency attributes that influence third party raters of the candidate's performance.

In the example presented here, an Oral Proficiency Interview (OPI) candidate has been guided through a series of unscripted tasks crafted by the interviewer to establish the candidate's base level, and to probe to a higher proficiency range in order to confirm that the candidate's proficiency level has been correctly identified. The penultimate task in the OPI is the role play. The role play task featured in this example is one whose validity claim is dependent on the degree to which the actual content of the performance unambiguously assesses the construct of interactive strategic competence. An OPI candidate who can succeed on such a role play task will have fulfilled one of the six tasks required for demonstrating that he can speak at Interagency Language Roundtable (ILR) Level 2—with "limited working proficiency." In relative terms, ILR 2 is an advanced level of proficiency and is widely considered as a threshold for using a second or foreign language in the workplace.

The warrant for a validity claim about interactive strategic competence is derived from the set of conventions established for the ILR rating system: "a limited working proficiency speaker can get into, through, and out of non-routine situations with complications, and interact successfully with native speakers not used to dealing with non-native speakers." The backing for this warrant is predicated on the assumption that candidates who can succeed on all performance tasks at a particular rating level can handle work-related interactions: "They can handle with confidence, but not with facility, most high-frequency social conversational conventions." The empirical basis for this backing statement is famously opaque (Lantoff and Frawley, 1988; Fulcher, 2003), but has nevertheless withstood the test of time, and remains in current circulation.

The empirical linkage between the claim, the backing and the warrant is the actual task performance. The evidence instantiated in the recording of the role-played situation with a complication provides the crucially important support for the claim that a successful role player demonstrates strategic competence at ILR Level 2 "limited working proficiency" threshold. In order for the claim to be warranted, supporting data need to be verified. The first line of evidence is the content validity of the task itself, since if the discourse in the simulated interaction does not sufficiently instantiate the warrant, a claim that the performance adequately justifies a valid inference about proficiency would be undermined.

The task is for the candidate (C) to ask a hotel concierge to arrange for a taxi to take him to the airport for a flight leaving the next morning. The interviewer plays the role of the concierge. For the task to have content validity, it has to be framed in such a manner that the candidate understands what the task is. This requirement is achieved by having the interviewer read out the task in the target language, and by allowing the candidate to read the task description in his native language.

Excerpt 1

5. I: tseh =>you are staying at hotel in Atlanta< and you have to catch a flight
   () to Buffalo()
6. I: early tomorrow morning

7. C: [uhuh
8. I: = the interviewer-that's me- will play the role of the concierge of the hotel-ok.
9. C: = ah
10. I: = Ok. so you would want to book a ()taxi early in the morning-ok.
11. C: uh bu-ah-book for a taxi.
12. I: = to go to the airport yeah
13. C: ahh
14. I: [Ok.
15. C: = ok.

In order for the task to be initiated, the candidate must immediately understand what the role play is about, and must be able to invoke a plausible schema in order to play the role of the hotel guest. Evidence of the candidate's understanding is tentative in Excerpt 1, with the confirmation in Line 15 as the evidence that C understands his role.

The concierge initiates the interaction with the hotel guest and creates the turn for the candidate to make his request for the taxi. As soon as the request is made, the "complication" is introduced. The complications make transactional role play tasks problematic, for such injected complications usually deny the availability of what is sought by the candidate. The construct of "strategic competence" is deemed assessable when the candidate can invent a pragmatically viable work-around for the problem at hand in a manner that leads to the desired outcome—in this case, getting to the airport in time for the flight.

Excerpt 2

16. I: Good morning sir-can I help you.
17. C: ()Good morning um I would like to take a taxi
18. I: [uh hah
19. C: = from here to airport
20. I: = okay
21. C: = tomorrow morning
22. I: = tomorrow morning() ahh okay th-there is a problem with that() from this afternoon
23. I: from six pm there is going to be a 24 hour()lightening city wide strike
24. C: = uh hum
25. I: = involving aa:ll the taxi cabs in the city
26. C: = ahum
27. I: ()they are striking for higher pay()so from six o'clock through six o'clock tomorrow
28. I: aft-evening there will be no taxis running in the city.
29. C: [uh huh

Strategic competence would be made evident in candidate turns in which an alternative to the originally requested service is nominated. As the rating of each task is a dichotomous pass or fail, the strategy used by the candidate is assessed for its viability in successfully getting the requested service. Candidates who can only repeat their requests, or ask for the interlocutor for advice in locating an alternative solution to the problem, run the risk of not passing the task if raters (the interviewer and an independent auditor) determine the work-around to the problem has been unrealistically assisted by the interviewer or pragmatically inappropriate.

Excerpt 3

30. C: ()so when's the taxi ()ahh start again.
31. I: tseh six o'clock tomorrow evening
32. C: tomorrow EVENing.
33. I: uhum
34. C: [ohh-is there ahh(.) is there any service in this hotel we- can take me to the airport.
35. I: well normally there is but the-the-the private drivers are also striking to support the taxi
36. I: drivers in the city() so there are no private()private cars for hire
37. C: [ca:z
38. I: for the twenty-four hour period from six o'clock

In Line 34 the candidate asks about the availability of a hotel shuttle to the airport. Consonant with the task specifications for a "situation with complication," the interviewer/concierge closes off that avenue in order to force the candidate to again access his strategic resources. At this juncture, it is possible to anticipate how a rater could construe the candidate's turn in Line 34 as a plausible strategy to get to the airport. If the interpretation is that a concierge would normally recommend practical solutions to problems hotel guests face, the request in Line 34 could be interpreted as weak evidence of strategic competence. There is nevertheless the complication for the candidate to deal with—even the hotel shuttle drivers will go on strike.

After two more turns in which the candidate again asks for suggestions for getting to the airport in the morning, and again hearing that bus drivers are going to be striking as well, the assessment point in the task is framed up. As a hint to the candidate, the interviewer queries the flight departure time, so as to remind him of the fact that the flight check in time is going to be early the next morning. Such hints are minor repairs by interviewers to reframe the salient facts for a candidate, who up to that point in the interaction may not provide evidence of understanding all of the relevant details. The candidate remains fixated on the idea that the flight leaves in the morning, and does not seem to consider alternatives in light of the relevant facts about the non-availability of means of transport in the morning.

Excerpt 4

53. I: = so:(.)there's no(1)feasible way to get there in the morning
54. C: = uhum
55. I: [hmmm
56. C: [hmmm (2) no bus no taxis
57. I: = not tomorrow morning-no()unfortunately yeah it seems to be bad timing there hmm
58. C: (3) hmm (3) a see tah(2)
59. I: what I could suggest is we havea we have a hotel-we have a sister hotel near the airport
60. C: [uhuh
61. I: >maybe you'd like to move there today
62. C: uhuh

The interviewer's summarization of the strike situation in Line 53 leads to a restatement by the candidate in Line 56. Evidence of a possible "breakdown" in the strategic competence task is made salient with the candidate's silent pause and sub-vocalization at Line 58. At this juncture, the candidate has not come up with a viable solution to his transportation problem. The interviewer/

concierge finally intervenes by nominating a solution to the problem—a move to an airport hotel before the strike begins.

The third excerpt offers empirical data to weakly support an interpretation that the candidate has sufficient strategic competence to succeed in ILR Level 2 situations with a complication. He repeated queries to the concierge for suggestions about how to get to the airport. The data available in the third excerpt are arguably consonant with the warrant statement *"can get into, through, and out of non-routine situations,"* assuming that a real-world concierge would be obliged to offer alternatives a hotel guest might not consider. The fourth excerpt provides data for a possible rebuttal to that inference. Even with several turns repeating the fact that drivers in general will go on strike in the early morning, the candidate cannot on his own think of a viable alternative. The verbalizations in Line 58 suggest that the candidate is indeed flummoxed, as his rejoinder tapers into long pauses and sub-vocalization until the interviewer intervenes in Line 59.

A key issue in performance assessment is how raters of candidate performances interpret the available evidence. The situation with complication example outlined above provides a typical interpretative problem for performance task raters as they decide whether the candidate's performance constitutes evidence in support of a claim that aligns with the backing and warrant, ergo, that the candidate demonstrates strategic competence in the role play task, or whether the rater interprets the performance as counterevidence to such a claim. The issue thus shifts to examining the role of the interlocutors and raters in arriving at inferences about candidates' task performances.

Interlocutor effects

Speaking assessment has gravitated to increasingly realistic performance tasks and simulations. In such tasks, interlocutors query, probe, and converse with candidates until a sufficient volume of data is available for rating. To the extent that interlocutors in transactional scenarios vary in communication style, the performance of any given candidate may be of questionable independence (McNamara, 1997). Even with considerable efforts to train interlocutors, stylistic differences emerge (Ross, 1996, 2007; Brown, 2003) and remain stable, suggesting there are systematic ways interviewers or interlocutors differ in verbosity, empathy with candidates, personality, attentiveness, and perhaps in short-term memory. Making speaking performance assessments optimally authentic often invokes a trade-off between fidelity with the real world and artifact-free measurement of proficiency. This dilemma presents one of the most vexing issues in performance assessment. Elimination of interlocutor variation to enhance the homogeneity of task delivery potentially reduces the authenticity of the performances used to infer proficiency assumed to generalize to the world outside of the assessment context.

As the OPI excerpts above suggest, the interlocutor can decide to withhold offering alternatives to the candidate in order to bring him to a point of strategic competence breakdown. Other interviewers in the same role play task might construct the complication in different ways—simply stating that the taxis are on strike, but not necessarily the buses or the subway system. With such an interlocutor, a candidate's access to a strategic solution is arguably less complex. Since OPI role plays are unscripted by design, no two are exactly alike. This fact opens the possibility that the interlocutor is an unmeasured facet and source of variance in candidate performance.

More amenable to empirical analysis and statistical adjustment is the rater or judge facet. Operational OPIs all have at least two raters, and therefore it is possible to trace the influence of the rater on tasks such as the situation with a complication. Tasks are normally scored by the second rater, who is blind to the interviewer's rating of each task, and to the identity of the candidate. The assessment is thus performed by the second rater, though the concordance of the first and second rater on each task provides the basis for diagnostic information about the degree to which raters differ in their proclivity to rate particular tasks leniently or severely (McNamara, 1996; Fulcher and Marquez-Reiter, 2003). By implication, more lenient task raters would more likely rate overall OPI performances higher than raters who look for evidence of breakdown such as that seen in Excerpt 4. Differences in rating outcomes on a particular performance task such as the role play with complication often reveal differences among raters in what portions of the interaction they attend to, and what particular pragmatic inferences are invoked in the rating process. A lenient rater would for instance hear the query about alternatives to taxies in Excerpt 3 as minimally sufficient evidence of strategic competence. A more severe rater would take into account the specifics of the constructed scenario—the fact that all drivers will be on strike in the morning. For such a rater, the evidence that the candidate had to be rescued (line 61) would probably rebut a claim that the candidate demonstrated strategic competence.

Variability in assessment criteria

Performance assessments typically reveal one of the most problematic aspects of language testing. To the extent design specifications call for authenticity and felicity with how language is used in real life, the more potentially confounding factors are likely to be introduced. Authenticity thus comes with a price. One cost is associated with the variability of the interlocutor, whose contribution to the candidate's performance is undeniably important. Another cost is that expended in assuring that the performance is rated in a consistent and unbiased manner. These two factors militate against the use of performance assessments when resources are limited, and when the stakes of the assessment are high.

Robust evidence of homogeneity in test delivery and rater agreement is a cornerstone of modern assessment methods. The need for parallelism across language assessment forms, and consensus in scoring has driven assessment system design for the last sixty years. The use of performance assessment brings into sharp focus the problems arising when authenticity confronts systematicity in language assessment. Authenticity invites more variation across contexts, interlocutors, and topics. It acknowledges that judges of performances have unique world views and may interpret evidence in different ways. The dilemma which assessment designers face is how to preserve realism in performance assessment while systematizing the delivery of assessments and rating of performances in a way that provides sufficient generalizability and fairness. Performance tasks on OPIs can vary across interviewers, though extensive training of raters generally produces sufficient concordance to satisfy most criterion-referenced inferences.

Benchmarks for determining agreement among raters of performances have been a point of controversy in recent decades. Rating hyper-homogeneity can invite a validity paradox. The more restrictive the rating rubrics, constrained until high levels of agreement are reached, the less valid and generalizable the results may become. The conventional view has maintained that rater disagreement is natural but is undesirable for measurement because rating error increases (DeGruijter, 1980) undermining inferences about candidates' ability. Rigorous rater training typically aims to standardize the rating process and thus reduce error. Broad (2003) and Charney (1984) have argued that high reliability among raters can be achieved when the focus of the assessment is limited to superficial aspects of language. The challenge for performance assessments is to maintain content validity and realism while providing evidence that can be judged with an acceptable degree of concordance among raters.

Accounting for variation

Bachman *et al.* (1995) examined the influence of task and rater variability with what have become the two main tools of performance assessment analysis, Generalizability theory (Brennan, 2001), and the

Many-Facet Rasch Model (Linacre, 1994). Generalizability theory provides the basis for simulations of the optimal number of tasks, occasions, and judges necessary to arrive at an acceptable level of generalizability for an assessment system. Generalizability studies typically start as experiments to model variation across the relevant facets of measurement. Based on the extent of variation associated with each facet, more or fewer tasks, retest occasions, or raters may be implied. Once a generalizability study is conducted, the assumption is that operational assessments conducted under the comparable conditions will maintain the same level of generalizability as that observed in the simulations.

Lynch and McNamara (1998) applied both generalizability theory and the many-facet Rasch model to an assessment designed for immigrants to Australia and point out the salient similarities and differences of the two approaches. While the G-theory approach can establish the parameters necessary for projecting consistently dependable ratings, assuming the conditions of the assessment remain constant, the many-facet Rasch approach identifies the actual differences in the difficulty across tasks and raters. As many performance assessment systems involve the use of tasks and raters assumed to be of parallel difficulty and severity, the many-facet Rasch approach can reveal how much tasks and raters vary in actual practice. While the generalizability theory approach is diagnostic and projective about the consistency of measurement, the Rasch approach attempts to account for task and rater variation by providing a compensatory estimate of candidate ability based on the particular calibrations of the actual task difficulties involved, and the relative differences in severity across the raters involved in the assessment of any particular candidate.

The introduction of the Rasch model into language assessment has made performance assessment more feasible than in the past (McNamara, 1996), and has gone a long way to revive performance assessments hitherto considered too variable for fair operational use. It provides the basis for compensatory estimations of candidate ability when the assumptions of task and rater homogeneity are not tenable, as is the usual case in performance assessment. Instead of rater training aiming at narrowing the focus of assessment to criteria optimally yielding interchangeable and homogeneous ratings from a pool of parallel raters, the Rasch approach has opened the door to the idea that raters of performances can differ from each other as long as they remain internally consistent and apply the same criteria to all candidates.

Two aspects of the Rasch approach have, however, dampened the enthusiasm seen in the years following its introduction. One is the logistical constraint in assessment design specifications for large-scale language assessment systems. The accurate estimation of a compensatory measure of a person is contingent on there being sufficient linkages or anchors across tasks and raters in a data matrix. For very large assessment systems, the orchestration and management of such linked or anchored matrices is often considered too costly for operational use. In such large-scale assessment systems, the results of generalizability study simulations are often the rationale for direct raw score interpretation.

A second shortcoming of the Rasch model as applied to performance assessment is in the diagnosis of bias. Inconsistencies within raters are normally not detectable in conventional approaches, but are readily diagnosable in the many-facet Rasch approach. Unfortunately, biased ratings cannot be repaired or compensated for, which leaves open the door to interpretive ambiguity when performance assessments are located in zones where high-stakes decisions are pending. In such cases, performance assessment interpretation takes on a degree of conditionality, as when one candidate with a lower ability estimate is compared with another candidate with a slightly higher calibrated ability, but with less fit to the Rasch model and consensus among the raters.

The fluency redux

The variability associated with performance assessments and the logistical costs of statistical adjustment of rater differences have increasingly constrained the use of performance assessments based on unscripted interviews and essays. The current trend is to replace human interlocutors and raters with computerized simulations and automated scoring systems (see Xi, this volume). Van den Branden *et al.* (2002), as a case in point, describe a computerized task-based assessment with tasks extracted from the target domain, and claim fidelity with samplings from the work-place context yielding rater-free unbiased reliability. In a similar work-related project, Van Moere *et al.* (2009) report on an automated system that can digitize candidate speech and auto-rate speech samples on pronunciation, structure, vocabulary, fluency, comprehension, and interaction. In the domain of academic English, Xi *et al.* (2009) describe the SpeechRaterSM system, which can score the fluency of non-native speakers on response tasks. Their studies suggest that automated scoring accuracy will eventually improve to the degree that it will rival the magnitude of correlations among human raters of speech samples—at least for a subset of criteria.

The current trend to automate the delivery and scoring of performance assessments, while improving the cost-effectiveness of large-scale language assessments, can be expected to reopen the debate on content validity and authenticity in performance assessment. The questions surrounding this debate are by no means new to language testing. Spolsky (1995) provides a detailed historical account of how some longstanding performance assessment methods such as translation eventually, and after delay and protestation from the Luddites of their time, gave way to machine-scored multiple-choice technology. The transition from constructed response to the selection of alternatives resulted in what became the standard technology for machine-scored testing of all sorts for decades.

It is well known that while live face-to-face performance assessments such as interviews, simulations, and role plays inject subjectivity and invite variation, they possess strong face and content validity as simulations of the world outside of the assessment context. In order to force the speaking construct into a computer-delivered and machine-scored format, content validity in particular may be sacrificed. Arguments used to justify compressing the speaking construct into performances that can be readily machine-scored tend to rely on concurrent validity evidence, primarily zero-order correlation coefficients, as the criterion for their validity. Correlation evidence has for decades been used as the basis for many validation claims, yet correlation evidence alone may be of tenuous substance, given the potential erosion of content validity if the speaking construct is reduced to its component parts to make machine scoring possible. The reduction of communicative competence to proxy indicators which can be scored automatically may well constitute an advance in the use of technology, but doing so concurrently invites a potentially serious threat of construct underrepresentation. While it can be argued that some interview tasks such as narratives and monologues can be scored automatically—when pause, hesitation, and verbosity are calibrated and scaled against native models, the nuances of the semantic content of rejoinders created interactively in discourse currently cannot be reduced to such proxy metrics.

Recent research suggests that indirect speaking tests sampling speakers' imitation of prompts, recall of synonyms, and speed of output provide some of the features that influence human raters when they assess speaking proficiency. Even with such indicators, until automated systems can decipher the semantics of speakers' discourse, they are unlikely to be valid as measures of communicative competence crafted through talk-in-interaction with live interlocutors. Human speech is meaning-laden thought conveyed through sounds. The reduction of language to normative sound-making makes this form of language assessment potentially meaning-less. Virtually none of the strategic competence features assessable in the situation with complication role play featured in the excerpts above are reducible to the mere verbosity of the candidate. The construct of strategic competence is situation-bound and dynamically related to the pragmatic details of the situation as they are negotiated by the participants. Whether performance assessments such as the situated role play can survive the current trend to compress language proficiency into automatic scoring formats remains to be seen.

The current state of automated scoring relies on low entropy tasks in which the speech provided by test candidates is constrained to have very few degrees of freedom to vary. The major hurdle proponents of automated scoring will face is the invention of a meaning-sensitive scoring system, one that can reliably deduce high entropy rejoinders more complex than fixed phrases or lexicalized sentences. The state-of-the-art speech-recognition software can impressively transcribe what is said with reasonable accuracy. Parsing of utterances into generative speech apropos the propositional content of realistic speech prompts is still apparently somewhere in the future. Without such a content-based system, regression equations used to predict human scoring outcomes will be limited to tallying the epiphenomena of verbosity, with little to do with creative and meaningful language. Future automated scoring research will eventually need to turn to the challenge of deciphering the meaningfulness of language in context. When such technology is invented, claims about the validity of automated scoring of performance assessments may be better justified.

Further reading

Chapelle, C., Enright, M. and Jaimeson, J. (2008). Test score interpretation and use. In C. Chapelle, M. Enright and J. Jamieson (eds), *Building a Validity Argument for the Test of English as a Foreign Language*. New York, NY: Routledge. Chapelle *et al.* present a readable formulation of the validity argument for the TOEFL in terms of the ECD (evidence centered design) framework. The article traces how test scores can relate to target language use for academic English based on validity evidence collected in a number of studies.

Williamson, D., Mislevy, R. and Bejar, I. (2006). *Automatic Scoring of Complex Tasks in Computerized Testing*. Mahwah NJ: Lawrence Erlbaum. This edited volume introduces the challenges facing test developers considering alternatives to human scoring, which is often costly, time-consuming, and variable. The chapters in the volume cover a wide range of automated scoring issues, and realistically lay out the current limitations as well as the future possibilities.

Xi, X., Higgins, D., Zechner, K. and Williamson, D. M. (2009). *Automated Scoring of Spontaneous Speech Using SpeechRater V.1.0*. Princeton, NJ: Educational Testing Service. Xi *et al.* present in this working paper the current state-of-the-art evidence supporting the limited use of automated scoring of low-entropy speaking tasks. The research alludes to the current problems with automated scoring systems, and the possible trade-offs faced when language is assessed automatically. The paper outlines future research on integrating more high-entropy tasks into SpeechRater.

Young, R. (2008). *Language and interaction: an advanced resource book*. London, UK: Routledge. Young presents a comprehensive introduction to the structural analysis of discourse in various social settings. The book provides several examples of how interaction can be analyzed from a sociolinguistic and conversation analytic perspective.

References

Bachman, L. (2002). Some reflections on task-based language performance assessment. *Language Testing* 19: 453–76.

——— (2005). Building and supporting a case for test use. *Language Assessment Quarterly* 2: 1–34.

Bachman, L., Lynch, B. and Mason, M. (1995). Investigating Variability in Tasks and Rater Judgments in a Performance Test of Foreign Language Speaking. *Language Testing* 12: 238–57.

Bachman, L. and Palmer, A. (1996). *Language Testing in Practice*. Oxford, UK: Oxford University Press.

Brennan, R.L. (2001). *Generalizability Theory*. New York, NY: Springer.

Broad, B. (2003). *What We Really Value: rubrics in teaching and assessing writing*. Logan, UT: Utah State University Press.

Brown, A. (2003). Interviewer variation and the co-construction of speaking proficiency. *Language Testing* 20: 1–25.

Chapelle, C., Enright, M. and Jamieson, J. (2008). Test score interpretation and use. In C. Chapelle, M. Enright and J. Jamieson (eds), *Building a Validity Argument for the Test of English as a Foreign Language*. New York, NY: Routledge.

Charney, D. (1984). The validity of holistic scoring to evaluate writing: A critical overview. *Research in the Teaching of English* 18: 65–81.

Cumming, A., Grant, L. Mulcahy-Ernt, P. and Powers, D. E. (2004). A teacher-verification study of speaking and writing prototype tasks for a new TOEFL. *Language Testing* 21: 107–45.

DeGruijter, D. N. M. (1980). The essay examination. In L. J. T. Vander Kamp, W. F. Langerak and D. N. M. DeGruijter (eds), *Psychometrics for Educational Debates*. New York, NY: John Wiley and Sons, 245–62.

Fulcher, G. (2003). *Testing Second Language Speaking*. London, UK: Pearson-Longman.

Fulcher, G. and Marquez-Reiter, R. (2003). Task difficulty in speaking tests. *Language Testing* 20: 321–44.

Lantoff, J. P. and Frawley, W. (1988). Proficiency: understanding the construct. *Studies in Second Language Acquisition* 10: 181–95.

Linacre, J. M. (1994). *Many-Facet Rasch Measurement*. Chicago, IL: MESA.

Lissitz, R. and Samuelsen, K. (2007). A suggested change in terminology and emphasis regarding validity in education. *Educational Researcher* 36: 437–48.

Lynch, B. K. and McNamara, T. F. (1998). Using G-theory and many-facet Rasch measurement in the development of performance assessments of the ESL speaking skills of immigrants. *Language Testing* 15: 158–80.

McNamara, T. F. (1996). *Measuring Second Language Performance*. London, UK: Longman.

—— (1997). "Interaction" in second language performance assessment: whose performance? *Applied Linguistics* 18: 446–66.

Mislevy, R., Steinberg, L. S. and Almond, R. G. (2002). Design and analysis in task-based language assessment. *Language Testing* 19: 447–96.

Norris, J. M., Brown, J. D., Hudson, T. D. and Yoshioka, J. (1998). *Designing Second Language Performance Assessments*. Honolulu, HI: University of Hawaii Press.

Norris, J. M., Brown, J. D., Hudson, T. D. and Bonk, W. J. (2002). Examinee abilities and task difficulty in task-based second language performance assessment. *Language Testing* 19: 395–418.

Oller, J. W. Jr (1979). *Language Tests at School*. London, UK: Longman.

Robinson, P. (2001). Task complexity, task difficulty, and task production: Exploring interactions in a componential framework. *Applied Linguistics* 22: 27–57.

Ross, S. J. (1996). Formulae and inter-interviewer variation in oral proficiency interview discourse. *Prospect* 11: 3–16.

—— (2007). A comparative task-in-interaction analysis of OPI backsliding. *Journal of Pragmatics* 39: 2017–44.

Spolsky, B. (1995). *Measured Words*. Oxford, UK: Oxford University Press.

Toulmin, S. E. (2003). *The Uses of Argument*. Cambridge, UK: Cambridge University Press.

Van den Branden, K., Depauw, V. and Gysen, S. (2002). A computerized task-based test of second language Dutch for vocational training purposes. *Language Testing* 19: 438–52.

Van Moere, A., Suzuki, M., Downey, R. and Cheng, J. (2009). Implementing ICAO language proficiency requirements in the versant aviation English test. *Australian Review of Applied Linguistics* 32: 1–27.

Wesche, M. B. (1987). Second language performance testing: the Ontario test of ESL as an Example. *Language Testing* 4: 28–47

Xi, X., Higgins, D., Zechner, K. and Williamson, D. M. (2009). *Automated Scoring of Spontaneous Speech Using SpeechRater V.1.0*. Princeton, NJ: Educational Testing Service.

Part V
Writing items and tasks

16

Item writing and writers

Dong-il Shin

Introduction

In the last few decades, positivistic worldviews and the related scientific techniques of testing have influenced the development and evaluation of second and foreign language tests (Hamp-Lyons and Lynch, 1998), and psychometrically approached research on scored/rated data was encouraged and well-connected to the professional literature of language testing. More effort has been given to rater reliability and rater characteristics than to item construction issues in validity.

The general procedure for item writing has been repeated and elaborated in language testing (Alderson *et al.*, 1995; Bachman and Palmer, 1996; Hughes, 2003; Spaan, 2006) and educational measurement literature (Downing and Haladyna, 2006). Some researchers (Davidson and Lynch, 2002; Fulcher and Davidson, 2007) approach item writing as consisting of the process of writing test specifications (or "test specs") and building validity arguments as a system. The actual process of how items are written from test specs and the people who write test items, however, are still areas of active enquiry. Research and development in the item writing process and writer training (Peirce, 1992 for example) have not been properly introduced to testing communities, while issues related to rating and rater training have often appeared in language testing literature.

The purpose of this chapter is to review different historical views of item writing and summarize critical issues and research topics surrounding item writing and item writers. This chapter will not, however, focus on the scoring aspect of item writing despite the intricate relationship between the two. When test items are developed to be objectively scored, the scoring will be, strictly speaking, a matter of item creation; for instance, if it is a multiple-choice formatted item, then the item writer's responsibilities include the crafting of good distractors linked to the item. If, however, an item is rater scored in direct tests of English speaking, or an admissions-related portfolio is expert evaluated, then there must be complicated steps taken beyond the item creation process. These types of items require the development of some kind of scoring rubric or training system. In these instances, the following questions remain complicated: Where does the responsibility of the item writer end? When does it shift to the province of test administration, scale calibration, rater training, and so forth? Although these are interesting and important questions, a discussion of them is beyond the scope of this chapter. Instead, I will focus on item writing in and of itself. Thus it should be noted that in this chapter, the term "item" will be interchangeable with "task".

Historical perspectives

Many books exist focusing on item development of second and foreign language testing. Some of these books detail item types and sample items that item writers can use to test vocabulary (Read, 2000), grammar (Purpura, 2004), listening (Buck, 2001), reading (Alderson, 2000), speaking (Fulcher, 2003; Luoma, 2004), writing (Cushing, 2002), and language for specific purposes (Douglas, 2000). These resource books list a number of different item types to operationalize the target test construct.

In this section, four different perspectives (psychometric, authentic, systematic, critical) are summarized to understand past and present approaches to item writing. It should be noted, however, that all four approaches are not mutually exclusive. Also, more recent perspectives have not necessarily made older ones obsolete. For instance, authentic test items are pervasive now, but the psychometric tradition remains strong. The systematic approach has made some advances in professionalizing the item writing process, but not much research has confirmed its meaningfulness or usefulness yet. The critical approach to testing has been deeply rooted in education, but micro-level issues in item design have received little coverage in the literature when compared to macro-level arguments.

The psychometric approach, or "Reproduce similar items in multiple-choice format. Do it objectively"

The way items are created is always influenced by the dominant paradigms, assessment culture, or set of assumptions behind the practice (see Lynch and Shaw, 2005 for examples). In the second half of the twentieth century, the language testing industry grew with a positivistic paradigm, which had a quantitative, objective, and outcome-oriented view of testing. This paradigm maintained that language testing and testers can and should be objective. Testers preferred context- and time-free inferences from well-standardized test items.

The multiple-choice format was preferred to test language proficiency in general as well as achievement in classroom contexts. True-or-false and matching item types were also welcomed. These formats were publicized as scientific. Much research was conducted related to testers' biases in written items to enhance test reliability (see McNamara and Roever, 2006: Chapter 4). The multiple-choice format was also powered by the tradition of discrete point testing. The psychometric approach to item development has continued to evolve not only to measure separate points of knowledge (e.g., grammar, vocabulary, or pronunciation) but to tactically infer advanced levels of the four language macro-skills (listening, reading, speaking, writing) in standardized testing. This tradition still remains a foundation for assessing language proficiency all over the world, and resources for test preparation (books, courses, multimedia products) are conventionalized in the same categories. Taxonomies of multiple-choice item writing guidelines (principles or technologies in other names) are widely available in the field of educational measurement (Haladyna and Downing, 1989; Haladyna et al., 2002; Roid and Haladyna, 1982).

During this period, the key principle of item writing was: "Reproduce similar items in multiple-choice format. Do it objectively." As elaborated by McNamara and Roever (2006: 1), it was the era in which "psychometric became the substrate discipline, prescribing the rules of measurement, and language was virtually poured into these preexisting psychometric forms"; the testing industry had poured separate points of language knowledge into a psychometrically efficient mold: the multiple-choice format of testing.

The authentic approach, or: "Search for authentic items. Avoid the multiple-choice format"

While the psychometric approach has remained influential, alternative paradigms (Hamp-Lyons and Lynch, 1998) emerged and diverse formats of language test items (e.g., authentic items in self- or peer-assessment, simulations, diaries) were associated with qualitative, subjective, and process-oriented views of testing (Brown and Hudson, 1998). The key principle of item writing under this approach was: "Search for authentic items. Avoid the multiple-choice format." Item writers tried to incorporate the real world, value practical language skills, and choose items which appear integrative, authentic, communicative, and pragmatic from real-world language use situations.

Because multiple-choice, discrete point testing had been criticized for giving too much weight to students' knowledge of the linguistic system, integrative test items were well-favored in the format of direct tests of speaking and writing (e.g., oral proficiency interviews), and comprehension tests of extended discourse. This approach was exposed to repetitious criticism (mostly from psychometric testers) for having subjective scales, unreliable raters, and impractical test administration (e.g., time-consuming procedures for test taking, scoring, and expert training). The proficiency movement in the United States, however, kept pushing this type of testing to assess productive skills for real-world communication. In the 1970s, the cloze test was a popular alternative format, in which test takers were asked to fill in the missing words of an extended text. The cloze test was researched and considered a substitute for integrative tests (Oller, 1972; Stubbs and Tucker, 1974, for example), but it functioned less pragmatically and contextually than expected (McNamara, 2000: 15). The communicative movement, theoretically approached from Hymes' theory of communicative competence, also made an impact on the way authentic items were developed. Assessments of second language pragmatics, such as discourse completion tests, also emerged (McNamara and Roever, 2006: Chapter 3).

Anti-psychometric approaches to test items, valuing multiple-constructed realities of inquiries, have been expanded and accompanied by humanism, hermeneutics, constructivism, or postmodernism. They did not seek one correct "true" answer for each test item. This type of item creation requires context-driven and value-bound approaches in item development and response interpretation. All the items which appeared in the name of authentic assessment, or performance assessment, have been positioned very far away from multiple-choice format.

The systematic approach, or "See the whole picture of test development. Do it systematically"

In the past decade, many language testers have not positioned themselves as either psychometric or authentic purists. They have realized that any specific item type cannot function perfectly to make inferences about test constructs. All items "have their particular strengths and weaknesses, and tend to engage different skills: some assess one set of skills and some another; some advantage one group of test takers, and some another. By using a variety of different task types, the test is far more likely to provide a balanced assessment" (Buck, 2001: 153). In order for test items to be comprehensively balanced, they need to be characterized, or coded, for specific features (for a literature review in testing of oral proficiency, for example, see Buck, 2001: Chapter 5; Fulcher, 2003: Chapter 3). Bachman and Palmer's non-test "target language use" (TLU) checklist is one of the most frequently referenced frameworks for comparing test tasks non-test settings (e.g., in the volumes of the Cambridge University Press Language Assessment series). It was believed that the situational authenticity of TLU-ness in test tasks is positively related to the validity argument.

Fulcher and Davidson (2007), however, following Fulcher (2000; 2003), challenged that emerging tradition. They stated that "authenticity, even conceived of as matching test method facets to facets of similar tasks in the real world (Bachman and Palmer, 1996), does not make test tasks automatically valid through directness." Instead, they tried to design test items as "the 'response as evidence' to the construct as language knowledge, or as ability for use within specified parameters laid out in a framework and test specification" (Fulcher and Davidson, 2007: 63). They endorsed a systematic framework called evidence-centered design (ECD), which has been well received by the testing community because of its solid chain of reasoning (Mislevy *et al.*, 2002, 2003; Chapter 14, this volume). The uniqueness of the ECD is that test items specified and the responses expected are systematically planned to claim "priori validity" arguments. Kim's (2008) empirical research is a good example of how ECD is utilized in test development and validation contexts. When designing an ESL diagnostic reading-to-write test in a university context, she conceptualized desirable effects of test items and considered how those effects could be achieved by using ECD as an assessment framework.

As ECD functions as a beginning platform in an overall system, test specifications can provide detailed information on each design of test items (Fulcher and Davidson, 2007: 70). It has been widely accepted that clear documentation of the test specification process contributes to formulating and evaluating the validity argument, and that test items need to be well-discussed and clearly characterized in the stage of test specification creation. Unlike those written in the 1970s and 1980s, many language testing books published in recent decades have included more space for test specifications (see Alderson *et al.*, 1995; Bachman and Palmer, 1996; Fulcher, 2003, for examples). Davidson and Lynch (2002: 4) drew on previous literature and conceived of an "efficient generative blueprint by which many similar instances of the same assessment task can be generated." Examples of research focusing on the value of test specifications still continue to appear (Fulcher and Davidson, 2009; Kim *et al.*, 2010; Walters, 2010).

The key principle of item writing in this approach is explicit: "See the whole picture of test development. Do it systematically." By taking a pragmatic stance, Fulcher and Davidson (2007), and Davidson and Lynch (2002: 114) approached test design and validation as a system. A pragmatic approach does not accept determinism outright, but instead conceives of testing practices as contingent, as unpredictable from complex variables, and as open to different methods of item creation and validation. It does not accept any unchanging, universal formula for test item development. Davidson and Lynch (2002: 2) stated that their "approach to test development is intended to be inclusive, open, and reflective," and that any test specifications "will fit all settings very rarely—or more likely never."

The critical approach, or "Create items to help test takers. Think socio-politically"

Item writing was once judged to be "an immature science" (Cronbach, 1970), and researchers reacted and finally placed the item writing process into a tightly organized set of guidelines or validity arguments. Some scholars (e.g., Lynch, 2001; Pennycook, 2001; Spolsky, 1995), however, tried to see the testing practice in a much bigger, and socio-political, picture. By articulating "critical language testing," for example, Shohamy, (2001: 131–32) saw tests as political tools within a context of power struggles. This approach challenges the dominant traditions of test uses and encourages an active, critical response from test takers. McNamara (2008), who has echoed critical perspectives on the misuse of language tests, subscribed to the views of many scholars who made major contributions to socio-political dimensions of language testing. Hamp-Lyons (1997, 2000), acknowledging political aspects embedded in the process of test design and use, called for ethical awareness in language testing and referred to "ethical language testing" with reference to the notion of "responsibility."

From the perspective of critical language testing, objective test formats, such as multiple-choice or true–false, are the features that grant language tests power. The assumption behind multiple-choice formatted test items is that they imply "one correct answer, i.e., one 'truth', one interpretation" (Shohamy, 2001: 24); thus, different approaches to item design are needed to allow for different meanings and interpretations for different test takers (see Shohamy, 2001: 27, 111 for more explanation). This criticism is different from the way other approaches to item writing have recognized multiple-choice items as meaningful or not meaningful: the psychometric approach sees them as scientific entities, the authentic approach distances itself from multiple-choice items in preference of acquiring real-world authentic tasks, and the systematic approach focuses on how items support inferences from the response evidence to the claims testers make about the test construct.

It should be noted that, while the systematic approach to test design is well connected to test use and its validation argument, the socio-political approach focuses on test misuse, that is, the negative impact of test use. It may be that each approach has its own strength for professionalizing test design and use as a theory, and the critical perspective may be functioning, not as "a placement for current testing practices, but as an additional approach to making decisions and judgments about individual language ability" (Lynch, 2001: 361). Critical language testers, however, need to pay more attention to the dimension of item design driven by intended or unintended misuses of the test. Even though the general features of critical language testing (e.g., a democratic system, an empowerment model, and multiple assessment procedure) have appeared in thought-provoking literature (e.g., Shohamy, 2001), the critical theorists have not yet suggested an alternative item creation protocol.

What would a critical-influenced test item look like? How would we develop critical language test items? It may be that certain rules of standardized test administration (e.g., the same questions and test-taking steps) are removed. The creation of the test could be heavily influenced by test takers and other stakeholders. For example, drawing on postmodernist notions of multiple interpretations, Yu (2007) invited test takers to contribute to the creation of a scoring template. Portfolio assessments of Lynch and Shaw (2005) also illustrated how students actively participate in the assessment process and reflect on their identities within a school context. Even if Lynch and Shaw (2005) used different terms, "alternative assessments operationalized from an interpretivist perspective," their Foucaultian framework of portfolio assessment offered a meaningful procedure for considering the critical approach as part of a larger picture of item design and validity argument. In their discussion of portfolio design and use, power relations were explicitly linked to the ethics and validity of assessment inferences.

Critical issues

Do we need a theory of test misuse?

Anyone who has worked in the testing industry may have seen inappropriate collaboration among testers and other stakeholders introduce hidden opportunities for impeding effect-driven assessment or biasing its appropriate use of tests. From a socio-political lens, we can find wrongly or socio-politically inappropriate intentions within testing systems. As identified by Fulcher (2009: 3), however, one "problem with the current discussion of test misuse is that examples are cited in isolation from a theory of why tests are misused." McNamara (2008: 423) acknowledged that "the lack of an appropriate model of the broader social context in which to consider the social and political functions of tests is true of work in validity theory in general." When item design and its negative impact do not feed each other in an on-going process of test development and validation, the viewpoint of why test items are misused cannot stand firm.

As different theories of test misuse are proffered, one conflicted question needs be discussed first: "Do we need a theory of test misuse?" This question could revolve around two competing poles. On one pole, many researchers, including critical language testers, shout "yes," arguing that language tests are misused socio-politically, and that a theory of test misuse needs to be situated with the responsibility of test/item designers (for accountability to test takers, see the review by Norton, 1997). On the other pole, many researchers will contradict that the misuse is not the responsibility of test/item designers, certainly, and maybe not the test publisher or supervisory authority either. Additionally, it might be that even if a test is mis/abused, it is only an open empirical question whether such mis/abuse matters (see Davidson, 1994), or whether such mis/abuse really happens. The current practice is to psychometrically and socio-historically report the misuse in later stages.

Theories of test misuse may allow for an expansive and self-inclusive range of the theory for language test development and validation. If a theory of test misuse is pervasive, however, socio-political concerns may have a destabilizing influence on item creation. Because any well-intended test can cause controversy in this "bad" world, many item writers may refuse to be targeted and politicized. If any theory on one pole becomes overvalued, the issues around the other pole could be marginalized. This rule applies to those both for and against theorizing test misuse, and between systematic and critical approaches to item design. Dichotomized viewpoints will most likely remain noticeable in the coming years.

Who are the item writers?

Another issue to consider is related to item writers. If recruiting and educating item writers are important stages in professional testing organizations, in-service teacher training programs, and also, perhaps, in testing courses, who are the individuals who develop test items? And who trains them? Although language testing research is awash with the development and administration of diverse tests, often based on the scrutiny of test items, interest in "who" produces test items remains a fairly under-researched area. The voices of item writers raising their own concerns (for example, Peirce, 1992 for an item-writer's experiences at the Educational Testing Service) have been even rarer. Unlike the other professionals of language testing, such as test designers, item spec directors, raters, rater trainers, data analysts, validity evaluators, etc., it seems that item writers are viewed as quasi-professional, and that item writing is a kind of abstract skill to be acquired in the testing world.

Davidson and Lynch (2002: 121) valued the importance of the human resource who generates and utilizes test specs and items: for example, "test development is most efficient when human resources are invested." It was also suggested that different roles be situated within the social reality of group dynamics. In the study by Kim et al. (2010), individual characteristics of item writers, such as their previous experience, nativeness–foreignness, cultural background, personality, and topic preference, were discussed to understand how those characteristics affected item writing. A more thorough investigation, or thick description, however, is still missing in research about item writers. Their characteristics can be quickly simplified into some conventional categories, like whether they are native speakers, have teaching experience, or have professional degrees. As the stories of learners and teachers are narratively described in many journals and books, language testers, including item writers, live their own complicated lives. Their item-writing practices often involve a complex decision-making process. Power, culture, and monetary issues are always of importance. Experience, education, and beliefs about how items should/can be constructed also matter. When item writers are underpaid, when parts of item writing jobs (e.g., searching for relevant passages on the internet, editing/proofreading item drafts) are unethically saddled upon part-time or freelance writers, when some cultures of communication do not allow group dynamics to be horizontal, when job coordinators or peers take too much power in decision-making, then any good test specs or well-qualified item writers cannot generate good items for what is to be tested. Item writing needs to be understood as a social practice.

What images flash through our minds when we think of item writers? Native speakers of the target language or full-time professional testers in collared shirts who drive to their offices each morning? Maybe their images or job descriptions are naively idealized, and little research has elaborated upon their socially constructed identities as (professional) testers. In testing companies and even school-based testing contexts, my suspicion is that they are weakly positioned in the social structure; thus, they are often tempted to leave the job, change their career path, or make ethically inappropriate decisions, like plagiarizing and releasing test materials unlawfully. In the Korean context I am daily exposed to, for example, the testing stakeholders, including item writers and reviewers, have appeared in newspaper articles for cheating. Little research has been reported on who they are and why they broke the law.

When Shohamy (2001) rethought language testing policies and practices from a Foucaultian lens as a way to empower test takers, the group of test takers was often dichotomously matched with a group of testers. As illustrated in Chapter 2 of her book (Shohamy, 2001), all the complaints, chagrin, and fears come from test takers, while testers are described as oppressing. However, this dichotomy needs to be carefully considered (see how Bachman (2000: 17) did not accept the perpetrator–victim relationships). This reductive dichotomy neglects the multifaceted and changing life of testing and tested individuals that modern theories have failed to adequately address. If test-taking students are categorized as a suppressed group of the testing industry, who are the suppressing individuals? Are the item writers also included in this group? More research needs be conducted concerning the relationship between item writers and their social world from poststructuralist perspectives (Morgan, 2007; Norton, 2000).

Is the multiple-choice item type still meaningful?

The third issue relates to whether the multiple-choice format is still meaningful, useful and even dominant in contemporary testing. This (arguably) most controversial item type has been criticized for mostly pursuing reliability and efficiency, at school or in the testing industry. One ever-present criticism is that the multiple-choice test has been maintained at the expense of using an overexposed format and content. However, it should be noted that the language testing industry was established in the era of efficiency. Testers lacked money, time, and professional partners, but thankfully they lived in a psychometric world. In that modernized era, they efficiently did what they were asked to do with multiple-choice items. The practice of testing language abilities in multiple-choice items has evolved in newly developed tests such as the TOEFL-IBT. All over the world, research on multiple-choice formatted tests has often appeared in educational measurement and language testing literature, most of which has viewed the features of the format neutrally (for example, see Shizuka et al., 2006, to review the effects of reducing the number of options per test item).

Critical language testers explicitly harbored antipathy against the multiple-choice format in the view of power emergence and maintenance. Investigative journalists have inflammatorily voiced the issues of how standardized testing emerged and the multiple-choice format survived in politically charged marketplaces. For example, Kohn (2000: 11) insisted that "the most damaging testing programs are characterized by certain readily identifiable features, beginning with the use of exams that are mostly multiple choice." It seems that more people now see multiple-choice items as an obstacle to good education, and, thus, researchers of language testing need to take a position on multiple-choice items: befriend or not.

Can we imagine the testing world without multiple-choice items? Or perhaps, taking a less extreme case, would we be happier with noticeably fewer multiple-choice items in a single test? Can we learn meaningfully without pursuing an efficiency-oriented testing culture? A variety of avenues of research are awaiting inquiry from integrative/alternative, systematic, and critical testing paradigms. If we guard against the efficiency paradigms behind the multiple-choice format, then principle-based testing (Shohamy, 2001) needs to be considered. In her discussion of alternative and democratic testing, she emphasized that "such methods must be more time consuming and costly. However, democratic practices are not chosen for their efficiency or costs; rather they are chosen because of their principles" (Shohamy, 2001: 139). Testers should not avoid taking responsibility for diverse educational needs by using formats beyond multiple choice.

Current contributions and research

Although some examples of empirical research focusing on the item writing process are beginning to appear, the issue "how are test items 'really' developed in the real world?" is still an area of research which has received too little attention. When item writing from test specifications is encouraged as part of a larger picture of test design, the spec-to-item process must be a reality to stakeholders, but do we all agree that better items are produced using test specifications? Is the spec-to-item flow applicable and feasible? Or are there any hidden sociocultural factors impeding the item writing process from test specs?

Non-native educators in the target language pedagogy, or from countries where many students prepare for these tests, need to be invited to participate in research and development teams for item writing. Interestingly, native educators are marginalized in foreign contexts, where a majority of non-native educators take responsibility for developing foreign language tests. In a discussion of empowerment, collaboration, and democracy, the opportunities to access the decision-making process need to be investigated in different contexts of test item development. One study demonstrating the values of using the spec-to-item mechanism as non-native educators is the work of Shin and Kim (2010). Data were collected from test writers' and reviewers' meetings to demonstrate the positive role of test specifications in item writing and revision processes. All the frequently used words and phrases from the meetings were categorized and matched with the language used in the test specs. A great mismatch was found between what was documented in specs and what was actually discussed in meetings.

In the case study by Kim et al. (2010: 163), negative feelings and attitudes toward test specifications were found among item writers, in their use of descriptive words such as "abstract," "mysterious," "difficult," "less transparent," "not helpful," "heuristics" when referring to specs. Why is this the case? When the systematic design of the spec-item fit was considered, why did the process still seem to fail on some levels? Kim et al. (2010) also found that item writers used their own internal guidelines for item writing: from their teaching experiences, other item writing practices, face-to-face meetings, as well as oral communications with item coordinators. Thus, different forms of test specifications or what are called "organic guidelines" are needed to utilize a spec-to-item work flow. This is just one worthwhile lesson from real people documenting the item writing process, and more questions should be proposed to challenge the taken-for-granted reality that the spec-item process always functions successfully: "Do item writers feel comfortable with the conventional format and content in test specs? Do they really need multiple (or specific) forms of test specifications?" Different stakeholders, different purposes, different cultures of testing can lead to different thinking.

A thorough documentation of item writers' voices does not yet exist, so it is still necessary to be hesitant in valuing the systematic feasibility of the item writing process printed in language testing literature. In the field of language testing, item writing is one of the most under-identified job descriptions, imposed as important, but not qualitatively elaborated upon and valued in case studies, action research, narrative inquiries or other value-embedded research. It is critical for future research efforts to address this topic.

Future directions

In language testing literature, there is an overabundance of information on types of test item formats and content, but it seems likely that language testers will continue to explore newly transformed items, such as in the tests of pragmatics, integrated abilities, process-oriented performance, and language for specific purposes (e.g., assessment for young learners). The use of classroom-based assessment items is likely to be the subject of much further research. High-stakes test items continue to measure general proficiency or a wide range of what one is supposed to know, and small-scale testing is still necessary to make direct connections to everyday learning. Additionally, it is expected that different stakeholders are empowered to magnify the meaningfulness of different testing purposes at school.

Item development and validation in computer-delivered environments will be another future direction of research which may continue within the discussion of test items. Multimedia technology holds affordable promise for item construction, test administration, and score reporting. It has been suggested that the use of computers and on-line technology have the potential to reflect authentic target language use situations. However, it is also argued that test items embedded in the multi-media environment do not function as being authentic or communicative, except in some limited situations (see Chalhoub-Deville, 1999; Bachman, 2000: 9, for more issues). People communicate on the internet, but language is still acquired, learned, and taught "off-line," spontaneously and interactively in most situations, especially in the novice and intermediate stages of language proficiency, and for young language learners of language—it should be noted that most test takers are from these levels. Semi-direct tests of speaking using a computer-based environment have been prevalent, but they seem to contradict the original purpose of being communicative or interactive through speaking. Talking to a computer is not a frequent event in real life. The meaningfulness of test items created and administered in a virtual space needs to be researched from the dimensions discussed in this chapter. The genuine originality of the language test construct should not be trivialized:

> In the dazzle of technological advance, we may need a continuing reminder of the nature of communication as a shared human activity, and that the idea that one of the participants can be replaced by a machine (in speaking test, for example) is really a technological fantasy.
>
> *(McNamara, 2000: 85)*

Work in language testing can be divided into two levels: macro-level studies that consider theories and systems of testing and micro-level studies of specific facets of test development and analysis. Item writers belong to the micro-level, and they need to use their professional experience to publish their own item-writing guidelines, or (in)validate current conventions introduced in language testing resources, or taught in workshops or training programs (see Haladyna et al., 2002 for research examples). Additionally, doors should be opened for item writers to be educated about and invited into macro-level discussions. Their perspectives may influence the way others see the testing world.

Different perspectives need to be collected as a philosophical foundation for item development and validation. Why are standardized items necessary? How do they function in society? Do we see the testing industry optimistically, pessimistically, or somewhere in between? Do we take the utilitarian/pragmatic, or critical/emancipatory worldviews of testing? Can we reconcile theories of neo-liberalism, pragmatism, globalization, poststructuralism, and Freirian pedagogy? Different ontological, epistemological, and methodological stances should be elaborated to follow the basis of each worldview of testing and to drive new test items teleologically (Lynch, 2001; Lynch and Shaw, 2005). Because it is agreed that the world of language testing is still open and incomplete, language testing researchers can play a role in creating and negotiating multiple test development realities or paradigms. Language testing has often been considered a science, and a disconnect exists between the practice of test development and its related philosophical debates. It is hoped that future directions of item development are related to macro-level discussions, leading ultimately to broader conversations about test items.

Further reading

Alderson, J. C., Clapham, C. and Wall, D. (1995). *Language Test Construction and Evaluation*. Cambridge, UK: Cambridge University Press. Chapters 2 and 3 of this volume have useful information on test specs, item types, and item writing. A few of their practical tips are (1) specs need to be adjusted to different audiences for different contexts and (2) item writing is best practiced in groups. Their guidelines remain effective for and relevant to recent discussions of item writing process.

Bachman, L. F. and Palmer, A. S. (1996). *Language Testing in Practice*. Oxford, UK: Oxford University Press. This book's strength is showing how the concept of "test usefulness" provides strong coherence for the whole process of test development and evaluation. The authors have summarized all useful information by presenting the nuts and bolts of test design and administration, and by illustrating test development examples for different contexts.

Davidson, F. and Lynch, B. K. (2002). *Testcraft: A Teacher's Guide to Writing and Using Language Test Specifications*. New Haven, CT: Yale University Press. This is a clearly written book on applying test specs to the creation of valid test items. Item writers' experience and wisdom, in the forms of principles or guidelines, are integrated into a unified system of specs-to-item writing process. This idea has been expanded in a recent publication on test retrofit (Fulcher and Davidson, 2009), much of which is metaphorically explained from architecture.

Norton, B. (2000). *Identity and Language Learning: Gender, Ethnicity, and Educational Change*. London, UK: Longman. By drawing on a feminism-poststructuralist philosophy of education, Norton argues that language learning is a complex social practice that engages an on-going construction of multiple identities. She has researched mostly outside of the testing world, but her approach to language learners and learning can be re-examined to include the issues of item writers and writing.

Shohamy, E. (2001). *The Power of Tests: A Critical Perspective on the Uses and Consequences of Language Tests*. London, UK: Longman. Although this book may appear to be disconnected from work containing guidelines/systems for item development, it effectively presents the issues as to why item writing should not be viewed only as a science. Her claims that intended effects can lead to unintended and unexpected consequences deserve thoughtful attention among all areas of test designers.

References

Alderson, J. C. (2000). *Assessing Reading*. Cambridge, UK: Cambridge University Press.
Alderson, J. C., Clapham, C. and Wall, D. (1995). *Language Test Construction and Evaluation*. Cambridge: Cambridge University Press.

Bachman, L. F. (2000). Modern language testing at the turn of the century: assuring that what we count counts. *Language Testing* 17: 1–42.

Bachman, L. F., and Palmer, A. S. (1996). *Language Testing in Practice*. Oxford, UK: Oxford University Press.

Brown, J. D. and Hudson, T. D. (1998). The alternatives in language assessment. *TESOL Quarterly* 32: 653–75.

Buck. G. (2001). *Assessing Listening*. Cambridge, UK: Cambridge University Press.

Chalhoub-Deville, M. (ed.), (1999). *Issues in Computer-Adaptive Testing of Reading Proficiency*. Cambridge, UK: Cambridge University Press.

Cronbach, L. J. (1970). Book Review. [Review of the book on *The Theory of Achievement Test Items*, by J. R. Bormuth] *Psychometrika* 35: 509–11.

Cushing, S. W. (2002). *Assessing Writing*. Cambridge, UK: Cambridge University Press.

Davidson, F. (1994). Norms appropriacy of achievement tests: Spanish-speaking children and English children's norms. *Language Testing* 11: 83–95.

Davidson, F. and Lynch, B. K. (2002). *Testcraft: A Teacher's Guide to Writing and Using Language Test Specifications*. New Haven, CT: Yale University Press.

Douglas, D. (2000). *Assessing Language for Specific Purposes*. Cambridge, UK: Cambridge University Press.

Downing, S. M. and Haladyna, T. M. (eds), (2006). *Handbook of Test Development*. Mahwah, NJ: Lawrence Erlbaum Associates.

Fulcher, G. (2000). The "communicative" legacy in language testing. *System* 28: 483–97.

—— (2003). *Testing Second Language Speaking*. London, UK: Longman.

—— (2009). Test use and political philosophy. *Annual Review of Applied Linguistics* 29: 3–20.

Fulcher, G. and Davidson, F. (2007). *Language Testing and Assessment: an advanced resource book*. London, UK: Routledge.

—— (2009). Test architecture. Test retrofit. *Language Testing* 26: 123–44.

Haladyna, T. M. and Downing, S. M. (1989). The validity of a taxonomy of multiple-choice item writing rules. *Applied Measurement in Education* 1: 51–78.

Haladyna, T. M., Downing, S. M. and Rodriguez, M. C. (2002). A review of multiple-choice item-writing guidelines for classroom assessment. *Applied Measurement in Education* 15: 309–34.

Hamp-Lyons, L. (1997). Ethics in language testing. In C. Clapham and D. Corson (eds), *Encyclopedia of Language and Education,* vol. 7. *Language Testing and Assessment*. Dordrecht, The Netherlands: Kluwer Academic Publishers, 323–33.

—— (2000). Social, professional and individual responsibility in language testing. *System* 28: 579–91.

Hamp-Lyons, L. and Lynch, B. K. (1998). Perspectives on validity: a historical analysis of language testing conference abstracts. In A. J. Kunnan (ed.), *Validation in Language Assessment: Selected Papers from the 17th Language Testing Research Colloquium, Long Beach*. Mahwah, NJ: Lawrence Erlbaum, 253–76.

Hughes, A. (ed.), (2003). *Testing for Language Teachers*. Cambridge, UK: Cambridge University Press.

Kim, J. (2008). *Development and Validation of an ESL Diagnostic Reading-to-write Test: An Effect-driven Approach*. PhD thesis, University of Illinois at Urbana-Champaign.

Kim, J., Chi, Y., Huensch, A., Jun, H., Li, H. and Roullion, V. (2010). A case study on an item writing process: Use of test specifications, nature of group dynamics, and individual item writer's characteristics. *Language Assessment Quarterly* 7: 160–74.

Kohn, A. (2000). *The Case Against Standardized Testing: raising the scores, ruining the schools*. Heinemann.

Luoma, S. (2004). *Assessing Speaking*. Cambridge, UK: Cambridge University Press.

Lynch, B. K. (2001). Rethinking assessment from a critical perspective. *Language Testing* 18: 351–72.

Lynch, B. K. and Shaw, P. (2005). Portfolio, power, and ethics. *TESOL Quarterly* 39: 263–97.

McNamara, T. (2000). *Language Testing*. Oxford, UK: Oxford University Press.

—— (2008). The socio-political and power dimensions of tests. In E. Shohamy and N. H. Hornberger (eds), *Encyclopedia of Language and Education,* Vol 7. *Language Testing and Assessment*, 2nd edn. New York, NY: Springer, 415–27.

McNamara, T. and Roever, C. (2006). *Language Testing: The Social Dimension*. London, UK: Blackwell Publishing.

Mislevy, R. J., Steinberg, L. S. and Almond, R. G. (2002). Design and analysis in task-based language assessment. *Language Testing* 19, 477–96.

—— (2003). On the structure of educational assessments. *Measurement: Interdisciplinary Research and Perspectives* 1: 3–62.

Morgan, B. (2007). Poststructuralism and applied linguistics: Complementary approaches to identity and culture in ELT. In J. Cummins and C. Davison (eds), *Springer International Handbook of Education,* Vol. 15. *International Handbook of English Language Teaching*. Norwell, MA: Springer, 949–68.

Norton, B. (2000). *Identity and Language Learning: gender, ethnicity, and educational change*. London, UK: Longman.

—— (1997). Accountability in language assessment. In C. Clapham and D. Corson (eds), *Encyclopedia of Language and Education, Vol 7: Language Testing and Assessment*. Dordrecht, The Netherlands: Kluwer Academic Publishers, 313–22.

Oller, J. W. (1972). Scoring methods and difficulty levels for cloze tests of proficiency in English as a second language. *Modern Language Journal* 56: 151–58.

Peirce, B. N. (1992). Demystifying the TOEFL reading test. *TESOL Quarterly* 26: 665–91.

Pennycook, A. (2001). *Critical Applied Linguistics: a critical approach*. Mahwah, NJ: Lawrence Erlbaum.

Purpura, J. E. (2004). *Assessing Grammar*. Cambridge, UK: Cambridge University Press.

Read, J. (2000). *Assessing Vocabulary*. Cambridge, UK: Cambridge University Press.

Roid, G. H. and Haladyna, T. M. (1982). *A Technology for Test-item Writing*. New York, NY: Academic Press.

Shin, D. and Kim, N. (2010). Munhang Kaebal Kwajungeseo Shihumjaksung Sepukyehwukseo Yuk-whalyeonKu [Investigating the role of test specifications in item development process]. *Foreign Languages Education* 17: 257–79.

Shizuka, T., Takeuchi, O., Yashima, T. and Yoshizawa, K. (2006). A comparison of three- and four-option English tests for university entrance selection purposes in Japan. *Language Testing* 23: 35–57.

Shohamy, E. (2001). *The Power of Tests: A Critical Perspective on the Uses and Consequences of Language Tests*. London, UK: Longman.

Spaan, M. (2006). Test and item specifications development. *Language Assessment Quarterly* 3: 71–79.

Spolsky, B. (1995). *Measured Words*. Oxford, UK: Oxford University Press.

Stubbs, J. B. and Tucker, G. R. (1974). The cloze test as a measure of English proficiency. *Modern Language Journal* 58: 239–41.

Walters, F. S. (2010). Cultivating assessment literacy: standards evaluation through language test specification reverse engineering. *Language Assessment Quarterly* 10: 317–42.

Yu, G. (2007). Students' voices in the evaluation of their written summaries: Empowerment and democracy for test takers? *Language Testing* 24: 539–72.

17
Writing integrated items

Lia Plakans

Introduction

In developing assessments that reflect language use in context, integration of the four skills has become an inviting direction for task design. Treating language as holistic or as an amalgamation of reading, writing, listening, or speaking, rather than as isolated abilities may allow for different or more substantive interpretations of performances that are transferrable to real world domains. However, claims about integrated items require more study and their development entails delving into multiple skill constructs and writing complex tasks. While integrating skills presents challenges for test developers and users, such tasks provide measures that may overcome some gaps left by independent skills assessment as well as introduce new directions for assessing language (Feak and Dobson, 1996; Plakans, 2008; Read, 1990; Weigle, 2004).

The term "integrated" has been applied fairly broadly to tasks that require more than one skill for completion. For example, an integrated item could entail reading a short text on a topic followed by writing a summary or it may involve listening to a conversation and commenting on the speakers' opinions. The following example illustrates an integrated writing task for an advanced level English language placement test.

Reading-to-write task

Read the following passage on an issue in education. Then consider your position on this topic. *Write an essay agreeing or disagreeing with the author.* Include the main points from the article in your essay and your opinion on each point. Do not copy exact phrases from the article. Your essay will be evaluated on the following:

- explanation of key ideas from the reading
- organization
- development of ideas
- clarity in grammar and vocabulary use

Evaluating teacher quality

Sometimes it seems that school reform is an annual event. Politicians and administrators continually seek to improve education through reform. One topic that appears in this area is teacher quality, in other words, how to make sure our children have the best teachers leading them in successful learning. A proposal suggested recently is to put parents in charge of judging teacher quality. This idea has several merits.

Parents, it may be argued, know what is best for their children. They see their young ones every day and can observe their learning and improvement. Parents know when their kids are excited about school and when they reach certain milestones in learning. It is also true that parents have the greatest stake in teacher quality. This should lead them to evaluate teachers with high motivation for strong results—school improvement. Unlike politicians, parents have their kids' best interests in mind, which should transfer into good assessment of teacher quality.

While this proposal might be controversial, it simply brings evaluation of teacher quality to the people who are impacted most, parents and children. Through their eyes, we might find new ideas and better ways to address teacher quality.

Integrated assessment is not an entirely new idea, but one that has regained momentum with current language teaching approaches, such as task-based language teaching (TBLT) and content-based/immersion instruction, which view language more holistically or functionally rather than as four separate skills. Outside of the classroom, large-scale language assessments are also including integrated assessment tasks to measure speaking and writing performances. While benefits exist for integrating skills in assessment, numerous challenges surface that warrant attention when developing and using such test tasks. This chapter will first discuss past work in integrative assessment, a precursor to integrated skills assessment, and then focus on current research, leading into issues and recommended practice in writing integrated tasks.

Historical perspectives

While tests that combine skills have had a recent surge in popularity, conceptually, the argument for assessing language as an integrated whole has a fairly extended history. The definition of language as four skills can be found in debates from the 1960s regarding testing language competence and use versus language knowledge (Cooper, 1965). Evolving from this debate, several hypotheses related to skill integration took shape: (a) language can be defined as an overarching ability, rather than as separate components, (b) skill integration is important for authentic language use, and (c) skills can be combined because they share processes. These perspectives can be found in the language testing literature since the 1960s, and are very much alive today in arguments for integrated skills assessment.

The first hypothesis operationalized the tenet that one could measure global language proficiency, rather than dividing it into components. This notion was written about extensively by Oller (1979) and termed "integrative." Research by Oller (1983), and others, supported the hypothesis that language proficiency was a unitary construct because all components or measures of language components share variance, and this global proficiency or unity construct was called "expectancy grammar." He claimed, "There are two kinds of empirical data which strongly suggest the possibility that all language skills are based on a rather unitary proficiency factor or internalized grammar" (Oller, 1983: 3). Examples of integrative test items include the cloze test, a kind of gap-filling item, or dictation tests. In relating expectancy grammar to integrated skills, it is important to note that assessing general language ability through "integrative tests" emerged from a response to discrete item testing of vocabulary and grammar (Farhady, 1979; Oller, 1983; Lewkowicz, 1997), rather than to encourage skill integration. The idea of expectancy grammar eventually met with diminished enthusiasm because of questions regarding the item types, such as the cloze, and critiques of the analysis used to support it (Chalhoub-Deville and Deville, 2005; Farhady, 1979, 1983); nevertheless, the contention that language should be assessed as a whole rather than as separated parts has contributed to the field of language testing and to integrated skills assessment.

The second hypothesis, rooted in authenticity, focused on including integration in assessment, because it occurs in real language use situations. In presenting fundamentals in language testing, Carroll (1961) recognized the usefulness of assessing areas of language knowledge, such as: knowledge of structure, knowledge of general-use lexicon, auditory discrimination, oral production, phonemic reading, and writing (spelling). However, he advocated integrated testing of rate and accuracy in four domains: listening comprehension, interactive speaking, reading comprehension, and writing comprehension. The rationale for integration in these areas was to facilitate transference to real language use, which Carroll articulated in the following:

> an ideal English language proficiency test should make it possible to differentiate, to the greatest possible extent, levels of performance in those dimensions of performance which are relevant to the kinds of situations in which the examinees will find themselves after being selected on the basis of the test.
>
> *(Carroll, 1961: 319)*

A third perspective on integration of skills appears somewhat later, and may be attributed to literature in first language (L1) domains such as educational and cognitive psychology (Fitzgerald and Shanahan, 2000), rather than in language testing specifically. This is a view that some processes involved in language skills are shared. In an empirical study, Shanahan and Lomax (1986) proposed three theoretical models of the reading–writing relationship and analyzed L1 data for each to determine which model was supported. The results of their study supported an interactive model, which holds that writing can influence reading development and reading can impact writing development. In another synthesis article, Eisterhold (1990) projected these ideas into second language reading and writing, illuminating important differences for second language learners, such as less established phonological systems in the second language and already developed first language reading–writing processes. However, she advocates for teaching that elicits the connections or transfer between the two skills, which can be further extended to integrated assessment.

While these three positions regarding integration of skills were initiated over forty years ago, they are still relevant today and appear in research seeking to elucidate the construct elicited by integrated tasks (e.g. Huang, 2010; Yang, 2009; Sawaki *et al.*, 2009).

Current research

Research on integrated assessment can be categorized into four overlapping domains: comparison of tasks, task characteristics, proficiency, and investigations of construct.

Comparing integrated and independent skills tasks

As interest in integrated assessment tasks increases, administrators, teachers, and language testing researchers have sought to understand the differences and similarities between these tasks and those that treat skills independently. Studies have compared scores and used correlations to determine if test takers differ in their performance on the two kinds of tasks, confirming that a relationship exists (Brown *et al.*, 1991; Gebril, 2009; Lee, 2006; Lewkowicz, 1994; Watanabe,

2001). However, when delving more deeply into the features of the products from writing-only and integrated writing tasks, differences have emerged. One area of divergence is in development. Cumming et al. (2005) found that independent tasks lead to longer essays. In contrast, Lewkowicz (1994) discovered that while there was no significant difference in word count (length), more points were introduced by writers on integrated tasks than on the independent tasks, leading her to conclude that writers were developing each point less on the former. Cumming et al. (2005) did not find significant differences in grammatical accuracy between the two tasks, but did find the independent task essays scored lower on a number of rhetorical features of persuasive writing. Watanabe (2001) found a difference in the quality of thesis statements from writing on the two tasks, with the independent tasks eliciting more originality than the integrated. While these studies have focused on comparing the products of independent and integrated assessment tasks, a few studies have looked at how test takers' processes relate in the two types of tasks. For example, Plakans (2008) found that one of the main differences was in planning, with independent tasks requiring more pre-writing planning and the integrated tasks leading to more planning while writing.

A large research study by Huang (2010) overlaps task comparison and test taker character-istics. His study investigated independent and integrated speaking tasks to determine if topic knowledge and anxiety impacted performance differentially. He found that for one topic, related to business, anxiety had comparable impact on both task types, while on the science-related topic, anxiety had a greater impact on integrated task performance. Huang suggests that intro-ducing reading or listening on a topic that a test taker is not familiar with might result in anxiety about comprehending the source material in addition to anxiety regarding performance. How-ever, in follow-up interviews, test takers were insistent that they experienced more anxiety with the independent speaking task. This study brings into question the assumption that providing content diminishes problems like test anxiety or background knowledge.

Despite the varied results in comparing integrated and independent tasks, when test takers have been asked their opinions, a preference for integration is resounding (Gebril and Plakans, 2009; Huang, 2010). Stakeholders report feeling more knowledgeable on the topic after reading or listening to content as well as finding the source texts useful for ideas, vocabulary, and organization. The research on comparison of these tasks has identified differences in planning, anxiety, and topic effect in the processes of completing the tasks as well as variation in development and rhetorical structure in the products.

Task characteristics

While a good deal of variation exists in integrated tasks, a few studies have looked at the differences across them. In a study that included test takers' process, Ascención (2005) compared summary writing with response writing, finding that the latter required more planning and monitoring than summarizing, which could be explained with the need to create one's own voice in response writing. In a study of the Test of English as a Foreign Language (TOEFL) speaking tasks, Swain et al. (2009) found differences in strategies used to complete integrated tasks that included two or three skills. They found an increase in skills related to an increase in strategy use, with tasks involving three strategies eliciting more strategies than those with two skills, and either integrated task revealing more strategies than the independent task.

Cumming et al. (2005) discovered differences in source text use between two task topics, one regarding political science and the other on cinema. Similar to Huang (2010), the challenge of topic in integrated tasks has been illuminated, but how to choose topics and what topics work well is yet to be determined by research. This struggle has existed with independent skills tasks as well, but given the potential for compounding background knowledge with reading or listening to source texts, integrated tasks may require additional care in topic selection.

Related to the issue of topic, the texts used in integrated tasks have generated little interest despite their importance. To address this issue, Yu (2009) investigated source text characteristics in summary writing and found that they had a greater impact on score than writers' proficiency. He compared the writers' use of three source texts of different domains and genres: an expository piece on education, a narrative about rivers, and an argumentative text on work. The texts also differed in other features such as having an introduction or no introduction and clear timeline or no detailed time frame. Lastly, readability, passivity, and lexical diversity were varied. While the source texts significantly affected the summary task score, it is not clear which features differentiated the texts' impact or if a combination of certain features was affecting test takers. However, in a follow up questionnaire and interview, the test takers reported that features such as organization, unknown words, length, and topic impacted their summarizing of a text. They felt that the education-related expository source text was easiest to summarize because of its clear organization and the low number of unfamiliar words. These studies are identifying the complexities in developing integrated tasks and continued work in this area will help to qualify the characteristics of task type, topic, and texts used in integrated assessment

Integrated tasks and proficiency

Research on integrated assessment tasks has considered the interplay between performance and proficiency level. Attention to general second language or writing proficiency has generated studies comparing essays across test scores for certain language features. Consistent with second language writing research, higher scoring integrated writing is longer, based on the metric of word count (Cumming *et al.*, 2005; Gebril and Plakans, 2009). Stronger integrated writing also has more accurate grammar and greater integration of sources than writing at lower levels. Interestingly, in a study by Gebril and Plakans (2009) closer comparison across three levels of scores revealed that linguistic features, such as grammatical accuracy, were stronger at differentiating between the lowest scoring group and the two higher scoring groups, than between the higher groups. Baba (2009) investigated how test takers' lexical proficiency impacted their scores on summary writing to explore whether general language proficiency or L2 lexical proficiency had an impact. The impact of lexical proficiency of summary writing score was weak compared to that of language proficiency, with receptive vocabulary indicators of size and depth having little impact and productive indicators of lexical density and definition ability showing more contribution to score. These results may illuminate integrated tasks taping test takers' ability to manipulate language.

The issue of source use and score level has appeared in a number of studies (Cumming *et al.*, 2005; Gebril and Plakans, 2009; Johns and Mayes, 1990). For example, examining summary writing, Johns and Mayes (1990) compared writing at two proficiency levels and found significant differences in the copying from the original text as well as how idea units from the original texts were combined in the summaries. These studies on language proficiency and score in integrated tasks are contributing to a picture of test taker performance at different levels and may, eventually, impact the design of rating scales as well as the interpretations made from the scores.

Seeking the construct

Given the importance of defining a construct for test development, it is not surprising that scholars have undertaken studies targeting the underlying abilities involved in integrated assessment. One question being pursued is whether the resulting score from an integrated task is a measure of *all* the skills that are integrated. Sawaki *et al.* (2009) analyzed the Internet-based TOEFL products to inform score interpretation. They found that scores on the integrated speaking and writing items were only slightly related to the less dominant skills in the tasks (listening, reading), and thus their scores were better interpreted as measures of writing or speaking. The skill of reading in reading–writing tasks has been studied from several angles. Two researchers correlated integrated reading–writing scores with separate measures of reading and writing, and in both cases determined that the variance in scores was determined more by writing and minimally explained by reading (Delany, 2008; Watanabe, 2001). In fact, Watanabe (2001) suggested that the variance attributed to reading may be related to general language proficiency. However, studies that have investigated the processes of writers during reading–writing tasks have found that reading is an important process in completing the assessment (Esmaeili, 2002; Plakans, 2009a).

Another approach to defining the construct in integrated tasks investigates the abilities that underlie integration and the synthesis of the skills, rather than individual skills added together. Ascención (2005) and Plakans (2009b) investigated the concept of "discourse synthesis" in second language integrated writing tasks using think-aloud verbal protocols. Discourse synthesis is a term used in English first language writing theory to describe the constructive meaning-making process of reading for writing that includes the sub-processes of organizing, selecting, and connecting (Spivey, 1990, 1997). In both studies, the results of recording writers' online processes revealed the sub-processes of discourse synthesis did occur in composing integrated writing tasks. These sub-processes also appeared in a writing strategy survey used by Yang (2009) to investigate reading–listening–writing tasks; her study concluded that higher scoring writers utilized organizing, selecting, and connecting strategies in their test taking process.

While the research so far has been ambitiously trying to define the construct of integrated assessment, more work is needed to identify and clarify the underlying abilities involved in the various kinds of integrated tasks and how scores reflect this. For example, listening has not been considered in the detail that reading has as a skill integrated with writing or speaking. In addition, construct investigation should be extended beyond a sum of skills to incorporate the overlapping and unique elements of skills integration.

Critical issues and guidelines for practice

In writing integrated tasks, several steps are required, most of which align with good test development practice in general; however, given their constructs and the complex processes they elicit, such items might require extra care. Several issues require consideration when writing or using integrated items in language assessment, which include defining what is being measured; considering appropriate and feasible input/output dimensions; choosing task type and developing items; carefully constructing instructions; establishing scoring criteria and rating materials; piloting repeatedly to test out the input, instructions, timing, and rating.

Needs analysis and defining the construct

In deciding whether to use integrated skills in assessment, the purpose of the test should be the first consideration, along with a needs analysis, to determine what the domain for language use entails. If a test will be used to identify language ability in contexts that require skill integration, then such tasks should appear in a test. However, the nature of the integration deserves careful consideration in the development phase. For example, how many texts do language users manage when integrating reading with writing or listening with speaking? What is the nature, length, and difficulty level of listening or reading texts? At what points in the process do the language users integrate skills? How fully are they integrated? Needs analysis at the beginning of the development process should attend closely to the nuances in integrated language use. Since a major argument for using such tasks is their authenticity, their fidelity claim needs verification.

Along with a needs analysis, test developers should consider what abilities underlie the integrated tasks being developed. Defining the construct is a major challenge for integrated assessment, as it is less clearly definable than separated skills testing. It may be that the constructs for these tasks are not just a sum of skills, but synthesized matrices. Once the tasks have been developed, data may need to be collected for validation to defend, further define, or discard the construct. Continual scrutiny of construct validity as well as updated needs analyses should be a regular part of any testing program using integrated skills tasks.

Considering task type

Given the broad definition of integrated assessment, many tasks reside under this umbrella, with room for further innovation. This variety makes integrating skills promising and, at the same time, complex (Leki *et al.*, 2008). The choice of integrated task type should be determined by the needs analysis and construct definition.

A common type of integration appears with content or "text responsible" tasks (Leki and Carson, 1997: 41) in which the test taker reads and/or listens to a text followed by speaking or writing a response that includes some of this content. A summary task is a common integrated task that would fall into this task type; related to summaries are review tasks, where the test taker summarizes the text and adds his/her commentary on the topic. An example of a text responsible task appears at the B2 Level of the DELF French language proficiency test administered by Centre international d'étude pédagogiques. To assess speaking, test takers read a short passage that is meant to create a reaction, and then they defend their reaction or opinion to the text in an extended spoken response. In content responsible tasks, test takers may be asked to comprehend and negotiate more than one text. For example, the integrated writing task on the internet-based TOEFL test includes reading and listening to two opposing views on a topic, followed by writing a comparative summary that explains the listening content and how it differs from the reading. Another example of an integrated task using multiple texts provides the test taker with two opinions on an issue and requires a persuasive response that is supported by the content (see example task below).

Example of a multiple text content-responsible task

Instructions: Read the two passages below presenting different opinions on children watching television. Then consider your viewpoint on this topic and write an essay giving reasons for your opinion. Use the readings appropriately to support your position.

The danger of television for children

Recent research has indicated that watching more than two hours a day of television can affect children's cognition and potentially lead to an increased chance of having attention deficit disorder. The way TV programs are designed for children, to be rapidly changing and exciting, may cause problems as they get older in terms of focusing on homework or extended tasks. Parents need to restrict the time that children watch as much as they attend to what is being watched. TV is not a babysitter.

The healthy impact of children's television

While there may be issues with watching extended hours of television, children can learn valuable lessons from educational programs. Recently, several programs, such as Sesame Street, have included healthy eating and exercise lessons to remind kids to get physical and not eat too many cookies. This kind of programming can have a great impact on what kids think about healthy choices, and open up this topic for discussion with their parents. If we lose this medium for influencing kids, they may not learn these valuable lessons.

Another task described as integrated is one in which input texts are provided for test takers but not required in the response. The content in the texts serves as an illustration or stimulus for the task topic. While the resulting score from this kind of task does not necessarily relate to the integration of skills, test takers will utilize more than one skill in their process. The example below shows an integrated stimulus task that provides the test taker with a conversation that introduces the topic for a short spoken response.

Example of a listening/speaking task

Instructions: Press the play button to listen to a conversation between two people waiting to buy a movie ticket. You will then have 30 seconds to plan a short response for the following: Recommend a movie that you like to these people, and explain why you suggest it. You will have 60 seconds to respond.

Audio transcript

Person 1: Which movie should we see? Do you feel like a comedy or something scary?

Person 2: Hmmmm. None of these looks very good to me. What do you think?

Person 1: Well, I know this movie is for kids and it's all animation. I don't want to see that. And the other three are too serious. I'd really like something more upbeat, like that movie we saw last week with the two travellers who kept having funny adventures. The characters were hilarious and the special effects, amazing.

Person 2: Yeah, or I liked your idea about something scary too. I don't really care what kind of movie it is, as long as it's good. I think we should find a movie to watch online or rent something instead of watching any of these. It would be cheaper for sure.

Choosing texts

The role of texts and topics in integrated tasks is a critical issue that exists in language tasks generally but has an elevated importance in integrating skills. The possible variety of topics in texts and performances in integrated assessment leads to several concerns: different constructs elicited by different texts, the interaction of previous experience or background knowledge, and the magnification of topic effect. While only a limited amount of research has looked at these issues, good practices in writing integrated tasks can be outlined.

The first step is choosing a topic. This decision could be guided by a needs analysis. If specific content areas are likely to be familiar to students, these topics are best. In addition, choosing texts in test takers' content area may allow for better assessment of integration in their field. For example, in integrated speaking and writing tasks at the C1 and C2 Level of *Diplôme approfondi de langue française* (DALF), test takers may choose between two areas: humanities and social science or science. However, often information about test takers' domain of interest or expertise is not available to test developers, in which case, more general topics may be selected. Once topics are chosen, texts can be developed or collected. Test developers may choose to find published texts on chosen topics, but should carefully pilot these texts and consider revising for difficult structures and challenging vocabulary. There may also be issues with copyrighted information and permissions should be sought on authentic texts used. The alternative is to develop new texts.

Once texts have been selected or developed, the level of difficulty should be evaluated. While not a perfect measure for difficulty, readability indices can provide some information regarding the grade level or difficulty level of a text based on word length, sentence length, and some other structural features. Online programs measure the readability of a text, and Microsoft Word includes this feature in the grammar/spellchecker. A more in-depth analysis can be conducted for lexical density or coherence of texts using online programs such as CLAN (childes. psy.cmu.edu) or CohMetrix (cohmetrix.memphis.edu/cohmetrixpr/index.html). If texts are found to be too difficult, they should be revised, although modification is not a clear direct path, as reading research has shown (Koda, 2004). Some features to modify include sentence length, unfamiliar or technical words, unclear subjects and main verbs, or adding cohesion devices such as transitions or topic sentences.

Composing instructions

Integrated tasks can be confusing for test takers if they have not experienced them before, and they may resort to interpreting the task in the same way as independent tasks. A number of studies have investigated task representation in reading-to-write tasks providing valuable insights into the nature of understanding the demands of these tasks. This research has revealed that task representation can be impacted by writers' experiences with prior writing tasks (Plakans, 2010; Ruiz-Funes, 2001; Wolfersberger, 2007). Obviously, test developers cannot control test takers' prior experience; however, carefully crafted instructions can, perhaps, minimize misinterpretation of the instructions. While this maxim is true of any assessment, one element specific to integrated task instruction demands heightened attention: use of source materials.

Mention of the source texts should appear in at least three parts of integrated task instructions. First of all, the intended purpose for the input texts should be explicit. The test takers need to know if they are responsible for the content of texts in their responses. Second, some mention regarding direct copying of phrases from the text and use of citation should be included, although this instruction is a greater issue with written than oral responses. While the wording for such instruction may be difficult, it can help minimize major problems for rating and interpreting the scores from the task. Lastly, test takers should be given the criteria on which they will be evaluated, not in detail, but to clarify what is important in their performance. If the sources are to be included in the products, then this integration should appear in the evaluation criteria. Below is an example of instructions for an integrated task (Gebril and Plakans, 2009):

> Read the question below, and then read the two passages to get more information about the topic. Write an essay on the topic giving your opinion in response to the question. Typically, an effective response will contain a minimum of 300 words. Your writing will be scored based on how well:

your **ideas** are explained
the **readings** support your argument
you **organize** your essay
you **choose words**
you **use grammar**
you **spell** and **punctuate**

IMPORTANT! READ CAREFULLY BEFORE WORKING ON THE TASK

- The two passages should help you get some ideas about the topic.
- You may go back to the passages to check information while writing.
- You can borrow ideas and examples from the text. However, you should mention the author's name if you do so.
- Also, if you take exactly the same phrases or sentences mentioned in the passage, put them between two inverted commas (" ").

Developing scoring rubrics

The rubric to score integrated tasks depends on the purpose of the task, the construct as it has been defined, and the constraints of the scoring sessions. Test developers should determine if the resulting scores are a sum of separate scores on different criteria, an analytic rubric, or one single score that represents the overall level of the performance, a holistic rubric. The example below illustrates the descriptor from a holistic rubric (Gebril and Plakans, 2009).

Level 4

A response:

- is good in clearly and correctly presenting ideas in relation to the relevant information in the reading texts. It may have weaknesses in connection to specific points made in the readings.
- uses clear organization and logical development.
- includes some minor language errors which occasionally create slight confusion, but not enough to lose the writer's meaning.

In addition to determining the form of the scale, the criteria and descriptors need development. Several approaches to this may be undertaken. First of all, a construct can help identify criteria for the scale; for example, if the construct includes reading comprehension, then the scale should have some wording regarding this skill. Another source for scale criteria can be found in the needs analysis. By scrutinizing the abilities required in a language use context, test developers may determine what criteria lead to successful integration of skills. A third method is to develop a data driven scale. In this case the test task is used with the target population to collect performance samples (see Fulcher, this volume). These samples are then divided into the score levels needed, and analyzed for language features. These features then become criteria and descriptors for the scale.

Research on integrated assessment scores has revealed an interesting challenge for future scale development. Studies have suggested the possibility that the features distinguishing high level performances may be dissimilar from those distinguishing lower level performances (Gebril and Plakans, 2009; Sawaki, *et al.*, 2009). In order to distinguish performances at all levels, it may be important to have different criteria across score levels.

Future directions

Certainly, the current interest in integrated tasks can spark new and innovative task types to support test takers' synthesis of skills. Along with this creative development will come better understanding of the constructs these tasks are eliciting. Several areas are beacons for future work. First of all, more investigation and advancement of constructs for integrated skill assessment holds promise. A tendency exists to conceptualize integrated skills as a summation of the skills; however, the benefit of these tasks may lie in recognizing higher-order processes that are measured by amalgamated skills or in defining the synthesis of skills as a unique ability. From such explorations, new tasks will evolve, which is another area for future endeavor. In recent integrated tasks, writing and speaking have remained the dominant skills, supported by listening and/or reading. However, tasks that require writing or speaking before reading or listening may have a good deal to offer in terms of integration for comprehension and scaffolding prior knowledge (Trites and McGroaty, 2005). These two areas, construct refinement and task innovation, require continued research to inform, support, and extend new ideas about the evolving concept of integrated skills assessment.

Further reading

Gerbril, A. (2010). Bringing reading-to-write and writing-only assessment tasks together: A generalizability study. *Assessing Writing* 15: 100–117. Using multivariate generalizability analysis, Gebril investigates reliability between independent and integrated tasks by comparing raters and task facets with the two tasks combined and with each task separately. His findings uncover similar results in reliability for the two combined and as separate tests, which provides evidence that the tasks are measuring the same construct. The results also exhibit similar results when different raters scored the two tasks and when the same raters scored the tasks. Gebril advocates for using independent and integrated tasks in combination when assessing writing to provide comprehensive information on second language writing ability.

Paltridge, B. (1992). EAP placement testing: An integrated approach. *English for Specific Purposes* 11: 243–69. This article describes the framework for an integrated English for Academic Purposes Placement test. The test intends to elicit "natural language" behavior through a series of tasks that integrate skills. An innovative aspect of this test is that it provides test takers with models for integration by using sources or language samples in the tasks that include integration of themes and rhetorical patterns. The author presents this test and the framework on which it was designed to encourage the study of integrated assessment tests.

Yu, G. (2008). Reading to summarize in English and Chinese: A tale of two languages? *Language Testing* 25: 521–51. Yu compares reading comprehension evidenced in the summary writing of 157 Chinese undergraduates in their first and their second languages (English). The study also collected interview and questionnaire data after writing. Yu found that the Chinese summaries were longer, but were consistently scored lower than the English summaries. The L1 summaries also appeared to be better indicators of the test takers' reading abilities, although the effect size was moderate. The follow up responses indicated that a majority of the writers preferred the English task and that they felt their reading impacted their ability to summarize.

References

Ascención, Y. (2005). *Validation of Reading-to-write Assessment Tasks Performed by Second Language Learners.* Unpublished doctoral dissertation, Northern Arizona University, Flagstaff, Arizona.

Baba, K. (2009). Aspects of lexical proficiency in writing summaries in a foreign language. *Journal of Second Language Writing* 18: 191–208.

Brown, J. D., Hilgers, T. and Marsella, J. (1991). Essay prompts and topics: minimizing the effect of mean differences. *Written Communication* 8: 533–56.

Carroll, J. M. (1961). *Fundamental Considerations in Teaching for English Language Proficiency of Foreign Students.* Washington, DC: Routledge.

Chalhoub-Deville, M. and Deville, C. (2005). Looking back at and forward to what language testers measure. In E. Hinkel (ed.), *Handbook of Research on Second Language Teaching and Learning.* Mahwah, NJ: Erlbaum.

Cooper, R. L. (1965). Testing. In H. B. Allen and R. N. Allen (eds), *Teaching English as a Second Language: A Book of Readings*. New York, NY: McGraw-Hill.

Cumming, A., Kantor, R., Baba, K., Erdosy, U., Eouanzoui, K. and James, M. (2005). Differences in Written Discourse in Writing-only and Reading-to-write Prototype Tasks for Next Generation TOEFL. *Assessing Writing* 10: 5–43.

Delaney, Y.A. (2008). Investigating the Reading-to-Write Construct. *Journal of English for Academic Purposes* 7: 140–50.

Eisterhold J. (1990). Reading-writing connections: toward a description for second language learners. In B. Kroll (ed.), *Second Language Writing: research insights for the classroom*. Cambridge, UK: Cambridge University Press.

Esmaeili, H. (2002). Integrated Reading and Writing Tasks and ESL Students' Reading and Writing Performance in an English Language Test. *Canadian Modern Language Journal* 58: 599–622.

Farhady, H. (1979). The disjunctive fallacy between discrete point and integrative tests. *TESOL Quarterly* 13: 347–57.

—— (1983). On the Plausibility of the Unitary Language Proficiency Factor. In J. W. Oller (ed.), *Issues in Language Testing Research*. Rowley, MA: Newbury House Publishers.

Feak, C. and Dobson, B. (1996). Building on the impromptu: source-based academic writing assessment. *College ESL* 6: 73–84.

Fitzgrerald, J. and Shanahan, T. (2000). Reading and writing relations and their development. *Educational Psychologist* 35: 39–50.

Gebril, A. (2009). Score generalizability of academic writing tasks: does one test method fit it all? *Language Testing* 26: 507–31.

Gebril, A. and Plakans, L. (2009). Investigating source use, discourse features, and process in integrated writing tests. *Spaan Working Papers in Second or Foreign Language Assessment* 7: 47–84.

Huang, H. T. (2010). *Modeling the Relationships among Topical Knowledge, Anxiety, and Integrated Speaking Test Performance: A Structural Equation Modeling Approach*. Unpublished doctoral dissertation, University of Texas at Austin, Austin, Texas.

Johns, A. M. and Mayes, P. (1990). An analysis of summary protocol of university ESL students. *Applied Linguistics* 11: 253–71.

Koda, K. (2004). *Insights into Second Language Reading: a cross-linguistic approach*. Cambridge, UK: Cambridge University Press.

Lee, Y. (2006). Dependability of Scores for a New ESL Speaking Assessment Consisting of Integrated and Independent Tasks. *Language Testing* 23: 131–66.

Leki, I. and Carson, J. (1997). Completely Different Worlds: EAP and the Writing Experiences of ESL Students in University Courses. *TESOL Quarterly* 31: 39–69.

Leki, I., Cumming, A. and Silva, T. (2008). *A Synthesis of Research on Second Language Writing in English*. New York, NY: Routledge.

Lewkowicz, J. A. (1994). Writing from Sources: does source material help or hinder students' performance? In N. Bird *et al.* (eds), *Language and Learning: Papers presented at the Annual International Language in Education Conference*. ERIC Document (ED 386 050).

—— (1997). The Integrated Testing of a Second Language. In C. Clapham and D. Corson (eds), *Encyclopaedia of Language and Education*. Dordrecht, The Netherlands: Kluwer.

Oller, J. W. (1979). *Language Tests at School: a pragmatic approach*. London, UK: Longman.

—— (1983). *Issues in Language Testing Research*. Rowley, MA: Newbury House.

Plakans, L. (2008). Comparing composing processes in writing-only and reading-to-write test tasks. *Assessing Writing* 13: 111–29.

—— (2009a). The role of reading strategies in L2 writing tasks. *Journal of English for Academic Purposes* 8: 252–66.

—— (2009b). Discourse synthesis in integrated second language assessment. *Language Testing* 26: 1–27.

—— (2010). Independent vs. integrated tasks: a comparison of task representation. *TESOL Quarterly* 44: 185–94.

Read, J. (1990). Providing relevant content in an EAP writing test. *English for Specific Purposes* 9: 109–21.

Ruiz-Funes, M. (2001). Task representation in foreign language reading-to-write. *Foreign Language Annals* 34: 226–34.

Sawaki, Y., Stricker, L. J., Oranje, A. H. (2009). Factor structure of the TOEFL internet-based test. *Language Testing* 26: 5–30.

Sawaki, Y., Quinlan, T. and Lee, Y. W. (2009). *Understanding Learner Strengths and Weaknesses: Measuring Performance on an Integrated Writing Task*. Paper presented at the 31st Language Testing Research Colloquium, March, Denver, Colorado.

Shanahan, T. and Lomax R. (1986). An analysis and comparison of theoretical models of the reading-writing relationship. *Journal of Educational Psychology* 78: 116–23.

Spivey, N. (1990). Transforming texts: constructive processes in reading and writing. *Written Communication* 7: 256–87.

Swain, M., Huang, L., Barkaoui, K., Brooks, L. and Lapkin, S. (2009). The Speaking Section of the TOEFL iBT (SSTiBT): Test-Takers' Reported Strategic Behaviors. *TOEFL iBT Research Report*, RR 09–30 (www.ets.org/Media/Research/pdf/RR-09-30.pdf).

Trites, L. and McGroaty, M. (2005). Reading to learn and reading to integrate: new tasks for reading comprehension tests? *Language Testing* 22: 174–210.

Watanabe, Y. (2001). *Read-to-Write Tasks for the Assessment of Second Language Academic Writing Skills: Investigating Text Features and Rater Reactions*. Unpublished doctoral dissertation, University of Hawaii.

Weigle, S. (2004). Integrating reading and writing in a competency test for non-native speakers of English. *Assessing Writing* 9: 27–55.

Wolfersberger, M. A. (2007). *Second Language Writing from Sources: An Ethnographic Study of an Argument Essay Task*. Unpublished doctoral dissertation, The University of Auckland, Auckland, New Zealand.

Yang, H. C. (2009). *Exploring the Complexity of Second Language Writers' Strategy Use and Performance on an Integrated Writing Test through SEM and Qualitative Approaches*. Unpublished doctoral dissertation, The University of Texas at Austin, Austin, Texas.

Yu, G. (2009). The shifting sands in the effects of source text summarizability on summary writing. *Assessing Writing* 14: 116–37.

Test-taking strategies and task design

Andrew D. Cohen

Introduction and definition of terms

The focus of this chapter picks up on a perspective voiced by Davidson (2000) when he warned against *statistical determinism* when validating language assessment measures:

> Any new development in language test statistics should not divert language testers away from the far more difficult and fundamental challenges of making valid assessments. Statistical determinism is a deceptively accessible *Weltanschaung* (world view); it is far too easy to allow items to survive trialing or editing based solely on their "p" or "d" value, just as it is far too easy to judge the work by an oral interview rater based solely on inter-rater reliability correlation coefficients. Statistical evidence of educational quality should be fused with and weighed against evidence that derives from other sources.
>
> *(Davidson, 2000: 615)*

Whereas determining the construct relevance or irrelevance of variance on a language test was traditionally based on psychometrics alone, in recent years it has become more fashionable to look beyond statistics to help understand test results. One such area of investigation has been that of test-taking strategies. In this chapter, I will take a non-psychometric approach to construct relevance in responding to the following question:

> In what ways might the study of construct-relevant and construct–irrelevant test-taking strategy use inform the design and construction of items and tasks on language assessment measures?

When designing and then constructing items and tasks for the purpose of language assessment, we are likely to make certain assumptions about them. One of them is that responding to the items and tasks correctly relies on a proper mobilization of certain cognitive processes. In line with this assumption, O'Sullivan and Weir (2011) include cognitive validity in their model for conceptualizing test validity and carrying out the validation of a measure. They see the *cognitive validity* of a measure as dependent upon the processes that respondents use in responding to language assessment items and tasks. With regard to this type of validity, they ask the following two questions:

1. Are the cognitive processes required to complete the tasks appropriate?
2. Are candidates likely to use the same cognitive processes as they would if performing the task in a "real-world" context?

If the test items and tasks are not measuring what they purport to measure, but rather something else which is "irrelevant" to the desired construct of focus, then we have a validity issue. Ideally, respondents are mobilizing strategies aimed at dealing with the construct being assessed rather than avoiding it. We will first consider strategies, then look at research from both an historical perspective and in terms of current efforts, and will consider practical applications as well.

Language learner strategies

The following is my own working definition of *language learner strategies*:

> Thoughts and actions, consciously chosen and operationalized by language learners, to assist them in carrying out a multiplicity of tasks from the very onset of learning to the most advanced levels of target-language (TL) performance.
>
> *(Cohen, 2011: 7)*

In order to carry out tasks on language tests, it is possible that learners will call upon their listening, speaking, reading, and writing skills, as well as the related skills of vocabulary learning, grammar, and translation. Hence, for example, a listening comprehension item could call for inferencing strategies while listening to a snippet of an interchange.

As an example, the listener hears: "Well, if you put it **that** way, then I guess I do owe you an explanation, but I think you're overreacting here … " and needs to indicate whether this is *most likely* part of an exchange between:

a. a boss and an employee
b. an auto mechanic and a patron
c. a husband and his wife or
d. a police officer and a suspected felon.

In this case, "c" is the appropriate choice, assuming that the man's tone of voice is slightly sarcastic with a touch of condescension. Thus, in responding to language assessment measures, respondents are using language learner strategies in consort with test-taking strategies, which will now be defined.

Test-management strategies

Test-management strategies are strategies for responding meaningfully to test items and tasks. These are the processes consciously selected to assist in producing a correct answer responsibly. They include logistical issues such as weighing the importance of responding to different items or tasks, keeping track of the time, and determining where to look for answers.

Test-management strategies on a reading test could deal with:

- going back and forth between a passage and a given question in order to obtain more information about just what to be looking for
- dealing with multiple-choice options systematically so as to give careful consideration to all the alternative choices and to craft a rationale for why one choice is better than the others

- time-management strategies that ensure sufficient attention to items and tasks, especially those with the highest point values on the test.

As an example, on an essay-writing task, a test-management strategy would be to outline the essay before writing it in order to ensure that it responds effectively to the writing prompt. Assume that the task is to write an essay requesting that the respondent take a stand, pro or con, on an issue such as the following from sample essay topics for the former *Test of Written English* published by Educational Testing Service:

> Do you agree or disagree with the following statement? Sometimes it is better not to tell the truth. Use specific reasons and details to support your answer.

Test-management strategies would include lining up arguments in outline form in advance—e.g., taking a position (in favor of white lies) listing instances where lying makes sense along with a rationale. Perhaps the essay would start with a justification for telling the truth as a preamble. In any case, good test-management strategies would ensure that the writing of the essay would be smooth, with a minimum of hesitation, since it had been adequately planned out in advance.

Test-wiseness strategies

Test-wiseness strategies involve using knowledge of testing formats and other peripheral information to answer test items without going through the expected cognitive processes (in this case, involving the selection of numerous language elements). Test-wiseness strategies would represent what were referred to above as construct-irrelevant strategies. They are strategies that assist respondents in obtaining responses—very possibly the correct ones—without engaging the second language (L2) knowledge and performance ability. So, for example, there are test-wiseness strategies that respondents can apply to multiple-choice items, such as the following:

- stem-option cues—where matching is possible between the stem and an option
- grammatical cues—where only one alternative matches the stem grammatically
- similar options—where several distractors can be eliminated because they essentially say the same thing
- item giveaway—where another item already gives away the information.

(Allan, 1992)

Presumably test constructors and language educators administering tests would want to restrict or avoid the possibility of responses to multiple-choice items being based on the use of these construct-irrelevant strategies. With regard to a reading test, it would mean using the process of elimination (i.e., selecting an option even though it is not understood, out of a vague sense that the other options couldn't be correct), using clues in other items to answer an item under consideration, and selecting the option because it appears to have a word or phrase from the passage in it—possibly a key word.

The following is an example of stem-option matching. Respondents did not have to look in the text for surface matches. They were able to match directly between the stem and the correct alternative:

> *Question*: The increased foreign awareness of Filanthropia has ...
>
> (a)   resulted in its relative poverty.
> (b)   led to a tourist bureau investigation.

(c) created the main population centers.

(d) caused its extreme isolation.

Students associated "foreign" in the stem with "tourist" in option (b), the correct answer in this case, without understanding the test item (Cohen, 2011: 313).

Historical origins of test-taking strategies

We will first take a look at some of the early studies on test-taking strategies to see what they taught us about item design. One such early study was that of Danish researchers who used introspection and retrospection to study the responses of high school and college EFL students to three multiple-choice test item types embedded in connected text. Students explained which alternatives they would choose and why they thought the selected alternative was the correct one (Dollerup *et al.*, 1982). Their findings that each item produced an array of strategies and that even erroneous decoding could produce the correct answer provided early evidence as to the importance of studying learner response processes in order to determine test validity.

Another influential early study dealt with strategy use in responding to random and rational-deletion cloze tests (Homburg and Spaan, 1981). In a preliminary phase, respondents were given four different types of cloze (two of them involving nonsense words instead of real words) and verbal report data were collected in order that they give their rationale as to how they responded. Based on the reports of strategy use and success with different random-deletion item types, a 23-blank rational-deletion cloze was constructed with four item types presumed to require different strategies:

- recognition of parallelism across phrases
- processing within a given sentence
- the use of cues in previous sentences
- the use of cues in subsequent sentences.

It was found that success at understanding the main idea among 39 EFL students at three levels was related to success at completing blanks requiring forward reading. The message to designers of rational-deletion cloze tests would be to include in the instructions the suggestion that respondents be sure to read beyond each blank before attempting to fill the gap, in order to reduce the use of construct-irrelevant strategies.

A series of studies were conducted in the early years to determine the closeness-of-fit between the tester's presumptions about what was being tested and the response processes that the test takers reported (Cohen, 1984). One such study investigating test method effect in EFL reading by Israeli high school students found differences in strategy use by low- and high-proficiency students (Gordon, 1987). The researcher used four response formats:

- multiple-choice questions in English
- multiple-choice questions in Hebrew
- open-ended questions in English
- open-ended questions in Hebrew.

A subgroup of respondents were asked to verbalize their thoughts while they sought answers to each question. Low-proficiency students were found to process information at the *local* (sentence/ word) *level*, without relating isolated bits of information to the whole text. They used individual word-centered strategies like matching alternative words to text, copying words out of the text, word-for-word translation, formulating global impressions of text content on the basis of key words or isolated lexical items in the text or in the test questions. High-proficiency students were seen to comprehend the text at the *global level*—predicting information accurately in context and using lexical and structural knowledge to cope with linguistic difficulties. As to performance, open-ended questions in the L2 (English) were found to be the most difficult and the best discriminator between the high- and low-proficiency students, since the low-proficiency students had difficulty with them. So this study had two messages for test designers:

1. They should construct reading tasks that challenge low-proficiency students to read text at the global level.
2. If discriminating across proficiency levels is important, then they should select formats that do a better job of discrimination, such as open-ended questions in the L2.

A final early study that deserves mention was one of the few not conducted with English. It looked at strategies used by students taking reading comprehension tests in Hebrew (their first language or L1) and French (their L2) (Nevo, 1989). A multiple-choice format was used to test comprehension of two reading passages each in Hebrew and French by 42 tenth graders. Students answered five multiple-choice items for each of the four texts (in the language of the text), marked alongside each item their primary and secondary strategies for answering that item (referring to a strategy checklist), responded to open-ended questions following each of the reading passages concerning the respondents' evaluation of the test items, and filled out a more general questionnaire at the end of the test. The study was groundbreaking in that it found it possible without undue disruption to get feedback from subjects immediately after responding to each item concerning the strategies used to select a response. The message here for test designers is to consider various means for piloting test measures to get a sense of their validity before finalizing them.

Critical issues and topics regarding test-taking strategies

The more recent research literature on test-taking strategies has delved into a number of topics related to the validation of the language assessment measures (Cohen, 2006):

*   conceptual frameworks for classifying test-taking strategies
*   the role that the test-takers' language proficiency and other characteristics play in the selection of and success in using test-taking strategies
*   the role that the test-takers' L1 (or dominant language) and the target language play in the selection and use of strategies
*   the impact of the testing format on the selection of test-taking strategies
*   the appropriateness of the research methods used to study test-taking strategies
*   the effectiveness of strategy instruction for improving respondents' performance on high-stakes standardized tests.

The assumption underlying many of the more recent studies is that the test is a valid measure of the construct. This is a departure from the earlier research which seemed more focused on whether a given approach to assessment was valid (Cohen, 2006).

Since the mandate in this chapter is to ask whether respondents are using construct-relevant strategies to produce their responses, the question of responsibility arises. If respondents do not use construct-relevant strategies, why is this?

- Is it because items or tasks on the given instrument are of questionable validity altogether and in need of revision?
- Is it because the respondents lack knowledge of how to respond to such items and tasks, and need clearer instructions or better prior test orientation?
- Is it because the students lack proficiency or have other characteristics which work to their detriment (e.g., their sociocultural background, gender, age, occupational status, and so forth) and would be better served by a more appropriate set of items or tasks?

Current research and implications for item design

To date, test-taking strategy research has provided insights in the following areas (see Cohen, 2006):

- the items on a test that would be susceptible to the use of test-wiseness strategies
- low-level versus higher-level processing on a test
- test takers' versus raters' understandings of and responses to language tasks
- the more effective strategies for success on tests as well as the least effective ones
- the impact of using authentic versus inauthentic texts in reading tests
- whether the strategies employed in L2 test-taking are more typical of L1 use, common to L1 and L2 use, or more typical of L2 use.

We will now take a look at some of these more current test-taking strategy studies—those dealing with the first four topics on the above list—in order to see what the studies tell us about how to design and construct items and tasks.

Studies focusing on the validity of the measures

Test-wiseness strategies on listening and reading tests

One study investigated the impact of test-wiseness—identifying and using the cues related to absurd options, similar options, and opposite options—in taking the paper-and-pencil test of English as a foreign language (TOEFL) (Yang, 2000). First, 390 Chinese TOEFL candidates responded to a modified version of Rogers and Bateson's (1991) Test of Test-Wiseness (TTW) (see Yang, 2000: 58–61) and the TOEFL Practice Test B (ETS, 1995). An item analysis of the TTW results for a subsample of 40 led to the selection of 23 respondents who were considered "test-wise" and another 17 who were deemed "test-naïve." All students were asked to provide verbal reports about the strategies that they were using while responding to a series of test-wiseness-susceptible items selected from the TTW and TOEFL. It was found that 48–64% of the items across the Listening and Reading Comprehension subtests of the TOEFL Practice Test B were identified as susceptible to test-wiseness strategies. It was also found that the test-wise students had a more meaningful, thoughtful, logical, and less random approach to the items than did the test-naïve students— which meant that they also had better test-management strategies. In addition, these students were more academically knowledgeable and used that knowledge to assist them in figuring out answers to questions. Finally, they extended greater effort and were more persistent in looking for test-wiseness cues, even when it involved subtle distinctions.

This study serves as a reminder that we need to keep performing test-wiseness studies as a means of checking whether tests are giving away the answers to items. I still remember the surprising results of a student study by Avi Israel, where the EFL respondents received just the title of an English passage and had to respond to multiple-choice questions about it (Cohen,

1984). The more proficient students, in particular, did far too well on the items for it to have been by chance. Even some of the less proficient students almost passed the test. The items were simply too guessable.

Validating a test of integrated reading and writing tasks

It is encouraging that bastions of traditional approaches to test validation, such as the Educational Testing Service, have in the last decade started funding test-taking strategy studies as part of the validation process. In fact, one such effort on a pilot reading-writing subtest for the internet-based (iBT) TOEFL resulted in eliminating the subtest altogether. The study looked at test-takers' understandings of and responses to what were referred to as Integrated Reading/Writing Tasks as these interacted with their English proficiency levels, and at related issues faced by raters (Lumley and Brown, 2004a, 2004b). The tasks in question on the prototype LanguEdge Courseware (ETS, 2002) not only required comprehension of the reading text, but also synthesis, summary, and/or evaluation of its content, all considered typical requirements of writing in academic settings. The study investigated how test takers at different writing proficiency levels interpreted the demands of these integrated tasks, and identified the strategies they employed in responding to them.

The study drew on verbal report data from tests taken by 30 Mandarin, 15 Cantonese, and 15 Korean students in Beijing, Hong Kong, and Melbourne, along with verbal reports by four raters in the act of rating. Score data and the student texts were also analyzed. Findings included students' responses to tasks and their descriptions of strategies used, as well as raters' reactions to the student's texts. Numerous problems with this subtest were reported. For example, raters were found to have a major problem identifying copied language versus students' own wordings. Furthermore, whereas the researchers had initially hoped to elicit detailed information on how students went about selecting information from the reading text, or in transforming the language of the input text into their own words, respondents had difficulty providing accurate insights as to how they had gone about producing their texts. The results of this study along with other in-house research led to the removal of a particular subtest from the exam. So here is a clear example of how the collecting of test-taking strategy data both from respondents and from raters of responses can lead to significant action, in this case, scrapping the test altogether.

Validating a test of reading

The second of the ETS validation studies entailed the description of reading and test-taking strategies that test takers used with different item types on the Reading subtest of the LanguEdge Courseware materials (ETS, 2002) developed to familiarize prospective respondents with the TOEFL iBT (Cohen and Upton, 2006). The investigation focused on strategies used to respond to more traditional *single-selection* multiple-choice formats (i.e., *basic comprehension* and *inferencing* questions) versus *selected-response* (i.e., multiple selection and drag-and-drop) *reading-to-learn* items, which were considered innovative at the time. The latter were designed to simulate the academic task of forming a comprehensive and coherent representation of an entire text, rather than focusing on discrete points in the text. The aim of the study was to determine whether the TOEFL iBT was actually measuring what it purported to measure, as revealed through verbal reports. In a test claiming to evaluate academic reading ability, it was felt that the emphasis needed to be on designing tasks calling for test takers to actually use academic reading skills, rather than rely on test-wiseness strategies.

Verbal report data were collected from 32 students, representing four language groups (Chinese, Japanese, Korean, and Turkish) as they did tasks from the Reading subtest in the LanguEdge

Courseware materials. Students were randomly assigned to complete two of the six reading tasks, each consisting of a 600–700 word text with 12–13 items, and subjects' verbal report accompanying items representing 10 different item formats was evaluated to determine strategy use.

The findings indicated that tasks on the TOEFL iBT Reading subtest did, in fact, call for the use of academic reading skills for passage comprehension—at least for respondents whose language proficiency was sufficiently advanced so that they not only took the test successfully, but could also report on how they did it as well. Nevertheless, it was also clear that subjects generally approached the TOEFL iBT Reading subtest as a test-taking task that required that they perform reading tasks in order to complete it. Thus, responding to selected passages from the Reading subtest of the LanguEdge test did not fully constitute an academic reading task for these respondents, but rather a test-taking task with academic-like aspects to it. Two reading strategies found to be common to all subtests were:

- reading a portion of the passage carefully
- repeating, paraphrasing, or translating words, phrases, or sentences (or summarizing paragraphs/the passage) to aid or improve understanding.

While the respondents were found to use an array of test-taking strategies, these were primarily test-management strategies. A caveat with respect to this finding is that the respondents were perhaps reluctant to use test-wiseness strategies because they knew that their behavior was being monitored. The six common test-management strategies were:

- going back to the question for clarification: rereading the question
- going back to the question for clarification: paraphrasing (or confirming) the question or task (except for *basic comprehension–vocabulary* and *basic comprehension–pronoun reference* items)
- reading the question and then reading the passage/portion to look for clues to the answer either before or while considering options (except in the case of *reading to learn–prose summary* and *reading to learn–schematic table* items)
- considering the options and postponing consideration of the option (except for *inferencing–insert text* items, calling for insertion of a new sentence into a displayed section of the text)
- selecting options through vocabulary, sentence, paragraph, or passage overall meaning
- discarding options based on vocabulary, sentence, paragraph, or passage overall meaning as well as discourse structure.

In terms of whether all the items and tasks were doing what the test designers had envisioned, the study found that the reading-to-learn and the inferencing items were not requiring different, more academic-like approaches to reading than the basic comprehension items. Because respondents were first required to consider words and sentences in the context of larger chunks of text and even whole passages, basic comprehension item types were found to reflect more academic-like tasks and elicit comparable strategies to those required by the inferencing and reading-to-learn tasks. By the time the respondents arrived at the reading-to-learn items, they already had a good sense of the passage as a whole and so found these items easy. As they read the five options for the prose summary item, they almost immediately knew which three statements to drag into a box in order to create a summary of the text.

The findings from this study would ideally lead to refinement of innovative item types in order that they better approximate the construct to be tested. Again, this study would serve as a warning to test designers not to assume that certain items, as innovative as they may appear, are eliciting the cognitive processes that they are intended to elicit.

The picture that emerges from test validation studies such as by Lumley and Brown and by Upton and myself is that the field has progressed beyond the days when tests were validated simply by statistical analysis of correct and incorrect responses. At present, respondents' verbal reports are also being collected in order to better determine what it actually entails to produce correct answers to various language assessment measures.

Studies focusing on language proficiency

As seen above with one of the early studies as well (Gordon, 1987) limited TL proficiency can prompt respondents to use construct-irrelevant strategies. This insight reflects on test validity in the sense that test constructors need to take into consideration the likely proficiency levels of the respondents and design the test accordingly, unless the test is intended for the purposes of gate-keeping—i.e., to ensure that only the highly proficient will pass.

Strategies on an objective test of writing

One study compared the test-taking strategies of 20 native English speakers and 20 limited-English-proficient (LEP) students on an objective writing skills test (Gavin, 1988). The students were enrolled in the first semester of college English composition. The study looked at the respondents' awareness of test item objectives, their test-taking strategies, and their test performance. Test performance showed that the test questions were generally more difficult for the LEP students than for the native speakers, and that consequently the LEP students responded to them at times with test-taking strategies that were construct-irrelevant. When aware of the objectives of the test items, the LEP students performed about equal to the natives. However, when unaware of the test item objectives, the LEP students focused more on rules dealing with grammar, mechanics, or style than did the natives, who were focused more on meaning. The LEP students were also more likely to choose answers at random or to perform lower-level analysis.

The study brings up the issue of intuition and how difficult it can be for someone with limited TL proficiency to perform the kind of intuiting that will ensure correct test answers. Perhaps prior orientation for the test could include suggestive guidance as to how to use powers of intuition profitably in determining the correct response. Some years ago I conducted a study comparing results when instructions as to how to read a Hebrew L1 and an English L2 text to summarize them (in the L1) and how to write the summary were either spelled out or not. The results showed that whereas more explicit instructions did not improve the summaries of the L1 text, they did make a significant difference when summarizing the L2 passages (Cohen, 1993).

Strategies on a test of listening comprehension

Another study looking at the influence of language proficiency on test-taking strategy use involved the assessment of listening comprehension among 75 Taiwanese college students in their third and final year of a mandatory three-year EFL course (Chang, 2009). The participants completed a listening test comprising four multiple-choice questions, three short answer questions, and three true-or-false questions about four stories, each three minutes long. The students completed a test-taking questionnaire before and after responding to the test. In addition, after each subtest they reported the strategies used based on a strategy list, and also added their own strategies not on the checklist. The most marked difference between the high-language-proficiency (HLP) and low-language-proficiency (LLP) students was *how* they used a strategy. For example, when the listening input was repeated, the LLP students reported listening just for the main ideas at the first hearing and paid attention to the details only at the second hearing. In contrast, the HLP students reported trying to understand as much as they could the first time and used the second hearing for confirmation only. Another difference was that while both HLP and LLP students used the strategy "trying to hear every word," their reported purpose was different. Whereas the HLP students tried to hear every word for fear of missing any information that might affect their scores, the LLP students tried to match the words that they had learned with the words that they heard. According to Chang (2009) this implied that students may use the same strategy but for a different purpose, and also may differ in the way that they use this strategy. Again, the message to the test designer may be to make the instructions (and prior test-taking orientation) clear as to the best way to deal with such listening tasks.

Strategies on reading and on reading–writing tasks

A third study explored the test-taking strategies of 52 HLP, MLP, LLP seventh-grade EFL students while they were completing five reading tasks and two integrated reading–writing tasks, locally constructed and assessed using the Common European Framework scale (Nikolov, 2006). The five reading tasks called for matching 10 questions with the correct 10 (out of 12) response choices. The reading–writing tasks involved identifying material in the passages and copying some of it:

Task 1: read a 60-word text about a pen pal and fill in a questionnaire about the person.
Task 2: complete a birthday party invitation with 8 or 10 well-chosen words.

The study was conducted to provide insights into how learners go about solving tasks and what they think and rely on while doing them. The results showed that the strategies that the children applied were not inherently effective nor ineffective, and that the successful use of the strategies depended on how appropriately they applied them on the actual item in the task (e.g., "guessing," "relying on cognates," "applying a rule," or "skipping the rubrics for an item"). The students provided concurrent verbal report as they did the tasks in two 45-minute sessions (without prompting from the 26 researcher assistants). The researcher noted that strategies differed in type and magnitude, some involving major cognitive processes and others referred to as "tiny tricks." More will be said about this study under "Research Methods" below.

Strategies on a gap-filling test

Yet another study comparing higher- and lower-proficiency learners involved 12 Japanese EFL university students (six skilled and six less-skilled readers) who completed a 16-item gap-filling test while thinking aloud about their test-taking processes (Yamashita, 2003). The text comprised 336 words and the items were all deemed to require text-level understanding for closure. Results showed that both skilled and less-skilled readers reported using text-level information more frequently than other types of information. Although there were several cases where the items were answered correctly with local grammatical clues and extra-textual background knowledge, overall, the gap-filling test generated text-level processing and differentiated well between skilled and less-skilled readers. Hence, the researcher concluded that the findings supported the claim that a gap-filling test can be used as a test to measure higher-order processing ability.

In taking a closer look at the data, it was found that the skilled readers reported using text-level information more frequently than the less skilled readers. Qualitative analysis of the protocols revealed further differences in the use of different types of information between the groups. Whereas the less-skilled readers had sensitivity about the type of information necessary to answer the items, they were less successful than the skilled readers in their attempts and resorted to other sources such as clause-level information and guessing. A key difference between the groups was in the way that the clause-level information was used. The skilled readers were able to give different weight to different types of information according to their importance in understanding the text. For them, clause-level information was only used as a source for confirming their answers. The less-skilled readers, on the other hand, were less able to use text-level information and put heavier emphasis on local grammatical information.

Research methods for investigating test-taking strategies

As seen above, collecting test-taking strategy data can help to determine the extent to which performance on a given assessment measure is reflective of L2 language knowledge and performance in the area assessed. It can also give us insights as to behaviors employed for the sake of getting through the test. A principal research tool for gathering such data is verbal report.

The use of verbal report

While efforts to be unobtrusive often leave us in the realm of speculation, it has sometimes proven to be a formidable task to obtain information about what respondents are doing without being obtrusive. Verbal report became a primary research tool for this endeavor in the early 1980s (see Cohen, 1984). Verbal reports include data reflecting one or more of the following approaches.

1. *Self-report*—learners' descriptions of what they do, characterized by generalized statements, in this case, about their test-taking strategies—for example, "On multiple-choice items, I tend to scan the reading passage for possible surface matches between information in the text and that same information appearing in one of the alternative choices."
2. *Self-observation*—the inspection of specific, contextualized language behavior, either introspectively, that is, within 20 seconds of the mental event, or retrospectively—for instance, "What I just did was to skim through the reading passage for possible surface matches between information in the text and that same information appearing in one of the alternative choices."
3. *Self-revelation*—"think-aloud," stream-of-consciousness disclosure of thought processes while the information is being attended to—for example, "Hmm … I wonder if the information in one of these alternative choices also appears in the text."

While verbal report continues to play a key role in test-taking strategy research, there have been changes in procedures for conducting such verbal report aimed at improving the reliability and validity of the results. One has been to provide a model for respondents as to the kinds of responses that are considered appropriate (see, for example, Cohen and Upton, 2006) rather than to simply let them respond however they wish, which has often failed to produce enough relevant data. In addition, researchers now may intrude and ask probing questions during data collection (something that they tended not to do in the past) in order to make sure, for instance, that the respondents indicate not just their rationale for selecting (for example) "b" as the correct alternative in multiple-choice, but also their reasons for rejecting "a," "c," and "d." Respondents have also been asked to listen to a tape-recording or read a transcript of their verbal report session in order to complement those data with any further insights they may have (Nyhus, 1994). The bottom line is that verbal report does not constitute a single approach, but rather is a vehicle for enlisting a number of different approaches.

The clustering of strategies and challenges in categorizing them

An important finding from the Nikolov (2006) study described above was that some strategies tended to occur in combination with others and that verbal report was needed to better understand these strategy clusters. For example, "reading the text in English" and "translating" were often combined with "phonetic reading of unfamiliar vocabulary items." Also, respondents varied as to how they used metacognitive strategies to approach the different tasks. For example, they tended to check the instructions for several tasks but neglected to do so for the others, or they read the example first in the first task and then proceeded to respond to the rest of the items without paying attention to the rubrics or the example in other tasks. Given the individual variation, Nikolov found that efforts to categorize the data were highly problematic as many strategies overlapped and others could be sub-divided into other strategies.

A survey of language learner strategy experts underscored the fact that strategies are often used in combination (Cohen, 2007: 35–36) even though they are often treated in the literature as if they occurred in an isolated fashion.

Recommendations for practice

With regard to test-management strategies, the message for test designers would be to make sure respondents are sufficiently informed (e.g., through clear instructions) as to how to make use of these:

1. read the instructions for the whole test and for each question carefully,
2. make use of clue words in the questions and underline them,
3. identify difficult questions that would require much thinking and longer time in processing, answer the easier questions first, and delay answering the difficult questions,
4. allocate appropriate time for each question according to its difficulty, and pay attention to time allotments indicated or make their own,
5. before handing in the test, check over the responses if time permits.

(Amer, 1993)

In this section, let us look at just a few illustrative test-taking strategies that emerge from this work with respect to a few of the prominent formats for assessing language (adapted from Cohen, 2011).

Strategies in taking cloze tests

Respondents could be alerted both in prior test-orientation sessions and perhaps even in the instruction to strategies such as the following:

- looking both at words and phrases immediately preceding and following a blank, as well as at the extended context for clues as to how to fill it in
- rephrasing sentences to make sure that the intended meaning is clear
- recalling knowledge of the passage and any other prior knowledge that could be of use in completing the blanks.

Strategies in dealing with multiple-choice items

The following are some test-management strategies for reading and listening tests that could be included in test-orientation sessions and perhaps in the instructions for the tests.

Test-management strategies for reading

- Going back to the question for clarification—rereading it carefully or paraphrasing it in order to verify or confirm understanding of the question or task, as the necessary clue may be in the wording of the question.
- Reading the question(s) first and then reading the passage/portion in order to expedite the search for the material in the text needed to answer the question.
- Selecting or eliminating options based on vocabulary knowledge or on the meaning of the sentence, paragraph, overall passage, or discourse structure.
- Performing a mental translation of parts of the text to see if the material makes sense in the L1, and then summarizing the passage as a check for comprehension.

Test-management strategies for listening items

- Verifying if the options match elements of the listening text or the question in terms of keywords, specific details, inferences about details, level of specificity.
- Checking back to part or all of a prior question as a guide to selecting a response to the item at hand.
- Determining the level of detail required in answering a question so as to reject an option that is either too general or too specific.
- Identifying relevant background knowledge and then utilizing it in an appropriate way.
- When uncertainty prevails, making an educated guess drawing on a combination of strategies such as those listed above.

Recommendations for test-taking strategy instruction

The study on test-taking strategies in listening by Chang (2009) reported on above, included recommendations for how to integrate strategy instruction for taking listening tests into regular adult EFL classroom instruction. While the following steps are intended just for listening assessment, they are meant to be illustrative of how to raise student awareness of how they can use test-taking strategies to their benefit:

1. The teacher provides students with a checklist of strategy use for a given task.
2. Before listening, students look at the strategy checklist for a minute and check off the strategies that they have ready for the task.
3. After listening, students spend a few minutes thinking about the strategies that they used for the task.
4. Students are provided a script so that they can confirm what they hear with what they read.
5. Students are encouraged to listen to the texts as many times as they wish without looking at the script.
6. More or less successful students are assigned to groups after a task so that they can compare and discuss the strategies used for a certain task.
7. Teachers pick one or two students (without revealing these students' names) who perform the best and share their strategy use with the whole class.

Further directions in research

Ideally, item and task designers will be increasingly cognizant of the need to prompt response strategies that call on the desired language knowledge and skills. To help keep these people on track, studies should continue to be undertaken describing test-taking strategies used to respond to items and tasks in various TLs and using a timely sampling of elicitation and response formats. Aside from TL and testing format, researchers would need to be mindful of:

- the respondents' TL proficiency level, gender, sociocultural group, and other characteristics
- the most appropriate methods for collecting the data
- means for meaningfully linking strategy use with performance on the language measures.

With regard to the final bullet point, we need to monitor the extent to which test takers who adopt their test-taking strategies to fit the demands of the assessment items and tasks actually perform better on the assessment. Another concern is the extent to which findings from research on test-taking strategies have contributed to making language tests more valid.

Finally, research should continue to investigate the impact on test performance of guides for respondents as to how to take high-stakes standardized tests. In a study of 43 students at a coaching school in Taiwan, for example, it was found that high scorers tended to focus on their understanding of the passages, to use the strategies taught by the coaching school only as an auxiliary to comprehension, and to stress the need to personalize these strategies (Tian, 2000). The low scorers, on the other hand, tended to focus on word-level strategies, to use the suggested strategies as a way of circumventing comprehension, and to follow the test-taking strategy instruction from the coaching-school staff mechanically. These findings should serve as a warning to test designers that strategy instruction materials may not necessarily help those who need them the most, and perhaps most benefit those who least need assistance.

By way of closing, what might we predict the field of test-taking strategies will look like in five years? What debates will remain? What issues will be unresolved? Predictably, there will always be new testing formats heralded in the literature, and so there will be a continuing need to do test-taking strategy research as a means for validating them. At present the debate is whether an approach such as Dynamic Assessment (DA) should be considered assessment at all, or rather a form on instruction. DA is based on the Vygotskyian perspective that assessment occurs not in isolation from instruction but as an inseparable feature of it. This approach to assessment challenges the widespread acceptance of independent performance as the privileged indicator of individuals' abilities and calls for assessors to abandon their role as observers of learner behavior in favor of a commitment to joint problem solving aimed at supporting learner development, whereby teachers collaborate with learners on increasingly complex tasks (Poehner, 2007, 2008; see also Chapter 7 of this volume). It remains to be seen just how widespread DA will be as a form of language assessment five years from now. In any event, this and other innovative approaches to language assessment need to be studied carefully from the test-taking strategy vantage point.

Further reading

Beare, K. (2010). Effectively taking the TOEFL, TOEIC, First Certificate, Proficiency or CAE. About.com: English as a 2d Language. esl.about.com/od/toeflieltscambridge/a/ht_taketest.htm (accessed 8/25/10). A website with strategies for taking standardized ESL tests, with links to numerous web pages with strategies for taking L2 tests: e.g., taking a multiple-choice reading comprehension exam, taking a word formation exam, taking a listening gap fill exam, and taking a vocabulary cloze test.

Bowles, M.A. (2010). *The Think-Aloud Controversy in Second Language Research*. Abingdon, UK: Routledge. The book aims to provide some answers to questions about the validity and use of verbal reports from learners during the performance of language tasks. It starts with theoretical background and empirical research on the validity of think-alouds, and then provides an overview of how think-alouds have been used in L2 language research, as well as a meta-analysis of findings from studies involving think-alouds on verbal tasks. The volume also offers guidance regarding the practical issues of data collection and analysis.

Brown, J. D. (ed.), (1998). *New Ways of Classroom Assessment*. Alexandria, VA: Teachers of English to Speakers of Other Languages. While not focused on test-taking strategies *per se*, the volume constitutes a compendium of everyday classroom assessment activities that provide a way of observing or scoring students' performances and giving feedback that is meant to inform students and teachers about the effectiveness of the teaching and learning taking place. Each activity comes with suggestions as to how to give feedback in the form of a score or other information (e.g., notes in the margin, written prose reactions, oral critiques, teacher conferences). Many of the entries utilize other possible feedback perspectives aside from that of the teacher, namely, self-assessment, peer assessment, and outsider assessment— often used in conjunction with teacher assessment. One entry on "Preparing students for tests" by Alastair Allan expressly deals with test-wiseness strategies (p. 199–203). Although not necessarily calling upon the teacher to be a collaborator in the assessment process as does Dynamic Assessment (Poehner 2007, 2008) the assessment activities in this volume are more aligned with DA than are traditional language assessment activities.

Green, A. J. F. (1998). *Using Verbal Protocols in Language Testing Research: a handbook*. Cambridge, UK: Cambridge University Press. Referring to verbal report as *verbal protocol analysis* (VPA) the author notes that it is a complex methodology, and that individuals choosing to use it require some degree of orientation in order to maximize the benefits in adopting this approach, and in order to avoid some of the more common misunderstandings and pitfalls associated with the use of verbal data. Her book aims to provide potential practitioners with the background to the technique (the design of data collection methods, the development of coding schemes for analyzing the data, and the actual analysis of the data) while focusing on what is entailed in using VPA in the specific context of language assessment.

Gass, S. M. and Mackey, A. (2000). *Simulated Recall Methodology in Second Language Research*. Mahwah, NJ: Lawrence Erlbaum. The book focuses on retrospective verbal report data prompted by an investigator, referred to as *stimulated recall*, and gives recommendations for how to collect and analyze the data, including a discussion of procedural pitfalls. They also consider issues of reliability and validity. In addition, they discuss possible uses for stimulated recall—for example, in comprehending and producing oral language, understanding the dynamics of L2 classroom interaction, looking at processes in L2 reading, and investigating L2 syntactic development, vocabulary acquisition, and pragmatics.

Landsberger, F. (2010). Tips for better test taking. Study Guides and Strategies. www.studygs.net/tsttak1.htm (accessed 8/25/10). A website with suggested strategies for preparing for a test, ten tips for terrific test taking, strategies for taking online tests, as well as strategies for taking true/false tests, multiple-choice tests, short-answer tests, open-book exams, oral exams, and essay exams.

References

Allan, A. (1992). Development and validation of a scale to measure test-wiseness in EFL/ESL reading test-takers. *Language Testing* 9: 101–22.

Amer, A. A. (1993). Teaching EFL students to use a test-taking strategy. *Language Testing* 10: 71–77.

Chang, A. C.-S. (2009). EFL listeners' task-based strategies and their relationship with listening performance. *TESL-EJ*, 13(2). www.tesl-ej.org/wordpress/issues /volume13/ej50/ej50a1 (accessed 8/9/10).

Cohen, A. D. (1984). On taking language tests: what the students report. *Language Testing* 1: 70–81.

—— (1993). The role of instructions in testing summarizing ability. In D. Douglas and C. Chapelle (eds), *A New Decade of Language Testing: Collaboration and Cooperation*. Alexandria, VA: TESOL, 132–60.

—— (2006). The coming of age of research on test-taking strategies: collaboration and cooperation. *Language Assessment Quarterly* 3: 307–31.

—— (2007). Coming to terms with language learner strategies: surveying the experts. In A. D. Cohen and E. Macaro (eds), *Language Learner Strategies: 30 years of Research and Practice*. Oxford, UK: Oxford University Press, 29–45.

—— (2011). *Strategies in Learning and Using a Second Language: research and practice*. Harlow, UK: Longman/ Pearson Education.

—— (2011). Test-taking strategies. In C. Coombe, P. Davidson, B. O'Sullivan and S. Stoynoff (eds), *The Cambridge Guide to Assessment*. Cambridge, UK: Cambridge University Press.

Cohen, A. D. and Upton, T. A. (2006). *Strategies in responding to the new TOEFL reading tasks* (Monograph No. 33). Princeton, NJ: ETS. www.ets.org/Media/Research/pdf/RR-06-06.pdf (accessed 8/12/10).

Davidson, F. (2000). The language tester's statistical toolbox. *System* 28: 605–17.

Dollerup, C., Glahn, E. and Rosenberg Hansen, C. (1982). Reading strategies and test-solving techniques in an EFL-reading comprehension test—a preliminary report. *Journal of Applied Language Study* 1: 93–99.

ETS (Educational Testing Sevice) (1995). *TOEFL Practice Test B in TOEFL Practice Tests, Vol. 1*. Princeton, NJ: ETS, 55–106. www.scribd.com/doc/47275686/TOEFL-Practice-Tests-Vol1 (accessed 21 July 2011).

—— (2002). *LanguEdge Courseware Score Interpretation Guide*. Princeton, NJ: Educational Testing Service.

Gavin, C.A. (1988). *The strategies of native and limited English proficient test-takers as revealed by think aloud protocols*. Unpublished EdD thesis, Rutgers University, New Brunswick, NJ.

Gordon, C. (1987). *The effect of testing method on achievement in reading comprehension tests in English as a foreign language*. Unpublished master of arts thesis, Tel-Aviv University, Ramat-Aviv, Israel.

Homburg, T. J. and Spaan, M. C. (1981). ESL reading proficiency assessment: testing strategies. In M. Hines and W. Rutherford (eds), *On TESOL '81*. Washington, DC: TESOL, 25–33.

Lumley, T. and Brown, A. (2004a). Test-taker and rater perspectives on integrated reading and writing tasks in the Next Generation TOEFL. *Language Testing Update* 35: 75–79.

—— (2004b). *Test taker response to integrated reading/writing tasks in TOEFL: evidence from writers, texts, and raters. Final Report to ETS*. Language Testing Research Centre, The University of Melbourne, Melbourne, Australia.

Nevo, N. (1989). Test-taking strategies on a multiple-choice test of reading comprehension. *Language Testing* 6: 199–215.

Nikolov, M. (2006). Test-taking strategies of 12-and 13-year-old Hungarian learners of EFL: why whales have migraines. *Language Learning* 56: 1–51.

Nyhus, S.E. (1994). *Attitudes of non-native speakers of English toward the use of verbal report to elicit their reading comprehension strategies*. Plan B Masters Paper, Department of ESL, University of Minnesota, Minneapolis.

O'Sullivan, B. and Weir, C. J. (2010). Language testing = validation. In B. O'Sullivan (ed.), *Language Testing: Theories and Practices*. Basingstoke, UK: Palgrave Macmillan.

—— (2011). Test development and validation. In B. O'Sullivan (ed.), *Language Testing: theories and practice*. Basingstoke, UK: Palgrave Macmillan, 13–32.

Poehner, M. E. (2007). Beyond the test: L2 dynamic assessment and the transcendence of mediated learning. *Modern Language Journal* 91: 323–40.

—— (2008). *Dynamic Assessment: a Vygotskian approach to understanding and promoting l2 development*. New York, NY: Springer.

Rogers, W. T. and Bateson, D. J. (1991). The influence of test-wiseness on the performance of high school seniors on school leaving examinations. *Applied Measurement in Education* 4: 159–83.

Tian, S. (2000). *TOEFL reading comprehension: strategies used by Taiwanese students with coaching-school training*. Unpublished PhD dissertation, Teachers College, Columbia University, New York.

Yamashita, J. (2003). Processes of taking a gap-filling test: comparison of skilled and less skilled EFL readers. *Language Testing* 20: 267–93.

Yang, P. (2000). Effects of test-wiseness upon performance on the Test of English as a Foreign Language. unpublished PhD dissertation, University of Alberta, Edmonton, CN.

Part VI
Prototyping and field tests

19

Prototyping new item types

Susan Nissan and Mary Schedl

Introduction

In this chapter we will begin by defining prototyping and differentiating it from other terms used to indicate tryouts of test materials before they are used operationally. Next, we will consider what the characteristics of a prototyping population should be, and, finally, we will discuss what kinds of information prototyping can provide. We will use extended examples to illustrate the issues addressed in the chapter. Although prototyping is carried out by many language testing programs, the examples in this chapter are from tests designed at Educational Testing Service (ETS) only. The authors, both on the test development staff of ETS, have worked on numerous prototyping projects and will draw on that experience to provide the examples in this chapter.

In a language testing context, prototyping refers to trying out new test materials for their appropriateness for use prior to field testing and making final decisions about the operational test content. Prototyping may provide information about the design of a new test or about revisions to an ongoing test. Before prototyping begins, a test construct must exist and the abilities to be measured that are part of the construct must be carefully considered and documented. By prototyping items we can investigate the extent to which our theories and expectations about what the items measure are accurate (e.g., by comparing performance of examinees to their performance on other measures of the construct) and the extent to which construct-irrelevant variance occurs because of item design (e.g., by interviewing examinees about their prototype experience).

Numerous factors contribute to decisions as to the amount and type of prototyping that is needed. If the item types are novel and little is understood about how examinees might perform on them, more extensive prototyping is likely to be necessary, and the issues to be addressed may be different than they would be for the introduction of a well-known item type into a revised test. For a revised test, the reasons for the revision (e.g., to improve reliability and/or discrimination, or to bring the test more in line with current understanding of the construct) will likely determine the types of prototyping questions to be addressed.

In addition to "prototyping," a number of other terms are used to describe various ways of trying out new items and tasks before they can be considered for use operationally. Some of these terms are used interchangeably with each other and with the term prototyping, and some indicate real differences in the purpose or stage of pre-operational administration.

"Usability testing" is a type of prototyping that focuses on interface features and directions in computer-based tests to see how easy it is to use the interfaces and how well examinees understand how to use them. A small group of examinees can provide useful information about these issues. Participants are observed as they interact with an interface, and a questionnaire can be used to obtain their feedback.

Additional terms used to describe trying out items prior to operational use are "field testing," "item trialing," "pilot testing," "pretesting," and "item tryouts." These terms sometimes indicate different stages in trying out new item types, directions, and scoring rubrics to provide feedback to test developers about their appropriateness and efficacy to gauge proficiency.

"Field testing" is generally more elaborate than prototyping. In a field study an example of an entire test is tried out to determine its feasibility as a full operational test form (see Kenyon and MacGregor, this volume). Whereas one of the major goals of prototyping is to determine the viability of new item types, field testing generally focuses on information about the functioning of the test as a whole, including such issues as test timing and reliability. Field testing is usually much more costly and time consuming than prototyping because it requires a large number of candidates that is fully representative of the target test population in order to obtain good item statistics and test timing information.

The terms "item trialing," "pilot testing," "pretesting," and "item tryouts" refer to trying out tasks or items on a large enough representative sample of the test population to provide information about item characteristics such as difficulty and discrimination. These tryouts may be part of a prototyping effort or may be part of operational test maintenance. Pretesting and item tryouts are for trying out specific exemplars of item types and tasks that already exist in the operational test specifications. The particular exemplars in the tryouts are analyzed for how well they perform as individual exemplars of the item types in use. Items with poor performance at this stage are revised or replaced. For these tryouts the sample of examinees must be large enough and representative enough to provide such statistics. This purpose is different from one of the major purposes of prototyping, which is to determine how well a proposed new item type or task works before it is considered for operational use.

Prototype population

In this section we discuss the size and characteristics of the prototype population, and explain the importance of these aspects of designing a prototype study.

The size of the prototyping population should depend on the questions the study is designed to address. Ultimately, it is preferable to have as large a prototype sample as possible, especially for multiple choice items, since large numbers are necessary for reliable statistical analyses. If the test will be a high-stakes test and performance on the test is likely to have important consequences for the examinees, this increases the responsibility of the test designer and test developer to ensure the most equitable and appropriate measurement possible. Examples of high-stakes tests for English language learners include such tests as TOEFL iBT and IELTS, tests of admission for foreign students to English language colleges and universities, TOEIC, a test of international workplace English, English tests required by foreign doctors and nurses working in English-speaking countries, etc. Prototyping for tests like these may require a large sample size at some point before they become operational.

Because the test populations for many high-stakes English language tests come from a variety of countries, the sample must be representative of a wide range of national and linguistic backgrounds. The better the prototyping population reflects the characteristics of the test population, the better it will predict performance on the test if these item types become operational, so each of the most important characteristics of the test population needs to be considered.

In some cases, it may be helpful to include native speakers (NSs), for example, if the intent is to measure a new aspect of a construct. During the design phase of TOEFL iBT, NSs were used in several prototyping studies, including one that investigated pragmatic understanding (PU), an aspect of the Listening construct that had not previously been systematically measured. Test designers included NSs in the prototype population to ensure that they would be able to answer these types of questions. It would not be appropriate to expect non-native speakers to perform tasks that were problematic for NSs.

However, a large population is not always necessary or appropriate. For example, in usability studies where examinees are observed interacting with computer interfaces, the population is usually relatively small (Fulcher, 2003). When trying out an item type to determine whether it provides appropriate evidence for a construct not previously measured, it may be worthwhile to initially try it out on a small number of participants, even as few as 10. If examinees understand the directions, and appropriate evidence is obtained, additional prototype studies can be undertaken with larger, more representative populations. This iterative approach is common during prototyping, as typically it is not possible to address every question with one prototyping study.

Usually the prototype population for the productive skills is smaller than for the receptive skills since human raters analyze the performance tasks, and human rating is costly and time consuming. Note that when a goal of prototyping is to develop a new scoring rubric (scoring guidelines), a larger prototype population may be necessary, as it is important that the prototype population reflects the full range of abilities of the operational test population to confirm that all of the score points of the rubric are appropriate.

Kinds of information prototyping can provide

Prototyping can provide information about many details of item development and scoring. In this section we provide examples of prototyping efforts that helped answer the following questions about the measurement of language constructs, scoring rubric development, and item difficulty for some ETS tests:

- Is measurement of a new part of the construct viable?
- How viable are alternative tasks in providing evidence for a new part of the construct to be measured?
- Is an integrated skills construct viable?
- Can a draft scoring rubric be used to successfully discriminate among examinees?
- Is item difficulty appropriate for the intended test population?

The first three examples of prototyping in this section are directly related to construct viability. We then discuss how prototyping can inform scoring rubric development and how it can help determine the difficulty of items.

Many additional types of information obtained through the prototyping efforts discussed below contributed to the answers to these questions. Issues related to item and rubric design and the wording of directions were prototyped, test development procedures were monitored to determine the feasibility of generating sufficient quantities of test materials for the maintenance of an ongoing testing program, and questionnaires were designed to interview examinees about their strategies and thought processes.

Viability of measuring a new part of a construct

The Listening Framework (Bejar *et al.*, 2000) recommended that the Listening measure in TOEFL iBT include a measure of Pragmatic Understanding (PU), so one early prototype study investigated the feasibility of systematically measuring PU in the new test (Jamieson and Denner, 2000). PU was defined as understanding speaker purpose (the function of an utterance), speaker attitude (or stance), and understanding whether an utterance was a fact or an opinion. One purpose of the study was to determine whether item types could be designed that measure this aspect of comprehension, and if so, whether examinees could answer them. Another purpose was to compare performance on these items to performance on basic comprehension items that measured main ideas and details, and to compare the types of strategies participants used to respond to the basic understanding (BU) and the PU items.

Six sets of items were developed, using a variety of stimulus types (e.g., lectures, classroom discussions, student conversations). Each stimulus was followed by 4–6 items: 2–3 BU items, which measure understanding of main ideas and details, and 2–3 PU items. Although all of the items were multiple choice, variations of the multiple choice format were trialed. For example, one item type included replaying a portion of the stimulus in the stem of the item to help examinees focus on the pragmatic features of a particular part of the stimulus.

An instrument was developed to collect usability information about the extent to which participants could answer the questions, e.g., whether examinees understood the directions, and to collect the thought processes that participants used to respond to the items. Retrospective interviews were employed to obtain this information (see Bowles, 2010).

The study materials were administered to 20 participants: 15 non-native speakers (NNSs), and five native speakers, all of whom were enrolled in a mid-sized university in the United States. The NNSs were placed into three ability groups according to their TOEFL paper-based test (PBT) scores. This study was administered to a very small number of participants because of the retrospective interviews, which require a great deal of time and effort and because it was the first time that these new item types measuring PU were administered.

Participants listened to the audio stimulus and responded to its items for all six sets. The participants were then shown the items a second time, and an interviewer asked questions about each item: Did you understand what you needed to do to respond to the item? Why did you choose that answer? These interviews were taped and transcribed.

Item development

Creating the 12 pragmatics items for the study and reviewing the performance data provided insight about potential feasibility issues. Items that asked about speaker function were fairly easy to write and it was recommended to explore several variations of this type in the next phase of prototyping. Participants reported that they often listened to intonation when responding to the speaker stance items. These items were not as easy to write, and required further investigation in subsequent prototype studies. There was only one fact versus opinion item, so it was not possible to draw conclusions about the challenges of writing this type of item. It was recommended that future prototyping studies include more examples of this item type to determine whether it was viable for numerous operational administrations.

Directions

The item directions were clear to the participants for the most part. Most of the items had a multiple choice format, with some variations that did not cause any confusion. However, one format had "audio options," where the options were not written on the screen but only presented orally. This format was attractive to some test designers, as no reading ability was required to respond, and it might be measuring listening ability more purely than other item formats. The first instance of this item format created some confusion for participants, but the second instance was not problematic for them. However, this item format was not pursued and not used operationally because items in this format took much longer to answer than did items with written options, and comparable evidence was obtainable with the written option format.

Comparison to basic comprehension questions

Analyses were conducted to compare the mean scores on the BU and the PU items to see whether these item types differed in difficulty and to compare the types and frequency of strategies used to respond to these different item types.

Results indicated that both BU and PU items were most difficult for the low-level ability group (based on TOEFL PBT scores), of medium difficulty for the mid-level group, and easiest for the high-level and native speaker groups. The total proportion correct was about the same for the two item types: 0.83 for all BU items, and 0.82 for all PU items. However, the pragmatic items separated the mid-level ability group more effectively than did the BU items. There was a 23% difference in proportion correct between the low-level group performance and the mid-level performance on the pragmatics items, and a 20% difference between the middle and high levels. With the BU items, there was a 30% difference between the low and middle levels, and only a 6% difference between the middle and high groups, suggesting that perhaps something different was being measured, and that these items could provide useful measurement information, particularly about examinees at the middle and higher levels of proficiency.

Strategy use

The retrospective interviews provided insight into the types and frequency of strategies used to respond to the items. For BU items, the most common strategies were to recall specific content, recall lexical information, recall general content, make inferences, and use a process of elimination. For the PU items, the most common strategies were to make inferences, recall lexical information, recall general content, recall the narrative, and use intonation. Although there is some overlap of strategies used, the differences support the hypothesis that the pragmatics items provide evidence about different aspects of the listening construct than do BU items.

Establishing an operational definition of PU was achieved by reanalyzing what the 12 PU items were measuring and the responses to the retrospective questions about these items. The outcome was a definition of PU that measures the understanding of speaker purpose (function of utterance), stance (speaker attitude), and recognizing whether a specific utterance was presented as a fact or an opinion. It was recommended that this definition of PU be confirmed and investigated further in a subsequent prototyping study.

In sum, participants were able to respond to the pragmatics items, and most of the items were answered correctly by a substantial number of the participants. Moreover, they seemed to contribute to distinguishing between ability groups. The differences between BU and PU were demonstrated by the different strategies used to respond to the items that measured those abilities.

Viability of texts and alternative tasks to provide evidence about a theoretical construct under two conditions

A major feasibility issue in early prototyping for ongoing testing programs where large numbers of forms are required is the question of whether or not the test can be maintained over time. For the TOEFL iBT reading section, one of the first questions addressed as part of prototyping was the question of whether a passage pool could be created with passages of appropriate length to create the kinds of tasks described in the reading test framework (Enright *et al.*, 2000). To allow measurement of an important part of the reading construct that had been defined for the new test, passages needed to be relatively long (~700 words) and to represent particular types of discourse. This issue was investigated by test development staff who were charged with creating a small pool of passages and tasks that could be used in prototyping and with evaluating the feasibility of finding sufficient passages to sustain these tasks in the operational test. A related issue addressed in this prototyping effort was whether such texts could be classified according to the specific features defined in the framework in such a way that they could be used to create comparable test forms.

A second goal of this TOEFL iBT reading prototyping study was to investigate alternative task types that could provide evidence for the purpose identified in the reading framework (Enright *et al.*, 2000) as "reading to learn." This purpose was further investigated and defined in Enright and Schedl (1999) as an academic purpose for reading that requires the reader to construct an organized mental framework of important information in texts. Tasks should require readers to show evidence of being able to both comprehend individual points and to use a framework such as a table or a summary to reconstruct the major ideas and important supporting information from the text. It was thought that if readers have such a mental framework, they should be able to reconstruct the major ideas and supporting information from the text.

Prototyping of reading-to-learn tasks began with an initial group of 475 candidates who were selected to match the characteristics of the international TOEFL test population in terms of their academic status (graduate/undergraduate), gender, first language, and English ability, based on their TOEFL paper-based test scores. This prototype study was relatively large, as the construct for reading to learn had already been defined and specific abilities associated with the construct had been identified. Several different types of items were initially designed and prototyped to determine their viability for measuring these reading-to-learn abilities. One of these was a schematic table (Figure 19.1) in which information about a topic was to be organized by selecting several answer choices from a longer list of possible choices and placing them into the correct categories in a table. This task was presented as the last item in a set of questions so that examinees would have a longer period of time to digest the information needed to answer this type of item. For this item type, examinees needed to both select the important ideas and to place them in the correct parts of the table to receive credit.

In an academic context, reading-to-learn involves remembering information, so some members of the design committee thought that participants should not be allowed to review the passage when responding to the reading-to-learn item. But other members of the committee were not certain that it was fair to withhold the text or that examinees would be able to remember the information in a test situation. Therefore, the prototyping of alternative task types was modified and expanded to include this concern. The revised goal was the prototyping of alternative task types under two conditions, with the texts available for review in one condition and not available in the other. Viewing the text was facilitated by the creation of a **View Text** link between the item and the passage text. An equal number of candidates of similar abilities were given the same test questions, one group with the texts available and one group with the texts unavailable for review.

A second reading-to-learn item type that was prototyped was a summary task (Figure 19.2) that required examinees to select three major ideas from the passage from six answer choices

Directions: Complete the table below by classifying each of the answer choices according to whether it is characteristic of

     1) the applied arts, or

     2) the fine arts

Not all of the phrases will be used.

Applied Arts	•
	•
	•
Fine Arts	•
	•

Answer choices:

Object's purpose is primarily aesthetic.

Objects serve a functional purpose.

Incidental details of objects do not vary.

Artists work to overcome the limitations of their materials.

Basic form of objects varies little across cultures.

Artists work in concert with their materials.

Object's place of origin is difficult to determine.

Figure 19.1 Schematic table

and place them in order in a summary format. The intended order was the order that a good reader would use in summarizing and remembering the information, i.e., the order of the mental framework for remembering the information. The item was presented to different but comparable groups of candidates with and without the passage available for review, as was done with the schematic table item.

A third reading-to-learn item type that was prototyped was an outline completion task (Figure 19.3). Answer choices were to be selected and placed into a partially completed outline. Again, the item was presented to comparable groups of candidates with and without the passage available for review.

The goals of the initial round of prototyping were (1) to investigate the feasibility and sustainability of creating ongoing exemplars of these types of texts and tasks, (2) to investigate the viability of alternative task types and to see how well they discriminated the examinees, under the two conditions (with and without text availability), and (3) to investigate the issue of how to score these more complex tasks, as it was thought that these item types should be weighted more heavily than the traditional four-option multiple-choice items because they would take more time and measure more global comprehension of the text.

Directions: The first sentence of a brief summary of the passage is provided below.

- **Select three additional sentences that represent the major ideas of the passage.**

- **Order the selected sentences to complete the summary.**

Not all of the sentences will be used.

This passage discusses fundamental differences between applied-art objects and fine-art objects.

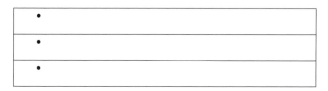

Answer choices:

The fine arts are only affected by the laws of physics because of the limitations of the materials that are used.

Applied-art objects are bound by the laws of physics in two ways: by the materials used to make them, and the function they are to serve.

The fundamental difference between the applied arts and the fine arts is found in the types of materials that are used to make the art objects.

In the fine arts, artists must work to overcome the limitations of their materials, but in the applied arts, artists work in concert with their materials.

We now tend to refer to the various crafts according to the materials used to construct them.

The fine art-objects of the twentieth century have often been modeled after earlier applied-art objects.

Figure 19.2 Summary task

Feasibility/sustainability

Test developers used a passage evaluation form to track the lexical, grammatical, rhetorical, and topical components of the passages they considered for use and were able to create a pool of passages that was representative of the types of passages described in the reading framework (Enright *et al.*, 2000). Moreover, they concluded that sustaining such a pool of passages would be possible. However, they found it difficult to find passages where the *order* of presentation of major ideas actually seemed to matter. For example, in the summary task presented in Figure 19.2, the order of the three major points of the text is not critical. If examinees select the three major points (#1, #2, #4), one would assume they had understood the major text information. For texts describing a process, the order matters, but a passage pool of texts describing processes would not be representative of academic texts in general. Prototype performance of examinees also supported the view that this requirement, noted in the item directions, was not well understood and not likely to discriminate well. The decision was made at this stage to drop the requirement to order the answer choices in subsequent rounds of prototyping.

Directions: Complete the following outline based on the information in the passage. Each answer choice will be used only ONCE.

- **Select the three general characteristics the author associates with each type of art.**
- **Select the specific examples the author uses in the discussion of each type of art.**

I. **Applied Arts**	**Answer choices:**
A. General Characteristics	**General Characteristics**
1. _____	• Artists work to overcome the limitations of their materials.
2. _____	
3. _____	• Primary purpose of objects is not functional.
B. Specific Examples	• Basic form of objects varies little across cultures.
1. _____	
2. _____	• Artists of ten treat materials in new ways.
II. **Fine Arts**	• Objects serve a functional purpose.
A. General Characteristics	
1. _____	• Artists work in concert with their materials.
2. _____	**Specific Examples**
3. _____	Painting
B. Specific Examples	Inca vase
1. _____	Shang Dynasty vase
2. _____	Bronze statues of horses

Figure 19.3 Outline completion task

Finding passages to support the creation of the schematic table seemed viable and the summary task was sufficiently discriminating to provide some evidence about reading-to-learn abilities. Therefore, this task was also retained for further prototyping.

Viability of task types and discrimination under two conditions

Test developers were able to create the summary task items and the schematic table items without great difficulty. Results of the initial round of prototyping indicated that performance of the two groups under the different test conditions—passage available vs. passage not available to complete the reading-to-learn tasks—was independent of the availability of the texts. In some cases candidates performed better with the texts available and in some cases they performed better with the texts unavailable. Therefore, a decision was made to allow access to the passages since this might make examinees more comfortable. The outline task was seen as focusing too much on details that could be better assessed by basic comprehension questions, and it was not continued.

Performance was also analyzed for consistency of scores with ability levels and different ways of scoring the items were considered. As mentioned above, it was thought that these item types should be weighted more heavily than the traditional four-option multiple-choice items because they would take more time and measure more global comprehension of the text. They could be scored all right or all wrong, the same as traditional multiple choice items. However, they covered more information and called on higher level skills. Since prototyping demonstrated that few participants selected all of the correct answers, the items would be very difficult if examinees needed to answer all parts correctly to receive credit. Thus, a simple partial credit model was used to score the initial prototypes and the number of points for each task depended on the number of correct answers that needed to be selected and the number of total answer choices. The details about awarding partial credit would be further investigated in subsequent prototyping efforts.

Viability of integrated skills construct

The design of the Writing section for TOEFL iBT defined the construct of writing as the ability to produce a sustained, coherent, appropriate and purposeful written text in response to an assigned task (Cumming et al., 2000). To determine whether evidence of this ability could be obtained by writing about various kinds of stimulus material, several prototype tasks were created in various iterations of prototyping, including Reading–Writing (RW) tasks and Listening–Writing (LW) tasks. The RW tasks included either a short (~350 words) or a longer (~650 words) reading passage, several multiple choice comprehension questions about the passage, and a writing prompt that asked about different aspects of the passage than did the multiple choice questions. This task design attempted to provide evidence of the ability to coherently and accurately write about previously unfamiliar content. The efficiency of using the same stimulus to obtain evidence about Writing ability as well as Reading (or Listening) ability was also explored here.

LW tasks included an excerpt from a university lecture or a campus-situated conversation, sometimes associated with several multiple choice comprehension items, and a writing prompt that asked about different aspects of the oral stimulus from what was asked about in the multiple choice questions. This task required the ability to write coherently and accurately about previously unfamiliar orally presented content. The rationale for including multiple choice (MC) items in these designs was to provide context and focus for the written responses (Chapelle et al., 2008: 135), and to explore the possibility of obtaining information about reading and listening abilities with these tasks in addition to writing ability.

In these early phases of prototyping integrated writing tasks, it was concluded that responses to shorter reading passages did not provide sufficient evidence of sustained writing ability. Similarly, writing about a conversation did not yield responses that elicited enough academic writing to give sufficient evidence of the desired construct. On a positive note, writing about the longer lectures provided evidence for the targeted claims about writing ability. In the prototypes where the passage was available to participants while writing, copying from the passage was identified as an issue which required further investigation.

As the results indicated that longer texts worked well, and the time allotted for writing the responses was sufficient, the responses to these tasks were used to develop initial scoring rubrics. The process of rubric development is described later in this chapter.

In a later design decision, writing tasks were separated from the reading and listening measures. Because it was decided that the integrated writing task would not inform the measurement in the Reading or Listening section, the next phase of prototyping compared the RW and LW tasks with longer texts to a new prototype task that incorporated writing about information that was both read and listened to. The Reading–Listening–Writing (RLW) task included a reading passage that presented an issue or an explanation, followed by a lecture that typically called into question the various points in the reading passage, and then a Writing prompt that asked examinees to explain the points called into question. This task design attempted to capture evidence of academic writing that reflects analysis of multiple sources and synthesis of complex information.

This task could be replicated in multiple forms, and numerous reading passages and accompanying lectures could be created. Moreover, it did not seem to be possible to "coach" examinees for this task, as examinees needed to use information from both the oral and written texts in their written response. Moreover, the topics discussed were academic, and even if there was some general familiarity, prior knowledge did not seem to assist with correctly completing these tasks. By using a prompt like "How did the information in the lecture call into question the information in the reading passage?", the advantage of copying from the reading text was minimized. The more proficient writing responses that were elicited included the kind of writing that was targeted in the construct and defined in the Framework (Cumming et al., 2000).

Development of a scoring rubric

To evaluate responses to new constructed response tasks, scoring rubrics (also referred to as scoring guidelines) need to be prototyped to see whether raters can use them to successfully separate examinees in the intended population into different ability levels. It may be necessary to refine the rubrics by clarifying the distinctions between different levels or to change the number of levels, either by decreasing the number, if the population cannot be sorted into the number of levels defined by the prototype scoring rubric, or by increasing the number, if examinees of clearly different abilities are being placed at the same rubric score point.

Responses to prototype tasks can be utilized to develop an appropriate scoring rubric for the construct to be measured. This approach was employed to develop the scoring rubric for the independent and integrated tasks in the speaking section of TOEFL iBT. Initially, four workshops were conducted, one with each of the following groups of experts: ESL instructors, oral proficiency raters, university administrators, and applied linguists. The purpose of these four initial workshops was to begin to identify characteristics of proficient academic speaking, which expanded on initial definitions in the Speaking framework (Butler et al., 2000). The groups listened to responses to prototype tasks and were asked to rank the responses into different levels according to proficiency. The groups then identified the salient features of the responses at the different levels. The discussion of these features and the levels they represented were summarized in a preliminary scoring rubric.

The fifth workshop included one representative from each of the groups of experts who listened to responses, described their salient features, and attempted to use the draft rubric. At this session, the preliminary rubric was refined into a four-point scoring scale for the integrated tasks and a five-point scale for the independent tasks. Subsequent prototyping efforts explored whether these scoring rubrics were appropriate (Chapelle et al., 2008: 122).

A similar approach was utilized to develop the scoring rubrics for the TOEFL iBT integrated writing tasks. Note that this approach does not prescribe the number of levels that will be on the operational scoring rubric. Rather, the number of levels is a direct result of the number of distinct bands or groupings of salient features of the responses that can be described by the panels of experts. Ultimately, this approach led to speaking rubrics with four levels and writing rubrics with five levels.

Scoring rubrics often undergo revisions even after the prototype phase of design. When additional tasks are created, when responses from additional examinees are obtained, and when additional raters attempt to use a new rubric, refinements in wording and level descriptions can be made, up to the first reporting of operational scores.

Item difficulty

Determining the appropriate difficulty of items for a particular population is also an important reason for prototyping potential new item types. In an experimental ETS adaptive test designed to place ESL students in appropriate level English classes in community colleges, prototype items were designed for six levels of difficulty. The material to be tested at each level was determined on the basis of what expert teachers identified as being commonly taught in courses at each level and what materials were covered in commonly used textbooks. Constructs for each of the four skills were developed and items to measure the abilities defined by the constructs were prototyped.

Around 3,000 community college students spread over six levels of ability participated in the study. It was realized that it was unlikely that the actual performance of examinees on items that were written for a specific level would fall exactly at the assigned level, even with close supervision of the item writing to specifications. This was one reason for prototyping. Based on the initial phase of prototyping, although the reading test items were fairly easy overall, they generally spanned the ability ranges from 1 to 6 and seemed to line up as expected in terms of difficulty with the levels predicted. Unfortunately, this was not the case for the Grammar and Listening items, which were too easy. The difficulty levels of these items did not line up as predicted (Schedl, 2007). It was observed that this population was quite different from the international test population with which the test designers were familiar. For example, this population had spent more time in the United States, they had better listening skills, and, on average, they were older. They also seemed to be much abler than anticipated. Items were created for six levels, but levels 1 and 2 were too easy for this population and levels 5 and 6 were not hard enough. Based on the first prototyping event, the language abilities to be measured at each level were reassigned to lower levels to match pilot test performance. In general, this involved revising test specifications for abilities to lower levels and recoding the items. As a result of this reassignment of items to lower levels, the pool of easy items was larger while the pool of difficult items was significantly smaller. Specifications for harder items were created for a second round of prototyping.

A second prototype effort was planned to create a large enough bank of items that performed well in order to produce a multi-stage adaptive package. In order to create the new items, examinee performance in the first prototype study was analyzed and new specifications for more difficult items were created.

Future developments

In this chapter, we began with a definition of prototyping, and emphasized that prototyping should begin only when a definition of the construct exists. The size of the prototyping population is determined by the number and nature of the questions being addressed, as well as by practical issues such as cost, time, and resources.

The examples illustrated how prototypes can inform decisions about the viability of measuring certain aspects of a construct and about the task types that provide the best evidence for a specific construct. A process for developing and trying out a scoring rubric based on prototype responses was provided. A prototype effort that investigated issues related to item difficulty and ability levels of ESL community college students was also described. That study illustrated the importance of prototyping on a population that is representative of the target operational test population.

What new directions might ESL prototyping take in the future? Until now, ESL prototyping has been carried out primarily for assessment purposes that focus on individual proficiency independent of access to and type of learning the individual has received. Given the importance of education and the recognition that the proportion of second language learners is growing throughout the world, a variety of learning situations and tasks to meet the learning needs of this expanding population will probably need to be researched and prototyped in the near future. Initial, small-scale prototyping efforts to inform teaching and learning might be carried out in the classroom in cooperation with, or led by, classroom teachers. In this context, it would be possible to construct more innovative communicative tasks that can provide teachers with information about students' instructional needs as well as assess how well students are able to use the information they have learned in class in communicative situations.

There may also be other components of assessment that should be taken into account. For example, the use of peer group work and various technologies in classrooms suggests that there may be a need to prototype new methods of assessing language abilities in these contexts.

There has also been a lot of interest in obtaining more feedback about examinees' abilities in order to inform the students themselves, their teachers, and institutions. Future efforts to develop assessments will most likely involve the prototyping of item types that have the potential to provide more of this type of information than current assessments do.

The expanded use of multi-media in language teaching and learning is an area where additional research is needed to determine what makes for effective learning materials and strategies in combination with these media. The analysis and prototyping of materials, activities, and tasks both for effective learning and assessment would be valuable in conjunction with such research.

Further reading

Chapelle, C., Enright, M. and Jamieson, J. (eds), (2008). *Building a Validity Argument for the Test of English as a Foreign Language*. New York, NY: Routledge. This volume provides a detailed description of the research and development efforts to revise the TOEFL test from 1990 to 2005. By describing this evolution, key principles in educational measurement are explained. The volume integrates the results of empirical studies and validity arguments that support the TOEFL iBT test. Early chapters of the volume present the rationales for the revisions and a description of the process used to define the construct. Middle chapters provide detailed accounts of numerous research studies and prototyping efforts that informed the design of the test. The volume concludes with a validity argument for the test.

Fulcher, G. and Davidson, F. (2007). *Language Testing and Assessment, An Advanced Resource Book*. New York, NY: Routledge. In the first section of this valuable resource book, the authors review issues of validity, test constructs, models and frameworks. They consider the relationship between these abstract models, the development of a test framework, and actual test specifications. They explain how items and tasks are written and prototyped. They also consider ethics and standards for testing, test validation and use. The second section of the book includes excerpts from highly influential papers by experts in these same areas. The third section focuses on group activities related to the core concepts of the book, such as analyzing items and tasks, creating arguments for test validation, and writing an assessment statement for a test.

Weir, C. and Milanovic, M. (eds), (2003). *Continuity and Innovation: Revising the Cambridge Proficiency in English Examination 1913–2002*. Cambridge, UK: Cambridge University Press. This comprehensive volume documents a revision of the Certificate of Proficiency in English (CPE) which took place from 1991 to 2002 to ensure that the test is aligned with current language testing and practice. CPE has been in use since 1913, and is the earliest assessment in the Cambridge suite of English as a foreign language examinations. A detailed description is provided of the issues addressed during the revision and the process used for making test design and construct decisions. Examples of the prototypes that informed the decisions are also provided.

References

Bejar, I., Douglas, D., Jamieson, J., Nissan, S. and Turner, J. (2000). *TOEFL® 2000 Listening Framework: A Working Paper* (TOEFL® Monograph No. MS-19). Princeton, NJ: Educational Testing Service.

Bowles, M. A. (2010). *The Think-Aloud Controversy in Second Language Research*. London, UK: Routledge.

Butler, F., Eignor, D., Jones, S., McNamara, T. and Suomi, B. (2000). *TOEFL® 2000 Speaking Framework: A Working Paper* (TOEFL® Monograph No. MS-20). Princeton, NJ: Educational Testing Service.

Chapelle, C., Enright, M. and Jamieson, J. (eds), (2008). *Building a Validity Argument for the Test of English as a Foreign Language*. New York, NY: Routledge.

Cumming, A., Kantor, R., Powers, D., Santos, T. and Taylor, C. (2000). *TOEFL® 2000 Writing Framework: A Working Paper* (TOEFL® Monograph No. MS-18). Princeton, NJ: Educational Testing Service.

Enright, M., Grabe, W., Koda, K., Mosenthal, P., Mulcahy-Ernt, P. and Schedl, M. (2000). *TOEFL® 2000 Reading Framework: A Working Paper*. TOEFL Monograph Series MS-17. RM-00-4. Princeton, NJ: Educational Testing Service.

Enright, M. and Schedl, M. (1999). *Reading for a Reason: Using Reader Purpose to Guide Test Design* (Internal Report). Princeton, NJ: Educational Testing Service.

Fulcher, G. (2003). Interface design in computer based language testing. *Language Testing* 20: 384–408.

Fulcher, G. and Davidson, F. (2007). *Language Testing and Assessment, An Advanced Resource Book*. New York, NY: Routledge.

Jamieson, J. and Denner, A. (2000). *Report on Prototype Project #7: Creation of tasks and observations for listening claim 2—Listening for pragmatic understanding in a variety of text types* (Internal report). Princeton, NJ: Educational Testing Service.

Schedl, M. (2007). *Summary of Placement Test Findings from Pilot 1* (Internal Report). Princeton, NJ: Educational Testing Service.

20

Pre-operational testing

Dorry M. Kenyon and David MacGregor

Introduction/definitions

Pre-operational testing is the thoughtful, deliberate, and systematic process of collecting and analyzing evidence to support the validity of an assessment *prior* to that assessment's operational use. Using quantitative and qualitative research methodologies, it is the process of conducting research to find answers to questions about, or to confirm the adequacy of, assessments, instruments, and tests currently under development. As such it shares much in common with all research endeavors, yet with a major and critical difference: its objective lens focuses ultimately on the *test* rather than the test takers and test score users, although all stakeholders may play a role in pre-operational testing.

While there are many terms used to describe aspects of pre-operational testing, in this article we will simplify the discussion by referring to two phases of the research. *Pilot testing* encompasses research on the test that is *exploratory*, conducted during a phase in which major or minor changes to the assessment and its accompanying pieces (e.g., scoring rubrics, test administration conditions, item and task formats) may still be made. *Field testing* refers to research on the test that is *confirmatory*, a final check that everything is working as intended and the test is ready to become operational within the context for which it is being developed. This latter definition by no means implies that research on the language test *qua* language test then ceases. Rather, it means that the test developer has made an evaluative judgment that sufficient evidence has been gathered to claim that the test can now be used for its intended purposes without further development. In other words, when pilot testing and field testing cease, the test developer implicitly claims that the instrument itself is now ready to be used to provide data which can lead score-users to making valid interpretations or taking appropriate actions about test-takers on the basis of their performances on the test. Together, pilot testing and field testing constitute *pre-operational testing*.

In this chapter, we embed the discussion of pilot testing and field testing as means of collecting evidence prior to the operational usage of a test to support claims about the relationship between test performance and assessment records, assessment records and interpretations, interpretations and decisions, and decisions and consequences following Bachman and Palmer's (2010) assessment use argument (AUA). With the framework of the AUA, test developers can optimize their limited resources as they plan for pre-operational testing in the real world.

We make a distinction here between the terms *items* and *tasks*. We use the term *item* to refer to discrete test questions that require the examinee to make a choice among given answers or to provide a short (usually one-word) answer. We use *task* to refer to questions that require an examinee to provide longer answers based on written or oral instructions and prompts (e.g., an extended writing sample).

Historical perspectives

Pre-operational testing happens. There is no identifiable academic literature on pre-operational testing as a content area, yet journal articles describing the development of a new instrument will describe the activities that took place during pre-operational testing in more or less detail. This finding is hardly surprising since pre-operational testing is so critical to establishing claims that an instrument is now ready for use. On the other hand, since the issues new assessments face vary widely, there is no one set procedure for pre-operational testing as understood in this article. Various stakeholders will also have their different concerns.

For example, some test developers may view pre-operational testing as the domain of psychometricians, or measurement specialists. For these stakeholders, the goal of pre-operational testing is "to ensure that items function as expected" (Wendler and Walker, 2006: 459). This is generally understood to mean: do we have evidence that the items are functioning *psychometrically*; that is, do the statistical properties of the items meet agreed upon criteria? While such evidence is absolutely *necessary* before a test becomes operational, in language testing at least, such evidence is not *sufficient* to cover all claims about the inferences and decisions that may be made on the basis of a test performance. For example, suppose test developers want to develop a test they can claim is only assessing aspects of linguistic ability and nothing else, such as background knowledge. While psychometric analyses may identify items that do not function as expected, qualitative and other quantitative research methods may need to be used to provide evidence that differences in background knowledge are not influencing performance on the test.

What little literature exists on pilot and field testing in regard to language testing suffers from inconsistent terminology. In their foundational book, Bachman and Palmer (1996) subsumes both under the name "pre-testing," with the additional note that at the late stages, pre-testing may include field trialing. In their follow-up book (Bachman and Palmer, 2010), they refer to the "trialing stage," with early trialing corresponding roughly to pilot testing, and late trialing corresponding roughly to field testing. Chapelle (2008) uses "prototyping" to describe the pre-operational testing phase (see Nissan and Schedl, this volume). Linn (2006) and Wendler and Walker (2006) appear to use the terms "item tryout" and "field testing" interchangeably.

In the interest of clear communication, we suggest that the field adopt a consistent terminology. Aside from any other merits that different terms may have, the terms "pilot testing" and "field testing" have the advantage of generally being used in technical reports for tests and of being understood in a wide variety of fields beyond language testing. When referring to pilot testing and field testing collectively, "pre-operational testing" is a descriptively adequate term. Thus, in this article, these three terms will be used.

Critical issues and topics

In this article we argue that pre-operational testing is an integral part of test development research and that Bachman and Palmer's AUA (Bachman and Palmer, 2010) provides a helpful framework in which to situate the issues involved in pre-operational testing. Using the AUA, test developers can develop a detailed plan for pre-operational testing and ensure that the necessary resources for carrying out this phase are available before committing to a test development project. In this section, we outline the AUA and the role of pre-operational testing within it, and then give some examples of how pre-operational testing fits within the AUA.

Mislevy *et al.* (2002, 2003; see also Kane, this volume, and Mislevy, this volume) argue for "evidence-centred design" with validity arguments based on Toulmin's (2003) argument structure. In this model of building argumentation, arguments are drawn linking *claims* to the *data*, that is, in language testing, the performance of the test-taker on a language assessment. Claims are supported by *warrants* that support the legitimacy of the steps in the arguments, while the warrants themselves are supported by *backing* that gives them authority. The argument also needs to take into account *rebuttals*, which are "*alternative explanations*, or *counterclaims* to the intended inference" (Bachman, 2005: 10, his emphasis). Rebuttals may be supported, weakened, or rejected by *rebuttal data*.

Bachman (2005) illustrates Toulmin's argument structure with the example of establishing the US citizenship of Marc. The claim is that Marc is a US citizen. The fact that Marc was born in the United States is used to support this claim. The warrant for that claim is that all individuals born in the United States are citizens. The backing for that warrant is the clause in the US Constitution that defines citizenship. A rebuttal to the claim is the fact that Marc has renounced his citizenship, and the rebuttal data consist of his affidavit renouncing his citizenship. In this case, then, the rebuttal data force us to reject the claim that Marc is a US citizen. In other words, the link between the data (Marc's being born in the United States) and the claim (Marc is a US citizen) is ultimately broken.

Embedding issues in pre-operational testing within the AUA leads to a more nuanced understanding of the important role that pilot and field testing play in test development and clarifies the type of data that should be collected. Are the data required to support the link between test performance and records, records and interpretations, interpretations and decision, or decision and consequences? The AUA forces us to spell out the claims directly and thereby sheds light on what data need to be collected and what analyses need to be undertaken. Within the AUA framework, the purpose of all pre-operational testing, then, is to establish links between data and claims, supported by warrants with backing, as well as to investigate and refute possible rebuttals to that link.

When considered in this framework, before developing test specifications and writing items and tasks that will undergo pre-operational testing, test developers need to have a clear understanding of the claims that will be made based on test results and the warrants and backing that support those claims. This will justify the kinds of data that need to be collected during pre-operational testing. Ultimately, the foundational data being used to make the claims are performance on the test; therefore, test items and assessment tasks must be designed to collect the kind of performance data needed, suggested by the theoretical models of linguistic competence being used.

Before designing pre-operational testing, test developers also need to consider the rebuttals to their claims and then design pre-operational testing that provides quantitative and/or qualitative data to refute those rebuttals, while allowing for the possibility that the data might actually support the rebuttal, thus requiring rethinking of the basic test design and specifications. Ultimately, whether and when a test becomes operational, along with which items and tasks are included on the test, will be determined by how well, in the judgment of the test developers, results from pre-operational testing support the claims being made and refute the rebuttals.

At the foundational level in the AUA, linking performance on items and assessment tasks to test records (scores, descriptions of performance), questions about individual items and tasks will be paramount. When innovative items and tasks are being developed, particularly performance-based tasks, iterative stages of pilot testing (i.e., exploratory research), collecting both qualitative data and quantitative data from examinees and raters, may be needed. The findings of the pilot testing may lead to several rounds of revisions to the items and tasks, not to mention scoring rubrics or to rater training, before field testing (i.e., confirmatory research) can take place. On the other hand, when new items are developed to replace items on an extant test, pilot testing is unlikely to be needed and more traditional psychometric understandings of field testing (that is, collecting item statistics to confirm that the new items are functioning similarly to the old) will be called for. Also at this foundational level evidence supporting the consistency (reliability) of the assessment items and tasks in producing scores will need to be collected (Bachman and Palmer, 2010).

Following Bachman and Palmer (2010), at the next AUA level, linking test records to interpretations, pre-operational testing may focus on collecting and analyzing data that relate to claims about the *meaningfulness* of test score interpretations, the *impartiality* of the test to all groups of test takers (i.e., questions of differential item functioning, item and test bias), the *generalizability* of the test score interpretations to language usage outside the testing context, and the *relevance* and *sufficiency* of the interpretations vis-à-vis their use. The degree to which these questions need to be (or can be) addressed in pre-operational testing will be highly contextual and depend on such factors as how novel the assessment and its use are, how high stakes the assessment is, and the amount of information that can be gathered via prior research or program experience, as well as resources available to the project. Each context will be different. However, we want to stress that the goal of pre-operational testing is to have sufficient evidence for the test developers to have confidence that the test is ready to go operational.

At the next AUA level, linking interpretations to decisions, Bachman and Palmer's (2010) framework suggests that pre-operational testing would focus on examining alignment of decisions to be made to values and legal requirements of the stakeholder context, as well as the equitability to all stakeholders of decisions made. Pre-operational testing at the final AUA level, linking decisions to consequences, would, following Bachman and Palmer's (2010) framework, call for examining evidence to support that consequences of decisions made are beneficial to all stakeholders involved. These last two levels of the AUA clearly stretch previous understandings of pre-operational testing and call for a wider variety of qualitative methodological approaches (e.g., focus groups, surveys, observations). Again, the degree to which any research in this area would actually be done pre-operationally will depend on the specifics of the testing context and the resources available. However, we believe that the existence of these levels must at least be acknowledged and addressed by test developers as they plan for pre-operational testing, even if it is only to describe potential issues that may arise and require examination in the future.

In summary, the ultimate goal of thinking through the AUA is not to make a black or white decision on whether an individual item or task can appear on a test or whether using test scores is valid for a given purpose. Rather, at the item and task level, the goal is to build a strong, evidence-based argument to support the decision and consequences to include certain items or tasks on a test. At the test level, the goal is to build a strong, evidence-based argument that can assure the test developer and test users that decisions made on the basis of performances on tests are defensible and their consequences beneficial. Within each test development context, the kind of data to be collected and analyses to be conducted will depend on a variety of factors and clearly quantitative data, qualitative data, and/or a mixture of the two may be required.

Thus, when planning for pre-operational testing, test developers need to make decisions about the timing of the testing, the type of data to be collected, the resources needed to conduct the testing, the analyses to be conducted, and the application of the results based on the questions to be answered in the research. In general, small-scale pilot testing, when called for, will occur in the early phases of pre-operational testing. Such testing is typically designed to investigate the functioning of items and tasks, item and task types, and the characteristics of the test as a whole.

At this stage, the test developer may investigate such questions as whether test directions are comprehensible, whether items and tasks are accessible and engaging, or whether performance-based (extended constructed response) tasks elicit the quantity and quality of language desired. Depending on the question being asked, pilot testing may involve a variety of qualitative research methods, including formal cognitive laboratories, observational instruments, think-aloud protocols, interviews, and surveys. Some questions that may be addressed at this stage include: identifying problems in item and task specifications and/or instructions that can lead to examinees not producing responses that match expectations, especially for constructed response tasks, or discovering how examinees respond to tasks, in terms of test-taking processes, perceptions of the tasks, and performance (Bachman and Palmer, 1996). After analyzing the results of pilot tests, test developers may decide to modify or scrap items or item types, clarify instructions, improve or remove illustrations, and so on. As mentioned earlier, pilot testing is exploratory and thus especially important when developing innovative item or task types to make sure that the demands are understandable, and that the items or tasks are eliciting the expected response.

In contrast to pilot testing, large-scale field testing is confirmatory in nature and thus more suitable for establishing statistical properties of items, such as fit to the measurement model, difficulty, and so on (Bachman and Palmer, 1996; Wendler and Walker, 2006). Because some items will almost inevitably fail to meet the pre-established criteria for inclusion on the test, test developers usually field test more items than are needed for the operational test. In this stage, environmental problems, such as excessive background noise from sources such as traffic or air conditioning, or procedural problems, such as inadequate training of test supervisors, can be identified (Bachman and Palmer, 1996). In addition, miskeyed or double-keyed items may be identified in this stage, and performance samples for performance-based tests can be collected that can be used to construct training sets for raters and to refine rating rubrics (Welch, 2006). Small modifications may be made to items after field testing if the field test is not used to establish item difficulty (such as in pre-equating test forms), but otherwise items that are field tested should either go on the operational test as is if the analysis confirms their suitableness, or be left off if their suitableness is not confirmed. Even at this stage, however, qualitative data can be collected to complement the quantitative results (see, for example, Kenyon and Stansfield, 1993).

In designing a confirmatory field test, it is important that the sample match closely the characteristics of the target population in order to ensure that the test is fully appropriate for all members of population who may take the test in the future. The Standards for Educational and Psychological Testing (American Educational Research Association/American Psychological Association/National Council on Measurement in Education, 1999) underscores the importance of carefully selecting a representative sample for field testing in Standard 3.8:

> **Standard 3.8:** When item tryouts or field tests are conducted, the procedures used to select the sample(s) of test takers for item tryouts and the resultant characteristics of the sample(s) should be documented. When appropriate, the sample(s) should be as representative of the population(s) for which the test is intended.

In addition, test developers must determine how to design the field test. Wendler and Walker (2006) (see also Welch, 2006) discuss three options regarding field test design, along with the benefits and drawbacks of each. The first two options involve embedding; that is, including new items that are being field tested in an operational administration of the test. In such cases, responses to items being field tested are recorded and analyzed in the same way as operational items, but they are not used to determine the examinees' test scores. The first embedding option is to embed a section of new items within an extant operational test form. This model helps to ensure that the sample of students taking the new items will be sufficiently large and will match the population of test takers, and allows for a large number of items to be field tested. However, if this approach is used, care must be taken to design the embedded section and the items within it so that they match the operational test sections as closely as possible; otherwise, test takers may identify the embedded section and not put as much effort into responding to those items. Because of this, embedded sections are not a good option when new item formats are being field tested.

Another option is to embed items within an extant test form. As with embedding sections, this technique helps to ensure a large and representative sample size, and it is useful when it is impossible or impractical to embed an entire section. However, embedding items lengthens the test and can force the test designer to choose among several unattractive choices: lengthening the test and increasing administration time proportionally, which may lead to fatigue on the part of the test takers; lengthening the test without increasing administration time, which gives test takers less time to respond to operational items; or decreasing the number of operational items, which can limit the content covered by the test and decrease reliability. Finally, as with embedded sections, this is not a good method to use for field testing new item types, as the test takers may identify the embedded items and not put their fullest effort into answering them.

The third option discussed by Wendler and Walker is not to embed items at all, but rather to try out new items in a special administration. This option can be used when embedding is impossible or impractical, such as when a new item or test format is being tested (and has already passed through extensive pilot testing). However, it can be difficult to find a large and representative sample size to participate in a special administration of a test, recruiting and administration can be expensive, and test takers may not feel motivated to perform their best if they know that they are participating in a field test rather than an operational test.

Pre-operational testing and the AUA: an example

As an example of how to approach pre-operational testing in terms of an AUA, consider a test designed to measure the proficiency of English language learners in writing academic English language at the middle school level. The claim is that ratings given to performances on the test tasks are predictors of the ability to write for academic purposes in an academic classroom where English is the medium of instruction. The data used for these claims, then, are the rating of performances; the warrant is that writing in response to prompts on a test is a good proxy for school writing; and the backing for this warrant would be prior research on the relationship between performance on writing tasks and overall writing proficiency.

Some rebuttals to the test design as a whole might include the following:

1. Students cannot produce a representative sample of their writing in the time allotted.
2. Students cannot produce a representative sample under the pressure of the testing situation.
3. Raters cannot reliably rate the samples produced.

Some rebuttals to individual tasks might include the following:

4. It is not clear from the task directions what the student must do.
5. The task is not engaging enough for students to produce a representative sample of their writing.
6. Student responses include too much copied text to allow for meaningful rating.
7. The task may require construct-irrelevant background knowledge about some topic beyond what is provided in the task directions.
8. The task favors one group (e.g., Latino students) over another group (e.g., non-Latinos).

Given this set of rebuttals, rebuttal data for both the test as a whole and for the individual tasks would include a mixture of quantitative and qualitative data. To provide data for 1 and 2, test developers may compare ratings of students' field test writing with independent measures of those students' writing, such as writing on classroom assignments. A high correlation would constitute a refutation of the rebuttal, and would indicate that students are able to produce a representative sample of writing under the test conditions, while a low correlation would be evidence that there is something about the conditions of the test that prevents students from producing a representative sample. In the latter case, test designers could use a variety of qualitative methods, such as student interviews in a cognitive laboratory setting, observations of student performance under testing conditions, or analysis of student writing, to pinpoint the source of the problem and adjust the test design accordingly.

To provide data for 3, a classic inter-rater reliability study is appropriate. If the inter-rater reliability is sufficiently high, that can be considered a refutation of the rebuttal. If it is low, test developers should consider revising the rubric used for rating, along with training materials and procedures.

For rebuttals to individual tasks, again a combination of quantitative and qualitative data is called for. Data addressing 4 might come from the number of responses rated as off-topic; if there is an inordinately large number of tasks so rated, there may be problems with the task instructions. Such problems can be pinpointed by examining student writing, as well as conducting student interviews in a cognitive laboratory setting. Similarly, low overall ratings on a task relative to other tasks on the test may be evidence that a task is not engaging. Again, that can be investigated by examining student writing and interviewing students, or by having teachers familiar with the students' writing provide feedback on student performance on that task. Likewise, Rebuttals 6 and 7 can be investigated using a combination of student writing and interviews. Finally, Rebuttal 8 is best addressed using a differential item functioning (DIF) analysis. Because of the large sample size necessary to conduct a DIF analysis, such an analysis may need to be conducted during the field testing stage. Any tasks that are found to have a high level of DIF should be investigated to see if there is a discernable reason for that high DIF and decisions will need to be made as to whether to include the task on an operational test form. For such reasons more items and tasks are generally included in field-testing than are required for operational purposes

This example list of rebuttals, and the evidence that can be used to address them, is meant to be illustrative, not exhaustive, and only partially covers levels 1, 2, and 3 of an AUA. The important point for test developers is to have a clear idea of rebuttals to their claims, and to consider how to address those rebuttals through pre-operational testing. Because pre-operational testing can be expensive and time consuming, it is also important to prioritize; that is, to consider which rebuttals are most important to address at the pre-operational stage given the resources available and the context of the test, including the stakes of the test. If test developers decide not to investigate a rebuttal in pre-operational testing, they should be prepared to defend their decision and, if necessary, to address it using operational data.

Current contributions and research

Given the lack of literature directly addressing pre-operational testing, it is difficult to describe the current state of the art. One notable exception is Chapelle *et al.* (2008). In that volume, the contributors detail in the context of an assessment use argument the in-depth pre-operational testing of a major revision of the Test of English as a Foreign Language, including the prototyping of new assessment tasks (Enright *et al.*, 2008), prototyping of measures of the four skills (listening, reading, writing, and speaking) (Enright *et al.*, 2008), prototyping the test as a whole (Huff *et al.*,

2008), and field testing the new form (Wang *et al.*, 2008b). Taken together these studies present an exemplary case of using a variety of qualitative and quantitative methods in conducting pre-operational testing in the context of an assessment use argument.

Chapelle *et al.* (2008) provides a good example of how to devise and carry out a pre-operational testing plan for a new (or newly revised) test. Such a plan is also vital when developing new items to go on an already existing test. In this section, we describe the pre-operational testing for refreshment tasks for the speaking section of a standards-based assessment of academic English language proficiency for English language learners in the United States in grades K–12. The assessment is one of a battery that also assesses listening, reading, and writing. The test is designed to assess proficiency in the language of four academic content areas (math, science, language arts, and social studies), as well as social and instructional language, without testing academic content knowledge.

Potential rebuttals to the tasks include: the tasks measure content area knowledge rather than (or in addition to) academic language; the language being tested does not reflect the language of the classroom; the content of the tasks can potentially give an unfair advantage or disadvantage to one group of students based on such factors as sex, ethnicity, geographic location, or first language; the tasks are not engaging; and the tasks do not allow students to produce a language sample that reflects their true proficiency.

In the annual refreshment cycle, we investigate the extent to which these rebuttals may be supported by rebuttal data. After raw tasks are developed by teachers in the field following detailed specifications, they go through a series of refinements, reviews, and pre-operational testing. All tasks are subject to reviews by two panels of teachers. The first panel, comprising subject-area teachers, investigates the question of whether the content of the tasks reflects content taught in classrooms. The second panel, comprising a mix of content-area teachers and ESL teachers, examines tasks to identify any bias or sensitivity issues. Any problems identified by these panels are addressed before tasks go on to the next stage.

The tasks then go through two rounds of pilot testing. In the first round, the test development team administers tasks to high proficiency students in a cognitive lab setting. After administering the tasks, they interview the students regarding the students' perceptions of the tasks. The purpose of this round is to gauge how well tasks are eliciting language at the targeted proficiency level and how engaging they are for the students.

In the second round of piloting, ESL teachers in the field administer the new tasks to their own students and then fill out an online questionnaire. The purpose of this round of piloting is to gauge how well the tasks allow students to produce language that reflects their current level of proficiency as demonstrated in their classroom work. ESL teachers are used for this stage because they are presumably more familiar with the abilities of their students, and so can provide informed feedback on the extent to which the tasks allow examinees to demonstrate their current level of proficiency. After each round of piloting, the tasks that are performing poorly are abandoned, while others are revised as needed based on the results.

Once the final tasks have been chosen and revised if necessary, they go through a small-scale field test. The primary purpose of this field test is to gather qualitative data on how well the tasks allow examinees to provide a sample of their current level of proficiency. The new speaking tasks are field tested together with the current operational tasks by the test development team to ensure that the task expectations are clear, that they elicit ratable samples from the students, and that performances on the new tasks are similar to performances on the tasks being replaced.

The intent behind this pre-operational testing is to ensure that the most serious potential rebuttals have been refuted by the time a task appears on an operational test. Addressing these rebuttals contributes to the creation of a defensible assessment use argument. When the revised operational test is released annually, the test developers are making the implicit claim that the new tasks can replace the old tasks and that the instrument can continue to provide data that test users can use to make valid interpretations about their students' proficiency in academic English language and take appropriate actions, such as allowing a student to proceed in a mainstream classroom without further language support.

Main research methods

Because the research questions addressed in pre-operational testing are very diverse, it is impossible to state that certain specific research methods will be used. Clearly, in conducting pre-operational testing, a combination of qualitative and quantitative methods should be used, as appropriate to answer specific research questions. In general, qualitative methods will predominate in the pilot testing phase since smaller numbers of examinees generally participate and understanding what is going on "behind the scenes" is of critical importance. Quantitative methods generally prevail in the field testing phase, where generally larger numbers of representative samples are tested and the psychometric properties of items and tests are to be confirmed. Nevertheless, in both phases a mix of qualitative and quantitative research methods (sometimes known as "mixed methods") can often provide a richer source of information than any single method alone.

In any event, the choice of research method should of course be driven by the question being asked. For example, to investigate whether a performance-based task is engaging to examinees, test developers could use a combination of observation and stimulated recall, in which researchers interview examinees soon after administering the task to gauge the examinees' attitude toward the task. To determine whether such a task successfully allows examinees to demonstrate how well they can use the language, test developers could have teachers administer the tasks to their own students, and then comment on whether the tasks allowed their students to show what they are capable of.

Kerlinger and Lee (2000) provide a good introduction to research methodology in the behavioral sciences, particularly more quantitatively oriented approaches. Mackey and Gass (2005) offer a good introduction to both quantitative and qualitative research methods for applied linguistics researchers, including such qualitative methods as ethnographies, case studies, interviews, observations, and diaries/journals. Gass and Mackey (2000) provides a detailed guide to using stimulated recall methodology. Finally, Creswell and Clark (2006) gives an introduction to mixed methods research.

Large-scale field tests are conducted when items are in their final form, and results are generally used to establish psychometric properties of items and test forms and to decide which items will appear on a test. Factors that influence whether an item will appear on a test include measures of item fit and point-biserial correlations, as well as measures of potential item bias such as DIF. In addition, field tests can provide information on item difficulty and can be used to establish the reliability of a test and equate parallel forms of the same test. Crocker and Algina (1986) provide a good introduction to measurement issues.

Recommendations for practice

Pre-operational testing is a critical phase in the development of a language test, and requires a great deal of thought and planning. In this section we provide a list of questions for test developers to consider when planning for pre-operational testing. This list of course is not meant to be exhaustive, nor will all of the questions apply to every testing project. Rather, the list is offered as a starting point. The questions are divided into questions more typically addressed in pilot testing and questions typically addressed in field testing; with each, they are divided into questions about the items and then questions about the test as a whole. Note that these questions correspond to the first level of the assessment use argument.

Illustrative questions typically addressed during pilot testing (exploratory)

a. Questions about individual items and tasks

    i.   Are multiple choice items correctly keyed, or are there any miskeyed or double-keyed items?

    ii.   Are any illustrations used clear and easily interpretable by examinees?

    iii. Are constructed response tasks engaging?

    iv. Do constructed response tasks allow students to produce performance samples that are truly representative of their current level of ability?

    v.   Do constructed response tasks allow students to produce rateable samples?

    vi. Are scoring rubrics easy to interpret by raters?

    vii. Can scoring rubrics be used consistently by raters?

    viii. Are there any items or tasks that are culturally sensitive or biased?

    ix. Do any items or tasks also assess a construct irrelevant to the target construct?

    x.   If there are any innovative item or task formats, do examinees clearly understand what they are to do?

b. Questions about the test as a whole

    i.   Are test administration procedures for test administrators clear and complete?

    ii.   Are test instructions for examinees clear and complete?

    iii. If the test includes manipulatives, are they easy to use?

    iv. If the test includes audio or video recordings, are they clear?

Illustrative questions typically addressed during field testing (confirmatory)

a. Questions about individual items and tasks

    i.   Are the psychometric properties of each item appropriate?

    ii.   Is the difficulty of the item as expected?

    iii. Is the item double-keyed or miskeyed?

    iv. Does the item fit to the measurement model being used?

    v.   Is there evidence that all the items and tasks are measuring the same construct?

    vi. Is a full range of performances elicited by the constructed response tasks?

    vii. Can raters score the constructed response tasks reliably?

b. Questions about the test as a whole

    i.   Is there evidence that the items and tasks assess the construct consistently (i.e., that the test is reliable)?

    ii.   If the test is a parallel or revised form, is there evidence that results are comparable to those on previous or alternate versions?

Future directions

In this chapter, we have argued that pre-operational testing, comprising both exploratory research in the pilot testing phase and confirmatory research in the field testing phase, is an integral element in constructing an assessment use argument. As such, pre-operational testing is a research enterprise, albeit one that focuses on the test itself as the subject of research, rather than on the performance of the examinees. The primary decision to be made and thus informed by pre-operational testing research is: is the test now ready to become operational?

Being a research enterprise, pre-operational testing merits the academic attention afforded all research enterprises. Unfortunately, while there is undoubtedly a great deal of pre-operational testing conducted, some of which may be innovative and of interest to the field, there is very little in the way of literature devoted to it as a separate topic *per se*, and very few conference presentations that discuss pre-operational testing methods. We urge test developers to present and publish work on pre-operational testing, and the field as a whole to give it due regard as an important research enterprise. We hope that in five to ten years' time there will be debates in the academic literature weighing the pros and cons of alternate approaches and discussing the most efficient and effective methods, so that all testers will understand the issues surrounding this overlooked topic and it will no longer be the underappreciated step-child of the test development process.

In addition, while traditional pre-operational testing has covered the foundational level of the assessment use argument (i.e., linking performances on test items to test records), given the more expanded understanding of validity, we would like to see more published examples of pre-operational testing that deal with the other levels of the AUA. This development will have the benefit of better contextualizing the important research done in pre-operational testing so that it may no longer be seen as just a technical requirement that needs to be fulfilled along the way to operationalizing a test.

Further reading

Bachman, L. and Palmer, A. (2010). *Language Assessment in Practice*. Oxford, UK: Oxford University Press. This edition is essentially a reworking of Bachman and Palmer (1996), this time approaching language assessment from the perspective of the assessment use argument first elucidated in Bachman (2005). In it, they offer a short discussion of field testing aimed at a broad audience of non-specialists with interest in language testing.

Chapelle, C. A., Enright, M. K. and Jamieson, J. M. (2008). *Building a validity argument for the Test of English as a Foreign Language^{TM}*. New York, NY: Routledge. The authors provide a detailed description of the pre-operational testing for a revision of a large-scale, high-stakes assessment, presented in the framework of an assessment use argument.

Crocker, L. and Algina, J. (1986). *Introduction to Classical and Modern Test Theory*. New York: Holt, Rinehart and Winston. This volume provides a foundational introduction to psychometric issues important to all testing.

Gass, S. M. and Mackey A. (2007). *Data elicitation for second and foreign language research*. Mahwah, NJ: Lawrence Erlbaum Associates. Mackey and Gass (2005) provides a good introduction aimed at an applied linguistics audience to qualitative research techniques that can be applied to pilot testing. The companion volume, Gass and Mackey (2007), provides a comprehensive review of data elicitation techniques.

Mackey, A. and Gass, S. M. (2005). *Second language research: Methodology and design*. Mahwah, NJ: Lawrence Erlbaum Associates.

References

American Educational Research Association/American Psychological Association/National Council on Measurement in Education (1999). *Standards for educational and psychological testing*. Washington, DC: American Educational Research Association.

Bachman, L. (2005). Building and supporting a case for test use. *Language Assessment Quarterly* 2: 1–34.

Bachman, L. and Palmer, A. (1996). *Language Testing in Practice*. Oxford, UK: Oxford University Press.

—— (2010). *Language Assessment in Practice*. Oxford, UK: Oxford University Press.

Chapelle, C. A., Enright, M. K. and Jamieson, J. M. (2008). *Building a validity argument for the Test of English as a Foreign Language^{TM}*. New York, NY: Routledge.

Creswell, J. W. and Clark, V. P. (2006). *Designing and Conducting Mixed Methods Research*. Thousand Oaks, CA: Sage Publications, Inc.

Crocker, L. and Algina, J. (1986). *Introduction to Classical and Modern Test Theory*. New York, NY: Holt, Rinehart and Winston.

Enright, M. K., Bridgeman, B., Eignor, D., Kantor, R. N., Mollaun, P., Nissan, S., Powers, D. E. and Schedl, M. (2008a). Prototyping new assessment tasks. In C. A. Chapelle, M. K. Enright and J. M. Jamieson (eds), *Building a Validity Argument for the Test of English as a Foreign Language*^{TM}. New York, NY: Routledge.

Enright, M. K., Bridgeman, B., Eignor, D., Lee, Y. W. and Powers, D. E. (2008b). Prototyping measures of listening, reading, speaking, and writing. In C. A. Chapelle, M. K. Enright and J. M. Jamieson (eds), *Building a validity argument for the Test of English as a Foreign Language*^{TM}. New York, NY: Routledge.

Gass, S. M. and Mackey, A. (2000). *Stimulated Recall Methodology in Second Language research*. Mahwah, NJ: Lawrence Erlbaum Associates.

—— (2007). *Data Elicitation for Second and Foreign Language Research*. Mahwah, NJ: Lawrence Erlbaum Associates.

Huff, K., Powers, D. E., Kantor, R. N., Mollaun, P., Nissan, S. and Schedl, M. (2008). Prototyping a new test. In C. A. Chapelle, M. K. Enright and J. M. Jamieson (eds), *Building a validity argument for the Test of English as a Foreign Language*^{TM}. New York, NY: Routledge.

Kenyon, D. M. and Stansfield, C. W. (1993). A method for improving tasks on performance-based assessments through field testing. In A. Huhta, K. Sajavaara and S. Takala (eds), *Language Testing: New Openings*. Jyväskylä, Finland: Institute for Educational Research, 90–102.

Kerlinger, F. N. and Lee, H. B. (2000). *Foundations of Behavioral Research*, 4th edn. Fort Worth, TX: Harcourt College Publishers.

Linn, R. (2006). The standards for educational and psychological testing: Guidance in test development. In S. Downing and T. Haladyna (eds), *Handbook of Test Development*. Mahwah, NJ: Lawrence Erlbaum Associates.

Mackey, A. and Gass, S. M. (2005). *Second Language Research: methodology and design*. Mahwah, NJ: Lawrence Erlbaum Associates.

Mislevy, R. J., Steinberg, L. S. and Almond, R. G. (2002). Design and analysis in task-based language assessment. *Language Testing* 19: 477–96.

—— (2003). On the structure of educational assessments. *Measurement: Interdisciplinary Research and Perspectives* 1: 3–62.

Toulmin, S.E. (2003). *The Uses of Argument* (updated edition). Cambridge, UK: Cambridge University Press.

Wang, L., Eignor, D. and Enright, M. K. (2008). A final analysis. In C. A. Chapelle, M. K. Enright and J. M. Jamieson (eds), *Building a Validity Argument for the Test of English as a Foreign Language*^{TM}. New York, NY: Routledge.

Welch, C. (2006). Item and prompt development. In S. Downing and T. Haladyna (eds), *Handbook of Test Development*. Mahwah, NJ: Lawrence Erlbaum Associates.

Wendler, C. and Walker, M. (2006). Practical issues in designing and maintaining multiple test forms for large-scale programs. In S. Downing and T. Haladyna (eds), *Handbook of Test Development*. Mahwah, NJ: Lawrence Erlbaum Associates.

21

Piloting vocabulary tests

John Read

Introduction

This chapter differs from the other two in Part VI of the book in two respects: first, it focuses on assessing a particular area of language knowledge, vocabulary, and second, it deals with the somewhat ill-defined topic of pilot testing. By contrast, the other chapters range more widely over types of items and tasks, and they deal with steps in the test development process that are better defined in language assessment, at least in these chapters themselves and in Fulcher and Davidson (2007: 76–90).

Let us take up the latter point first. Various authors (see, e.g., Bachman and Palmer, 1996: 248; Moussavi, 1999: 284) have pointed out that there is a confusing array of terms which are partly if not fully synonymous – 'pilot', 'pre-test', 'trial' and 'tryout' – referring to a particular event or activity, along with the corresponding set of verbal forms – 'piloting', 'pre-testing', etc. – that refer to a more general process. As it happens, the two sources just cited take 'pre-test/ing' to be the default term, as do Alderson *et al.* (1995: 74), although the latter authors see it as a cover term for two distinct phases, which they call 'pilot testing' and 'main trials'. To add to the confusion, another popular testing book for teachers (Hughes, 2003) identifies the same two phases as Alderson *et al.* but refers to them both as 'trials'. In their dictionary, Davies *et al.* (1999) have separate main entries for 'pre-test' and 'trial(ling)', but they acknowledge that the terms are not clearly distinguished in the literature. Thus, unfortunately, as in so many other areas of applied linguistics, we have to live with a lack of standardization in the terminology that is used. I will adopt the cover terms 'pilot test' and 'pilot testing' here, but they should be understood as referring broadly to the same kinds of activity as the other terms. What is probably more important is to be aware of how these activities are planned to improve the quality of draft test material before it is used for assessment purposes. Of that, more later.

It is also necessary to define the scope of vocabulary testing. Vocabulary is obviously an indispensable component of language use, to the extent that almost any kind of language test is in a sense measuring the test-takers' vocabulary ability, even if this ability is not an explicit focus of the scoring or rating. I distinguish between 'discrete' and 'embedded' assessments of vocabulary knowledge and use (Read, 2000: 8–10). The embedded type involves a focus on vocabulary as part of the assessment of a broader construct, as when a reading comprehension test includes some items that measure whether the test-takers can understand particular words or phrases that occur in the reading passages, or when the raters in a speaking test evaluate the range and accuracy of vocabulary use as one of the criteria for rating each candidate's performance. However, normally vocabulary tests are a discrete form of assessment, in that they are intended to focus specifically on some aspect of vocabulary knowledge or use, based on a pre-selected set of words. This chapter will be limited to the discussion of discrete vocabulary testing in this sense.

Historical perspective

Vocabulary tests in the multiple-choice format were the classic type of test item in foreign language tests during the middle decades of the twentieth century when, at least in the United States and its international sphere of influence, the purely psychometric approach to test design and analysis was at its height (Spolsky, 1995). For example, I have traced elsewhere (Read, 2000: 138–47) the history of vocabulary assessment in the Test of English as a Foreign Language (TOEFL) from 1964 until the late 1990s. In the original version of the test, multiple-choice vocabulary items presenting the target words in isolation or very short sentence contexts were highly reliable and efficient measures which correlated well with the reading section of the test. It was only under external pressure from applied linguists and language teachers that the TOEFL Program progressively moved to more contextualised formats for assessing vocabulary knowledge, and eventually it was embedded in the assessment of reading comprehension. Numerous other large-scale language proficiency and achievement tests also took advantage of the good psychometric qualities of multiple-choice and other types of objectively scorable vocabulary test items.

This means that a number of the early textbooks on language testing (e.g. Lado, 1961; Clark, 1972; Valette, 1977; Heaton, 1988) have substantial sections on vocabulary tests, including a range of sample item types and advice on both the writing and piloting of items. Such coverage of vocabulary testing is less of a standard feature in more recent texts, with some exceptions being Read (2000: Chapter 6) and Hughes (2003: Chapter 13). In addition, Fulcher and Davidson (2007: 76–90) use some sample vocabulary items to illustrate the processes of prototyping and field testing.

More generally, piloting is a somewhat hidden element of test design and development, in the sense that it is mentioned only in passing in most published papers on vocabulary tests. For instance, in a short article for teachers on the Vocabulary Size Test, Nation and Beglar (2007) state that '[a] lot of care was put into making the distractors [of the multiple-choice items] so that they were genuine choices and they were carefully checked in pilot testing' (p. 12). However, there is no specific information on how many people participated in the pilot and who they were, what the procedure was, what kind of feedback was obtained, or what changes were made to the draft items.

Piloting conventional test items

The basic principle of most conventional vocabulary test items is to require the learners to show that they can make a link between a word in the target language and its meaning, as expressed by a synonym or definition in L2, a translation equivalent in L1 or a picture. For this purpose, the most common format is probably the familiar multiple-choice type, with its numerous variants:

I was astonished to hear what happened.

a. eager   b. quite sad   c. very pleased   d. very surprised

Sonia has always been a friendly person, but recently she has been _____ kind and generous.

a. mostly   b. particularly   c. primarily   d. fully

The other widely used format is word–definition matching, as in:

1. environment
2. principle   _____ close detailed study of something
3. response   _____ money received regularly
4. factor   _____ surrounding area or conditions
5. analysis
6. income

These item types require the test-takers to select responses from the options given. In the piloting of such items, the kind of questions we need to consider are:

- Is there in fact only one correct response for each item?
- Is the correct response clearly expressed, and not easily guessed by being longer or noticeably more specific than the other options?
- Is each of the non-correct options functioning effectively by attracting at least some of the less proficient test-takers?
- Is the item at an appropriate level of difficulty?

Apart from selected-response items, there are others which require the test-takers to supply a response, the most common of which is the gap-filling (or completion) task. In gap-filling items, the simplest case is that the target word is deleted from a single sentence:

Land that can produce good crops is _____.

They went out to _____ the people on the sinking boat.

A gap-filling sentence needs to provide the clues needed to figure out what the missing word is. Thus, in the second sample item, the test-takers need to know what 'sinking' means in order to have a reasonable chance of supplying the appropriate word. Sometimes the sentences are more or less definitions, as in the first example above, rather than the more natural sentential context for the word represented by the second item. Gap-filling items may also be created from whole paragraphs or longer texts, by selectively deleting content words at regular intervals. These are often called 'cloze' tests, although strictly speaking the standard cloze procedure involves deleting both content and function words at a fixed interval of, say, every seventh word.

Where the learners share a first language, the gap-filling items can be bilingual, as in this example (based on Clark 1972: 100), which is intended to elicit the English word 'summit' from French learners:

L'endroit le plus élevé d'une montagne s'appelle le _____
[The highest point on a mountain is called the _____]

The main issues with gap-filling items are:

- Is it possible for the test-takers to supply an acceptable response based on the contextual information provided?

- Given that very often more than one word can fill a blank, which responses actually supplied by the participants in a trial are correct? For the second example above, the intended answer may be 'rescue', but words like 'save', 'help' and 'assist' can presumably also be accepted. But what about 'welcome' or 'see'? A pilot test can elicit a range of responses to be evaluated, so that decisions can be made as to which words will be included in the answer key. If the intention is to elicit just one target word, the sentence will need to be revised to try to rule out other possible answers; alternatively, the first letter of the target word may be supplied.
- Do the words supplied by the test-takers need to be correct in terms of grammar and spelling? For instance, can some credit be given for 'rescuing' or 'reskue' in the above example? One can argue either way on this issue but the point is that it should be resolved at the piloting stage, so that those who score the operational test can be given clear guidelines.

Piloting a new format: word associates

Vocabulary test formats that are used in operational tests for assessment purposes, such as those discussed in the previous section, tend to be variations on a theme. The more innovative types of test are likely to be developed and used by researchers interested in investigating how vocabulary knowledge expands (or is lost), how words are stored and accessed in the brain, and other research questions of that kind. If they show some initial promise, these research instruments are often explored by a number of researchers in succession as measures in their own right. This can be seen as a process of 'serial piloting', in which a format is tried out in several variants and in a variety of educational contexts, with the result that over time the potential of the format is thoroughly explored.

Devising the format: the initial studies

I can illustrate this process by reference to a type of vocabulary test that I devised in 1990: the word associates format. The test is based on the concept of word association, which has long had a significant role in psychological and psycholinguistic research. The basic research technique is a simple elicitation procedure: participants are presented with a series of words one by one and asked to supply the first word they think of in response to each stimulus word. For native speakers the responses to particular words are remarkably stable and there are published norms for word associations in English (Palermo and Jenkins, 1964; Deese, 1965). On the other hand, research by Meara (2009) and his students in the 1980s showed that second language learners produced responses that were much less consistent or interpretable, so that the standard technique seemed an unpromising basis for either gaining an understanding of the learners' lexical networks (which was Meara's concern) or assessing the depth of their vocabulary knowledge (my own interest).

Working with Meara in London at the time, I took an alternative approach to my research objective by creating a test format that required learners to *select* words associated with particular stimulus words rather than supplying them. After drafting an initial set of items, discussing them with a group of graduate students and trying them out with a class of ESL students in London, I settled on the following item format:

edit

arithmetic	film	pole	publishing
revise	risk	surface	text

Four of the words were associates of 'edit' ('film', 'publishing', 'revise', 'text'), whereas the other four were distractors. There were three types of relationship between the target word and the associates:

- *paradigmatic*:
  the two words were either synonyms or similar in meaning, and belonged to the same word class e.g. 'edit' and 'revise' (both verbs)
- *syntagmatic*:
  the two words could occur one after the other, as a collocation, e.g. 'edit' and 'text' (verb + noun).
- *analytic*:
  the associate represents one aspect of the meaning of the target word and is likely to form part of its dictionary definition, e.g. 'edit' and 'publishing'.

One of the first things I found out from the initial pilot was the test-takers needed to know what kinds of association they were looking for and thus for subsequent piloting I prepared a practice sheet containing instructions and sample items which illustrated the three types of relationship. I went on to write two forms of a 50-item word associates test based on samples of items from the University Word List (UWL) (Xue and Nation, 1984).

After my return to New Zealand, I took a number of steps to pilot the test further. I asked 10 English for academic purposes (EAP) teachers at the English Language Institute (ELI) of my university to work through the items individually and record what they thought were the correct answers. I made two interesting observations: some of the teachers reported that the test took longer to complete than they expected; and often they could find two or three associates for an item quite readily but had more difficulty in finding the fourth one. The latter observation strengthened my belief that test-takers should be told in the instructions that there were four associates to be found in each item. Of the 100 items, 27 were revised because more than one of the teachers chose a distractor or could not find one of the associates. Five of the teachers checked the revised items and no further problems were found.

Both forms of the revised test were administered to over 100 students in the intensive English for academic purposes (EAP) programme at the ELI on separate days. The full details of the analysis can be found in Read (1993), but briefly the two forms proved to be reliable (KR-20: 0.92) and they correlated reasonably well with a longer test of the UWL words that used a matching format (Form A: $r = 0.76$; Form B: $r = 0.81$). A Rasch partial credit analysis showed that 12 students were 'misfitting' on at least one form of the test, in the sense that their response patterns did not fit the norm established by the pilot participants as a whole. An inspection of the test papers indicated that most of these test-takers scored well overall but did not respond to certain items, presumably because they did not know the target word. This suggested that willingness to guess might be a significant factor in the learners' response behaviour.

Another step in the piloting was to ask eight learners individually to work through a selection of the items and provide a verbal report on why they chose each of their responses. This proved to be quite revealing. Those who were less proficient tended not to attempt any responses to an item if they did not recognise the target word. However, some more proficient learners were not so inhibited, as in this explanation by one of them for his responses to the 'denominator' item:

denominator

| common | develop | divide | eloquent |
| fraction | mathematics | species | western |

John Read

RESEARCHER (R): Do you know this word?

LEARNER (L): I don't know this word ... but I'm trying to look at all the words that ... what are the similar in meaning because I know that four words can go together ... [Pause] I'm not sure that my idea will be right ...

R: You've circled 'fraction' ... 'divide' ... 'species' ...

L: Or 'develop' ... So do you want my reason?

R: Yeah.

L: Because I don't know this word before and I tried to looking for some words that have similar in meaning. I think it's a guess – 'fraction', 'divide', 'species' – all things are cut in smaller – yeah – and then it develop bigger amount ... but I don't know ...

(Read, 1993: 366)

The learner applied a strategy that allowed him to identify two of the four associates correctly, while emphasising that he was just guessing. Another learner was able to choose three of the four associates of 'diffuse' in a similar manner. Thus, the verbal report evidence called into question the inference I wanted to make at the item level, that the selection of associates was a measure of how well the target word was known.

In order to address some of these concerns, I undertook a second study based on a redesigned item format (Read, 1998). Since the original study had shown that words entered into some-what different semantic relations according to their part of speech, the new format was intended specifically to assess knowledge of adjectives. The associates and distractors were presented in two clusters, with possible paradigmatic and analytic associates on the left side and possible syntagmatic associates on the right, as in this example:

Conscious	
awake healthy knowing laughing	face decision effort student

In this case, there were two associates on the left ('awake' and 'knowing') and two on the right ('decision' and 'effort'), but in other items the pattern was either one and three, or three and one, in order to reduce the prospects of successful guessing. The variant patterns also took account of the fact that the different uses of some adjectives could be better represented by three col-locates, e.g. 'broad – river', 'broad – shoulders', 'broad – smile', whereas three distinct meanings of 'secure' were appropriately expressed through three paradigmatic associates: 'confident', 'fixed' and 'safe'. A draft set of 46 items was tried out with a class of 16 Japanese learners and with four language teachers. Based on the problems revealed by this feedback, six items were discarded and another four were revised. This illustrates a useful guideline for piloting, that a draft test should contain more items than are needed for the operational version, so that poorly performing items can be removed without making it necessary to pilot replacement items.

Two trials were conducted with students in an intensive EAP programme, both involving concurrent measures of the learners' knowledge of the target adjectives. In the first trial 84 learners took both the word associates test and another test that required them to match words and definitions. The correlation between the two tests was quite high, at .86. In the second, smaller trial, 15 learners not only took the two written tests but also participated in an interview based on the Vocabulary Knowledge Scale (Wesche and Paribakht, 1996) to probe their knowledge of the target adjectives in greater depth. The results showed that the interview scores correlated more highly with the matching test (0.92) than the word associates test (0.76). Although these findings were based on a small sample, they suggested – along with some other evidence – that the revised format was still affected by the test-takers' willingness to guess what the associates of the target word might be.

Two North American studies

Since these two initial studies, a number of other researchers have carried out further piloting of the word associates format, adapting it for different learner populations and investigating variations in the design features.

Qian (1999) adopted an edited version of the Read (1998) test as his Depth of Vocabulary Knowledge (DVK) measure in a study of the relative contributions of breadth and depth of vocabulary knowledge to reading comprehension performance. His participants were 74 Chinese and Korean students taking an intensive ESL course at a university in Canada. He conducted his own piloting of the test, which resulted in the replacement of eight of the original items because of concerns that some of the associates were not unambiguously correct.

Subsequently, the same DVK format was used in a larger scale project (Qian and Schedl, 2004) to investigate the possibility of including the word associates format as an efficient measure of vocabulary knowledge in the Test of English as a Foreign Language (TOEFL). The original target words were replaced by 40 adjectives that had been tested in the multiple-choice format in an earlier (pre-1995) version of TOEFL. In this case, there were 207 ESL students from a much wider range of language backgrounds, again taking an intensive university course in Canada. A time limit of 35 minutes was set, reflecting the time taken by the test-takers in Qian's (1999) study, and almost all the test-takers were able to complete the items within that period. After the test had been administered, 30 randomly selected participants were interviewed about their experience of taking it. All but two of them reported that they were able to understand the nature of the test task, once they had read the instructions, and an inspection of all the test papers showed that only 10 test-takers had responded inappropriately by, for instance, selecting more than four responses for numerous items. Furthermore, all except one of the interviewees stated that they were reluctant to guess what the associates were for items with a target word that was unfamiliar to them. The researchers concluded that the DVK test was comparable in quality to the existing TOEFL multiple-choice vocabulary test and was worthy of further evaluation. One concern they raised was that the TOEFL item writers had found it difficult to select nouns as syntagmatic associates that were indisputably the correct responses, which would have been a problem in producing multiple forms of the test. However, in the end the DVK format did not fit the design of the new internet-based TOEFL and was not put to operational use.

Extending the format: French learners in the Netherlands

A number of researchers in the Netherlands have adapted the word associates format for their purposes and have explored several variations in the basic design. In particular, Tine Greidanus and her associates (Greïdanus and Nienhuis, 2001; Greidanus et al., 2004; Greidanus et al., 2005) saw the format as a potentially useful means of assessing the vocabulary knowledge of Dutch students who were advanced learners of French. Greidanus and Nienhuis (2001) considered it more appropriate for such learners to write word associates items in which the distractors as well as the associates were semantically related to the target word. They selected a sample of 50 words from the most frequent 5,000 words in French and wrote pairs of items like this for *rive* (bank):

rive	*artificiel* (artificial)	*rive*	*bord* (edge)
	bord (edge)		*fleuve* (river)
	côté (side)		*gauche* (left)
	fleuve (river)		*paquet* (parcel)
	gauche (left)		*prudent* (careful)
	vague (wave)		*tombe* (tomb)

First, note that there are just three associates and three distractors for each item, so that each associate represents one of the three semantic relationships identified in my original study (Read, 1993): paradigmatic, syntagmatic and analytic. The three associates in both of these items are *bord*, *fleuve* and *gauche*; the difference is that the distractors in the item on the left are related in meaning to the target word to some degree, whereas the distractors in the item on the right are quite unrelated.

Preliminary versions of the two 50-item tests (each with half related and half unrelated items) were tried out with four university teachers of French, two of whom were native speakers. Items were modified when these judges did not select the intended associates. Clearly the use of semantically related distractors increases the likelihood of debate over whether the associates are really more acceptable responses than the distractors. The revised tests were taken by 54 undergraduate students at two universities in Amsterdam. Collectively the items with semantically unrelated distractors were significantly easier than those with related distractors, as might be expected. The researchers also calculated separate scores for the syntagmatic and paradigmatic associates and found the means for the paradigmatic associates were always significantly higher than those for the syntagmatic ones. This finding, which was confirmed by Greidanus *et al.* (2005), contrasted with Qian and Schedl's (2004) study, where the means for the two types of associate were virtually the same.

In a follow-up study, Greidanus *et al.* (2004) introduced a new variable: a differing number of associates in the items. They initially prepared test items for 65 French words, 22 with two associates, 34 with three associates and nine with four associates. In order to ensure that they considered each of the six words in an item, the test-takers were required to explicitly accept or reject each word as an associate, and their total score included both the number of associates and the number of distractors correctly identified. Another innovation was to include students who were native speakers of French in the trialling. The test was piloted twice and after each pilot the researchers applied item analysis statistics to the responses of the French-speaking students as the basis for revising or discarding items containing associates that were not selected frequently enough or distractors that proved too attractive. In both trials the mean scores showed a consistent pattern of variation according to the frequency level of the words (from first 1,000 to fifth 1,000) and the proficiency level of the students (e.g. third to second to first-year Dutch university students).

The third study (Greidanus *et al.*, 2005) built on the earlier ones in various ways. The items assessed less common vocabulary, in the fifth 1,000 to tenth 1,000 range of French words, and the participants included not only French and Dutch students but also British students studying French at the University of Edinburgh. Once again, the distractors were semantically related to the target words. As the authors acknowledged, it was 'not easy to find distractors semantically related to each possible stimulus word because these distractors risk being too "attractive" to the participants who may consider them associate words too easily' (Greidanus *et al.*, 2005: 224). Thus, they piloted a preliminary version of the test with five university teachers of French and three university students, and found that they needed to replace a number of distractors with less appealing alternatives. A total of 18 items had to be modified.

In the third study, the researchers wanted to investigate the effects of having a variable number of associates from another angle. The actual test consisted of 50 items with three associates and three distractors, but it was presented to the test-takers in two 60-item versions. Test A had 10 filler items added, also with three associates and distractors, whereas in Test B the additional 10 items had a variable number of associates. The instructions for the test version stated that the number of associates in each item was fixed and variable respectively. The results showed that there was no significant difference between the two versions, except for the most proficient group of native speakers (third-year linguistics students in France). The authors were a little puzzled by this result because they had hypothesized that Version A would be easier, since it could encourage guessing by making it easier to identify associates by a process of elimination. It suggests that test-takers take each item on its merits and mostly do not adopt the kind of strategic approach to responding that the researchers expected.

Adapting the format for Dutch children

Two other Dutch researchers, Schoonen and Verhallen (2008), have applied the word associates format in a rather different educational context. Their interest has been in assessing the deep word knowledge of primary school children in the Netherlands. In an earlier study (Verhallen and Schoonen, 1993), they used an elaborate interview procedure to demonstrate that children with Dutch as a first language not only had larger vocabularies but also richer semantic concepts associated with individual words than children for whom Dutch was a second language. However, the interview procedure was time-consuming and they wanted to find a more practical alternative. They adapted Read's (1993) word associates format, first by reducing the number of associates and distractors from eight to six and then presenting them visually as a 'word web', as in the example in Figure 21.1.

The target word 'banana' is at the centre and the test-takers' task is to draw lines from there to the three associates, as shown in the figure. Note that, like Greidanus and her colleagues, Schoonen and Verhallen decided that the distractors should also be semantically related to the target word. They argue that depth of knowledge should be conceived as the ability to define words in the decontextualized manner that is important for school learning. Thus, the associates represent the core meaning of the word, whereas the distractors are related to it in a more context-specific way. It is true that bananas are 'nice' to eat, for humans and for 'monkeys', and circus clowns tend to 'slip' on banana skins, but the associates 'fruit' (paradigmatic), 'peel' (syntagmatic) and 'yellow' (analytic) are more basic elements of the meaning. The children had

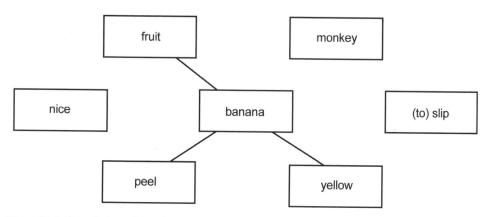

Figure 21.1 Sample item from the WAT for Dutch children
Source: Schoonen and Verhallen, 2008: 219

to mark all three associates correctly in order to be given one point for the item; there was no partial-credit scoring.

The researchers wrote an experimental test comprising 27 items and conducted a pilot study with 133 children in Grades 3 and 5. In order to introduce the test to the children, the test administrator worked through two practice items with each child on a blackboard to discuss the kind of relationships they should look for and to prompt the child to draw the lines. In addition to analysing the responses, the researchers recorded children 'thinking aloud' as they worked through the test items, to gain a better understanding of the strategies the children were following in selecting their responses. Some items were revised and more were added to make a total of 50, which were divided into two test forms of 25 items each because of a concern that a 50-item test might be too long for nine-year-old children, the youngest participants in the study. The full study involved 822 nine- and 11-year-old students in 19 primary schools in the Netherlands, who took the test in class groups in school after receiving standardized instructions from a test assistant.

More research on the design features

More recently, Schmitt *et al.* (2011) have gone back to the Read (1998) format, using adjectives as target words, and they conducted two pilot studies which represent the most comprehensive investigation of design features of the word associates format to date. In Study 1 they wrote their own 40-item test of adjectives from the Academic Word List. After taking the whole test, the participants, who were 18 EAP students in Japan, were interviewed to elicit an independent measure of their knowledge of 10 of the target words. The results provided support for Read's (1993) original concerns about the validity of item scores as measures of knowledge of the target words. On the one hand, test-takers with scores of 0 or 1 were shown to have little if any knowledge of the word in the interview and those who scored 4 generally had good knowledge. However, item scores of 2 or 3 could indicate anything from no understanding to good knowledge of the target word. Overall, in nearly half of the cases, the test appeared to be overestimating the learners' knowledge of the target words. In addition, the researchers recorded think-aloud protocols as the test-takers worked through ten further items. From their analysis of the strategies that the learners adopted, they concluded that a score of 3 or 4 was a good indicator that the test-takers had at least partial knowledge of the target word meaning; otherwise, they were more likely to be making guesses based on knowledge of word parts, loose semantic associations or connections among the associates and distractors.

The second study by Schmitt *et al.* (2011) used another set of academic English adjectives as target words. The participants, 28 international students at the University of Nottingham, took 20 word associates items as a pen-and-paper test and worked through another 14 items in an interview, which broadly confirmed the findings in Study 1. The authors suggest that the format 'appears to be better at indicating what learners do know rather than what they do not know' (Schmitt *et al.*, 2011: 11). Test-takers who had no knowledge of the target word (according to what they revealed in the interview) tended to make inferences based first on what they knew about the meanings of the associates and distractors and then on the orthographic form of the words. Other variables in this study were as follows:

- Both six-option and eight-option items, which seemed to perform at a similar level.
- Three different scoring methods. The 'all-or-nothing' method used by Schoonen and Verhallen (2008) worked better for six-option items, whereas awarding one point for each associate correctly identified seemed preferable for eight-option items. The more complex method used by Greidanus *et al.* (2004) did not appear to be worth the extra effort involved in applying it.

- Three types of relationship between the target word and the distractors: unrelated, related in meaning, and related in form (e.g. 'special' and 'obvious' as distractors for 'spurious'). The form-based distractors did not perform satisfactorily at all. On the other hand, the semantically related distractors worked better with six-option items, and the unrelated distractors gave better results with the eight-option items.
- The distribution of the associates between the paradigmatic and syntagmatic types: 1–3, 2–2, or 3–1. The researchers found the 2–2 pattern produced the highest correlation between the word associates and interview results. They suggested that the 1–3 pattern was more susceptible to successful guessing because three nouns that could all collocate with a particular target adjective tended to be similar to each other in meaning.

Conclusion

Thus, the word associates test is a very interesting case of an apparently simple test format which turns out to raise multiple design issues and has generated a considerable amount of research involving three target languages (English, French and Dutch) and a variety of learners in several different settings. In some respects the various studies can be regarded as investigations of the validity of this kind of test rather than pilot studies in the conventional sense, but they are generally small-scale projects that address the same sort of questions – and adopt similar methods – to those that should be used in piloting new types of vocabulary test. One interesting point about all this work on the word associates format is that, to the best of my knowledge, none of the studies has yet led to the adoption of the format as a vocabulary measure in a large-scale operational test. Nevertheless, collectively the research provides very useful guidelines for any test designer considering the use of the format for an operational assessment purpose, although of course it does not obviate the need to pilot any such test in the educational context for which it is intended.

Let us review the procedures described above by summarizing the key elements involved in piloting vocabulary tests:

1 Test developers are faced with multiple decisions in determining the particular form that their test will take: the criteria for selecting the target words; the presentation format of the items; how many response options there will be; whether the distractors will be related in meaning or form to the target word; whether there will be the same number of associates for each item; and how the responses will be scored.
2 Once a draft set of items has been written, it is the normal practice to ask a number of native speakers or other proficient users of the target language – particularly language teachers – to work through the items, to see if they can readily identify the intended responses and spot any problems with the way the items have been written.
3 The next stage in piloting is to administer a revised version of the test to learners who are similar in educational background, target language proficiency and other respects to the intended population of test-takers. No single pilot study can address all the potential issues and so more than one is likely to be needed if the test is to be used for formal assessment purposes.
4 Since the test-takers will almost certainly have had no previous experience with the word associates format, it is essential to brief them thoroughly through written and oral instructions, so that they understand what kind of relationships they are looking for, and the adequacy of the briefing needs to be monitored as part of the pilot. There should also be some practice items for them to work through.

5   In addition to administering the pen-and-paper test on a group basis, it is desirable to ask some test-takers to provide individual verbal reports as they work through the items, in order to gain insights into their response behaviour.

6   A trial with a reasonable number of learners (at least 30, but the more the better) will generate the data required to estimate the reliability of the test and to apply item analysis statistics to the individual items.

7   Another helpful means of evaluating the pilot test results is to have some independent measure of the test-takers' knowledge of the target words, through giving a separate written test in a different format or by interviewing the learners individually.

Steps 4 and 5 are not so necessary with more standard test items, such as the multiple-choice and gap-filling types, but the other steps can be applied to any kind of vocabulary testing. The higher the stakes involved in the assessment for the test-takers, the more important it is to ensure that the test material is adequately piloted before it is used for decision-making purposes. However, even in the lower stakes environment of the language classroom, teachers can engage in a form of serial piloting by treating the first administration of a test that they give to their students as a pilot, which provides the basis for revising and improving the test progressively as it is used with subsequent groups of students.

Future developments

The basic procedures just outlined for piloting vocabulary tests are unlikely to change a great deal in the foreseeable future, but the tests themselves and the contexts in which they are used will be influenced by a number of developing trends. The first is the increasing use of computers to administer language tests. The item types that are typically chosen for vocabulary tests lend themselves well to computer delivery, which allows for rapid scoring and analysis of the test-takers' responses. In addition, the computer can be programmed to record data which is useful at the piloting stage, such as test-taker keystrokes, changes made to responses, and the time taken to respond to particular items or the test as a whole.

The precise measurement of reaction time may play a role in another emerging area: diagnostic language assessment. Diagnosis is receiving fresh attention as a purpose for language assessment (see, e.g., Alderson, 2005; Jang, this volume) and, although various approaches are being explored, it is likely that measures of vocabulary and grammar knowledge will play a significant part in identifying areas of weakness needing attention by learners and their teachers. Traditionally test-takers have been assessed on their ability to recognise and supply the correct language forms without time pressure, but from a diagnostic perspective learners' speed of access to their lexical knowledge is also important for fluency in all four skills. Thus, language testers developing diagnostic measures of this kind will need to draw on the expertise of psycholinguists, for whom reaction time has long been a basic measurement tool. This in turn will make new demands on the piloting of such tests, to ensure that the timing measures can be meaningfully interpreted without being contaminated by extraneous variables.

A third trend in vocabulary studies is the increasing interest in collocations and other kinds of multi-word lexical items. Since there has been little systematic work on how such lexical units should be assessed, it is not clear whether new forms of piloting will be required to accommodate this development. Until now researchers investigating learners' collocational knowledge have mostly employed conventional test formats, such as gap-filling and various selected-response tasks (Barfield and Gyllstad, 2009: Part III). Some types of multi-word lexical items can be assessed in the same way as single words, but others will require contextualized test formats which go beyond the scope of this chapter.

Further reading

Milton, J. (2009). *Measuring Second Language Vocabulary Acquisition*. Bristol, UK: Multilingual Matters. Milton has written an up-to-date review of issues in the development of suitable measures to assess various aspects of the vocabulary knowledge of foreign language learners. He discusses work conducted in numerous countries, including Greece, Hungary, the United Arab Emirates and Japan, as well as the UK. In particular, he draws extensively on his own vocabulary research and that of his colleagues and the doctoral students at Swansea University, which has emerged as a major international centre for L2 vocabulary studies under the leadership of Paul Meara.

Read, J. (2000). *Assessing Vocabulary*. Cambridge, UK: Cambridge University Press. This volume in the authoritative Cambridge Language Assessment series was the first book-length treatment of second language vocabulary testing. It reviews relevant theory and research in language testing and second language acquisition; discusses the validity of four influential vocabulary tests; and offers practical advice on the issues involved in designing and scoring vocabulary measures for a variety of purposes. It is an essential reference for anyone who wishes to develop vocabulary tests that meet the standards of contemporary language testing theory.

Schmitt, N. (2010). *Researching Vocabulary: A Vocabulary Research Manual*. Basingstoke, UK: Palgrave Macmillan. This book offers a comprehensive guide to research on vocabulary learning. It discusses both the substantive research questions to be investigated and the methodological issues that arise in designing good studies. There is a substantial section on measuring vocabulary knowledge which includes a critical review of many published vocabulary tests and guidance on how to develop new tests for various purposes. The author also outlines 10 vocabulary research projects that new researchers could usefully undertake.

References

Alderson, J. C. (2005). *Diagnosing Foreign Language Proficiency*. London, UK: Continuum.

Alderson, J. C., Clapham, C. and Wall, D. (1995). *Language Test Construction and Evaluation*. Cambridge, UK: Cambridge University Press.

Bachman, L. F. and Palmer, A. S. (1996). *Language Testing in Practice*. Oxford, UK: Oxford University Press.

Barfield, A. and Gyllstad, H. (eds), (2009). *Researching Collocations in another Language: multiple interpretations*. Basingstoke, UK: Palgrave Macmillan.

Clark, J. L. D. (1972). *Foreign Language Testing: theory and practice*. Philadelphia, PA: Center for Curriculum Development.

Davies, A., Brown, A., Elder, C., Hill, K., Lumley, T. and McNamara, T. (1999). *A Dictionary of Language Testing*. Cambridge, UK: Cambridge University Press.

Deese, J. (1965). *The Structure of Associations in Language and Thought*. Baltimore, MD: Johns Hopkins Press.

Fulcher, G. and Davidson, F. (2007). *Language Testing and Assessment: an advanced resource book*. London, UK: Routledge.

Greidanus, T., Beks, B. and Wakely, R. (2005). Testing the Development of French Word Knowledge by Advanced Dutch and English-speaking Learners and Native Speakers. *The Modern Language Journal* 89: 221–33.

Greidanus, T., Bogaards, P., Van der Linden, E., Nienhuis, L. and Wolf, T. (2004). The construction and validation of a deep word knowledge test for advanced learners of French. In P. Bogaards and B. Laufer (eds), *Vocabulary in a Second Language: selection, acquisition, and testing*. Amsterdam, The Netherlands: John Benjamins.

Greidanus, T. and Nienhuis, L. (2001). Testing the quality of word knowledge in a second language by means of word associations: types of distractors and types of associations. *The Modern Language Journal* 85: 567–77.

Heaton, J. B. (1988). *Writing English Language Tests*, 2nd edn. London, UK: Longman.

Hughes, A. (2003). *Testing for Language Teachers*, 2nd edn. Cambridge, UK: Cambridge University Press.

Lado, R. (1961). *Language Testing*, London, UK: Longman.

Meara, P. (2009). *Connected Words: word associations and second language vocabulary acquisition*. Amsterdam, The Netherlands: John Benjamins.

Moussavi, S. A. (1999). *A Dictionary of Language Testing*, 2nd edn. Tehran, Iran: Rahnama Publications.

Nation, I. S. P. and Beglar, D. (2007). A vocabulary size test. *The Language Teacher* 31: 9–13.

Palermo, D. and Jenkins, J. (1964). *Word Association Norms*. Minneapolis, MN: University of Minnesota Press.

Qian, D. D. (1999). Assessing the roles of depth and breadth of vocabulary knowledge in reading comprehension. *Canadian Modern Language Review* 56: 282–308.

Qian, D.D. and Schedl, M. (2004). Evaluating an in-depth vocabulary knowledge measure for assessing reading performance. *Language Testing* 21: 28–52.

Read, J. (1993). The Development of a new measure of L2 vocabulary knowledge. *Language Testing* 10: 355–71.

—— (1998). Validating a test to measure depth of vocabulary knowledge. In A. Kunnan (ed.), *Validation in Language Assessment*. Mahwah, NJ: Lawrence Erlbaum.

—— (2000). *Assessing Vocabulary*. Cambridge, UK: Cambridge University Press.

Schmitt, N., Ng, J. W. C. and Garras, J. (2011). The word associates format: validation evidence. *Language Testing* 28: 105–126.

Schoonen, R. and Verhallen, M. (2008). The Assessment of Deep Word Knowledge in Young First and Second Language Learners. *Language Testing* 25: 211–36.

Spolsky, B. (1995). *Measured Words*. Oxford, UK: Oxford University Press.

Valette, R. M. (1977). *Modern Language Testing*, 2nd edn. New York, NY: Harcourt Brace Jovanovich.

Verhallen, M. and Schoonen, R. (1993). Word definitions of monolingual and bilingual children. *Applied Linguistics* 14: 344–65.

Wesche, M. and Paribakht, T. S. (1996). Assessing second language vocabulary knowledge: breadth vs. depth. *Canadian Modern Language Review* 53: 13–39.

Xue, G. and Nation, I. S. P. (1984). A university word list. *Language Learning and Communication* 3: 215–29.

Part VII
Measurement theory and practice

22

Classical test theory

James Dean Brown

Introduction/definitions

Classical test theory (CTT) was first developed and predominated in measurement circles during the early to middle twentieth century and is "a measurement theory which consists of a set of assumptions about the relationships between actual or observed test scores and the factors that affect these scores, which are generally referred to as error" (Association of Language Testers in Europe, 1998: 138). "At the heart of CTT is the assertion that an observed score is determined by the actual state of the unobservable variable of interest plus error contributed by all other influences on the observable variable. The actual state of the unobserved variable is its hypothetical true score" (DeVellis, 2006: S50). Clearly, the notions of error and true scores are central to CTT and therefore to all else that follows in this chapter.

The recognition that all measurement contains errors can be traced back at least as far as Spearman (1904: 76), who observed that individuals created "accidental deviations" in any measurement which become "variable errors" for groups of individuals. Put in the parlance of CTT, *observed scores* (i.e., the examinees' actual scores on a test) contain *errors* (unsystematic effects due to factors not being measured), which in turn contribute to *error variance* (unsystematic variation in the scores that is due solely to random errors). Such error variance is taken to be random because it can arise from a variety of extraneous, non-systematic sources, which typically have nothing to do with the purposes for which the test was designed, for example, sources of error arise in the environment (e.g., noise, heat, lighting, etc.), administration procedures (e.g., directions, equipment, timing, etc.), scoring procedures (subjectivity, math errors, scorer biases, etc.), test items (e.g., item types, item quality, test security, etc.), the examinees themselves (e.g., health, fatigue, motivation, etc.), and so forth (Brown, 2005: 171–75).

Unless the scores on a particular test are completely random (i.e., 100% error), some proportion of the observed score variance that results from the test will be attributable to the construct that the test was designed to measure. *True scores* are hypothetical representations of the scores that would result if there were no errors in measurement. Variation among examinees in their hypothetical true scores is called *true score variance*. Logically, any set of observed scores will be made up of both true score variance and error variance. Let's represent these relationships as follows:

Total test variance = true score variance + error variance

$$Var_{Total} = Var_{True\ Score} + Var_{Error} \tag{1}$$

This notion that observed score variance is made up of true score variance plus error variance underlies the entire framework of CTT.

Historical perspective

There are two historical perspectives through which to view CTT: the history of testing in education and psychology, and the history of language testing.

The history of CTT in education and psychology

By the beginning of the twentieth century, Pearson (1896) had shown that the best value for the correlation coefficient was the covariance of the two sets of numbers divided by the product of the standard deviations for those two sets of numbers. In addition, scientists had widely accepted the notion that errors occurred in measurement. Thus the stage was set for the beginnings of CTT, the development of which can be traced through a number of landmarks. In 1904, Spearman formulated the correction for attenuation using reliability estimates for the first time. Spearman (1910) and Brown (1910) showed how to calculate what is commonly called split-half reliability adjusted by the Spearman–Brown prophecy formula from a single set of test items. Kuder and Richardson (1937) critiqued existing methods of reliability estimation (split-half, and test–retest) and derived the K-R20 and K-R21 formulas. Later, Guttman (1945) showed that reliability estimates from one administration of a test are *lower bounds* estimates (i.e., underestimates) of the actual correlation between observed and true scores. All of these CTT trends and others discussed below are best summarized in Lord and Novick (1968).

The history of CTT in language testing

Based on Spolsky (1978) and Hinofotis (1981), Brown (2005) briefly traces the history of language testing through three central movements: psychometric/structuralist testing, integrative testing, and communicative testing. Classical test theory (as exemplified by Lado, 1961) dominated all three of those movements, but has been overshadowed during the last 30 years or so among expert language testers by additional theories and techniques, especially criterion-referenced testing (CRT), generalizability theory (G theory), and item–response theory (IRT). Indeed, the label *classical theory* surfaced and became necessary only in the presence of these alternative theories. From the perspective of the expert language testers doing research using CRT, G theory, and IRT, *classical* is sometimes used pejoratively to mean *old fashioned*, which of course is really not the case given the rarity of genuine instances of use of CRT, G theory, and IRT in operational testing situations in language programs around the world. Indeed, outside of the major test development institutions (e.g., Educational Testing Service, University of Cambridge Local Examinations Syndicate, the Society for Testing English Proficiency, etc.) and the language testing professional organizations (e.g., the International Language Testing Association, the European Association for Language Testing and Assessment, etc.), classical testing theory is probably the dominant psychometric theory actually applied to the problems of language testing in real-world language teaching situations.

Critical issues and topics

Other crucial notions in the development of CTT include the concepts of strictly parallel items and item variance, as well as parallel tests. Let's consider each of these in turn before combining them with the ideas of true score variance and error variance discussed above. The phrase *strictly parallel items* describes a set of conditions that were necessary to logically derive CTT procedures for estimating the reliability and standard error of measurement for a test. Thus this notion underlies much of CTT. The conditions or assumptions of strictly parallel items are that they must

1. be related to some true score (i.e., be unidimensional)
2. be independent of all other items in terms of error
3. be independent of true scores in terms of error
4. have equal variances
5. be equally good indicators of true scores.

As a matter of practice, in piloting and revising language tests under CTT, all items are designed to test a single construct equally well (thus, test developers are striving to meet Assumptions 1 and 5). Furthermore, test development and administration procedures are used that minimize the degree to which items' errors might be correlated to each other and to true scores (thus addressing Assumptions 2 and 3). Then, by selecting those items for the final version of a test that are most highly correlated with the total scores (and therefore probably most highly correlated with true scores) and within a desired range of item facility (e.g., from 0.30 to 0.70), the test developer maximizes the degree to which items discriminate well, the degree to which they discriminate similarly, the degree to which they produce equal variances (Assumption 4), and the degree to which they are equally good indicators of true scores (Assumption 5).

Another concept is important to any discussion of CTT: *item variance* is the standard deviation squared of the item responses. In the special case where items are scored right/wrong and coded 1 for correct and 0 for incorrect, the item variance for each item can be calculated by simply multiplying the proportion of correct answers (symbolized by p) times the number of incorrect answers (symbolized by q, which is equal to $1 - p$). Thus item variance $= p \times q = p(1 - p)$ for each item. For example, a difficult item with $p = 0.20$ would mean that only 20% of the examinees answered correctly; the proportion of incorrect answers would be $q = (1 - p) = (1 - 0.20) = 0.80$; and the item variance for that item would be $p \times q = 0.20 \times 0.80 = 0.1600$.

The idea of *parallel tests* describes the tests that will result if sets of strictly parallel items are repeatedly developed (to measure a construct) and compiled into tests (with equal numbers of items). Any two such tests can theoretically be said to be parallel tests. More importantly from a CTT point of view, the average of each examinee's score on an infinite number of such tests, at least theoretically, would provide that examinee's true score.

Once this theoretical idea of examinee true scores is accepted, it is a small step to argue that a correlation coefficient calculated between the observed scores on a single operational test and the true scores for that construct or domain (i.e., the average scores across an infinite number of parallel tests) would indicate the proportions of the total variance in observed scores that are related to true score variance and error variance. Under CTT, it is assumed that total variance (Var_{Total}) is the sum of true score variance ($Var_{True\ Score}$) plus error variance (Var_{Error}) and, therefore, that the variance that is not accounted for as true score variance must be error variance. Since true scores have no error variance, this error variance must be associated with the operational test. In CTT, reliability can be defined in terms of true score variance and error variance as follows:

$$reliability = \frac{Var_{True \atop Score}}{Var_{True \atop Score} + Var_{Error}} = \frac{Var_{True \atop Score}}{Var_{Total}} \qquad (2)$$

Thus reliability is the true score variance on a test divided by the total variance on that test (which consists of true score variance plus error variance).

Current contributions and use

Often when language testers (especially young ones) talk or write about CTT, they refer to it as though it is a thing of the past. I would argue that CTT is alive and well.

First, many (even most) people who take any university courses in language testing are trained primarily in CTT. Brown and Bailey (2008) show that the vast majority of topics (and probably course hours) is spent on topics that are within the general area of CTT.

Second, a number of textbooks are available to help language teachers and administrators do language testing. For example, the four most commonly used textbooks written for MA level SLS teacher training programs (according respondents in Brown and Bailey, 2008) appear to be: Bachman and Palmer (1996); Brown (2005); Alderson *et al.* (1995); and Hughes (2002). Brown (2005) covers both norm-referenced and criterion-referenced analyses. It is therefore at least 50% based on CTT. The other three books, insofar as they cover statistical testing theory, do so from the CTT perspective.

Third, perhaps because of the first and second points above, most language teachers and administrators doing proficiency or placement testing in their programs are doing it on the basis of their training in CTT during MA or PhD programs (again, see Brown and Bailey, 2008).

Fourth, while expert language testers seem to naturally take an interest in CRT, G theory, IRT, and so forth, understanding CTT is clearly a prerequisite for comprehending and using any of the more exotic forms of analysis. Indeed, articles reporting research based on the above forms of analysis sometimes start by contrasting the newer analyses with CTT, or by explaining the newer concepts with reference to CTT concepts (e.g., Brown and Ross, 1996; Henning, 1984).

CTT, then, appears to be alive and well because it continues to contribute to the actual operational testing in language programs and because it serves as the basis for understanding all aspects of language testing.

Main research methods

The main research methods used in CTT include at least item analysis (item facility, item discrimination, and distractor efficiency analysis), reliability estimates, the standard error of measurement, and various validity analyses (including criterion-related, content, and construct validity strategies). This section will end by stressing the importance of calculating descriptive statistics and attending to the distributions they describe when interpreting any other testing statistics.

Item analyses

Item facility (also known as *IF, item difficulty, item easiness,* or *p* for proportion correct) is usually expressed as the proportion, or percentage, of examinees who answered a particular item correctly. If 95% of the examinees answer an item correctly, that item is viewed as very easy. If only 11% of the examinees answer an item correctly, the item is considered very difficult. Ideal items in CTT (which is essentially norm-referenced in focus) would be items of intermediate facility, that is, items between 0.30 and 0.70 in facility, or put another way, items that 30–70% of the examinees answered correctly. In addition to the fact that testers do not want to wastefully require examinees to breeze through items that are too easy or suffer through items that are too difficult for them, items with difficulties within the range of 0.30 to 0.70 generally discriminate better than items outside that range.

Item discrimination (also called *ID*, *item–total correlations*, *point–biserial correlation coefficients*, *d-value*, or simply r_{pbi}) indicate in one way or another the degree to which the examinee performances on a given item are related to their performances on the test as a whole. Given that the sum of the information provided by all the items on a test is assumed to be more reliable than the information on any single item, examining the *ID* in a form such as item-total correlations indicates the degree to which each item is testing what the more reliable total score is testing. For instance, a point-biserial correlation coefficient (r_{pbi}) of 0.26 would indicate that the particular item in question was not very highly correlated with the total test scores, that is, this item is not very highly related to whatever the ensemble of items is testing. In contrast, an r_{pbi} of 0.87 would indicate that the item is doing very much what the rest of the test is doing. Put another way item discrimination indicates the degree to which an item is spreading the examinees out similarly to the way the total scores spread out the examinees. Thus items with high item discrimination indexes are viewed from the classical theory perspective as desirable to include in revised versions of a test. Including items with high discrimination indexes in a revised version of a test will lead to more reliable measurement overall, whereas including items with low discrimination will lead to less reliable measurement.

One simple and quick way to estimate item discrimination (*ID*) is by calculating the *Item facility (IF)* for the top scoring group of examinees (e.g., the top 30% of examinees based on their total scores), also calculating the *IF* for the bottom scoring group of examinees (e.g., the bottom 30% of examinees based on their total scores), and then subtracting the *IF* for the top group minus the *IF* for the bottom group as follows: $ID = IF_{top} - IF_{bottom}$. For example, if 90% of the top group answered an item correctly, but only 20% of the bottom group did so, the *ID* would be as follows: $ID = IF_{top} - IF_{bottom} = 0.90 - 0.20 = 0.70$. Such an item seems to discriminate well between the high scoring and low scoring examinees.

Distractor efficiency analysis (also known as "*distractor analysis*") is used to investigate the degree to which the internal parts of items are working well. This form of analysis is most commonly used with multiple-choice items, so any discussion of this topic will necessarily involve related terminology like *item stem* (the stimulus part of the item at the top), the *options* (the alternative choices presented to the examinee), the *correct answer or choice* (the option that will be scored as correct), and the *distractors* (the options that will be counted as incorrect). The incorrect options are called distractors because they are meant to divert, or pull the students away, from the correct answer if they do not know which is correct. The primary goal of distractor efficiency analysis, then, is to investigate the degree to which the distractors are attracting students who do not know which answer is correct. To do this for a given item, the percentages of students who choose each option are analyzed. If this analysis can also compare the percentages choosing each option in the upper, middle, and lower groups, the analysis will be even more useful. In any case, the goal is to investigate the degree to which the distractors are functioning efficiently.

After dividing the examinees on a test into high, middle, and low thirds based on their total scores, a sound item in CTT would be one where most (e.g. 100%) of the high group select the correct answer, about 50% of the middle group, and little or none of the lower group. However, distractor efficiency analysis focuses on how well the other options, the distractors, are doing their jobs. For example, the distractors can only be said to be working efficiently if they are all drawing at least some examinees away from guessing the correct answer without knowing it. Thus a distractor that nobody selects is contributing nothing to the functioning of the item because it is not attractive enough; in contrast a distractor that many high group students are selecting may indicate that the distractor is too attractive, or indeed that the answer key is wrong, or even that there are two possible answers; and so forth. Common sense examination of the percentages of students selecting each option can lead the test developer to revise and improve the internal functioning of individual items.

Reliability estimates

Recall the CTT argument above that test score reliability is the true score variance divided by the total variance (which, remember, consists of true score variance plus error variance). Clearly, it is impossible to develop and administer an infinite number of parallel tests and determine the examinees' actual true scores. Fortunately, CTT provides a number of short cuts, one of which involves calculating the correlation coefficient between two sets of observed scores on two parallel tests. Then, because these tests both contribute error variance to the correlation coefficient, we know that the resulting correlation coefficient will be lower (i.e., an underestimate) than the correlation coefficients between either of those operational tests and the true scores (which, after all, have no error variance). We therefore interpret the correlation coefficient between the two operational parallel tests as an underestimate of the proportion of true score variance in either of the tests. This set of procedures is sometimes called *equivalent forms reliability estimation*, which gives us an idea of the consistency of results across parallel test forms (where true scores are theoretically based on an infinite number of parallel tests).

Similar procedures used to analyze the correlation between two administrations of the same test (say, two weeks apart) are called *test–retest reliability estimation*, which gives us information about the stability of the same test over time (where true scores are theoretically based on an infinite number of administrations of the same test). In reality, even these CTT short cut methods of estimating test reliability (across forms or across administrations) are so cumbersome (requiring two tests in the one case and two test administrations in both cases) that they are rarely used in practice.

Hence, easier short-cut methods for calculating CTT reliability were developed. One such method has the unwieldy moniker of *split-half reliability (adjusted by the Spearman-Brown prophecy formula)*. Split-half reliability, as it is sometimes known, artificially creates two forms of a test from a single test. Typically, the two forms are created by scoring the odd and even numbered items separately. Then the correlation coefficient between the half-test scores for the even-numbered items and those for the odd-numbered items is calculated. The resulting correlation coefficient provides an estimate of the half-test reliability, that is, the reliability of the even-numbered items or the odd-numbered items, but not both combined. The full-test reliability will logically be higher than the half-test reliability because more observations are typically more reliable then fewer observations. Hence the half-test correlation coefficient must be adjusted using the Spearman–Brown prophecy formula for a test of double the half-test length. One formula for this adjustment is as follows: S–B prophecy $= (2 \times r_{half\text{-}test})/(1 + r_{half\text{-}test})$. For example, if the half-test correlation ($r_{half\text{-}test}$) turned out to be 0.50, the S–B prophecy adjustment would be $(2 \times r_{half\text{-}test})/(1 + r_{half\text{-}test}) = (2 \times 0.50)/(1 + 0.50) = 1.00/1.50 = 0.67$. Thus the split-half reliability adjusted for full-test reliability would be 0.67.

Other internal consistency estimates have been developed within CTT that are even easier to calculate. These include at least Kuder-Richardson (K-R) formulas 20 and 21, and Cronbach alpha.

K-R21 is perhaps the simplest to calculate because it requires only that the tester know the number of items on the test (k), the mean (M), and standard deviation (S) of the scores as follows:

$$K\text{-}R21 = \frac{k}{k-1}(1 - \frac{M(k-M)}{kS^2}) \tag{3}$$

However, K-R21 assumes that the items on the test have been scored right or wrong and that they are all of equal facility. If those assumptions are tenable, K-R21 gives a reasonable estimate of reliability. For a test with 30 items, with a mean (M) of 15, and a standard deviation (S) of 8, K-R21 would be calculated as follows:

$$K - R20 = \frac{k}{k-1}(1 - \frac{M(k-M)}{kS^2}) = \frac{30}{30-1}(1 - \frac{15(30-15)}{30(8^2)}) = 1.034(1 - \frac{225}{1920})$$
$$= 1.034(1 - .117) = 0.913 \approx 0.91$$

$$\tag{4}$$

K-R20 is a bit more difficult to calculate by hand (though it is fairly straightforward to calculate using a Microsoft Excel spreadsheet on a computer) because it requires that the tester know not only the number of items on the test (k) and standard deviation of the test scores (S_t), but also the p and q values for all items (i.e., where p = item facility, or the proportion of examinees who answered correctly, and $q = 1 - p$, or the proportion of examinees who answered incorrectly). For example, an item that 40% of the examinees answered correctly would have $p = 0.40$ and q would $= 1 - p = 1 - 0.40 = 0.60$. Based on the above definitions of the symbols in the formula, K-R20 is calculated as follows:

$$K - R20 = \frac{k}{k-1}(1 - \frac{\Sigma pq}{S_t^2}) \tag{5}$$

The only tedious part of this equation is the Σpq in the numerator on the right side. To calculate Σpq, the tester needs to multiply p times q for each item (e.g., for the example item in the previous paragraph, $pq = 0.40 \times .60 = 0.2400 \approx 0.24$ and then sum up the pq values for all the items on the test). K-R20 assumes that the items on the test have been scored dichotomously (right or wrong). If that assumption is tenable, K-R20 provides a good estimate of reliability. For a test with 30 items, with $\Sigma pq = 7.5$, and with a standard deviation of 8, K-R20 would be calculated as follows:

$$K - R20 = \frac{k}{k-1}(1 - \frac{\Sigma pq}{S_t^2}) = \frac{30}{30-1}(1 - \frac{7.5}{64}) = 1.034(1 - 0.117) = 0.913 \approx 0.91$$

$$\tag{6}$$

Cronbach suggested another more flexible formula (i.e., one that is not restricted to dichotomously scored tests and can therefore be used with weighted items), which is called alpha (α). Cronbach α requires that the tester know not only the number of items on the test (k) and standard deviation of the test scores (S_t), but also the item variances for each individual item (S_i^2) (i.e., the standard deviation squared for each item; these values can be calculated fairly simply in Excel spreadsheet using the = VARP(range) function). With those quantities in hand (and summing up the S_i^2 values for all the items), for a test with 30 items, with $\Sigma S_i^2 = 7.5$, and with a standard deviation of 8, calculating Cronbach α is accomplished as follows:

$$\alpha = \frac{k}{k-1}\left(1 - \frac{\Sigma S_i^{\,2}}{S_i^{\,2}}\right) = \frac{30}{30-1}\left(1 - \frac{7.5}{64}\right) = 1.034(1 - 0.177) = 0.913 \approx 0.91 \tag{7}$$

On a test with items that are all scored dichotomously, the results for K-R20 and Cronbach α will be the same.

Interpreting CTT reliability estimates is straightforward because reliability estimates indicate the proportion of observed score variance on a test that is true score variance. For example, if Cronbach alpha turns out to be 0.91, that means that 91% of the total variance is true score variance and by extension 9% is error variance (i.e., $1.00 - 0.91 = 0.09$). Expanding on the CTT conception of reliability discussed above, the relationships between true score and error variance would be as follows:

$$reliability = \frac{Var_{True\;Score}}{Var_{True\;Score} + Var_{Error}} = \frac{0.91}{0.91 + 0.09} = \frac{0.91}{1.00} = 0.91 \tag{8}$$

Since reliability is often defined as the degree to which a set of test scores measure consistently, we sometimes interpret CTT reliability estimates as indicating the proportion of observed score variance that is consistent. In addition, because all of the reliability estimates described above are viewed as underestimates, none of them should overestimate the actual state of reliability in the test scores involved—as long as the assumptions are tenable.

Remember that CTT reliability estimates are calculated from the scores of a particular group of examinees taking a particular set of items. Hence, any reliability estimate is linked to that particular group and that specific set of items. Put another way, we can only make claims about the reliability of a test with reference to that particular group of examinees and that set of items. In practice, testers often cautiously make claims about the probable level of reliability if the test were administered to a *very similar* group of examinees with about the same characteristics and range of abilities.

The standard error of measurement

Reliability estimates like those described above are one useful CTT strategy for investigating test consistency. Such estimates can be used to express the reliability of a set of test scores in percentage terms, which is useful when we are arguing for the quality of a test (i.e., trying to sell it to a group of stakeholders in one way or another). However, a more concrete strategy for looking at the consistency of a set of test scores, especially when making decisions about who should pass or fail, is called the *standard error of measurement* (SEM), not to be confused with the SEM for structural equation modeling). The SEM provides a concrete estimate in test score values of the amount of unreliable score variation in a set of scores. This statistic is calculated as follows (where S = the standard deviation of the test scores, and $r_{xx'}$ = reliability estimate):

$$SEM = S\sqrt{1 - r_{xx'}} \tag{9}$$

For a set of test scores with an $S = 6.00$ and $= 0.91$, the SEM would be as follows:

$$SEM = S\sqrt{1 - r_{xx'}} = 6.00\sqrt{1 - .91} = 6.00\sqrt{0.09} = 6.00 \times .30 = 1.80 \approx 2 \tag{10}$$

The *SEM* can be used to estimate the average error in score points across all the examinees who took the test. Using the *SEM*, we can estimate with certain probabilities how far examinees' scores are likely to vary by chance alone. We can predict that error alone can cause examinees' scores to vary within a band of plus or minus of one *SEM*, that is, about ± 2 points in the example above (rounded because these scores are only interpretable as whole numbers) with 68% accuracy (based on the expected percentages under the normal bell-shaped distribution of test scores). Thus for a particular examinee whose score is 65, the *SEM* of 2 means that her scores could vary by chance alone between 63 and 67 points (65 − 2 = 63; 65 + 2 = 67) 68% of the time if she were to take repeated administrations of the test. If we want to be even more confident in predicting where her score is likely to be on repeated administrations, we can go out two *SEMs* (2 + 2 = 4) and say that her scores could vary by chance alone between 61 to 69 (65 − 4 = 61; 65 + 4 = 69) with 95% confidence.

An *SEM* of only 2 points indicates that we can expect relatively small fluctuations in the examinees' scores if they take repeated administrations of the test, while an *SEM* of 15 points would indicate larger fluctuations. Generally, the narrower (or smaller) the *SEM*, the narrower the band of random fluctuations will be, or put another way, the smaller the *SEM*, the more consistently the scores will represent the examinees' true abilities. Some testers find *SEMs* to be easier to interpret than reliability estimates because they represent score bands rather than the more abstract percentage of true score or consistent variance interpretations typically applied to reliability estimates.

Validity analyses

Under CTT, validity is typically defined as the degree to which a test is measuring what it claims to measure. Three types of validity arguments are used in CTT: criterion-related validity, content validity, and construct validity.

Criterion-related validity arguments are built in two ways. First, the tester can administer a new test (e.g., English Proficiency Test X) and give the same group of test-takers a well respected test, or *criterion measure*, of the same construct (e.g., TOEFL iBT, see www.ets.org/toefl/ibt/about) and then calculate a correlation coefficient between the two measures. Doing so investigates the degree to which the new test is producing scores that are spread out very much like the scores on the criterion measure (this form of criterion-related validity is also known as *concurrent validity*). The second approach is to administer the new test (e.g., Academic Ability Test X) and gather subsequent post-test information about the criterion construct (e.g., academic ability as measured by grade point average of the examinees in the two years following the test administration) and then calculate a correlation coefficient between the two measures to investigate the degree to which the new test is producing scores that predict the variation in the academic ability construct as measured by grade point average (this form of criterion-related validity is also known as *predictive validity*).

Content validity arguments are built by asking content experts to judge, in one way or another, the degree to which the items measure the construct that the test designer is claiming the items assess. For example, a panel of experts in communicative language teaching might be assembled to judge each of the tasks on a communicative English proficiency test using a rating scale ranging from 5 (high degree of match to the construct) to 1 (no match) in each of three categories (authenticity of the language input, unpredictability of the language input, and amount of productive language required).

Construct validity arguments are built by setting up an experiment to investigate the degree to which the new test is measuring what it claims to measure. The experiment can take numerous forms: (a) a *differential groups study*, in which the test is administered to two groups (one group that is known to have relatively high levels of the construct and another group that is known to have relatively low levels of the construct) and the results are compared in terms of the degree to which the results for the group with the construct are superior to those for the group lacking the construct; (b) an *intervention study*, in which the test is administered as a pre-test and post-test to a group of examinees who are taught or otherwise led to acquire the construct to demonstrate that the scores increase after the examinees acquire the construct; (c) a *multi-trait multi-method study*, in which data from tests of different constructs (e.g., reading, listening, and writing) are gathered using three very different testing methods (e.g., multiple-choice, graded classroom assignments, and self-assessment) for a group of examinees so that the pattern of all possible correlation coefficients can be compared to see if correlations are higher among tests of the same *trait* (i.e., the same construct) as opposed to among tests using the same *method* (i.e., the same testing method); and (d) a *factor analysis study*, in which data from tests of different constructs (e.g., reading, listening, writing, and speaking) are gathered from different test batteries (for example, the TOEFL iBT (see www.ets. org/toefl/ibt/about) and *Eiken Grade 1* (see stepeiken.org/grade_1)) taken by the same examinees so that the results indicate whether a four factor solution (one for each construct) makes sense and, if so, whether the loadings for the subtests suggest that each of the four factors represents a different construct.

In the last three decades, studies of test validity have moved historically from the three pronged approach described here, to a unified theory of validity, and then further to the expanded set of validity responsibilities assigned to testers by the Messick model (e.g., Messick, 1989, 1996). Nonetheless, the strategies developed under CTT can still serve well as part of the evidential basis for validity (though not the consequential basis that Messick argued for).

Importance of descriptive statistics and normal distribution in CTT

It is important to recognize that calculating and examining the descriptive statistics (i.e., the mean, standard deviation, range, etc.) are crucial steps in interpreting all of the other testing statistics discussed in this chapter. The bottom line is that correlational statistics like item discrimination indexes, reliability estimates, as well as the numerous validity arguments that are dependent on correlation coefficients (i.e., both types of criterion-related validity, as well as construct validity based on multitrait-multimethod or factor analysis studies) are highly reliant on (indeed, they all assume) normal distribution of scores on whatever tests are involved. Thus, as with most statistical studies, it is crucial to present the descriptive statistics that underlie all the other more exotic statistics whenever those other statistics are to be interpreted, understood, or explained. Note that well-designed criterion-referenced tests that have been carefully developed to fit a particular curriculum may not, indeed most often should not, produce the normal distribution in their scores at the beginning or end of instruction. For this reason, separate statistical analyses outside of CTT have been developed for CRTs (see Brown, 2005; Brown and Hudson, 2002).

Recommendations for practice

Given the general bias in most fields for doing research and publishing in new, exotic areas of analysis, it seems likely that most important psychometric developments in language testing will take place within the frameworks of CRT, IRT, G theory, SEM, and Messick's expanded view of validity. Nonetheless, particularly at the local level in areas of proficiency and placement testing, where the target classes and examinees have fairly stable characteristics, CTT will probably continue to thrive. Testers working at that level should consider the advantages and disadvantages of CTT as a framework for developing their tests and decide for themselves if CTT will be adequate to their needs.

Advantages of CTT

There are numerous advantages to working within the CTT framework when doing test development. First, the concepts of CTT are widely taught and understood. Second, CTT concepts are relatively easy to learn, use, and explain. The very useful descriptive statistics (e.g., the mean, standard deviation, range, etc.) and item analysis statistics (especially item facility and item discrimination) can all be calculated fairly easily in spreadsheets or in widely available computer programs. Third, the CTT model fits many measurement needs, particularly for the development of proficiency and placement measures that can aid admissions, program comparisons, and placement decisions. Fourth, right or wrong, CTT accommodates and allows interpretation of examinee scores of 0% and 100% and item facility estimates of .00 and 1.00—results that do occur in the real world. Such examinee scores (aka, person ability estimates) and item difficulty estimates are generally considered misfitting in IRT models.

Disadvantages of CTT

However, working within CTT carries certain disadvantages as well. First, CTT tests tend to be long and necessarily have homogeneous items. Second, examinees taking tests developed through CTTs may have to slog through numerous items that are far too easy or too difficult for them as individuals. Third, the results on CTT tests only apply to the sample at hand, or very similar samples. Fourth, CTT results only apply to the current selection of items. Fifth, because of its dependence on the normal distribution, CTT is only useful for developing norm-referenced tests. Sixth, because of the correlational nature of item discrimination, reliability, and some validity estimates, CTT items and tests often end up being sensitive to differences between the extremes on the scale. Seventh, while in actuality the measurement errors on a test vary across the range of all possible scores on a CTT test (i.e., the *SEM* is larger at or near the mean and becomes increasingly smaller as scores get further from the mean in both directions), the standard error of measurement that is estimated in CTT is an *average* across that range.

Caveats

Given the disadvantages listed in the previous paragraph, testers using CTT should keep at least the following caveats in mind while using it:

1. Don't write tests that are too long (i.e., pilot and revise for shorter tests).
2. Don't forget to use item analysis to fit a given test as closely as possible to the range of abilities in the examinees being tested.
3. Don't continue to use a particular CTT test (without re-validating it) if the examinees' abilities are changing on average from semester to semester or year to year.
4. Don't assume that items in different forms of a test are the same because they look similar (be sure to pilot and equate test forms).
5. Don't use CTT for criterion-referenced purposes because CRTs are not designed to spread students out and are therefore not referenced to a normal distribution.
6. Don't interpret CTT item discrimination estimates, reliability estimates, and validity statistics as characteristics of the test itself, but rather as characteristics of that set of items when administered to the examinees in the particular distribution involved.
7. Don't assume that the standard error of measurement is the same at all points in the range of possible scores.

Future directions

The disadvantages of CTT listed above appear to be more numerous than the advantages. However, from the local perspective, the disadvantages may, in most cases, be more theoretical than real. For example, I have item analyzed tests using IRT (Rasch analysis to be specific) and CTT techniques and found little practical difference in the item-level test-development decisions that I would make based on the two models (see also Henning, 1984). All in all, I predict that CTT is sufficiently accurate, easy-to-learn, and practical to continue in use for years to come in real (especially local) testing situations.

I further believe that CTT item statistics and distractor efficiency analysis will continue to provide useful feedback to item writers and test developers about their items and their test specifications. In particular, I cannot imagine that distractor efficiency analysis will be replaced by the new forms of analysis. Indeed, some IRT software packages acknowledge this possibility by providing CTT item statistics and distractor efficiency analyses right along with their IRT difficulty, discrimination, and guessing parameter estimates (e.g., the *Xcalibre* software described at www.assess.com/xcart/product.php?productid=270).

Since CTT excels at showing test developers which items and/or tasks discriminate when they are administered to a given group of examinees, developers are tempted to focus only on and select only those items or tasks that fit the abilities of the particular population and spread them out into a nice, neat, normal distribution. After all, doing so often produces high reliability estimates for the resulting scores. However, in the interest of test validity, it has long been important to temper the use of item statistics by close analysis of item content and quality. In view of the increasing importance in recent years of validity concerns, I predict that item specifications will become progressively more important, especially in classroom and program level diagnostic, progress, and achievement testing. As a consequence, the roles of item/task content and item/task writers will rise in importance, and decisions will increasingly be informed by common sense aspects of CTT like item facility and distractor efficiency analysis in ways that will at least supplement the newer forms of analysis like IRT. Such trends may foster research and debate on the authority of item/task writers, especially in terms of the need for clear item specifications in all testing situations and the role of item/task writers in creating and judging the match of test items to test specifications, as well as the match of test specifications to construct definitions or curriculum content.

True, technology has opened up many new possibilities, some or all of which may lead some testers to abandon CTT in favor of IRT analyses. Holland and Hoskens (2003: 123) view "classical test theory as a very general version of IRT, and commonly used IRT models as detailed elaborations of CTT for special purposes," and it is these special purposes that naturally nudge language testers away from CTT toward IRT models. Such special purposes include but are not limited to the following: item banking, automated test construction, sample and test equating, and computer adaptive testing.

Regardless of all these special purposes and tendencies toward newer forms of analysis, it appears that CTT will live on as the basis for the training we give teachers and administrators to help them develop and understand local institutional (especially proficiency and placement) tests. As such, CTT will serve as the base knowledge needed by language testers who want to learn, understand, and use the other more specialized forms of analysis listed above. In that sense, CTT is the cake, and all else is the icing.

Further reading

Bachman, L. F. (2004). *Statistical Analyses for Language Assessment*. Cambridge: Cambridge University.
Further detailed descriptions and explanations of the statistical methods included in this chapter.

Brown, J. D. (2005). *Testing in Language Programs: a comprehensive guide to english language assessment* (new edition). New York, NY: McGraw-Hill.

Salsburg, D. (2001). *The Lady Tasting Tea: How Statistics Revolutionized Science in the Twentieth Century*. New York, NY: Henry Holt. A more general and very readable history of the development of statistical methods.

Traub, R. E. (1997). Classical test theory in historical perspective. *Educational Measurement Issues and Practice* 16: 8–14. An historical overview of CTT.

References

Alderson, C. J., Clapham, C. and Wall, D. (1995). *Language Test Construction and Evaluation*. Cambridge, UK: Cambridge University.

Association of Language Testers in Europe (1998). *Studies in Second Language Testing 6: Multilingual Glossary of Language Testing Terms*. Cambridge, UK: Cambridge University.

Bachman, L. F. and Palmer, A. S. (1996). *Language Testing in Practice: Designing and Developing Useful Language Tests*. Oxford, UK: Oxford University.

Brown, J. D. (2005). *Testing in Language Programs: a comprehensive guide to English language assessment* (new edition). New York, NY: McGraw-Hill.

Brown, J. D. and Bailey, K. M. (2008). Language testing courses: what are they in 2007. *Language Testing* 25, 3: 349–83.

Brown, J. D. and Hudson, T. (2002). *Criterion-referenced Language Testing*. Cambridge, UK: Cambridge University.

Brown, J. D. and Ross, J. A. (1996). Decision dependability of item types, sections, tests and the overall TOEFL test battery. In M. Milanovic and N. Saville (eds), *Performance Testing, Cognition and Assessment*. Cambridge, UK: Cambridge University.

Brown, W. (1910). Some experimental results in the correlation of mental abilities. *British Journal of Psychology* 3: 296–322.

DeVellis, R. F. (2006). Classical test theory. *Medical Care* 44: S50–S59.

Guttman, L. (1945). A basis for analyzing test-retest reliability. *Psychometrika* 10: 255–82.

Henning, G. (1984). Advantages of latent trait measurement in language testing. *Language Testing* 1: 123–33.

Hinofotis, F. B. (1981). Perspectives on language testing: past, present and future. *Nagoya Gakuin Daigaku Gaikokugo Kyoiku Kiyo* 4: 51–59.

Holland, P. W. and Hoskens, M. (2003). Classical test theory as a first-order item response theory: application to true-score prediction from a possibly nonparallel test. *Psychometrika* 68: 123–49.

Hughes, A. (2002). *Testing for Language Teachers* (revised). Cambridge, UK: Cambridge University.

Kuder, G. F. and Richardson, M. W. (1937). The theory of estimation of test reliability. *Psychometrika* 2: 152–260.

Lado, R. (1961). *Language Testing: the construction and use of foreign language tests*. New York, NY: McGraw-Hill.

Lord, F. M. and Novick, M. R. (1968). *Statistical Theories of Mental Test Scores*. Reading, MA: Addison-Wesley.

Messick, S. (1989). Meaning and values in test validation: the science and ethics of assessment. *Educational Researcher* 18: 5–11.

—— (1996). Validity and washback in language testing. *Language Testing* 13: 241–56.

Pearson, K. (1896). Mathematical contributions to the theory of evolution-III. Regression, heredity and panmixia. *Philosophical Transactions, A* 187: 252–318.

Spearman C. (1904). The proof and measurement of association between two things. *American Journal of Psychology* 15: 72–101.

—— (1910). Correlation calculated from faulty data. *British Journal of Psychology* 3: 171–95.

Spolsky, B. (1978). Introduction: linguists and language testers. In B. Spolsky (ed.), *Advances in Language Testing Series: 2*. Arlington, VA: Center for Applied Linguistics.

Item response theory

Gary J. Ockey

Introduction/definitions

Item response theory (IRT) is an approach used to estimate how much of a latent trait an individual possesses. The theory aims to link individuals' observed performances to a location on an underlying continuum of the unobservable trait. Because the trait is unobservable, IRT is also referred to as latent trait theory—the literal meaning of "latent" is hidden. An example of a latent trait is a test taker's English reading ability. The construct of reading ability is not observable, so measuring this ability requires observable performances designed to assess it. For instance, test takers could read short passages and then answer multiple-choice questions designed to measure their comprehension of the passages. IRT can then be used to relate these observable performances, scores on the multiple-choice reading test items, to test takers' underlying reading abilities. IRT can be used to link observable performances to various types of underlying traits. For instance, it can be used to connect individuals' observed or self-reported anxiety about an assessment to their underlying levels of test anxiety.

The following definitions are helpful for understanding IRT concepts as discussed in this chapter. *Latent variables* are unobservable traits like second language listening ability, which influence observable behaviors, such as individuals' responses to items on a second language listening assessment. The term latent variable is used synonymously with the terms construct and underlying trait throughout the chapter. A *model* is a mathematical equation in which independent variables are combined to optimally predict dependent variables (Embretson and Reise, 2000). Various IRT models, some of which are discussed in this chapter, are used to estimate individuals' underlying traits on language ability constructs. *Parameter* is used in IRT to indicate a characteristic about a test's stimuli. For instance, a 1-parameter (1PL) model mathematically defines only one characteristic of a test item (Osterlind, 2010).

Historical perspective

The concepts and mathematics which underlie IRT are not new. Linacre contends that the foundations of item response theory "go back to ancient Babylon, to the Greek philosophers, to the adventurers of the Renaissance" (Bond and Fox, 2007: *x*). Current IRT practices can be traced back to two separate lines of development. Thurston's (1925), "A method of scaling psychological and educational tests," is the paper often cited as the "intimations" of IRT for one line of development. The paper describes how to place items designed to assess children's mental achievement on an age-graded scale (Bock, 1997). Roughly 30 years later, Fredrick Lord (1952) provided the foundations of IRT as a measurement theory by outlining assumptions and providing detailed models. Lord and Novick's (1968) monumental textbook, *Statistical theories of mental test scores*, outlined the principles of IRT that they and others had developed in the previous two decades. Owing to Lord's access to large data sets as an employee of the Educational Testing Service, the authors were able to develop IRT principles with real data sets.

George Rasch (1960), a Danish mathematician, is also credited with developing IRT principles. The primary focus of his research was to use probability to separate test taker ability and item difficulty. Rasch inspired Benjamin Wright, who was a professor at the University of Chicago, to teach these principles in his graduate courses. Wright became an avid proponent of Rasch's approach, and he and his graduate students are credited with many of the developments of the family of Rasch models.

Although the two lines of IRT development have led to quite similar practices, they can be distinguished by at least one major difference. Rasch models are prescriptive. If data do not fit the model, the data must be edited or discarded. The other approach (derived from Lord's work) promotes a descriptive philosophy. Under this view, a model is built that best describes the characteristics of the data. If the model does not fit the data, the model is adapted until it can account for the data.

IRT became prominent in the language testing literature in the 1980s. The first article published in the journal *Language Testing* was written by Grant Henning (1984). His article, "Advantages of latent trait measurement in language testing," discusses the advantages of IRT as compared to CTT. The following year, three papers in an issue of *Language Testing* (Davidson and Henning, 1985; Henning *et al.* 1985; Woods and Baker 1985) further established IRT in the language testing field.

While language assessment researchers and practitioners have benefited from both lines of IRT research, the majority have used Rasch models. About a decade after IRT appeared in the journal *Language Testing*, a particularly influential book on the subject was written by Tim McNamara (1996), *Measuring Second Language Performance*. The book provides an introduction to the many-facet Rasch model and FACETS (Linacre 1987–2009) software used for estimating ability on performance-based assessments. This book influenced many language testing researchers to use the many-facet Rasch model (MFRM) developed by Wright and the FACETS program created by Mike Linacre, who worked with Wright at the University of Chicago. Soon after the publication of McNamara's book, studies which used MFRM began to appear in the language testing literature. Some of these studies are mentioned in the *current contributions and research* section, below.

Critical issues and topics

Conceptualization of IRT

The purpose of IRT is to link test takers' observed performances, such as scores on a multiple-choice listening test, to a location on an underlying continuum of the latent trait, such as listening ability. This is made possible by relating the probability of test takers' correct responses to items and the ability of the test taker.

IRT assumes an underlying ability continuum with the least amount of ability at the far left and the greatest ability at the far right. Each test taker has an ability which can be located at a point along this continuum. On this scale, by convention, average ability is set to 0 and located at the middle of the continuum. Test takers with below average ability have negative estimates, and test takers with above average abilities have positive estimates. In practice, abilities of most test takers can be located between –4 (little ability) and 4 (very able) on this scale. This continuum can be seen as the horizontal axis in Figure 23.1. This figure is described in detail in the *Item Characteristics Curves* section.

Observable performances aimed at assessing the ability of interest must be used to locate test takers' abilities on this latent continuum. Correct and incorrect responses of 20 test takers on 15 multiple-choice items designed to assess listening comprehension are presented in Table 23.1. These responses represent the observable performances used to locate test takers' listening abilities on an underlying listening ability continuum. It should be noted that in practice, more test takers would be needed to use IRT techniques.

In Table 23.1, 1 indicates a correct response and 0 an incorrect response, so, for example, Keiko, the first test taker, answered items 3, 1, 4, 12, and 10 correctly and all of the other items incorrectly.

The ordering of the test takers and items and the resulting patterning of correct and incorrect responses help to demonstrate the theory underlying IRT. Progressing from left to right in the table, items become more difficult, and progressing from top to bottom, test takers possess more listening ability. The bottom left-hand corner is filled with mostly correct responses because this is where test takers with the most listening ability are answering the easiest items. In contrast, the top right-hand corner is filled with incorrect responses because this is the area in the table where test takers with the least amount of listening comprehension are answering the most difficult items. It should be noted that the pattern is not completely predictable. It might better be described as probabilistic since not all responses in the matrix would have been predicted from the pattern. It should be emphasized that real-world data are not (of course) arranged in such an ordered manner. The data here are arranged that way to illustrate the principles of IRT.

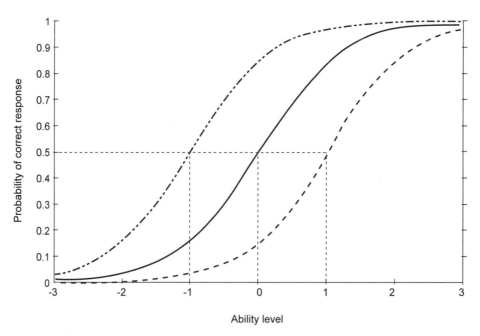

Figure 23.1 Item characteristic curves for three items from the 1PL Rasch model

Table 23.1 Test taker response on a multiple-choice listening test

Test Taker	Item														
	3	1	5	4	7	12	8	10	14	13	9	2	6	15	11
Keiko	1	1	0	1	0	1	0	1	0	0	0	0	0	0	0
Sally	1	1	1	1	1	1	0	0	0	0	0	0	0	0	0
Steve	1	1	0	1	1	1	0	1	0	0	0	0	0	0	0
Pierre	1	1	1	1	1	0	0	0	0	1	0	0	0	0	0
Don	1	1	1	1	1	0	0	0	1	0	1	0	0	0	0
Maia	1	1	1	1	1	1	0	0	1	1	0	0	0	0	0
Trang	1	1	1	0	1	1	1	0	0	1	1	0	0	0	0
Srey	1	0	1	1	1	1	0	1	1	0	0	0	0	0	0
Junko	1	1	1	0	1	1	1	0	1	0	1	0	1	0	0
Lee	1	1	1	1	1	1	1	0	0	0	1	1	0	0	0
Sam	1	1	1	1	0	1	1	0	1	0	1	0	1	0	0
Yasu	1	1	1	1	1	1	1	0	1	1	0	0	0	0	0
Tara	1	1	1	1	1	0	1	1	0	0	0	0	1	1	1
Inma	1	1	1	1	1	0	0	0	1	1	1	1	1	0	0
May	1	1	1	1	1	0	1	1	1	1	0	1	0	1	0
Anna	1	1	1	1	1	0	1	1	0	0	0	1	1	1	1
Ning	1	1	1	1	1	1	1	1	1	0	1	0	1	0	1
Mina	1	1	1	1	1	1	1	1	0	1	0	1	0	1	1
Jack	1	1	1	1	1	1	1	1	1	1	1	1	0	1	1
Ali	1	1	1	1	1	1	1	1	1	1	1	1	1	1	1

A practical advantage of probabilistic modeling should be pointed out at this juncture. Response patterns found in the data that are highly unlikely can be identified. Test takers or items that produce unlikely response patterns are often referred to as "misfitting" (McNamara, 1996). Once identified, misfits can be investigated and decisions can be made about how to handle them. For instance, if a test taker correctly answers most hard items, but incorrectly answers many easy items, it may be that the test taker was unfairly distracted during the exam, and should be given an opportunity to retake it.

The least predictable responses in Table 23.1 are in a strip from the top left hand corner to the bottom right hand corner. In this section of the matrix, it appears that the responses are correct or incorrect in a quite random manner. In these cases, test takers' listening abilities are at about the same level as the difficulty of the items. Thus, roughly half of the time the test takers respond correctly, and the other half of the time, they respond incorrectly. Put another way, these test takers have about a 0.5 probability of answering these items successfully. By capitalizing on these probabilities, the test taker's ability can be defined by the items that are at this level of difficulty for the test taker. This is central to IRT because it means that test taker ability and the difficulty of items can be placed on the same latent ability scale.

The 1PL Rasch model

Relating test taker ability to the difficulty of items makes it possible to mathematically model the probability that a test taker will respond correctly to an item. The most fundamental IRT model, the Rasch or 1-parameter (1PL) logistic model is presented as Equation 1.

$$\text{Probability of correct answer} = \frac{exp\ (\textit{test taker ability} - \textit{item difficulty})}{(1 + exp\ (\textit{test taker ability} - \textit{item difficulty}))} \tag{1}$$

Readers should focus on the relationship between the probability of the correct answer, test taker ability, and item difficulty. Item difficulty is subtracted from test taker ability to arrive at the probability of the test taker answering the item correctly. The rest of the equation, including exp, the exponential function, is based on probability statistics and is beyond the scope of this introductory chapter. However, to demonstrate this relationship, an example calculation is provided. Embretson and Reise (2000) provide an explanation of the mathematics underlying IRT models.

The example will predict the probability of Melanie, a new test taker with a listening ability of 1 on the underlying ability scale answering an item with a difficulty of 0, an item of average difficulty. The number 1 would replace test taker ability in the top and the bottom of the right hand side of the equation, and 0 would replace item difficulty on the top and bottom of the right hand side of the equation. To make the calculation, it is necessary to begin by subtracting Melanie's ability estimate from the difficulty of the item in both the numerator and the denominator of the right hand side of the equation, that is, 1 - 0 equals 1. The exponential function (available on many calculators) of 1 is then calculated to give a value of 2.72 in the numerator and 1 + 2.72 in the denominator. The 2.72 in the numerator is then divided by the 3.72 in the denominator to give a probability of 0.73, indicating that Melanie has about a 73% chance of answering an item with a difficulty level of 0 correctly. It's not surprising that Melanie has a good chance of answering the item correctly because her listening ability is greater than the difficulty of the item.

Item characteristic curves

The relationship between the probability of a test taker answering an item correctly and the test taker's ability can also be presented in graphic form in an item characteristic curve (ICC). These graphs can be used to understand IRT principles as well as differences among various IRT models. In addition, ICCs are commonly used to help test developers understand how specific items function on an assessment. Being able to interpret ICCs is important for making decisions about which items to maintain, modify, or discard for a particular assessment instrument.

ICCs present the characteristics of each item as a trace line on probability and ability continuums. As previously discussed, the ability of the test taker and the difficulty of the item are on the same scale. ICCs for three items from the 1PL Rasch model are presented in Figure 23.1.

The furthest left curve (the dash dotted line) represents one item, the solid line another, and the furthest right (dashed) another. The probability of a test taker correctly responding to an item is presented on the vertical axis. This scale ranges from zero probability at the bottom to absolute probability at the top. The horizontal axis displays the estimated ability level of test takers in relation to item difficulties, with least at the far left and most at the far right. The measurement unit of the scale is a logit, and it is set to have a center point of 0. A test taker with an ability of 0 logits would have a 50% chance of correctly answering an item with a difficulty level of 0 logits.

ICCs express the relationship between the probability of a test taker correctly answering each item and a test taker's ability. As a test taker's ability level increases, moving from left to right along the horizontal axis, the probability of correctly answering each item increases, moving from the bottom to the top of the vertical axis. For instance, for the item represented by the solid line, a test taker with an ability level of 0 on the logit scale would have a 0.5 probability of answering the item correctly. This can be seen by drawing a vertical line from the 0 ability level on the horizontal axis to the ICC and then noting where this intersection occurs on the vertical axis. Lines have been drawn in Figure 23.1 from the solid line to the horizontal axis and the vertical axis to illustrate this point.

The three ICCs shown in Figure 23.1 were chosen because they demonstrate some characteristics of ICCs of the 1PL Rasch model. First, the ICCs are somewhat S-shaped, meaning the probability of a correct response changes considerably over a small ability level range. For example, the ICC represented by the solid line indicates that the probability of a correct response increases quite gradually for test takers with abilities at the low end, below –1, and high end, above +1, of the scale. Test takers with abilities ranging from –3 to –1 have less than a 0.2 probability of answering the item correctly, whereas, for test takers with abilities levels in the middle of the scale, between roughly –1 and +1, the probability of correctly responding to that item changes from quite low, about 0.1 to quite high, about 0.9. This probability should also be apparent from the pattern of correct and incorrect responses in Table 23.1.

Inflection points are at the location on ICCs where the slope of the line is at a maximum and a test taker's chances of answering an item correctly are 0.5 (for the 1PL and many other models). Inflection points are indicated by the thin dotted lines that have been drawn from the middle of the ICCs, that is, half the distance from the upper and lower extremes, to the vertical and the horizontal axes. The inflection point also indicates the difficulty of the item. The thin dotted vertical lines drawn from the ICCs inflection points to the horizontal axis indicate the difficulties of the three items. The dash dotted line has a difficulty level of –1, the solid line, 0, and the dashed line is the hardest item with a difficulty level of 1.

Knowing the location of an inflection point can assist test designers to improve the measurement properties of the test. Information about all of the items on a test are often combined and presented in test information function (TIF) plots. The TIF indicates the average item information at each ability level. The TIF can be used to help test developers locate areas on the ability continuum where there are few items. Items can then be written that target these ability levels. For instance, if the TIF indicated that few items discriminate well at the –2 to –1 ability level on a listening test, item writers could craft additional items targeted at assessing listening ability at this level.

Two and three parameter models

In two parameter models (2PLs), unlike 1PLs, the shapes of the ICCs can vary. Stated differently, items are not all modeled to discriminate equally. The equation for the 2PL logistic model is as follows:

$$
\begin{aligned}
&\textit{Probability of correct answer} \\
&= \frac{exp\left[\textit{item discrimination (test taker ability} - \textit{item difficulty)}\right]}{\left(1 + exp\left[\textit{item discrimination (test taker ability} - \textit{item difficulty)}\right]\right)}
\end{aligned} \tag{2}
$$

Compared with Equation 1, Equation 2 is identical except item discrimination has been included in the model. Item discrimination refers to the slope of the ICC. With the 1PL, the discrimination parameter is fixed, and all items are assumed to be equally related to the ability (that is to say, equal slopes). With the 2PL, the relationship between each item and the listening ability of the test taker can be different.

The three parameter model (3PL), which includes a parameter to control for guessing, is also often encountered in language assessments. When test takers have a significant chance of guessing the correct answer, such as in a multiple-choice format, the 3PL may be appropriate. The equation for this model is as follows:

$$Probability\ of\ correct\ answer =$$
$$guessing + (1 - guessing)\frac{exp\left[item\ discrimination\ (test\ taker\ ability - item\ difficulty)\right]}{(1 + exp\left[item\ discrimination\ (test\ taker\ ability - item\ difficulty)\right])}$$

(3)

As can be seen, a guessing parameter has been added to the model. The differences in the 1PL, 2PL, and 3PL are evident when the three ICCs in Figure 23.2 are compared. All have item difficulties of 0 on the logit scale.

The solid line presents an ICC which was estimated with a 1PL. The estimate of person ability from this item is based only on the difficulty of the item and whether or not the item was answered correctly. The discrimination and guessing parameters are not included in the model, so the item is constrained to have a certain slope (1.0 for the Rasch model) and a guessing parameter of 0. Because it does not include a discrimination parameter, the shape of the ICC follows the S-shaped pattern of 1PL ICCs, and because it does not have a guessing parameter, it crosses the vertical axis near 0.

The dash dotted line represents an item that used a 2PL for estimation, which models the difficulty of the item as well as discrimination or slope of the line. This ICC does not follow the S-shaped pattern because the slope of the line has been modeled, or put another way, allowed to vary according to the actual relationship between the probability of a correct response and the

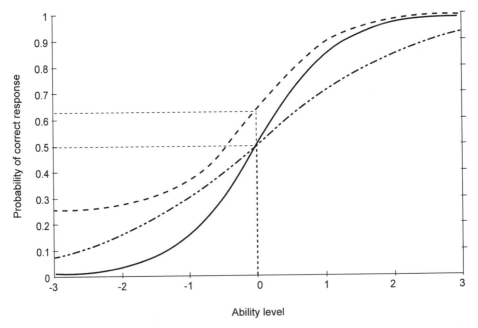

Figure 23.2 Item characteristic curves for 1PL, 2PL, and 3PL

test taker's ability. When the 2PL is used, ICCs for each item will have varying slopes, whereas, when the 1PL is used, all items will have the same slopes. Because the 2PL does not include a guessing parameter, the ICC for this item also crosses the vertical axis near 0.

Information about the actual relationship between the probability of a correct response and test taker ability can also be useful for test developers. Items that have steep slopes are generally considered better than ones that gradually increase across a wide ability range. This is because items with steep slopes discriminate well at certain ability level locations. Items which rise gradually provide little information about where a test taker should be located on the underlying ability continuum, and are therefore not very useful. Items with steep slopes can be selected for use, and less discriminating items can be modified or discarded.

Like the other two lines in Figure 23.2, the dashed line represents an ICC of an item with a difficulty of 0 on the logit scale. However, unlike the item represented by the solid line, it includes a discrimination parameter and unlike both the items represented by solid and dashed dotted lines, it includes a guessing parameter. Because it models guessing, it is not constrained to cross the vertical axis near 0. In the figure, it crosses the vertical axis well above 0, at roughly 0.25, indicating that even test takers with no listening ability are able to correctly respond to the item about 25% of the time. This is because with multiple-choice items, even test takers with little or no ability on the construct to be assessed have a probability of a correct response of roughly 0.25 on a test with four answer options. It should be noted that although item difficulty occurs at the inflection point, it is not at 0.5 as is the case with the 1PL and 2PL. In this example, it is a little above 0.6, which is indicated by the horizontal thin dotted line which connects the ICC to the vertical axis.

Estimation procedures

Person ability estimation is determined through an iterative process and for most IRT models is based on the pattern of correct and incorrect responses. For instance, in Table 23.1, Keiko, the first test taker, answered items 3, 1, 4, 12, and 10 correctly and all of the other items incorrectly. The estimation of Keiko's ability is conceptually the same as asking which ability level has the highest probability of producing Keiko's pattern of correct responses. The question is answered with an iterative process that involves multiple steps. In the first step, the probability of each response in the pattern is calculated based on one of the IRT formulas, such as Equation 23.2. In the second step, the probability of the response pattern is estimated by multiplying the probabilities of correctly answering each item. In step 3, steps 1 and 2 are repeated for a range of ability levels. That is, points along the ability continuum are selected and the likelihood of each response pattern of producing each ability estimate is compared. The process is iterative, and an ability estimate is produced when the desired degree of precision has been reached (de Ayala 2009).

Many-facet Rasch measurement model

The many-facet Rasch measurement (MFRM) model has been used in the language testing field to model and adjust for various assessment characteristics on performance-based tests. MFRM is a one parameter model, but because test taker ability and item difficulty are treated as measurement facets, other characteristics of the measurement process, such as raters and scales, can be included in the model (Bond and Fox, 2007). When raters assign scores for performance-based assessments, the scores may be affected by various factors. For example, test takers may be required to write an academic essay to demonstrate their academic writing ability. The essays could then be rated on a five-point scale. In large-scale assessments, it may be necessary to use different raters, prompts, and times of the day for the assessment, and as a result, the scores may be affected by factors like rater severity, the difficulty of the prompt, or the time of day that the test is administered. MFRM can be used to identify such effects and adjust the scores to compensate for them. The MFRM model used for modeling test taker ability, rater severity, and item difficulty for a rating scale can be expressed as follows:

$$\text{Probability of correct answer} = \frac{\exp\,(\text{test taker ability} - \text{item difficulty} - \text{rater severity} - \text{rating step difficulty})}{(1 + \exp\,(\text{test taker ability} - \text{item difficulty} - \text{rater severity} - \text{rating step difficulty}))} \tag{4}$$

Like the models for items scored as either right or wrong previously discussed, item difficulty is subtracted from test taker ability to arrive at a rating. The difference between this MFRM and the 1PL Rasch model for items scored as correct or incorrect is that the severity of the rater and the rating step difficulty is also subtracted from the test taker ability. Rater severity denotes how strict a rater is in assigning scores to test takers, while rating step difficulty refers to how much of the ability is required to move from one step on a rating scale to another. For example, on a five-point writing scale with 1 indicating least proficient and 5 most proficient, the level of ability required to move from a rating of 1 to 2, or between any two scales would be difficulty of rating step. Figure 23.3 presents the category response curves (CRCs), which are used when rating scales are employed, for a five-point scale.

CRCs are analogous to ICCs. The probability of assignment of a rating on the scale, the five-point scale in this example, is shown on the vertical axis, and test taker ability is shown on the horizontal axis. Each rating on the five-point scale appears as a hill. Progressing from left to

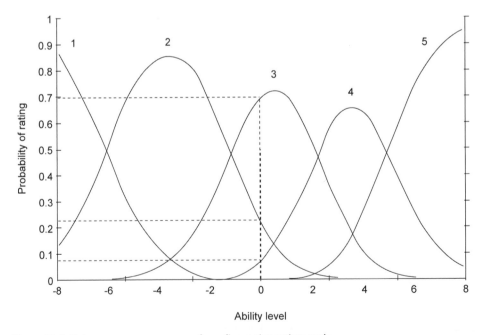

Figure 23.3 Category response curves for a five-point rating scale

right, the far left peak indicates a 1 on the five-point scale, and the far right peak indicates a rating of 5. The numbers 1 to 5 have been written above the curve for the writing scale that they represent. By comparing the point on each rating category to the vertical and horizontal axes, it is possible to determine the probability of a test taker with a particular ability being assigned a particular rating on the five-point scale. Figure 23.3 includes dotted lines for an ability level of 0 on the logit scale to each rating category which has a probability of being assigned for this ability level. A test taker with an ability level of 0 would have virtually no probability of a rating of 1 or 5, a little above a 0.2 probability of a rating of 2, and about a 0.7 probability of a rating of 3.

The five-point writing scale in Figure 23.3 indicates that a score of 2 is the most commonly assigned since it extends the furthest along the horizontal axis. Ideally, rating categories should be highly peaked and equivalent in size and shape to each other. Test developers can use the information in the CRCs to revise rating scales. For instance, faced with the CRC in Figure 23.3, if the goal is to spread test-takers along the ability continuum as is usually the case, it may be appropriate to revise the 2 rating scale to define less of the ability range in the descriptor, and include more ability in the 1 and 3 rating scale descriptors. The desired effect would be for raters to assign an increased number of 1s and 3s and a decreased number of 2s.

Current contributions and research

IRT is currently used for various purposes in the language testing arena. Probably its most commonly reported use in the field over the past two decades is for investigating task characteristics and their effects on various types of performance-based assessments. The majority of this research has focused on tasks designed to assess speaking and writing ability. For instance, MFRM has been used to investigate the effects of rater bias (Kondo-Brown, 2002), rater severity (Eckes, 2005), rater training (Weigle, 1998), rater feedback (Elder *et al.*, 2005), task difficulty (Fulcher, 1996), and rating scale reliability (Bonk and Ockey, 2003).

Applications of IRT to computer adaptive testing (CAT) are not commonly reported in the language assessment literature, likely because of the large number of items and test takers required for its feasibility. However, it is used in some large-scale language assessments and is considered one of the most promising applications of IRT. Computer adaptive tests are designed to deliver assessments that are tailored to the ability levels of test takers. The approach capitalizes on the fact that items near test takers' ability levels are most useful for ability estimation. A computer is programmed to deliver items increasingly closer to the test takers' ability levels. In its simplest form, if a test taker answers an item correctly, the IRT-based algorithm assigns the test taker a more difficult item, whereas, if the test taker answers an item incorrectly, the next item will be easier. The test is complete when a predetermined level of precision of locating the test taker's ability level has been achieved. Sawaki provides further explanation of CAT in Chapter 29.

Language testers also use IRT techniques to identify and understand possible differences in the way items function for different groups of test takers. Differential item functioning (DIF), which can be an indicator of biased test items, exists if test takers from different groups with equal ability do not have the same chance of answering an item correctly. IRT DIF methods compare ICCs for the same item in the two groups of interest. When the ICCs are different, the items are flagged for DIF. Some IRT DIF studies can be found in the language assessment literature. Three particularly useful articles on the topic can be found in volume 4, issue 2, of *Language Assessment Quarterly*. Ferne and Rupp (2007) discuss DIF techniques and studies that have been conducted in language testing. Ockey (2007) reports on the use of IRT DIF techniques to identify items on a National Assessment of Educational Progress math test that functioned differently for English learners and non-English learners. Geranpayeh and Kunnan (2007) used IRT DIF techniques to investigate whether or not items on the listening section of the Certificate in Advanced English examination functioned differently for test takers from different age groups.

Recommendations for practice

When deciding whether or not to use IRT for language assessment projects, assumptions about the data necessary for appropriate application, along with the advantages and disadvantages of using IRT techniques for the intended purpose should be considered.

Assumptions underlying IRT models

For the results of an IRT analysis to be meaningful, the data must conform to assumptions that underlie the theory. The first assumption relates to dimensionality: most IRT models require unidimensionality. In a unidimensional data set, a single ability can account for the differences in scores. For example, a second language listening test would need to be constructed so that only listening ability underlies test takers' responses to the test items. A violation of this assumption would be the inclusion of an item that measured both the targeted ability of listening as well as reading ability not required for listening comprehension.

A second assumption underlying IRT, referred to as local independence, is that responses to each item on a test are independent of responses to all other items. This means that each item should be assessed independently of all other items. The assumption of local independence could be violated on a reading test when the question or answer options for one item provide information that may be helpful for correctly answering another item about the same passage.

A third assumption underlying IRT, sometimes referred to as certainty of response, is that test takers make an effort to demonstrate the level of ability that they possess when they complete the assessment (Osterlind, 2010). Test takers must try to answer all questions correctly because the probability of a correct response in IRT is directly related to their ability. This assumption is often violated when researchers recruit test takers for a study, and there is little or no incentive for the test takers to offer their best effort.

It is important to bear in mind that almost all data will violate one or more of the IRT assumptions to some extent. It is the degree to which such violations occur that determines how meaningful the resulting analysis is (de Ayala, 2009). Diagnostic analyses should therefore be conducted and reported on each assumption, so stakeholders can make informed decisions when placing trust in the reported ability estimates. Embretson and Reise (2000) provide a description of how to assess assumptions for various types of assessment data.

Sample size

Although not generally conceived of as an underlying assumption, a requirement of the effective use of IRT is a sufficient sample size. Many factors should be considered when determining the number of cases needed for a sound analysis. In general, smaller samples provide less accurate parameter estimates, and models with more parameters require larger samples for accurate estimates. High stakes tests require more accurate estimates than low stakes tests, and users must decide how much inaccuracy they are willing to tolerate. A minimum of about 100 cases is required for most testing contexts when the simplest model, the 1PL Rasch model, is used (McNamara, 1996). As a general rule, de Ayala (2009) recommends that the starting point for determining sample size should be a few hundred.

Advantages of IRT

IRT has advantages over classical test theory. First, provided that ability estimates are drawn from the population of interest, they are group independent. This means that ability estimates are not dependent on the particular group of test takers that complete the assessment. Second, IRT can be used to aid in designing instruments that target specific ability levels based on the TIF. For instance, an assessment for the purpose of English certification of international airline pilots would require a specific cut-score targeted to separate qualified and unqualified individuals. Using IRT item difficulty parameters makes it possible to design items with difficulty levels near the desired cut-score, which would increase the accuracy of decisions at this crucial ability location. Third, IRT provides information about various aspects of the assessment process, including items, raters, and test takers, which can be useful for test development. For instance, raters can be identified that have inconsistent rating patterns or are too lenient. These raters can then be provided with specific feedback on how to improve their rating behavior. Fourth, test takers do not need to take the same items to be meaningfully compared on the construct of interest.

Disadvantages of IRT

Two decades ago, it was believed that the use of IRT would become increasingly prevalent in the language testing field (Garret, 1991). However, so far, IRT has been minimally used both in language assessment projects and as a language assessment research tool. This lack of widespread use is likely due to practical and technical disadvantages of IRT when compared to CTT. First, the necessary assumptions underlying IRT may not hold with many language assessment data sets. Second, lack of agreement on an appropriate algorithm to represent IRT-based test scores (to users) leads to distrust of IRT techniques. Third, understanding of the somewhat technical math which underlies IRT models is intimidating to many. As a result, training in the theory and practice of IRT is not always accessible. Fourth, the relatively large samples sizes required for parameter estimation are not available for many assessment projects. Finally, although IRT software packages continue to become more user friendly, most have steep learning curves which can discourage fledgling test developers and researchers.

Future directions

To date, IRT has not gained widespread use in the language testing field. However, given its advantages, it is likely that it will become more prevalent in the coming years. Techniques, such as item bundling (Keller *et al.*, 2003), which have been developed to help certain types of data sets meet the assumption of local independence will likely become increasingly accessible. The development of techniques which require fewer cases for accurate parameter estimation, as has occurred in the area of structural equation modeling (Bentler, 2008), will also likely emerge.

As a relatively new approach, few language testers have received training in IRT techniques. Consequently little literature written specifically for language testers is available to provide guidance on using IRT. An increasing number of written resources specific to the needs of language testers, like McNamara's (1996) book *Measuring Second Language Performance* will almost certainly appear to fill this void.

Advancements in computer technology will also likely lead to greater use of IRT techniques. The lack of computer-friendly programs has limited the use of IRT among language testers. As Osterlind (2010) states, "IRT programs are not designed for the casual user. Individuals must be willing to invest a significant amount of time to learn a given program's individual features and peculiarities." As IRT software packages become more accessible to the wider language assessment community, it is likely that the use of IRT techniques will become more prevalent in the field.

Further reading

Bond, T. and Fox, C. (2007). *Applying the Rasch model: fundamental measurement in the human sciences*. Mahwah, NJ: Lawrence Erlbaum Associates Inc. The authors provide an extremely readable introduction to the Rasch model. The book is written for an audience without advanced mathematical knowledge. Various examples are described and many are accompanied by interpreted computer output. An emphasis of the book is to convince readers that the 1PL Rasch model is appropriate for all situations.

de Ayala, R. J. (2009). *The Theory and Practice of Item Response Theory*. New York, NY: The Guilford Press. This book provides a rather comprehensive introduction to IRT. It includes the mathematics which underlies the theory as well as practical examples, computer output and detailed explanations. It is highly recommended for individuals with some math background who want to further understand the theory and practice of IRT.

Embretson, S. E. and Reise, S. P. (2000). *Item Response Theory for Psychologists*. London, UK: Lawrence Erlbaum Associates, Inc. The first chapter in this book provides a must read mathematical and conceptual comparison of IRT and CTT for persons interested in understanding how IRT is different than CTT. The book also provides a rather comprehensive description of the models used for rating scales.

McNamara, T. F. (1996). *Measuring Second Language Performance*. London, UK: Addison Wesley Longman Limited. This book is a must read for language assessment researchers who are interested in performance-based assessments and/or IRT. It likely influenced the field of language testing to use the many-facet Rasch measurement model for analyzing performance-based assessments. The book is both conceptual and practical. It provides a very clear introduction to the principles underlying the Rasch model as well as interpretations and explanations of output from the FACETS program.

References

Bentler, P. M. (2008). *EQS Structural Equations Program Manual*. Encino, CA: Multivariate Software, Inc.

Bock, R. D. (1997). A brief history of item response theory. *Educational Measurement: Issues and Practice* 16: 21–33.

Bond, T. and Fox, C. (2007). *Applying the Rasch Model: fundamental measurement in the human sciences*. Mahwah, NJ: Lawrence Erlbaum Associates Inc.

Bonk, W. and Ockey, G. J. (2003). A many-facet Rasch analysis of the second language group oral discussion task. *Language Testing* 20: 89–110.

Davidson, F. and Henning, G. (1985). A self-rating scale of English difficulty: Rasch scalar analysis of items and rating categories. *Language Testing* 2: 164–79.

de Ayala, R. J. (2009). *The theory and Practice of Item Response Theory*. New York, NY: The Guilford Press.

Eckes, T. (2005). Examining rater effects in TestDaF writing and speaking performance assessments: A many-facet Rasch analysis. *Language Assessment Quarterly* 2: 197–221.

Elder, C., Knoch, U., Barkhuizen, G. and von Radow, J. (2005). Individual feedback to enhance rater training: Does it work? *Language Assessment Quarterly* 2: 175–96.

Embretson, S. E. and Reise, S. P. (2000). *Item Response Theory for Psychologists*. London, UK: Lawrence Erlbaum Associates, Inc.

Ferne, T. and Rupp, A. (2007). Synthesis of 15 years of research on DIF in language testing: Methodological advances, challenges and recommendations. *Language Assessment Quarterly* 4: 113–48.

Fulcher, G. (1996). Testing tasks: issues in task design and the group oral. *Language Testing* 13: 23–51.

Garret, N. (1991). Technology in the services of language learning: Trends and issues. *The Modern Language Journal* 75: 74–101.

Geranpayeh, A. and Kunnan, A. J. (2007). Differential functioning in terms of age in the certificate in advanced English examination. *Language Assessment Quarterly* 4: 190–222.

Henning, G. (1984). Advantages of latent trait measurement in language testing. *Language Testing* 1: 123–33.

Henning, G., Hudson, T. and Turner, J. (1985). Item response theory and the assumption of unidimensionality for language tests. *Language Testing* 2: 141–54.

Keller, L., Swaminathan, H. and Sireci, S. (2003). Evaluating scoring procedures for context-dependent item sets. *Applied Measurement in Education* 16: 207–22.

Kondo-Brown, K. (2002). A FACETS analysis of rater bias in measuring Japanese second language writing performance. *Language Testing* 19: 3–31.

Linacre, J. M. (1987–2009). *Many facets Rasch measurement, version 3.66.1.* Chicago IL: Mesa Press.

Lord, F. M. (1952). A theory of test scores. *Psychometric Monograph No 7.*

Lord, F. M. and Novick, M. (1968). *Statistical Theories of Mental Test Scores.* Reading, MA: Addison-Wesley.

McNamara, T. F. (1996). *Measuring Second Language Performance.* London, UK: Addison Wesley Longman Limited.

Ockey, G. J. (2007). Investigating the validity of math word problems for English language learners with DIF. *Language Assessment Quarterly* 4: 149–64.

Osterlind, S. J. (2010). *Modern Measurement: theory, principles and applications of mental appraisal.* Boston, MA: Pearson.

Rasch, G. (1960). *Probabilistic Models for some Intelligence and Attainment Tests.* Chicago, IL: University of Chicago Press.

Thurston, L. L. (1925). A method of scaling psychological and educational tests. *Journal of Educational Psychology* 16: 433–51.

Weigle, S. (1998). Using FACETS to model rater training effects. *Language Testing* 15: 263–87.

Woods, A. and Baker, R. (1985). Item response theory. *Language Testing* 2: 117–40.

24

Reliability and dependability

Neil Jones

Reliability as an aspect of test quality

This chapter offers a non-technical discussion of the concept of reliability intended to complement the presentation in the remaining chapters of this section of a number of theories of measurement applied to testing language proficiency. These models are to an extent related, and reliability is a concept common to them all.

This chapter looks at measurement and the limits of the measurement metaphor. Because these limits impact on the interpretations we can make of test scores, my central concern is with the relationship of reliability and validity.

Reliability and validity are classically cited as the two most important properties of a test. When Bachman (1990) identified four key qualities – *validity*, *reliability*, *impact* and *practicality*, he was proposing that in any testing situation validity and reliability should be maximised to produce the most useful results for test users, within practical constraints that always exist. As will be further discussed below, reliability and validity have often been portrayed as potentially in conflict. Here, reliability will be presented rather as an integral component of validity, and approaches to estimating reliability as potential sources of evidence for the construct validity of a test.

Measurement

So what is measurement? Examples like measuring temperature with a thermometer, or length with a ruler, spring to mind – some instrument used to quantify a physical property of an object on some conventional scale, such as degrees Celsius or millimetres. The idea that quantification is the way to understanding was memorably expressed by Kelvin in 1883:

> … when you can measure what you are speaking about, and express it in numbers you know something about it; but when you cannot measure it, when you cannot express it in numbers, your knowledge is of a meagre and unsatisfactory kind.
>
> *(Kelvin, quoted by Stellman, 1998: 1973)*

Does this apply to the case of language proficiency? In some ways it does, as the chapters in this section on measurement theory make clear. But measuring a person's temperature with a thermometer is very different to measuring their proficiency with a language test. We should be wary of taking this metaphor too literally, for two reasons.

First, it suggests that language proficiency is an enduring real property that resides in a person's head and can be quantified, like their height or weight. This recalls an outdated behavioural psychology view of abilities or features of personality such as 'intelligence' as stable *traits*, quantitative in nature. Indeed, all the approaches to measurement presented in this section can be described as *trait-based*. A measurement approach that views language as a stable trait is increasingly out of tune with our current understanding of human abilities. Currently language assessment takes a more socio-cultural view of proficiency, as something which is situated in the variability of social use and interaction, and to some extent inseparable from it.

Second the metaphor implies that language proficiency, like temperature, has a single unique meaning, and can be precisely quantified. If this were true then simple valid comparisons of proficiency measures could be made across all different groups of learners and contexts of language learning. Language proficiency is a hugely complex phenomenon, and every context of learning needs to be treated on its own terms. We cannot take a one-size-fits-all approach to language assessment.

Such trait-based approaches presented in this section share the same basic view of educational measurement. They represent the current mainstream. However, it is interesting to note that theorists have been progressively expanding the concept of measurement to include a wider range of practices, emphasising the notion of information: 'the descriptive power effected by measurement, as distinct from the process of obtaining a quantity of something in relation to the observed' (Ferris, 2004: 104).

Something of this is reflected in criticisms of current approaches, and possible future developments, which we will consider later. These criticisms concern the shortcomings of trait-based measurement models for describing the complexity of learners' cognition. But a measurement model need not be a psychological model. The technical apparatus of trait-based measurement, as presented in the chapters in this section, still has much to offer language testing. It enables us to construct measurement scales for language proficiency, and even link different scales into frameworks such as the Common European Framework of Reference for Languages (CEFR; Council of Europe, 2001), achieving some broad comparability across different contexts. If such constructions are found practically useful it is partly due to their metaphorical power as accessible, communicative representations of a complex reality. This chapter attempts to analyse the relation of the metaphor to the reality.

The concept of reliability

Reliability equals consistency

Reliability in assessment means something rather different to its everyday use. 'Reliable' in common parlance is a synonym of 'trustworthy' or 'accurate'. Feldt and Brennan (1989: 106) point out that 'in everyday conversation, "reliability" refers to a concept much closer to the measurement concept of *validity*', that is, it implies that a test gives accurate and correct results. However, in testing reliability has the narrower meaning of 'consistent'. This is indeed one aspect of trustworthiness, as when we speak of a reliable friend, car or train service. But usages such as 'trust John to make a mess of things,' or 'you can rely on the trains breaking down in winter' remind us that consistency has no inherently positive connotation. Ennis (1999) argues that simple misunderstanding of the term on the part of test users has led to a damaging focus on reliability at the expense of other test qualities. He proposes that 'reliability' should be renamed 'consistency', although there is no evidence of this proposal catching on.

A reliable test is consistent in that it produces the same or similar result on repeated use; that is, it would rank-order a group of test takers in nearly the same way. But the result need not be a correct or accurate measure of what the test claims to measure. Just as a train service can run consistently late, a test may provide an incorrect result in a consistent manner. High reliability does not necessarily imply that a test is good, i.e., valid. Nonetheless, a valid test must have acceptable reliability, because without it the results can never be meaningful. Thus a degree of reliability is a necessary but not sufficient condition of validity.

Reliability and error

> Quantification of the consistency and inconsistency in examinee performance constitutes the essence of reliability analysis.
>
> *(Feldt and Brennan, 1989: 105)*

When a group of learners takes a test their scores will differ, reflecting their relative ability. Reliability is defined as the proportion of variation in scores caused by the ability measured, and not by other factors. This proportion is typically described as a correlation (or correlation-like) coefficient. Depending on the type of reliability being analysed, what is correlated with what will change; however, all reliability coefficients are interpretable in the sense of repeated measurement that I describe above. A perfectly reliable test would have a reliability coefficient (r) of 1. Figure 24.1 illustrates this: about three-quarters of the variability is caused by ability, so this test has an r of about three-quarters, or 0.75.

The variability caused by other factors is called *error*. Like the term 'reliability', the choice of the term 'error' is unfortunate, because of connotations which attach to its everyday meaning. 'Error'

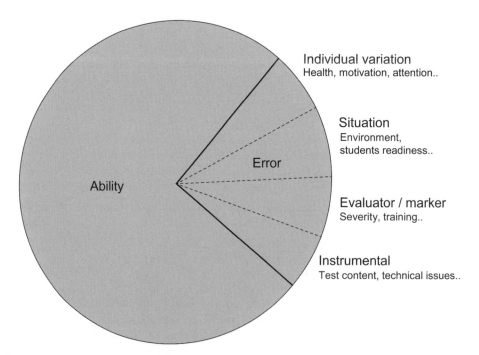

Figure 24.1 Some sources of error in a test

is often an antonym of 'truth', though we have pointed out that results may be reliable but not truthful. 'Error' also strongly implies negligence or incompetence on somebody's part, something which has moved at least one ministry of education to refuse any sensible public discussion of it. But the fact is, of course, that even the best tests contain error, in its psychometric sense.

Figure 24.1 illustrates four major sources of error which are discussed by Feldt and Brennan (1989: 107). There is inherent variability in individual test takers' performance, depending on the day of the test. On another day the weather, the test administration conditions, and the students' psychological preparedness might be more or less favourable. A range of factors affect the judgment of markers. The tasks in the test version may perform differently to those in another version, and so on.

Figure 24.1 breaks down error into different sources, but shows ability as a single factor. However, the third and fourth sources of error could also be seen as potentially affecting the very nature of the ability which is tested, and thus impact on validity as much as reliability. We will return to this below.

Replications and generalisability

'A person with one watch knows what time it is; a person with two watches is never quite sure.' Thus Brennan (2001: 295) introduces a presentation of reliability from the perspective of replications. Information from only one observation may easily deceive, because unverifiable, while to get direct information about consistency (i.e., reliability) at least two instances are required. Replications in some form are necessary to estimate reliability.

Even more importantly, Brennan argues, 'they are required for an unambiguous conceptualization of the very notion of reliability.' Specifying exactly what would constitute a replication of a measurement procedure is necessary to provide any meaningful statement about its reliability. Figure 24.1 can serve to illustrate this. The individual variation in test-takers from one day to another is difficult to measure, because the test is taken only once. Thus its impact is very likely ignored, leading to an overestimate of reliability, unless we can do specific experiments to replicate the testing event in a way that will provide evidence. Variable severity in markers will contribute undetected error unless steps are taken to control this by extra training, multiple marking or scaling. In a writing test one test version might set an imaginative task and another an argumentative essay. Whether these are seen as replications of the same test procedure depends on how the writing construct has been defined. This is an issue of validity no less than one of reliability. Stating what would constitute a replication of a test forces the test designer to be absolutely specific about which facets are relevant. Brennan's purpose is to locate reliability within the framework of generalisability theory, which offers an alternate and perhaps better approach to decomposing error into its constituent facets (see Schoonen, this volume).

Reliability and dependability

Dependability is a term sometimes used (in preference to reliability) to refer to the consistency of a classification – that is, of a test-taker receiving the same grade or score interpretation on repeated testing.

The way the term is used relates to the distinction made between *norm-referenced* and *criterion-referenced* approaches to testing (see the chapters by Davidson and by J.D. Brown, this volume). Taken literally, norm-referencing means interpreting a learner's performance relative to other learners, i.e., as better or worse, while criterion-referencing interprets performance relative to some fixed external criterion, such as a specified level of a proficiency framework like the CEFR. The term dependability is used in a criterion-referencing context where the aim is to classify learners, for example as masters or non-masters of a domain of knowledge.

But if dependability relates to a particular criterion-referenced approach to interpretation we should not conclude that reliability relates only to norm-referenced interpretations. True, reliability is defined in terms of the consistency with which individuals are ranked relative to each other, but in many testing applications it is no less concerned with consistency of classification relative to cut-off points that have well-defined criterion interpretations. Item response theory has the particular advantage that it models a learner's ability in terms of probable performance on specific tasks (see Ockey, this volume). Henning (1987: 111) argues that IRT reconciles norm- and criterion-referencing. Even large-scale assessments within the older classical test theory (CTT) model will very often use judgmental or statistical approaches to try and maintain a fixed standard from session to session. All approaches to testing may be concerned with dependability of classification, whatever the terms or the procedures used.

The standard error of measurement

The standard error of measurement (SEM) is a transformation of reliability in terms of test scores, which is useful in considering consistency of classification (see J.D. Brown, this volume). While reliability refers to a group of test-takers, the SEM shows the impact of reliability on the likely score of an individual: it indicates how close a test-taker's score is likely to be to their 'true score', e.g. in raw marks, to within some stated confidence. SEM is conceived in different ways in the measurement theories presented in this section. One difference often cited between CTT and IRT is that CTT SEM is a single value applied to all possible scores in a test, while the IRT SEM is conditional on each possible score, and is probably of greater technical value. However, as Haertel (2006: 82) points out, CTT also has techniques for estimating SEM conditional on score.

Estimating reliability

So far so good, but we cannot directly observe reliability or distinguish error from ability. We can only estimate it. J.D. Brown (this volume) presents the range of approaches to estimating reliability developed within the framework of classical test theory, reaching back more than a century. That development started with more direct approaches to replication, based on comparing different tests or test administrations: *test-retest*, or *parallel forms*. These were followed, and in practice largely replaced, by more indirect or 'contrived' (Brennan, 2001: 295) forms of replication, based on the notion of *internal consistency*, that is, on comparing the performance of items within a single version of a test. Internal consistency estimates reflect the extent to which all items test 'the same thing' and for this reason have also been called indices of *homogeneity* (Gulliksen, 1950: 220).

Internal consistency approaches have the great practical advantage that they require response data from a single operational test administration, unlike test-retest or parallel forms approaches, which require specific experimental studies. Thanks to their practicality, internal consistency estimates of reliability are by far the most commonly used.

Internal consistency as the definition of a trait

It is important to note that internal consistency is conceptually quite unrelated to the definition of reliability given earlier. This can be easily demonstrated. Think of a short test consisting of items on, say: your shoe size, visual acuity, the number of children you have, and the distance from your house to work. Assume that with appropriate procedures each of these can be found without error, for a group of candidates. The reliability of this error-free test will be a perfect 1. But these items are completely unrelated to each other, and so an internal consistency estimate of their reliability would be about zero. For this reason too, it is impossible to put a name to this test, that is, to say what it is actually a test *of*.

Now suppose the test contained, say, items on shoe size, height, gender. This time it is likely that on administering the test the internal consistency estimate of reliability would be found to be considerably higher than zero. The difference is that this time the items *are* related to each other. Study them and you could probably name what it measures: something like 'physical build'.

So the trait which a test actually measures is whatever explains its internal consistency. An example of internal consistency defining a trait can be found in Coe (2008), who analysed data on exam grades in UK schools to investigate the question of standards: are different exam subjects graded to the same standard? This might seem a curious question: what would it mean to say that French, for example, was a more difficult subject than Maths? Coe's approach within the general approach of IRT (Ockey, this volume), was to apply a Rasch model. He was able to fit most subjects to a scale, showing, according to this approach, that some subjects were more difficult than others, and hence that the standards applied to the harder subjects were more stringent than those applied to the easier subjects. The fact that it was possible to construct a coherent trait linking such a variety of subjects suggests that the test takers had something in common which could be measured. But what is it? How would you name it? 'General academic ability', or 'propensity to do well at tests' are two equally valid possibilities.

Reliability and validity

Validity (see Chapelle, this volume) nowadays tends to be judged in terms of whether the uses made of test results are justified (Messick, 1989). This implies a complex set of arguments that go well beyond the older and purely psychometric issue of whether the test measures what it is believed to measure; yet this narrower issue is key to any interpretative argument.

Coherent measurement and construct definition

In the trait-based, unidimensional approaches which are treated in this section, conceptions of validity and reliability emerge as rather closely linked. They both relate to the same notion of coherent measurement – of focusing in on 'one thing' at a time. Typically this means identifying skills such as Reading, Writing, Listening and Speaking as distinct traits, and testing them separately. Each of these traits requires definition: what do we understand by 'Reading' or 'Listening' ability, and how is it to be tested? Such construct definition provides the basis of a validity argument for how test results can be interpreted. Defining constructs encourages test developers to identify explicit models of language competence, enables useful profiling of an individual learner's strengths or weaknesses, and helps to interpret test performance in meaningful terms.

There are two basic approaches to testing language skills. The performance skills of Writing and Speaking are tested by eliciting a small number of complex samples of performance, which are evaluated in a complex way by expert raters. In this approach, validity depends in part on eliciting performances which give interpretable evidence of the ability to be measured. Both reliability and validity depend on the consistency of *standardisation*: the test tasks must be comparable from session to session, and the evaluation must apply the same criteria, to the same standard.

In contrast, tests of Reading and Listening often are composed of a large number of objectively marked items – the more items, the higher the reliability (other things being equal). It is this kind of test where high internal consistency of items tends to be valued. Each item contributes only a small amount of information, but by ensuring that the items 'collaborate' with each other, the learner's location on a proficiency scale may be quite accurately measured. By the same line of trait-based reasoning, low internal consistency may imply not just that a test is unreliable, but that the construct itself lacks clear definition, that is, validity.

Should validity really be associated with internal consistency in this way? After all, language ability is a very complex phenomenon, which reflects the interaction of many different factors both within and beyond the test taker: competences, communicative tasks, topics, situations, and so on. Should we expect valid tests to demonstrate high internal consistency? In fact we observe that, however complex and contingent the nature of language ability, test items can elicit responses which fit a simple trait model quite well. This is because different aspects of language competence are interrelated and tend to correlate with each other. Thus a test can demonstrate good internal consistency and reliability, even if it contains tasks which focus on different aspects of the same skill, or elicit different kinds of response. As Wood (1991: 138) points out, high internal consistency need not imply homogeneity.

One might also question whether unidimensionality can be reasonably expected in a trait which spans several proficiency levels. When we look at level descriptors, as in the CEFR, it is striking how the skill descriptors change from level to level. Each has different salient features. Reading at A1 seems a completely different activity to Reading at C2. Can we really treat Reading (or any skill) as a coherent unidimensional trait? In fact, it turns out to be quite practical to do so. While it is impossible to compare directly A1 learners with C2 learners, because there is no single task on which both could demonstrate their ability, it *is* possible to compare individuals at every small incremental step along the path from A1 to C2, and this is how proficiency scales are constructed. Unidimensionality has meaning only within the range of ability where individuals can reasonably be compared.

Focusing on specific contexts

The conclusion is thus that the trait-based measurement models presented in this section enable approaches to language proficiency testing which can work well, achieving a useful blend of reliability, validity and practicality. However, there is a condition: each testing context must be treated on its own terms, and tests designed for one context may not be readily comparable with tests designed for another context.

Language tests differ because every aspect of test design requires choices to be made. For example, Weir (2005) presents a socio-cognitive model for test validation in which 'context validity' concerns how features of the test design elicit responses from the test taker that validly reflect the ability to be measured. Bachman (1990) discusses 'test method facets', which encompass essentially all the features of a test and its administration. Bachman's use of the term 'facet' refers to Guttman's (1970) theory of 'facet design', which presents methods for studying and optimising the impact of such facets on validity and reliability, within the framework of generalisability theory (see Schoonen, this volume). Above all the decisions made reflect the construct and the purpose of the test, and systematic features of the candidate population such as age, level, professional group, first language, purpose in seeking accreditation, and so on. Explicit consideration of these enable the construction of valid and reliable measurement scales for a particular context and population of learners, but the downside is that each of these scales is to an extent *sui generis*, and the population of learners that it measures is not necessarily comparable with that from another test context.

Mislevy (1992: 22) identifies four possible levels at which tests can be compared:

- Equating – the strongest level: refers to testing the same thing in the same way, e.g. two tests constructed from the same test specification to the same blueprint. Equating such tests allows them to be used interchangeably.

- Calibration – refers to testing the same thing in a different way, e.g. two tests constructed from the same specification but to a different blueprint, which thus have different measurement characteristics.
- Projection – refers to testing a different thing in a different way, e.g. where constructs are differently specified. It predicts learners' scores on one test from another, with accuracy dependent on the degree of similarity. It is relevant where both tests target the same basic population of learners.
- Moderation – the weakest level: can be applied where performance on one test does not predict performance on the other for an individual learner, e.g. tests of French and German.

The first three of these use statistical methods. The last can only be a judgmental process, although if one were comparing tests of French and German in terms of, say, their functional proficiency level, such a judgment could be based on various kinds of empirical evidence.

Proficiency frameworks such as the CEFR offer ways of comparing different languages and contexts of learning in terms of a general notion of functional level. The widespread adoption of the CEFR's reference levels confirms that they are practically useful. But the judgments and arguments that relate different tests to CEFR levels remain subjective, and grow out of the specific context and design of each test.

Issues with reliability

So far I have presented an essentially supportive view of trait-based measurement and the role of reliability in assuring test quality. This part presents some more critical views, and leads into the final part where possible future developments are considered.

Reliability versus validity

There is almost a tradition of seeing reliability as in conflict with validity. Spolsky (1995: 5) identifies 'two major ideologies' underlying testing: a traditional 'humanist-scepticist descriptive approach', associated with the British university style, and relying typically on essays, and a 'rationalist–empiricist approach', associated with the United States and with multiple-choice tests. He finds both problematic: 'To oversimplify, with the traditional examination we think we know what we are assessing, but remain happily or unhappily uncertain about the accuracy or replicability of our assessment; with the modern examination, we are sure enough of our measurement, but are, or should be, uncertain as to what exactly we have measured.'

This is, of course, a caricature, and whatever the original justice of this statement, it is certainly no longer the case that language testing can be neatly classified into the reliable but invalid, or the valid but unreliable. The increasing use of performance tests in the United States, and of psychometrics in Europe, the general movement in education towards criterion-based goals and interpretations, and above all, the evolution of the concept of validity in language assessment (see Chapelle, this volume) has put interpretation and use of test results squarely at the centre, with reliability as an integral aspect of this.

In practice language testing seeks to achieve both reliability and validity within the practical constraints which limit every testing context. The aim should be to optimise both, rather than prioritise one over the other. If reliability is prioritised, then indeed it may conflict with validity. Internal consistency estimates of reliability make it possible to drive up the reliability of tests over time, simply by weeding out items which correlate less highly with the others. This, as Ennis (1999) points out, is potentially a serious threat to the validity of a test, as it leads to a progressive narrowing of what is tested, without explicit consideration of how the content of the test is being modified. A classic way of narrowing the testing focus is to restrict the range of task types used and select items primarily on psychometric quality – the discrete item multiple-choice test format which Spolsky questioned.

The one-time practice of testing Writing through multiple-choice items was very much a case of reliability being prioritised above validity. Arguably the automated assessment of Speaking by computer is a current case where high reliability may or may not compensate for a deficit in validity (to the extent that the current technology cannot measure speech in terms of its actual communicative effectiveness).

Trait-based measures versus cognitive models

The trait-based measurement approach is most useful in *summative* assessment, where at the end of a course of study the learner's achievements can be summarised as a simple grade or proficiency level. *Formative* assessment, which aims to feed forward into future learning, needs to provide more information, not simply about *how much* a learner knows, but about the *nature* of that knowledge. As Mislevy (1992: 15) states: 'Contemporary conceptions of learning do not describe developing competence in terms of increasing trait values, but in terms of alternative constructs.'

Reliability limits the forms of assessment

Moss (1994) asks this question in her title: 'Can there be validity without reliability?' Her concern is about 'the influence of measurement *practices* on the quality of education', arguing more recently that 'conventional operationalisations of reliability in the measurement literature … unnecessarily privileged certain assessment practices over others' (Moss, 2004: 245, emphasis in original). As an alternative approach she endorses hermeneutics, 'a holistic and integrative approach to interpretation of human phenomena that seeks to understand the whole in light of its parts, repeatedly testing interpretations against the available evidence until each of the parts can be accounted for in a coherent interpretation of the whole' (Moss, 1994: 7).

Mislevy's response to Moss (Mislevy, 1994, 2004) is to define reliability more broadly than in trait-based measurement theory: 'if by reliability we mean credibility of evidence, where credibility is defined as appropriate to the inference, the answer is no, we cannot have validity without reliability' (Mislevy, 1994: 11). He accepts the case for extending the range of forms of assessment, but points out that this is already happening. His broader conception of reliability aims to deal with the more complex evidence that these new assessments provide. 'This is not "reliability" in the sense of accumulating *collaborating* evidence, as in classical test theory, but in the sense of *converging* evidence – accumulating evidence of different types that support the same inference' (Mislevy, 1994: 8).

Future directions

The above discussion indicates several respects in which current assessment practices are coming under pressure to change. I would like to suggest two possible development paths that may be emerging for assessment and for conceptions of reliability. What they have in common is the aim to change the relationship between educational assessment and the process of learning and teaching. They differ over the nature of the change. The first sees the power of standardised psychometric testing reduced, and shared with more heterogeneous, classroom-based approaches to assessment, while the second looks to implement far more sophisticated models of competence, supported by even more powerful statistical methods.

Turning first to the latter programme: it is by no means new. In *Test Theory for a New Generation of Tests* (Frederiksen *et al.*, 1993: 19), Mislevy states: 'Educational measurement faces today a crisis that would appear to threaten its very foundations. The essential problem is that the view of human abilities implicit in standard test theory – item response theory as well as classical true-score theory – is incompatible with the view rapidly emerging from cognitive and educational psychology.' The claim is that while trait-based measures serve well for many practical purposes, they fail to capture the complexity of abilities in the way necessary to understand and impact on the process of learning. For this purpose detailed cognitive models are needed, and approaches to measurement that can deal with them.

This programme has been pursued through two major projects at Educational Testing Services (ETS): work on Evidence-Centred Design (ECD), and on Cognitive Diagnostic Analysis (CDA) (see, respectively, the chapters by Mislevy and by Jang in this volume).

ECD (Mislevy *et al.*, 2003, Mislevy *et al.*, 2002) proposes a formal framework for constructing a validity argument for an assessment. The framework includes a *student model* (the skills to be measured), *task models* (schema for how to elicit relevant evidence) and an *evidence model* (comprising an *evaluation model* for how to score tasks, and a *measurement model* for how to combine scores to develop interpretations). It reflects validity theories advanced by Kane (1992, 2004). Similar schemes have been proposed specifically for language testing (Weir, 2005; Jones and Saville, 2010). Its most striking innovation is the measurement model, which combines different kinds of observations using probability-based reasoning, implemented through Bayesian networks.

Cognitive Diagnostic Analysis concerns explicit modelling of the elements of a skill to be tested, specifying which elements are tested by a given task and how the elements collaborate to produce a right or wrong response. *Language Assessment Quarterly* Volume 6: 3 (2009) is devoted to examples of CDA in language testing. A key issue that emerges (Lee and Sawaki, 2009, 2010; Alderson, 2010) is what kind of elements or subskills can be identified and validated, and how one would construct test items that test certain subskills and not others.

While the focus on cognition offers new ways of defending the validity of summative proficiency assessments, its obvious application is to formative assessment. Pellegrino *et al.* (2001) identify three elements of an 'assessment triangle': cognition, observation and interpretation. They argue that better understanding of how learners represent knowledge and develop competence, and advances in computer-based assessment technology which enable us to observe process as well as outcomes, as well as statistical models to provide sophisticated interpretation, create new opportunities to devise assessments that can impact directly and positively on learning. They stress the importance of basing assessment on an explicit model of cognition. They see applications to classroom teaching as well as to building intelligent tutoring systems.

Not all are convinced by that argument. Shavelson (2008, 2009) warns against premature applications of cognitive development models, particularly for specifying learning progressions. He cites research to undermine the assumption that development is neatly describable, or follows predictable paths. Successful formative assessment is difficult to reduce to rules, and depends, of course, on a high level of teacher training.

We should also bear in mind the special nature of language learning. The cognitive approach as presented by Pellegrino *et al.* is illustrated chiefly by examples from maths and science, which stress the process of problem-solving. Language learning is unique among school subjects in the range of learner attributes – cognitive, psycho-motor and affective – which it engages (Coleman, 2004). There is far more to it than intellectual understanding.

Thus the major doubt raised by the work described above is whether it can actually impact learning at the classroom level. Diagnosis is only a starting point for formative action. When we consider the nature of formative interactions within the classroom it becomes clear that learners' states of understanding or mastery can hardly be analysed in isolation from the interactions themselves (Teasdale and Leung, 2000). Cognition is socially constructed and begins in interaction. Model-based diagnosis of cognitive attributes requires stable observations, something hardly to be expected at the growing point where learning is happening. It is easier to see the relevance to summative than to formative assessment.

The attempt to extend the concept of measurement beyond the unidimensional trait to more complex configurations of skills is undoubtedly important and promises to push back the limits of measurement. Nonetheless those limits remain, where the attributes of interest are too unstable, varied or contingent to be measured.

An alternative programme would recognize the limits of measurement and seek complementary roles for quantitative and qualitative methods. This is a procedural and pedagogic conception more than a psychometric one. Quantitative information – measurement – allows teaching to hone in on the general skills profile of an individual or a group and hence to find the optimal level for effective language learning. The CEFR can be seen as a quasi-measurement construct which provides useful reference points for goal-setting. Given this orientation a teacher can then target formative procedures on qualitative aspects of a learner's competence and understanding. The learner's development of autonomous learning skills is also favoured. *Learning oriented assessment* is a term we might use to subsume summative and formative assessment, treating these as complementary elements of a complex system aimed at supporting learning.

In my personal view this alternative is the one which offers most practical ways for language testing bodies to engage with language teaching and learning. However, it presents a number of challenges, first to develop formative processes which teachers will be willing or able to incorporate in classroom work (Shavelson, 2008), and second to demonstrate the validity and efficacy of these processes – that is, formative assessment *is* assessment and both its methods and its effect require empirical validation (Bennett, 2010).

Formative assessment is the area where I see a clear need for language testing to explore new forms of engagement. Otherwise, I am not convinced (at least as far as language testing is concerned) that the trait-based measurement paradigm is really in urgent need of reform. It is still very much the norm, and for most purposes remains quite appropriate. Highly complex inter-related systems such as language still tend to elicit performance which can be described quite well by simple trait models. Thus the notion of language proficiency levels, which can be characterised in linguistic and functional ways, remains essentially sound, and of practical value for framing learning objectives, designing curricula and assessing outcomes. CDA offers one answer, but if any cognitive diagnosis approach is to succeed it will require test constructors reliably to identify the subskills tested by test items, something which has baffled generations of language testers, and which may not be a realistic ambition within communicative approaches to testing.

At the same time, it is good to remember that individual learners differ in a range of attributes which the most reliable trait-based measurement cannot reveal, but which are relevant to characterising their knowledge and helping them to learn. As testing engages more closely with language learning and teaching we can expect to see interesting new developments, and further re-evaluation or reconceptualisation of reliability.

Further reading

In this chapter I have focused on measurement and reliability from a more theoretical point of view, and the references reflect this. The different chapter which I might have written would have linked theory to exemplification of how language testers may go about the practical business of constructing measures of proficiency, valid, reliable and dependable enough to serve their purpose. Here are some suggestions for further reading offering this complementary practical perspective. They are recent additions to the Studies in Language Testing (SiLT) series published by Cambridge University Press.

Hanan, K. and Weir, C. J. (2009). *Examining Reading: research and practice in assessing second language reading.* SiLT Volume 29. This volume develops a theoretical framework for validating tests of second language reading ability. The framework is then applied through an examination of tasks in Cambridge ESOL reading tests from a number of different validity perspectives that reflect the socio-cognitive nature of any assessment event. As well as providing an up-to-date review of relevant literature on assessing reading, it also offers an accessible and systematic description of the key criteria that differentiate one proficiency level from another when assessing second language reading.

Shaw, S. D. and Weir, C. J. (2007). *Examining Writing: research and practice in assessing second language writing.* SiLT Volume 26. A similar approach applied to assessing the skill of writing.

Taylor, L. (ed.), (2011). *Examining Speaking: research and practice in assessing second language speaking.* SiLT Volume 30. An edited collection of papers on issues in assessing the skill of speaking.

References

Alderson, J. C. (2010). Cognitive diagnosis and q-matrices in language assessment: a commentary. *Language Assessment Quarterly* 7: 96–103.

Bachman, L.F. (1990). *Fundamental Considerations in Language Testing.* Oxford, UK: Oxford University Press.

Bennett, R. (2010). *Formative Assessment: A Critical Review.* Cambridge Assessment Network Seminar, Cambridge, UK, February 18, 2010.

Brennan, R. L. (2001). An essay on the history and future of reliability from the perspective of replications. *Journal of Educational Measurement* 38: 295–317.

Coe, R. J. (2008). Comparability of GCSE examinations in different subjects: an application of the Rasch model. *Oxford Review of Education* 34: 609–36.

Coleman, J. A. (2004). Modern languages in British universities: past and present. *Arts and Humanities in Higher Education* 3: 147–62.

Council of Europe (2001). *Common European Framework of Reference for Languages, Teaching, Learning, Assessment.* Cambridge, UK: Cambridge University Press.

Ennis, R. H. (1999). Test reliability: a practical exemplification of ordinary language philosophy. In R. Curren (ed.), *Philosophy of education.* Urbana, IL: The Philosophy of Education Society, 242–48.

Feldt, L. S. and Brennan, R. L. (1989). Reliability. In R. L. Linn (ed.), *Educational Measurement*, 3rd edn. New York, NY: Macmillan, 105–46.

Ferris, T. L. J. (2004). A new definition of measurement. *Measurement* 36: 101–9.

Frederiksen, N., Mislevy, R. J. and Bejar, I. (eds), (1993). *Test Theory for a New Generation of Tests.* Hillsdale, NJ: Erlbaum.

Gulliksen, H. (1950). *Theory of Mental Tests.* New York, NY: Wiley.

Guttman, L. (1970). Integration of test design and analysis. In *Toward a Theory of Achievement Measurement. Proceedings of the 1969 Invitational Conference on Testing Problems.* Princeton, NJ, 53–65.

Haertel, G. D. (2006). Reliability. In R. L. Brennan (ed.), *Educational measurement.* National Council on Measurement in Education. Westport, CT: Praeger Publishers.

Henning, G. (1987). *A Guide to Language Testing: development, evaluation, research.* Cambridge, MA: Newbury House.

Jones, N. and Saville, N. (2010). Scales and frameworks. In B. Spolsky and F. M. Hult (eds), *The Handbook of Educational Linguistics.* Malden MA: Blackwell.

Kane, M. T. (1992). An argument-based approach to validity. *Psychological Bulletin* 12: 527–35.

—— (2004). Certification testing as an illustration of argument-based validation. *Measurement: interdisciplinary research and perspectives* 2: 135–70.

Lee, Y. and Sawaki, Y. (2009). Cognitive diagnosis approaches to language assessment. *Language Assessment Quarterly* 6: 172–89.

—— (2010). Cognitive diagnosis and Q-matrices in language assessment: the authors respond. *Language Assessment Quarterly* 7: 108–112.

Messick, S. (1989). Validity. In R. L. Linn (ed.), *Educational Measurement*, 3rd edn, New York: American Council on Education and Macmillan, 1–103.

Mislevy, R. J. (1992). *Linking Educational Assessments Concepts, Issues, Methods, and Prospects*. Princeton, NJ: ETS.

—— (1994). *Can There be Reliability Without 'Reliability'?* Princeton, NJ: Educational Testing Service.

—— (2004). Can there be reliability without 'reliability?' *Journal of Educational and Behavioral Statistics* 29: 241–44.

Mislevy, R. J., Almond, R. G. and Lukas, J. F. (2003). *A Brief Introduction to Evidence-Centred Design*. Research Report RR-03–16. Princeton, NJ: Educational Testing Service.

Mislevy, R. J., Steinberg, L. S. and Almond, R. G. (2002). Design and analysis in task-based language assessment. *Language Testing* 19: 477.

Moss, P. (1994). Can there be validity without reliability? *Educational Researcher* 23: 5–12.

—— (2004). The meaning and consequences of 'reliability'. *Journal of Educational and Behavioral Statistics* 29: 245–49.

Pellegrino, J. W., Chudowsky, N. and Glaser, R. (2001). *Knowing What Students Know: the science and design of educational assessment*. Washington, DC: National Academy Press.

Shavelson, R. J. (2009). *Reflections on Learning Progressions*. Paper presented at the Learning Progressions in Science (LeaPS). Conference, June 2009.

—— (2008). Guest editor's introduction. *Applied Measurement in Education* 21: 293–94.

Spolsky, B. (1995). *Measured Words: development of objective language testing*. Oxford, UK: Oxford University Press.

Stellman, J. M. (1998). *Encyclopaedia of Occupational Health and Safety,* 4th edn. Geneva Switzerland: International Labor Office.

Teasdale, A. and Leung, C. (2000). Teacher assessment and psychometric theory: a case of paradigm crossing? *Language Testing* 17: 163.

Weir, C. (2005). *Language Testing and Validation*. Basingstoke, UK: Palgrave Macmillan Ltd.

Wood, R. (1991). *Assessment and Testing: a survey of research*. Cambridge, UK: Cambridge University Press.

The generalisability of scores from language tests

Rob Schoonen

Introduction

One of the important features of an empirical study is the quality of its measurements, i.e., are the constructs measured appropriately (i.e., validity, Chapelle, this volume) and are these measurements trustworthy (i.e., reliability, J. D. Brown, this volume). We expect the scores on a testing instrument to be a reflection of the construct we intend to measure, for example language proficiency, and nothing else. However, in practice, other factors influence test performance as well. For example, if we test a candidate's writing proficiency by means of a writing prompt, eliciting a written composition, the writing score the candidate receives will be the result of the candidate's writing proficiency, the characteristics of the writing prompt, the rating criteria, the rater's severity, the interactions between these factors and probably some random other factors as well. If, shortly afterwards, the candidate has to take a new writing test, all these characteristics and their effects on the writing score are likely to be somewhat different, except for the candidate's writing proficiency. So, the comparability of the scores will largely depend on the size of the effects of the factors mentioned and their interactions, compared to the candidate's proficiency. Classical test theory (CTT, see J.D. Brown, this volume) focuses on the subdivision of the variance in test takers' scores into variance due to proficiency differences ('true score' variance) and variance due to other, random factors (error variance). Generalisability theory (G-theory) aims at teasing apart the effects of different factors, such as writing prompt and rater, and thus determining the generalisability of test scores across, for example, prompts and raters. As such, G-theory can be seen as an extension of CTT, but G-theory also adds a number of interesting possibilities of evaluating the quality of (complex) measurements and designing new assessments.

In the next sections, we will introduce a few applications of G-theory. The flexibility of this approach comes at the cost of computational complexity. Here, we will confine ourselves to the basic elements of G-theory. The interested reader is referred to suggested readings at the end of this chapter.

Generalisability theory

Framework and terminology

When we want to determine the generalisability of an assessment or test score, the first question that needs to be addressed is to what domain do we want to generalise, and thus: what is the *universe of admissible observations* from which we consider our measurement to be a (random) sample. When measuring writing proficiency, we might consider our writing assignment and the subsequent expert rating as appropriate. At the same time we probably acknowledge that another writing assignment and the rating by another expert could have been used equally well. Actually, we assume that our current assessment score has predictive value for the performance on other (similar) assessments. This predictive value may concern just the ranking of the candidates (*relative decisions*) or the actual level of the scores (*absolute decisions*). In all cases, we have to consider what the construct is we intend to measure, and what we consider admissible observations or measurements of that construct. G-theory is often presented as just another approach to reliability, but its concerns and questions about the facets of a measurement, underscore that generalisability is very much intertwined with validity issues.

Assessments for a given construct can be described in terms of one or more aspects of the testing conditions, such as writing prompts, text types and raters. Each aspect of the testing conditions is called a *facet* and has its own categories. For instance, the facet of text types may consist of persuasive, descriptive and narrative texts. A facet can be considered a set of similar conditions (Brennan, 1992). The facets involved in a study define the universe of admissible observations. For example, in a study with a three-faceted operationalisation of writing proficiency, this universe is determined by combinations of the different (acceptable) prompts, the different (acceptable) text types, and the different (acceptable) raters.

In CTT the test taker is assumed to have a 'true' score, that with some error determines the actual observed scores. G-theory's counterpart of the true score is defined as a person's mean score across all admissible observations, that is the mean score over an infinite number of writing prompts for an infinite number of text types with ratings by an infinite number of raters. Of course, this is a theoretical definition. The actual measures in an assessment are taken as a sample of all possible measures that allow us to estimate a person's mean score over all admissible scores. This mean score is called the *universe score* and can be seen as the analogue of a person's 'true score' in CTT. G-theory is concerned with the generalisability of actual observations to all admissible scores and thus to a person's universe score. Most commonly in applied linguistic research, the language learners are the so-called *objects of measurement* and for convenience we will take our examples from these types of studies, but obviously the following also applies to studies with other objects of measurements, such as schools or sentences.

Evaluating the generalisability of scores, we need to be aware of the kind of information we want to include in our generalisation. In some studies the absolute level of the scores is not very meaningful or relevant. In those cases we are mainly interested in the ranking of candidates, for instance, for correlational analyses. We make so-called *relative decisions* about candidates. For example, two raters who differ in severity, but rank the candidates in the same way, will still come to the same relative decisions. However, if the absolute level of a candidate's score is meaningful or relevant, and we want to make claims about candidates' level of performance, we make *absolute decisions*. This could be the case in forms of criterion-referenced testing where candidates have to reach a certain preset score level for admission or immigration (Davidson and J. D. Brown, this volume, both discuss criterion-referenced testing; see Glaser, 1963, for the origin of the concept). It is not hard to imagine that in these latter situations raters of different severity are not interchangeable, and that when (severity) differences are large, the generalisability of single ratings is limited. So, the kind of decisions we want to make based on our scores determines the kinds of differences between raters, tasks and such we have to take into account when we evaluate the generalisability of the scores. Below we will introduce separate generalisability indexes for relative and absolute decisions.

So far, we have assumed that the conditions within a facet are random. We consider our raters as a random sample of all acceptable raters. When, for example, we employ two raters in our studies and we consider them interchangeable with any other two acceptable raters, raters is a *random facet* of our measurement. The same reasoning can be applied to a set of items in a reading test: items as a random sample of all possible items, and interchangeable with another set of items. However, in cases where the conditions of a facet are limited and exhausted by the observations in the measurement, the facet is considered a *fixed facet* (Shavelson and Webb, 1991; Brennan, 2001). For example, when we administer writing tasks for fictional writing and for factual writing, and we intend to generalise to a universe consisting of these two conditions, fictional and factual writing, the facet of factualness is a fixed facet. Since the *universe of generalisation* is restricted, there is no longer a concern about generalisation across sorts of writing.

The generalisability of the observed scores is determined by on the one hand the kind of decisions (relative or absolute) and generalisations (over random or fixed facets) we want to make, and on the other hand by the sample of measurements we have to work with. G-theory uses analysis of variance to estimate both the variance due to individual differences in proficiency (the facet *person* representing the objects of measurement) and the effects of different facets of the assessment on score variance. The first stage of calculating the variance components of the different facets and their interactions is called a G(*eneralisability*)-study. The results of the G-study, i.e., the variance estimates, can be used to design future assessments and to make decisions about number of tasks, raters and such. This second stage of designing a new assessment and estimating its expected generalisability is usually referred to as a D(*ecision*)-study. In the next sections, we will present some of the statistical underpinnings of G- and D-studies by discussing a few examples in more detail.

Some examples: one and two (random) facets

We will use a one-facet design to briefly introduce the basic formulae that are used in G-theory to compute the generalisability. This will then be extended to two-facet designs. As examples, two small datasets will be analysed.

Example with one facet

Consider a person (p)'s score on a test item (i) to be X_{pi}. This score can be rewritten as the result of several effects, and as such, as deviations of the grand mean, i.e., the mean score for all persons over all items. If all persons were equally proficient and all items were equally difficult, everyone would score the grand mean on all items. However, persons differ if we look at their average performance on (all) items, and items differ in difficulty if we look at the average performance of (all) test takers. The effect due to the level of a person p compared to other persons is the person effect, the difficulty (or facility) of an item i compared to the other items is the item effect, and then there remains a residual effect. The residual effect can be the specific response of person p to item i (interaction of $p \times i$) and/or random error. The $p \times i$ interaction cannot be discerned from random error when we do not have multiple observations of the same person p performing the same item i. More formally:

$$X_{pi} = \mu \qquad \text{(grand mean)}$$
$$+ \, \mu_p - \mu \qquad \text{(person effect, i.e., a person's deviation from the grand mean)}$$
$$+ \, \mu_i - \mu \qquad \text{(item effect, i.e., an item's deviation from the grand mean)}$$
$$+ \, X_{pi} - \mu_p - \mu_i + \mu \qquad \text{(residual effect, i.e., a score's deviation from the grand mean and the person and item effect)}$$

$$(25.1)$$

(cf. Cronbach et al., 1972: 26)

The residual is a rewrite of the difference between the observed score (X_{pi}) and the grand mean and the other known effects, $(\mu_p - \mu)$ and $(\mu_i - \mu)$: $X_{pi} - \{\mu + (\mu_p - \mu) + (\mu_i - \mu)\}$. A person's level or μ_p, i.e., a person's expected mean score over all possible items, is called the *universe score* and is G-theory's analogue for CTT's 'true' score. The grand mean is a constant, but the person, item and residual effect vary with the sample of persons and items under investigation, and the size of the variance components can be estimated when we study multiple persons and multiple items. Thus, the observed score variance $(\sigma^2_{X_{pi}})$ can be decomposed in terms of the aforementioned effects:

$$\sigma^2_{X_{pi}} = \sigma^2_p + \sigma^2_i + \sigma^2_{pi,e} \tag{25.2}$$

(Cronbach et al. 1972: 27)

where $\sigma^2_{pi,e}$ refers to the residual variance as being the confound of the interaction between person and item, and the random error. The variance components can be derived from the mean squares in an analysis of variance. The computational derivations can be found in Cronbach *et al.* (1972), Shavelson and Webb (1991) and Brennan (2001).

To make it more concrete, let us assume a study with 10 persons taking a seven-item multiple-choice test (Table 25.1). As the marginal means show, items differ in their difficulty (0.03–0.09) and persons differ in their level of performance (0.143–1.00).

For the G-study, an analysis of variance with item as a repeated measure provides the mean sum of squares and thus the estimated variance components (Table 25.2, upper panel). The size of the variance components indicates that Person interacts with Item, which means that the ranking of persons is affected by the items that are administered. There is also an effect of Item which implies that the items differ in difficulty, as was indicated above. This latter effect is especially relevant when we plan an assessment in which we make claims about the absolute level of performance of the test takers.

The variance components of the G-study can be used in a D-study to estimate the generalisability with a given number of items, either for the current dataset or future test development. In our example, the person-by-item interaction, residual variance component is large compared to the person variance component (0.066 versus 0.147). To cancel out the person-by-item interaction effects to some extent, it might be wise to administer several items. This way the generalisability of the *test*

Table 25.1 Scores for 10 persons on a seven-item test (fictitious data)

Person	Item 1	Item 2	Item 3	Item 4	Item 5	Item 6	Item 7	Person's mean
1	1	0	1	0	0	0	0	0.286
2	1	1	1	1	0	1	1	0.857
3	0	0	0	0	0	0	1	0.143
4	1	1	0	1	1	0	1	0.714
5	1	1	1	1	1	1	1	1.000
6	1	1	0	0	0	0	1	0.429
7	1	0	1	1	0	1	1	0.714
8	1	1	0	0	0	0	1	0.429
9	1	1	1	0	0	1	1	0.714
10	1	1	1	1	1	1	1	1.000
Item's mean	0.9	0.7	0.6	0.5	0.3	0.5	0.9	0.629

Table 25.2 Analysis of variance table for the sample data (Table 25.1)

Source (facet)	G-study			
	Sums of squares	Degrees of freedom	Means of squares	Estimated variance component
Person (p)	5.486	9	0.610	0.066
Item (i)	2.943	6	0.490	0.034
Person x item, error (pi,e)	7.914	54	0.147	0.147
D-study (seven items)				
σ^2_δ	0.021		Eρ^2	0.759
σ^2_Δ	0.026		Φ	0.719

score will increase. Equations 25.3 and 25.4 define how, in a single-faceted design, the number of items reduces the 'error' variance in relative decisions (σ^2_δ or σ^2_{rel}) and absolute decisions (σ^2_Δ or σ^2_{abs}), respectively. The more items of a given quality we use, the smaller the error variance (σ^2_δ and σ^2_Δ) due to item effects will be, and the more generalisable the test score based on the set of items will be. For claims about the absolute performance level of candidates, all variance components due to items are taken into account (Equation 25.4); for decisions about test-takers' relative standing, only those variance components that interact with persons are of concern (Equation 25.3).

$$\sigma^2_\delta = \frac{\sigma^2_{pi,e}}{n_i} \tag{25.3}$$

and

$$\sigma^2_\Delta = \frac{\sigma^2_i}{n_i} + \frac{\sigma^2_{pi,e}}{n_i} \tag{25.4}$$

where n_i indicates the number of items.

If, in our example, we decide to use a test with seven items, we can thus compute the relative and absolute error variance for this test design, and subsequently the two corresponding generalisability coefficients. For relative decisions the generalisability is denoted by *generalisability coefficient* Eρ^2 which is the ratio of the variance due to person (universe score variance) and the variance due to person plus the relative error variance (Equation 25.5). This coefficient can be interpreted as the 'expected value [E] (over randomly parallel tests) of the squared correlation between observed scores and universe scores' (Brennan, 1992: 17). It is also the analogue of Cronbach's alpha in CTT.

$$E\rho^2 = \frac{\sigma^2_p}{\sigma^2_p + \sigma^2_\delta} \tag{25.5}$$

$$\Phi = \frac{\sigma^2_p}{\sigma^2_p + \sigma^2_\Delta} \tag{25.6}$$

For absolute decisions, the generalisability is indicated by the *index of dependability*, coefficient Φ. The equation of the index of dependability formula is similar to that of the generalisability coefficient; the difference is that the relative error variance estimate σ_δ^2 is replaced by the absolute error variance estimate σ_Δ^2 (Equation 25.6). The absolute error variance estimate also takes into account the differences in difficulty of the items, σ_i^2 (compare Equations 25.3 and 25.4).

In a G-study, we compute the 'average' effect of items. Based on these outcomes and using Equations 25.3–25.6, we can, in a D-study, compute what we can expect the generalisability to be, deploying seven items, or any other number of items. If we stick to the seven items of this example, the relative and absolute error variance for this given number of observations or items – usually indicated by capital letter in the subscript, so X_{pI} and n_I – would be as follows: the relative error variance $(\sigma_\delta^2) = 0.147/7 = 0.021$ and the absolute error variance $(\sigma_\Delta^2) = (0.034/7) + (0.147/7) = 0.026$. The corresponding generalisability coefficients are $E\rho^2 = 0.759$ and $\Phi = 0.719$, respectively (Table 25.2, lower panel).

Compared to CTT, G-theory so far is much the same. CTT makes the assumption of parallel tests/items, which implies that variance due to differences in item difficulty is presumed to be zero, and thus the distinction between relative and absolute error variance is non-existent. In G-theory, this variance component is estimated, and can be taken into account when required. Interestingly, the relative error variance component is the square of what is known from CTT as the standard error of measurement (cf. Jones, this volume).

Example with two facets

G-theory shows its flexibility in more complex measurement settings, where the assessment is multifaceted, as usually is the case in performance testing. Candidates may have to perform several tasks, maybe on several occasions, and performances might be rated by several raters. The question is to what extent are raters interchangeable, or are tasks or occasions interchangeable. If they are, one or two raters or tasks or occasions might suffice, respectively. However, if, for example, raters differ substantially in their ratings, then we need a larger number of raters to get a good estimate of the universe score that is generalisable across new panels of raters. It is also important to figure out whether the raters differ in just their leniency or whether they (also) differ in their ranking of the candidates. As the performance assessments are clearly multifaceted, so are the sources of variance. In a G-study, the score variance is decomposed along the lines of its sources, and the size of the variance components is estimated. Again, in a D-study, these estimates can be used to compute the (expected) generalisability in the current (or a new) testing situation. The design of the D-study can be different from the G-study that provides the estimates.

Table 25.3 lists sample data from a fully crossed design with two raters who rated all performances of two speaking tasks; Table 25.4 shows the computational results. In this two-faceted universe, it turns out that person variance is the major component. Additionally, there are variance components indicating that the relative ranking of the test takers is affected by task and rater $(\sigma_{pt}^2, \sigma_{pr}^2$ and $\sigma_{ptr,e}^2)$, though smaller than the component for person. There are also effects that do not affect the relative ranking of the persons, but do affect the absolute level of the scores $(\sigma_t^2, \sigma_r^2$ and $\sigma_{tr}^2)$. However, these variance components are also relatively small compared to the individual differences component. From the estimated variance components in this G-study (Table 25.4, upper panel), we can estimate the expected generalisability for a given number of tasks and/or a given number of raters in D-studies (Table 25.4, lower panel). For the sample data presented in Table 25.3 (two tasks, two raters), the generalisability coefficient and the index of dependability are 0.926 and 0.900, respectively. (For these computations, Equations 25.3 and 25.4 need to be extended to include both item or task effects and rater effects (Brennan, 2001; Shavelson and

Table 25.3 Scores for 15 persons on two speaking tasks rated twice on a 30-point scale (fictitious data)

Person	Task 1		Task 2		Person's mean
	Rater_1	Rater_2	Rater_1[a]	Rater_2[a]	
1	16	19	13	17	16.25
2	25	27	21	24	24.25
3	19	21	23	23	21.50
4	16	18	17	20	17.75
5	23	23	23	21	22.50
6	22	29	20	29	25.00
7	19	17	16	18	17.50
8	17	17	14	13	15.25
9	28	27	23	24	25.50
10	9	12	5	9	8.75
11	12	12	11	13	12.00
12	15	18	12	17	15.50
13	12	11	10	12	11.25
14	17	16	15	17	16.25
15	12	10	10	11	10.75
Task by Rater's mean	17.47	18.47	15.53	17.87	17.33

[a] In the next example (Table 25.5), the same data will be used, but Task 2 performances are considered to be rated by new rates, i.e., rater 3 and 4.

Webb, 1991)). These two indexes can be computed for all kinds of combinations of tasks and raters. The relationship between the number of conditions within facets involved and the generalisability or dependability of the scores can be depicted in a graph (Figure 25.1). The graph allows researchers to make optimal decisions for the design of their assessments. For example, researchers can *a priori* consider their budget constraints and decide to hire more raters or to administer more speaking tasks (cf. Parkes, 2000; Lee, 2006). Each extension of the data collection will of course have a repercussion on the research budget as well as on the workload of test takers, raters, and researchers.

Nested factors

A fully crossed design as in Table 25.3 is rather straightforward, but G–theory also applies to more complex designs of data collection, such as nested designs. In our example, we can imagine that for reasons of efficiency we want other raters than rater 1 and rater 2 to rate the second task. So, raters 3 and 4 are hired to rate the performances on the second task. Now, raters are 'nested' in task $(p \times (r{:}t))$, which slightly complicates the computations, but essentially the same kinds of estimates are made. Some variance components are 'confounded' and cannot be computed independent of other facets. For example, rater differences cannot be estimated across all tasks and thus rater effects are confounded with the task they have rated. One could say that such confounded effects are taken together. Brennan (2001) and Shavelson and Webb (1991), among others, provide the derivations and corresponding computations of the variance components. In

Table 25.4 Analysis of variance table (p×t×r) for the sample data 2 (Table 25.3)

Source (facet)	G-study			
	Sums of squares	Degrees of freedom	Means of squares	Estimated variance component
Person (p)	1640.33	14	117.17	27.11
Task (t)	24.07	1	24.07	0.48
Rater (r)	41.67	1	41.67	1.01
Person x task (pt)	53.93	14	3.85	1.52
Person x rater (pr)	79.33	14	5.67	2.43
Task x rater (tr)	6.67	1	6.67	0.39
Person x task x rater, error (ptr,e)	11.33	14	0.81	0.81
D-study (2 tasks, 2 raters, fully crossed)				
σ_δ^2	2.18		$E\rho^2$	0.926
σ_Δ^2	3.02		Φ	0.900

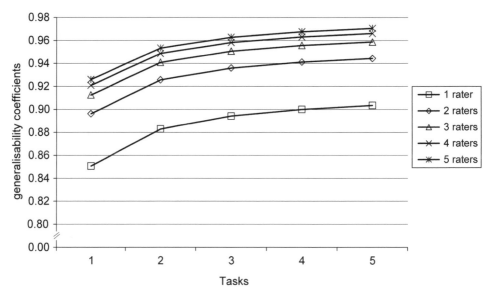

Figure 25.1 Generalisability coefficients ($E\rho^2$) for different numbers of tasks and raters (cf. Table 25.4)

Table 25.5, the estimated variance components are reported for the Table 25.3 data presuming that Task 2 is rated by raters 3 and 4.

Comparing the results for the two analyses (Table 25.4 and 25.5), we can make a few observations. It is obvious that a fully crossed G–study design yields more information than a nested G–study, that is, for all individual variance components estimates are available. In a nested design, some facets are confounded, and this is reflected in a smaller number of variance estimates. For example, in the nested design we have an estimate for raters within tasks (r:t), which basically is the variance attributable to the raters (r) and to the rater by task interaction (tr).

Table 25.5 Analysis of variance table (p×(r:t)) for the sample data 2 (Table 25.3), with raters nested within task

Source (facet)	G-study (nested design)			
	Sums of squares	Degrees of freedom	Means of squares	Estimated variance component
Person (p)	1640.33	14	117.17	28.33
Task (t)	24.07	1	24.07	0[a]
Rater within task (r:t)	48.33	2	24.17	1.40
Person x task (pt)	53.93	14	3.85	0.31
Person x rater within task (pr:t,e)	90.67	28	3.24	3.24

D-study (2 ratings, 2 tasks, raters nested within tasks)			
σ^2_δ	0.963	$E\rho^2$	0.967
σ^2_Δ	1.312	Φ	0.956

Note: [a] This variance estimate was slightly negative. This might be due to sampling error in small samples. Negative estimates are usually considered to be zero (see Brennan 2001: 84–85).

This confound limits the range of different D-studies for which estimates can be produced, because from a nested G-study no estimates of these separate effects can be made. Conversely, departing from a fully crossed G-study, we can make estimations for nested D-studies (cf. Webb *et al.*, 2007).

When we compare the generalisability and dependability indices in Tables 25.4 and 25.5, we see that an assessment design with nesting can lead to better generalisable scores ($E\rho^2$: 0.926 versus 0.967, and Φ: 0.900 versus 0.956). This happens when the nested facet shows a relatively large variance. The rater variance component in Table 25.4 is relatively large, also compared to the task variance component. This means that scores are fairly dependent on the raters involved. In the fully crossed design just two raters are employed who rate both task performances. However, in the nested design when two new raters are hired for the second task, four raters 'contribute' to the overall score of the candidates, which leads to a more generalisable score. In this case, nesting provides the opportunity to get more raters involved or, more generally speaking, more conditions of a nested facet, which will reduce the effect of condition-specific variance or 'error' caused by those conditions.

Random or fixed

So far we have treated all conditions of a facet as random samples of that facet; that is, the two raters (Table 25.3) as a random sample of all admissible raters, and the two tasks as a random sample of all admissible tasks. In most language studies this is presumed to be the actual situation, because tasks and raters are considered to be interchangeable with any other (set of) admissible task(s) and admissable rater(s), respectively. Yet, there might be situations in which all conditions of a facet are already present in the study or in which conditions are purposefully chosen without the intention to generalise beyond these conditions. This might also be the case in operational assessments where there is no opportunity to change conditions, e.g. raters. However, if in such cases raters are treated as a fixed facet, then one must realise that no generalisations beyond the given raters can be made. Another example with a fixed facet would be a study in which reading ability for two text types, narrative and expository, is assessed. The two text types should be considered a fixed facet, when the researcher does not want to generalise beyond the two genres and thus the universe of generalisation is limited to those two genres. Shavelson and Webb (1991) suggest two different, practical approaches to assess the generalisability across a fixed facet. One is quite straightforward and simple: do a separate G-study for each condition of the fixed facet. In our example, it would mean estimating the generalisability for items of the narrative reading test and a similar analysis for the items of the expository reading test. The second approach is to average over the conditions of the fixed facet, and is appropriate when it makes sense to average over the conditions. Starting from an analysis with all facets treated as random, adjusted variance components can be estimated for a fixed effect design; Shavelson and Webb (1991: 66ff), among others, provide the computational details.

Software and computations

The basic elements of a G-study and subsequent D-studies are variance components that are related to effects of different conditions of a facet in the assessment. Thus, it is important to be able to correctly compute the estimates of variance components. These computations depend on the right specification of the design of the G-study and D-study (nested or crossed, random or fixed, etc.). In the following we will make a few brief general remarks concerning the computations and software that might be helpful to do a G- and D-study.

General statistical packages as SPSS (www.spss.com) can provide estimates of variance components, certainly for common crossed and nested designs. These estimates can be inferred from repeated measures analyses of variance (ANOVAs), but the readers should bear in mind that ANOVA considers (and denotes) the variance in individual scores as error, which in G-theory and from an assessment perspective usually is the variance of interest. However, another analytical procedure might be used in SPSS as well: *Variance components*. The analytical procedure used determines the way the data should be organised. For example, our sample data in Table 25.3 can be treated as 15 cases (15 rows in a data file) with each four scores (four columns) in a repeated measures ANOVA, but also as a long list of 60 scores that are coded for person (being a random facet), task and rater. The SPSS variance components procedure requires the data to be organised the latter way. Computational procedures become more complicated when designs are more complex, such as in cases when nested facets have a different number of conditions at the levels of the nesting facet, i.e., so-called unbalanced designs.

Another general technique to estimate variance components is structural equation modelling (Marcoulides, 1996; Raykov and Marcoulides, 2006a). Structural equation modelling is a generic and flexible data analysis technique that allows for different estimation procedures. Ullman (2007) and Raykov and Marcoulides (2006b) are general introductions to structural equation modelling. Schoonen (2005) is an example of a generalisability study of writing assessment that uses structural equation modelling.

Brennan and colleagues developed a suite of three computational programs, directed to the analysis of variance components for different kinds of balanced and unbalanced designs and for the estimation of generalisability coefficients (Brennan, 2001: Appendices F, G and H; www.education.uiowa.edu/casma/GenovaPrograms.htm). The first program GENOVA (Crick and Brennan, 1983) deals with balanced designs with a maximum of six facets, including the facet of the objects of measurements (usually 'persons'). The GENOVA program provides all sorts of intermediate outcomes and can provide both generalisability ($E\rho^2$) and dependability (Φ) indices for different D-studies. The second program, urGENOVA, is an extension to deal with unbalanced designs, mentioned earlier, and mGENOVA is geared to multivariate G-studies. Multivariate G-studies have been part of G-theory from the beginning (Cronbach *et al.*, 1972) and address the generalisability of persons' multiple scores or profiles of scores. The power and flexibility of these analyses are, as Brennan (2001) stated, 'purchased at the price of challenging conceptual and statistical issues' (op. cit.: 267), issues that are beyond the scope of this chapter. Brennan (2001: 245ff) compares procedures and assumptions of several statistical packages, i.e., SAS (www.sas.com), S-Plus (spotfire.tibco.com/products/s-plus/statistical-analysis-software.aspx), SPSS and urGENOVA.

Language testing and generalisability

In all its complexity, language performance is multifaceted, and so is the assessment of language proficiency. The assessment of productive abilities, speaking and writing, lends itself especially well for a decomposition of sources of variance in a G-study. The effects of self-evident facets such as task (or topic) and rater are difficult to deal with simultaneously within the CTT framework (J. D. Brown, this Volume; Jones, this Volume). In the last three decades of language testing research, a number of G-studies have been conducted; below we will outline a few of them. One of the first applications in the realm of language testing dates back to the early 1980s. Bolus et al. (1982) investigated the oral English proficiency of non-native-speaking teaching assistants. Six raters evaluated videotaped speech samples of ten teaching assistants twice on a nine-point scale. Consequently, the universe of admissible observations consisted of two facets, rater and occasion, and teaching assistants comprise the objects of measurement. Although the raters were consistent in their ratings (cf. intra-rater reliability), the scores showed a large person-by-rater variance component, indicating a different appreciation of the performances by the raters (cf. inter-rater reliability). A number of subsequent D-studies illustrated that the error variance was better reduced by hiring more raters than having multiple ratings from the same raters: for example, 10 raters rating once was expected to lead to a higher generalisability ($E\rho^2 = 0.88$) than five raters rating twice ($E\rho^2 = 0.84$).

Van Weeren and Theunissen (1987) studied different procedures ('atomistic' and 'holistic') for the assessment of pronunciation of German and French as foreign languages. Reading text aloud, test takers were rated for their pronunciation of certain 'items'. The researchers found a substantial item-by-person interaction for the French test with hardly any rater effects, contrary to the German test scores, which showed a relatively large person-by-item-by-rater residual effect and a smaller person-by-item effect. The study showed that the test format worked much better for the French test than for the German test.

Generalisability of speaking proficiency scores has been the focus of several studies that were concerned with the variability due to speaking tasks in addition to rater variability. Bachman et al. (1995) investigated the speaking part of a large test battery (LAAS), measuring proficiency in Spanish as a foreign language. Students were administered two speaking tasks and the speech samples of 218 of them were scored by two raters on five aspects: pronunciation, vocabulary, cohesion and organisation on a four point scale, and grammar on a seven point scale. All generalisability coefficients for the two ratings and the two tasks were relatively high ($E\rho^2 > 0.86$), except for pronunciation ($E\rho^2 = 0.75$). The authors further explored the variance components for the grammar scores (two ratings and two tasks, $E\rho^2 = 0.92$) and found that – apart from person variance – the rater-by-person interaction was the largest variance component, and that the task-by-person and the task-by-rater-by-person, residual components were negligible. For a more extensive (multivariate G-) analysis of all the subscales, see Sawaki (2007). The finding of a small person-by-task effect is not very common. Other studies of speaking assessment most often report large task effects compared to rater effects (Lee, 2006; Van Moere, 2006).

Lee (2006) analysed the performances on 11 speaking tasks of 261 ESL students, rated on a five-point scale by two raters from a pool of 22 raters, and found a large person-by-task interaction (and an even larger person-by-task-by-rater, residual interaction). Van Moere (2006) used (among

373

other techniques) G-theory to study the scores of 113 Japanese EFL students taking group oral tests twice. He also reports substantial three-way person-by-rater-by-occasion, residual interaction and two-way person-by-occasion interaction compared to small rater effects. Occasion in this study was the confound of topic, interlocutors in the group test and the accompanying group dynamics.

Similar findings have been reported for the generalisability of writing proficiency scores. Using structural equation modelling, Schoonen (2005) studied the scores of 89 young writers, grade 6, on four writing tasks. Two scales were employed, one for content and organisation and one for language use, and ratings were given either holistically (general impression) or analytically (i.e., counting features). Holistic ratings were more generalisable than analytic scorings, and language use scores were more generalisable than content and organisation scores, but in all cases there were large person-by-task variance components. Large person-by-task interactions were also reported by Gebril (2009), both for independent writing tasks and integrated tasks (i.e., reading-to-write tasks). He investigated the writing performance of 115 Egyptian students, using two independent and two integrated writing tasks of the Test of English as a Foreign Language (TOEFL), and had the performances rated holistically by three raters. Besides the person-by-task interaction, the three-way interaction of person, task and rater, including the residual variance, was large as well; the rater-by-person interactions were small for both types of tasks. The relatively large person-by-task interactions and small person-by-rater interactions might be interpreted as that raters usually recognise proficient performance, but that test-takers are to some extent dependent on the task to be able to show their proficiency. These person-by-task effects have been reported in the assessment of other (language) skills and behaviour as well. For example, Brennan, et al. (1995) report substantial effects in the assessment of listening and writing (as connected tasks) and Shavelson, et al. (1993) report similarly large effects for person-by-task in three subject matters in primary school assessments. They concluded that performance assessment requires a large number of tasks to be generalisable. Huang's (2009) meta-analysis of studies of performance assessment corroborates this conclusion. In this study an average standardised effect size of .26 is reported for 68 person-by-task components (i.e., 26% of the score variance is attributed to this interaction).

G-theory can be used for all kinds of assessments and related reliability and validity issues. Brown (1999) studied the effect of language background on the generalisability of former TOEFL scores for vocabulary and reading, listening, and structure and writing, and thus investigated a form of test-fairness. In a similar vein, Zhang (2006) studied the test-fairness of the listening and reading section of the Test of English for International Communications (TOEIC) with persons nested within the variable language background and found, as Brown (1999), only very small effects for language background in interaction with test features (items, sections).

Since G-theory can be used to evaluate the effect of measurement features on the absolute level of scores, it is a very suitable approach for criterion-referenced testing and related issues as evaluating the consequences of decisions on standard setting and cut-off scores (e.g. Kozaki, 2004; Sawaki, 2007; Brennan, 2000b). Most applications of G-theory concerned the generalisability of a single dependent variable, i.e., univariate G-theory. However, as was mentioned above, G-theory can also be employed in multivariate research contexts in which a researcher wants to investigate the generalisability of multiple scores or score profiles, and the correlation between the scores. The interested reader is referred to Cronbach et al. (1972) and Brennan (2001) for the theoretical foundations; Brennan et al. (1995), Lee (2006) and Sawaki (2007) are applications of multivariate G-theory.

Future directions: reliability, generalisability and validity

G-theory is often perceived as an extension of CTT, although the focus of G-theory is slightly different (Brennan, 2000a). CTT focuses on the relation between the observed score variance and the presumed 'true' score variance; G-theory focuses on the expected accuracy of generalisations based on a certain measurement (Cronbach *et al.*, 1972: 15). In either case, researchers are (and should be) concerned about unwanted variance due to measurement procedures. However, G-theory raises the question what to consider unwanted and what to consider relevant score variance. Deville and Chalhoub-Deville (2006) question the distinction between variability and error, and wonder whether it is justified to look upon the person-by-task interaction as error. Tasks differ and language learners might respond differently to task features. However, the distinction between 'good' and 'bad' variability (Deville and Chalhoub-Deville, 2006: 12–13) is not for psychometrics to decide. G-theory is a very convenient tool to analyse variability, but is does not pass judgments on the meaningfulness of the universe of admissible observations. As a researcher we need to theorise about the universe of admissible observations, for example: What do we consider 'admissible observations' for writing proficiency? If in such a case the interaction between person and task is relatively large, we must be aware that generalising about a person's writing proficiency on the basis of a single task is 'ill-advised'. On the other hand, if the large person-by-task interaction is considered 'good' variance as Deville and Chalhoub-Deville suggest, we may need to reconsider our universe of admissible observations and thus the constructs we want to distinguish. That is, writing a narrative might be very different from writing an application letter, and thus the universe of admissible observations for each type of writing should be distinguished. If that is the case, we also should be able to show that writing application letters is a meaningful universe of generalisation and that we can sample tasks that measure 'application letter-writing' proficiency. A G-study of the latter domain should no longer show a large person-by-task interaction. To understand person-by-task interactions we should be able to define a narrower universe of generalisation that precludes large person-by-task interactions. Generalising to a broader domain or construct requires a larger number of observations than generalising to a narrowly defined domain or construct (cf. Chapelle, 2006: 57). Deville and Chalhoub-Deville's (2006) call for the study of 'ability-in-language user-in-context' is not at odds with G-theory. Actually, G-theory could be helpful in a more fundamental study of context and context effects. The researcher will have to define which contexts belong to the universe of generalisation and thus what the admissible observations are, that is, which features of context should be taken into account and which not. Obviously, the distinction between reliability and validity blurs; for some researchers features or facets of the measurement are related to reliability and for other researchers they are related to validity (Cronbach *et al.*, 1972; Brennan, 2000a; Jones, this volume). A language proficiency theory about the construct concerned should provide the necessary insights about linguistic knowledge and processes involved to decide in such matters (cf. Schoonen, 2011), which is reminiscent of Borsboom *et al.*'s (2004) call for a theory of response behaviour.

It is important to bear in mind the constructs we intend to measure and the kinds of generalisations we want to make. Chapelle (2006) extensively discusses the different kinds of generalisations we make in doing research, going from observed performance to theoretical constructs ('construct inference') or to performance on similar tasks ('generalisation inference') and performance beyond the assessment tasks ('extrapolation inference'), and she stresses the importance of a construct definition as central to our interpretation of performance. (Bachman (2006) also provides an extensive discussion of all kinds of generalisability in applied linguistic research.) G-theory can thus be used to evaluate reliability of performance assessments (i.e., scores from different raters, similar tasks or at different occasions), but also to evaluate the convergent validity of rather different tasks. Shavelson *et al.* (1993) explicitly introduced a method facet (e.g., observations, computer, short answer) in their research design to study the convergent validity of the methods. In open-ended tasks, language learners' response behaviour can be manifold. From a more diagnostic, second language acquisition (SLA) perspective, it is important to know whether all measures researchers are inclined to use in their studies, are equally sensitive to task or context conditions. In this case the multivariate extension of G-theory that can evaluate the generalisability of (linguistic) score profiles might be an interesting avenue to go.

In sum, Deville and Chalhoub-Deville (2006: 23) 'suggest that person x task investigations might offer promise for examining the L2 construct'; G-theory might turn out to be a very convenient and flexible analytic tool to do so and thus can help to provide the empirical basis for theoretical claims about language proficiency and the appropriateness of measurements thereof.

Acknowledgement

The author wishes to thank Sible Andringa, Jan Hulstijn and the editors for their helpful comments on an earlier draft. All remaining errors are the author's.

Further reading

Brennan, R. L. (2001). *Generalizability Theory*. New York, NY: Springer. This is a comprehensive book on G-theory. This book deals with all the statistical underpinnings, from simple one-faceted models to complex multivariate models, including different procedures for estimating variance components and brief introductions to the programs of the GENOVA suite.

Cronbach, L. J., Gleser, G. C., Nanda, H. and Rajaratnam, N. (1972). *The Dependability of Behavioral Measurements: Theory of generalizability for scores and profiles*. New York, NY: John Wiley and Sons, Inc. This seminal book is often considered the starting point for G-theory. It provides an extensive discussion of the multi-facetedness of measurements and the way in which generalisability of these measurements can be assessed. This early publication already deals with multivariate assessments and how generalisability of score profiles can be determined.

Shavelson, R. J. and Webb, N. M. (1991). *Generalizability Theory. A primer*. London, UK: Newbury Park; New Delhi, India: Sage Publications, Inc. This book provides a very good introduction to G-theory, starting from simple examples the procedures are explained very clearly. The authors also discuss procedures for nested and fixed facets, and nicely include conceptual considerations in their discussions.

References

Bachman, L. F. (2006). Generalizability. A journey into the nature of empirical research in applied linguistics. In M. Chalhoub-Deville, C. A. Chapelle and P. Duff (eds), *Inference and Generalizability in Applied Linguistics. Multiple perspectives*, Amsterdam, The Netherlands: John Benjamins Publishing Company, 165–207.

Bachman, L. F., Lynch, B. K. and Mason, M. (1995). Investigating variability in tasks and rater judgements in a performance test of foreign language speaking. *Language Testing* 12: 238–57.

Bolus, R. E., Hinofotis, F. B. and Bailey, K. M. (1982). An introduction to generalizability theory in second language research. *Language Learning* 32: 245–58.

Borsboom, D., Mellenbergh, G. J. and Van Heerden, J. (2004). The concept of validity. *Psychological Review* 111: 1061–71.

Brennan, R. L. (1992). *Elements of Generalizability Theory*, 2nd rev edn. Iowa: The American College Testing Program.

—— (2000a). (Mis)conceptions about generalizability theory. *Educational Measurement: Issues and practice* 19: 5–10.

—— (2000b). Performance assessments from the perspective of generalizability theory. *Applied Psychological Measurement* 24: 339–53.

—— (2001). *Generalizability Theory*. New York, NY: Springer.

Brennan, R. L., Gao, X. and Colton, D. A. (1995). Generalizability analyses of Work Keys listening and writing tests. *Educational and Psychological Measurement* 55: 157–76.

Brown, J. D. (1999). The relative importance of persons, items, subtests and languages to TOEFL test variance. *Language Testing* 16: 217–38.

Chapelle, C. A. (2006). L2 vocabulary acquisition theory: The role of inference, dependability and generalizability in assessment. In M. Chalhoub-Deville, C. A. Chapelle and P. Duff (eds), *Inference and Generalizability in Applied Linguistics. Multiple perspectives*. Amsterdam, The Netherlands: John Benjamins Publishing Company, 47–64.

Crick, J. E. and Brennan, R. L. (1983). *Manual for GENOVA: A generalized analysis of variance system* (No. ACT Technical Bulletin No. 43). Iowa City, IA: ACT, Inc.

Cronbach, L. J., Gleser, G. C., Nanda, H. and Rajaratnam, N. (1972). *The Dependability of Behavioral Measurements: Theory of generalizability for scores and profiles.* New York, NY: John Wiley & Sons, Inc.

Deville, C. and Chalhoub-Deville, M. (2006). Old and new thoughts on test score variability: Implications for reliability and validity. In M. Chalhoub-Deville, C. A. Chapelle and P. Duff (eds), *Inference and Generalizability in Applied Linguistics. Multiple perspectives.* Amsterdam, The Netherlands: John Benjamins Publishing Company, 9–25.

Gebril, A. (2009). Score generalizability of academic writing tasks: Does one test method fit it all? *Language Testing* 26: 507–31.

Glaser, R. (1963). Instructional technology and the measurement of learning outcomes: Some questions. *American Psychologist* 18: 518–21.

Huang, C. (2009). Magnitude of task-sampling variability in performance assessment: A meta-analysis. *Educational and Psychological Measurement* 69: 887–912.

Kozaki, Y. (2004). Using GENOVA and FACETS to set multiple standards on performance assessment for certification in medical translation from Japanese into English. *Language Testing* 21: 1–27.

Lee, Y.-W. (2006). Dependability of scores for a new ESL speaking assessment consisting of integrated and independent tasks. *Language Testing* 23: 131–66.

Marcoulides, G. A. (1996). Estimating variance components in generalizability theory: The covariance structure analysis approach. *Structural Equation Modeling* 3: 290–99.

Parkes, J. (2000). The relationship between the reliability and cost of performance and cost performance assessments. *Education Policy Analysis Archives* 8: 16.

Raykov, T. and Marcoulides, G. A. (2006a). Estimation of generalizability coefficients via a structural equation modeling approach to scale reliability evaluation. *International Journal of Testing* 6: 81–95.

—— (2006b). *A First Course in Structural Equation Modeling*, 2nd edn. Mahwah, NJ: Erlbaum.

Sawaki, Y. (2007). Construct validation of analytic rating scales in a speaking assessment: reporting a score profile and a composite. *Language Testing* 24: 355–90.

Schoonen, R. (2005). Generalizability of writing scores: An application of structural equation modeling. *Language Testing* 22: 1–30.

—— (2011). How language ability is assessed. In E. Hinkel (ed.), *Handbook of Research in Second Language Teaching and Learning, Volume II*, New York and London, UK: Abingdon, UK: Routledge, 701–16.

Shavelson, R. J., Baxter, G. P. and Gao, X. (1993). Sampling variability of performance assessments. *Journal of Educational Measurement* 30: 215–32.

Shavelson, R. J. and Webb, N. M. (1991). *Generalizability Theory. A primer.* London, UK: Newbury Park; New Delhi, India: Sage Publications, Inc.

Ullman, J. B. (2007). Structural equation modeling. In B. G. Tabachnick and L. S. Fidell (eds), *Using Multivariate Statistics*, 5th edn. Boston, MA: Pearson/Allyn and Bacon, 676–780.

Van Moere, A. (2006). Validity evidence in a university group oral test. *Language Testing* 23: 411–40.

Van Weeren, J. and Theunissen, T. J. J. M. (1987). Testing pronunciation: An application of generalizability theory. *Language Learning* 37: 109–22.

Webb, N. M., Shavelson, R. J. and Haertel, E. H. (2007). Reliability coefficients and generalizability theory. In C. R. Rao and S. Sinharay (eds), *Handbook of Statistics*. Vol. 26 Psychometrics. Amsterdam, The Netherlands: Elsevier Sience B.V., 81–124.

Zhang, S. (2006). Investigating the relative effects of persons, items, sections, and languages on TOEIC score dependability. *Language Testing* 23: 351–69.

26

Scoring performance tests

Glenn Fulcher

Introduction and definitions

A rating scale is typically a series of hierarchical levels, with each level providing a proficiency descriptor against which learner performance is measured. Each level (or *band*) in the rating scale is characterized by a verbal descriptor which, taken together, constitute the operational definition of the construct that the test developer claims to be assessing (Fulcher, 1996: 227; Davies *et al.*, 1999). Recent variations in performance data-based scales have included empirically derived, binary-choice, boundary definition scales (EBBs) (Upshur and Turner, 1995) and performance decision trees (Fulcher, 2010; Fulcher *et al.*, 2011).

Rating scales can be oriented towards the examiner, the test taker or the test constructor (Alderson, 1991). They can be holistic, analytic, primary-trait or multiple-trait (Hamp-Lyons, 1991); and they can be 'real-world' or 'interaction/ability' focused (Bachman, 1990). Most rating scales are designed for the use of raters (judges) who match writing or speaking performances to descriptors in order to arrive at a score. These are 'examiner-oriented' scales, and are the focus of this chapter. Holistic scales require the rater to make a global, holistic judgment about a performance, so that there is no counting or 'tallying' of particular features or errors. These scales seek to get at the general 'quality' of the performance, in much the same way that judges rate skating or diving performances in the Olympics (Pollitt, 1990). Conversely, an analytic scale requires the enumeration of specific features in a performance, such as the number of errors or of appropriate second-parts of adjacency pairs, and so on. A primary-trait scale asks the rater to make a single judgment about the performance on a single construct, such as 'communicative ability'. Each descriptor in the rating scale must therefore describe a level within this construct. Multiple-trait rating scales assume that multiple constructs underlie a performance, and therefore require separate scores for each trait or construct. These are most useful when assembling profiles in classroom assessment. Any of these scale types may have a real-world focus, where the descriptors attempt to describe what the learner 'can do' in the real world, or have an ability focus, where the descriptors describe the underlying abilities that a learner needs to have acquired in order to do the test task successfully, and which are also needed for successful task completion in a defined real-world context. These dimensions may be used to describe most rating scales currently in use (Fulcher, 2003: 91).

The kind of rating instrument we choose to design will depend upon test purpose and the claims we wish to make about the meaning of scores for a particular decision-making process. The rating instrument serves as the construct definition and is the scoring component of the evidence model within an evidence centred design approach to test development (Mislevy *et al.*, 2003; Mislevy and Yin, this volume). An interpretive argument for the usefulness of test scores for the intended purpose will therefore set out the claims and assumptions that are likely to justify the inferences we make about the observed score, including how we generalize score meaning to the universe of possible performances, and to extrapolate it to what the test taker is capable of doing in real-life domains (see Kane, this volume).

Historical perspectives

Early scales and performance tests

The conceptualization of score meaning as inference occurred much earlier than is often recognized. This represented a revolution in testing theory, as it made possible the idea that scores provide only approximate measurements of abilities. In turn, this led to the view that careful performance test and rating scale design would lead to sounder, if imperfect, inferences. This 'inferencing breakthrough' came when researchers began to think about the practical issue of how a rating scale could be constructed in a principled way to aid the process of decision making.

Thorndike (1912: 290) reported 'Scales, graded standards, by which to report knowledge of German, ability to spell... any educational fact you may think of, are now where the thermo-meter, spectroscope and galvanometer were three hundred years ago – they do not exist.' He argued the task was to create scales to describe 'performance ability' that (a) describe the ability (and only the ability) in question, (b) over a number of levels that describe relative amounts of the same ability, where (c) each level of the scale contains a unit of difference (it is an interval scale), and (d) that there should be a zero point on the scale (it is a ratio scale).

By saying that 'his knowledge is about equivalent to that required for passing intermediate German', or 'his English is a grade C', Thorndike argued that we are making statements 'on a level with the statement that a glass of water is "tepid".' Thorndike recommended the collection of samples of performance, giving the example of writing, and asking expert judges to agree which samples were characteristic of a level, 'then we should have one point on a scale thereby defined' (ibid.: 292). In order to achieve an interval scale, he also recommended using essay samples to characterize levels based on the percentage of judges that had judged one essay to be in a level higher than another by an equally high decision rate in a set of binary decisions: 'in a very important, and, with certain limitations, true sense, we can say that the difference between 1 and 2 is equal to the difference between 3 and 4, because it is equally often noted by equally competent judges' (ibid.: 295). Such a scale with examples of levels from 0 to 93 was given as an example (Thorndike, 1913: 19–21). The use of these scales was rejected in the United Kingdom. Ballard (1923), for example, argued that the samples which defined the levels were tied to the context in which they had been collected, thus making their use elsewhere inadvisable: ' ... its merits are not so obvious as to lead to its adoption in other countries. If it ever comes to England it must put on English garb. The sample pieces must be taken from English schools and standardized afresh... There is, in fact, no help for it: we must, for the present at least, fall back upon the method of personal impression' (ibid.: 216). The notion of a 'universally applicable scale' was questioned from the start.

Nevertheless, the practice of looking at what 'better' and 'poorer' performers do in the context to which inferences were to be made quickly became very common when attempting to investigate score meaning. This was certainly the case with the first large-scale standardized language test developed during the First World War as a screening instrument to decide which US Army recruits should be sent to development battalions to learn English. While the group test was generic, the individual verbal test was based on an analysis of military content (Yerkes, 1921: 355). Scores from both the individual and group tests were clustered into levels (Table 26.1) using correlational procedures, from which inferences were drawn in the following way:

> In language the rating E means inability to obey the very simplest commands unless they are repeated and accompanied by gestures, or to answer the simplest questions about name, work, and home unless the questions are repeated and varied. Rating D means an ability to obey very simple commands, or to reply to very simple questions without the aid of gesture or the need of repetition. Rating C is the level required for simple explanation of drill; rating B is the level of understanding of most of the phrases in the Infantry Drill Regulations; rating A is a very superior level. Men rating D or E in language ability should be classified as non-English.
>
> *(Yerkes, 1921: 357)*

There is little or no discussion of how the test designers established the number of levels, or the tentative descriptions of what a person can do with the language in each level. However, in a little known text Yerkes (1920: 382–385) does provide a short description of the process used to develop the Army 'trade' tests for placing recruits into suitable jobs, and it is reasonable to assume that similar procedures would have been used for the development of the individual language test. The steps are summarized as follows:

1. Conducting an analysis of the tasks required of the person in the target domain, attempting to define 'the elements of skill and information and judgment which combine to constitute real proficiency' (Yerkes, 1920: 382).
2. Identification of 'typical tasks' through interviews with experts, and those responsible for standards of performance in the target domain. This kind of consultation was carried out to ensure what we would refer to today as bringing to bear 'indigenous criteria' (see Jacoby and McNamara, 1999).
3. Construction of a prototype test, which could take one of three forms: a performance test, in which a test taker does a sample task from the domain; an oral test in which questions are asked to discover if he could perform in the target domain; or present images or objects from the target domain about which the test taker is asked questions. The examiner is required to match a performance against a 'standard rating' (Yerkes, 1920: 383), or prose descriptor.

Table 26.1 Clustering scores by levels

Rating	Individual test	Group test
A	40 and up	23 and up
B	28 to 39	12 to 20
C	20 to 27	5 to 11
D	9 to 19	Up to 4
E	Up to 8	

4. Initial test 'try-out' using ' … from five to twenty men whose high-proficiency … is known. During this preliminary tryout the test undergoes progressive revision and refinement. Ambiguities and localisms of terminology are eliminated. Elements that require too much time or that prove to be repetitive of other elements, or that are not sufficiently diagnostic, are dropped' (ibid.: 384). This process sounds remarkably like alpha testing in modern prototyping studies (see Fulcher and Davidson, 2007: 76–84; Nissan and Schedl, this volume).

5. Remarkably, 'The revised test is now subjected to a second and much more thorough tryout' (Yerkes, 1920: 384), using a much larger sample, including some who are known to be proficient 'experts', some are 'learners' on the way to proficiency, and some are 'novices'.

6. Statistical analysis is conducted to discover which tasks discriminate most effectively between the three groups, referred to as the computation of the test's 'diagnostic value'. 'This stage of the process we have called "calibrating" the test' (ibid.: 385), and only those tasks which survive this process are retained for the final test. This step coincides with modern approaches to piloting and field testing, combined with a group-differences approach to standard setting (see Fulcher, 2010: 179–85, 240–41; Kenyon and MacGregor, this volume).

These procedures are extremely sophisticated for the time, and show that the technical aspects of test development and scoring procedures were highly developed. Despite the very real problems (social, ethical and philosophical) identified with early testing practices (e.g. Lipman, 1922; Gould, 1997), it is still possible to recognize the technical and methodological advances that were made both generally, and more specifically in scoring performance tests:

> Not infrequently the tentative formulation of the test has proved inadequate, and after all the labour and expense of an elaborate tryout it had to be thrown into the waste-basket and a fresh start made.
>
> *(Yerkes, 1920: 385)*

The inter-war years

The rapid expansion of education in the post-war era brought with it the need for a much larger testing industry to provide data in the emerging accountability environment. Language testing was no longer driven solely by the need to predict likely real life performance, but by the economics of mass assessment. In the first book specifically on language testing, Wood (1928) argues for the use of 'new-type' (multiple-choice) tests in the assessment of modern foreign languages. The most important rationale was cost. Wood estimated that performance tests cost between $0.78 and $1.24 to score, whereas a multiple choice test of the time cost $0.07. The argument: 'These differences are too large to need comment' (Wood, 1928: 312). As a result, there was little work on rating scales, although within the context of school-based diagnostic assessment there is some evidence that rating scales were developed to score task-specific language tasks (Burt, 1922; Fulcher, 2010: 130–34). We should also add that the same pressures on the cost of scoring performance assessments exist today (Barton, 2009).

The Second World War and beyond

It took another war to bring scoring performance tests back into focus, as the aim once again became to relate the test score directly to an ability to perform. This change is clearly seen in the work of Kaulfers (1944: 137–38):

Scores on the measurement scale must be interpreted in terms of 'performance norms' or statements of what an examinee who reaches a certain point on the scale can specifically be expected to *do* with the foreign language in real life communication situations. (Italics in the original)

Scores on the 'new-type tests' were seen as surrogates for performance test scores, and no matter how highly the two correlated, Kaulfers argued that sound inferences regarding likely success in the field could only be drawn from performance tests. The innovations that took place at this time grew out of the Army Specialized Training Program (ASTP) established in 1942 to produce the linguists needed for the war effort (Barnwell, 1996; Vellemann, 2008). Primitive rating scales were developed to assess performance on newly developed speaking tests. A scale suggested by Kaulfers consisted of levels related to the 'scope' (content) of production, and its 'quality' in terms of intelligibility. The most significant evidence for the rapid evolution of rating scales comes from Agard and Dunkel (1948). They report on a number of prototype tests that had been developed at Queen's College. The tests had three components:

(1) the ability to report a single, simple act or situation in precise words, (2) the ability to express a sequence of ideas fluently, (3) the ability to converse. As will be noted in the rating scales reported below, the major criterion in all three aspects was intelligibility.

(Agard and Dunkel, 1948: 56)

In the second part, the test taker was given a topic and was required to 'discourse without interruption for two to three minutes' (Agard and Dunkel, 1948: 57). The production was scored on multiple-trait holistic scales as follows:

Fluency

2 – Speaks smoothly, phrasing naturally according to his thoughts
1 – Occasionally hesitates in order to search for the right word or to correct an error
0 – Speaks so haltingly that it is difficult to understand the thought he is conveying

Vocabulary

2 – Vocabulary adequate for expressing the ideas he wishes to convey
1 – Manages to convey his ideas in part, but in serveral instances uses an incorrect word or fails to find any word to use
0 – Cannot communicate his thought because he does not have an adequate vocabulary

Pronunciation and enunciation

2 – Sufficiently approaches native speech to be completely understandable.
1 – Can be understood, though with difficulty, because there are sounds which he does not utter correctly.
0 – Would not be understood by natives because his pronunciation is so different from theirs.

Grammatical correctness

2 – Speaks correctly with no serious errors in correct grammatical usage
1 – Speech is understandable, but there are serious grammatical errors.
0 – Speech is not readily understandable because it is so full of grammatical errors.

Agard and Dunkel (1948: 97) report that the tests were not ready for use until late 1945 or early 1946, by which time they were no longer necessary. We are told, however, that in piloting part II (the only section requiring sustained speech) ' … despite the rating scale supplied, examiners necessarily relied on the standards of excellence they were accustomed to set for their own students' (ibid.: 99–100).

The development of rating scales continued to be linked to military need, with the Korean War and the Cold War giving impetus to the development of the Foreign Service Institute (FSI) scale between 1952 and 1958, and the war in Vietnam leading to the evolution of the FSI into a standardized scale for use by all US military and intelligence agencies in 1968, called the Interagency Language Roundtable (ILR) (Wilds, 1975; Sollenberger, 1978). This is still in use today. These scales were then adopted and adapted by educational institutions, with both the structure and wording appearing in later influential scales like the American Council on the Teaching of Foreign Languages (ACTFL) Guidelines, and the Australian Second Language Proficiency Ratings (Fulcher, 1997). Indeed, the influence of these early US scales can be seen in most subsequent scales listed in the compilation of North (1993), which were used to select descriptors in the creation of the patchwork quilt that is the Common European Framework of Reference (CEFR) illustrative scales. Only recently have alternatives to these hierarchically structured scales been explored.

Current contributions and research methods

There are five clearly definable methodologies for the construction of rating scales, listed in chronological order of development:

1. Intuitive and experiential
2. Performance data-based
3. Empirically derived, binary-choice, boundary definition (EBB)
4. Scaling descriptors
5. Performance decision trees (PDTs)

(Fulcher, 2010: 209–15)

Methods 1 and 4 represent a measurement-driven approach, which ' … prioritizes the ordering of descriptors onto a single scale. Meaning is derived from the scaling methodology and the agreement of trained judges as to the place of any descriptor on the scale.' Methods 2, 3 and 5 represent the performance-data driven approach, in which 'Meaning is derived from the link between performance and description' (Fulcher et al., 2011: 5).

For the most part, rating scales have been constructed using the intuitive and experiential method, or what I have called the '*a priori*' or 'armchair' method of construction (Fulcher, 1993: 33). Descriptors are arrived at by expert committees who bring their experience and knowledge to the task. The basis of a validation claim is primarily experience, and over time, the socialization of users into what a band means through practice. Thus, Lowe (1986: 392) states that 'The essence of the AEI [ACTFL, ETS, ILR] proficiency lies not in verbal descriptions of it, but in its thirty-year-long tradition of practice – making training in AEI proficiency testing a desideratum.' Elsewhere, Lowe (1985: 16) states that 'the use of the system remains implicit', whereas high rater agreement is reached through continuous use of the scales and long-term institutional socialization (Barnwell, 1996). This is why the tradition of AEI evaluation 'must continue unbroken' (Lowe, 1986: 396).

The similarity between the *a priori* approach and scaling descriptors is remarkable. *A priori* scales have been criticized for being circular and a-theoretical (Lantolf and Frawley, 1985; Fulcher,

2008), and it is generally agreed that the Common European Framework of Reference (CEFR) which relies upon scaling descriptors has no basis in second language acquisition theory (Fulcher, 2003; Fulcher, 2008; Hulstijn, 2007; North and Schneider, 1998: 242–43). The only difference between the two is that the CEFR descriptors, drawn from other extant rating scales, are placed at a particular level on the basis of Rasch analysis of teachers' perceived difficulty for a group of imagined typical learners.

As measurement-driven approaches they also share a common mandate (Davidson and Lynch, 2002). Clark (1980) says that the purpose of the FSI scale was to have a 'common measure' that could be used across languages for the purpose of comparability, and as Schultz (1986: 373) said of ACTFL, to provide language testers and curriculum developers with a 'common language' with which to communicate. Similarly, the purpose of the CEFR is to provide a 'common meta-language' for testing and teaching languages in Europe (North, 2007: 659). It is claimed that the CEFR scales are 'natural levels', which means 'the conventional, recognized, convenient levels found in books and exams' (North, 1992: 12) rather than having anything to do with how languages are learned.

The measurement-driven approaches share these features because ultimately they are both grounded in the use of socialization, or 'social moderation' (Mislevy, 1992) for their meaning and usefulness.

> Social moderation is the process whereby a group of raters establish a common under-standing of a set of standards by discussion and training… The challenge with applying standards-oriented assessment across different institutions or areas is to achieve a situation in which all groups come to share the same common frame of reference, rather than each staffroom or region developing its own, separate consensus.
>
> *(North, 2000: 566–67)*

Whether the descriptors or the scale have any basis in language use or acquisition is largely irrelevant, as long as through training and socialization the scores have acceptable psychometric properties. As North (2000: 573) makes clear: ' … what is being scaled is not necessarily learner proficiency, but teacher/raters' perception of that proficiency – their common framework.' The purpose of the CEFR scales is to provide the basis for extending this view of the linguistic world through socialization and training (Council of Europe, 2001: 182), so that participants are no longer capable of seeing it through any other lens. The new CEFR 'adepts' (a term intro-duced by Lowe, 1986, to describe AEI followers) must be trained and socialized into ' … a common understanding of the CEFR' which is 'maintained over time', through arriving at 'correct' or 'truthful' decisions in the use of the scales (Council of Europe, 2009: 37). This is social con-structivism at work on a grand scale. Instead of using the concept to separate out social products from reality (Hacking, 1999), the measurement-driven approach uses the scale to socially construct a linguistic myth in support of a political identity (Fulcher, 2009).

By contrast, the performance-data driven approach does not seek to provide grand solutions to the horrendously difficult task of comparing performances across languages, or the construc-tion of a meta-system through which large numbers of people are expected to view the world. Rather, they are designed to score performance samples drawn from specified communicative domains. In the performance data-based method, samples of speech or writing are drawn from responses to particular tasks sampled from the domain, and discourse analysis employed to identify key features of performances at identifiable levels of proficiency. Discriminant analysis can be used to estimate the accuracy with which these features can be used to separate levels, thus providing empirical evidence for the number of levels and the content of descriptors. It is noteworthy that the fluency descriptors developed within this paradigm (Fulcher, 1993: 1996) were included in the descriptor bank for the development of the CEFR, which in turn showed that 'empirically, the fluency descriptors proved to have a rock-solid interpretation of difficulty across sectors, regions, and languages … ' and so were used as anchor items (North, 2007: 657). In other words, the most recent measurement driven approach was dependent for its psychometric properties on a scale developed within another paradigm. It is therefore not surprising that data-based scales are now frequently constructed for use in domain-specific tests (Inoue, 2009), exhibiting as they do high content representativeness and stable measurement properties.

The disadvantage to the performance data-based method is that it tends to generate level descriptors that can be too complex for use in live operational rating. This problem was avoided in the development of EBBs, which sets out a series of binary decisions arrived at by asking judges to write questions that would separate speech or writing samples produced in response to a specific task into levels (Turner, 2000; Turner and Upshur, 2002; Upshur and Turner, 1995, 1999).

The construction method does not require an analysis of the performance samples per se, but an evaluation of what makes one sample superior or inferior to another. Other techniques that have been used in this kind of analysis include Thurstone's method of paired comparisons and Kelly's repertory grid technique (Pollitt and Murray, 1996). In the former, judges are presented with all possible pairs of samples, and asked to rate one higher than the other. From this the samples are ordered onto a rank order scale. In the latter, judges are asked to verbalize why they make a sequencing judgment in terms of the quality of the two samples. This is used to create binary questions or descriptors for the scale, similar to that in Figure 26.1.

While EBBs are very practical, they lack the descriptive richness of data-based scales, and hence the close relationship between score and score meaning in terms of what a learner is

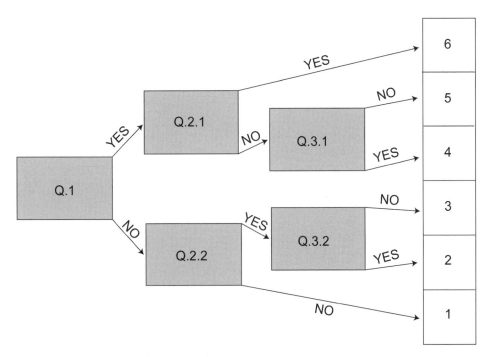

Figure 26.1 Empirically derived, binary-choice, boundary definition scale schematic

likely to be able to do in the target domain. In order to produce a rating instrument that combines the simplicity of the EBB with the descriptional adequacy of a data-based methodology Fulcher *et al.* (2011) have developed a prototype of a performance decision tree (PDT). This approach uses an analysis of discourse in context to generate binary questions with regard to the presence of obligatory discourse elements, discourse features that mark quality of communication, and the use of pragmatic features to establish relationships and achieve goals. The instrument and its design also incorporate and extend insights from LSP assessment (Douglas, 2001), layered discourse analysis (Young, 2002) and indigenous assessment (Jacoby and McNamara, 1999).

Critical issues and topics

Rating instruments and language acquisition

Rating scales are traditionally structured hierarchically, and measurement-driven scales could not be constructed in any other way. These give the impression that they also represent an acquisitional hierarchy with each level describing the next 'step' in language acquisition and learning. Indeed, some writers talk about learners 'climbing the ladder' with each scale descriptor representing a rung (Westoff, 2007). This is entirely misleading, and there remains a paucity of empirical evidence for any link between hierarchical scale descriptors and second language acquisition (Brindley, 1998; Fulcher, 2008, 2010: 77–79). The problem is avoided in the non-hierarchical EBBs and PDTs, which make no claim to represent such sequences.

Prose descriptors

Wilds (1979: 1) was among the first to observe that frequently used terms in rating scales like 'good' and 'fluent' are extremely vague and are open to as many interpretations as there are raters. Typical descriptors are far from self-explanatory (Barnwell, 1996), and as Matthews (1990: 119) notes, levels on scales 'are described in only vague and general terms and abound in qualifiers, so that only gross distinctions can be made with any confidence.' This problem has not abated over the years (Weir, 2005; Fulcher *et al.*, 2011), but within the context of recent data-driven scoring instruments it does seem possible to make progress in this area by explicitly linking the language used to describe abilities to observational attributes, which in turn are tied to domain specific inferences, and tasks sampled from a relevant universe of generalization (Fulcher, 2010: 149–154).

Assessment focus

Scoring instrument designers can be pulled in two seemingly conflicting directions. On the one hand, there is the desire to establish a clear link between the score and what the test taker can do in an identifiable 'real-life' context. On the other hand, the score is seen to be indexical of the presence, absence, or strength, of some trait that is assumed to be essential to performance in one or more real life contexts. In practice, this dilemma has led to scoring systems that focus either on 'observable attributes' (Kane, 2009) that are sampled from in some way from the real life context of interest, or abstractions (traits) that can be scaled and used to describe abilities from which inferences can be made to likely real world performances. However, in practice it has been exceptionally difficult to keep the two apart. For example, an essay scoring system may prioritize what can be observed, such as effective use of grammar and lexis or cohesive and linking devices, but still describes scores in terms of 'style' or 'rhetorical development'. Testers seem unhappy to leave observable attributes unexplained by theory, or to have trait labels undefined by observational attributes. Although either theory or observation may take precedence, it is in fact very difficult to find a scoring system that does not have a dual focus. This is most clear in PDTs (Fulcher *et al.*, 2011), where raters' attention is drawn to observable attributes such as discourse markers or marked topic transitions, but these are interpreted in terms of traits such as discourse or pragmatic competence. The relationship between observable attributes and the constructs of which they are part will remain an area of research for many years to come, and this should in turn impact upon the descriptors used in rating instruments of all types.

The centrality of inference

This tension between observable attributes and their interpretation in terms of constructs dates back to the very beginning of performance testing, and remains the most fundamental problem with which we still wrestle: how we make an inference from a score based on observable attributes to an ability that generalizes to performance in a real-life context. Here is how Latham set out this problem:

> Now we cannot lay bare the intellectual mechanism and judge it by inspection, we can only *infer* the excellence of the internal apparatus and the perfection of its workmanship from the quality of the work turned out: this work, in the case of young people, is represented by the knowledge they have attained, and the powers they have acquired… Examinations for judging about them are confessedly insufficient, and we can only give our conclusions as approximations …
>
> *(Latham, 1877: 155–157, italics added)*

We should also note in this quotation the awareness of the fundamental uncertainty that resides in all testing. Further, it was the constructs that were valued, such as 'cultivated taste', 'creativity' or 'wisdom', which had to be inferred from a work product; but Latham says elsewhere:

> … we can only *infer* their presence in greater or less degree by the amount we discover of certain concomitants, which usually accompany these precious but imponderable elements more or less, but in no fixed proportion that we can determine.
>
> *(ibid.: 63–54, italics added)*

In other words, whether the outcome of the assessment process is a numerical score or an impressionistic categorical judgment, the meaning of the score or category is an inference from this outcome to a trait or ability, via observable evidence of its presence.

Conclusions and future directions

The purpose of sound inferencing is extremely practical. It allows a score user to make some decision about an examined individual. Decisions may be high stakes in nature. Is this person able to guide pilots through air space safely and get them onto the ground without incident? Is that person capable of explaining a medical condition to a patient, discussing and selecting alternative treatments, and writing a case history? Is the other able to interpret for the military when on patrol in a peace keeping operation, winning hearts and minds rather than alienating those they are supposed to serve? For Peirce (1903: 212) 'The act of inference consists in the thought that the inferred conclusion is true because in any analogous case an analogous conclusion would be true.' In this definition we can see that reliability and validity are conjoined and fluid, as the inferences must be consistent across instances of assessment, and lead to good decisions: the intended outcome of testing should be to the benefit of both the individual, and those who would put their lives in his or her hands. 'The only thing that induction accomplishes is to determine the value of a quantity. It sets out with a theory and it measures the degree of concordance of that theory with fact' (ibid.: 218). This 'only' has been at the heart of language testing since Latham's discussion of inference in the nineteenth century, and remains so today.

Inferences may only be made from scores, through observable attributes to constructs, and on to predictions of likely performance, if the target domain is specified. Without that there is no value to the quantity represented in a test result, for there is no theory to relate it to fact. Or in much more down to earth language, 'All tests are for a purpose. A test that is made up without a clear idea of what it is for, is no good' (Ingram, 1968: 70). This is why global claims for score meaning lead to validity chaos (Chalhoub-Deville and Fulcher, 2003: 502). It is also why retrofitting tests for new uses must be done with the utmost care (Fulcher and Davidson, 2009).

More recent approaches to rating scale development from a data-driven tradition ground the scores in specific domains. To this extent they draw upon a long tradition of observing successful performance in context as a key methodology in the construction of the scoring instrument. An early example of this is found in Yerkes (1920: 383) ' ... no amount of this accumulated material [discussion with experts] could take the place of analysis made by actual observation of skilled and partly skilled tradesmen at their work.' Similarly, the analysis of successful, border-line, and unsuccessful communicators in a particular context, undertaking specific tasks, provides the data with which the scale constructor works. This is the way forward for the development of scoring instruments for performance tests, which allies the task of measurement to applied linguistic research. This is the first part of our work for the future. Measurement in language testing is not simply a matter of establishing good psychometric properties, as Messick (1995: 6–7) knew only too well: ' ... the theory of the construct domain should guide not only the selection or construction of relevant assessment tasks but also the rational development of construct-based scoring criteria and rubrics.'

If there is some truth to the preceding argument, why does the world continue to use mea-surement driven systems and indulge in generalizing score meaning to contexts which reasonable inference will not bear? The inferences we make are directly related to a criterion that we wish to predict, and so all score meaning is therefore criterion referenced. The cut score, once arrived at, cannot be altered at whim, but only by changes in the complexities of tasks in the target domain, or a reassessment of risks associated with borderline pass scores. This is inconvenient for policy makers, who wish to move cut scores up or down in order to achieve their policy goals, as frequently happens with tests that are used for immigration purposes. In times of financial crisis when international workers are not required the pass level is raised; it is easily reduced when the economy recovers. Similarly, it is easy to decide that B1 on the CEFR is required for immigration to a European country, and then to select a test and score that reflects B1-ness in order to reduce immigration levels. The decisions cannot be challenged if validity chaos reigns, and if conditions change other tests can be used, their difficulty levels manipulated, or the CEFR level altered.

Our future work also requires vigilance about claims for score meaning that serve purely political or policy aims. Rating scales and their descriptors can be used to establish barriers to mobility and employment as well as to provide fair access. They can be used to create artificial identities, control educational systems, and hold teachers accountable. There is a growing need for social critiques of rating scale use, and research into their impact upon institutions and individuals (Fulcher, 2004; Vallax, 2010). This extends to the providers of examinations, where there is always the temptation to follow policy makers in generalizing score meaning beyond reasonable inference to drive up test volume and therefore increase profit margins, a danger of which some are well aware (Wendler and Powers, 2009). We must insist that there are boundaries to score meaning (Messick, 1995: 7) to avoid validity chaos, for it may trigger gross unfairness to test takers through the inevitability of poor decision making.

The issues surrounding rating instruments and scoring performance tests have become much wider in a very short period of time. There is much work here for the language testing profession, language teachers, and postgraduate researchers, for many years to come.

Further reading

Fulcher, G. (1996). Does thick description lead to smart tests? A data-based approach to rating scale construction. *Language Testing* 13: 208–38. With reference to the construct of 'fluency', this paper describes the data-based methodology that was developed to relate observational variables to the construct. It focuses on analysis of discourse from speaking tasks to generate observable categories that can predict student level. These categories are then used with a new sample of learners in order to investigate the usefulness of the categories for future use.

Fulcher, G., Davidson, F. and Kemp, J. (2011). Effective rating scale development for speaking tests: Performance decision trees. *Language Testing* 28: 1. Performance decisions trees represent a recent development in the design of scoring instruments that combine the 'thick description' of data-based methods, with the practicality of EBBs. This article presents a prototype PDT for service encounters and explains the procedures used for arriving at its structure and content. As a prototype further research and refining is required, and it will be necessary to create PDTs for other contexts in order to investigate the extent of their usefulness.

Messick, S. (1995). Standards of validity and the validity of standards in performance assessment. *Educational Measurement: Issues and Practice* 14: 5–8. Within the framework of Messick's 'aspects of validity', he explores central issues for scoring performance assessments, drawing particular attention to the need to base scoring criteria on analyses of task and domain structure. The paper is concerned with the extent to which scores can be generalized beyond the specific domain envisaged in the test, or restricted by the boundaries of the domain and test purpose.

Pollitt, A. (1990). Giving students a sporting chance: Assessing by counting and by judging. In J. C. Alderson and, B North (eds), *Language Testing in the 1990s*. London: Modern English Publications and the British Council, 46–59. Pollitt considers two paradigms for scoring performance tests: marking and judging. The first is situated within the normative psychometric paradigm, while the latter draws on practices from sport, particular events such as free-style figure skating. The exploration of the two paradigms provides ideas and challenges for designers of scoring instruments without being prescriptive.

Upshur J. and Turner C.E. (1995). Constructing rating scales for second language tests. *English Language Teaching Journal* 49: 3–12. In this article Upshur and Turner first proposed and demonstrated the value of EBBs, which have subsequently been used in a variety of contexts. EBBs are fundamentally tied to the tasks and domains delimited in the statement of test purpose, as discussed by Messick (1995). They are relatively easy to use, and have the added advantage of being easy to construct by teachers for local assessments needs.

References

Agard, F. and Dunkel, H. (1948). *An investigation of second language teaching*. Chicago, IL: Ginn and Company.

Alderson, J. C. (1991). Bands and scores. In J. C. Alderson and B. North (eds), *Language Testing in the 1990s*. London, UK: Modern English Publications and the British Council.

Bachman, L. F. (1990). *Fundamental Considerations in Language Testing*. Oxford, UK: Oxford University Press.

Ballard, P. B. (1923). *Mental Tests*. London, UK: Hodder and Stoughton.

Barnwell, D. (1996). *A History of Foreign Language Testing in the United States*. Tempe, AZ: Bilingual Press.

Barton, P. E. (2009). *National Education Standards: getting beneath the surface*. Policy Information Center, Princeton NJ: Educational Testing Service. www.ets.org/Media/Research/pdf/PICNATEDSTAND.pdf (8/2/11).

Brindley, G. (1998). Describing language development? Rating scales and SLA. In L. F. Bachman and A. D. Cohen (eds), *Interfaces Between Second Language Acquisition and Language Testing Research*. Cambridge, UK: Cambridge University Press, 112–140.

Burt, C. (1922). *Mental and Scholastic Tests*. London, UK: P. S. King and Son Ltd.

Chalhoub-Deville, M. and Fulcher, G. (2003). The oral proficiency interview and the ACTFL Guidelines: A research agenda. *Foreign Language Annals* 36: 498–506.

Clark, J. L. D. (1980). Toward a common measure of speaking proficiency. In J. R. Frith (ed.), *Measuring Spoken Language Proficiency*. Georgetown University Press, 15–26.

Council of Europe (2001). *Common European framework of reference for language learning and teaching*. Cambridge, UK: Cambridge University Press. www.coe.int/t/dg4/linguistic/Source/Framework_EN.pdf (accessed 8/2/11).

—— (2009). *Relating Language Examinations to the Common European Framework of Reference for Languages: learning, teaching, assessment (CEFR): a manual*. Strasbourg, France: Council of Europe Language Policy Division. www.coe.int/t/dg4/linguistic/Manuel1_EN.asp#TopOfPage (accessed 8/2/11).

Davidson, F. and Lynch, B. K. (2002). *Testcraft: a teacher's guide to writing and using language test specifications*. New Haven, CT: Yale University Press.

Davies, A., Brown, A., Elder, C., Hill, K., Lumley, T. and McNamara, T. (1999). *Dictionary of Language Testing*. Cambridge, UK: Cambridge University Press.

Douglas, D. (2001). Language for specific purposes assessment criteria: where do they come from? *Language Testing* 18: 171–85.

Fulcher, G. (1993). *The Construction and Validation of Rating Scales for Oral Tests in English as a Foreign Language*. University of Lancaster, UK. Unpublished PhD thesis.

—— (1996). Does thick description lead to smart tests? A data-based approach to rating scale construction. *Language Testing* 13: 208–38.

—— (1997). The testing of speaking in a second language. In Clapham, C. and Corson, D. (eds), *Encyclopedia of Language and Education*, Vol 7: *Language Testing and Assessment*. Dordrecht, The Netherlands: Kluwer Academic Publishers, 75–85.

—— (2003). *Testing Second Language Speaking*. London, UK: Longman/Pearson Education.

—— (2004). Deluded by artifices? The Common European Framework and harmonization. *Language Assessment Quarterly* 1: 253–66.

—— (2008). Criteria for Evaluating language quality. In E. Shohamy and N. H. Hornberger (eds), *Encyclopedia of Language and Education*, 2nd edn. Vol. 7: *Language Testing and Assessment*. New York, NY: Springer, 157–76.

—— (2009). Test use and Political Philosophy. *Annual Review of Applied Linguistics* 29: 3–20.

—— (2010). *Practical Language Testing*. London, UK: Hodder Education.

Fulcher, G. and Davidson, F. (2007). *Language Testing and Assessment: an advanced resource book*. London, UK: Routledge.

—— (2009). Test architecture, test retrofit. *Language Testing* 26: 123–44.

Fulcher, G., Davidson, F. and Kemp, J. (2011) Effective rating scale development for speaking tests: performance decision trees. *Language Testing* 28: 1.

Gould, S. J. (1997). *The Mismeasure of Man*. London, UK: Penguin.

Hacking, I. (1999). *The Social Construction of What?* Cambridge, MA: Harvard University Press.

Hamp-Lyons, L. (1991). Scoring procedures for ESL contexts. In L. Hamp-Lyons (ed.), *Assessing Second Language Writing in Academic Contexts*. Norwood, NJ: Ablex, 241–76.

Hulstijn, J. A. (2007). The shaky ground beneath the CEFR: quantitative and qualitative dimensions of language proficiency. *Modern Language Journal* 91: 663–67.

Ingram, E. (1968). Attainment and diagnostic testing. In A. Davies (ed.), *Language Testing Symposium: a psycholinguistic approach*. Oxford, UK: Oxford University Press.

Inoue, M. (2009). Health sciences communications skills test: the development of a rating scale. *Melbourne Papers in Language Testing* 14: 55–91.

Jacoby, S. and McNamara, T. (1999). Locating competence. *English for Specific Purposes* 18: 213–41.

Kane, M. (2009). Validating the interpretations and uses of test scores. In R. W. Lissitz (ed.), *The Concept of Validity*. Charlotte, NC: Information Age Publishing, 39–64.

Kaulfers, W. V. (1944). War-time developments in modern language achievement tests. *Modern Language Journal* 70: 366–72.

Lantolf, J. P. and Frawley, W. (1985) Oral proficiency testing: a critical analysis. *Modern Language Journal* 69: 337–45.

Latham, H. (1877). *On the Action of Examinations Considered as a Means of Selection*. Cambridge, UK: Dighton, Bell and Company.

Lipman, W. (1922). The Mental Age of Americans. *New Republic* 32, no. 412 (October 25), 213–15; no. 413 (November 1), 246–48; no. 414 (November 8), 275–77; no. 415 (November 15, 1922), 297–98;

no. 416 (November 22), 328–30; no. 417 (November 29), 9–11. historymatters.gmu.edu/d/5172 (accessed 8/2/11).

Lowe, P. (1985). The ILR proficiency scale as a synthesizing research principle: The view from the mountain. In James, C. J. (ed.), *Foreign Language Proficiency in the Classroom and Beyond*. Lincolnwood, IL: National Textbook Company, 9–53.

—— (1986). Proficiency: panacea, framework, process? A reply to Kramsch, Schulz, and particularly Bachman and Savignon. *Modern Language Journal* 70: 391–97.

Matthews, M. (1990). The measurement of productive skills: doubts concerning the assessment criteria of certain public examinations. *English Language Teaching Journal* 44: 117–21.

Messick, S. (1995). Standards of validity and the validity of standards in performance assessment. *Educational Measurement: Issues and Practice* 14: 5–8.

Mislevy, R. J. (1992). *Linking Educational Assessments. Concepts. Issues. Methods and Prospects*. Princeton NJ: Educational Testing Service.

Mislevy, R. J., Almond, R. G. and Lukas, J. F. (2003). *A Brief Introduction to Evidence-Centred Design*. Research Report RR-03–16. Princeton, NJ: Educational Testing Service.

North, B. (1992). Options for scales of proficiency for a European Language Framework. In R. Scharer and B. North (eds), *Toward a Common European Framework for Reporting Language Competency*. Washington, DC: National Foreign Language Center, 9–26.

—— (1993). *Scales of language proficiency: a survey of some existing systems*. Strasbourg: Council of Europe, Council for Cultural Co-operation, CC-LANG (94) 24.

—— (2000). Linking language assessments: an example in a low stakes context. *System* 28: 555–77.

—— (2007). The CEFR illustrative descriptor scales. *The Modern Language Journal* 91: 656–59.

North, B. and Schneider, G. (1998). Scaling descriptors for language proficiency scales. *Language Testing* 15: 217–62.

Peirce, C. S. (1903). *Pragmatism as a Principle and Method of Right Thinking*. The 1903 Harvard Lectures on Pragmatism. Edited by Patricia Ann Turrisi (1997), New York: State University of New York Press.

Pollitt, A. (1990). Giving students a sporting chance: Assessing by counting and by judging. In J. C. Alderson and B. North (eds), *Language Testing in the 1990s*. London, UK: Modern English Publications and the British Council, 46–59.

Pollitt, A. and Murray, N. L. (1996). What raters really pay attention to. In M. Milanovic and N. Saville (eds), *Performance Testing, Cognition and Assessment*. Cambridge, UK: Cambridge University Press, 74–91.

Schulz, R. A. (1986). From achievement through proficiency through classroom instruction: some caveats. *The Modern Language Journal* 70: 373–79.

Sollenberger, H. E. (1978). Development and current use of the FSI oral interview test. In Clark, J. L. D. (ed.), *Direct Testing of Speaking Proficiency: Theory and Application*. Princeton, NJ: Educational Testing Service, 1–12.

Thorndike, E. L. (1912). The measurement of educational products. *The School Review* 20, 5: 289–99.

—— (1913). *An Introduction to the Theory of Mental and Social Measurements*, 2nd edn. New York, NY: Teachers College, Columbia University.

Turner C.E. (2000). Listening to the voices of rating scale developers: Identifying salient features for second language performance assessment. *Canadian Modern Language Review* 56: 555–84.

Turner C.E. and Upshur J. (2002). Rating scales derived from student samples: Effects of the scale marker and the student sample on scale content and student scores. *TESOL Quarterly* 36: 49–70.

Upshur J. and Turner C.E. (1995). Constructing rating scales for second language tests. *English Language Teaching Journal* 49: 3–12.

—— (1999). Systematic effects in the rating of second-language speaking ability: Test method and learner discourse. *Language Testing* 16: 82–111.

Vallax, P. (2010). *The Common European Framework of Reference for Languages: A critical analysis of its impact on a sample of teachers and curricula within and beyond Europe*. Unpublished PhD thesis. New Zealand: University of Waikato.

Velleman, B. L. (2008). The 'scientific linguist' goes to war: the United States A.S.T. program in foreign languages. *Historiographia Linguistica* 35: 385–416.

Weir, C. J. (2005). Limitations of the Common European Framework for developing comparable examinations and tests. *Language Testing* 22: 28–300.

Wendler, C. and Powers, D. (2009) *What does it mean to repurpose a test? R&D Connections No. 9*. Princeton NJ: Educational Testing Service. www.ets.org/Media/Research/pdf/RD_Connections9.pdf.

Westhoff, G. (2007). Challenges and opportunities of the CEFR for reimagining foreign language pedagogy. *The Modern Language Journal* 91: 676–79.

Wilds, C. (1975). The oral interview test. In R. L. Jones and B. Spolsky (eds), *Testing language Proficiency*. Arlington, VA: Center for Applied Linguistics, 29–44.

—— (1979). The measurement of speaking and reading proficiency in a foreign language. In M. L. Adams and J. R. Frith (eds), *Testing Kit: French and Spanish*. Department of State: Foreign Services Institute, 1–12.

Wood, B. (1928). *New York Experiments with New-Type Modern Language Tests*. New York, NY: Macmillan.

Yerkes, R. M. (1920). What psychology contributed to the war. In R. M. Yerkes (ed.), *The New World of Science: its development during the war*. New York, NY: The Century Co., 364–89.

—— (1921). *Psychological Examining in the United States Army*. Memoirs of the National Academy of Sciences, Vol. XV. Washington, DC: Government Printing Office.

Young, R. F. (2002). Discourse approaches to oral language assessment. *Annual Review of Applied Linguistics* 22: 243–62.

Part VIII
Administration and training

Quality management in test production and administration

Nick Saville

Introduction

This chapter presents and discusses the core processes required in developing and administering language tests and makes the case for adopting a quality management (QM) approach to improve testing and to ensure that appropriate professional standards are met. In this respect, language test developers need to adopt the kind of managerial practices which enable successful organisations to implement error-free processes.

In making this case, it is important to define what quality means in the context of language assessment and to describe how an approach based on QM can help to achieve the required quality goals and at the same time to enhance a validity argument (see Kane, this volume). By adopting that QM approach, it is possible to ensure that processes are continually improved and standards raised; this is in keeping with the concept of validation as a long-term, ongoing activity (Kane, 2006).

A key point is the necessary convergence between the twin concepts of quality and validity. I argue that QM provides an appropriate basis for guaranteeing the consistency of the processes which underpin a validity argument and provides the tools and techniques for linking theoretical concerns with the practical realities of setting up and administering assessment systems.

The principles of QM and the link with validation can be widely applied in many different test development contexts with the aim of improving the quality of assessment systems. A number of explicit stages need to be followed from production of the test materials to the issuing of the test results. This applies whether the test development team is a group of teachers producing language tests for students within their own classes, or whether they are specialised staff within a testing agency responsible for developing and administering high stakes, international language examinations in many countries.

To illustrate the applicability of the approach, these two contexts – classroom assessment and large-scale assessment – will be referred to throughout this chapter. In both cases the validity of the assessment needs to be ensured and the integrity of the results guaranteed for the intended purposes, even if these may be very different. To achieve the required validity profile for the intended purpose and use, the quality of the development and administration procedures have to be checked and monitored at each stage of the assessment cycle (see Figure 27.1). What differs between the school context and the large-scale assessment operation is the complexity of the organisational structure within which the activities take place and, most obviously perhaps, the resources available for achieving the intended assessment goals, i.e., the human, material and time-related factors which are available to meet the intended objectives. Other factors may relate to the intended uses of the test results and the importance attached to decisions made about the test takers. In other words whether the test is considered to be high or low stakes by the users and whether this may offer opportunities to increase the resources available (e.g. in order to achieve adequate reliability of test scores to support high stakes decisions about test takers).

Practical considerations are always important. The test developer must attempt to match the ambitions of the assessment sponsors to the 'real world' considerations and constraints which exist in their context. This inevitably requires judgments to be made about deploying the available resources in the most effective way at all stages of the cycle. Careful planning is required at the outset, and appropriate management systems need to be set up to allocate and manage resources throughout. Leadership and communication skills are important and those involved in a test development project need to employ techniques for managing successful projects and to be aware of critical issues related to the management of change within organisations.

Bachman and Palmer (1996: 35–37) discuss practicality as an important 'test quality' and Bachman and Palmer (2010: 411–27) dedicate a chapter to the identification, allocation and management of resources. These points are taken up below when considering aspects of organisational management.

Definition of terms

In the recent literature on quality a distinction is usually made between the detailed procedures for checking and assuring the quality of a *product* or service (*quality control* and *quality assurance* – QC and QA), and the overarching concept of QM which is concerned with the management of *processes* within the organisation responsible for developing the product or service. These distinctions are maintained in this chapter and the history of QM systems will be reviewed to illustrate how the strands have developed and why they are now relevant to language assessment systems. The finer grained distinction between quality control and quality assurance is addressed below.

Historical perspectives

Language assessment

Interest in developing high-quality language tests for practical purposes has increased since the 1980s and a large number of textbooks have been written to provide guidance to aspiring practitioners (Hughes, 2003; Alderson *et al.*, 1995; Bachman and Palmer, 1996, 2010; Weir, 2005). This has also been reflected to some extent in the literature on educational and psychological measurement; see for example Downing and Haladyna (2006).

A common feature of these textbooks is that the process of test development is conceived of as a series of logical steps, starting with the test design and item writing, progressing through to administration and reporting of results, and ending with some form of evaluation. I refer to this as *the assessment cycle*.

Bachman and Palmer (1996), for example, set out to 'enable the reader to become competent in the design, development and use of language tests' (1996: 3) and in their approach to 'test usefulness', they outline a three stage model: *design, operationalisation and test administration*.

In their updated edition entitled *Language Assessment in Practice* (2010), they switch their focus to the development and support of 'assessment use arguments (AUA)', but nevertheless they still recommend a process-based approach to the assessment cycle which starts with a 'design statement' for the intended assessment and its uses and concludes with the language assessments being *used responsibly* in practice. See Bachman and Palmer (2010: 247–439), 'Developing and using language assessments in the real world'.

Downing (2006: 3–25) in his introductory chapter to Downing and Haladyna (op. cit.) discusses 'a systematic test development model organised into twelve discrete tasks or activities'; he lists these in a table as 'Twelve Steps for Effective Test Development' (op. cit.: 5).

It is less common in the testing textbooks to find a discussion of the institutional parameters which need to be addressed in order to set up and manage an organisation which is capable, not only of designing good quality test materials, but also of maintaining an assessment system over an extended period of time.

In rare instances when the operational management of a testing system is covered in the literature, it tends to be discussed in relation to test *administration*, which is taken as only one part of the overall assessment cycle. For example, Fulcher and Davidson (2007: 115) in their chapter on Administration and Training state that: 'The delivery of tests requires an infrastructure, and a set of procedures that are usually followed', and they go on to discuss 'getting things done'. They make a case for 'doing things consistently' and suggest that: 'For language testing, part of the validity claim is that the test administration and all the processes used by the testing agency are done according to standardized procedures' (2007: 127). In the same section of their chapter, they briefly refer to 'quality management systems' as a way of ensuring that consistency and dependability can be achieved within a company by *defining, controlling and evaluating* what gets done.

The role of the 'testing agency' (whether this is interpreted as the team of school teachers or the large-scale testing company) and 'the processes' required to manage a valid assessment system are two key points. Although not widely discussed, the organisational structure and the processes employed by those responsible for developing and administering tests (the staff) are essential elements in a quality model. Both of these aspects are discussed in more detail below.

In the literature on educational and psychological measurement, attention has recently been given to the concept of quality. An important contribution is the volume entitled *Improving Testing: Applying Process Tools and Techniques to Assure Quality* edited by Wild and Ramaswamy (2008). This volume is structured around the notion of a quality model and the so-called *'quality triangle'*, the three sides of which are: planning and design; monitoring and improvement; and implementing standards. The next section deals with these points within the general discussion of QM.

Quality management

In taking an historical perspective on QM, it is informative to start by reviewing developments in the manufacturing sector, especially in production processes and in the development of approaches to organisational management within companies. However, although the quality movement originated in manufacturing, the same approach is now employed across many types of organisation, including those which provide services rather than products. The developments in the service sector have also been extended to educational systems and to educational assessment, as described by Wild and Ramaswamy (op. cit.). A case is made in this chapter for applying the model in language assessment too.

The concept of quality may appear to be a modern development but practices related to consumer protection, standards and inspection have been with us for hundreds of years, e.g. through the development of trades and guilds in the Middle Ages. However, the industrial and scientific advancements in the past two hundred years shifted the focus from *maintaining* standards, to *improving* standards and the central notion of *continual improvement* emerged. This has now become axiomatic within all QM systems.

The founders of this field, for example Taylor (1911) and Shewhart (1931, 1939) emphasised the link between effective management of the organisation (e.g. the company producing the products) and the quality of the products themselves (the outputs from the company). They saw management as a science and began to show how systems could be experimented with and improved in order to get better results. Processes were defined in terms of their *inputs* and *outputs* and this in turn enabled the *links* between different parts of an organisation to be seen more clearly, and as a result to be managed more effectively. Furthermore, the high cost of relying on inspections to check on quality *post hoc*, with the subsequent reworking of a product to ensure its quality, became apparent. The recommended solution was for more effort to go into reducing the number of defective items *before* the product reached the final stage of the process.

W. Edwards Deming (1900–1993) emerged in the mid-twentieth century as the leading figure in this movement; he built on these evolving views of quality to create one of the first coherent 'quality management systems', known as Total Quality Management (TQM). Deming's 1986 volume *Out of the Crisis* has had a major influence on the development of modern management standards and influenced all the other QM methods which have been developed over the years. Kemp (2006: 177) lists the following six approaches which are now in use: the Capability Maturity Model (CMM); Six Sigma; the Zero Defect Movement; Gemba kaizan; Just-in-time (lean) Manufacturing; and ISO 9000.

Deming's influence is often illustrated by the Japanese experience where his ideas were taken up whole heartedly in the attempt to rebuild Japanese industry in the 1950s in the aftermath of the Second World War. By the 1960s industrial companies which implemented TQM, such as Sony, Toyota and Hitachi, had already achieved a global reputation for the consistently high quality of their products. Competitors in other parts of the world were obliged to take note.

Along with the development of quality as a concept within organisational management, the notion of *quality standards* also emerged as a mechanism of accountability and as the guarantee of quality for consumers. This notion also has a long history and dates back over100 years to the establishment of the first manufacturing standards with external accreditation. One of the earliest examples is the British Standards Institution (BSI), which was founded as the Engineering Standards Committee in London in 1901. The original quality mark known as the BSI 'kite mark' was introduced in 1903 (known as such because the design of the logo resembles a kite).

These days we are all familiar with the *quality marks* which appear on the products we buy, and we may be influenced in our purchasing decisions by the type of quality mark we see, e.g. cycle helmets are manufactured to resist impact according to particular safety standards.

Most recently, an important international influence has come from the International Organization for Standardization (ISO) and the ISO quality standards, such as the ISO 9000 range (see below). It is important to note that this kind of accreditation is not primarily designed to guarantee the quality of the end product or service; the intention is to certify that processes are being applied consistently and effectively to meet the stated objectives of an organisation. We will see below how the approach to QM represented by ISO 9000, combined with the appropriate principles of good practice in language assessment, provide the basis for auditable processes and the achievement of professional standards, for example, as set out by the AERA/APA/NCME *Standards for Educational and Psychological Testing* (1999) or in the international Codes of Practice for language assessment (see Further Reading below).

When adopted and implemented in conjunction with one another, these two elements can help ensure that assessment systems are developed and administered to meet the demanding requirements of regulatory authorities, and at the same time to provide the basis for fair testing practices which meet the needs of the language test users.

In the rest of this chapter, the ISO approach will be used as an example of how standards form part of a QM system. The International Organization for Standardization itself is a non-governmental organisation (NGO) founded in 1947 with headquarters in Switzerland. It is composed of representatives from various national organisations concerned with standards of the kind noted above. The standards, such as the 9000 range, are maintained centrally by ISO but are administered by the accreditation and certification bodies at a national or regional level (e.g. American National Standards Institute (ANSI); Deutsches Institut für Normung (DIN); British Standards Institution (BSI); Canadian Standards Association; Standards Australia; etc.).

The ISO 9000 group of standards is particularly relevant to organisations involved in educational systems, including those responsible for test development and administration. The requirements for accreditation are updated periodically by ISO; so, for example, the requirements for ISO 9001, one of the standards in the ISO 9000 group, were updated in 2001 and again in 2008. ISO 9001: 2008 is now the world's most widely used QM standard and it is particularly applicable to our discussion because it can be applied to all types of organisation, no matter what the size. Its stated purpose is to provide a framework for any organisation to control its processes in order to achieve its objectives, including customer satisfaction, regulatory compliance and continual improvement.

Any organization which aspires to meet the ISO standard can apply to be independently audited and certified in conformance with the standard in question (e.g. ISO 9001: 2008). Once the organisation has been accredited, it can claim to be 'ISO 9001 certified' or 'ISO 9001 registered'.

The ISO approach exemplifies clearly the underlying principles of QM with the aim of continual improvement. While compliance to external standards and external accreditation are benefits that accrue, the main focus is on meeting objectives and getting the job done properly. The principles and the techniques to assure quality can be applied even within a small-scale testing operations such as a school or university department.

Critical issues

Definition of quality management

QM is an overarching term; it includes the planning and management of processes, which over time lead to improvements being implemented (c.f. the key concept of continual improvement noted above).

In organisational terms, the aim should be for quality to become synonymous with what the organisation does – normally referred to in QM discourse as the organisation's 'mission'. A prerequisite is a clear understanding and statement of the organisation's aims and objectives. This means that leadership and good management underpin a quality approach.

Simon Feary, CEO of the Chartered Quality Institute, suggests that quality ' ... *is an approach, a set of tools, a philosophy, the substance of which is no more than an articulation of what all good managers recognise to be good business practices*' (retrieved from CQI website 2009).

The effective achievement of organisational objectives will of course vary, depending on the type of organisation. A school which provides language assessment as part of its educational mission will have different objectives than a testing company which specialises in large-scale assessment.

From the assessment perspective both types of organisation need to be able to guarantee 'fitness for purpose', or in Bachman and Palmer's usage, to develop and administer 'useful' tests (1996: 17).

Customer or client satisfaction is another key concept here. Products or services which can be considered 'high quality', adequately meet or exceed the expectations of the customers or clients who buy or make use of those products or services. Identification of customer/client needs is therefore an important initial consideration.

In language testing, the main clients are the test users; the *primary users* are the test takers themselves and the *secondary users* are those who sponsor the test takers (parents, teachers, employers, etc.) or make use of the test results to make decisions (educational institutions, employers, government bodies etc.). For discussion of the terms primary and secondary user see the Code of Fair Testing Practices (1988/2004) and ALTE's Code of Practice (1994).

Quality control and quality assurance

QM encompasses quality control and quality assurance activities, which have related but discrete functions.

The broad meaning of quality control is synonymous with checking. In other words it entails carrying out systematic checks to ensure that all aspects of a work flow meet the stipulated standards as defined and described in relevant documentation.

Quality control activities involve the detailed checking of the components which make up a product and services *at each stage* of the overall process. The checks need to be carried out by the people who have the responsibility for doing the tasks. Quality control activities, therefore, form an integral part of a person's job and are not something carried out by a separate 'quality control department'.

In the assessment cycle these kind of checks are essential to ensure that basic mistakes are not made which could threaten validity (e.g. introduce construct-irrelevant variance into scores), disrupt the smooth administration of the assessment, or lead to mistakes such as the wrong result being issued to a test taker.

Quality checks may focus on important details such as:

- the quality of the tests materials themselves – in other words the test items and other features of the assessment procedures;
- the quality of the information and support provided to the clients (the test takers, teachers and other users);
- the quality of the documentation needed to support the administration of the tests at the testing venues;
- the quality of the data collected and stored for assessment purposes and for producing the test results.

Quality assurance activities, on the other hand, are carried out to monitor, evaluate and improve processes; the aim is to ensure that all processes are maintained to the required standard.

Quality assurance activities differ in that they are normally carried out in order to monitor and adjust processes when they are operational within a system. Procedures for monitoring need to put in place to evaluate whether core processes are working adequately (see core processes in Figure 27.1). It is crucial that relevant evidence (i.e., data and information) can be collected through QA mechanisms, such as periodic audits, inspections and formal reviews, so that the evaluation can take place.

The required standard which is quality assured may be set by:

(a) an external regulatory body, such as a government agency;
(b) a professional organisation responsible for a specific domain of activity (e.g. law, medicine, educational assessment, etc.);

(c)   an external standards organisation (e.g. ISO);
(d)   the organisation itself and its internal rules and regulations.

In some cases related to (a) or (b) above, the need to demonstrate compliance may be a statutory requirement. Voluntary accreditation is normally associated with (c) and (d). In a QM system it is important to recognise, however, that quality cannot be imposed from outside, but must be established and monitored within an organisation in the first instance. Detailed illustrations of QC and QA activities in language test development and administration are given below.

Quality management within an organisation

Let us return for a moment to the nature of organisations and the two extreme examples introduced above: the classroom teachers in a school context and the staff within a testing agency. In both cases, the assessment cycle needs to be effectively managed, and all those involved need to have a clear understanding of the objectives and how they will be achieved.

The people involved in the test development and administration processes (the staff) need to understand their roles and how to operate effectively within their own institutional context. The identification and allocation of the non-human resources available to get the job done also needs to be managed effectively and the time-frame for carrying out the processes must be clearly communicated to all concerned.

The importance of the people – the staff

The lessons to be learnt from QM suggest that staff are a key asset in assuring quality and that senior managers within an organisation must take responsibility for ensuring that each member of staff is qualified to carry out their own responsibilities. Support for the recruitment and training of qualified specialists, as well as effective communication across teams, is central to this.

Given the cost of recruiting and training staff, successful organisations seek to retain those who have acquired relevant skills and to provide regular in-service training for them to ensure that up-to-date knowledge is maintained. For example, it will be important for any organisation involved in language assessment to maintain a good level of assessment literacy throughout the organisation, as well as specialist knowledge for carrying out specific tasks, such as item writing, rating and test analysis.

However, many organisations involved in developing assessment systems cannot afford to retain *all* the expertise they need on their permanent staff and so they need to employ temporary staff or specialised consultants to carry out some tasks within their processes. This might include the following kinds of task: item writing; rating; rater training; professional support coordination for teachers; administration at test venues (as the proctors or invigilators); and so on.

As these tasks play an essential part in core processes, the assessment provider has a responsibility to ensure that these external stakeholders are also appropriately recruited and trained. Relevant quality control and quality assurance procedures can be used to guarantee that their contributions meet specified quality standards and that they contribute to the overall quality of the assessment system. The monitoring and evaluation of the work of staff and consultants over time can be used to identify threats to validity, as well as to identify where processes can be made more efficient. Where necessary staff changes can be made or additional training provided. See Saville and Hargreaves (1999: 42–51) for a discussion of rater training and monitoring systems in language assessment; also Fulcher and Davidson (2007: 129–32) on administration and training.

Setting up the structure for managing the staff and monitoring their performance is the responsibility of senior managers, but the QM model also requires *all staff* within an organisation to take responsibility for their *own* role and the contribution they make to quality. They should seek to gain a sound understanding of how their role fits within the overall organisation and its stated objectives (its mission and goals).

Individuals must be able to connect their own jobs to those of others working in their team or work group, and they should identify professional development and training requirements in order to improve their knowledge and skills over time.

Linking quality management to the assessment cycle

In this section we will look in more detail at how the concepts of QM can be directly linked to the assessment cycle and at ways that test development projects can be effectively managed by an organisation. Specific quality control and quality assurance techniques are illustrated in relation to the *core processes* within the assessment cycle. In doing so, the core processes are distinguished from *wider processes* within an organisation which support the assessment activities, and the *support processes* which are needed to manage the organisation as a whole.

Wider processes include activities such as: document control and record keeping; internal audits and liaison with external regulators and auditors; conformance to relevant statutory regulations and standards (e.g. equal opportunities, health and safety, data protection, financial regulation, etc.); risk management and continuity planning (e.g. contingency for when things go wrong), etc.

Support processes within a company would include recruitment and training of all staff (including administrators, cleaners, etc.); finance systems, including payment of salaries, purchase payments, issuing of invoices, collection of fees and credit control; technical support service related to IT and communications; project management; and so on.

Although many of these wider and support processes are best demonstrated in large-scale assessment providers (such as testing companies), many are also relevant in other contexts where tests are developed and administered by smaller organisations or groups of individual (e.g. in schools, university departments, etc.). In order to ensure quality of the core processes, appropriate attention needs to be given to all these areas as they impact on important considerations, such as resource allocation and management, which affect the quality of the assessment system.

The importance of defining processes

I return here to the language testing frameworks which I referred to above and which address practical test development issues within the assessment cycle. From among the many suggested frameworks and models, five main steps or stages can be identified in a basic assessment cycle:

- Planning and design following a decision to develop a test;
- Development, including initial development and systems for test assembly;
- Delivery, including routine test assembly and the administration of the assessment;
- Processing, including marking and grading and issue of results;
- Review and evaluation.

These are the *core processes* commonly found in the handbooks on testing (although the names given to them may vary) and they represent the day-to-day reality for any organisation which undertakes to develop and administer assessment systems.

The convergence between QM and the principles of language assessment can be illustrated through the assessment cycle shown in Figure 27.1.

I have already noted that defining processes is a crucial part of a QM approach. It can be argued that it is only when the processes are adequately defined and appropriately documented that the necessary quality control and quality assurance procedures can be carried out. The QC and QA procedures ensure that the defined processes are being followed effectively and efficiently and provide the necessary information to make improvements.

Figure 27.1 shows five *core processes* and four *outputs* in the assessment cycle. In QM terminology this is the central part of a *process interactions map* which shows how the core processes fit together and enable an organisation to manage the interaction between them to meet its objectives.

The core processes (design, production, administration, processing, review and evaluation) are supplemented by the wider and support processes noted above. These vary considerably depending on the nature of the organisation within which the core processes are being implemented.

The outputs which the core processes generate are:

- Specifications
- Assessment materials and procedures
- Completed assessments (test takers' responses)
- Results and interpretive information

In implementing this model, the relevant processes are defined by senior managers who can then coordinate the links between those processes as effectively as possible and ensure that the staff are capable of carrying out their tasks effectively.

To achieve this within a QM model, *process owners* are appointed to ensure that the critical interactions in the map are identified and documented appropriately. Each core and support process should be described in a process document and each sub-process is described in a *standard operating procedure (SOP)*. Ultimately each task to be carried out should be described in detailed *work instructions* which must be explicit enough to ensure that the activity can be performed without mistakes being made and to meet the quality standard.

The documents, such as the SOPs and work instructions, need to be stored so that they can be readily accessed by members of staff and so that they can be kept up to date when improvements are made to the processes. In assessment systems some of these documents may need to be stored so that only certain people can have access to them to meet requirements for security and confidentiality.

Within the ISO approach, it is recommended that some documents should be stored in a *central document register*; this applies to documents which are needed by groups of staff across the organisation. In addition, *local document registers* can be complied to store the documents needed for

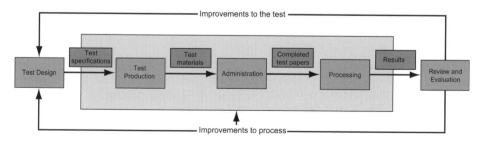

Figure 27.1 Core processes

carrying out particular activities by specific groups of staff. These include the detailed work instructions, manuals, standardised forms, guidelines, checklists, etc. which are particularly important for quality control purposes.

Quality assurance techniques are needed to monitor whether the procedures for document production, document control and records management are being followed effectively. Procedures such as internal audits can be implemented for this purpose.

The continual improvement cycle is also central to QM, as illustrated by the ISO 9001 Standard in which it is characterised as the *Plan, Do, Check, Act* model. The feedback loop in this model requires action to be taken after the checking takes place to ensure that well-specified improvements are made to the operational system.

Figure 27.2 illustrates this iterative process within the assessment cycle; each iteration allows feedback to be used to evaluate effectiveness and efficiency and to enable improvements to be made in subsequent iterations.

The planning stage begins with the perceived need for a new (or revised) test or assessment system. The aim is to define the intended context and use of the prospective assessment and the key output of this stage is a set of specifications defining the requirements for the validity argument and its operational procedures (see Davidson, this volume). This stage occurs when the assessment system is developed for the first time or is being significantly modified.

Each test version or administration of the test needs to be delivered according to the required quality standards. There are typically three stages in this process: the assembly of test forms; the administration of the test at testing venues; and the processing of test takers' responses, including the rating and grading procedures, to produce and issue the results to users.

As part of the operational system, the quality control and quality assurance procedures noted above should be implemented to ensure that the design features are maintained effectively under operational conditions and that unexpected threats to validity are not introduced.

The aims and outputs of each core process is shown in Figure 27.2.

How does this work in practice?

To illustrate how this can work in practice in this section I will look in more detail at QC and QA activities related to two processes in the operational system: assembling tests and test administration.

QC and QA procedures in assembling test materials

At the development stage, the production of test specifications and instructions for item writers which can be used in assembling tests is an essential prerequisite. Checking against the specifications must be done at various stages of the operational cycle before the assessment is finalised and ready to be administered.

To ensure that test materials are controlled for quality, the test provider must set up a system to collect, store and process the test tasks and associated materials. This is particularly important if a large number of items and tasks are involved.

All test materials should go through standardised quality control processes, which will involve editing and try out (piloting or pre-testing). Technical characteristics such the level of difficulty of items, any actual or potential bias in the materials, the content coverage of the tasks (topic, genre, etc.) and conformance to the required format of tasks and items (in terms of length, type of item, etc.) must be checked.

It is important to be able to track progress and to know at any time what stage a tasks or item has reached in this process. The work-flow therefore has to be managed efficiently and, if

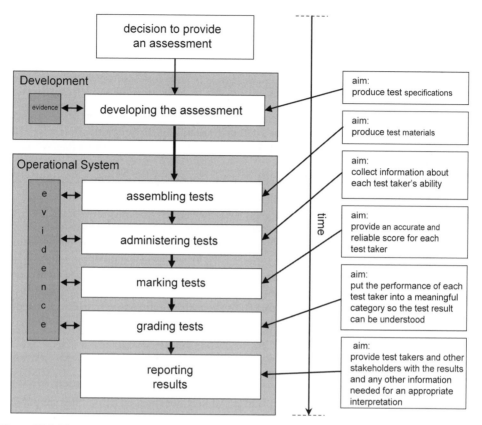

Figure 27.2 The assessment cycle

necessary appropriate technology should be employed to deal with the complexity. This becomes increasingly important as the number of items and range of people involved increases and will usually entail using item-banking techniques.

A basic system for managing the test materials might include the following:

- an identification number and description of each task or set of materials produced;
- a checklist to track progress and to provide a complete record of the stages completed, the changes made and other relevant information about decisions taken;
- a system to ensure the stored materials are readily accessible along with
- relevant management information which is accrued during the editing process.

QC and QA procedures in administering tests

The test developer needs to be confident that assessments are administered in a standardised way. Consistency is important as uncontrolled variation can undermine validity. Standardisation between testing locations, if different venues and groups of people are involved, and over time from one session to the next needs to be guaranteed. Quality control and quality assurance techniques can be used to ensure that the administration of an assessment, whether in a classroom context or as part of a large-scale assessment system, is based on a set of standard operating procedures which are susceptible to monitoring and improvement.

In large-scale operations the administration of the assessment will be delegated to personnel at the testing venue. This means that the administrative procedures need to be clearly and comprehensively described and produced in a format which can be used under operational conditions.

For example, the following areas should be covered:

- the physical setting – how the venue is selected and how the rooms where the assessments take place are managed, including the safety and security of the premises;
- the storage and handling of secure and confidential materials and information (before, during and after the event);
- the type and number of personnel needed to oversee the administration on the day of the assessment to ensure safety and guarantee test security;
- the procedures for recruitment, training and management of invigilators/proctors and examiners, including practical aspects (such as payments for travel and subsistence);
- the management of the interaction between test takers and administrators before, during and after the assessment takes place – including the arrival at the venue of the test taker, the checking of their identities and eligibility, the seating arrangements, provision of accommodations to meet special needs or requirements;
- the management of the assessment procedures themselves – providing instructions, handing out and collecting test papers and answer sheets, monitoring for malpractice (including all kinds of cheating), ensuring that timings are respected;
- the handling of unforeseen eventualities and catering for specific circumstances (illness, fire alarms, power cuts, minor accidents, disruption from outside the venue).

All these procedures need to be carefully planned and fully documented before they are put into practice and must be turned into operational documents, such as instructions, regulations, checklists, etc.

The staff involved must be accountable for carrying out the quality control checks to ensure that each time the assessment is administered at a venue things run efficiently and unfair outcomes are avoided.

To ensure that the administrative procedures are implemented effectively at *all venues*, quality assurance techniques also need to be implemented on a wider scale. These might include monitoring visits or inspections carried out on behalf of the assessment provider across a range of venues. This form of monitoring can have a dual function; it can identify and deal with irregularities (non-conformances) where standard procedures are not followed effectively and it can identify opportunities for improvement.

Large-scale testing agencies can employ data-informed forensic techniques to monitor test taker behaviour and to identify possible cases of malpractice including cheating. This cannot usually happen in real-time as the analysis is based on test-response data (see Foster *et al.*, 2008 for a discussion of this).

Quality improvements resulting from QA monitoring might include:

- better conditions for administering listening tests (CDs rather than tapes; improved audio systems, use of headphones, etc.);
- improved security procedures to cut down on fraud, such as identity checks using biometric techniques (test day photos, etc.);
- better ways to accommodate test takers with special needs (e.g. improved access at venues for wheelchairs).

Quality and validation

Current thinking on validity emphasises the importance of *validation* as a process of accumulating evidence to support inferences made using the results of tests. This accrual of evidence should take place at all stages in the cycle (as shown in Figure 27.2).

Good practice also requires an assessment system to be reviewed regularly based on the monitoring of operational processes. QM methodology suggests that improvements can always be made; they may be small in nature and implemented in an ongoing way, or they may require a major revision project to carry them out. During routine monitoring, the need for a full-scale revision may be identified and if so, the planning and design stages are repeated.

Fulcher and Davidson (2009) use the metaphor of a building to consider those parts of a test which must be changed more regularly and those which may be changed infrequently.

Kane's chapter on validation in the fourth edition of *Educational Measurement* (2006) makes the case for 'validity as argument'. He suggests that in developing and presenting *a validity argument*, an examination provider must provide an overall evaluation of the intended interpretations and uses of the test or examination which is being validated based on evidence (Kane, 2006: 23). As validation needs to be maintained over time, we see a synergy between test validation and the QM concept of continual improvement.

Kane builds on the seminal paper by Messick (1989) which presented the *unitary concept of validity* and construct validation remains central to his approach. Validating inferences about a construct requires attention to be paid to all aspects of the assessment cycles. Failure to maintain the quality of any aspect of the system may threaten validity and lead to the assumptions of the validity argument being undermined. For example, undetected problems within the assessment system may lead to construct-irrelevant variance being introduced which may affect all test takers, groups of test takers, or individuals and thus lead to unfair outcomes (see Kunnan 2000, 2004).

Staff whose work contributes directly to the development of a validity argument for a particular assessment system, have a responsibility to ensure that they understand the concepts involved and that they are able to supply the required evidence from their own area of work (see above for discussion of the role of staff in a quality model).

By adopting the QM approach test developers are in a better position to build an appropriate validity argument and the rigor imposed means that they can be held to account by their stakeholders and other interested parties.

Recommendations for practice

In this chapter, we have seen that an effective QM system within organisations involves a clear statement (in the form of a mission statement or charter) of the aims and objectives to be achieved. The adoption of an internationally recognised Code of Practice can provide this function for many language test providers, especially smaller organisations (such as schools) or those whose main function is not language assessment (university departments, cultural bodies, etc.). It is recommended that all those involved in providing language tests should become familiar with one of the recognised Codes of Practice listed in the references and should review their aims and objectives in light of the underlying principles. If appropriate, those principles should be integrated into working practices.

Doing so is often easier said than done as well-established procedures might need to be changed, with implications for resources and how they are deployed. The *management of change* therefore is an important consideration here and the timescale for bringing about necessary improvements must be taken into account. Introductory textbooks on *organisation theory* and *innovation* are recommended for readers who are interested in this aspect of organisational management (e.g. Hatch and Cunliffe, 2006).

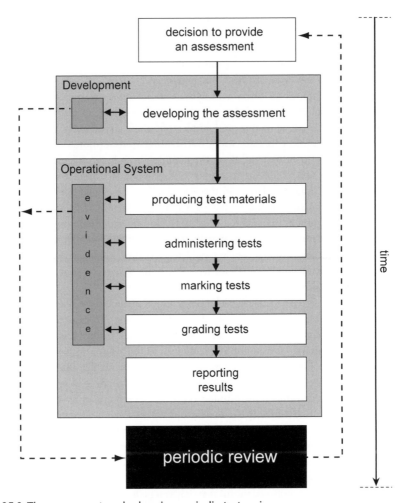

Figure 27.3 The assessment cycle showing periodic test review

QM systems require a commitment to *change processes* and so the adoption of a QM approach can be helpful in bringing about change and continual improvement in a well-managed and principled way. It is axiomatic that improvement is always possible, even where cases of good practice may already exist. It is recommended, therefore, that test developers should become familiar with QM principles, and where appropriate, seek to implement QM systems.

It should be remembered that quality standards cannot be imposed from outside, but must be established and monitored within an organisation in the first instance. This means that awareness raising and self-evaluation should proceed any form of external monitoring, which can be introduced at a later stage to check and confirm that the required standards are being met and to achieve external accreditation. This is consistent with the notion of validation based on the accrual of evidence over time.

Any test provider can introduce a typical QM sequence into their working practices, as exemplified by the following bullet points.

- Define your assessment objectives (mission), including the role of your institution, it goals and future ambitions.

- Assess what you currently do.
- Identify areas in most need of improvement.
- Decide on measures of improvement and an action plan to bring about the changes.
- Carry out the planned action to implement the improvements.
- Review progress and revise the action plan.
- Carry out new action to bring about further improvements.
- Repeat the cycle.

As QM systems provide the basis for wider accountability, organisations employing this approach can be confident of meeting requirements for accountability and should consider accreditation by an external agency.

An example of this is practice is the ALTE Quality Management System which provides a range of materials which can be accessed from the ALTE website.

ALTE adopted a quality model and adapted its Code of Practice (ALTE, 1994) to function as a QM tool (van Avermaet, 2003; Kuijper, 2003; van Avermaet et al., 2004; Saville, 2005, 2010).

This redesigned format (as Microsoft Excel-based checklists) reflected the assessment cycle which test developers are very familiar with, as discussed above (development; administration; processing; analysis and review). Taking both the Code of Practice and QM checklists into account, parameters were established for setting *minimum standards*. ALTE members (which include small test providers in university departments as well as international examinations boards) are now required to make a formal claim that a particular test or suite of tests has a quality profile appropriate to the context and use of the test. Members build a reasoned argument explaining how the minimum standards are met and provide relevant evidence to back up this claim. The formal scrutiny of these parameters takes place during an auditing process which is intended to ensure that adequate standards are achieved. Auditing has both a consultancy and a quality control role; if quality standards are not being met, the audited organisation is required to implement an action plan aimed at working towards and ultimately reaching the required standards.

Conclusions

In this chapter I have illustrated how a QM approach can help to improve language assessment and how the monitoring of quality through auditing procedures can enhance professional standards. I have noted that a QM approach can be helpful in fulfilling obligations for accountability to key stakeholders (especially the test takers and users of the test results) and to regulatory bodies. A validity argument and supporting evidence which has been constructed using QM principles can be readily scrutinised during an audit or inspection in order to verify whether appropriate industry standards are being met and/or statutory regulations are being adhered to (e.g. the code of practice of a regulatory body).

In recent years Codes of Ethics and Codes of Practice have been available for language testers to guide their practices, but these are not designed to assist practitioners in carrying out the day-to-day work of writing and administering tests, or for establishing minimum standards for their work. While an understanding of the ethical concerns and the underlying principles of assessment provide necessary conditions for developing fair and valid assessments, a QM approach can help link these concerns to practicable ways of doing things effectively. By adopting a QM approach, it is possible to connect the principles of good practice in language assessment with operational procedures which are transparent and accountable. In other words, it provides a practical approach to putting *principles into practice*.

Future developments

In future, it is likely that language test providers will experience increasing demands to account for their assessment practices with reference to theory, as well as pressure from stakeholders to provide evidence to back up the claims they make about the quality of their tests. Already there is a debate emerging over the nature of regulation and who is best qualified to set and monitor professional standards; does the responsibility lie within the language testing profession itself (e.g. through self-regulation) or is there a need for an independent regulator of some kind? If so, how might regulation operate on an international level, and who would 'guard the guards themselves'?

This chapter has suggested that whatever the jurisdiction for regulation, the basis for accountability needs to derive from a clear understanding of the principles of assessment coupled with a capacity to ensure that tests are developed and maintained effectively over time within organisations. First and foremost, the responsibility lies with the test providers themselves. This will mean that the larger test providers (testing agencies and examinations boards) will increasingly need to employ QM techniques to ensure that they can meet the demands of the regulatory environment.

To keep up with these demands, access to specialist knowledge and skills will become increasingly relevant, and more attention will need to be given to the professional development of language testers working within their own organisational contexts (whether teachers in schools or staff in testing agencies). In terms of staff training, a greater focus on management skills (e.g. covering the administrative aspects of the assessment cycle), is likely to be necessary.

As the debate over regulation develops and calls for greater accountability increase, a realistic way forward is to ensure that 'best practice' models which employ QM techniques are identified and shared, in order to help test providers to develop workable systems and for tangible improvements to be made incrementally. The sharing of expertise and know-how is essential, and in this regard, the professional language testing associations and international discussion forums will play an increasingly important role in enhancing awareness of quality within the wider concept of *assessment literacy*.

Acknowledgements

I am grateful to my colleagues Dittany Rose for her input to this chapter and for comments on an earlier draft, and Michael Corrigan for his help in designing the figures.

Further reading

Quality in educational assessment

Wild, C. L. and Ramaswamy, R. (2008). *Improving Testing. Applying process tools and techniques to assure quality*. London, UK: Routledge. This is an edited volume of 18 chapters focusing on a range of process tools and techniques to assure quality and to improve testing. It is wide-ranging in coverage, and although not specifically aimed at language testing, it deals with many of the issues raised in this chapter in an accessible way. The editors themselves set the scene by discussing the risks and the costs of poor quality in testing and they round off the volume with thoughts on the future of quality in the testing industry.

Background to quality management systems

There are numerous textbooks available which explain the principles of quality management. One readily available text which is aimed at non-specialist readers is *Quality Management Demystified* by Sid Kemp (2006, New York: McGraw-Hill). It defines the basic concepts and describes the tools for defining and measuring quality. In its historical review it covers Total Quality Management, as well as more recent schemes such as Six Sigma. Anderson (2008) in Wild and Ramaswamy also describes the use of Six Sigma in a large-scale testing company. Rose (2010) describes the ISO-based approach to quality management which has been adopted by Cambridge ESOL in the context of English Language assessment: Setting the standard: Quality management for language test providers. *Research Notes 39 (2–7)*. www.cambridgeesol.org/rs_notes/offprints. Useful information on quality management is available on many QM websites; e.g. Chartered Quality Institute (CQI): www.thecqi.org. The ISO standards can be accessed from the ISO website: www.iso.org which also provides many useful documents related to quality. National sites, e.g. British Standards Institute www.bsigroup.com also provide helpful advice and accessible explanations. See for example documents such as: ISO 9001: 2008 *Quality Management System Requirements*; ISO 9000: 2005 *Quality Management Systems – fundamentals and vocabulary*.

Codes of Practice

Codes of Practice in language testing emerged relatively recently starting in the 1990s. A more general *Code of Fair Testing Practices in Education*, was published in 1988 by the Joint Committee on Testing Practices (JCTP) by the American Psychological Association, and was particularly influential as it deliberately provided an approach which could be adapted to a wide range of testing contexts. See: www.apa.org/science/fairtestcode. For example, the Association of Language Testers in Europe (ALTE) produced its *Code of Practice* (1994) based on the JCTP model. ALTE also provides a range of other resources based on their Code of Practice and have developed an approach to quality management which employs techniques such as auditing to improve quality. See the ALTE website: www.alte.org. Reference materials which can be downloaded include: *Minimum standards for establishing quality profiles in ALTE Examinations* (2007); *The ALTE Quality Management and Code of Practice Checklists* (2008); *Manual for test development and examining* (2010). Produced by members of ALTE on behalf of the Council of Europe to accompany the CEFR.

Other associations have developed Codes of Practice and guidance for test providers in regional contexts, including the Japanese Language Testing Association (JLTA) and the European Association for Language Testing and Assessment (EALTA). See: www.ealta.eu.org – *EALTA Guidelines for Good Practice in Language Testing and Assessment* (2006).

The International Language Testing Association (ILTA) promotes ethical standards in language testing through its *Code of Ethics* (adopted in 2000) and through its *Guidelines for Practice* (2007). These resources are available from the ILTA website: www.iltaonline.com.

References

AERA, APA and NCME (1999). *Standards for Educational and Psychological Testing*. Washington DC: AERA Publishing.

Alderson, J. C., Clapham, C. and Wall, D. (1995). *Language Test Construction and Evaluation*. Cambridge, UK: Cambridge University Press.

Bachman, L. F. (1991). *Fundamental Considerations in Language Testing*. Oxford, UK: Oxford University Press.

—— (2005). Building and supporting a case for test use. *Language Assessment Quarterly* 2: 1–34.

Bachman, L.F. and Palmer, A. (1996). *Language Testing in Practice*. Oxford, UK: Oxford University Press.

—— (2010). *Language Assessment in Practice*. Oxford, UK: Oxford University Press.

Deming, W. E. (1986). *Out of the Crisis*. Cambridge, UK: Cambridge University Press.

Downing, S. M. (2006). Twelve steps for effective test development. In S. M. Downing and T. M. Haladyna (eds), *Handbook of Test Development*. Mahwah, NJ: Lawrence Erlbaum.

Downing, S. M. and Haladyna, T.M. (2006). *Handbook of Test Development*. Mahwah, NJ: Lawrence Erlbaum.

Feary, S. (2009). Time for quality. www.thecqi.org (accessed 8/2/11).

Foster, D., Maynes, D. and Hunt. B. (2008). Using data forensic methods to detect cheating. In C. L. Wild and R. Ramaswamy (eds), *Improving testing. Applying Process Tools and Techniques to Assure Quality*. London, UK: Routledge.

Fulcher, G. and Davidson, F. (2007). *Language Testing and Assessment – an advanced resource book*. Abingdon, UK: Routledge.

—— (2009). Test architecture, test retrofit. *Language Testing* 26: 123–44.

Hatch, M. J. and Cunliffe, A. L. (2006). *Organization Theory: modern, symbolic and post-modern perspectives*, 2nd edn. Oxford, UK: Oxford University Press.

Hughes, A. (2003). *Testing for Language Teachers*, 2nd edn. Cambridge, UK: Cambridge University Press.

Kane, M. (2006). Validation. In R. L. Brennan (ed.), *Educational Measurement*, 4th edn. Washington, DC: American Council on Education/Praeger.

Kemp, S. (2006). *Quality Management Demystified*. New York, NY: McGraw Hill.

Kuijper, H. (2003). QMS as a continuous process of self-evaluation and quality improvement for testing bodies. www.alte.org/qa/index.php (accessed 8/2/11).

Kunnan, A. J. (2000). Fairness and justice for all. In A. J. Kunnan (ed.), *Fairness and Validation in Language Assessment*. Cambridge, UK: Cambridge University Press, 1–13.

—— (2004). Test fairness. In M. Milanovic and C. Weir (eds), *Studies in Language Testing* 18.

Messick, S. (1989). Validity. In R. Linn (ed.), *Educational Measurement*, 3rd edn. New York, NY: Macmillan, 13–103.

Saville, N. (2005). Setting and monitoring professional standards: a QMS approach. *Research Notes* 22, 2–5. Cambridge: Cambridge ESOL.

—— (2010). Auditing the quality profile: From code of practice to standards. *Research Notes* 39, 24–28. Cambridge: Cambridge ESOL.

Saville, N. and Hargreaves, P. (1999). Assessing speaking in the revised FCE. *ELT Journal* 53: 42–51.

Shewhart, W. A. (1931). *Economic Control of Quality of Manufactured Product*. New York, NY: D. Van Nostrand Company.

—— (1939). *Statistical Method from the Viewpoint of Quality Control*. Washington, DC: The Graduate School, the Department of Agriculture.

Taylor F. W. (1911). *The Principles of Scientific Management*. New York, NY: Harper and Brothers Publishers.

van Avermaet, P. (2003). *QMS and The Setting of Minimum Standards: issues of contextualisation variation between the testing bodies*. www.alte.org (accessed 8/2/11).

van Avermaet, P., Kuijper, H. and Saville, N. (2004). A code of practice and quality management system for international language examinations. *Language Assessment Quarterly* 1: 137–50.

Weir, C. J. (2005). *Language Testing and Validation: an evidence-based approach*. Basingstoke, UK: Palgrave Macmillan.

Interlocutor and rater training

Annie Brown

Introduction

The focus in language learning on the development of communicative competence, and the centrality of speaking and writing in second language use contexts, means that it is common for language tests to involve the measurement of oral and written language proficiency. Such assessments typically require the involvement of trained personnel to assess the performance and, in the case of speaking assessments, to elicit the performance. The recruitment of sufficient numbers of suitably qualified people can be a challenge in itself; to ensure that they perform their required task to the same standard is another.

To the test takers, it should not matter who scores their performance, or who interviews them. One examiner should be interchangeable with another. Inconsistency or lack of equivalence in scoring or eliciting test performances by its very nature has an impact on validity in terms of the inferences one is able to draw about learners on the basis of their scores. Nevertheless, that unwanted variation in ratings exists due to variability among and within raters and interlocutors is well known. There is a considerable body of research which indicates that raters differ in the way they go about the task of rating, that they follow different procedures to arrive at a score, and that they can – consciously or unconsciously – be influenced by their background when judging test taker proficiency. It has also been shown that the behaviour of interviewers and other speaking test interlocutors can be influenced by their background or orientation to their role. McNamara (1996) argues that the rating may tell as much about the rater or the interlocutor as it does about the test taker.

Given this, the need for the careful selection and training of examiners is well understood. Rater training is an act of socialization into the standards set by the test owner (Lumley, 2002), and its purpose is to ensure that ratings derive from a consideration of the features defined within the construct and to ensure a high degree of comparability, both inter- and intra-rater. As far as the content and methodology of rater training is concerned, there is very little public description of the procedures adopted by specific examination boards or test developers, although a review of the research literature suggests that most seem to follow a similar approach, loosely corresponding to the six steps proposed by Bachman and Palmer (1996: 222):

a. Read and discuss the scales together.
b. Review language samples which have been previously rated by expert raters and discuss the ratings given.
c. Practice rating a different set of language samples. Then compare the ratings with those of experienced raters. Discuss the ratings and how the criteria were applied.
d. Rate additional language samples and discuss.
e. Each trainee rates the same set of samples. Check for the amount of time taken to rate and for consistency.
f. Select raters who are able to provide reliable and efficient ratings.

In training, raters are typically introduced to the purpose and format of the test first. Then the rating scales are explained and clarified so that the raters become aware of the aspects of performance that form part of the construct. A review of and practice with benchmarked exemplar performances brings raters to a common interpretation of the scales and understanding of the standards. It also allows the trainers to deal with atypical or problematic cases such as borderline cases, off-topic or seemingly rehearsed or memorized responses, inadequate length responses, or unclear (illegible or inaudible) responses. The final stage of the training is accreditation, where raters assess a further set of samples independently. These ratings are typically compared with those awarded by expert markers, and raters failing to meet a defined level of agreement with the benchmark ratings or those failing to meet defined level of consistency and severity as identified in a many-facet Rasch measurement (MFRM) analysis may be excluded. Regular retraining and/or standardization before each assessment period is also argued to be necessary to achieve reliable ratings and to ensure that the first stage of the operational rating does not become the practice session (Lumley, 2002).

Although raters and ratings have been the focus of many studies over the years, it is only recently that the potential of the *interlocutor* to affect the quality of the test taker's performance has come to be seen as an important issue affecting the fairness of tests and been empirically examined. It has been found that differences in the way that interlocutors interact with test takers can indeed impact on the quality of the test takers' performance, and that this can affect the ratings awarded for those performances (Brown, 2003, 2005). Ironically, much of the current awareness of the impact of the interlocutor on performance has arisen as a result of increasing focus on paired and group orals where the interlocutor is not a trained (or trainable) examiner, but another test taker.

In formal test contexts at least, there is generally some attempt to ensure the standardization of interviewers' technique through the use of an interview schedule or outline, or a role-play outline. In training, prospective interviewers are introduced to the format of the test and the expected test taker performance. They typically view and discuss sample speaking tests with standard and non-standard interlocutor behaviour, and participate in and observe simulated tests. They may also be trained in strategies for dealing with communication and performance problems.

Historical perspectives

Historically, different language test traditions in the UK and USA led to different perspectives on the role of the examiner, and hence training requirements (Spolsky, 1995). In the UK, large-scale language testing was begun in the early twentieth century by Cambridge University. The principal role of the Cambridge exams was to control the instructional process rather than measure proficiency *per se*, so standardization of test format and assessment criteria was not the main priority. In the oral interview, examiners would lead learners in conversation on one or more of a list of syllabus-related topics. Assessment was largely impressionistic, and both reliability and validity were taken for granted. Weir (2005: 5) comments that the 'the notion of the "connoisseurship" of an elite group of examiners prevailed'.

Despite this prevailing culture, concerns were at times raised and suggestions made about the training of examiners. An internal Cambridge report (Roach, 1945) raised concerns about the equivalence of standards and criteria used by examiners in different testing centres, and argued that reliability could be improved by the use and discussion of marking schemes, review of sample papers, regular meetings of examiners, and supervision by a chief examiner. Roach even experimented in 1944 with the use of speech samples recorded on gramophone records to train examiners, but his recommendations regarding the introduction of standard criteria and examiner training were not taken up (Spolsky, 1995).

In contrast, the US testing movement, which developed largely during the Second World War, was built on psychometrics and privileged reliability. For tests of spoken language, examiner training was provided which included practice with trial ratings of phonographic recordings on the one hand, and training in interviewing behaviour, including demeanour and pitch of questions, on the other (Spolsky, 1995). An influential tradition of oral interviewing began in the early 1950s with the Foreign Service Institute (FSI) oral interview and accompanying scales which described increasing levels of proficiency in terms of typical functional language use requirements and levels of linguistic performance (Clark and Clifford, 1988). Because of the incorporation of the functional and topical dimension into the assessment, and the interaction between the interview structure and the scoring checklist, the interview was necessarily more structured and required more standardization of examiners than had previously been the case. Reliability in the assessment of writing was also first taken up as a major concern in the USA, initially in studies involving first language composition with later research focusing also on second language writing. Lumley (2005) provides a detailed review of the major research studies. Despite these initial differences, this broad contrast between the UK and the US approaches to reliability, validity and training has not been maintained in more recent times (Chalhoub-Deville and Deville, 2005). Certainly now, we see in both contexts a strong focus on researching and ensuring consistency in the administration and rating of speaking and writing tests.

Critical issues and topics

Recent theoretical perspectives have begun to challenge the psychometric orthodoxy of measurement theory, with its attendant privileging of reliability. At the same time, the increasing use of qualitative research methods in test validation has allowed us to examine closely what happens in the interactions between the test performance and the rater on the one hand, and, in oral tests, the test taker and interlocutor on the other. Issues that have emerged from these alternative perspectives as relevant to the training of raters and interlocutors include a concern that training raters to agree may enhance reliability at the expense of validity; a growing understanding of the complexity of the rating process, and a growing understanding of the ways in which the discourse produced in a speaking test is a mutual achievement of all participants, and not just the test taker in isolation.

The general belief that raters must be brought into agreement in their assessments implies that their own perspectives are idiosyncratic or naïve at best, and wrong at worst. Variability in ratings is also interpreted as evidence of disagreement over the trait to be assessed, and thus impacting on the construct validity of the assessment. However, a different perspective sees this view as denying the status of raters as 'readers' and the value of the personal response (Moss, 1994; Lumley, 2002; Erdosy, 2004). Yet while this argument privileges the validity of the rater's perspective, from the traditional measurement standpoint it can be argued to lead to unfairness, as the fact of which rater a test taker encounters can impact on the score he or she is awarded. There is a fundamental difference in the way validity is understood in the two perspectives. On the one hand, validity derives from the expertise of the individual raters; raters might disagree but their perspectives are equally valid, and consensus-building is the approach taken to establish agreement. On the other – the measurement perspective – validity derives from the ability to draw accurate inferences about what test takers can and cannot do on the basis of their scores, which requires transparency of the criteria, and stability in their interpretation across raters. The debate is usually conducted from across the divide of the assessment context: those arguing for the primacy of raters' intuitions are generally working within the context of teacher-led, classroom-based assessment, whereas those arguing the importance of standardization of rater assessments are usually working within the context of high stakes, standardized assessments.

The heightened awareness in recent years of the role of the *interlocutor* in the construction of the test performance derives from an increasing acceptance of the interactionist model which sees test interaction as mutually achieved rather than solely the achievement of the test taker (McNamara, 1997; Chalhoub-Deville, 2003). This co-constructivist view is based on the work of Vygotsky (1978, 1986) and socio-cultural theory on the one hand, and on linguistic communication theories such as conversation analysis (Psathas, 1995) and interactional competence theory (Young, 2000) on the other. Empirical research into test interaction undertaken within these theoretical perspectives has demonstrated how the performances of the participants – examiner and test taker – are inextricably linked and 'how intimately the interviewer is implicated in the construction of candidate proficiency' (Brown, 2003: 1). These findings pose a challenge to language testers because of the implications for validity, reliability and fairness to test takers (Brown, 2005). The view presented by interactional competence theory in particular is challenging for the field of language assessment, as it questions the generalizability of assessment not only from one context to another, but also from one performance to another, and one interlocutor to another. It also challenges the accepted wisdom that a test taker's performance can be attributed to an individual internal, cognitive competence.

A response to research illustrating the integral role of the interlocutor in the test taker's performance has been to attempt to constrain undue interlocutor variability in order to reduce any unfairness associated with individual interlocutors. However, Brown (2005) argues that while this might enhance the reliability of the measure, it can lead to a reduction in validity on the other, as interlocutor frames disallow the relatively natural interaction and broader range of interactional moves which characterize less structured interviews.

Just as discourse analysis has demonstrated the inherent complexity and variability of interlocutor behaviour, so also verbal report analysis has revealed the inherent complexity of rater behaviour. It has been pointed out that 'if we do not know what raters are doing ... then we do not know what their ratings mean' (Connor-Linton, 1995: 763), and that understanding the rating process can inform the development of effective training procedures (Milanovic *et al.*, 1996; Weigle 1994, 1998; Furneaux and Rignall, 2007). To this end, a number of studies have employed techniques such as verbal protocol analysis to investigate how raters go about the task of rating, what aspects of the performance they privilege, and how they decide on a rating. While earlier studies focused on writing assessment (e.g. Vaughan, 1991; Huot, 1993; Cumming, 1990), more recently there has also been a focus on oral assessment (e.g. Lumley and McNamara, 1995; Brown, 2000, 2006; Brown *et al.*, 2005). Differences have been found in the reading styles of raters of L2 writing (Milanovic *et al.*, 1996; Smith, 2000) and in the importance they attach to different aspects of the performance (Brown, 2000; Sakyi, 2000; Cumming *et al.*, 2001; Eckes, 2008).

The aim of these types of study is generally said to be to investigate the validity of what raters do and to improve rater training (see, for example, Cumming, 1990; Weigle, 1998; Eckes, 2008). However, while such research has certainly illuminated the cognitive processes involved in the rating process, perhaps because of the broad range of processes, strategies, and influences that have been identified, and the lack of any clear relationship between these and rating skill, it has been less successful in identifying how the findings can be incorporated into training programs in order to improve them. Nevertheless, while the studies provide little general guidance for the development of training programs it seems that test specific studies may help inform training procedures for that particular test. For example, Taylor (2007) reports that knowing what criteria raters have problems with in a particular testing context means the test developers can clarify them and/or increase the focus in training. Similarly, the finding by Brown *et al.* (2005) that raters struggled to evaluate the content of integrated reading/writing tasks in a study involving prototype Test of English as a Foreign Language (TOEFL) tasks led the test developers to include, as recommended, some text-specific information in the scoring guide.

Current contributions and research

Despite a widespread recognition that training improves the quality of ratings, there is limited research into how, or why, this happens. An analysis of verbal protocols produced by raters before and after training (Weigle, 1994) indicated that the changes could be attributed to three factors arising from the training: clarification of the rating criteria, modification of expectations in terms of the characteristics of student writing and the demands of the task, and provision of a reference group of other raters with whom to align one's ratings. However, it has consistently been found that the effects of training do not persist, and that over time raters tend to become more lenient (Weigle, 1998; Shaw, 2002; Song and Caruso, 1996). There is also evidence that severity can fluctuate across rating sessions (Lumley and McNamara, 1995; Congdon and McQueen, 2000). Lumley and McNamara argue that this not only indicates the need for a moderation session before each operational rating session, but also calls into question the appropriateness of basing judgments of test takers on a single rating.

There has been little research into the relative efficacy of different types of training methodology. A comparison of training methods for the assessment of L1 compositions (Moon and Hughes, 2002) found that training raters on a number of different writing prompts at the same time resulted in higher inter-rater agreement than training them separately on each prompt. They argue that this may be because it grounds the standard to the score scale, whereas the use of single prompt allows more for comparison of student performance. In L2 writing, Rethinasamy (2006) investigated the impact of three different training procedures on the quality of ratings: reviewing a set of exemplar essays with their official scores, assessing a set of exemplar essays and comparing own scores with official scores, and a combination of both. The second method was the most effective, having a significant impact on accuracy both immediately following the training and a month later. The first approach had a significant positive effect on accuracy immediately following training, but this faded with time and became insignificant after a month, which Rethinasamy infers was due to the lack of hands-on rating practice. The third approach did not have a significant immediate effect but had significant follow-up effect, interpreted as the result of the length of the training and consequent fatigue when completing the first set of ratings.

Rater variability can be caused by a number of different rating behaviours, including severity or leniency, the use of restricted range of scores, halo effect, randomness or inconsistency in rating behaviour, and bias with regard to particular facets of the testing situation. Therefore, some researchers are now investigating whether the provision of feedback on these different aspects of rating behaviour can enhance training and lead to improvements (Wigglesworth 1993; Elder *et al.*, 2005). The lack of agreement in the findings of these studies may be attributable to the different methodologies for providing feedback. Moreover, two studies designed to test the hypothesis that feedback delivered systematically over a period of time may result in more consistent and reliable examiner performance than a single instance of feedback (O'Sullivan and Rignall, 2007; Shaw, 2002) both found little to support the value of regular feedback.

Technological advances have led to the development of online rater training programs. Online rater training is argued to have practical advantages over conventional face-to-face training as bringing people together for group training is sometimes impracticable because of time limitations or geographical spread. There are also arguments that online training might be more effective for people who find group training sessions intimidating or who need more time to read and evaluate writing samples than is typically provided in a group session (Charney, 1984; Elder *et al.*, 2007). On the other hand, there are concerns that a lack of ease with computer technology and the lack of opportunity to engage with other markers may mean that online training is less effective for some people. Elder *et al.* (2007) point out that 'it cannot be assumed that individualised feedback will have the same impact as peer pressure, which may be what produces convergence in rater judgments in a group training context.' Comparisons of the two modes of training have produced mixed results. Whereas Knoch *et al.* (2007) found that online training was marginally more successful in improving reliability, this contrasts with Brown and Jaquith's (2007) findings that online raters performed less well. Elder *et al.* (2007) found that while raters who were more positive about an online training program for L2 writing generally showed more improvement than raters who were not, there was little improvement in severity, intra-rater consistency and bias overall.

In addition to training, the careful selection of raters is said to be important in achieving high inter-rater consistency. Erdosy (2004) claims that similarities in background are likely to lead to shared views of the nature of language proficiency, which in turn means that judgments will be based on a shared construct. To some, native speakers who are experienced teachers are the gold standard. Others argue that there may be contexts where non-native speakers or, particularly in ESP testing contexts, non-teaching background raters may be at least equally acceptable, if not more appropriate (Brown, 1995; Hill, 1997, Brown and Lumley, 1994). In a university context, there is concern that ESL faculty will value different aspects of performance than faculty from other subject areas, and that their assessments may not reflect those of mainstream academic staff. Not surprisingly, given these concerns, there is a substantial body of research comparing different types of rater.

While three background factors – mother tongue, professional experience, and gender – have been well-researched, in general both rater and interlocutor background studies have found that group-based effects are minimal, and findings are also at times contradictory (see, for example, Brown, 1995; Lumley, 1995; Santos, 1988; Shi, 2001; Kim, 2009, O'Loughlin, 2002). Brown and McNamara (2004) point out that the conflicting results are perhaps not surprising, especially given that such studies tend to be small scale and exploratory, looking at a single factor at a time. They also argue that analysing the impact of specific variables such as gender in isolation, without considering the possible impact of other potential social identity variables, is a weakness of such studies. While research does not suggest the greater suitability of one particular group over another, what it does perhaps suggest is that raters need careful training in order to bring them into line initially, and regular re-standardization in order to ensure that they do not drift away from the original standard to which they were trained.

Despite the fact that there has long been disquiet about the effect of the choice of interviewer on ratings awarded to test takers in oral tests, particularly in tests where test takers are assessed whilst engaging in relatively natural or unscripted interaction with an examiner (Clark, 1978; McNamara,

1996, *inter alia*), until very recently interlocutor training has not been given the same attention as rater training. Re-standardization in particular tended to focus only on rating behaviour. The assumption was that once trained, interviewers remained faithful to their training. There is, however, considerable evidence that individual interviewers do differ, sometimes quite markedly, in the way they conduct interviews. Ross (1996) argues that employing a consistent approach to the organization of the interview and presentation of prompts, what he terms a *procedural script*, allows interviewers to release their attention from managing the interaction to monitoring the test taker. Differences in these scripts have been claimed to derive from raters' cultural background (Ross, 1996), their level of experience or expertise (Morton *et al.*, 1997), or their attitude to their role (Brown and Lumley, 1997). Brown (2005) provides a comprehensive survey of the literature, and reports that interviewers have been found to vary with respect to several key aspects of speech and interactional behaviour, including: the level of rapport that they establish with test takers; their functional and topical choices; the ways in which they ask questions and construct prompts; the extent to which or the ways in which they accommodate their speech to that of the test taker; and the ways in which they develop and extend topics.

A number of studies have tackled the question of whether different interviewers can lead to different ratings outcomes for test takers, and have done so from a variety of perspectives. Some have examined score variability in relation to interviewer *type*, focusing on background variables such as gender or ethnicity. However, as Brown and McNamara (2004) point out, the fact that the findings are inconclusive indicates that these sorts of categorical variables may not have stable or predictable effects. Other studies have established that scores can vary for individual interviewers (Shohamy, 1983; Reed and Halleck, 1997; Brown 2003, 2005). Yet others (Morton *et al.*, 1997; McNamara and Lumley, 1997; Brown, 2005) have related score differences to raters' perceptions of interviewer competence or helpfulness.

As is the case for studies of rater behaviour, studies of interviewer behaviour have been claimed to provide input for the development of examiner training and standardization procedures. For example, findings from Brown's (2003, 2005) study directly informed changes to the IELTS interview (Taylor, 2007). The interview, which until then had been conducted on relatively informal, conversational lines, was replaced with a more structured format in which interviewers were required to follow a script. This was argued to allow for 'greater standardization of examiner behaviour... and hence comparability of the challenge presented to IELTS candidates' (Taylor, 2007: 186). However, as Brown (2005) points out:

> While such a shift in approach does appear to limit the extent of variability, a move to constrain what the interviewer does necessarily limits unpredictability of interaction and removes some of the opportunities for candidates to display the types of interactional skills assessed in the earlier interview. Increasing reliability, therefore, may lead to a decrease in validity, if these skills are considered a necessary part of the construct.
>
> *(Brown, 2005: 261–62)*

Brown suggests that in tests where variability is desirable, more explicit articulation of the construct will go some way to removing unwanted variation while still allowing some flexibility because it will allow the trainers to clearly define which interactional behaviours will lead to the elicitation of construct relevant behaviours and which will interfere with this. Fulcher (2000: 491) also makes this point:

> Not only can careful specification of the construct lead to less variable interviewer behaviour, it can also lead to more precise targeting of construct-relevant skills. This is particularly the

case for the less narrowly linguistic aspects of performance – communicative or interactional ability – which are typically described and understood in vague and imprecise terms.

Main research methods

As we have seen in the review of the literature in this chapter, many-facet Rasch measurement in particular has facilitated the analysis of rater and interlocutor variables in performance tests and allows for the sophisticated modelling of a range of rater behaviours, including leniency and severity, central tendency, randomness, and halo effect (Myford and Wolfe, 2003). Using MFRM, rater or interviewer behaviour can be examined in relation to personal variables, such as professional background or gender, or bias in raters' judgments can be examined with regard to particular contextual features, such as test taker variables, task, or assessment criteria (see, for example, Lynch and McNamara, 1998; Wigglesworth, 1993; Schaefer 2008). Such analyses can inform examiner selection or can form the basis of feedback to raters about the quality of their performance.

While language testing research typically involves the analysis of score data, recent years have seen an increase in the use of qualitative research methodologies to examine issues of interest in test validation and language testing research in general. Two qualitative research methods which have proven value for understanding the meaning of scores, and are of relevance to the training of interlocutors and raters, are protocol analysis and discourse analysis. Protocol analysis, or verbal report analysis, is of particular use in exploring the cognitive processes of raters, and has been used to investigate such questions as how raters go about assigning a rating to a performance, what aspects of the performance they privilege, whether experienced or novice raters rate differently, whether raters of different backgrounds rate differently, how training changes the rating process, and how raters deal with problematic performances. Discourse analysis, on the other hand, has been of particular use for examining test taker and interviewer speech. Discourse analysis is not, of course, a single method reflecting a single approach to the data; how the analysis will be carried out is dependent on the research question and the theories underpinning it. For example, Ross (1992) used Speech Accommodation Theory, a social psychological approach to language, to examine the ways in which interviewers accommodated their speech to the test taker, and Brown (2003, 2005) demonstrated the value of Conversation Analysis in examining the interplay of communication between interviewer and candidate. By identifying interactional strategies which seem to lead to differential performance by candidates, such studies can feed into interlocutor training and help to minimize unwanted interlocutor variability.

Recommendations for practice

In the early 1990s, a survey was undertaken of the practices of examination boards responsible for language tests in the UK (Alderson and Buck, 1993). The authors painted a somewhat concerning picture of the state of examiner training. While most boards provided some sort of standardization for markers, its intensity varied. Only half the boards included the marking of sample scripts or interviews and discussion of criteria with other examiners, and it was not reported how often standardization meetings were held. Moreover, it transpired that there was little attempt to monitor reliability on a regular basis. Alderson and Buck concluded that 'little systematic attention seems to be paid to establishing whether the training and monitoring procedures have indeed been effective. Reliability should be measured, not asserted' (p. 20). The extent of interviewer training also seemed to be limited: only three boards who examined oral English provided 'guinea-pig candidates' to be interviewed by examiners during the standardization meeting.

While it is not known to what extent examiner training procedures have changed in the intervening years, what has happened since Alderson and Buck's article was published is the development of codes of practice such as those of the International Language Testing Association and the Association of Language Testers in Europe. The need for such codes was foreshadowed by Alderson and Buck as a means of ensuring that all examination boards administering language tests, and all language testers adhered to the same set of standards. However, while these do describe recommendations for practice, they are just that – recommendations – and there is, as yet, no system or process for enforcing good practice.

So what is good practice in interlocutor and rater selection and training? First, it is evident from the research that anyone, regardless of background, has the potential to become a good examiner. Selection does not seem to be justified on the basis of examiner background. Second, research has shown that while basic training which includes discussion of the criteria and the opportunity to review samples and practice rating in a group does lead to a shared understanding of the standards, it also needs to be followed up at regular intervals to ensure that standards are maintained. It is less clear, however, whether detailed feedback on rating performance can enhance rating quality. Having said this, we must recognize that training cannot be expected to remove all variability. Raters will continue to disagree about the meanings of the scale and the relationship of students performances to that scale. Ultimately, the important thing is to ensure that interpretations are as equivalent as possible and inconsistencies are minimized. Further than that, in high stakes contexts at least, basing the final score on two ratings, with adjudication in the case of large discrepancies can deal with these inevitable disagreements.

As far as interviewing or role-playing is concerned, examiners will inevitably display their own characteristic interactional styles. Yet research on interviewer variability has shown that differences in technique can impact on candidate performance. What is needed, therefore, is for test developers to incorporate the findings of this research into their training programs, and also to be more explicit about the speaking construct so that examiners can learn which differences in interviewing technique are likely to impact on the construct-relevant quality of candidate performance, and which are less likely to. It also seems important to provide regular restandardization of interviewers in order to avoid the subsequent adoption of non-standard, idiosyncratic techniques.

Future directions

In terms of research into interlocutor and rater training, there are some as yet under-researched questions. First, while there has been considerable research into the impact of the mode of delivery of training and the value of individualized feedback, there has as yet been little research into the relative efficacy of different training formats. While recognizing that trainings are naturally test specific and what works in one context may not necessarily work in another, exploring different training methods may provide some input into improving the effectiveness of training. Furthermore, while studies of rater behaviour have revealed different approaches to the rating task and different decision-making strategies, we have as yet little evidence of whether certain of these are associated with better raters. Such research may indicate whether certain rating behaviours are more or less desirable, thus allowing them to be built into training models.

Another area where additional research is required is in the format of rater feedback. The feedback described in research studies is typically based on IRT analyses, but how can this be made meaningful to raters? Relative overall severity, even if couched in terms of bands rather than logits, being general may be of little help. What does it mean to be quarter of a band too lenient? How is a rater to deal with that knowledge? A more promising approach, suggested by Wilson and Case (1997), might be to compare the distribution of scores assigned by individual raters with that of the average rater which, as they point out, allows for a more nuanced view of scoring patterns across all the levels. It may also help to review aberrant ratings to help raters understand what their inconsistencies derive from.

In terms of practice, one could ask what the future is of live interviewing and human rating, given the realistic options these days of tape-based or computer-mediated speaking tests, and automated rating of written or spoken performances. In short, can the need for the recruitment, training and monitoring of examiners be circumvented by technology. Certainly semi-direct oral testing, which has been found to result in statistically equivalent scores when compared with face-to-face testing, is now acceptable in many contexts, at least in those where the speaking construct does not involve interactive skills. In contrast, while the automated rating of test performances has been well researched, and typically found to correlate highly with human ratings (e.g. Bernstein *et al.*, 2004; Chodorow and Burstein, 2004; Balogh *et al.*, 2008), it does not seem to have reached the same level of public acceptance, and this seems to be more the case for assessment of spoken language than written. Also, where tasks are less constrained or convergent, automated assessment appears not to be as reliable as human judgements (McCurry, 2010). Given these validity and reliability concerns, in addition to the practical constraint of the time and cost involved in developing automated rating systems, it seems that human ratings will continue to be the norm for some time to come. It remains, therefore, to ensure that this is done as effectively and as efficiently as possible.

Further reading

Brown, A. (2003). Interviewer variation and the co-construction of speaking proficiency. *Language Testing* 20: 1–25. Brown's article explores the inter-relatedness of interviewer, candidate and rater behaviour in a test of oral proficiency. It provides an in-depth picture of the impact of interviewer variation on candidate performance, and the further impact on raters' perceptions of the performance and on the scores they award.

Fulcher, G. (2003). *Testing Second Language Speaking*. London, UK: Pearson Education. Chapter 6 'Raters, training and administration' provides an extended discussion of issues pertaining to rater and interlocutor reliability and training.

Lumley, T. (2002). Assessment criteria in a large-scale writing test: what do they really mean to the raters? *Language Testing* 19: 246–76. Lumley's research draws on think-aloud protocols to illustrate the complexity of the rating process, in particular the tension that raters face in trying to reconcile their impressions of the text, the specific features of the text, and the wordings of the rating scale, in order to produce a set of scores. He shows that in spite of this tension and indeterminacy, raters can succeed in yielding consistent scores as long as they are supported by adequate training.

McNamara, T. (1996). *Measuring Second Language Performance*. London, UK: Longman. This book provides an accessible introduction to the use of many-facet Rasch analysis in the development and validation of performance tests, focusing in some detail on its use in research into rater and interviewer behaviour, and its role in monitoring and enhancing the quality of operational ratings.

References

Alderson, J. C. and Buck, G. (1993). Standards in testing: a study of the practice of UK examination boards in EFL/ESL testing. *Language Testing* 10: 1–26.

Bachman, L. F. and Palmer, A. (1996). *Language Testing in Practice*. Oxford, UK: Oxford University Press.

Balogh, J., Bernstein, J., Suzuki, M. and Lennig, M. (2008). *Automatically Scored Spoken Language Tests for Air Traffic Controllers and Pilots*. www.ordinate.com/technology/featured/Developmental_Paper_AET_I ATS2006-reformatted.pdf (accessed 8/2/11).

Bernstein, J., Rosenfeld, E., Townshend, B. and Barbier, I. (2004) An automatically scored spoken Spanish test and its relation to OPIs. Paper presented at IAEA 2004, Pennsylvania, PA. www.ordinate.com/technology/featured/IAEA.Full-Paper.Ordinate-reformatted.pdf (accessed 8/2/11).

Brown, A. (1995). The effect of rater variables in the development of an occupation-specific language performance test. *Language Testing* 12: 1–15.

—— (2000) An investigation of the rating process in the IELTS Speaking Module. In R. Tulloh (ed.), *IELTS Research Reports,* Vol. 3. Sydney: ELICOS, 49–85.

—— (2003). Interviewer variation and the co-construction of speaking proficiency. *Language Testing* 20: 1–25.

—— (2005). *Interviewer Variability in Oral Proficiency Interviews.* Frankfurt, Germany: Peter Lang.

—— (2006). An examination of the rating process in the revised IELTS speaking test. In P. McGovern and S. Walsh (eds), *IELTS Research Reports,* Vol. 6, Canberra, Australia: IELTS Australia.

Brown, A. and Jaquith, P. (2007). *On-line rater training: perceptions and performance.* Paper presented at Language Testing Research Colloquium, Barcelona, April, 2007.

Brown, A. and Lumley, T. (1994). How can an English proficiency test be made more culturally appropriate? A case study. In S. K. Gill (ed.), *National and International Challenges and Responses. Proceedings of the International English Language Education Conference.* Kuala Lumpur, Malaysia: Language Centre University Kebangsaan.

—— (1997). Interviewer variability in specific-purpose language performance tests. In A. Huhta, V. Kohonen, L. Kurki-Suonio and S. Luoma (eds), *Current Developments and Alternatives in Language Assessment.* Tampere, Finland: Universities of Tampere and Jyväskylä.

Brown, A. and McNamara, T. (2004). 'The devil is in the details': researching gender issues in language assessment. *TESOL Quarterly* 38: 524–38.

Brown, A., Iwashita, N. and McNamara, T. (2005). *An Examination of Rater Orientations and Test-taker Performance on English for Academic Purposes Speaking Tasks* (TOEFL Monograph series, MS-29). Princeton, NJ: Educational Testing Service.

Chalhoub-Deville, M. (2003). Second language interaction: current perspectives and future trends. *Language Testing* 20: 369–83.

Chalhoub-Deville, M. and Deville, C. (2005). A look back at and forward to what language testers measure. In E. Hinkel (ed.), *Handbook of Research in Second Language Teaching and Learning.* Mahwah, NJ: Lawrence Erlbaum Associates.

Charney, D. (1984). The validity of using holistic scoring to evaluate writing: a critical overview. *Research in the Teaching of English* 18: 65–81.

Chodorow, M. and Burstein, J. (2004). *Beyond Essay Length: evaluating e-rater's performance on TOEFL® essays* (TOEFL Research Rep. No. TOEFL-RR-73). Princeton, NJ: Educational Testing Service.

Clark, J. L. D. (1978). *Direct Testing of Speaking Proficiency: theory and application.* Princeton, NJ: Educational Testing Service.

Clark, J. L. D. and Clifford, R. T. (1988). The FSI/ILR/ACTFL proficiency scales and testing techniques: development, current status, and needed research. *Studies in Second Language Acquisition* 10: 129–47.

Congdon, P. J. and McQueen, J. (2000). The stability of rater severity in large-scale assessment programs. *Journal of Educational Measurement* 37: 163–78.

Connor-Linton, J. (1995). Looking behind the curtain: what do L2 composition ratings really mean? *TESOL Quarterly* 29: 762–65.

Cumming, A. (1990). Expertise in evaluating second language compositions. *Language Testing* 7: 131–51.

Cumming, A., Kantor, R. and Powers, D. E (2001). *Scoring TOEFL® Essays and TOEFL 2000 Prototype Writing Tasks: An Investigation into Raters' Decision Making and Development of a Preliminary Analytic Framework* (TOEFL Monograph No. TOEFL-MS-22). Princeton, NJ: Educational Testing Service.

Eckes, T. (2008). Rater types in writing performance assessments: a classification approach to rater variability. *Language Testing* 25: 155–85.

Elder, C., Barkhuizen, G., Knoch, U. and Von Randow, J. (2007). Evaluating the Utility of online training for L2 writing assessment: how responsive are ESL raters? *Language Testing* 24: 37–64.

Elder, C., Knoch, U., Barkhuizen, G. and Von Randow, J. (2005). Individualized feedback to enhance rater training: does it work? *Language Assessment Quarterly* 2: 175–96.

Erdosy, M. U. (2004). *Exploring Variability in Judging Writing Ability in a Second Language: a study of four experienced raters of ESL compositions* (TOEFL Research Rep. No. TOEFL-RR-70). Princeton, NJ: Educational Testing Service.

Fulcher, G. (2000). The 'communicative' legacy in language testing. *System* 28: 483–97.

Furneaux, C. and Rignall, M. (2007). The effect of standardisation-training on rater judgments for the IELTS writing module. In L. Taylor and P. Falvey (eds), *IELTS Collected Papers: Research in Speaking and Writing*

Assessment, Studies in Language Testing, Vol. 19. Cambridge, UK: Cambridge University Press/Cambridge ESOL.

Hill, K. (1997). Who should be the judge? the use of non-native speakers as raters on a test of English as an international language. In A. Huhta, V. Kohonen, L. Kurki-Suonio and S. Luoma (eds), *Current Developments and Alternatives in Language Assessment.* Tampere, Finland: Universities of Tampere and Jyväskylä.

Huot, B. A. (1993). The influence of holistic scoring procedures on reading and rating student essays. In M. M. Williamson and B. A. Huot (eds), *Validating Holistic Scoring for Writing Assessment: theoretical and empirical foundations.* Cresskill, NJ: Hampton Press.

Kim, Y.-H. (2009). An investigation into native and non-native teachers' judgments of oral English performance: a mixed methods approach. *Language Testing* 26: 187–217.

Knoch, U., Read, J. and von Randow, J. (2007). Re-training writing raters online: how does it compare with face-to-face training? *Assessing Writing* 121: 26–43.

Lumley, T. (1995). The judgements of language-trained raters and doctors in a test of English for health professionals. *Melbourne Papers in Language Testing* 4: 74–98. www.ltrc.unimelb.edu.au/mplt/index.html (accessed 8/18/10).

—— (2002). Assessment criteria in a large-scale writing test: what do they really mean to the raters? *Language Testing* 19: 246–76.

—— (2005). *Assessing Second Language Writing: The Rater's Perspective.* Frankfurt, Germany: Peter Lang.

Lumley, T. and McNamara, T. (1995). Rater characteristics and rater bias: implications for training. *Language Testing* 12: 54–71.

Luoma, S. (2004). *Assessing Speaking.* Cambridge, UK: Cambridge University Press.

Lynch, B. K. and McNamara, T. F. (1998). Using G-theory and many-facet Rasch measurement in the development of performance assessments of the ESL speaking skills of immigrants. *Language Testing* 15: 158–80.

McCurry, D. (2010). Can machine scoring deal with broad and open writing tests as well as human readers? *Assessing Writing* 15: 118–29.

McNamara, T. (1996). *Measuring Second Language Performance.* London, UK: Longman.

—— (1997). 'Interaction' in second language performance assessment: whose performance? *Applied Linguistics* 18: 444–66.

McNamara, T. F. and Lumley, T. (1997). The effect of interlocutor and assessment mode variables in overseas assessments of speaking skills in occupational settings. *Language Testing* 14: 140–56.

Milanovic, M., Saville, N. and Shen, S. (1996). A study of the decision-making behaviour of composition markers. In M. Milanovic and N. Saville (eds), *Performance Testing, Cognition and Assessment.* Cambridge, UK: Cambridge University Press.

Moon, T. R. and Hughes, K. R. (2002). Training and scoring issues involved in large-scale writing assessments. *Educational Measurement: Issues and Practice* 21: 15–19.

Morton, J., Wigglesworth, G. and Williams, D. (1997). Approaches to the evaluation of interviewer performance in oral interaction tests. In G. Brindley and G. Wigglesworth (eds), *Access: Issues in English Language Test Design and Delivery.* Sydney, Australia: National Centre for English Language Teaching and Research.

Moss, P. A. (1994). Can there be validity without reliability? *Educational Researcher* 23: 5–12.

Myford, C. M. and Wolfe, E. W. (2003). Detecting and measuring rater effects using many-facet Rasch measurement. *Journal of Applied Measurement* 4: 386–422.

O'Loughlin, K. (2002). The impact of gender in oral proficiency testing. *Language Testing* 19: 169–92.

O'Sullivan, B. and Rignall, M. (2007). Assessing the value of bias analysis feedback to raters for the IELTS writing module. In C. Weir (ed.), *IELTS Collected Papers: Research in Writing and Speaking, Studies in Language Testing,* Vol. 19. Cambridge, UK: Cambridge University Press/Cambridge ESOL.

Psathas, G. (1995). *Conversation Analysis: the study of talk-in-interaction.* Thousand Oaks, CA: Sage.

Reed, D. J. and Halleck, G. B. (1997). Probing above the ceiling in oral interviews: what's up there? In A. Huhta, V. Kohonen, L. Kurki-Suonio and S. Luoma (eds), *Current Developments and Alternatives in Language Assessment.* Jyväskylä, Finland: University of Jyväskylä and University of Tampere.

Rethinasamy, S. (2006). *The effects on rating performance of different training interventions.* Unpublished PhD thesis, Roehampton University.

Roach, J. O. (1945). *Some Problems of Oral Examinations in Modern Languages: An Experimental Approach Based on the Cambridge Examinations in English for Foreign Students, Being a Report Circulated to Oral Examiners and Local Examiners for Those Examinations.* Cambridge, UK: Cambridge University Press.

Ross, S. (1992). Accommodative questions in oral proficiency interviews. *Language Testing* 9: 173–86.

—— (1996). Formulae and inter-interviewer variation in oral proficiency interview discourse. *Prospect* 11: 3–16.

Sakyi, A. A. (2000). Validation of holistic scoring for ESL writing assessment: how raters evaluate compositions. In A. J. Kunnan (ed.), *Fairness and Validation in Language Assessment*. Cambridge, UK: Cambridge University Press.

Santos, T. (1988). Professors' reactions to the writing of nonnative-speaking students. *TESOL Quarterly* 22: 69–90.

Schaefer, E. (2008). Rater Bias patterns in an EFL writing assessment. *Language Testing* 25: 465–93.

Shaw, S. (2002). The effect of training and standardization on rater judgement and inter-rater reliability *Research Notes* 8: 13–17. www.cambridgeesol.org/rs_notes (accessed 8/18/10).

Shi, L. (2001). Native- and nonnative-speaking EFL teachers' evaluation of Chinese students' English writing. *Language Testing* 18: 303–25.

Shohamy, E. (1983). The stability of oral proficiency assessment on the oral interview testing procedures *Language Learning* 33: 527–40.

Smith, D. (2000). Rater judgments in the direct assessment of competency based second language writing ability. In G. Brindley (ed.), *Studies in Immigrant English Language Assessment,* Vol. 1. Sydney, Australia: National Centre for English Language Teaching and Research, Macquarie University.

Song, B. and Caruso, I. (1996). Do English and ESL faculty differ in evaluating the essays of native English-speaking and ESL students? *Journal of Second Language Writing* 5: 163–82.

Spolsky, B. (1995). *Measured Words: the development of objective language testing*. Oxford, UK: Oxford University Press.

Taylor, L. (2007). The impact of the joint-funded research studies on the IELTS writing module. In L. Taylor and P. Falvey (eds), *IELTS Collected Papers: Research in Speaking and Writing Assessment, Studies in Language Testing,* Vol. 19. Cambridge, UK: Cambridge University Press/Cambridge ESOL.

Vaughan, C. (1991). Holistic assessment: what goes on in the rater's mind? In L. Hamp-Lyons (ed.), *Assessing Second Language Writing in Academic Contexts*. Norwood, NJ: Ablex.

Vygotsky, L. S. (1978). *Mind in Society*. Cambridge, MA: Harvard University Press.

—— (1986). *Thought and Language*. Cambridge, MA: MIT Press.

Weigle, S. C. (1994). Effects of training on raters of ESL compositions. *Language Testing* 11: 197–223.

—— (1998). Using FACETS to model rater training effects. *Language Testing* 15: 263–87.

Weir, C. J. (2005). *Language Testing and Validation: An Evidence Based Approach*. Oxford, UK: Palgrave Macmillan.

Wigglesworth, G. (1993). Exploring bias analysis as a tool for improving rater consistency in assessing oral interaction. *Language Testing* 10: 305–36.

Wilson, M. and Case. H. (1997). *An Examination of Variation in Rater Severity Over Time: A Study in Rater Drift*. BEAR Report Series, CD-97-1, Berkeley, CA: University of California, Berkeley.

Young, R. (2000). *Interactional Competence: challenges for validity*. Paper presented at The Language Testing Research Colloquium, March 11, 2000, Vancouver. citeseerx.ist.psu.edu/viewdoc/download?doi=10.1.1.37.9903&rep=rep1&type=pdf (accessed 8/2/11).

29

Technology in language testing

Yasuyo Sawaki

Introduction

With the ever-increasing advancement of computer technology the number of language assessments that utilize computer technology in designing, developing, and delivering test content as well as scoring and reporting examinee test performance is growing steadily and rapidly. Many test authoring systems are currently available to language teachers in various forms, while taking a language test on a computer is becoming a familiar activity for language learners as well. Traditionally, various types of technologies other than computer technology have been utilized in language assessment. For example, audio, video, and telephone have been used for delivering speaking tests, recording examinee responses in oral interviews, and delivering stimuli in listening assessments. However, because many of these existing technologies are being replaced with computer technology, this chapter focuses primarily on the use of computer technology in language assessment. Following Chapelle and Douglas (2006), the term computer-assisted language testing (CALT) will be employed throughout to refer to language assessments that utilize computer technology in various ways. During the last few decades, language testers have been exploring the possible usage of CALT in order to make language assessment efficient and to design language tests that can provide us with more useful information about the L2 ability of learners than in traditional assessments. This chapter provides a brief overview of the historical development of CALT and current issues of concern, along with directions for future CALT research in the field of language assessment.

Historical perspectives

The introduction of CALT to language assessment dates back to the early 1980s. Chapelle and Douglas (2006) refer to a 1981 publication that describes a CALT developed as part of a French-as-a-foreign-language curriculum at the University of Illinois. The theme of the Language Testing Research Colloquium (LTRC) in 1985 was technology and language testing, and selected papers from the conference were published as a volume edited by Stansfield (1986). Since then, applications of and research into CALT have been increasing steadily in the field. In this section the historical development of CALT will be described in terms of two phases, roughly following Jamieson's (2005) review of CALT advancements and Bennett's (2000) scenario for the advancement of computer-based testing (CBT) in large-scale educational assessment.

In the initial phase of the CALT development, existing test items are "mounted" on computers, while the test content remains mostly unchanged. One of the main goals of this type of computerization of a test would be to "automate an existing process" (Bennett, 2000: 3), so that language tests could be administered more efficiently than before. Previous CALT works belonging to this phase can be seen in test development efforts in which existing paper-based tests (PBTs) were converted to CBT formats. These projects typically involved tests based on selected-response items for discrete-point testing. This is partly because selected-response items can more readily be converted to a CBT format than complex constructed-response tasks. For example, Fulcher (1999) reported on a project in which an existing ESL placement test at a university in the UK was computerized. A primary goal of the project was to minimize the time required to score examinee responses to the multiple-choice section of the test. Accordingly, the grammar part, comprising 80 multiple-choice items, was converted to a CBT format, while the essay questions were administered on paper.

As can be seen in the number of computer adaptive tests (CAT) development projects in language assessment conducted in the 1980s and 1990s reviewed by Chalhoub-Deville and Deville (1999), quite a few early forms of CALT were CATs, a special type of CBT in which the test content is tailored to the ability level of each examinee. In a conventional test, all examinees receive the same, fixed set of items presented all together in a test booklet, regardless of ability levels. In contrast, in a typical CAT, test items are presented on the computer screen one by one. First, the examinee's rough ability estimate is obtained based on his/her performance on an initial set of items. Then, an item with the difficulty level suited to the examinee's ability estimate is chosen from an item bank and presented as the next item. The examinee's ability estimate is updated as he/she responds to the item, followed by presentation of the next item matched to the examinee's latest ability estimate. This process continues until an accurate enough estimate of the examinee's ability level is obtained. An algorithm behind a full-fledged CAT is typically based on item response theory (IRT), a measurement model that allows estimation of examinee ability level and item difficulty on the same scale (see Ockey, this volume).

While both advantages and disadvantages of CAT were discussed in the field from early on (e.g., Stansfield, 1986), the efficiency of CAT in particular was thought to bring distinct advantages to language assessment. For instance, CAT sessions are relatively short compared to those in existing assessments. Test administration schedules would be flexible because examinees can take the test individually. The availability of a precise examinee ability estimate immediately after a test session is another often-cited CAT advantage. Moreover, administering test items matched to individual examinees' ability levels might make the test session less stressful for examinees because they are not exposed to too easy or too difficult items. Taking advantage of various strengths of CAT, TOEFL CBT, which included listening and structure sections implemented in CAT forms, was launched worldwide in 1998. Currently, various other commercial tests with CAT capabilities are available as well (e.g., Business Language Testing Service (BULATS) from Cambridge ESOL; COMPASS/ESL from American College Testing; and Computerized Assessment System for English Communication (CASEC) originally developed by the Society for Testing English Proficiency and currently managed by the Japan Institute of Educational Measurement).

While the advantages that a CAT can bring to an assessment context seem to recommend its use whenever possible, CAT is not without its limitations. One thing that the field has learned is that developing and maintaining a CAT is extremely expensive. CAT requires continuous item development and large scale pretesting efforts so that an item bank can constantly be refreshed by adding new items with item parameter estimates (see Nogami and Hayashi, 2010, for a discussion of this issue). Furthermore, a CAT format is not necessarily compatible with other design features of an assessment required to test important aspects of examinee ability in a specific assessment context. For example, TOEFL Internet-based Test (iBT), which does not employ a CAT format, replaced TOEFL CBT in 2005. Jamieson *et al.* (2008) discuss several reasons for the return to the non-adaptive format. One was that new task types that integrate modalities for assessing academic speaking and writing skills in authentic academic language use contexts were not compatible with a psychometric assumption of IRT. Another was the need for human scoring of speaking and writing responses, which did not allow on-the-fly estimation of examinee ability levels during test sessions.

Meanwhile, CALT with new types of adapting capabilities that alleviate the resource-intensiveness of IRT-based adaptive algorithms emerged in the field as well. The Computer-based OPI (COPI) developed by the Center for Applied Linguistics is a simulated version of the ACTFL Oral Proficiency Interview (Kenyon and Malabonga, 2001). A speaking test requiring human scoring after a test session is not compatible with on-the-fly estimation of examinee ability level based on IRT. Thus, COPI has the examinee choose the difficulty level of the task based on results of a self-assessment administered at the beginning of a test session. Concerns were raised as to whether learner self-assessment can serve as a valid adaptive algorithm (e.g., Norris, 2001). However, Malabonga *et al.*'s (2005) validation study showed high correlations of examinee self-assessment with final examinee ability estimate and faculty rating of examinee speaking ability, supporting the validity of the adaptive algorithm. DIALANG, a web-based self-assessment of 14 European languages designed for diagnosis, takes a similar approach in that it combines a screening test of vocabulary and a self-assessment of overall language ability based on the Common European Framework of Reference (Council of Europe, 2001) to deliver a set of test items suited to each examinee's ability level (Alderson and Huhta, 2005; see Read, this volume).

The second phase of CALT is characterized by taking advantage of functionalities available only on computers, resulting in substantive changes to various aspects of testing including task design, test delivery, and response scoring. This is consistent with Bennett's (2000) second phase of the development of computerized testing and Jamieson's (2005) next and future steps entailing advancements in various aspects of testing. Although there are a significant number of publications that explore new-style tests, empirical evidence on their qualities is still rather limited. First, various new task types taking advantage of computer capabilities have been proposed to enhance the authenticity of a test, i.e., the degree to which the design of a test task reflects characteristics of real-life language use tasks. For example, a telephone message listening task proposed as part of the Japanese version of WebLAS, a web-based placement test developed at the University of California, Los Angeles (www.weblas.ucla.edu), allowed a full control over replay of the listening stimuli on the part of the examinee similar to when he/she listens to a voice message left on an answering machine. Functionalities available on computers make innovative response formats possible as well. In one task type in the TOEFL iBT Reading section the examinee drags and drops appropriate options to complete a prose summary of the stimulus text. Moreover, the use of a computer enhances control over the timing for presentation of different parts of a complex task. An example can be found in the TOEFL iBT speaking and writing tasks that integrate different modalities. In the integrated task in the Writing section, for instance, the examinee reads a written academic text first. After the text disappears, a lecture on the same topic is presented. After the lecture is complete the written text reappears. At this point the examinee starts writing a summary to synthesize information from both texts.

Bennett (2000) stated that this phase may witness changes in CBT delivery modes, which has indeed happened to CALT over the years. In early CBT applications, test content was distributed to individual computer platforms via CD-ROMs or closed local networks, as can be seen in examples such as TOEFL CBT and CD-ROM versions of the Cambridge ESOL Suite of language tests. Meanwhile, there were concerns about the compromised security of web-based test delivery for high-stakes purposes. Roever (2001) suggested that, although high-stakes assessments might eventually be delivered on the web, the then-available web-based systems were not yet suitable for delivering high-stakes assessments. Likewise, Alderson (2000b) specifically mentioned the advantage of the low-stakes environment of DIALANG, which allowed the developers of the test to experiment with innovative task types on the web. However, improvements in computer security have led to the introduction of high-stakes large-scale language assessments (e.g., TOEFL iBT and the TOEIC Speaking and Writing Tests, and tests from Pearson Assessment). This greatly improves test access for examinees taking tests in locations with internet access.

Another area of ongoing work is automated scoring of constructed responses (see Xi, this volume). As predicted by Jamieson (2005), there have been notable advancements in the development and evaluation of automated systems for scoring L2 learners' writing as well as speech samples.

Two other areas discussed by both Bennett (2000) and Jamieson (2005) are the application of multimedia and virtual reality to CALT. Although the use of multimedia would lead to the development of innovative test tasks, language testers have been proceeding rather cautiously (see Wagner, 2010). Using virtual reality would contribute greatly to designing performance-based test tasks with enhanced authenticity. According to Oskoz and Chalhoub-Deville (2009) some work utilizing virtual reality such as Second Life for teaching and testing L2 speaking is emerging. Before one can contemplate the use of these technologies in anything other than low-stakes classroom assessment, however, a great deal of research will be required.

Although the field is well into the second phase of the CALT development with ongoing experimentation in the use of functionalities only available on the computer, some possibilities, such as the use of multimedia and virtual reality, are progressing relatively slowly. Changes in the use of CALT have been, and may continue to be, "incremental evolutions" (Chapelle and Douglas, 2006). That is, the advancements are still short of what one might call a true innovation that would fundamentally change the ways in which we do testing. Many available tests in CALT formats still rely largely on traditional assessment techniques, despite the emergence of some research that may lead to genuine innovation.

Critical issues and topics

Critical issues of consideration are those that would take us beyond the "incremental evolutions" to make CALT innovative. The third phase in Bennett's (2000) scenario for the development of CBT is a generation of tests that are radically different from traditional assessments. Here, we are concerned with what truly innovative CALT may look like. A "curriculum-embedded, distance assessment" proposed by Bennett is administered frequently as an integral part of a curriculum, accommodating the diverse needs of individual learners. Such testing may be available in the form of learning tools with virtual reality simulations for both individual and collaborative work accessed through the internet by learners from various locations. Such innovations require a considerable amount of substantive work on the part of applied linguists. First, the success of a curriculum-based testing or an integration of instruction and assessment like the one proposed by Bennett hinges on how well we understand the nature of the constructs we teach and assess. On the one hand, this would require a careful analysis of characteristics of language use tasks that learners are exposed to in real life. In today's highly computerized society, many language use activities take place in computer-mediated environments, while others continue to take place in non-technology-mediated conditions. On the other hand, we need to use results of such a domain analysis to identify various abilities required to be successful in language use tasks in today's digitized society. Chapelle and Douglas (2006) suggest a direction by proposing a context-sensitive definition of language ability for communication through technology. Their definition of the construct comprises three components: linguistic competence, technological competence, and strategic competence. When the L2 learner engages in L2 communication, various technological choices are available to them. Thus, what is required of the learner is to make a decision as to what type of technology is appropriate for a particular purpose, and what linguistic resources and technological skills are required for successful completion of a task. For example, when missing an important business meeting due to illness, the learner may choose to use e-mail to inform a client of their absence. Completing this task would require word-processing skills and the ability to construct a fairly formal apology, following conventions of e-mail communication. The learner has to deploy different strategies from other contexts, such as telephoning a friend to cancel a get together.

Defining the L2 ability construct for communication through computer technology leads us to a second issue: how we go about evaluating the qualities of CALT usefulness. Like any traditional assessment, qualities of the usefulness of a test for CALT should be evaluated systematically. This is because no matter how attractive such a test may look, what is critical is the quality of information about examinee language ability the test provides. As pointed out by Bachman and Palmer (1996), the decision as to which qualities of test usefulness—reliability, construct validity, authenticity, interactiveness, impact, and practicality—to prioritize depends on a particular test context. However, if the overall quality of test usefulness required for a specific context cannot be maintained, the information obtained from the CALT might not be interpreted in a meaningful manner, potentially leading to inappropriate test score use. This has led to a concern with developing frameworks for evaluating CALTs and the claims made for their usefulness.

Current contributions and research

Approaches to evaluating CALT

In examining the qualities of CALT a number of frameworks for test validation have been employed. Bachman and Palmer's (1996) qualities of test usefulness framework is a prime example, which has been applied to analyses of general characteristics of CALT (Chapelle and Douglas, 2006), a low-stakes web-based ESL test (Chapelle *et al.*, 2003), and Versant (e.g., Chun, 2006, 2008; Downey *et al.*, 2008), a telephone-based speaking assessment developed by Pearson (formally known as Ordinate SET-10). Meanwhile, test validation theory itself is in a transition as argument-based approaches come to the fore (Bachman, 2005; Kane, 2006; Kane, this volume). In this approach test validation is conceptualized as a long-term process where various types of evidence are collected systematically to build an argument for a specific test score interpretation and use. Some sample applications of this argument-based test validation to CALT include Chapelle *et al.*'s (2008) volume on the documentation of the development and early validation of TOEFL iBT as well as Xi *et al.*'s (2008) conceptualization and validation of SpeechRater, an automated scoring engine being developed by Educational Testing Service (ETS) for evaluating spontaneous speech. In addition, Chapelle and Douglas (2006) adapt frameworks developed by Noijons (1994) and Fulcher (2003) to create a systematic approach to CALT evaluation, embedded within an argument-based approach to validation.

CALT validity: PBT versus CBT score comparability

Along with overall analyses of CALT qualities, individual studies focusing on specific qualities of test usefulness have been published. A CALT validity issue that has attracted some attention of researchers, particularly during early years of CALT development, is the comparability of scores obtained across the PBT and CBT modes, a test method effect on examinee test performance (see Sawaki, 2001 for a literature review on this topic in reading assessment). Chapelle and Douglas (2006) argue that whether a method effect becomes a hindrance or not depends on the test purpose. When we develop a new CBT, which is often expensive, we typically aim at designing a better assessment, taking advantage of functionalities available only on computers. In this context it is unlikely that a paper-based form of the test is designed. In contrast, in contexts where PBT and CBT versions of the same test are used concurrently for decision-making, psychometric equivalence of scores across the modes must be established in consideration of test fairness. The same applies to a case where CAT items are pretested in a PBT form and then added to an item bank, because the difficulty of the items should not change across the modes.

Although the number of score comparability studies is still small, this issue has been examined from two perspectives. One is the effects of computer familiarity on examinee test performance. This is because examinees should not be disadvantaged by taking a CBT simply because they are not familiar with using or taking tests on computers. For example, a series of such studies was conducted by ETS prior to the introduction of the first computer-based version of the TOEFL test in 1998. In Taylor et al.'s (1998) study, scores on the CBT version of the TOEFL were compared between computer-familiar and computer-unfamiliar groups after the examinees had completed a computer tutorial. After adjusting CBT scores for English ability, the mean score of the computer-familiar group was found to be significantly higher, but the difference was too small to be considered practically important. Similarly, Trites and McGroarty (2005) found that computer familiarity did not affect scores on two TOEFL iBT prototype reading tasks where examinees summarized a single text or multiple texts on the same topic.

Even if computer familiarity is not an issue, examinees may still perform differently between PBT and CBT conditions. This is because displaying existing PBT items on the computer screen often introduces qualitative changes to the task. For example, a fairly long reading text can be presented on a page in a PBT, but the text may require scrolling or dividing up into multiple pages when presented on a screen. However, results of empirical studies suggest that the text presentation mode might not affect examinee reading comprehension test scores. In Choi et al.'s (2003) study, a PBT group performed significantly better than a CBT group on multiple-choice reading comprehension items. However, the two versions of the test were highly correlated with each other, and the factor structure of the test was invariant across the modes, suggesting that the two versions of the test tapped psychometrically the same constructs. No statistical differences between PBT versus CBT groups were found on examinee performance on constructed-response reading-comprehension items for summarizing source text content either (Trites and McGroarty, 2005; Yu, 2010).

The lack of meaningful differences in examinee performance on reading tests does not necessarily mean that we can now safely conclude that neither computer familiarity nor presentation mode is a validity concern, however. First, as rightly pointed out by Douglas and Hegelheimer (2007) and Yu (2010), group-level comparisons do not tell us much about how the presentation mode affects individual examinees and specific subgroups. Second, the picture looks quite different when it comes to the effects of response mode on writing performance. When a performance-based writing assessment is included in a CBT, three scenarios are possible: (1) all examinees are required to write their responses by hand, (2) all examinees are required to word process their responses, or (3) examinees are given a choice of handwriting or word processing their responses. Although previous findings are not entirely consistent, it has generally been found that mean essay scores do not differ between those submitting handwritten essays and those submitting word processed essays when a choice is given (e.g., Blackhurst, 2005; Breland *et al.*, 2004; Wolfe and Manalo, 2004). However, an important ability-group difference emerged in the studies by Breland, *et al.* (2004) and Wolfe and Manalo (2004) when test scores were adjusted for differences in English ability: while performance of high-ability examinees did not differ across the modes, low-ability examinees performed worse when they word-processed their responses. Wang *et al.* (2008) report that mitigating the response mode differences found in such studies was a reason, among others, for requiring all examinees to word process their writing responses when TOEFL iBT was introduced in 2006. Possible explanations of the results above include a higher cognitive demand imposed on lower-level learners when word processing in L2 (Wolfe and Manalo, 2004) and raters' tendencies to compensate for poor hand-writing during the rating process, assigning higher scores to hand-written essays (Brown, 2003). Another possibility is qualitative differences in the composing process, where word processing meant less advanced planning and more extensive text revision compared to handwriting, as demonstrated in a study by Lee (2002).

CALT authenticity and validity: What does multimedia do to the construct?

Many real-life listening tasks include visual information. For example, in a face-to-face conversation, an interlocutor's facial expressions and gestures would help the listener understand the utterance of the interlocutor. Likewise, when a student listens to an academic lecture in a classroom, a professor might provide visuals while delivering a lecture orally. Audio content can readily be integrated into CALT to enhance its authenticity. As already noted, however, integration of multimedia into CALT is progressing rather slowly. This is because the availability of additional information while listening may change the nature of the construct the test was designed to assess. Recent research has focused primarily on two areas. The first is examinees' video viewing behaviors, namely, the extent to which examinees actually look at the video monitor. Results vary greatly, ranging from studies in which only a small percentage of participants looked at the video monitor because they found it distracting (e.g., Coniam, 2001) to those where participants were oriented toward a monitor for as long as about 70% of the testing time, on average (e.g., Wagner, 2007, 2010). Another line of investigation has investigated how the presence or absence of visual information affects examinee performance on listening comprehension. A study conducted by Ginther (2002) suggested that the presentation of visuals in the TOEFL CBT may facilitate listening comprehension when the images supplemented the content of the audio. However, studies that compared audio and video listening conditions showed that L2 listening test scores were not affected by the video vs. audio viewing conditions (e.g., Coniam, 2001).

Given that the findings of examinees' viewing behaviors as well as the effects of visuals on listening comprehension performance are rather mixed, the question of the extent to which multimedia elements impact on the construct remains open. Some research does suggest, however, that the answer may depend on the type of visuals presented. In a small-scale study of examinees' test-taking behaviors under still photo vs. video conditions, Ockey (2007) found that his participants in a still photos condition looked at the visuals only at the beginning of the test, while examinees in the video condition varied in the degree of engagement in and the use of visual information while processing information presented aurally. Thus, Ockey suggested that listening with still photos would minimally affect the construct assessed in a listening test, while listening with video would assess a broader construct. Similarly, Wagner (2008, 2010) found that visual information presented in videos (e.g., hand gestures, body language, context information) did affect processing of information, although the participants varied in the extent to which they used the visual information for text processing, suggesting that a video-based listening test may assess something that cannot be assessed in an audio-only test. A key issue that requires future exploration is the extent to which individuals utilize visual information from video. If it transpires that there is a great deal of individual variability in how this is done, and the extent to which it helps or hinders comprehension (as suggested by Buck, 2001), significant validity questions will remain regarding the use of multimedia content.

Assessing speaking: How best to utilize computer technology

The use of computers in the assessment of speaking has been particularly problematic (Chalhoub-Deville and Deville, 1999), primarily due to technical challenges in replicating an important feature of real-life human interactions: the unpredictable and reciprocal nature of the discourse. Accordingly, concerns are continually raised as to whether a computer can be a suitable medium for assessing speaking, and if so, in what circumstances CALT for speaking assessment is meaningful (e.g., Norris, 2001; Ericsson and Haswell, 2006). A number of different approaches have nevertheless emerged (see also Xi, this volume).

In one approach, CALT speaking assessments are based on tasks where the examinee responds orally to various types of prompts that provide fairly authentic language use contexts. In some task types the examinee provides a monologue, such as a solution to a problem presented as a voice message (e.g., TOEIC Speaking Test), while others elicit examinee responses to a series of questions in a simulated conversation (e.g., AP Japanese Speaking section). An advantage of these approaches, characterized by computer delivery of tasks and digital response capturing, is that every examinee can be tested under the same conditions, unlike when a human examiner interacts with examinees individually in one-on-one interviews (e.g., Kenyon and Malabonga, 2001).

In another approach, CBT speaking tasks are designed to elicit information about aspects of speaking ability that cannot be readily evaluated in existing speaking assessments. For instance, Versant tests are designed to assess psycholinguistic processes that underlie speaking performance on contextualized speaking tasks that learners may encounter in real life. The test consists of seven types of speaking tasks such as reading aloud and repeating sentences, giving antonyms of words presented, and responding to short-answer questions. Examinees' responses are analyzed by an automated scoring engine to yield an overall score as well as four subscores: pronunciation, fluency, sentence mastery, and vocabulary. Although the authenticity of these decontextualized tasks is relatively low (Chun 2006, 2008), the Versant score has shown meaningful correlations with other language proficiency tests, supporting the view that these tasks tap into skills underlying more contextualized speaking performance (Downey et al., 2008; Bernstein et al., 2010). As Fox and Fraser (2009) rightly pointed out, the variables the speech recognizer extracts for calculation of the four subscores seems to have potential for the diagnosis of learner strengths and weaknesses.

Recommendations for practice

Given the rapidly developing nature of computer technology it may be tempting for the test designer to focus on the appearance of a test, or constantly trying to use new functionalities. However, it should be remembered that what is critical is the quality of information about the learner's L2 ability level that the CALT offers. Any language test should go through a rigorous, systematic investigation of its qualities of usefulness, and a test designed for CALT is no exception. Toward this end, it is important to start planning carefully how to go about evaluating CALT qualities in the early stages of test development. It is recommended that the test designers refer to previous CALT validation studies as well as applications of frameworks for evaluating L2 test validity and use, such as those reviewed above. In particular, Fulcher (2003) argues that often little attention is paid to various interface issues despite the fact that they have important implications for the qualities of test usefulness. A careful examination of various issues raised would help the test developer alleviate a situation where intended test score interpretation and use are undermined due to suboptimal test design decisions.

Future directions

This discussion shows that while notable incremental advances in CALT have been made in the field of language assessment, there is still a lot more work to be done to pave the way toward developing truly innovative CALT. Various tests for CALT have been designed and developed, and some documentation on these efforts as well as early validation studies are available (e.g., Alderson, 2005; Alderson and Huhta, 2005; Chapelle *et al.*, 2008). However, there is room for a great deal of more empirical research, including studies based on operational data, as well as long-term investigations into how CALT might impact on individuals, society, and language instruction.

Two other areas of investigation should proceed in tandem. First, we need to explore ways to design test tasks that are engaging and reflective of the characteristics of real-life language use tasks. One such area to explore is the use of virtual reality. Language testers do not yet have a satisfactory solution as to how to emulate real-life human communication involving reciprocal interaction with computers. However, it might be possible, for instance, to replicate such a situation if the examinee could play the role of an interlocutor in a conversation in a virtual reality community. Another important area for consideration is how new media other than computers (e.g., mobile phones, games) may contribute to implementing CALT as part of an L2 curriculum in a seamless manner.

Second, we need to deepen our understanding of substantive theory. For instance, an application of virtual reality to CALT would not succeed without a thorough understanding of the characteristics of real-life language use tasks in various technology-mediated contexts. Toward this end, clearly defining the construct of L2 ability along the lines of Chapelle and Douglas's (2006) three-part definition of the target construct should be an ongoing research endeavor. Furthermore, we need to find ways to assess the target constructs in a more comprehensive manner. For instance, latency of learner performance in reading was mentioned by Alderson (2000a) as an area that can readily be assessed with computer technology. Moreover, as Chapelle and Douglas suggested, collaborating with second language acquisition (SLA) researchers might help us design tests for CALT that are sensitive to how L2 ability develops in the long term.

Another substantive issue is to actively seek for ways to better link assessment with instruction (Alderson, 2005; Jang, this volume). Offering elaborate performance feedback that may help examinees and their teachers identify learner strengths and weaknesses in new CALT systems is consistent with the growing interest in diagnostic assessment as well. A particularly fruitful approach would be the collaboration of applied linguists and measurement specialists to explore new approaches such as cognitive diagnosis, which integrate cognitive psychology and measurement theory to obtain diagnostic information from assessment data. Despite various challenges associated with application of cognitive diagnosis to L2 testing (Lee and Sawaki, 2009), such collaboration might allow tighter definitions of the target ability. Another promising area is dynamic assessment (DA), a type of classroom assessment based on socio-cultural theory (Antón, this volume). According to Lantolf and Poehner (2008) the interventionalist approach to DA employs relatively standardized assessment procedures to provide the learner with various pre-programmed feedback based on human teacher behaviors. Lantolf and Poehner argue that this approach might be amenable to implementation on computers, which seems to have exciting implications to enhancing capabilities for learner diagnosis and instruction. Although there are a lot of challenges ahead, focused efforts to enhance our substantive knowledge would help us take a step forward in designing truly innovative tests for CALT that transform the conventions of L2 assessment.

Further reading

Chalhoub-Deville, M. (ed.), (1999). *Issues in Computer-adaptive Testing of Reading Proficiency*. Cambridge, UK: Cambridge University Press. This volume is a must-read for those who are interested in how to assess L2 comprehension in CALT environments. While the volume focuses primarily on CAT, the insightful, critical discussions on the constructs of L2 comprehension presented by various distinguished authors in the field highlight many important issues to consider when determining whether CALT is appropriate for a particular test purpose and defining target constructs for CALT. Moreover, chapters on empirical studies on existing CATs and relevant measurement issues are helpful for those who are planning to develop their own CATs.

Chapelle, C. A. and Douglas, D. (2006). *Assessing Language through Computer Technology*. Cambridge, UK: Cambridge University Press. This Cambridge Language Assessment Series volume offers an excellent introduction to various aspects of CALT for students and professionals that are new to the topic. The authors start their discussion by identifying notable features of CALT as well as similarities and differences of CALT against conventional assessments. Various issues raised in chapters on the threat of CALT, evaluating CALT, and the impact of CALT are particularly eye-opening. The authors' proposal of a context-sensitive definition of language ability for communication through technology marks an important step forward in enhancing our understanding of L2 abilities required to communicate successfully in technology-mediated environments.

Chapelle, C. A., Enright, M. K. and Jamieson, J. M. (2008). *Building a Validity Argument for the Test of English as a Foreign Language^{TM}*. New York, NY: Routledge. Chapelle, Enright, and Jamieson offer an overview of the history of the TOEFL test as well as a comprehensive account of how the TOEFL iBT was designed and developed. Discussions on rationales behind various aspects of the test design and research studies conducted as part of the test development process and for initial validation of the test are valuable for the reader to understand the complexity and extensiveness of the work involved in the development of the high-volume, high-stakes CALT over the years. In addition, the TOEFL validity argument framework presented in the final chapter illustrates how a argument-based approach can be applied to CALT validation.

Douglas, D. and Hegelheimer, V. (2007). Assessing Language Using Computer Technology. *Annual Review of Applied Linguistics* 27: 115–32. This is the most recent review article in *Annual Review of Applied Linguistics* on computer technology with the focus on L2 assessment. Douglas and Hegelheimer provide an overview of the nature of the language construct and test validation issues relevant to CALT. However, they also offer a review of a variety of computer-based and web-based test authoring systems as well as computer-based systems for scoring examinee responses and providing feedback to test users, along with relevant current research, which would prove informative for those involved in the development of CALT.

References

Alderson, J. C. (2000a). *Assessing Reading*. Cambridge, UK: Cambridge University Press.
—— (2000b). Technology in testing: the present and the future. *System*, 28: 593–603.
—— (2005). *Diagnosing Foreign Language Proficiency: the interface between learning and assessment*. New York: Continuum.
Alderson, J. C. and Huhta, A. (2005). The development of a suite of computer-based diagnostic tests based on the common European framework. *Language Testing* 22: 301–20.
Bachman, L. F. (2005). Building and supporting a case for test use. *Language Assessment Quarterly* 2: 1–34.
Bachman, L. F. and Palmer, A. (1996). *Language Testing in Practice*. Cambridge, UK: Cambridge University Press.
Bennett, R. E. (2000). *Reinventing Assessment: speculations on the future of large-scale educational testing*. Princeton, NJ: ETS.
Bernstein, J., van Moere, A. and Cheng, J. (2010). Validating automated speaking tests. *Language Testing* 27: 355–77.

Blackhurst, A. (2005). Listening, reading, and writing on computer-based and paper-based versions of IELTS. University of Cambridge ESOL Examinations. *Research Notes* 21: 14–17.

Breland, H., Lee, Y.-W. and Muraki, E. (2004). *Comparability of TOEFL CBT Writing Prompts: Response Mode Analyses* (TOEFL Research Report No. RR-75). Princeton, NJ: ETS.

Brown, A. (2003). Legibility and the rating of second language writing: an investigation of the rating of handwritten and word-processed IELTS task two essays. *IELTS Research Reports* 4. IELTS Australia.

Buck, G. (2001). *Assessing Listening*. Cambridge, UK: Cambridge University Press.

Chalhoub-Deville, M. and Deville, C. (1999). Computer adaptive testing in second language contexts. *Annual Review of Applied Linguistics* 19: 273–99.

Chapelle, C. A. and Douglas, D. (2006). *Assessing Language through Computer Technology* Cambridge, UK: Cambridge University Press.

Chapelle, C. A., Enright, M. K. and Jamieson, J. M. (2008). *Building a Validity Argument for the Test of English as a Foreign Language*. New York, NY: Routledge.

Chapelle, C. A., Jamieson, J. and Hegelheimer, V. (2003). Validation of a web-based ESL test. *Language Testing* 20: 409–39.

Choi, I.-C., Kim, K. S. and Boo, J. (2003). Comparability of a paper-based language test and a computer-based language test. *Language Testing* 20: 295–320.

Chun, C. W. (2006). An analysis of a language test for employment: the authenticity of the phonepass test. *Language Assessment Quarterly* 3: 295–306.

—— (2008). Comments on 'Evaluation of the usefulness of the versant for English test: a response: the author responds'. *Language Assessment Quarterly* 5: 168–72.

Coniam, D. (2001). The use of audio or video comprehension as an assessment instrument in the certification of English language teachers: a case study. *System* 29: 1–14.

Council of Europe (2001). *Common European Framework of Reference for Languages: Learning Teaching and Assessment*. Cambridge, UK: Cambridge University Press.

Douglas, D. and Hegelheimer, V. (2007). Assessing language using computer technology. *Annual Review of Applied Linguistics* 27: 115–32.

Downey, R., Farhady, H., Present-Thomas, R., Suzuki, M. and van Moere, A. (2008). Evaluation of the Usefulness of the Versant for English Test: A Response. *Language Assessment Quarterly* 5: 160–67.

Ericsson, P. F. and Haswell, R. (eds), (2006). *Machine Scoring of Student Essays: truth and consequences*. Logan, UT: Utah University Press.

Fox, J. and Fraser, W. (2009). The versant Spanish test. *Language Testing* 26: 313–22.

Fulcher, G. (1999). Computerizing an English language placement test. *ELT Journal* 53: 289–98.

—— (2003). Interface design in computer-based language testing. *Language Testing* 20: 384–408.

Ginther, A. (2002). Context and content visuals and performance on listening comprehension stimuli. *Language Testing* 19: 133–67.

Jamieson, J. (2005). Trends in computer-based second language assessment. *Annual Review of Applied Linguistics* 25: 228–42.

Jamieson, J., Eignor, D., Grabe, W. and Kunnan, A. J. (2008). Frameworks for a New TOEFL. In C. Chapelle, M. K. Enright and J. Jamieson (eds), *Building a Validity Argument for the Test of English as a Foreign Language*^{TM}. New York: Routledge.

Kane, M. (2006). Validation. In R. Brennan (ed.), *Educational Measurement,* 2nd edn. Westport, CT: American Council on Education and Praeger Publishers.

Kenyon, D. M. and Malabonga, V. (2001). Comparing examinee attitudes toward computer-assisted and other oral proficiency assessments. *Language Learning Technology* 5: 60–83.

Lantolf, J. P. and Poehner, M. E. (2008). Dynamic assessment. In E. Shohamy and N. H. Hornberger (eds), *Encyclopedia of Language and Education,* 2nd edn, Vol. 7, *Language Testing and Assessment*. New York, NY: Springer.

Lee, Y.-J. (2002). A Comparison of composing processes and written products in timed-essay tests across paper-and-pencil and computer modes. *Assessing Writing* 8: 135–57.

Lee, Y.-W. and Sawaki, Y. (2009). Cognitive diagnosis approaches to language assessment: an overview. *Language Assessment Quarterly* 6: 172–89.

Malabonga, V., Kenyon, D. M. and Carpenter, H. (2005). Self-assessment, preparation and response time on a computerized oral proficiency test. *Language Testing* 22: 59–92.

Nogami, Y. and Hayashi, N. (2010). A Japanese adaptive test of english as a foreign language: developmental and operational aspects. In W. van der Linden and C. A. W. Glas (eds), *Elements of Adaptive Testing*. New York, NY: Springer.

Noijons, J. (1994). Testing computer assisted language tests: Towards a checklist for CALT. *CALICO Journal* 12: 37–58.

Norris, J. M. (2001). Concerns with computerized adaptive oral proficiency assessment. *Language Learning and Technology* 5: 99–105.

Ockey, G. J. (2007). Construct implications of including still image or video in computer-based listening tests. *Language Testing* 24: 517–37.

Oskoz, A. and Chalhoub-Deville, M. (2009). Test review: assessing language through computer technology by Chapelle and Douglas (2006). *Language Testing* 26: 149–54.

Roever, C. (2001). Web-based Language Testing. *Language Learning and Technology* 5: 84–94.

Sawaki, Y. (2001). Comparability of Conventional and Computerized Tests of Reading in a Second Language. *Language Learning and Technology* 5: 38–59.

Stansfield, C. W. (ed.), (1986). *Technology and Language Testing*. Washington, DC: TESOL.

Taylor, C., Jamieson, J., Eignor, D. and Kirsch, I. (1998). *The Relationship between Computer Familiarity and Performance on Computer-based TOEFL Test Tasks* (TOEFL Research Report No. 61). Princeton, NJ: ETS.

Trites, L. and McGroarty, M. (2005). Reading to learn and reading to integrate: new tasks for reading comprehension tests? *Language Testing* 22: 174–210.

Wagner, E. (2007). Are they watching? test-taker viewing behavior during an l2 video listening test. *Language Learning and Technology* 11: 67–86.

—— (2008). Video listening tests: what are they measuring? *Language Assessment Quarterly* 5: 218–43.

——(2010). The effect of the use of video texts on ESL listening test-taker performance. *Language Testing* 27: 493–513.

Wang, L., Eignor, D. and Enright, M. K. (2008). A final analysis. In C. Chapelle, M. K. Enright and J. Jamieson (eds), *Building a validity argument for the Test of English as a Foreign Language™*. New York, NY: Routledge.

Wolfe, E. W. and Manalo, J. R. (2004). Composition Medium Comparability in a Direct Writing Assessment of Non-native English Speakers. *Language Learning & Technology* 8: 53–65.

Xi, X., Zechner, K., Higgins, D. and Williamson, D. M. (2008). *Automated Scoring of Spontaneous Speech using Speechrater v1.0* (ETS Research Report No. 08–62). Princeton, NJ: ETS.

Yu, G. (2010). Effects of presentation mode and computer familiarity on summarization of extended texts. *Language Assessment Quarterly* 7: 119–36.

Validity and the automated scoring of performance tests

Xiaoming Xi

Introduction

In recent decades, the trend toward more communicative approaches to language teaching and a growing demand for more authentic measures for assessing language abilities have given rise to the revival of performance-based language tests (McNamara, 1996). Performance-based tasks elicit authentic performance samples that are evaluated based on pre-established scoring criteria. They are often referred to as "constructed response" tasks (Bennett, 1993; Kane *et al.*, 1999), which require responses other than selecting from fixed options.

The past two decades have seen an increasing use of performance-based tasks in large-scale testing (Bennett, 1993), which has helped to generate greater demand for more efficient, affordable and reliable scoring approaches. Increasingly, automated scoring is becoming a part of the solution to meet this demand. For example, e-rater is used as a quality control on the scores assigned by human raters for the Analytical Writing section of the Graduate Record Examinations (GRE) General Test used for admission into English-medium graduate schools (Powers *et al.*, 2002a). The Pearson Test of English (PTE) Academic, a new test of English proficiency required for participation in English-medium post-secondary education, uses automated scoring alone to score both written and spoken responses (Pearson, 2009).

Research into the automated scoring of constructed responses began more than four decades ago, when Page investigated the use of automated scoring for scoring essays with a view to provide immediate, reliable writing score feedback to students, and to relieve classroom teachers of the burden of scoring a large number of essays (Page, 1966). This initial work was in suspension for almost three decades, partly due to limited computing power and lack of access to computers, a major obstacle in applying the research to real-world practice. Automated scoring research regained momentum in the early 1990s with advances in computer technologies and a rising demand for more efficient procedures for scoring essays in large-scale standardized testing (Page, 1994; Page and Dieter, 1995; Page and Peterson, 1995; Shermis *et al.*, 1999). With the increasing prevalence of computer-based tests that use constructed response tasks and the growing maturity of computer scoring technologies, automated scoring is gaining in popularity. The growing use of automated scoring underscores the need for investigating and building shared understanding of relevant validity issues, which is the focus of this chapter.

In contrast to the general positive acceptance in computational linguistics and general educational measurement, automated scoring has met strong resistance from many language and literature teachers and professionals from the outset (Coombs, 1969; Macrorie, 1969). In an early review of Page and Paulus's essay scoring program, Project Essay Grade, an English professor mocked that students would be likely to write to the computer and produce "Engfish," boring and dull prose (Macrorie, 1969). Hostility toward automated scoring arose again once automated scoring regained momentum in the 1990s (Roy, 1993). Fitzgerald (1994) wrote passionately in his response to Roy, who had argued for the use of a computer scoring for writing placement purposes:

> The recognition that "writing" is a rhetorical act inseparable from its content, contexts, has been hard-won. It would be a mistake now to undo these admittedly partial victories in the name of seemingly "new," but, no doubt, "authoritative" technologies.
>
> *(Fitzgerald, 1994: 17)*

Deep skepticism from the teaching profession persisted as automated scoring systems evolved. Recently, Cheville (2004) raised the following question while reflecting on the growing influence of automated essay scoring and feedback tools on the learning and instruction of writing:

> How might the context of high-stakes assessment privilege technologies that actually impoverish students' understanding of language conventions and writing?
>
> *(Cheville, 2004: 47)*

In the field of second language testing, computer technologies have helped transform conceptual thinking and practice about test delivery, definition of test constructs, measurement models, and task design (Chalhoub-Deville, 2001; Jamieson, 2005; Ockey, 2009). The reactions to automated scoring technologies, however, have been mixed from language testers; the general sentiment can be characterized as *cautiously optimistic* (Xi, 2010). On the one hand, language testers understand the challenges of training, monitoring and retaining a large number of human raters for large-scale testing programs and are appreciative of the potential benefits scoring technologies could offer in terms of producing faster and more reliable scores. On the other hand, they are keenly aware of the limitations of automated scoring technologies, which put constraints on the contexts and ways in which the technologies should be used. Language testers, many of whom have language teaching experience, also empathize with teachers' concerns that computer scoring technologies might erode good practice in language learning and teaching.

The vastly different ways and contexts in which automated scoring has been implemented have fueled some of the controversy over automated scoring. In some applications the use of automated scoring may be easier to justify whereas in others it may be strongly disputed. Ignoring the differences in how automated scoring is applied may lead to undifferentiated resistance to automated scoring. Consequently, a particular challenge is to establish what validity means for different contexts and uses of automated scoring. A general validity framework geared toward practice with flexibility to accommodate particular applications of automated scoring is much needed. Language testers, with an interdisciplinary training in linguistics, measurement and testing theories, and statistics, possess the requisite knowledge and skills to address the challenge of engaging experts in other areas to advance research on validity frameworks for automated scoring for language tests and to make recommendations for best practice.

This chapter will chart the evolution of validity theories and practice in relation to automated scoring for performance-based language tests. It reviews historical perspectives on the validity of automated scoring, discusses the current trends and issues in both conceptual and empirical work with a view towards establishing practical guidelines for best practice, and points to some future directions.

Historical perspectives

The quest for the validity of automated scoring has drawn on evolutions in validity paradigms. Initially, automated scoring validity research focused primarily on the agreement between human and automated scores (Page, 1966). This was consistent with the dominant view in the 1950s and 1960s that conceptualized validity as the extent to which test scores are related to criterion scores that are considered the gold standard (Cureton, 1951). Although both the system and the validation approach may seem primitive in the backdrop of today's landscape of automated scoring, Page's work was pioneering in that it opened up a whole new world of possibilities for utilizing computer technologies. The human–machine score comparison, although not the sole criterion for evaluating an automated scoring system, continues to be a highly relevant and intuitive criterion both in academic publications and publications which target the general public.

This initial approach to validation has been improved or expanded in a number of ways. A wide array of evaluation statistics that are complementary in nature have been combined for human–automated score comparison (Yang *et al.*, 2002), including percentage of agreement, correlation, kappa, and comparisons of means and standard deviations. Research has also emerged that compares the generalizability of automated versus human scores (Clauser *et al.*, 2000).

Since automated scoring research was reenergized in the 1990s, a new generation of validity research has been examining the relationship between automated essay scores and independent measures of language or other abilities, as well as human essay scores (Attali *et al.*, 2010; Landauer *et al.*, 1998; Petersen, 1997; Powers *et al.*, 2002a; Weigle, 2010). The purpose of this work is to understand the extent to which automated and human scores relate to other measures of similar or distinct constructs. These studies have provided some insights into whether automated scores reflect similar constructs as human scores.

The effect of automated scoring on test-taker behavior is an important consideration from a validity perspective. Powers and his colleagues conducted an innovative study on how e-rater may be fooled by writing experts to improve the quality of e-rater and to understand the interactions between the scoring engine and the writer (Powers *et al.*, 2002b). They concluded that the state-of-the-art technologies did not support the use of computer scoring alone to score essays because they can be manipulated in ways that could defeat the fidelity to the writing construct. Their findings also helped enhance future versions of e-rater which have included mechanisms to flag and exclude from scoring responses that may be associated with commonly used techniques to fool e-rater (e.g., repeating the same paragraph many times or exceedingly long essays).

Critical issues and topics

As discussed in the previous section, validity research on automated scoring has gradually moved beyond human-automated score agreement. However, as Yang *et al.* have pointed out, previous work has applied particular validation approaches without embedding them in a comprehensive validation framework. The previous work focused on one or more of the following three areas: (1) comparing scores produced by automated scoring systems and by human scorers, (2) examining patterns of relationships between automated scores, human scores and scores on external measures, and (3) understanding the scoring processes that automated scoring systems employ (Yang *et al.*, 2002). These different aspects of validity could potentially be marshaled to support an argument for using automated scoring in an assessment; however, a framework is needed to help us conceptualize the relevant validity issues systematically and organize them in a coherent manner. This framework should guide practitioners to determine the critical evidence needed keeping in mind the way in which automated scoring is implemented and the targeted use of the automated scores. It should also provide a mechanism for synthesizing and evaluating existing evidence for using automated scoring in a particular assessment context.

Although validity research on automated scoring has broadened in scope, an underexplored yet critical area of research is the consequences of automated scoring, in particular how test consequences can be integrated into an overall validity argument. Important topics include the acceptance of automated scoring by users; the effect of the use of automated scoring on test-taking strategies; the impact of automated scoring on how scores are perceived, interpreted, and used; the impact on how the test is prepared; and, more broadly, its impact on how languages are taught and learned.

Current contributions and research

Conceptual work

When automated scoring is integrated into an assessment, its most immediate impact seems to be on the accuracy of the resulting scores. This is also the aspect of automated scoring that has attracted the most research. However, because automated scoring introduces unique challenges that are typically not associated with human scoring (e.g., failure to assess all essential qualities of the performance samples, susceptibility to cheating, constraining the kind of tasks that can be used), the effects of automated scoring may extend beyond the accuracy of scores and be evident in the generalizability, interpretation and use of the scores.

On the conceptual front, Bennett and Bejar's work (1998) represents the earliest attempt to position automated scoring in the larger context of an assessment, rather than seeing it merely as a substitute for human scoring. They argued that while automated scoring should be designed in alignment with other aspects of the assessment process including construct definition, test and task design, test taker interface, and reporting methods, it also influences design decisions related to all these aspects. Bennett and Bejar's conceptual approach is particularly useful for driving the development of a valid computerized assessment that involves automated scoring. By seeing automated scoring as a dynamic component in a computerized assessment system consisting of interrelated components, this framework emphasizes the importance of evaluating the scoring system in the context of a validity argument for the assessment. This framework allows issues beyond score accuracy to be framed and investigated such as the meaning of automated scores and the consequences of automated scoring. Consequently, it broadens the scope of validity investigations regarding automated scoring. Although the relationship of automated scoring to the overall validity argument of the assessment is not emphasized, their paper unveils the complexity of validation work related to automated scoring and provides a foundation for the subsequent work that shifts the focus to an overall validity argument.

Based on a critical analysis of empirical validity work on automated scoring, Yang et al. (2002) proposed a comprehensive validation approach, drawing largely on Bennett and Bejar (1998). Using this broadened validation framework as the reference point, they noted two gaps in the existing literature. The first one was the dearth of literature that conceptualized potential threats posed by the use of automated scoring for construct relevance and representation. They also highlighted the role of the consequences of using automated scoring in a validity argument.

Kelly (2001), in his work on the overall validity of using automated scoring to complement human scoring in large-scale writing tests, adopts Messick's (1995) unitary concept of validity that encompasses six facets: content, structural, substantive, external, generalizability and consequential.

In framing automated scoring validity research in a general validity framework for an assessment, Kelly has implicitly endorsed Bennett and Bejar's view that an automated scoring system is not just replacing the human rater; rather it interacts with the other assessment components in complex ways. Drawing on Messick's validity framework that emphasizes test consequences as part of validity, Kelly has effectively extended the boundaries to include the impact of automated scoring on stakeholders' interpretation and use of the scores.

Research by Bennett and Bejar, Yang and his colleagues, and Kelly represents an important step towards the development of an overarching, coherent framework for integrating automated scoring into the overall assessment process. Nevertheless, a mechanism is needed to weigh, combine, and synthesize different lines of evidence to support a validity argument.

Clauser et al. (2002) responded to the need for such a mechanism. Motivated by the shift to an argument-based approach to test validation (Kane, 1992), they proposed to investigate the validity of automated scoring in the larger context of an assessment validity argument. Their approach subsumes and coherently integrates the various areas of validation reviewed in Yang et al. (2002) into a larger validity argument for the whole assessment. It also extends these areas to include decisions based on automated scores and consequences that result from the use of automated scoring. It thus provides a working framework for weaving automated scoring into the validity argument for the whole assessment. They argue that multiple pieces of evidence need to be provided regarding score generalizability, score interpretation, score-based decisions, and consequences of score use to support the use of automated scoring in an assessment. Their framework is useful for guiding the development and synthesis of evidence to support the proposed interpretation and use of automated scores.

With this approach, validation unfolds in two stages: developing an interpretative argument and evaluating a validity argument (Kane, 2006). In the first stage, for each intended use of test scores, an interpretive argument is articulated through a logical analysis of the chain of inferences linking performance on a test to a score-based decision, and the assumptions upon which these inferences rest. The second stage involves an evaluation of the plausibility of the interpretive argument within a validity argument given existing evidence.

In applying this framework to automated scoring, Clauser et al. (2002) discussed how decisions regarding automated scoring may strengthen the overall validity argument or potentially weaken it. Their discussion focused on the potential threats to the strength of each inference in the chain that may be introduced by automated scoring, pointing to the critical areas of research that are needed to discount or reduce the threats. Although Clauser et al. (2002) may not cover all the potential validity issues introduced by automated scoring, they provide a working model for integrating automated scoring into this network of inferences used to justify the intended interpretation and use of test scores.

Xi (2008) took this work further by discussing how the Clauser et al. (2002) framework can guide practical validation efforts related to automated systems used for performance-based language tests in particular. Using an actual automated scoring application as an example, she conducted a thorough analysis of the kinds of threats automated scoring may introduce and the types of evidence that need to be put forward to minimize or reduce these threats. In particular, she proposed that validation priorities may be determined by how automated scoring is used (e.g., used alone or in conjunction with human scoring) and the kind of decisions the assessment intends to support (e.g., low-stakes practice purposes versus medium- or high-stakes decisions). Later, in her introduction to a special issue on automated scoring and feedback systems in *Language Testing* (Xi, 2010), she summarized the validity questions that should be asked in validating automated scoring systems for language tests and linked them to specific inferences in the argument-based validation framework (Chapelle et al., 2008; Kane, 2006).

Empirical work

Although the earlier empirical validation work on automated scoring for performance-based language tests focused on the agreement between human and automated scores, more recent work has started to show more sophistication and breadth, inspired by advances in conceptual frameworks. Specifically, validation work has been expanded to address the relationships between automated scoring features in relation to the constructs of interest (Enright and Quinlan, 2010; Xi *et al.*, 2008) and the consequences of automated scoring (Kelly, 2001; Xi *et al.*, 2011). In addition, a piecemeal approach, where a single validity aspect is investigated without connections to other evidence, has evolved into a more complex, integrated approach that synthesizes multiple pieces of evidence to support the use of automated scoring for a particular assessment (Bernstein *et al.*, 2010; Enright and Quinlan, 2010; Kelly, 2001; Xi *et al.*, 2008).

Recommendations for practice

Given the many different areas of expertise required to fully understand the complexity of automated scoring systems it seems a daunting task for practitioners to attempt to validate the use of automated scoring. A useful practice is to raise the relevant validity issues and then determine which issues need to be prioritized. In setting validation priorities, it is crucial to ask the following two questions to determine the types of evidence that should be prioritized and the standards against which the results should be evaluated to support the use of the automated scoring system.

- For what purpose are the scores intended to be used?
- How is the automated scoring system used to produce the scores? As the sole rater? As a check for human scores? Or as a contributory score in the final reported score?

Asking relevant validity questions

This section provides a list of the relevant questions to be asked that address the accuracy, generalizability, meaningfulness, and usefulness of the scores, and the consequences of using automated scoring (Xi, 2010). The questions correspond to the specific inferences in a validity argument that need to be supported (Chapelle *et al.*, 2008; Kane, 2006). For each question, a brief discussion of the issues and the relevant evidence needed is included.

- *Does the use of assessment tasks constrained by automated scoring technologies lead to construct under- or misrepresentation?* (Domain Definition)

There is a tension between task types included in an assessment and automated scoring capabilities, especially when the computer is intended as the only rater. Automated scoring for simple, constrained tasks may lead to higher agreement with human scores and score reliability but heavy reliance on these tasks in high-stakes testing may lead to construct underrepresentation and incur negative washback on teaching and learning. In contrast, systems designed to score more complex, performance-based tasks lack the level of sophistication and maturity that is required for accurate evaluation of the quality of the performance if used as the only rater. In designing and validating an assessment that uses automated scoring, this trade-off between test design and automated scoring capabilities needs to be taken into account.

Currently automated scoring technologies are not mature enough to support using computers as the sole rater to score responses to constructed response tasks in high-stakes testing. Using automated scoring in combination with human scoring may be a way forward to explore the benefits of automated scoring without having fully addressed all of these concerns associated with automated scoring, as the presence of human scoring will negate the importance of some of them. This approach can potentially improve the reliability and efficiency of scoring while not constraining the type of tasks used to measure communicative language abilities.

To evaluate whether computer scoring has resulted in a more limited domain representation, a critical analysis of the test tasks in relation to the target language use domain involving both the characteristics of the tasks and the knowledge, skills, and processes involved will provide the relevant evidence.

- *Do the automated scoring features under- or misrepresent the construct of interest?* (Explanation)
- *Is the way the scoring features are combined to generate automated scores consistent with theoretical expectations of the relationships between the scoring features and the construct of interest?* (Explanation)
- *Does the use of automated scoring change the meaning and interpretation of scores provided by trained raters?* (Explanation)

Although automated scoring may allow some degree of "control" of the constructs we intend to measure, systematic errors or deficiencies may be introduced that result in construct under-representation or construct-irrelevance. The tendency to extract easily computable, quantifiable aspects of the performance due to the limitations of current technologies would potentially result in construct-irrelevant features or features that do not represent the full construct. For example, the construct in an oral assessment might include a subconstruct for topic development, further defined by a number of features, not all of which are yet adequately captured by the automated scoring system (e.g., logic and coherence). In addition, although it is a desirable goal to combine automated features in a principled, construct-relevant way to produce automated scores, given the complexity of human raters' decision-making processes, it obviously is not an easy task to design a scoring system that adequately reflects those processes.

Evidence required to answer these related questions is conceptual and judgmental in essence.

In particular, two essential qualities need to be verified to ensure that automated scoring captures relevant and meaningful aspects of performance: the construct relevance and coverage of the features, and the defensibility of the manner in which features are combined. The evidence largely involves judgments of these qualities by experts who have an intimate understanding of the construct the assessment is designed to measure, the conceptual meaning of each scoring feature used, and the way the scoring features are combined through a statistical model to produce a score that indicates the overall quality of performance.

- *Does automated scoring yield scores that are accurate indicators of the quality of a test performance sample? Would examinees' knowledge of the scoring logic of an automated scoring system impact the way they interact with the test tasks, thus negatively affecting the accuracy of the scores?* (Evaluation)

The relevant evidence includes the association between human and automated scores indicated by traditional measures of agreement such as percentage of agreement, correlation and kappa. Different scoring methodologies that are used to produce automated scores based on automatically extracted features can be compared based on the strength of the association between the model predicted scores and the human scores. The soundness of the statistical principles underlying each methodology is also an important consideration in employing a particular scoring methodology.

When evaluating the strength of the relationship between human and automated scores, care must be taken to verify the conditions under which test takers produce the performance samples used for human–automated score comparison (e.g., whether they are aware of computer scoring; whether they have any knowledge about the logic of the computer scoring). Evaluation statistics obtained by running performance samples produced for human graders through an automated scoring engine are likely to be misleading indicators of the quality of the automated scores on performance samples produced for a computer grader.

- *Does automated scoring yield scores that are sufficiently consistent across measurement contexts (e.g., across test forms, across tasks in the same form)?* (Generalization)

Two types of evidence can help address this question. One concerns the procedures for developing and evaluating the scoring models such as the adequacy of the sample size, representativeness of the sample, and absence of similarity in candidates between the scoring model training and evaluation data. The second type of evidence includes the reliability of the automated scores across different tasks and test forms. The score reliability estimates could be compared to those obtained for human scores and typical figures acceptable for a particular context.

- *Does automated scoring yield scores that have expected relationships with other test or non-test indicators of the targeted language ability?* (Extrapolation)

The potential evidence for answering this question is the association between automated scores and scores on other relevant test or non-test indicators of language ability. It is helpful to compare the strengths of relationships for human scores and automated scores with scores on these indicators to see if these human and automated scores relate to the other indicators in similar ways. This information will help us decide whether weak relationships between automated scores and scores on these relevant indicators are due to differences in the test measures or in the scoring method.

- *Do automated scores lead to appropriate score-based decisions?* (Utilization)
- *Does the use of automated scoring have a positive impact on examinees' test preparation, teaching and learning practices?* (Utilization)

Replacing or complementing human scoring with automated scoring may change users' perceptions of the assessment, the way they interact with the assessment tasks, and the way languages are learned and taught. Knowing that scores are produced by automated means or by a combination of automated and human scoring means rather than solely by human raters, users may also interpret and use the scores differently.

Arguments for the usefulness of automated scores are supported by an analysis of the magnitude of the error associated with the intended score-based decision. Arguments about potential consequences of using automated scoring may be supported by investigations of user perceptions, e.g., to what extent the awareness of the scores being produced by a machine impacts the way a user interprets and uses the scores, as well as the impact of using automated scoring on test preparation, teaching and learning practices.

Determining validation priorities

Both the way automated scoring is implemented and the intended use of the scores determine the validation priorities. Different aspects of the validity argument may have differential importance depending on the stakes of score use and how automated scoring is implemented. The burden of evidence required to support each aspect of the validity argument is also higher for high-stakes use. For example, the areas of emphasis for validating an automated scoring system intended for a practice environment may differ from those for a system employed in an assessment for high-stakes decisions. If automated scores are intended to support high-stakes decisions, satisfactory answers need to be provided to all of the questions raised above. The domain representativeness of the test tasks (or the Domain Definition inference) and the meaningfulness of the scores (or the Explanation inference) are critical yet are most likely to be compromised by automated scoring— if the assessment tasks or automated scoring models under- or misrepresent the construct of interest, the assessment scores may be inadequate indicators of candidates' language ability. It may also make the assessment more susceptible to cheating and test-gaming strategies that would negatively impact the trustworthiness of the scores. An automatically scored test that under- or misrepresents the construct of interest either as a result of constrained task designs or deficient scoring models may also incur negative washback effects on teaching and learning and hurt the credibility of the testing program. Such inappropriate use may serve to stigmatize any use of automated scoring by further strengthening the skepticism of its critics.

If an automated scoring system is intended to be used to check the accuracy of human scores (i.e., to flag potentially inaccurate human scores for re-scoring by another human rater) or to contribute to the final score along with human scoring, the test design need not be constrained by limitations of automated scoring technologies. Therefore, the use of automated scoring is not expected to introduce additional issues related to the Domain (Definition) inference. However, the Evaluation and Generalization inferences would require adequate backing. It is less critical for the other three inferences, Explanation, Extrapolation, and Utilization to be fully supported given the concurrent use of human scoring.

In evaluating the evidence put forward, different criteria should be used for determining the strength and sufficiency of the evidence for the intended use. Automated scoring used for high-stakes purposes obviously should be subject to higher standards than for low-stakes purposes, with regard to (a) the level of score accuracy in comparison to a gold standard (e.g., high-quality human scores), (b) generalizability of scores, (c) in how the scores represent the essential qualities of the performance samples, (d) in how the scores relate to scores on external criterion measures, (e) how the scores support decision-making, and (f) the consequences of using automated scoring.

Because automated scoring may impact more than one aspect of the validity argument, in developing an automated scoring system we frequently need to reconcile different priorities and determine a design that maximizes the overall quality of the assessment. Correspondingly, in evaluating a system, we also need to be cognizant that some design decisions may strengthen particular aspects of the validity argument while compromising others. For example, automated scoring may reduce task specificity by capturing aspects of performance that are relatively stable across tasks, thus improving the score generalizability. However, it may also reduce task specificity in undesirable ways. It may compromise the explanatory power of the scores in representing the constructs by failing to include some aspects that are construct-relevant but are less stable across tasks, thus weakening the Explanation inference.

Based on the process discussed above, the relevant evidence pertaining to each question or inference can be integrated and evaluated. Then the overall strength of the validity argument can be evaluated in light of the critical inferences that need adequate backing to support the intended claims of automated scoring.

Future directions and developments

Validity research on automated scoring has come a long way from its initial focus on human-machine score comparison. The increasing use of automated scoring in high-stakes contexts necessitates heightened attention to related validity issues and accelerating the maturation of research in this area. We expect to see more depth in the conceptual thinking about validation frameworks, more sophistication in the validation methods, and more breadth in the kind of issues investigated. Additionally, new conceptions of best practice for using automated scoring in class-room assessments are expected to emerge. Rather than being deeply rooted in the conventional validity frameworks for large-scale testing, these new conceptions are likely to draw heavily on the unique characteristics of classroom assessments (e.g., diagnostic, formative, and criterion-referenced).

Establishing standards for evaluating typical applications of automated scoring

As discussed earlier there have been a number of approaches to combining and synthesizing multiple types of evidence to develop validity arguments for automated scoring. As our understanding evolves for different contexts and uses of automated scoring it is imperative to develop standard structures for validity arguments for typical applications of automated scoring. For example, an assessment may use automated scoring alone, as a check or as a contributing score, or use both computers and human raters to score *different* aspects of the same performance samples to generate scores used for high-, medium- or low-stakes decisions. Established standards for expected system performance in different use contexts can then facilitate the practical work of evaluating aggregated evidence. Adopting widely accepted models of validity arguments does not necessarily suppress innovation and creativity in automated scoring work as these models do not constrain the ways in which computer scoring algorithms are developed. Rather, these established models prompt thinking about the highly relevant validity issues and commonly accepted levels of performance given the particular application of automated scoring.

Perceptions by different stakeholders and group-related perception differences

Among other factors, the rigor with which an automated scoring system is developed for a test and its technical and substantive quality may directly impact stakeholders' (e.g., test takers, score users, and teachers) perceived confidence in the scores and their use of them. Each group of stakeholders also brings in their own background and training, and their interests and priorities associated with the test. Therefore, their levels of confidence in and acceptance of the scores may also differ. Even within a group of stakeholders (for example, test takers), perceptions of and interactions with automated scoring may depend on their culture, age, discipline, exposure to and attitude toward technology, and their knowledge about the specific scoring system. Research has started to address some of the open questions through surveys, interviews and focus groups (Kelly, 2001; Xi et al., 2011). More research is certainly needed to address many of the remaining questions.

Test-taking strategies adapted to computer scoring

Test takers may adapt to the grading system for the purpose of getting higher scores. They may adapt their test-taking strategies in systematic or idiosyncratic ways based on their understanding of the grading criteria. Writing or speaking to a computer is likely to trigger more systematic changes in test-taking strategies if the scoring logic is known, because computer scoring logic is typically systematic. This possibility raises intriguing research questions such as how test takers might respond to the test tasks differently because of computer scoring or computer scoring combined with human scoring in some fashion.

Survey methods have been used to gather this kind of information from test takers (Xi et al., 2011). More direct methods are needed such as stimulated recall that allows insights into the actual test-taking processes engaged by test takers when writing to the human rater, the computer, or to a combination of human and computer scoring. Correspondingly it will be useful for us to understand how candidates' performance samples may have been altered by test-taking strategies specific to computer scoring, and how human raters would interact with these samples. Some alterations may result from construct-relevant strategies (i.e., monitor one's pronunciation more closely) while others may not be consistent with the intended construct (e.g., keep talking even if the speech makes little sense or write long essays without much concern for the content). For the construct-relevant strategies it would be interesting to explore how they impact the manifestation of other qualities of the performance samples and whether similar strategies would emerge in response to human scoring. For example, how would a greater focus on pronunciation impact speech accuracy and fluency given the contention for resources during real time speech production and thus the overall speech quality?

A look into both the processes and the products in relation to automated scoring will offer insight into the extent to which changes in test-taking strategies lead to changes in score accuracy, meaning, and interpretations.

Impact on language learning and teaching in different contexts

The increasing use of automated scoring for performance-based language tests either in high-stakes environments or for practice and diagnostic feedback is expected to impact the teaching and learning of language skills in profound ways. Changes in test-taking strategies in response to computer scoring may be prompted by the motivation to "trick" the computer into giving higher scores or may be due to more sustained effects introduced by automated scoring on test preparation, coaching and language teaching.

As an initial step, it is necessary to understand how language learning and teaching theories and practices might adapt to the use of automated scoring in tests with high-stakes decisions, and whether the adaptations are positive or negative from the perspective of learning. Surveys of teachers' classroom teaching techniques geared toward the use of computer scoring may reveal interesting issues to be further explored through direct contact with teachers in interviews, focus groups and classroom observations.

The reactions to automated scoring and feedback capabilities targeted for classroom use on classroom teaching may be mixed, depending on the perceived quality and sophistication of the capabilities, how they are integrated into classroom teaching, the contexts of teaching (e.g. ESL versus EFL) and the qualifications of the language teachers (e.g. native versus non-native speakers of the target language). In studying the impact of automated scoring and feedback capabilities on teaching, factors such as the actual and perceived performance of the capabilities, teachers' competence in the target language, their teaching philosophies and methodologies, their level of knowledge and understanding of the specific automated scoring system need to be taken into account in the design and interpretation of the findings.

Validity frameworks for using automated scoring in large-scale testing versus classroom assessment

Most of the current validity frameworks focus on validity issues related to automated scoring used in large-scale testing, which is typically norm-referenced, aiming to spread out the test takers. However, as Moss pointed out (Moss, 2003), classroom assessments serve different purposes, e.g., whether individual students have mastered certain content, knowledge and skills. She further argued that conventional validity frameworks conceptualized for large-scale standardized testing may be ill-fitted to classroom assessments that are formative, criterion-based (Moss, 2003). As automated scoring systems are making inroads into classrooms, new conceptions of good practice are much needed for use of automated scoring in formative, classroom-based assessments. Chapelle and Chung (2010) and Xi (2010) have raised some validity issues regarding the use of automated feedback systems, but they are framed in Kane's argument-based validation framework that is best-suited to large-scale testing. Automated scoring and feedback systems may be embedded in classroom instruction and assessment activities that serve drastically different purposes than standardized testing. Therefore, any validity frameworks for this context should highlight the prominent characteristics of classroom assessments. Language teaching professionals have much to offer in helping validity theorists think through the most relevant issues for using automated scoring in classroom contexts.

Concluding remarks

To conclude we expect to see validation frameworks for automated scoring continue to grow and to mature, and empirical research to expand into less explored areas such as test takers' interactions with the scoring system and the consequences of automated scoring on test preparation, on teaching and on learning. In the next decade, we may see some consensus developed for the criteria used for evaluating the use of automated scoring in high-stakes contexts given heightened attention to this controversial area of research. The use of automated scoring and feedback capabilities in classroom assessments may also gather more traction because of the increased participation from language teaching professionals in this debate. The coming decade may see a greater clarification with regard to the prominent validity issues and unique challenges in this context. However, debates will continue as to what constitutes acceptable performance for other applications of automated scoring (e.g., automated scoring used for medium-stakes purposes).

The use of automated scoring is expected to have considerable impact on how language abilities are defined, assessed, learned and taught. As language testers, we have the obligation to actively engage in validation research and practice, and to fully participate in cross-disciplinary conversations that inform best practices. Ultimately, it should be the human who harnesses the technology to realize its positive potential for users.

Further reading

Bennett, R. E. and Bejar, I. I. (1998). Validity and automated scoring: it's not only the scoring. *Educational Measurement: Issues and Practice* 17: 9–17. This article provides the first comprehensive treatment of automated scoring as an integral part of an assessment, which is a departure from seeing it as merely a substitute for human scoring. A central argument in this article is that automated scoring should be designed as a dynamic component in the assessment process, interacting with the construct definition, test and task design, test taker interface and reporting methods.

Clauser, B. E., Kane, M. T. and Swanson, D. B. (2002). Validity issues for performance-based tests scored with computer-automated scoring systems. *Applied Measurement in Education* 15: 413–32. This is the first attempt to integrate automated scoring into an argument-based validation framework, thus highlighting the complex and expanded effects that automated scoring may have on the overall validity argument for the entire assessment. It discusses potential validity threats to the strength of each inference in the validity argument that may be introduced by automated scoring, pointing to the critical research that is needed to discount or reduce the threats.

Kane, M. (2006). Validation. In R. L. Brennan (ed.), *Educational Measurement*, 4th ed. Washington, DC: American Council on Education/Praeger, 18–64. This chapter provides an excellent overview of the historical perspectives and the evolution of the concepts of validity, with a focus on the current widely-accepted argument-based approach to test validation. In this approach, a series of inferences that lead to score-based interpretations and decisions are articulated in an interpretive argument developed in the first stage. In the second stage, the plausibility of the interpretive argument is evaluated in terms of the relevance, sufficiency and strength of the evidence to support a validity argument.

Xi, X. (2010). Automated scoring and feedback systems—Where are we and where are we heading? *Language Testing* 27: 291–300. This introduction to a special issue offers a critical review of the research and development work in automated scoring and feedback systems for language assessment and learning. It raises a series of relevant validity questions for automated scoring and feedback systems respectively. These validity questions are linked to the inferences in the argument-based validation framework. It also provides a brief overview of the seven articles featured in the special issue.

References

Attali, Y., Bridgeman, B. and Trapani, C. (2010). Performance of a generic approach in automated essay scoring. *The Journal of Technology, Learning, and Assessment*, 10(3). www.jtla.org (accessed 10/11/10).

Bennett, R. E. (1993). On the meaning of constructed response. In R. E. Bennett and W. C. Ward (eds), *Construction versus Choice in Cognitive Measurement: Issues in Constructed Response, Performance Testing, and Portfolio Assessment*. Hillsdale, NJ: Lawrence Erlbaum Associates, 1–27.

Bennett, R. E. and Bejar, I. I. (1998). Validity and automated scoring: it's not only the scoring. *Educational Measurement: Issues and Practice* 17: 9–17.

Bernstein, J., Van Moere, A. and Cheng, J. (2010). Validating automated speaking tests. *Language Testing* 27: 355–77.

Chalhoub-Deville, M. (2001). Language testing and technology: Past and future. *Language Learning and Technology* 5: 95–97.

Chapelle, C. A. and Chung, Y.-R. (2010). The promise of NLP and speech processing technologies in language assessment [Special issue]. *Language Testing* 27: 301–15.

Chapelle, C. A., Enright, M. K. and Jamieson, J. M. (eds), (2008). *Building a Validity Argument for the Test of English as a Foreign Language^{TM}*. Mahwah, NJ: Lawrence Erlbaum.

Cheville, J. (2004). Automated scoring technologies and the rising influence of error. *English Journal* 93: 47–52.

Clauser, B. E., Kane, M. T. and Swanson, D. B. (2002). Validity issues for performance-based tests scored with computer-automated scoring systems. *Applied Measurement in Education* 15: 413–32.

Clauser, B. E., Swanson, D. B. and Clyman, S. G. (2000). A comparison of the generalizability of scores produced by expert raters and automated scoring systems. *Applied Measurement in Education* 12: 281–99.

Coombs, D. H. (1969). Review of the analysis of essays by computer by Ellis B. Page and Dieter H. Paulus. *Research in the Teaching of English* 3: 222–28.

Cureton, E. F. (1951). Validity. In E. F. Lindquist (ed.), *Educational Measurement*, 1st edn. Washington, DC: American Council on Education, 621–94.

Enright, M. K. and Quinlan, T. (2010). Complementing human judgment of essays written by English language learners with e-rater® scoring [Special issue]. *Language Testing* 27: 317–34.

Fitzgerald, K. R. (1994). Computerized scoring? A question of theory and practice. *Journal of Basic Writing* 13: 3–17.

Jamieson, J. (2005). Recent trends in computer-based second language assessment. *Annual Review of Applied Linguistics* 24: 228–42.

Kane, M. (1992). An argument-based approach to validity. *Psychological Bulletin* 112: 527–35.

—— (2002). Validating high-stakes testing programs. *Educational Measurement: Issues and Practice* 21: 31–35.

—— (2006). Validation. In R. L. Brennan (ed.), *Educational Measurement*, 4th edn. Washington, DC: American Council on Education/Praeger, 18–64.

Kane, M., Crooks, T. and Cohen, A. (1999). Validating measures of performance. *Educational measurement: Issues and Practice* 18: 5–17.

Kelly, P. A. (2001). *Automated scoring of essays: evaluating score validity*. Unpublished dissertation, Florida State University.

Landauer, T. K., Foltz, P. W. and Laham, D. (1998). An introduction to latent semantic analysis. *Discourse Processes* 25: 259–84.

Macrorie, K. (1969). Review of the analysis of essays by computer by Ellis B. Page and Dieter H. Paulus. *Research in the Teaching of English* 3: 222–36.

McNamara, T. F. (1996). *Measuring Second Language Performance*. London, UK: Longman.

Messick, S. (1995). Validity of psychological assessment: Validation of inferences from persons' responses and performances as scientific inquiry into score meaning. *American Psychologist* 50: 741–49.

Moss, P. A. (2003). Reconceptualizing validity for classroom assessment. *Educational Measurement: Issues and Practices* 22: 13–25.

Ockey, G. J. (2009). Developments and challenges in the use of computer-based testing for assessing second language ability. *The Modern Language Journal* 93: 836–47.

Page, E. B. (1966). The imminence of grading essays by computers. *Phi Delta Kappan* 47: 238–43.

—— (1994). Computer grading of student prose, using modern concepts and software. *Journal of Experimental Education* 62: 127–42.

Page, E. B. and Dieter, P. (1995). *The Analysis of Essays by Computer, Final Report of U.S. Office of Education Project No. 6–1318*, Storrs. CT: University of Connecticut. ERIC ED 028 633.

Page, E. B. and Petersen, N. S. (1995). The computer moves into essay grading: Updating the ancient test. *Phi Delta Kappan* 76: 561–65.

Pearson (2009). *PTE Academic Automated Scoring*. pearsonpte.com/research/Pages/AutomatedScoring.aspx (accessed 8/2/11).

Petersen N. S. (1997). *Automated scoring of writing essays: Can such scores be valid?* Paper presented at The Annual Meeting of the National Council on Education, Chicago, IL. March.

Powers, D. E., Bursterin, J., Chodorow, M. S., Fowles, M. E. and Kukich, K. (2002a). Comparing the validity of automated and human scoring of essays. *Educational Computing Research* 26: 407–25.

Powers, D. E., Burstein, J. C., Fowles, M. E. and Kukich, K. (2002b). Stumping e-rater: Challenging the validity of automated essay scoring. *Computer in Human Behavior* 18: 103–34.

Roy, E. L. (1993). Computerized scoring of placement exams: a validation. *Journal of Basic Writing* 12: 41–54.

Shermis, M. D., Koch, C. M., Page, E. B., Keith, T. Z. and Harrington, S. (1999). *Trait ratings for automated essay grading*. Paper presented at The Annual Meeting of National Council on Measurement in Education, Montreal, Canada, April.

Weigle, S. C. (2010). Validation of automated scores of TOEFL iBT tasks against non-test indicators of writing ability. *Language Testing* 27: 335–53.

Xi, X. (2008). What and how much evidence do we need? Critical considerations in validating an automated scoring system. In C. A. Chapelle, Y. R. Chung and J. Xu (eds), *Towards Adaptive CALL: Natural Language Processing for Diagnostic Language Assessment*. Ames, IA: Iowa State University, 102–14.

—— (2010). Automated scoring and feedback systems—Where are we and where are we heading? *Language Testing* 27: 291–300.

Xi, X., Schmidgall, J. and Wang, Y. (2011). *Examinee perceptions of automated scoring of speech and validity implications*. Paper presented at the Language Testing Research Colloquium, June. Michigan: Ann Arbor.

Xi, X., Higgins, D., Zechner, K. and Williamson, D. M. (2008). *Automated Scoring of Spontaneous Speech Using SpeechRater v1.0* (ETS Research Rep. No. RR-08-62). Princeton, NJ: ETS.

Yang, Y., Buckendahl, C. W., Juszkiewicz, P. J. and Bhola, D.S. (2002). A review of strategies for validating computer automated scoring. *Applied Measurement in Education* 15: 391–412.

Part IX
Ethics and language policy

Ethical codes and unexpected consequences

Alan Davies

Codes

Codes of ethics and of practice across all sectors have proliferated in recent years. This increase raises three questions:

1. Why has there been such a rapid increase?
2. Has the increase improved ethical standards?
3. Do the Codes provide protection for the profession from misuse of their products?

As part of its development as a profession, language testing has published several codes (Jia, 2009). In this chapter I will first consider these codes and then attempt answers to the three questions set out above, paying particular attention to the third question which is very much a current issue within the profession, involving, as it does, an ethical concern about the profession's own ethics.

If a Code of Ethics is 'a public statement by an organisation of its principled approach to its professional and/or business activities.' (Davies, 2005), a Code of Practice is less abstract and more concerned with everyday issues requiring behavioural judgments by language testers. It could be said that a code of practice instantiates the code of ethics, setting out in detail how it should be interpreted across the range of situations encountered by language testers. The term Standards or Code of Standards is also used (mainly in North America) as an alternative to Code of Ethics, thus a Code of Standards sets out the agreed upon rules of ethical conduct. There is a further confusion in that the terms Code of Ethics (or Standards) and Code of Practice are used in some contexts interchangeably. In this chapter the terms Code of Ethics and Code of Practice will be used in distinction from one another, the Code of Ethics to refer to the more abstract formulation and the Code of Practice to the more practical rules.

'Ethics codes', write Leach and Oakland (2007), 'are designed to protect the public by prescribing behaviors professionals are expected to exhibit'. And their spread is clear: 'of the two hundred largest corporations in the world, 52.5% have some sort of ethical code' (Helin and Sandstrom, 2007: 253). However, these same authors conclude at the end of a review of corporate codes of ethics: 'we still lack knowledge on how codes work, how they are communicated and how they are transformed inside organizations' (ibid: 253).

Language testing has in the last 30 years or so sought to professionalize itself. To that end, it has provided itself with both national and international professional associations such as the International Language Testing Association (ILTA, 2000, 2007), the Association of Language Testers of Europe (ALTE, 2000, 2001), the European Association for Language Testing and Assessment (EALTA, 2006), the Japan Language Testing Association (JALT, 2007), three regional associations in the USA, the Mid West Association of Language Testers (MWALT, 2010), the East Coast Organization of Language Testers (ECOLT, 2010) and the Southern California Association for Language Assessment Research (SCALAR, 2010).

> The basic concerns of language testing, that its work should be reliable, valid and practical and that it should take responsibility for its impact, fall on different sides of the two explanations for acting ethically. The first explanation is the deontological (following the philosopher, Kant) which takes account of its intrinsic value, the second is teleological (following the philosopher, Hobbes) which takes account only of consequences. Thus we could crudely align validity and practicality with the deontological explanation and reliability and impact with the teleological explanation, which means that we cannot choose between the deontological and the teleological because we must take account of both present value and of future effects.
>
> *(Davies, 2008)*

This claim is unlikely to be disputed – although the division between deontological and teleological may be queried. But the issue which needs discussion is what exactly is meant by impact. I come to this in the latter part of the chapter.

International Language Testing Association

When the International Language Testing Association (ILTA) was established in the early 1990s, one of the early projects was to develop a Code of Standards (also known as a Code of Practice). A draft Code was produced in 1997 but the project was not taken further, largely, it seems, because it appeared too difficult to agree on a single ILTA code. ILTA may have been a small organization but it had a global membership and therefore wished to reach agreement on a single – global – Code. Somewhat later the project was restarted. It was decided that in the first instance a Code of Ethics should be developed and not a Code of Practice on the grounds that it would be more abstract and therefore more likely to gain universal acceptance. The Code of Ethics was developed and accepted by ILTA in 2000.

Several years later, ILTA decided that a Code of Practice was also necessary. A new committee was established in 2003 to develop a Code of Practice for ILTA. The Japanese Association (JLTA) agreed to develop its own code and to share its thinking with ILTA. It would then be possible for ILTA either to develop the JLTA Code of Practice in full or amended form, or to consider an alternative if the JLTA Code was thought too local. Such an alternative might be to encourage local associations and groups to adopt their own Code of Practice in conformity to the ILTA Code of Practice, on the understanding that such local Codes of Practice would be submitted for approval by ILTA. In any event, the Code of Practice committee agreed to recommend to the ILTA AGM in Ottawa in 2005, that an amended version of the JLTA Code should be accepted. The draft was finally adopted as the ILTA Code of Practice in 2007.

As a global body, ILTA had a more difficult task in reaching this agreement than did EALTA or ALTE. It is true that both are Europe-wide bodies, but the intercultural links are probably less difficult to make than the global ones of ILTA.

The Codes of ALTE and EALTA are, in any case, quite different. ALTE, unlike both ILTA and EALTA, is an association of test/examination organizations and providers while ILTA and EALTA are both associations of individual language testers.

The ILTA Code of Ethics justifies itself thus:

> [it] … is a set of principles which draws upon moral philosophy and serves to guide good moral conduct. It is neither a statute nor a regulation, and it does not provide guidelines for practice, but it is intended to offer a benchmark of satisfactory ethical behaviours by all language testers.

It mentions sanctions and it makes clear that good professional behaviour is dependent on judgment; there are no formal rules and what the Code of Ethics relies on in the absence of sanctions is the willingness of ILTA members to act responsibly in accordance with the Code of Ethics because they are professionals. In other words, professional training and experience equip you to behave responsibly. Those who fall short may be stripped of their ILTA membership. That mirrors the procedure in, for example, law and medicine, but in those professions the sanctions are very much more effective. Without membership of the relevant legal and medical professional bodies it is not possible to practise as a lawyer or a doctor. That is just not the case in language testing where the sanctions are weak and not supported by statute or binding regulation. Thus there is nothing to prevent an ex-member of ILTA from continuing to practise as a language tester. While the law and medicine are strong professions, language testing is a weak profession where the burden of being professional is more an individual than a collective responsibility.

While the Code of Ethics stays aloof at the abstract level, the ILTA Code of Practice attempts to fill in the detail. Thus Principle 8 of the Code of Ethics states:

> language testers shall share the responsibility of upholding the integrity of the language testing profession.

which is followed by Part B of the Code of Practice, entitled:

> Responsibilities of test designers and test writers

followed by such detailed instructions as:

> Test materials should be kept in a safe place, and handled in such a way that no test taker is allowed to gain an unfair advantage over other test takers.

Association of Language Testers in Europe

The Association of Language Testers in Europe (ALTE) distinguishes between the responsibilities of ALTE members and the responsibilities of examination users. What ALTE members are enjoined to do is to follow orthodox language testing principles and procedures in the design of their tests, to publish those principles and procedures for test users, to interpret examination results for the benefit of test users and test takers, to take the necessary measures to ensure fairness and where necessary make appropriate accommodations on behalf of handicapped candidates and to provide candidates with full disclosure on the level and content of the examination and on the rights of candidates. The Code also sets out the responsibilities of examination users. This responsibility concerns the appropriate use of the information provided to the test users by the examination developers. I return to this component of the ALTE Code later when I consider Question 3 at the head of this chapter but it is hard to see how the ALTE organization can exercise control over test users – it is not clear how this could be implemented.

In recent years, ALTE have revised their Code of Practice as detailed questionnaires in the form of checklists. These self-assessment checklists are set out in the areas of test design and construction, administration, processing (marking, grading of results) and analysis and review. The questioning method is somewhat similar to the method employed in the EALTA Code, to which I come shortly. But it needs to be emphasized first that the rationale of the ALTE Code is quite different from that of the ILTA Code and Guidelines and indeed from the EALTA Code in that it presents ethics as a matter of professional test development, with particular reference – as is to be expected with a membership of test providers – to responsible and accountable test construction, delivery and analysis. It does, as noted earlier, embrace examination users (and of that more later). What is omitted from the ALTE Code is the individual language tester and the ethical questions s/he may pose. The ILTA and the EALTA Codes concern individual behaviours by members of their organisations; the basic question they pose to a member is: what is expected of me as a professional member of ILTA or EALTA? In contrast, the basic ALTE question is: what are the technical requirements of a responsible testing/examination organization?

European Association of Language Testing and Assessment

The European Association of Language Testing and Assessment (EALTA)'s mission statement is as follows:

> The purpose of EALTA is to promote the understanding of theoretical principles of language testing and assessment, and the improvement and sharing of testing and assessment practices throughout Europe.

EALTA's Guidelines for Good Practice are introduced thus:

> Reflecting its policy of inclusiveness, EALTA wishes to serve the needs of a very broad membership. EALTA's guidelines for good practice in testing and assessment are accordingly addressed primarily to three different audiences: those involved in (a) the training of teachers in testing and assessment, (b) classroom testing and assessment, and (c) the development of tests in national and institutional testing units or centres.

> For all these groups, a number of general principles apply: respect for the students/examinees, responsibility, fairness, reliability, validity and collaboration among the parties involved.

EALTA's own guidelines to good practice in language testing and assessment contain 71 questions addressed to EALTA members. They cluster under three main headings relevant to the three audiences set out in the rationale quoted above:

a.   considerations for teacher pre-service and in-service training in testing and assessment
b.   considerations for classroom testing and assessment
c.   considerations for test development in national or institutional testing units or centres

These EALTA Guidelines cover some of the same ground as found in the ILTA Guidelines for Practice and as in the ALTE Code. EALTA are less concerned than the ILTA Code of Ethics with ethical principles but they give wide coverage to ethical practices, although they do not consider the conflict of interest that language testers can find themselves in. They cover much of the same territory – albeit in terms of individual language testers – as the ALTE Code. The most striking difference of the EALTA Code is that it is wholly presented in question format. Does that mean that there is no EALTA view of appropriate conduct and behaviour of its members? The answer is probably no, since in many cases the expected response to a question in the Guidelines is fairly obvious, for example:

> C 3/2: 'Are the tests piloted?'

It would be a brave (misguided?) language tester who would answer 'no' that that question.

The EALTA questions, like the ALTE checklists, contain the issues that language testers need to think about and, where appropriate, act on. What they do not do, except in so far as the expected response is obvious and self-evident – is provide an account, a narrative to EALTA members – of what is normally expected, what type of ethical behaviour constitutes EALTA behaviour. There are two responses to this, the first is that by not providing a set of EALTA norms, there is allowance for a variety of legitimate replies which empower individual members. The second response is that this question format assumes that EALTA takes its professional responsibility seriously through its workshops, conferences and other meetings and its publications, thereby making clear to the members what the issues are and what responses could be expected from a serious member of the association. From that point of view, the 71 questions are indeed an aide-memoire, a checklist to make sure that all relevant matters have been taken care of.

American Educational Research Association

By way of comparison, I turn to the American Educational Research Association (AERA), which is a very much larger body than the three language testing organizations discussed so far. It is much broader in scope, although it does include testing and assessment within its brief. It is a very important organization and its Ethical Standards are influential.

The Standards (also referred to as the Code) contain six sections:

1. Responsibilities to the field
2. Research populations, educational institutions and the public
3. Intellectual ownership
4. Editing, reviewing and appraising research
5. Sponsors, policymakers and other uses of research
6. Students and student researchers

Two examples of these Standards follow:

> 2 B.8: Researchers should carefully consider and minimize the use of research techniques that might have negative consequences, for example, experimental interventions that might deprive students of important parts of the standard curriculum.

> 5 B.9: Educational researchers should disclose to appropriate parties all cases where they could stand to benefit financially from their research or cases where their affiliations might tend to bias their interpretation of their research or their professional judgments.

The Standards are intended

> to stimulate collegial debate and to evoke voluntary compliance by moral persuasion … it is not the intention of the Association to monitor adherence to the Standards or to investigate allegations of violation of the Code.

'[V]oluntary compliance by moral persuasion' could be read as the slogan/motto of all weak professions. The closest any of the organisations discussed here comes to asserting its strengths as a responsible and authorized professional body is the ILTA annotation to Principle 6:

> Failure to uphold this Code of Ethics will be regarded with the utmost seriousness and could lead to severe penalties, including withdrawal of ILTA membership.

These are fine and necessary words but it would be difficult to take action against an individual for not upholding the Code of Ethics – difficult to demonstrate and difficult to prove. And would an individual care, given that ILTA is a tiny and not hugely influential organization? AERA is influential but takes what is surely the more mature position on 'voluntary compliance by moral persuasion' – in other words putting the responsibility on professionals to act as professionals. No doubt, it would be desirable for ILTA and the other language testing associations to be stronger and to be in a position to impose sanctions on those members who fail to uphold their Code of Ethics. But for that to happen, it is first necessary for the external stakeholders to recognise their need for a trusted and authoritative and accountable organization.

Such development comes in two ways, first, from within, by pursuing the principles and procedures of good practice in developing, delivery, analysis and interacting with tests and clients (all included in the ALTE Code); and second, from without, through public awareness of their need for the services they can trust, and where they can obtain those services, which is the case for doctors and lawyers.

Three questions

I return now to the three questions I posed at the beginning of this chapter. The first is:

> 1. Why has there been such a rapid increase (in the publication of Codes of Ethics)?

It has been suggested that everyone today wants to be a professional, that every work activity now desires to professionalize itself for purposes of prestige and to secure greater control over those involved in the activity. Indeed, in Western societies it could be argued that the familiar distinction between professions and trade unions is now blurred. And as professions have multiplied, so have Codes of Ethics or Practice by the newer professions, anxious to claim their status as a profession and to do so in the public way that publishing a Code permits.

Siggins comments:

> Codes of ethics and codes of practice have multiplied without pause in the last decades of this century, not only in the professions but in business, industry and social services, largely in response to the successful growth of consumer movements and their demand for accountability to the public interest.
>
> *(Siggins, 1996: 53)*

Siggins goes on to explain that those commercial activities that have issued codes are wholly concerned 'to acknowledge legal and moral rights of their customers and their duty towards them' (ibid.). Codes of the learned professions, on the other hand, have always 'declared the virtue and competence of the select members of a distinguished class' (ibid.).

The concept of a 'code' takes its origin in the oath taken in law and medicine.

> When in the nineteenth century, medical associations in Britain, the US, Australia and elsewhere called their corporate ethical standards 'code of ethics', they intended to echo the prescriptive force of this usage to express what the Hippocratic oath had already called the 'law of medicine' (ibid.: 156). The learned professions' use of codes always differed from the more recent commercial use by their declaration of the virtue and competence of their members who are 'select members of a distinguished class'
>
> *(Siggins, 1996: 55)*

For language testers, caught up in their rush to professionalize, the question has been: is language testing a 'learned' profession or a social/commercial activity? The answer has to be that it is both: for those members who are academics, they see themselves as belonging to a learned profession, while those in more business-like bodies regard themselves (or perhaps their organisations) as more commercial. To an extent, this explains the difference between the ILTA/EALTA codes (more learned profession) and the ALTE Code (more business-oriented).

2. Has the increase in Codes improved ethical standards?

    There is no easy answer to this question. What can be said is that:

    > A professional grouping risks being characterised as unethical if it does not now espouse a set of principles enshrined in a Code of Ethics
    >
    > *(Freckelton, 1996: 131)*

What a code does is to clarify to the members of the profession what it stands for – it acts as a unifying statement; at the same time, it makes clear to the public what may be expected of members of this profession. It is, indeed, a modern version of an oath.

But codes have their critics, that they are elitist and exclusive, that they are hypocritical by claiming what no-one in reality practises, that they act as good public relations and that they provide the profession with a moral screen to hide behind; once the code has been published, it can be set aside and ignored while 'professional' practice continues as brokenly as before.

It is necessary to emphasize that a Code of Ethics or Practice, or Guidelines for Practice or Ethical Standards are not rules and they are certainly not laws. The most we can expect of them is that they 'make a contribution to improving behaviour in the areas they deal with' (Coady, 1996: 287). Where there are sanctions leading to loss of membership and subsequent inability to practise the profession (as in law and medicine), then the Code comes nearer to a law. But this is not possible for most professions, and it is not possible, so far, for language testing.

3. Do the Codes provide protection for the profession from misuse of their products?

    > [T]ests are not developed or used in a value-free psychometric test-tube; they are virtually always intended to serve the needs of an educational system or of society at large. Cronbach (1984) has succinctly stated this fact as follows: testing of abilities has always been intended as an impartial way to perform a political function – that of determining who gets what.
    >
    > *(Bachman, 1990: 279–80)*

And Spolsky has no doubt about the main purpose of tests: 'From the beginning, public tests and examinations were instruments of policy' (Spolsky, 2009: vii).

Tests, then, are used for political purposes, language tests as much as, perhaps more than, other tests, because they perform a social function. Those who use tests are being political: the question I address in this section is who makes those political decisions about the use of language tests, and to what extent those language testers who develop tests are responsible, ethically if not legally, for that use (Shohamy, 2001).

Fulcher and Davidson (2007) agree with Messick (1989) that decisions about test use need to be considered in terms of their consequences, very much a teleological approach:

> The intention of a decision should be to maximize the good for the democratic society in which we live, and all the individuals within it. We may define any test as its consequences.
>
> *(Fulcher and Davidson, 2007: 142–3)*

But tests, like every other action, have both intended and unintended consequences. Must a test be judged only by its intended consequences? That, after all, is the nature of validity. Tests are developed for a particular purpose, for a particular audience. But what about unintended consequences? Are language testers, ethically (if not legally) responsible for the unintended consequences of the tests they develop? What does taking responsibility for one's actions mean? If I write a book, how far does my responsibility for its use go? If the book is a ghost story, can I be responsible if a reader has nightmares after reading my book? If the book is a biography of a famous religious leader, am I responsible for the actions of devotees who burn my book and attack my family?

In the case of the infamous Dictation test (Davies, 2004; McNamara, 2006), employed in Australia in the first half of the twentieth century for the purpose of excluding unwanted immigrants, those who developed the test like those who used it were clearly responsible, ethically responsible, because its explicit use as a method of exclusion was intended. Bachman and Palmer (2010) balance the demands on the test developer and the test user and make no mention of unintended test use. This is only to be expected, given the comments by Fulcher and Davidson (2007):

> ... an unintended use may take one of two forms: (1) an unintended use that the test developers do not know about or do not approve of, or (2) an unintended use that the test developers know about and approve of... Both are equally invalid unless a new argument is constructed for the new testing purpose and evidence collected to show that the retro-fitting is valid, so that the same test may be shown to be useful in a new decision-making context ... retrofitting test purpose without the construction and investigation of a new validity and utilization argument constitutes an implicit claim that any test can be used for any purpose, which is to introduce validity chaos.
>
> *(ibid.: 175)*

McNamara and Roever (2006) consider a range of language tests used for establishing social identity, ranging from the celebrated biblical story of the shibboleth (Lado, 1949; McNamara, 2005; Spolsky, 1995) to present-day language tests used to determine the claims of asylum seekers. They write:

> The politics and ethics of the use of these tests are complex... The procedures involved are widely used in Europe, Australia and elsewhere in the pioneering of claims of undocumented

asylum seekers … the lack of validity considerations in their implementation leads to serious injustice, a situation that would be remedied in large part by attention to the quality of the testing procedure.

(McNamara and Roever, 2006: 165)

The objection, then, that McNamara and Roever have to these procedures, which involve assessing whether the claimant really does come from the country which s/he claims to come from by matching his/her accent/dialect to that country or region, is in terms of their validity. They criticize the sociolinguistic construct which all too commonly assumes a homogeneity of accent/dialect where none exists and they criticize the methods used in the assessment. In other words, they have no objection to the testing of asylum seekers to determine their honesty. This is what they write:

Although some applied linguists and language testers have objected to the use of such procedures altogether, it is reasonable to think that the evidence that they provide, when that evidence is properly obtained and interpretable, might be as useful in supporting a valid claim to asylum as in denying an invalid one.

(ibid.: 172)

McNamara and Roever refer to the guidelines for the proper use of language analysis in relation to questions of national origin in refugee status (Language and National Origin Group, 2004). Where does this leave their assertion, already quoted, that 'the politics and ethics of these tests are complex' (p. 165)?

The politics of their argument is straightforward: it concerns the national decision to offer asylum only to those who are genuine refugees and to exclude those who aren't. The implementation of that intention in the procedures they discuss is a matter of validity and, as they show, they fail that test. Where, then, are the ethical concerns? Presumably they have to do with the use of such procedures and are a judgment on the exclusion measures. As McNamara and Roever have shown, there is no agreement on this in the language testing profession – and it may be (as the ILTA Code of Ethics makes clear) that while the profession accepts the need for such testing, which is, after all, quite legal, there will be acceptance of those individuals in the profession who choose not to participate on grounds of conscience. So are these tests ethical? It would seem that, according to McNamara and Roever, they are potentially externally valid but they lack internal ethicality, that is they are not valid.

Related to the choice of code in which to test asylum seekers is the wider question of the World Englishes speakers. For the most part, first language tests in education make use of a standard code: they do not provide a range of assessment according to regional and national varieties. And for World Englishes, the practice is similar, except that the standard selected is a metropolitan one. Thus to test the English of schoolchildren in, say, Singapore, the model will be the Standard English of the UK. The same holds for international English language proficiency tests such as TOEFL and IELTS. And although postcolonial voices are heard to object to what seems a continuation of colonial hegemony, it does appear that World Englishes speakers and their education authorities do not object. Institutional uses require formal arrangements, they require norms and standards, including a standard language which is clear to everyone. Using Standard English in these situations is not unethical as long as World English communities do not desire change. Such change to local norms will come about only when the speech community itself accepts its dialect or vernacular as the new standard (Haugen, 1966; Davies, 2009).

Can a language test be fair and is fairness an ethical consideration? McNamara and Roever (2006) discuss fairness in the context of the ETS Fairness Review Guidelines (ETS, 2003) and of the various Codes of Ethics and Practice discussed earlier. They recognize the difficulty of setting a global norm for fairness (ibid.: 137). Fairness, McNamara and Roever propose, is a professional obligation. If fairness is an ethical component, they are right. But what exactly is fairness? Examining Rawls (2001) on fairness and justice, Davies (2010) argues that in language testing it is validity rather than fairness which must be the criterion:

> A test that is valid for group A (say adults) cannot be valid for group B (say children) because they belong to different populations. It is not whether such a test is fair or unfair for group B: the test is just invalid for group B. The search for test fairness is chimerical.
>
> *(Davies, 2010: 175)*

This leads back to the earlier discussion on language testing for asylum seekers and raises the issue of language tests for citizenship. The proposed UK legislation for pre-entry language tests was debated in the House of Lords on 25 October 2010. Briefing points were quoted from Adrian Blackledge of the University of Birmingham who argued that such tests were not valid for purpose. Charles Alderson was also mentioned in the debate. He commented that:

> the UK Border Agency's August 2010 list of approved providers of the English test has been developed by unknown agencies with absolutely no evidence of their validity, reliability etc.
>
> *(Hansard, 2010: 1101,1102)*

These two critics approach the issue from the two different ethical positions discussed earlier, one from the point of view of ethics for use (no test for this purpose could be valid) and the other from the point of view of the internal validity of the test (this test lacks the necessary requirements of a language test). Alderson appears to claim, unlike Blackledge, but like McNamara and Roever on the testing of asylum seekers – that such a test could be ethical if it were a satisfactory test.

The moral philosopher, Peter Singer, contends:

> what is it to make moral judgments or to argue about an ethical issue or to live according to ethical standards? Why do we regard a woman's decision to have an abortion as raising an ethical issue but not her decision to change her job?
>
> *(Singer, 2002: 13)*

Singer's answer is the golden rule: an ethical belief or action or decision is one that is based on a belief that it is right to do what is being done. Ethics, Singer argues, is a set of social practices that has a purpose, namely the promotion of the common welfare. 'Moral reasoning, therefore, is simply a matter of trying to find out what is best for everyone, achieving the good of everyone alike – the golden mean' (Davies, 2004: 98).

Professional ethics, therefore, is about the ethics of the profession, not about morality which is a matter for the individual. In becoming a member of a profession, the new entrant agrees to uphold the ethics of the group – with which his/her own conscience may not always agree. The various Codes (of Ethics, of Practice, of Standards …) make public what it is members are prepared to agree to, what it is they 'swear' by, and they reach this agreement through compromise. They accept responsibility for the development of the language tests they work on and for the intended consequences of those tests. But they do not accept responsibility for any unintended consequences. Nor should they.

The prisoner's dilemma in game theory presents the role, both theoretical and practical, of ethics, placing the emphasis on the importance of being unselfish:

> Two prisoners, A and B, are arrested for complicity in the commission of a crime (they are in fact both guilty). They are put in cells between which no communication is possible and then offered a deal. The deal is as follows:
>
> 1. If A confesses and B does not (or vice versa) then A is released and B gets ten years.
> 2. If both A and B confess they each get five years in prison.
> 3. If neither confesses, they each get one year in prison.

The best (selfish) strategy for A is to confess. Then, if B does not confess, B gets ten years and A is released. However, A does not know what B will do: it is possible that B will also confess, in which case, they both get five years. The best strategy might therefore not work, indeed it could work to A's disadvantage. The best result would be obtained if neither A nor B confesses. However, this is still risky as a strategy for A since B may confess, in which case A would get ten years and B be released. What is necessary is for both A and B to think not of the best strategy for themselves alone (the selfish approach) but of the best outcome for them both (for 'the profession'). If they each take concern for the other then neither will confess, in which case they will both get one year (Davies, 1997: 329–330).

Discussing this dilemma, Scriven (1991) concludes:

> The only solution is through prior irreversible commitment to treat the welfare of each other as comparable to their own, and this reflects the reason for ethical training of the young. Being ethical comes at a cost to oneself (both A and B would have to go to prison for one year) but for the group/society/company/profession etc., the cost is worth while since an ethical society has better survival rate value than a society of rational egoists.
>
> *(Scriven, 1991: 276)*

Codes do not protect the profession from misuse. This is surely a matter for the law and would require some kind of legal measure to protect misuse. A Code presents the commitment of the profession as a whole to professional behaviour by its members and it has nothing to say about the actions of non-members. Of course, misuse by members is taken care of: this is implicit *passim* in the ILTA Code of Ethics and explicit in Principle 9:

> Language testers shall regularly consider the potential effects, both short and long term on all stakeholders of their projects, reserving the right to withdraw their professional services on the grounds of conscience.

And the ILTA Code of Practice offers advice in (D), entitled:

> Obligations of those preparing and administering publicly available tests.

and in (E), entitled:

> Responsibility of users of test results.

These are worthy attempts but remain advisory rather than admonitory. What control does ILTA have over unscrupulous test users?

ALTE has a major section entitled:

Responsibility of examination users.

It may be that the members of ALTE are in a stronger position than the members of ILTA or EALTA in that they can embargo an errant user and prevent him/her from using their products or name. They can do this because of their individual power and prestige (such as Cambridge ESOL) not because of the strength of ALTE.

EALTA has an entry on Washback (Alderson *et al.*, 1995; Hamp-Lyons, 1989) and so there is concern for test use by EALTA members. AERA comes close to a concern for the use of its research by non-members, writing in section VB4 of 'improper influence' and of 'research that conflicts with academic freedom'. But in none of these limited cases is there protection for the profession: righteous indignation, yes, but not constructive sanction.

The ALTE Code does show concern for the effects of ALTE made tests on examination users so again there is advice to members that they should be concerned about impact. EALTA, as has already been noted, mentions washback. Once again, as with misuse, these Associations have proper concern for the possible effect of their tests but no control over it.

Conclusions and future directions

So what are the Codes for, what is their value, what is their role?

What they do is limited. They are not a set of rules, not a legal document. What they are is a promise, an oath, to which members bind themselves, a way of asserting and claiming fraternity and sorority, not in secret but in public. But the onus is on individual members to demonstrate their professionalism, their status as professionals by adherence to the Code. Paradoxically, while the ethics are group related, their upholding is a matter for individual morality.

As for responsibility for test use, this must be limited, as Fulcher and Davidson (2007) point out, to the purpose for which the designer has validated the test. Where does this leave tests for asylum and citizenship, and the use by government agencies of invalid tests (ILPA, 2010)? In the case of the first (asylum and citizenship) what is ethical in language testing – what the Codes require – is that the tests should be properly designed, valid for their purpose. The profession does not oppose such tests. However, as ILTA Code of Ethics Principle 9 quoted above make clear, while not opposing such tests, the profession does not require members to take part in their construction if they have a conscientious objection against them. The imposition of such tests is a political matter and the Codes have nothing to say about politics. What is ethical for the profession is not necessarily moral for every individual member. In the case of the second (government use of invalid tests) the Codes again insist that it is professionally irresponsible to use invalid tests. However, correct though that argument is, it can succeed only if government and other agencies are willing to heed professional advice. Otherwise, like the Australian government's attitude to the Dictation Test, what decides is politics and not ethics.

Further reading

Davies, A. (1997). Demands of being professional in language testing. *Language Testing* 14: 328–39. The need for a professional ethic in addition to public and individual moralities is proposed and its importance to individual members and other stakeholders is explained. Given the weakness of sanctions for a social science profession, such as Language Testing, what members can do is create an 'ethical milieu' through professional training and professional activities (forming an association, establishing journals and web pages, issuing codes of ethics and practice, developing qualifications). Such explicitness shows both the reach and the limits of the profession's ethics.

Freckleton, I. (1996). Enforcement of ethics. In M. Coady and S. Bloch (eds), *Codes of Ethics and the Professions*. Carlton, Victoria: Melbourne University Press, 130–65. The whole Coady and Bloch volume, which contains this chapter by Freckleton, is an essential point of reference for consideration of codes of ethics. Freckleton considers the difficult issue of sanctions. He insists that professions require sanctions; professionals who behave unethically 'can be denounced and they can be punished by being suspended from practice' (p. 165). How far Freckleton has weak professions in mind is unclear. However, it is encouraging that he allows for the possibility of rehabilitation, tempering justice with mercy.

McNamara, T. and C. Roever (2006). *Language Testing: the Social Dimension*. Oxford, UK: Blackwell Publishing. The book provides a comprehensive overview of the social consequences of language testing. Chapter 5 ('Fairness Reviews and Codes of Ethics') is of particular relevance to my paper. McNamara and Roever take a usefully critical view of codes of ethics, arguing that language testing should adopt the AERA's 'Standards for Educational and Psychological Testing' which, they maintain, are far more specific than any of the current language testing codes. Even so, the authors accept that 'codes of ethics are important steps in strengthening the identity of language testing as a profession' (p. 147). Codes of ethics provide a 'moral framework for testers' work' (ibid).

Rawls, J. (2001). *Justice as Fairness: A Restatement*. Cambridge, MA: Harvard University Press. Rawls puts forward two principles. The first is that everyone has the same claim to the basic liberties. The second is that where there are inequalities, they must satisfy two conditions, that offices and positions must be open to everyone on the basis of equality of opportunity, and that the least advantaged members of society should benefit more from these inequalities. In other words, what justice does is to ensure that those who lose out through that very equality of opportunity will be accorded positive discrimination. The strength of Rawls's very influential argument is that he ties fairness to an ideal legal system which provides justice.

References

AERA (1992). *Ethical Standards*. www.aera.net. (accessed 10/30/10).

Alderson, J. C., Clapham, C. and Wall, D. (1995). *Language Test Construction and Evaluation*. Cambridge, UK: Cambridge University Press.

ALTE: Association of Language Testers in Europe (2001). Principles of good practice for ALTE examinations. www.alte.org (accessed 10/30/10).

Bachman, L. F. (1990). *Fundamental Considerations in Language Testing*. Oxford, UK: Oxford University Press.

Bachman, L. F. and Palmer, A. (2010). *Language Assessment in Practice*. Oxford, UK: Oxford University Press.

Coady, C. A. J. (1996). On regulating ethics. In M. Coady and S. Bloch (eds), *Codes of Ethics and the Professions*. Melbourne: Melbourne University Press: 269–87.

Cronbach, L. J. (1984). *Essentials of Psychological Testing*, 4th edn. New York, NY: Harper and Row.

Davies, A. (1997). Demands of being professional in language testing. *Language Testing* 14: 328–39.

—— (2004). Introduction: Language testing and the golden rule. *Language Assessment Quarterly* 1–3: 97–107.

—— (2005). *A Glossary of Applied Linguistics*. Edinburgh, UK: Edinburgh University Press; and Mahwah, NJ: Lawrence Erlbaum Associates.

—— (2008). Ethics, professionalism, rights and codes. In E. Shohamy and N. H. Hornberger (eds), *Encyclopedia of Language and Education*, 2nd edn. Vol. 7. *Language Testing and Assessment*. New York, NY: Springer Science + Business Media, 429–43.

—— (2009). Assessing World Englishes. *Annual Review of Applied Linguistics* 29: 80–89.

—— (2010). Test fairness: a response. *Language Testing* 27: 171–76.

EALTA. European Association for Language Testing and Assessment (2006). *EALTA Guidelines for Good Practice in Language Testing and Assessment*. www.ealta.eu.org (accessed 10/30/10).

ECOLT (2010). Validity, Opportunities and Challenges. www.cal.org/ecolt (accessed 8/2/11).

ETS (Educational Testing Service) (2003). *Fairness Review Guidelines*. Princeton, NJ. www.ets.org/Media (accessed 8/2/11).

Freckelton, I. (1996). Enforcement of ethics. In M. Coady and S. Bloch (eds), *Codes of Ethics and the Professions*. Melbourne, Australia: Melbourne University Press, 130–65.

Fulcher, G. and Davidson, F. (2007). *Language Testing and Assessment: an advanced resource book*. London, UK: Routledge.

Hamp-Lyons, L. (1989). Language testing and ethics. *Prospect* 5: 7–15.

Hansard. (2010). 25 October. (1101), (1102) (ILPA) (2010). www.publications.parliament.uk/pa/cm/cmse (0910).htm (accessed April 2011).

Haugen, E. (1966). Dialect language, nation. *American Anthropologist* 68: 922–35.

Helin, S. and Sandstrom, J. (2007). An inquiry into the study of corporate codes of ethics. *Journal of Business Ethics* 75: 253–71.

ILPA: Immigration Law Practitioners' Association (2010). House of Lords Motion re: Statement of Changes in Immigration Rules (Cm (7944)) 25 October (2010). www.ilpa.org.uk (accessed 30/10/10).

ILTA (2000)a. *Code of Ethics for ILTA* (CoE). www.iltaonline.com (accessed 30/10/10).

—— (2000)b. *ILTA Guidelines for Practice* (CoP). www.iltaonline.com (accessed on 30/10/10).

JALT (2010). jalt.org/test/join.htm (accessed 8/2/11).

Jia, Y. (2009). Ethical standards for language testing professionals: a comparative analysis of five major codes. *Shiken: JALT Testing and Evaluation SIG Newsletter* 13: 2–8.

Lado, R. (1949). *Measurement in English as a Foreign Language*. Unpublished doctoral dissertation. University of Michigan, Ann Arbor.

Language and National Origin Group (2004). Guidelines for the use of language analysis in relation to questions of national origin in refugee cases. *The International Journal of Speech, Language and the Law* 11: 261–166.

Leach, M. M. and Oakland, T. (2007). Ethical standards impacting test development and use: a review of 31 ethical codes impacting practices in 35 countries. *International Journal of Testing* 7: 71–88.

McNamara, T. (2005). 21st century shibboleth: Language tests, identity and intergroup conflict. *Language Policy* 4: 1–20.

—— (2006). Validity in language testing: the challenge of Sam Messick's legacy. *Language Assessment Quarterly* 3: 31–51.

McNamara, T. and Roever, C. (2006). *Language Testing: The Social Dimension*. Oxford, UK: Blackwell Publishing Ltd.

Messick, S. (1989). Validity. In R. L. Linn (ed.), *Educational Measurement*, 3rd edn. Washington, DC: The American Council on Education and the National Council on Measurement in Education, 13–103.

MWALT (2010). mwalt.public.iastate.edu (accessed 8/2/2011).

Rawls, J. (2001). *Justice as Fairness: a restatement*. Cambridge, MA: Harvard University Press.

SCALAR (2010). scalarActivities.googlepages.com (accessed 8/2/2011).

Scriven, M. (1991). *Evaluation Thesaurus*, 4th edn. Newbury Park, CA: Sage.

Shohamy, E. (2001). *The Power of Tests*. Harlow, UK: Pearson Education.

Siggins, I. (1996). Professional codes: some historical antecedents. In M. Coady and S. Bloch (eds), *Codes of Ethics and the Professions*. Melbourne, Australia: Melbourne University Press, 55–71.

Singer, P. (2002). *Writings on an Ethical Life*. New York, NY: Harper Collins.

Spolsky, B. (1995). *Measured Words*. Oxford, UK: Oxford University Press.

—— (2009). Editor's Introduction. *Annual Review of Applied Linguistics* Vol. 29. *Language Policy and Language Assessment*: vii–xii.

32

Fairness

F. Scott Walters

Introduction

Among language testing researchers, the notion of *fairness* has accumulated a number of complex, technical definitions over the years. However, since the word has such a widespread, everyday usage, consulting a dictionary can be a good starting-point for discussion. For example, Your-Dictionary.com (2011) states that to be *fair* is to be "just and honest," "impartial," and "unprejudiced," specifically, "free from discrimination based on race, religion, sex, etc." Merriam-Webster (Mish *et al.*, 2003) states similarly that fairness is "marked by impartiality or honesty" and is "free from self-interest, prejudice, or favoritism." As this volume deals with second/foreign/other language testing, it would seem appropriate (or perhaps one should say, *fair*) to include a dictionary definition crafted for L2 learners, as is this one from Cambridge (Walter *et al.*, 2006): "Treating someone in a way that is right or reasonable, or treating a group of people equally and not allowing personal opinions to influence your judgment."

Such common-sense notions can be contrasted with more technical definitions, which, as mentioned above, can actually be somewhat complex (Camilli, 2006). In fact, the various technical definitions of fairness proposed by language testing scholars evince sharp differences as well as overlap. For example, Kunnan (2000) argues that fairness embraces three concerns: validity, accessibility of tests to test takers, and justice. Spaan (2000) first defines fairness as an ideal "in which opportunities are equal," but then argues that "in the natural world, test writers and developers cannot be 'fair' in the ideal sense, but … they can try to be equitable." This equitability is "the joint responsibility of the test developer, the test user, and the examinee, in a sort of social contract" (Spaan, 2000: 35). Not only do language testing scholars disagree somewhat on the meaning of the word, but L2 test takers can have variable and fluid views of L2 testing fairness as well. For example, Jang reports on a study into "folk fairness" among English as a second language (ESL) learners (2002). She provides evidence that "fairness is not derived [psychometrically] from a test itself, but it is constructed, interpreted and practiced in different ways by various stake holders." Davies (2010) argues that in a language testing context achieving "fairness" is impossible and even unnecessary. The purpose of this chapter will be to accommodate and to discuss such differences and similarities of conceptualization in an orderly way for those with an interest in language testing.

Fairness can be seen as a *system* or *process* – as distinct from a quality. In contrast, *ethics* is a broader concept than fairness; indeed, language testers can be seen generally as understanding ethics as being broader than fairness (e.g., Xi, 2010). For the purposes of this chapter, *fairness* will be understood as something that may, but not necessarily, be synonymous with justice, and may be subsumed under the broader concept of ethics. Nevertheless, it will be seen that although fairness can be so subsumed, formulations of the concept by language testing researchers are not simple.

What is fairness?

What most language testing views of fairness have in common is a desire to avoid the effects of any *construct-irrelevant factors* on the entire testing process, from the test-design stage through post-administration decision-making. The word *construct* may be understood as referring to a piece of knowledge or skill that a test taker may (or may not) possess and which we might be interested in testing for; an example would be ESL oral proficiency. However, certain factors, such as an unconscious bias by a rater against certain non-native accents, may be said to be *irrelevant* to the construct, and might distort the test results. Thus, *not* eliminating the effects of these phenomena on the testing process could result in an administration or use of a test that is unfair.

In this context, one dimension of fairness concerns the *roles* of the major stakeholders in achieving language testing fairness. These stakeholders, to use Spaan's (2000) tripartite "social-contract" scheme, are test developers, L2/FL learners, and test users (i.e., teachers, administrators, etc.). The role of test developers is manifold. They must try to ensure the validity, reliability, and practicality of their test methods. They must also provide test users with easily under-standable guidelines for the use of their tests. Moreover, since test developers are engaged in a social contract with test users and test takers, they must also solicit feedback *from* them, to effect further test improvements. In this social contract, Spaan points out that test takers have a role to play in test fairness as well: They must become familiar with the testing format and overall test content before taking the test, and they must also try to make sure that the level of the test matches their own skill/knowledge level. Finally, test administrators must give tests to students for whom the tests were designed; to do otherwise would be an instance of test abuse.

Viewing test developer, test taker, and test user as parties to a social contract highlights a second issue, namely the phenomenon of *power relations* in testing. Shohamy (2001) points out that language tests have often been used by powerful agencies such as governments, educational bureaucracies, or school staff for reasons other than the assessment of language skills. For example, tests have been used to establish discipline, to impose sanctions on schools or teachers, or to raise the prestige of the subject matter being tested. She offers a set of principles organized under the heading of *critical language testing*, as a way to engage language testers "in a wider sphere of social dialogue and debate about ... the roles tests ... have been assigned to play in society" (Shohamy, 2001: 132–33). One principle is that critical language testing "encourages test takers to develop a critical view of tests as well as to act on it by questioning tests and critiquing the value which is inherent in them." She also "calls for a need to question the purposes and actual uses of tests. Are they intended to measure and assess knowledge or are they used to define and dictate knowledge?" (Shohamy, 2001: 131–32). Such extra-linguistic purposes may even be at variance with purposes stated in official policy documents. A critical language testing perspective asks that all parties to the contract remain vigilant.

Approaches to language testing fairness have evolved over the years. Traditionally, fairness has been conceived relatively narrowly in testing, with a focus being a concern for fairness in the construction of test questions; accordingly, this traditional view is rather technical. Although this view has been somewhat supplanted, it is useful to review it, because it is still part of the landscape of language test development.

From this technical perspective, one approach to examining whether or not test questions are fair is through a *test sensitivity review*. Such reviews are performed by trained judges employed by test-development organizations, who examine test tasks to determine whether they contain language or content that may be considered stereotyping, patronizing, inflammatory, or otherwise offensive to test takers belonging to subgroups defined by culture, ethnicity, or gender (AERA/APA/NCME, 1999: 82). An offensive test prompt may adversely affect test-taker performance on such an item. Often such biases in language are subtle (Ramsey, 1993), which is why a panel of experts is needed.

Another concept related to fairness in test questions is *test bias*. This is a technical term indicating a testing situation in which a particular test use results in different interpretations of test scores received by cultural, ethnic, gender, or linguistic subgroups (AERA/APA/NCME, 1999: 81). A frequent synonym for test bias is *differential item functioning*, or DIF. Bias or DIF is considered to be present when a test item is differentially difficult for an ethnic, cultural, or gender-related subgroup which is otherwise equally matched with another subgroup in terms of knowledge or skill (Willingham and Cole, 1997). Among the statistical methods used to uncover DIF are the Standardization Procedure (Dorans and Kulick, 1986) and the Mantel–Haenszel method (Holland and Thayer, 1988).

More recently, however, researchers have tended to conceptualize fairness rather more broadly and less technically than have earlier testing researchers, crucially with regard to its relationship with validity. Kane (2010) points out that the relationship between fairness and validity depends on how the two concepts are defined: Narrowly defining validity and broadly defining fairness will result in validity being considered a component of fairness. On the other hand, a broad definition of validity and a narrow conceptualization of fairness will result in fairness being understood as a part of validity. Such considerations are non-trivial. In fact, arriving at an understanding of fairness in relation to validity is essential, as validity is "the most fundamental consideration in developing and evaluating tests" (AERA/APA/NCME, 1999: 9).

Xi (2010) points out that some researchers regard fairness as a test characteristic that is *independent* of validity. One example of this is the *Standards for Educational and Psychological Testing* (AERA/APA/NCME, 1999) which define it as having, at minimum, three components: lack of item bias, the presence of equitable treatment of all test-takers in the testing process, and equity of opportunity of examinees to learn the material on a given test. While fairness here is not linked directly with validity, these 1999 *Standards* do mention that fairness "promotes the validity and reliability of inferences made from test performance" (AERA/APA/NCME, 1999: 85). Another example is the *Code of Fair Testing Practices in Education* (2004). This Code focuses on the respective responsibilities of test developers and test users to ensure fairness by engaging in a sort of dialogue. In this dialogue, the test developer provides "evidence that the technical quality, including reliability and validity, of the test meets its intended purposes." On the other hand, the test users "[e]valuate evidence of the technical quality of the test provided by the test developer and any independent reviewers" (Code, sect. A-5). Briefly, test developers and test users must exercise fairness in four major areas of the testing process – creating and selecting tests, administering and scoring them, reporting and interpreting results, and providing certain information to test takers. Such information should include "the nature of the test, test taker rights and responsibilities, the appropriate use of scores, and procedures for resolving challenges to scores." While fairness is considered to be "a primary consideration in all aspects of testing," it is "not an isolated concept, but must be considered in all aspects of the testing process" (Code, introductory section).

Another approach to conceptualizing language testing fairness, as Xi (2010) further points out, is as an all-embracing concept that *subsumes* validity. Kunnan (2000) articulates a framework in which fairness includes issues of validity, accessibility to test takers, and justice. Under *validity*, Kunnan includes issues such as construct validity, DIF, insensitive test-item language, and content bias. An example of the latter might be a dialect of English employed in the test prompts that differs in some respects from another English dialect that may constitute the L2 of the test taker. Under *accessibility*, Kunnan indicates issues such as affordability, geographic proximity of test taker to the testing site, accommodations for test takers with disabilities, and opportunity to learn. "Opportunity to learn" is closely connected with the notion of *construct under-representation* (Messick, 1989), which indicates the ability of a test to measure some aspects of a construct or skill, but not others. A test may be measuring aspects of a construct, such as knowledge of a particular rule of language pragmatics, that certain test takers will not have had the opportunity to learn and thus score poorly on the test, despite the fact that they may be proficient in other relevant areas of the construct. Finally, Kunnan's facet of *justice* embraces the notion of whether or not a test contributes to social equity. Kunnan (2004) later modified this model to include absence of bias, and test-administration conditions.

A third approach, that of Kane (2010), sees fairness and validity as *overlapping* concepts, neither being completely included within the other, but as closely-related ways of considering the same issue. Kane's definition of test fairness draws on political and legal concepts. One, *procedural due process*, states that the same rules should be applied to everyone in more or less the same way. Kane also bases his definition on *substantive due process*, which states that the procedures applied should be reasonable both in general and in the context in which they are applied. In applying this twin-definition of fairness to assessment, Kane gives two principles: The first is *procedural fairness*, in which test takers are treated "in essentially the same way ... take the same test or equivalent tests, under the same conditions or equivalent conditions, and ... their performances [are] evaluated using the same (or essentially the same) rules and procedures." The second is *substantive fairness*, in which the score interpretation and any test-based decision rule are reasonable and appropriate for all test takers (Kane 2010: 178).

A fourth conceptualization, articulated by Willingham and Cole (1997), views fairness as "an important aspect of test validity" and more specifically, as *comparable validity* for all test takers and test-taker groups (Willingham and Cole, 1997: 6–7). In this context, a fair test is one for which both the (preferably, small) extent of statistical error of measurement, and the inferences (hopefully, reasonable ones) from the test results regarding test-taker ability, are comparable from individual to individual and from subgroup to subgroup. Willingham and Cole (1997) state that comparable validity must be met at all stages of the testing process – when designing the test, developing the test, administering the test, and using the test results. Comparable validity must be achieved by selecting test material that does not give an advantage to some test takers for reasons that are irrelevant to the construct being measured; by avoiding difficulties in the testing situation that are unrelated to the construct, such as unnecessary inclusion of technical terms in the test prompts; and by employing equivalent scoring procedures. Thus, Willingham and Cole see fairness as having three qualities linked to validity: (1) comparable opportunities for test takers to show their knowledge and skills, (2) comparable test tasks and scores, and (3) comparable treatment of test takers in test interpretation and use.

Current contributions and research

In the first decade after the turn of the millennium, two approaches to fairness in testing were proposed, which will be summarized below. One is a proposal from Xi (2010) and the other is the Test Context Framework by Kunnan (2009).

Xi both expands the definition of test fairness and offers a new framework for investigating fairness issues. The definition builds on that offered by Willingham and Cole (1997; see above), namely, comparable validity for all subgroups, by stating that fairness is "comparable validity for *identifiable* and *relevant* groups across all stages of assessment, from assessment conceptualization to use of assessment results," where "construct–irrelevant factors, construct under-representation, inconsistent test administration practices, inappropriate decision-making procedures or use of test results have no *systematic* or *appreciable* effects on test scores, test score interpretations, score-based decisions and consequences for all *relevant* groups of examinees" (Xi, 2010: 154; italics in original).

After offering this definition, Xi then outlines a framework for language testing fairness research, consisting of a *fairness argument* embedded within a *validity argument*. A validity argument is a chain of inferences that leads a test user to appropriate interpretations of test results. Xi's validity argument framework consists of six successive sub-arguments, that: (1) there is evidence that the domain of L2 use which is of interest, provides a meaningful basis for our observations of test-taker performance on the test; (2) there is evidence that the observed test scores reflect that domain of L2 use and not construct-irrelevant factors; (3) there is evidence that the observed scores on the test are generalizable over similar language tasks on other, similar tests; (4) there is evidence that the abovementioned generalization of observed scores can be linked to a theoretical interpretation (i.e., the construct, the theoretical skill) of such scores; (5) there is evidence that the theoretical construct can explain the L2 use in actual situations envisioned by the users of the test; and (6) there is evidence that the language-test results are "relevant, useful, and sufficient" (Xi, 2010: 157) for determining the level of L2 ability. Each of these sub-arguments is supported by certain *assumptions*. To take one example, for sub-argument (1) above, which claims an inferential link between observations of test-taker performance and a certain domain of L2 use, there may be one or more assumptions: (a) the assessment tasks on the test represent the intended L2 domain (in this case, academic English skills on the collegiate level), or (b) critical language skills, knowledge, and processes needed for collegiate study are represented on the test.

Embedded in the above chain of sub-arguments and underlying assumptions, Xi proposes, can be a *fairness argument*, which consists in part of a series of rebuttals, one or more posed to each of the validity sub-arguments. One can conceive of such rebuttals as research questions into the degree of fairness of a given language test, i.e., each rebuttal serves as a practical check on the claims of each sub-argument. For example, to the first of the sub-arguments above, one can ask whether or not the domain of L2 use actually provides a meaningful basis for observations of test-taker performance. More specifically, a rebuttal may challenge a specific assumption underlying the sub-argument: Are all the test tasks on the test *equally* representative of the intended collegiate-level, academic English L2 domain for *all* test-taker groups? If not, then one could say that the fairness argument has been weakened. As another example, Xi suggests that one might formulate rebuttals to the sub-argument regarding construct-irrelevant factors. Such rebuttals could address issues such as inconsistent test administration, lack of accommodations for test takers with disabilities, or rater bias against certain groups. In short, one or more rebuttals would be used to determine any weaknesses in each sub-argument and hence in the overall validity argument, that is, to see whether or not there are systematic or appreciable effects of construct-irrelevant factors on test scores or score-based decisions.

Another recent proposal for investigating language testing fairness issues is Kunnan's (2009) Test Context Framework. This approach is intended to consider the wider political, educational, cultural, social, economic, legal, and historical aspects of a test. In this it differs somewhat from other, more psychometrically focused approaches considered above, such as DIF, or even Xi's fairness-argument framework. It has a certain overlap with Kane's (2010) applications of political and legal concepts to language testing, and it also resonates with the analyses of power relations in language testing offered by Shohamy (2001), both mentioned above.

Kunnan's approach is here briefly illustrated by way of an example dealing with versions of the Naturalization Test, a tool used by the US federal government to screen non-native English-speaking applicants for US citizenship. The stated purpose of this test is to assess prospective citizens on their "civic nationalism" and potential for "social integration," as well as their English language ability. The test asks the prospective citizen to listen, speak, read, and write short English sentences dealing with facts about US history and government. After giving a break-down of the components and uses of the Naturalization Test, Kunnan (2009) asks a set of questions that throw light on the degree of fairness involved: (1) "Test Requirement and Purpose: Is the requirement and purpose meaningful?" (2) "Test conceptualization, content, and operations: Can the test assess English language ability and knowledge of U.S. history and government?" (3) "Test Consequences: Can the test bring about civic nationalism or social integration?"

To the first question, for example, Kunnan takes a politico-historical perspective, pointing out that the Naturalization Test is a holdover from the anti-communist furor of the 1950s in the United States. It also reflects anti-immigration and voting policies in the early twentieth century, for which literacy requirements had been instituted. Kunnan points out that these older policies had become irrelevant by the 1990s, and moreover, recent US legal and court rulings had made the literacy requirement meaningless. Thus, he implies, current use and administration and use of the Naturalization Test is unfair. As another example, Kunnan responds to the same question regarding test purpose and meaningfulness by pointing out that the test as currently constituted simply cannot test the constructs of "civic nationalism" or "social integration." This is because the measures of English ability or of knowledge of US history and government are, at best, indirect assessments of those constructs and not direct measures of actual community participation. Hence, one may conclude, use of the Naturalization Test is unfair to test-taking, prospective citizens. Kunnan's approach thus brings wider social factors into consideration when evaluating the fairness of a language test.

Future directions

At this point, one may well ask how language testing fairness might be conceived and addressed over the next decade from the time of this writing. To make a few predictions, it is reasonable to assume that test bias will be a continual concern as long as unequal societal and educational divisions continue, as along gender, ethnic, or racial lines. One might also hope that the theoretical dispute over the relationship between fairness and validity will begin to wind down toward consensus. As can be seen from the discussion in this chapter, researchers and practitioners can indeed conceptualize the two as being different, even to the point of being able to craft research questions into fairness independent of validity. Thus, one may predict that in ten years' time most scholars will agree that they are not synonymous, but rather are distinct, related aspects of test construction and use.

Yet another prediction involves the evolution of current approaches to fairness research. It would seem that at the present time we have two general ways of approaching L2 testing fairness. Examination of each general approach reveals an apparent divergence. One, exemplified by Xi's (2010) model, uses a technical-formalistic approach, which may conceivably be informed by focused, test-development tools such as DIF as well as procedural-fairness concerns outlined by Kane (2010). This is a manifestly *micro*-analytic approach suited to scientific investigations of fairness, and as such is not, apparently, able to accommodate wider social, historical, or political contextual issues. In contrast, the other general approach to test fairness takes a broad-based, societal perspective, exemplified by Kunnan's (2009) Test Context Framework, Shohamy's (2001) principles of critical language testing, and certain substantive-fairness concerns suggested by Kane (2010). This latter approach offers qualitative, *macro*-analyses of test requirements, purposes, and consequences, and thus seems better suited for evaluating social and political issues pertaining to language testing fairness.

There are at least two productive responses to this seeming divergence between the two approaches. One is to consider the framework for validation argued by Messick (1988, 1989). This framework outlines consequential bases for validity that encompass *value implications* and *social consequences*. These are two concerns arguably relevant to a qualitative, interpretive, social justice-oriented approach to language testing fairness. Moreover, Messick's formulation of *consequential bases* for validity posits "test use" as comprising two fairness-related elements (see also Bachman, 1990: 242). One is *construct-related evidence for validity*, which can be an issue amenable to technical, micro-analysis. The other element is *social consequences*, which clearly overlaps with a socially broad approach to fairness. With this theoretical perspective, one could modify a given technical-formalistic approach to fairness to accommodate broader social aspects of language-testing contexts. For example, one might craft rebuttals to assumptions in an initial, inferential step involving domain definition. Other rebuttals would be relevant to inferential steps regarding test use (Xi in her model calls it *utilization*), challenging claims regarding the relevance and usefulness of test results for making decisions.

With these suggestions in mind, we might make a prediction that language testing scholarship in the area of fairness will evince a principled synthesis of such "macro" and "micro" approaches to fairness, drawing on Messick's (1988, 1989) unitary model of validity. Thus, a formalistic model could integrally provide meaningful structure for both scientific-technical, micro-analytic research efforts as well as ethico-social, macro-analytic investigations. Achieving such an integrated practice will no doubt take time, given differing theoretical views of fairness vis-à-vis validity. One may hypothesize, however, that as validity arguments may draw upon multiple and canonical types of validity evidence (e.g., content-related, construct-related, consequence-related), so too might a fairness argument integrated with a validity argument draw on different evolving theoretical models of test fairness.

Recommendations for practice

In effect, this entire chapter has been about defining the very thing it seeks to explain: fairness. As can be surmised from the above survey of thought and research, this definition is still very much in flux. Accordingly, this section of the chapter will offer some exercises, which, it is hoped, will help form a definition of fairness of practical use to the reader.

Practical exercise 1

With a group of colleagues, consider an L2 test with which some or most of you are familiar. It may be a test of writing ability used to screen applicants to a university graduate school program, or a test of pronunciation given to non-native-speaking graduate students who wish to be university teaching assistants, or perhaps a standardized exit test taken by secondary-level students and promulgated by the testing agency of the national, state, or provincial government. Try to determine the author(s) and stated purpose(s) of the test. If you can obtain a test-user's manual, or some statement as to test purposes and characteristics online, this may be helpful for ascertaining sub-arguments and their underlying assumptions.

Then, using Xi's (2010) model as a guide, first construct a six-step validity argument with sub-arguments and assumptions. Afterward, examine the test items closely, and possibly interview anyone in your group or class who may have taken the test in question, and then try to construct a series of rebuttals in a fairness argument for as many of the six inferential steps as you can. It may help if you conceive of this as an "anti-fairness" argument. As far as you are able to determine, how fair is the test or test use? You or your group may find a worksheet grid such as the one shown in Figure 32.1 useful in organizing your thoughts.

Keep in mind that the points in the cells are only examples to get you started. You may well find *more* than one assumption, or *more* than one rebuttal, per inferential step.

Practical exercise 2

Regarding the relationship between fairness and validity, Davies (2010: 171) expresses the opinion that everything that can be claimed about fairness is already covered by validity, and that attempts to integrate fairness into validity are meaningless. Read (or re-read) the chapter on validity in this volume (by Chapelle), paying attention to the descriptions of consequential evidence for validity. Do you agree with Davies' opinion? Why or why not? Is "fairness" just another name for "validity"? Might Kane (2010: 177), mentioned above, be correct in saying that they are just "closely related ways of looking at the same basic question"?

Practical exercise 3

In the "Future Directions" section above, it was suggested that micro-analytic approaches to fairness such as that of Xi (2010) and macro-analytic approaches such as that of Kunnan (2000) could be both integrated by virtue of Messick's (1989) unitary model of validity. Do you think this possibility is workable? Why or why not? In a group, discuss the pros and cons of this idea, keeping in mind that Kunnan's view of the relationship between validity and fairness differs from Xi's view.

Name of test: _____

Test purpose(s): _____

Sub-arguments	Underlying assumptions	Rebuttals
The domain of L2 use (describe here) provides a meaningful basis for our observations of test-taker performance	According to the online test user's manual, test tasks represent the domain (describe)	We feel that the L2 domain is only partly represented by the tasks (for example...)
The observed test scores reflect that domain of L2 use and not construct-irrelevant factors	Reasonable accommodations given to test takers with disabilities (describe)	Rubric is vaguely worded, so construct-irrelevancy is possible Rater training uneven across semesters

Figure 32.1 Worksheet grid
Source: based on Xi (2010)

Further reading

Kunnan, A. J. (2008). Using the Test Fairness and Wider Context frameworks. In L. Taylor and C. Weir (eds), *Multilingualism and Assessment: achieving transparency, assuring quality, sustaining diversity*. Papers from the ALTE Berlin Conference. Cambridge, UK: Cambridge University Press. This is a presentation of Kunnan's Test Context Framework, giving an example of a "macro-analytic" approach to investigating test fairness.

Lee, Y. (2010). Identifying suspect item bundles for the detection of differential bundle functioning in an ESL reading comprehension test: a preliminary study. In A. J. Kunnan (ed.), *Fairness and Validation in Language Assessment: selected papers from the 19th Language Testing Research Colloquium, Orlando, Florida: Studies in Language Testing 9*. Cambridge: Cambridge University Press, 105–27. This paper presents an example of a "micro-analytic" fairness study, taking concepts and techniques of differential item functioning (DIF) and applying them to the "test bundle", i.e., a group of related items on a test.

Toulmin, S., Rieke, R. and Janik, A. (1984). *An Introduction to Reasoning*, 2nd edn. New York, NY: Macmillan. This is a good resource for understanding the formal antecedents of Xi's (2010) embedded fairness/validity argument structure.

Willingham, W. W. (1999). A systemic view of test fairness. In S. Messick (ed.), *Assessment in Higher Education: issues in access, quality, student development, and public policy*. Mahwah, NJ: Lawrence Erlbaum Associates, 213–42. This book chapter is a good, short exploration of fairness issues at all stages of the test development process, from test design and item writing to test administration, interpretation, and use.

References

AERA/APA/NCME (American Educational Research Association, American Psychological Association, and National Council on Measurement in Education) (1999). *Standards for Educational and Psychological Testing*. Washington, DC: Author.

Bachman, L. F. (1990). *Fundamental Considerations in Language Testing*. Oxford, UK: Oxford University Press.

Camilli, G. (2006). Test fairness. In R. Brennan (ed.), *Educational Measurement*, 4th edn, Westport, CT: American Council on Education and Praeger, 221–56.

Code of Fair Testing Practices in Education (2004). *The Code of Fair Testing Practices in Education*. Washington, DC: Joint Committee on Testing Practices. www.apa.org/science/programs/testing/fair-code. aspx (accessed 18 April 2010).

Davies, A. (2010). Test fairness: a response. *Language Testing* 27: 171–76.

Dorans, N. J. and Kulick, E. (1986). Demonstrating the utility of the standardization approach to assessing unexpected differential item performance on the Scholastic Aptitude Test. *Journal of Educational Measurement* 23: 355–68.

Holland, P. W. and Thayer, D. T. (1988). Differential item performance and the Mantel-Haenszel procedure. In H. Wainer and H. Braun (eds), *Test Validity*. Hillsdale, NJ: Lawrence Erlbaum Associates, 129–45.

Jang, E. (2002). Folk fairness in language testing. Paper presented at the Southern California Association for Language Assessment Research conference (SCALAR 5), May 15–16.

Kane, M. (2010). Validity and fairness. *Language Testing* 27: 177–82.

Kunnan, A. J. (2000). Fairness and justice for all. In A. J. Kunnan (ed.), *Fairness and Validation in Language Assessment: selected papers from the 19th Language Testing Research Colloquium, Orlando, Florida: Studies in Language Testing 9*. Cambridge, UK: Cambridge University Press, 1–14.

—— (2004). Test fairness. In M. Milanovic and C. Weir (eds), *European Language Testing in a Global Context: proceedings of the ALTE Barcelona conference*. Cambridge, UK: Cambridge University Press.

—— (2009). Testing for citizenship: The U.S. Naturalization Test. *Language Assessment Quarterly* 6: 89–97.

Messick, S. (1988). The once and future issues of validity: assessing the meaning and consequences of measurement. In H. Wainer and H. I. Braun (eds), *Test Validity*, Hillsdale, NJ: Lawrence Erlbaum.

—— (1989). Validity. In R. L. Linn (ed.), *Educational Measurement*, 3rd edn, New York, NY: American Council on Education and Macmillan, 13–103.

Mish, F. C. (ed.), (2003). *Merriam-Webster's Collegiate Dictionary*, 11th edn, Springfield, MA: Merriam-Webster, Incorporated.

Ramsey, P. A. (1993). Sensitivity review: the ETS experience as a case study. In P. W. Holland and H. Wainer (eds), *Differential Item Functioning*. Hillsdale, NJ: Lawrence Erlbaum, 367–88.

Shohamy, E. (2001). *The Power of Tests: a critical perspective on the uses of language tests*. Harlow, UK: Longman.

Spaan, M. (2000). Enhancing fairness through a social contract. In A. J. Kunnan (ed.), *Fairness and Validation in Language Assessment: selected papers from the 19th Language Testing Research Colloquium, Orlando, Florida: Studies in Language Testing 9*. Cambridge, UK: Cambridge University Press, 35–37.

Walter, E. (ed.), (2006). *Cambridge Advanced Learner's Dictionary*, 3rd edn. Cambridge: Cambridge University Press. dictionary.cambridge.org/dictionary/british/fair_1 (accessed 4/1/11).

Willingham, W. W. and Cole, N. (1997). *Gender and Fair Assessment*. Mahwah, NJ: Lawrence Erlbaum Associates.

Xi, X. (2010). How do we go about investigating test fairness? *Language Testing* 27: 147–70.

YourDictionary.com (2011). *YourDictionary.com*. Burlingame, CA: LoveToKnow Corporation. www.yourdic tionary.com/fair (accessed 4/1/11).

33

Standards-based testing

Thom Hudson

Introduction

Standards serve to outline expectations and to encourage consistency. Humans have created and utilized standards of various sorts throughout history. For example, cultures have standard calendars, countries have standards for railroad track gauges, screws and bolts have standard thread depth and pitch, appliances have standard electrical requirements, and schools have standards for language learning outcomes. The International Organization for Standardization (ISO) sets international standards for such areas as mechanical and physical qualities of toys, natural gas cylinders, units of measurement, and language translation. Standards provide criteria against which to judge as well as descriptions of completeness and mechanisms for articulation.

Language learning standards make content, goals, conditions, and expected outcomes of language learners explicit to all potential stakeholders. A primary expectation in establishing standards is that explicit standards can promote cohesion among instruction, curriculum design, and assessment. As will be noted, however, language learning standards do not have, indeed cannot have, the precision of the ISO standards linked to the physical world. Indeed, one of the most problematic facets of language ability standards is the lack of precision in linking relatively abstract definitions to test scores.

Development of standards and standards-based testing

There have been a number of paths through which foreign and second language standards have emerged. They have been developed historically through a myriad of instructional approaches labeled variously *objectives, competency, communicative, performance, proficiency and standards* based. Some have developed through school centered initiatives, and others have been produced through needs identified by governmental agencies or professional organizations. Standards-based testing applies both to foreign language education (where language is a school subject) and to second language contexts (where the language is the language of instruction and the broader social context). Aspects of such standards initiatives will be addressed below.

The literature about standards-based assessment identifies both content standards and performance standards (Lachat, 2004). Content standards spell out what the student should know.

They present the knowledge and skills that are needed to reach proficiency in a content area. They are curriculum related in that they identify what is to be taught and learned. Performance standards, on the other hand, indicate the levels of performance that are expected on each of the skills. They specify the proficiency level that is expected. In the area of language learning, there are instances of content standards being articulated systematically, and instances of performance standards being articulated in order to drive the curriculum.

Within the US educational systems, there is a long history of concern with standards-based instruction and, consequently, standards-based assessment. Standards-based instructional concerns across the curriculum gained interest in the late 1970s and early 1980s, and were given impetus with the federal educational objectives presented in *Nation at Risk: The Imperative for Educational Reform* (National Commission on Excellence in Education, 1983). Many parents and educators were troubled by the dismal results of students on international measures of science and mathematics. Much of the focus in education changed from seat time and number of courses or credits to the quality and results of the curriculum. This was followed by the Goals 2000: Educate America Act. In 1990, President G. H. W. Bush called for national standards in English, math, science, history, and geography. As a practical matter, this proposal was attached to a reauthorization of the Elementary and Secondary Education Act (ESEA), an act initially passed during the Lyndon Johnson administration in 1965 containing vague requirements for testing and having vague standards for assessment. Goals 2000 became law in 1994 and was amended in 1996. The Goals 2000 Act was designed to assist states in developing clear and rigorous standards delineating what every child should know and be able to do. It also assisted with planning for the implementation of the standards in an effort to improve student achievement. Subsequently, the passage of the No Child Left Behind Act (NCLB), required tests that measured performance against state-adopted academic content standards.

Throughout this period of growth in the standards-based orientation to general education, language education in the United States was also disillusioned with seat time as an indicator of student language learning. In 1979, a US government report *Strength Through Wisdom: A Critique of U.S. Capability* (President's Commission on Foreign Language and International Studies, 1979) lamented the status of foreign language education in the United States and recommended the establishment of a National Criteria and Assessment Program for foreign language study. It recommended that the program, among other endeavors, should "assess the proficiency of both students and teachers in existing as well as new or experimental foreign language programs; monitor application of language skills by students on completion of their training; determine the language skills required to function in a variety of contexts; establish language proficiency achievement goals for the end of each year of study at all levels, with special attention to speaking proficiency" (p. 42). Developing common achievement goals, then, became an important goal.

FSI/ACTFL/ILR standards

The development of a common scale of standards emerged from the interaction of the Foreign Service Institute (FSI), the American Council on the Teaching of Foreign Languages (ACTFL), and the Educational Testing Service (ETS). The original FSI oral interview (Foreign Service Institute, 1979) is the model for the guidelines developed by ACTFL and ETS. Although the scale was initially focused on oral language skills, it has been extended to include language skills other than speaking. Also, the scales were extended to other governmental agencies, and are at times referred to as the Interagency Language Roundtable (ILR) scales.

The FSI/ILR/ACTFL scales have been of importance in language testing for many years. These scales are the outgrowth of forty to fifty years of research and development of measurement instruments intended to determine the extent of an examinee's ability to function successfully in a variety of "real-world" communication contexts. In reaction to the prevalence of indirect non-performance testing in the 1950s and 1960s, the US Foreign Service conceived of a set of verbal descriptions defining six levels of general language proficiency. These ranged from no functional proficiency in the language (a rating of 0) up to a proficiency equivalent in all respects to that of an educated native speaker (a rating of 5). In the oral tests, the testing technique used to place examinees at the appropriate level within this scale was a structured face-to-face interview. A basic claim is that this interview solicits responses that reflect the language behaviors associated with real-life communicative exchanges, while also providing sufficient information about the examinee's speaking abilities in the target language to permit the accurate assessing of the candidate's performance. The possible ratings (for speaking) are indicated in Table 33.1 along with selected associated contexts.

Further steps in the development of FSI process involved collaboration by ETS and ACTFL in which language educators from around the United States reviewed and discussed the FSI approach to assessment in order to evaluate its potential as a common yardstick for speaking ability assessment within schools and colleges (Hiple, 1987). Again, educators were dissatisfied with *seat time* being the only indicator of progress in language learning. The FSI scale was examined, but it became clear that the complete scale ranging from 0 through 5 was not sensitive enough to reflect the relatively small gains in overall language proficiency that could reasonably be expected over one to two years of high school or college level language study. Further, it was clear that the higher levels represented ability levels that were only rarely found in school or college language contexts. A modified scale was developed, and subsequently adopted by ACTFL. The new scale basically subsumed the original FSI/ILR scale as shown in Table 33.2 (Liskin-Gasparro, 1989). This scale was seen as more applicable to secondary and tertiary levels of foreign language education. Note that the three top FSI levels are all assigned the single global rating of Superior.

Table 33.1 Interagency Language Roundtable Levels and selected contexts – speaking

Level	Label	Description
Speaking 0	No proficiency	
Speaking 0+	Memorized proficiency	Formulaic utterances for immediate needs
Speaking 1	Elementary proficiency	Predictable, simple, personal and accommodation needs
Speaking 1+	Elementary proficiency, plus	Make travel arrangements
Speaking 2	Limited working proficiency	Routine social demands and limited work requirements
Speaking 2+	Limited working proficiency, plus	Communicate on topics of particular interest
Speaking 3	General professional proficiency	Answer objections
Speaking 3+	General professional proficiency, plus	Satisfy professional needs in wide range of tasks
Speaking 4	Advanced professional proficiency	Fluency and accuracy in all levels of professional needs
Speaking 4+	Advanced professional proficiency, plus	Near native ability
Speaking 5	Functionally native proficiency	Educated native speaker

Source: Adapted from ILR Speaking Skill Scale www.govtilr.org/skills/ILRscale2.htm

Table 33.2 The Interagency Language Roundtable (ILR) to the American Council on the Teaching of Foreign Languages (ACTFL) concordance

ILR	ACTFL
Level 0	No ability whatsoever
	Novice-low
	Novice-mid
Level 0+	Novice-high
Level 1	Intermediate-low
	Intermediate-mid
Level 1+	Intermediate-high
Level 2	Advanced
Level 2+	Advanced plus
Levels 3–5	Superior

Source: Adapted from Liskin-Gasparro (1989)

Table 33.3 presents a sample of the FSI scale descriptor, and Table 33.4 presents a sample of the corresponding ACTFL scale descriptor that is based on the initial FSI scale. Note that these scales include such specific situations as casual conversations, current events, work, family, everyday topics, well-known current events, etc. This formulation of language scales attempts to utilize "real-world" contexts in the standards. The FSI/ILR/ACTFL scales are not empirically derived. They represent intuitive notions of how texts, tasks, and skills should be implicationally related. Further, note that this incarnation of the behavioral scale includes negatively directed descriptions such as in Table 33.3 where it states at the end of the first paragraph that the candidate " … does not have thorough or confident control of the grammar."

The *ACTFL Proficiency Guidelines* gained widespread application as proficiency indicators for assessing learners' functional competency across a variety of levels. Further, as performance standards, they were promoted as part of the base for a proficiency oriented curricular approach to formal language instruction (Omaggio, 1986; James, 1988; Higgs, 1989). Institutions (such as the University of Minnesota) began requiring foreign language students to take a proficiency test following their second year of instruction (Johnson, 1997). When a program adopts the ACTFL proficiency guidelines as the standard for meeting undergraduate foreign language requirements, it is under a great deal of pressure to change its curricula such that students are taught materials relevant to the standards against which they will be evaluated. Furthermore, it can cause foreign language curricula to become little more than a reflection of the language proficiency test rubric.

Many foreign language educators conceive of the role of foreign language education to be more broadly conceived than the descriptors embodied in the ACTFL guidelines, particularly as it applies to K-12 educational settings. In 1993 foreign language education became the final subject area to receive US federal funding for developing national standards for K-12 students (National Standards in Foreign Language Education Project, 1999). A task force was established to develop content standards in a variety of languages for grades four, eight, and twelve. The task force based its developments on an examination of the broad goals of foreign language education, and disseminated its drafts throughout the foreign language education community. In 1996 and 1999 this work resulted in the publication of *Standards for Foreign Language Learning: Preparing for the 21st Century*. This publication presented content standards for foreign language learning within five interconnected goal areas: communication, cultures, connections, comparisons,

Table 33.3 Foreign Service Institute descriptor for Level 2 speaking

Speaking 2	Able to satisfy routine social demands and limited work requirements. Can handle with confidence but not with facility most social situations including introductions and casual conversations about current events, as well as work, family, and autobiographical information; can handle limited work requirements, needing help in handling any complications or difficulties; can get the gist of most conversations on non-technical subjects (i.e., topics which require no specialized knowledge, and has a speaking vocabulary sufficient to respond simply with some circumlocutions; accent, though often quite faulty, is intelligible; can usually handle elementary constructions quite accurately but does not have thorough or confident control of the grammar.
	Examples: While these interactions will vary widely from individual to individual, the individual can typically ask and answer predictable questions in the workplace and give straightforward instructions to subordinates. Additionally, the individual can participate in personal and accommodation-type interactions with elaboration and facility; that is, can give and understand complicated, detailed, and extensive directions and make non-routine changes in travel and accommodation arrangements. Simple structures and basic grammatical relations are typically controlled; however, there are areas of weakness. In the commonly taught languages, these may be simple markings such as plurals, articles, linking words, and negatives or more complex structures such as tense/aspect usage, case morphology, passive constructions, word order, and embedding

Table 33.4 American Council on the Teaching of Foreign Languages Advanced descriptor

Advanced: Able to satisfy routine social demands and limited work requirements. Can handle with confidence but not with facility most social situations including introductions and casual conversations about current events as well as work, family, and autobiographical information; can handle limited work requirements, needing help in handling any complications or difficulties. Has a speaking vocabulary sufficient to respond simply with some circumlocutions; accent, though often quite faulty, is intelligible; can usually handle elementary constructions quire accurately but does not have thorough or confident control of the grammar.

Source: ACTFL (1989: 220)

and communities. As such, the standards include not only language itself, but areas of: (1) communicating in languages other than English; (2) gaining knowledge and understanding of cultures that use the target language; (3) connecting to additional knowledge areas; (4) comparing and contrasting which provide insight into the student's own language and culture; and (5) participating in multilingual communities at home and around the world in a variety of contexts. Each of the goal areas has two to three content standards and each content standard presents sample progress indicators for grades four, eight, and twelve. Two of the goal areas and standards are presented in Table 33.5.

In 1998, ACTFL released the ACTFL Performance Guidelines for K–12 Learners (Swender and Duncan, 1998). Swender and Duncan (1998) state that

> Standards for Foreign Language Learning are the **content standards** that define the "what" of foreign language learning in American classroom. The ACTFL Performance Guidelines for K–12 Learners are the **performance standards** that define the "how well."
>
> *(p. 479) (emphasis in original)*

Table 33.5 Example standards for foreign language learning

Communication: Communicate in languages other than English	
Standard 1.1	Students engage in conversations, provide and obtain information, express feelings and emotions, and exchange opinions.
Standard 1.2	Students understand and interpret written and spoken language on a variety of topics.
Standard 1.3	Students present information, concepts, and ideas to an audience of listeners or readers on a variety of topics.
Connections: Connect with other disciplines and acquire information	
Standard 3.1	Students reinforce and further their knowledge of other disciplines through the foreign language.
Standard 3.2	Students acquire information and recognize the distinctive viewpoints that are only available through the foreign language and its cultures.

Source: Adapted from National Standards in Foreign Language Education Project (1999: 9)

The Standards for Foreign Language Learning characterize the communication of learners as representing three modes. The interpersonal mode involves active negotiation of meaning among interlocutors. The interpretive mode involves appropriate cultural understanding and inferencing. The presentational mode represents the ability to create messages that can be understood by members of the target culture without negotiation. The ACTFL K-12 guidelines utilize these three modes in evaluation and description of language performance. The guidelines evaluate language performance under the analytic areas of: comprehensibility, comprehension, language control, vocabulary use, communication strategies, and cultural awareness. The ACTFL Performance Guidelines for K-12 Learners are used as the basis for assessment by many state education departments in the United States. Examples of the performance standards for the Intermediate Learner Range are presented in Table 33.6.

Canadian language benchmarks

Canada developed the Canadian Language Benchmarks (CLB) to establish a common framework of standards across national and provincial concerns in the description and assessment of adult immigrants (Peirce and Stewart, 1997, 1999). It was a response to the fact that various language programs did not use consistent terminology in describing language levels and that it was difficult for immigrant learners to transfer from one program to another due to a lack of common descriptors describing what students have learned. In 1991, Canada's immigration agency committed to improve the language training of immigrants through improved assessment and common types of training across the country. The CLB are task-based assessments and descriptors based on a functional view of language, language use, and language proficiency.

The CLB address five functions: (1) a descriptive scale of communicative proficiency; (2) a set of descriptive standards; (3) statements of communicative knowledge competence and skill; (4) a framework of reference for learning, teaching, programming and assessing adult English as a second language in Canada; and, (5) a national standard for planning second language curricula for a variety of contexts and a common "yardstick" for assessing the outcomes (Pawlikowska-Smith, 2000: viii). The CLB is structured with three levels of proficiency with four subdivisions within each of those levels. An example for the speaking and listening competencies is shown in Table 33.7.

Table 33.6 Example descriptors for the intermediate learner range of American Council on the Teaching of Foreign Languages K-12 Guidelines

Comprehensibility	Interpersonal	Express their own thoughts using sentences and strings of sentences when interacting on familiar topics in present time; Are understood by those accustomed to interacting with language learners; Use pronunciation and intonation patterns which can be understood by a native speaker accustomed to interacting with language learners;
	Presentational	Express their own thoughts, describe and narrate, using sentences and strings of sentences, in oral and written presentations on familiar topics; Make false starts and pause frequently to search for words when interacting with others;
Comprehension	Interpersonal	Comprehend general concepts and messages about familiar and occasionally unfamiliar topics; May not comprehend details when dealing with unfamiliar topics;
	Interpretive	Understand longer, more complex conversations and narratives as well as recorded material in familiar contexts; Use background knowledge to comprehend simple stories, personal correspondence, and other contextualized print.

Source: Adapted from Schwender and Duncan (1998)

The CLB standards have global performance descriptors and performance conditions for each benchmark. Table 33.8 shows these for Benchmark 8.

Community, academic, and workplace tasks are associated with each skill area in each benchmark. In this way, score users can take the learner's context into account in determining which particular tasks to use.

Common European framework of reference

The standards-based instruction and assessment movement has also been pursued to some degree in the UK. In 1988, the UK introduced the Education Reform Act, which required the Secretary of State for Education and Science to establish a National Curriculum, "specify program of study, set attainment targets for each subject, and assess student achievement" (Walton, 1993: 154.) The central subjects of mathematics, English, and science were the first areas to be developed. The UK introduced its National Curriculum in 1992. State schools were required to adhere to it until students reach age 16. National Curriculum core subjects are: English, mathematics and science; Welsh is a core subject in Welsh-speaking schools. Foundation subjects are design and technology; information and communication technology; history; geography; modern foreign languages; music; art and design; physical education; religious education; and citizenship. The National Curriculum is a framework employed by schools to ensure that teaching and learning take place. It provides: (1) the subjects to be taught; (2) the skills and understanding expected in each subject; (3) the standards or attainment targets in the subjects; and (4) the ways each child's progress is assessed.

Table 33.7 Canadian Language Benchmarks speaking and listening competencies

An overview		
Benchmark	Proficiency Level	Speaking and Listening Competencies
Stage I: basic proficiency		
1	Initial	Creating/interpreting oral discourse in routine non-
2	Developing	demanding contexts of language use in:
3	Adequate	Social interaction
4	Fluent	Instructions
		Suasion (getting things done)
		Information
Stage II: intermediate proficiency		
5	Initial	Creating/interpreting oral discourse in moderately
6	Developing	demanding contexts of language use in:
7	Adequate	Social interaction
8	Fluent	Instructions
		Suasion (getting things done)
		Information
Stage III: advanced proficiency		
9	Initial	Creating/interpreting oral discourse in very demanding
10	Developing	contexts of language use in:
11	Adequate	Social interaction
12	Fluent	Instructions
		Suasion (getting things done)
		Information

Source: Adapted from Pawlikowska-Smith (2000)

Table 33.8 Example global performance descriptor and performance conditions from the Canadian Language Benchmarks

Listening: Stage II Benchmark 8

Global performance descriptor	Performance conditions
Learner can comprehend main points, details, speaker's purpose, attitudes, levels of formality and styles in oral discourse in moderately demanding contexts.	Tasks are in a standard format, with items to circle, match, fill in a blank, and complete a chart.
Can follow most formal and informal conversations and some technical work related discourse in own field at a normal rate of speed.	Learner is adequately briefed for focused listening.
Can follow discourse about abstract and complex ideas on a familiar topic.	Communication is face to face, observed live, or video- and audiomediated (e.g., tape, TV, radio). Speech is clear at a normal rate. Instructions are clear and coherent.

Source: Adapted from Pawlikowska-Smith (2000: 82)

In terms of language education, work through the Council of Europe demonstrated early orientations toward standards-based instruction and assessment in the development of Threshold Level (van Ek, 1975). The Threshold involved a unit–credit system by which learners studied units of work and received credits for the completion of the units. Units were related to notional–functional components rather than specifically linguistic based syllabus items. The units were communicatively based and practically oriented. In order to define the learning objective for a group of learners, situations in which the learners will need a foreign language were identified. The approach was seen to satisfy the needs of a European system in that it lent itself to learning objectives for all languages and to the comparison across languages (van Ek, 1975).

Throughout the 1980s and 1990s, the Council of Europe developed several projects expanding and refining the principles in the Threshold Level. In 1991, Trim (2001: 5) notes,

> An International Symposium … agreed to the Swiss Government's suggestion that the mutual recognition of qualifications and communication concerning objectives and achievement standards would be facilitated if they were calibrated according to agreed common reference standards, purely descriptive in nature.

The Common European Framework of Reference for Languages (CEFR) was presented in 2001 (Council of Europe, 2001). The framework involves three bands, each of which has two levels. These are presented in Table 33.9. The framework represents a "can do" approach that recognizes the functional and communicative usefulness of the language represented across all levels. The Council of Europe, hence, recognizes that the partial and functional abilities at the lower levels will promote plurilingualism through the learning of a wider variety of European languages (pp. 1–2). The CEFR standards do not regard native speaker ability as the ultimate model. Further, the descriptors of performance do not have negative directionality as with the ACTFL Guidelines and the CLB. Thus, there are no statements such as with the CLB "Often has difficulty following rapid, colloquial/idiomatic or regionally accented speech between native speakers" (Table 33.8).

The development of the CEFR across all levels of language ability was seen as desirable in order to: (1) promote and facilitate co-operation among educational institutions in different countries; (2) provide a sound basis for the mutual recognition of language qualifications; and (3) assist learners, teachers, course designers, examining bodies and educational administrators to situate and co-ordinate their efforts. (Council of Europe, 2001: 5–6). The CEFR is designed with the view that, "by providing a common basis for the explicit description of objectives, content and methods, the Framework will enhance the transparency of course syllabuses and qualifications" (p. 1). The descriptors provide common standards for identifying what learners should be able to do at the designated levels on the scale.

In the construction of a pool of descriptors, the developers surveyed over 30 existing language scales describing spoken interaction and/or global proficiency. The components of the scales were divided into sentences. Then, each of the sentences was analyzed to determine what descriptive category (such as pragmatic fluency, communicative interaction, etc.) it seemed to be describing. The more than 2,000 potential descriptors that were identified were converted into statements that could be answered either yes or no. Teachers evaluated the descriptors and indicated which were useful and which were not. The descriptors were used to rate examinee videotaped performance. Teachers rated learners from a variety of first language backgrounds on each of the descriptors. The descriptors were then analyzed with the

Table 33.9 Common European Framework—global scale

Proficient user	C2	Can understand with ease virtually everything heard or read. Can summarise information from different spoken and written sources, reconstructing arguments and accounts in a coherent presentation. Can express him/herself spontaneously, very fluently and precisely, differentiating finer shades of meaning even in more complex situations.
	C1	Can understand a wide range of demanding, longer texts, and recognise implicit meaning. Can express him/herself fluently and spontaneously without much obvious searching for expressions. Can use language flexibly and effectively for social, academic and professional purposes. Can produce clear, well-structured, detailed text on complex subjects, showing controlled use of organisational patterns, connectors and cohesive devices.
Independent user	B2	Can understand the main ideas of complex text on both concrete and abstract topics, including technical discussions in his/her field of specialisation. Can interact with a degree of fluency and spontaneity that makes regular interaction with native speakers quite possible without strain for either party. Can produce clear, detailed text on a wide range of subjects and explain a viewpoint on a topical issue giving the advantages and disadvantages of various options.
	B1	Can understand the main points of clear standard input on familiar matters regularly encountered in work, school, leisure, etc. Can deal with most situations likely to arise whilst travelling in an area where the language is spoken. Can produce simple connected text on topics which are familiar or of personal interest. Can describe experiences and events, dreams, hopes ambitions and briefly give reasons and explanations for opinions and plans.
Basic user	A2	Can understand sentences and frequently used expressions related to areas of most immediate relevance (e.g. very basic personal and family information, shopping, local geography, employment). Can communicate in simple and routine tasks requiring a simple and direct exchange of information on familiar and routine matters. Can describe in simple terms aspects of his/her background, immediate environment and matters in areas of immediate need.
	A1	Can understand and use familiar everyday expressions and very basic phrases aimed at the satisfaction of needs of a concrete type. Can introduce him/herself and others and can ask and answer questions about personal details such as where he/she lives, people he/she knows and things he/she has. Can interact in a simple way provided the other person talks slowly and clearly and is prepared to help.

Source: Council of Europe, 2001

Rasch model using the computer program Facets. Items that did not fit the model or did not scale well were dropped from the subsequent development process. This analysis provided a scale for the descriptors from least difficult to most difficult, and the level descriptors were created from this ordering. Through this process, an empirically based scale was developed, in contrast to the previous approaches which developed the standard scale conceptually.

Examples of the descriptors can be seen in Table 33.10. The scale is made up of "can do" statements that address positive aspects of the learner's language ability. Rather than focusing on any language deficits, this scale emphasizes the positive functional abilities of the learners.

The CEFR provides a set of standards against which different languages can develop language assessment and curricula.

Table 33.10 Example descriptors for the Common European Framework of Reference for Languages

C1
Can communicate spontaneously, often showing remarkable fluency and ease of expression in even longer complex stretches of speech. Can relate own contribution skillfully to those of other speakers. Can use circumlocution and paraphrase to cover gaps in vocabulary and structure. Can carry out an effective fluent interview, departing spontaneously from prepared questions, following up and probing interesting replies.

A2
Can write simple notes to friends. Can ask and answer questions about personal details, such as where they live, people they know, and things they have. Can reply in an interview to simple direct questions spoken very slowly and clearly in direct non-idiomatic speech about personal details. Can indicate time by such phrases as next week, last Friday, in November, three o'clock.

Source: Adapted from North, 2000

English language development standards for California public schools K-12 and others

The overview of standards-based education and assessment above noted some of the impetuses for development and use of standards. Within US public school systems, there are forms of educational standards in every state. The California Department of Education (CDE), along with those in most other states, has developed English language arts content standards for its public schools. However, California has over 1.4 million English language learners whose first language is not English. Thus, California developed the English–Language Development (ELD) Standards for California Public Schools (California Department of Education, 1999). The standards are designed to explicitly state what all students need to know and be able to do in order to become proficient in the English language arts. The standards are presented in Table 33.11.

The CDE states that the ELD standards are written as benchmarks of the English-language arts standards that are to be achieved by all learners, regardless of first language. In fact, it notes that at the more advanced levels, the skills addressed by the ELD standards begin to resemble those of the English-language arts standards.

The California English Language Development Test (CELDT) is aligned with the ELD standards. This test is the test used to fulfill state and federal requirements for identifying and assessing English language learners. The purpose of the test is to identify students who are English language learners, determine the level of English proficiency, and assess progress toward becoming proficient in English. Students must take the test each year until they are determined to be English proficient. The test includes listening, speaking and writing strategies and applications, as well as written English-language conventions and the reading components of word analysis, fluency and systematic vocabulary development, comprehension and literary response analysis (California Department of Education, 2008, 2010). As an example, the blueprint for the grade 2 CDELT is presented in Table 33.12. The blueprint indicates the proficiency level of each standard.

It should be noted that there are frameworks for language standards other than that of California within the United States. One set of standards that is gaining influence is the

Table 33.11 California English Language Development Standards Listening and Speaking Strategies and Applications

English-language arts substrand	Beginning ELD level
Comprehension	Answer simple questions with one- to two-word responses. Respond to simple directions and questions by using physical actions and other means of nonverbal communication (e.g., matching objects, pointing to an answer, drawing pictures). Begin to speak with a few words or sentences by using a few standard English grammatical forms and sounds (e.g., single words or phrases). Use common social greetings and simple repetitive phrases independently (e.g., "Thank you," "You're welcome"). Ask and answer questions by using phrases or simple sentences. Retell stories by using appropriate gestures, expressions, and illustrative objects.
Organization and delivery of oral communication	Begin to be understood when speaking, but usage of standard English grammatical forms and sounds (e.g., plurals, simple past tense, pronouns [he or she]) may be inconsistent. Orally communicate basic personal needs and desires (e.g., "May I go to the bathroom?").
English-language arts substrand	Intermediate ELD level
Comprehension	Ask and answer instructional questions by using simple sentences. Listen attentively to stories and information and identify important details and concepts by using both verbal and nonverbal responses. Ask and answer instructional questions with some supporting elements (e.g., "Which part of the story was the most important?").
Comprehension and organization and delivery of communication	Participate in social conversations with peers and adults on familiar topics by asking and answering questions and soliciting information.
Organization and delivery of communication	Make oneself understood when speaking by using consistent standard English grammatical forms and sounds; however, some rules are not followed (e.g., third-person singular, male and female pronouns).
English-language arts substrand	Advanced ELD level
Comprehension	Demonstrate understanding of most idiomatic expressions (e.g., "Give me a hand") by responding to such expressions and using them appropriately.
Organization and delivery of communication	Negotiate and initiate social conversations by questioning, restating, soliciting information, and paraphrasing the communication of others.

Source: CDE (1999)

multi-state WIDA (World-class Instructional Design & Assessment) language proficiency set of standards (WIDA, 2007). The standards cover the English language proficiency standards for language of instruction, language arts, mathematics, science and social studies. Within each of the standards there is a focus on listening, speaking, reading, and writing. (The reader is referred to www.wida.us for further information.)

Table 33.12 California English Language Development Test blueprint from grade 2

Reading–Total Number of Items: 35	
Word Analysis	
ELD Standard	ELD Proficiency Level
Recognize English phonemes that correspond to phonemes students already hear and produce in their primary language.	Beginning
Recognize English phonemes that do not correspond to sounds students hear and produce (e.g., *a* in *cat* and final consonants).	Early intermediate
Recognize sound/symbol relationships and basic word-formation rules in phrases, simple sentences, or simple text.	Intermediate
Recognize and name all uppercase and lowercase letters of the alphabet.	Intermediate
Use common English morphemes to derive meaning in oral and silent reading (e.g., basic syllabication rules, regular and irregular plurals, and basic phonics).	Early advanced
Recognize sound/symbol relationship and basic word-formation rules in phrases, simple sentences, or simple text.	Early advanced
Apply knowledge of common morphemes to derive meaning in oral and silent reading (e.g., basic syllabication rules, regular and irregular plurals, and basic phonics).	Advanced

Source: CDE (2010)

Advantages and potential issues with standards-based assessment

We have seen four example standards initiatives above. All standards are designed in some way to assure that instructional practice is aligned with desired learning outcomes. Standards-based education is seen to present a method to ensure that all learners receive challenging curricula which prepare them for success.

Positive features

In general, there are a host of positive aspects for testing and assessment within a standards-based framework. First, standards provide a common vocabulary for the myriad of stakeholders within the educational context. Learners, teachers, administrators and materials developers can refer to common levels of ability and can reference mutual expectations. Users of the ACTFL guidelines, for example, can refer to different proficiency levels and infer a common understanding of the abilities that are being discussed. Additionally, the availability of common standards may allow the object of assessment to be more open and accessible than assessment in more traditional standardized assessment developed through norm-referenced test development methods.

Further, standards are seen as a means for improving instruction and learner achievement. They provide a compelling explicit approach to organizing instruction and assessment. In principle, a standards-based model provides a process that aids in answering the question, "What do we want our learners to be able to do?" Each standard offers an opportunity to evaluate its truth or falseness. Standards are seen as a means to bring about change in faltering educational systems.

As such, they are seen a means for enabling educational institutions to address falling standards, and to provide more accountability to all stakeholders. They provide opportunities to focus on performance and proficiency rather than seat time.

Negative features

The questionable aspects of standards tend to result from the specific application of the standards-based framework in particular contexts. Perhaps the most controversial issue with standards is whether or not they are mandatory. Most of the standards frameworks discussed above do not claim to constrain the curriculum or to present prescriptive syllabus descriptors. They do tend, however, to note that classroom instruction will change in order to move students along the ability continuum. Thus, when used, they tend to have strong impacts on how a curriculum is viewed. State school standards, such as the California ELD standards discussed above, however, are mandatory. Such standards often show a fundamental distrust of teachers and other educators. Overly specific mandatory standards can be dispiriting to teachers and stifling of creativity.

A further criticism leveled at many of the standards-based scales in foreign language education and research is that they are atheoretical, and not based on cognitive or linguistic models. They tend to present a sampling of operational definitions of performance, not models of language use and communication. This absence of a firm theoretical grounding casts questions about the construct validity of the assessment process. For example, the CEFR found certain descriptors that did not scale or fit the statistical model, and they were thus deleted from the CEFR standards. These included such areas as pragmatic strategies and literary appreciation. The absence of language components that are statistically uncooperative may lead to construct underrepresentation. Without a theoretical perspective, the creators of standards are left to rely solely on statistical analysis. Users or prospective users of particular systems of standards should not only demand clearly articulated statements of the basis for how standards are determined, but also require thorough construct validity studies.

In some standards-based settings there are too many standards to be adequately covered in either instruction or assessment. While there may be a long list of standards, only a few can be adequately covered. The proliferation of standards is particularly problematic in public school settings. Global standards may be vague and too general to be specified in measurement terms. Each standard is then subdivided into benchmarks or performance objectives, and the numbers of these benchmarks become excessively large and specific (Popham, 2001). This can lead to inconsistencies in teaching and grading across programs.

Standards often take on political roles and serve social agendas, and are developed to achieve social outcomes. Fulcher (2004) notes that the CEFR was developed in part to encourage mobility, to promote understanding and cooperation, and to overcome prejudice and discrimination within Europe. The ACTFL/FSI scales are widely employed within the US government and its educational context. They are often the benchmarks used in grant writing. Such political support makes them immune from challenges to their validity. This reification makes them the definition of the language construct, and almost necessarily causes them to underrepresent the construct of language use. English language standards in schools are often fairly explicitly anti-bilingual education and English-only in nature. California's English development standards state explicitly, "The ELD standards integrate listening, speaking, reading, and writing and create a distinct pathway to reading in English rather than delaying the introduction of English reading" (California Department of Education, 1999: 12). In short, these standards see language diversity as a problem.

Future directions

Standards have become a part of the educational landscape and are not likely to soon diminish their hold. They have great potential for keeping assessment tasks transparent and productive. However, they also have the possibility of proliferating and weighing down the educational enterprise in a bureaucratic accountability stalemate that homogenizes and stifles creativity. Several future developments, both positive and negative, appear possible.

First, with the development of the Standards for Foreign Language Learning in the twenty-first century (National Standards in Foreign Language Education Project, 1999) which expand content standards beyond the ACTFL scale itself, there is the opportunity to move beyond the narrow conception of foreign language education and measurement that has resulted from the overreliance on these scales. New types of performance-based assessment related to the content standards may be developed which go beyond a four skills approach.

Second, given the growing focus on assessment across all levels of education, it is very likely that there will be an increasing interest in standard-based assessment. However, given the continual lack of resources in education, there is likely to be an increase in the negative effects of assessment on successful application of standards-based assessment. That is, robust standards-based assessment requires a lot of testing time and time resources. This creates a dilemma around what areas of programs actually get covered in the assessment process. For example, educators can continue to develop standards across all areas of the school curriculum. Yet if institutions focus only on one or two standards, math and reading for example, because those are the areas that are being tested, little attention is allocated to the areas that are not assessed. Thus, regardless of the standards for subjects such as geography or physical education, teachers align their instruction to assessment and teach to the test.

Finally, it seems clear that there will continue to be development of standards because there is a need for benchmarks that are external to any particular setting. Currently, we see language materials, courses, research subjects, etc. described as "beginning" or "intermediate". There is a need to anchor these descriptors across studies and programs. Well articulated standards will be able to accommodate these needs.

Further reading

Horn, R. A. (2004). *Standards Primer*. New York, NY: Peter Lang. Horn presents an in depth treatment of content standards reform and accountability.

Lachat, M.A. (2004). *Standards-based Instruction and Assessment for English Language Learners*. Thousand Oaks, CA: Corwin Press. This is a detailed treatment of standards as they relate to public schools and English language learners.

Morrow, K. (ed.), (2004). *Insights from the Common European Framework*. Oxford, UK: Oxford University Press. This publication presents a review of the implementation of the CEFR and issues that have emerged.

References

ACTFL (1989). The ACTFL provisional proficiency guidelines. In T. V. Higgs (ed.), *Teaching for Proficiency, the Organizing Principle*. Lincolnwood, IL: National Textbook Company, 219–26.

California Department of Education (1999). *English-language development standards for California Public Schools: Kindergarten through Grade Twelve*. www.cde.ca.gov/be/st/ss/documents/englangdevstnd.pdf (accessed 4/23/10).

—— (2008). *Questions and Answers About the California English Language Development Test*. cia.banning. schoolfusion.us/modules/groups/homepagefiles/gwp/911238/992418/File/Testing%20and%20Accountab ility/celdt08brosp.pdf?sessionid=241b04638f5a18cfe2304f405af375ce (accessed 5/20/10).

—— (2010). *CELDT blueprints*. www.cde.ca.gov/ta/tg/el/resources.asp (accessed 5/20/10).

Thom Hudson

Council of Europe (2001). *Common European Framework of Reference for Languages: Learning, Teaching, Assessment.* Cambridge, UK: Cambridge University Press.

Foreign Service Institute (1979). Absolute language proficiency ratings. In M. L. Adams and J. R. Frith (eds). *Testing Kit: French and Spanish.* Washington, DC: Department of State, 13–15.

Fulcher, G. (2004). Deluded by artifices? The Common European Framework and harmonization. *Language Assessment Quarterly* 1: 253–66.

Higgs, T. V. (ed.), (1989). *Teaching for Proficiency, the Organizing Principle.* Lincolnwood, IL: National Textbook Company.

Hiple, D. V. (1987). A progress report on the ACTFL proficiency guidelines 1982–86. In H. Byrnes and M. Canale (eds), *Defining and Developing Proficiency: Guidelines, Implementations and concepts.* Lincolnwood, IL: National Textbook Company, 5–14.

James, C. J. (ed.), (1988). *Foreign Language Proficiency in the Classroom and Beyond.* Lincolnwood, IL: National Textbook Company.

Johnson, Y. (1997). Proficiency guidelines and language curriculum making ACTFL proficiency guidelines effective in furthering Japanese language proficiency. *Applied Language Learning* 8: 261–84.

Lachat, M. A. (2004). *Standards-based Instruction and Assessment for English Language learners.* Thousand Oaks, CA: Corwin Press.

Liskin-Gasparro, J. E. (1989). The ACTFL proficiency guidelines: A historical perspective. In Higgs, T. (ed.), *Teaching for Proficiency, the Organizing Principle.* Lincolnwood, IL: National Textbook Company, 11–42.

National Commission on Excellence in Education (1983). *A Nation at Risk: The Imperative for Educational Reform.* Washington, DC: Superintended of Documents, U.S. Government Publishing Office.

National Standards in Foreign Language Education Project (1999). *Standards for foreign language learning in the 21st century.* Lawrence, KS: Allen Press, Inc.

North, B. (2000). *The Development of a Common Framework Scale of Language Proficiency.* New York, NY: Peter Lang.

Omaggio, A. C. (1986). *Teaching Language in Context: proficiency-oriented instruction.* Boston, MA: Heinle & Heinle Publishers, Inc.

Pawlikowska-Smith, G. (2000). *Canadian language benchmarks: English as a second language for adults.* The Center for Canadian Language Benchmarks. www.language.ca (accessed 5/20/10).

—— (2002). *Canadian Language Benchmarks 2000: theoretical framework.* The Centre for Canadian Language Benchmarks. www.language.ca (accessed 5/20/10).

Peirce, B. N. and Stewart, G. (1999). Accountability in language assessment of adult immigrants in Canada. *Canadian Modern Language Review* 56: 223–44.

—— (1997). The development of the Canadian Language Benchmarks assessment. *TESL Canada Journal/ La revue TESL du Canada* 14: 17–31.

Popham, W. J. (2001). *Standards-based assessment: Solution or charade?* Paper presented at the annual meeting of the American Educational Research Association, Seattle, Washington, April 10–14.

President's Commission on Foreign Language and International Studies (1979). *Strength Through Wisdom: A Critique of U.S. Capability.* Washington, DC: U.S. Department of Health, Education, and Welfare. Office of Education.

Swender, E. and Duncan, G. (1998). ACTFL Performance Guidelines for K-12 Learners. *Foreign Language Annals* 31: 479–91.

Trim, J. (2001). *The work of the Council of Europe in the field of modern languages, 1957–2001.* Paper presented at symposium on the European Day of Languages 26 September 2001 at the European Centre for Modern Languages, Graz. www.ecml.at/efsz/files/Trim.pdf (accessed 5/15/10)

Van Ek, J. A. (1975). *Threshold Level English.* Oxford, UK: Pergamon Press.

Walton, K. D. (1993). The British National Curriculum in Mathematics and the American NCTM Standards – A contrast of strategies. *Teaching Mathematics and its Applications* 12: 154–58.

WIDA (2007). *WIDA's English Language Proficiency Standards for English Language Learners in Pre-Kindergarten through Grade 12: Frameworks for Formative and Summative Assessment and Instruction.* www.wida.us (accessed 8/2/11).

34

Language testing and language management

Bernard Spolsky

The chicken or the egg?

I have been puzzling about a title for this chapter, and it will become clear in the course of the chapter that I remain uncertain—confused, even—about the relationship between language testing and language policy, which is why I have chosen the neutral connector "and". My first thought was to consider language testing as a method of language management (Spolsky, 2009), that is to say, a way in which some participants in a speech community attempt to modify the language beliefs and language practices of others. Let us take a simple example: a school class in language, in which the teacher sets and marks tests that require pupils to use a version of the school language (or other language being taught) that he or she hopes that pupils will use. In essence, this assumes a belief, unfortunately widespread among those responsible for education, that testing is a good way to teach, rather than a way to gather data that needs further interpretation. Rather than take on the difficult problems of dealing with circumstances such as poverty which interfere with school success, a politician can simply propose that students who fail to pass a test (whatever that means) should be punished or even that their teachers who fail to bring them to some arbitrary standard should be fired. The general level of ignorance about testing displayed by politicians, the press, and the public is sometimes hard to believe (Taylor, 2009). How, for example, is a "pass" determined? I even recall a newspaper headline that complained half the students had failed to reach the average.

Krashan (2010) regularly draws our attention to the huge gap in achievement between middle class and lower class schools in the United States: the former produce results as good as any other nation, while the latter pull down the national average, and international ranking results from the high percentage of child poverty in the United States. Under successive presidents of all political persuasions, US education policy has followed a brutally ineffective approach, testing and punishing rather than teaching (Menken, 2008). The same strange but convenient belief can be applied to all educational levels and topics, whether reading in the early years or mathematics in high school, so that its application to language specifically is not the point. Additionally, a decision to write a test in the standard language, whether pupils know it or not, is simply a consequence of an earlier decision to use it as the medium of instruction. A high-stakes test in the national language may modify the sociolinguistic ecology of a community, but language management may not have been the first direct goal of the testing (Shohamy, 2006).

Some historical examples

In this light, the significant effect that the Chinese Imperial Examination system had in establishing the status of written Chinese and the Beijing way of pronouncing it as the ideal version of language, paving the way for the *Putonghua* (common language) campaign (Kalmar *et al.*, 1987) that is now seen as a method to unite a multilingual society, was not its original intended result, but rather an inevitable outcome of the choice of language in which this restricted higher-status elite examination was written (Franke, 1960). While the purpose of an examination may be neutral as to language, the choice of language will promote a particular variety of language and so advance its wider use. As long as the Cambridge *tripos* was an oral examination in Latin, it bolstered the status of those able to speak Latin: when it became a written examination, it recognized the significance of the English vernacular. We must be prepared therefore to distinguish between the language-related *results* of testing and the *intention* to use a test to manage language policy.

This may also be illustrated by the Indian Civil Service examination which helped establish the power and importance of examinations in nineteenth-century England. In arguing for the value of an examination as a method of replacing patronage in selecting candidates for government office, Macaulay (1853, 1891) made clear his neutrality on language issues. If the English public schools taught Cherokee rather than Latin and Greek, he said in his speech in Parliament, the candidate who could compose the best verse in Cherokee would be the ideal cadet. In practice, the examination when it was established did not include Cherokee, but besides Latin and Greek, it incorporated compulsory papers in German, French, Italian, Arabic and Sanskrit (Spolsky, 1995: 19). Similarly, the testing system which the Jesuits brought back from China for their schools in the seventeenth and eighteenth century had tested a syllabus that was determined centrally and did not focus in particular on attempting to change language choice, although of course it rewarded use of the appropriate version of the school languages and punished incorrect grammar (de La Salle, 1720).

But the Jesuit system was later adapted to language management during and after the French revolution. Under the Jacobins, the secularized school system was given the specific task of making sure that all pupils in schools under French rule inside France or its empire came out speaking and writing Parisian French, a task that took some seventy or eighty years to realize in schools of all but a few peripheral regions, and was never finally achieved in the colonies (Ager, 1999). This was a clear case of language management as I define it. Cardinal Richelieu's goal of uniting the multidialectal provinces of France under a Parisian king, implemented by his establishment of the Académie Française (Cooper, 1989), was taken over by the Jacobins and carried on by Napoleon and successive French governments to establish monolingualism not just in continental France but ideally in the many colonies that France came to govern during the nineteenth century. The French example, with its many government committees and agencies responsible for promoting *francophonie*, and its timely constitutional amendment setting French as the sole language of the Republic passed just before Maastricht when the establishment of the European Community threatened to encourage other languages, showed the nationalist language focus of these activities quite clearly. Accepting the close tie between language and nationalism, a policy that insisted on the use of a single language and that used an elaborate high-stakes examination system to achieve it was clearly an example of language management.

Tests for language diffusion

My own first experience of language management testing was when I was at secondary school in New Zealand and took part in the oral examinations conducted by the *Cercle Française*, which, I have since learned, was an agency of the French language diffusion enterprise (Kleineidam, 1992). The New Zealand school examinations, including the national examinations conducted towards the end of secondary school, did not include oral testing in foreign languages. The *Cercle Française* tests were given outside school to selected pupils at two or three levels; they consisted of a dictation and a short conversation, and were conducted not by schoolteachers but by lecturers from the local university. Participation as far as I recall was voluntary, but it was an honor to be selected. This international program was part of French government efforts to encourage the learning of French even in those countries that had not come under French colonial rule. It was distinct from the normal examination of language subjects associated with regular schooling.

Although school-based testing of national and foreign languages can be seen as an attempt to force or encourage the learning of the language, it is simply the application of testing to another school subject: it is the decision on which languages to include as school subjects (just like the decision on medium of instruction) that is language management rather than the test itself. Thus, the European Union's policy calling for the teaching of two foreign languages is a management practice intended to ensure that a language other than English is included in the syllabus (Ammon, 2002). When testing is used to manage (or replace) teaching for all subjects, it is somewhat stretching the scope to include it in this chapter. In other words, it is a matter of the power of *testing* rather than of the power of *language testing* (Shohamy, 1993). The voluntary French oral tests were focused specifically on a language goal, and significantly, were under the direction of a foreign agency.

The gatekeeping function of high-stakes tests

When many years later I became directly involved in the testing of the English language proficiency of foreign students in or seeking admission to US universities, I became aware of the further management potential of language testing. I came to realize the non-educational effect of requiring English language competence in students applying to American universities, and wrote a paper drawing attention to the probable way in which it limited admission to those potential students whose parents' financial or political standing had given them an opportunity to attend a school which taught English efficiently (Spolsky, 1967). Later, as I carried out research on the development of the Test of English as a Foreign Language (Spolsky, 1995), I learned more about this phenomenon, marked by the tendency of students from European countries to do better on the test (I discount, as some Canadian and other universities have learned to do, the distorted results of some Asian candidates who memorize possible examination questions).

The Test of English as a Foreign Language (TOEFL) is a clear case of a high-stakes test with social effects, and with a language management origin (Spolsky, 1995: 55–59). It was the third attempt to comply with a request from the US Commissioner of Immigration to correct a loophole in the 1923 US Immigration Act, the purpose of which had been to exclude immigrants from Asia, Africa, and eastern and southern Europe by setting quotas based on the years in which most immigrants had come from northern Europe. The loophole was a provision granting automatic student visas to candidates coming to study in the United States; the Commissioner feared (rightly) that many would use this as a way to enter the country and then remain illegally. The US government was not yet prepared (as the Australian government had been some years earlier) to establish its own testing system, but asked the College Entrance Examination

Board, an association established by elite private schools to standardize admissions procedures, to develop a test which would guarantee that candidates planning to study in the United States had already achieved proficiency in English. In 1926, the Commissioner requested "that all schools indicate in the certificate of admission the exact knowledge of the English language a student must have before he can be accepted"; this led to a request the following year to the College Board to develop a special examination. A committee set up by the Board suggested an outline for the examination, and a grant of US $5,000 from the Carnegie Endowment for International Peace helped to cover costs. With the hesitant assistance of some American embassies, in 1930 30 candidates took the examination in eight different countries; the following year, 139 candidates were examined in 17 countries including a group of 82 engineering students in Moscow. In 1932, the test was offered in 29 countries but in the increasingly difficult world economic depression, there were only 30 candidates; in 1933, the number dropped to 17 and in 1934, after only 20 students could afford the US$10 fee, the examination was "at least temporarily" discontinued, as no one could afford to prepare a new form. (We may also add that it was thus not available to certify the English proficiency of Jewish professionals seeking to escape from Nazi Germany.) There are a number of interesting features about this first attempt: the dependence on the support of foundations, the intelligent design of the test but practical limitations in its implementation, and the lack of willingness on the part of prospective users to pay for it.

The second attempt to plug the immigration loophole came in 1945, again with encouragement and limited support from the Department of State. Advised by leading language testers (including Charles Fries and his young student Robert Lado), one form of the English examination for Foreign Students was prepared in 1947 and administered overseas at some Department of State Cultural Centers. The test, developed by the College Board, was passed on to the newly independent Educational Testing Service at Princeton and available for a few years until financial problems led it too to be dropped (Spolsky 1995: 155–57).

In 1961, there was a new attempt. In the meantime, several American universities had developed English tests of their own. Lado's Michigan tests were the best known, but the American University Language Center tests, originally written by A. L. Davis but later improved by David Harris, were also widely used by the US government. Many US consulates conducted their own primitive tests before granting student visas, but all these tests lacked the financial resources to guarantee security by offering new forms at each administration. To consider a possible solution, a meeting of interested parties was called by the newly established Center for Applied Linguistics in 1961 which developed a plan for what eventually became the TOEFL (Center for Applied Linguistics, 1961). After a few years of independence, and as a result of complicated maneuvering, the test was taken over completely by Educational Testing Service and grew into a major source of income (Nairn, 1980). Under user pressure, tests of spoken and written proficiency were later added, followed by a computerized version of the test. But the underlying problem continues: an Associated Press report in *The New York Times* on 8 March 2010 says that "A California man was charged Monday with operating a ring of illegal test-takers who helped dozens of Middle Eastern citizens obtain United States student visas by passing various proficiency and college-placement exams for them, federal authorities said." This is a story repeated throughout the world, for all high-stakes tests.

Exploiting the demands for English tests

This corroborates how the value of the test finally became apparent to prospective users: the status of English as the major international language for education and commerce moved the demand for the test to the public, so that by now there are competing international English tests offered by public and private organizations. The first of these was the English Language Testing Service test (later renamed International English Language Testing Service test) developed in the late 1970s by the University of Cambridge Local Examinations Syndicate at the request of the British Council, with the participation later of the International Development Program of Australian Universities (Criper and Davies, 1988; Alderson and Clapham, 1992). This test and its later forms have proved financially successful, and others have rushed into the business, including Pearson Education, a major international firm selling teaching and testing materials. There are now English testing businesses in many Asian countries.

At this stage, we have moved beyond the organized language management situation (Neustupný and Nekvapil, 2003), with governments attempting to encourage people to learn their language, and to a stage where the demand for testing comes from the learners. That is to say, whereas the French oral examination that I took was supported by the French government to encourage pupils in other countries to learn French, these major industrial testing services intend to profit from demand from people in non-English speaking countries who see the value of learning the language and having a way of certifying that proficiency. These commercial tests then serve what Nekvapil and Nekula (2006) would call *simple* management, namely an individual seeking to improve his language and communication skills, rather than the complex management envisioned in the title of this chapter which assumes an authority aiming to manage the language choice of others: we are dealing then with top-down exploitation of bottom-up demand.

A similarly neutral attitude to language management lay behind the development of the Council of Europe Framework of Language Learning and Teaching (Council of Europe, 2001). While the Council and the European Union do have a language management policy, namely that all should learn two additional languages, they do not specify which languages they should be. True, calling (unsuccessfully as it turns out) for two additional languages is an effort to make sure that European foreign language learning should not be restricted to English teaching. But it is a weak management plan, as compared say to the Soviet insistence on satellite countries teaching Russian or the French willingness to accept bilingualism provided only that it includes French.

Phillipson (1992) has proposed that the spread of English is the result of imperialism of the core English-speaking countries rather than the result of the growing demand for knowledge of a useful language. Many argue against his position (Fishman *et al.*, 1996). For me, the clearest evidence is the weakness of government diffusion agencies. The British Council for some years now has seen the teaching of English as a source of income rather than as a political and cultural investment, although admittedly in the 1930s there were a few who saw it as a way of spreading English influence; and the US Information Agency discouraged those centers which allocated too large a proportion of the budget to English teaching. This contrasts with other diffusion agencies like the network of activities encouraging Francophonie, or the language-teaching programs of the Goethe Institute, or the developing community of Lusophone countries with its post-imperial concerns, or the growing number of Confucius Institutes set up by the Chinese government to persuade Africans to replace English and French by Mandarin Chinese.

An instructive exception was the attempt of John Roach, assistant secretary of the University of Cambridge Local Examinations Syndicate who in the 1920s and 1930s concentrated on the development of the English language test, which, he argued before he left the Syndicate in 1945, would be an acceptable way of spreading English and its associated way of life (Roach, 1986). His ideas were ahead of his time, opposed by the establishment including the British Council: but he managed to keep the test alive into the 1940s so that it was ready for its later profitable growth as the demand for English spread.

School examinations for language management

I need to return to the general issue of school examinations as a potential language management device. My argument is that language tests and examinations can serve to focus attention in situations where society accepts the decision of government to require the learning of the language and even more in those cases where education is conducted in a language other than the home language of the pupils. Members of minority groups and children of immigrants can be forced by these examinations to attempt to change their language practices; otherwise, their failures can be blamed on them rather than on a misguided educational policy.

Few educational systems allow for the fact demonstrated in many research studies that students need several years of instruction in a language before they can learn in it efficiently (Walter, 2003, 2008). In these circumstances, language tests become a powerful method of filtering out all but a select elite of immigrants and minority children; in Africa, in most countries where the medium of instruction is English or French, it reduces the possibility of providing a good education to the mass of speakers of indigenous languages (Heugh, 2005; Heugh *et al.*, 2007). There are of course other ways of forcing the learning of the school language: American Indian children were punished for using their own home languages (McCarty, 1998, 2002), just as the enforcement of English in Welsh schools was accomplished by corporal punishment rather than testing (Lewis, 1975). In school then, language testing is one of several methods of implementing language management policies. Phillipson is right in his judgment of the effect of these policies, but perhaps overstates the intentionality.

Language tests to manage immigrants and asylum seekers

A similar analysis may be applied to the use of language tests in non-school situations. The infamous Australian immigrant language test (Davies, 1997) is a case in point (see Kunnan, this volume). As a number of studies have shown, the test was intended to exclude prospective immigrants who were judged unsuitable on other grounds by the immigration official. He was instructed to give a dictation test in a language which he assumed the immigrant did not know. The test failed if the immigrant passed. While the circumstances and results were similar, this was quite different from two other kinds of language tests administered to prospective immigrants, the test given to an asylum seeker to check his or her identity, and the test given to a prospective citizen to guarantee knowledge of the official language.

The asylum seeker's test, now becoming common in Europe and providing employment for self-certified dialect experts (Eades *et al.*, 2003; McNamara, 2005), is perhaps the closest thing to the shibboleth test in the Bible. I quote the passage from the book of Judges:

> The men of Gilead defeated the Ephraimites for they had said, "you Gileadites are nothing but fugitives from Ephraim ... " The Gileadites held the fords of the Jordan against the Ephraimites. And when any fugitive from Ephraim said, "let me cross," the men of Gilead would ask him, "are you an Ephraimite?"; if he said, "no," they would say to him, "then say shibboleth"; that he would say "'sibboleth" not being able to pronounce it correctly thereupon they would seize him and slay him by the fords of the Jordan. Forty-two thousand Ephraimites fell at that time.
>
> *(Judges, 12: 14)*

In the current European asylum tests, the experts claim to be able to determine the origin of the asylum seeker from aspects of his dialect (Blommaert, 2008; Reath, 2004). As pointed out by

Kunnan (this volume) the identifications are doubtful and clearly miss such facts as that the speaker may pick up a particular pronunciation from a short stay in another country or from a foreign teacher. Again, in the asylum seeker's test, the test is a method of implementing an immigration decision to refuse admission to a person who cannot prove that he or she is from a specific country or group.

Similarly, language tests for citizenship depend on a government decision to require knowledge of the national language. The relationship between language and citizenship has been widely debated. Those who argue for multicultural citizenship favor linguistic diversity, but linguistic homogenization has been a common method of establishing civic identity (Patten and Kymlicka, 2003: 11–12). Our concern however is not specifically with multilingual societies, but with immigrants seeking citizenship in a new society. It is commonly agreed that in the long term they should integrate by learning the national language. But there are those who argue that excessive emphasis on language as a gateway to community membership is associated with "old-fashioned cultural assimilation." To expect immigrants to develop fluency in the state language rapidly is seen by liberals as a challenge to their civic rights. The question then becomes, at what point in the process should the system require proficiency in the state language: in order to emigrate, in order to receive voting rights, or as in some Constitutions (this is notable in the linguistic clauses of the constitution of former British colonies in the West Indies) in order to be a candidate for legislative office. Whichever decision is made, one way of implementing it is likely to be a language test. The tests then will be seen by some as a barrier to immigrant rights (Milani, 2008; Nic Shuibhne, 2002).

Language tests to manage employment

Related to the case of language proficiency for citizenship, there are complex issues in requiring language proficiency for employment in various positions. There are occupations that seem to require specific language proficiency. I start with one that has been quite recently recognized: the ability of airplane pilots and ground personnel, especially traffic controllers, to communicate with each other (see Moder and Halleck, this volume). The International Civil Aviation Organization has established a policy requiring air traffic controllers and pilots to have certified proficiency in English or in a relevant national language. This step was taken only after a number of cases of accidents attributable to communication failure. Setting the requirement has been comparatively simple, but finding a way to implement it has led to a complex and largely unsatisfactory search for appropriate instruments. Alderson (2009, 2010) has been studying the process, and finds a multiplicity of tests, few with evidence of standards, reliability, or validity.

This is perhaps the appropriate point to comment on the quality of any of the tests used for language management. I have already raised questions about the validity of the test used for asylum seekers. Serious questions can in fact be raised about many tests used in education. Apart from the normal questions about test validity, special problems arise when the same test is expected to measure the language proficiency of native speakers and of language learners, as currently in the United States. The range is simply too large to develop an appropriate instrument: this is one of the most significant flaws in the current attempt to use test results to judge the efficiency of various schools and teachers. It is a fundamental principle that a poor test is a useless or dangerous way to manage language policy. This tendency will be exacerbated if countries, like the United States, adopt a policy that establishes a "common core" of educational standards (focused on English and Mathematics), and if as anticipated national examinations are developed to assess students, schools, and states in meeting those standards. If this happens, the result will be a major revolution in further centralization of US education and the kind of narrowness of focus that central standardized tests have produced, a fact bewailed 140 years ago by an English educator (Latham, 1877) who saw this as an emulation of the French policy.

Returning to occupational language qualification tests, one area where language proficiency is or should be a requirement is the health profession. Doctors and nurses need to be able to communicate with their patients both for satisfactory diagnosis and monitoring of treatment. The question then arises, who should be tested? Many health agencies put the burden on the patient, who is expected to bring a child or other bilingual capable of answering questions and passing on instructions. Foreign and foreign-trained doctors and nurses are regularly expected to pass language tests, although the focus of these tests remains a serious problem. Should they be tested in medical language, or in communication in the various vernaculars with patients? Having listened to an Israeli doctor (fluent in Arabic and Hebrew) trying to take a medical history in an emergency room from an elderly patient limited to Russian and depending on a relative who could manage English, one realizes the attraction of requiring plurilingual proficiency in health personnel: the other choice is of course the expense of providing qualified interpreters in a large range of languages (Roberts et al., 2001).

Similar problems are faced by police departments in increasingly multilingual cities. In 2005, for instance, 470 New York police department employees were reported to have passed tests in more than 45 languages, including Arabic, Urdu, Hindi, Pashtu, Farsi, Dari, and Punjabi: another 4,000 were waiting to be tested. A number of US police departments encourage certification in sign language. Again, qualified personnel reduce the need for extensive and expensive interpretation services. In a related policy, the European Union required new candidates for membership to ensure that officials (especially border and customs officials) were proficient in Western European languages as well as in the Russian they needed during Soviet rule.

In the business world, international firms and companies with dealings with speakers of other languages commonly have a language policy usually implemented by hiring employees with relevant language proficiency. Occasionally, they may have specially designed language tests to measure the kinds of proficiency associated with the task, but they are just as likely to rely on casual interviews or the results of academic language tests. There have so far been only a few studies of language management in the workplace; they show the complexity of situations and include cases where testing is used (Neustupný and Nekvapil, 2003).

Language tests—whether and whither?

Putting all this together, one might ask about its relevance to this Handbook and to language testing practice. For prospective language testers, it might be read as a warning that you are heading into a dangerous field, one where there will be jobs, but where you will face, like workers in the armament industry, ethical problems. Tests, like guns, can be and regularly appear to be misused. For students of language policy, it shows the existence of a powerful instrument to manage other people's language, to force them to learn and use new varieties, to trap them into authority-valued or -condemned identities. For all of us, it raises serious issues in educational, civil and political spheres, cautioning us that tests are as easily misused as employed for reasonable goals.

I would certainly not want to be interpreted as claiming that testing is necessarily bad: just as there are morally and ethically justifiable uses for guns, so there are morally and ethically justifiable uses for language tests. The problem seems to be rather that both tests and guns are potentially so powerful as to be commonly misused. If we analyze the problem of the US educational system in the twenty-first century, there is good reason to suspect that it can be cured only by serious social and economic engineering and the eradication of the poverty that produces the most serious failures. It is readily understandable but regrettable that educators, politicians, and the naive general public are attracted to a much simpler approach: raise the standards of school tests and punish any teacher or school that fails to achieve good results. This approach may seem more attractive, but in the long run it will not work. I am therefore depressed about the short-term future, and can only hope for greater wisdom in the future. Similarly, it is beginning to seem logical to deal with the demographic changes produced by immigration and asylum seeking by setting barriers controlled by tests rather than developing intelligent plans for teaching necessary language skills to immigrants and their families and providing appropriate support until they are gained. Again, the short term solution is unlikely to succeed, but it will take some time before the general public and politicians are prepared to undertake more basic solutions.

Thus, I deplore the misuse of language tests for management as a superficially attractive but fundamentally flawed policy. Language tests can play a major role when used diagnostically in improving language teaching or in planning for language support systems, making them an excellent instrument for intelligent and responsible language management, but the misuse remains a "clear and present danger".

Further reading

McNamara, T. and Roever, C. (2006). *Language testing: the social dimension*. Malden, MA: Blackwell Publishing. While language tests are usually analyzed using statistical measures and citing psychometric principles, this important work adds social dimensions, thus giving sociolinguistics a role in testing alongside statistics.

Shohamy, E. (2006). *Language policy: hidden agendas and new approaches*. New York, NY: Routledge. Having earlier argued for the power of tests (especially language tests) to effect language policy, Shohamy here deals with the various innocent-seeming language management policies used to establish boundaries and gatekeeping mechanisms to control immigrants and other minorities.

Spolsky, B. (1995). *Measured Words: the development of objective language testing*. Oxford, UK: Oxford University Press. The first half of the book is a history of language testing up to 1961, the year that a meeting took place in Washington, DC that led to the creation of TOEFL. The rest of the book tracks the meeting and its results, and shows how what started as a test controlled by language testers became part of a major testing industry. It traces the early years of the industrialization of language tests.

References

Ager, E. D. (1999). *Identity, Insecurity and Image: France and language*. Clevedon: Multilingual Matters Ltd.

Alderson, C. J. (2009). Air safety, language assessment policy and policy implementation: the case of aviation English. *Annual Review of Applied Linguistics* 29: 168–88.

—— (2010). A survey of aviation English tests. *Language Testing* 27: 51–72.

Alderson, C. J. and Clapham, C. (1992). Applied linguistics and language testing: a case study of the ELTS test. *Applied Linguistics* 13: 149–67.

Ammon, U. (2002). *Present and future language conflict as a consequence of the integration and expansion of the European Union (EU)*. Paper presented at the XXXVI Congresso Internationale di Studi della Societa di Linguistica Italiana, Bergamo.

Blommaert, J. (2008). *Language, Asylum, and the National Order*. Washington, DC: American Association of Applied Linguistics.

Center for Applied Linguistics (1961). *Testing the English proficiency of foreign Students. Report of a conference sponsored by the Center for Applied Linguistics in cooperation with the Institute of International Education and the National Association of Foreign Student Advisers*. Washington, DC: Center for Applied Linguistics.

Cooper, Robert L. (1989). *Language Planning and Social Change*. Cambridge, UK: Cambridge University Press.

Council of Europe (2001). *Common European Framework of Reference for Languages: learning, teaching, assessment*. Cambridge, UK: Cambridge University Press.

Criper, C. and Davies, A. (1988). *ELTS Validation Project Report*. The British Council and the University of Cambridge Local Examinations Syndicate.

Davies, A. (1997). Australian immigrant gatekeeping through English Language Tests: how important is proficiency? In A. Huhta, V. Kohonon, L. Kurki-Suonio and S. Luoma (eds), *Current Developments and Alternatives in Language Assessment: Proceedings of LTRC 96*. Jyväskylä, Finland: Kopijyva Oy, University of Jyväskylä, 71–84.

de La Salle, Saint Jean-Baptists (1720). *Conduite des Ecoles chrétiennes*. Avignon: C. Chastanier.

Eades, D., Helen, F., Siegel, J., McNamara, T. and Baker, B. (2003). Linguistic identification in the determination of nationality: a preliminary report. *Language Policy* 2: 179–99.

Fishman, J. A., Rubal-Lopez, A. and Conrad, A. W. (eds), (1996). *Post-Imperial English*. Berlin, Germany: Mouton de Gruyter.

Franke, W. (1960). *The Reform and Abolition of the Traditional Chinese Examination System*. Cambridge, MA: Harvard University Center for East Asian Studies.

Heugh, K. (2005). Language education policies in Africa. In Keith Brown (ed.), *Encyclopaedia of Language and Linguistics*, Vol. 6. Oxford, UK: Elsevier, 414–22.

Heugh, K., Benson, C., Bogale, B. and Yohannes, M. A. G. (2007). *Final report study on Medium of Instruction in Primary Schools in Ethiopia*. Addis Ababa, Ethiopia: Ministry of Education.

Kalmar, I., Yong, Z. and Hong, X. (1987). Language attitudes in Guangzhou, China. *Language in Society* 16: 499–508.

Kleineidam, H. (1992). Politique de diffusion linguistique et francophonie: l'action linguistique menée par la France. *International Journal of the Sociology of Language* 95: 11–31.

Krashen, S. D. (2010). *Comments on the Learn Act*. www.sdkrashen.com/articles/Comments_on_the_LEARN_ Act.pdf (accessed 8/2/11).

Latham, H. (1877). *On the Action of Examinations Considered as a Means of Selection*. Cambridge, UK: Deighton, Bell and Company.

Lewis, G. E. (1975). Attitude to language among bilingual children and adults in Wales. *International Journal of the Sociology of Language* 4: 103–25.

Macaulay, T. B. (1853). *Speeches, Parliamentary and Miscellaneous*. London, UK: Henry Vizetelly.

—— (1891). *The Works of Lord Macaulay*. London, UK: Longmans, Green and Co.

McCarty, T. L. (1998). Schooling, resistance and American Indian Languages. *International Journal of the Sociology of Language* 132: 27–41.

—— (2002). *A Place to be Navajo: rough rock and the struggle for self-determination in indigenous schooling*. Mahwah, NJ: Lawrence Erlbaum Associates.

McNamara, T. (2005). 21st century shibboleth: Language tests, identity and intergroup conflict. *Language Policy* 4: 351–70.

Menken, K. (2008). *Learners Left Behind: standardized testing as language policy*. London, UK: Multilingual Matters.

Milani, T. M. (2008). Language testing and citizenship: A language ideological debate in Sweden. *Language and Society* 37: 27–59.

Nairn, A. (1980). *The Reign of ETS: the corporation that makes up minds*. The Ralph Nader Report. Washington, DC: Ralph Nader.

Nekvapil, J. and Nekula, M. (2006). On language management in multinational companies in the Czech Republic. *Current Issues in Language Planning* 7: 307–27.

Neustupný, J. V. and Nekvapil, J. (2003). Language management in the Czech republic. *Current Issues in Language Planning* 4: 181–366.

Nic Shuibhne, N. (2002). *EC Law and Minority Language Policy: culture, citizenship and fundamental rights*. Boston, MA: Kluwer Law International.

Patten, A. and Kymlicka, W. (2003). Introduction: language rights and political theory. In W. Kymlicka and A. Patten (eds), *Language Rights and Political Theory*. Oxford UK: Oxford University Press, 1–51.

Phillipson, R. (1992). *Linguistic Imperialism*. Oxford, UK: Oxford University Press.

Reath, A. (2004). Language analysis in the context of the asylum process: procedures, validity, and consequences. *Language Assessment Quarterly* 1: 209–33.

Roach, J. O. (1986). *On leaving the Syndicate, 1945*. Personal papers of J. O. Roach.

Roberts, R. P., Carr, S. E., Abraham, D. and Dufour, A. (eds), (2001). *The Critical Link 2: interpreters in the community*. Selected papers from the Second International Conference on interpreting in legal, health and social service settings, Vancouver, BC, Canada, 19–23 May 1998. Amsterdam, The Netherlands: John Benjamins Publishing Company.

Shohamy, E. (1993). *The Power of Tests: the impact of language tests on teaching and learning*. Washington, DC: National Foreign Language Center.

—— (2006). *Language Policy: hidden agendas and new approaches*. New York, NY: Routledge.

Spolsky, B. (1967). Do they know enough English? In D. Wigglesworth (ed.), *ATESL Selected Conference Papers*. Washington, DC: NAFSA Studies and Papers, English Language Series.

—— (1995). *Measured Words: the development of objective language testing*. Oxford, UK: Oxford University Press.

—— (2009). *Language Management*. Cambridge, UK: Cambridge University Press.

Taylor, L. (2009). Developing assessment literacy. *Annual Review of Applied Linguistics* 29: 21–36.

Walter, S. L. (2003). Does language of instruction matter in education? In M. R. Wise, T. N. Headland and R. M. Brend (eds), *Language and Life: essays in memory of Kenneth L. Pike*. Dallas TX: SIL International and the University of Texas at Arlington, 611–35.

—— (2008). The language of instruction issue: Framing an empirical perspective. In B. Spolsky and F. M. Hult (eds), *Handbook of educational linguistics*. Malden, MA: Blackwell Publishing, 129–46.

Index